THE PRESOCRATIC PHILOSOPHERS

The Arguments of the Philosophers

EDITOR: TED HONDERICH
Reader in Philosophy, University College London

The group of books of which this is one will include an essentially analytic and critical account of each of the considerable number of the great and influential philosophers. Each book will provide an ordered exposition and an examination of the contentions and doctrines of the philosopher in question. The group of books taken together will comprise a contemporary assessment and history of the entire course of philosophical thought.

Already published in the series

Plato	J. C. B. Gosling
Meinong	Reinhardt Grossman
Santayana	Timothy L. S. Sprigge
Wittgenstein	R. J. Fogelin
Hume	B. Stroud
Descartes	Margaret Dauler Wilson
Berkeley	George Pitcher
Kant	Ralph Walker

THE PRESOCRATIC PHILOSOPHERS

Jonathan Barnes

Fellow of Balliol College, Oxford

Routledge & Kegan Paul
London, Boston, Melbourne and Henley

First published in two volumes in 1979
This revised edition in one volume first published in 1982
by Routledge & Kegan Paul Ltd
39 Store Street, London WC1E 7DD,
9 Park Street, Boston, Mass. 02108, USA,
296 Beaconsfield Parade, Middle Park,
Melbourne, 3206, Australia and
Broadway House, Newtown Road,
Henley-on-Thames, Oxon RG9 1EN
Photoset in 11 on 12pt Garamond
and printed in Great Britain by
Ebenezer Baylis & Son Ltd
Worcester, and London

ISBN 0-7100-9200-8

Contents

Preface

Anyone who has the temerity to write a book on the Presocratics requires a remarkably good excuse. The surviving fish from the Presocratic shoal, fortuitously angled from Time's vast ocean, have been gutted, anatomized, and painstakingly described by generations of scholars; and it might reasonably be supposed that further dissection would be a vain and unprofitable exercise.

The lucubrations of scholars have for the most part dwelt upon the philological and historical interpretation of Presocratic philosophy: the sources have been studied, weighed, and analysed; the fragments have been microscopically investigated, their every word turned and turned again in the brilliant light of classical scholarship; and the opinions and doctrines of those early thinkers have been labelled and put on permanent exhibition in the museum of intellectual history.

Yet if the linguistic expression and the historical context of the Presocratics have been exhaustively discussed, the rational content of their thought has been less thoroughly scrutinized. By and large, scholars have asked what the Presocratics said, and what external circumstances may have prompted their sayings; they have not asked whether the Presocratics spoke truly, or whether their sayings rested on sound arguments.

It is those latter questions with which my book is primarily concerned. My main thesis is that the Presocratics were the first masters of rational thought; and my main aim is the exposition and assessment of their various ratiocinations. The judicious reader will decide for himself the value of that essay and what success it may have achieved: it constitutes my sole excuse for offering this volume to his perusal.

My aim has imposed certain restrictions on the scope and nature of my treatment of early Greek philosophy; and it is proper for a Preface to acknowledge those limitations.

First, then, the book presents little in the way of philological scholarship. No writer on ancient philosophy can entirely forego scholarly suggestions; and any investigation of Presocratic thought will constantly make philological judgments and take sides in scholarly controversies. But classical scholars have raised great monuments to their art over the bones of the Presocratics. I rely largely on that work; indeed, I should not have had the audacity to write on the Presocratics at all had they not been richly provided with wise and learned philological commentary.

Second, I have little concern with history. It is a platitude that a thinker can be understood only against his historical background; but that, like all platitudes, is at best a half-truth, and I do not believe that a detailed knowledge of Greek history greatly enhances our comprehension of Greek philosophy. Philosophy lives a supracelestial life, beyond the confines of space and time; and if philosophers are, perforce, small spatio-temporal creatures, a minute attention to their small spatio-temporal concerns will more often obfuscate than illumine their philosophies. History, however, is intrinsically entertaining. A few external facts and figures may serve to relieve the reader from a purely abstract narrative: I hope that my occasional historical paragraphs may be of use to that end, and may do something to placate the historically minded reader.

Third, my treatment of early Greek philosophy is discriminatory. I shall, it is true, say something about most of the inmates of Diels-Kranz' *Fragmente der Vorsokratiker*; and Diels-Kranz' magisterial volumes are customarily taken to define the extension of early Greek thought. Yet such a definition is not wholly felicitous: it gives an artificial unity to a body of thought and doctrine that is, in reality, disparate in conception and various in purpose and intent; and it excludes those early thinkers—I have in mind the Hippocratic doctors, Euripides, and Thucydides—whose works had the good fortune to survive intact. I adhere to the convention that 'the Presocratics' are the men in the *Fragmente*; and the convention is, after all, not wholly without merit. But it follows that I cannot pretend to give a comprehensive account of early Greek philosophy.

Fourth, I shall have nothing to say about many of the interests of the Presocratics. We know a vast amount about Presocratic 'meteorology' and very little about Presocratic epistemology: I have little to do with the former subject, and much to say about the latter. The Presocratics did not work in departments and faculties as we do, and they saw nothing incongruous in treating ethics and astronomy in a single book. For the most part I have restricted myself to topics which would now be classified as philosophical. I shall not be greatly moved by the charge that my classification seems at times to be arbitrary; for in the last resort I have chosen to deal with those issues which happen to interest me and to fit my notion of what a philosopher might reasonably busy himself about.

My debt to the published literature on the Presocratics is incalculable; and it is only in part acknowledged in the Notes and the Bibliography. It would be invidious to pick out a short list of names from the long and learned catalogue of Presocratic scholars; but no one, I think, will object if I say that the writings of Gregory Vlastos have always proved a source of particular stimulation; and I wish also to confess an especial indebtedness to Professor Guthrie's invaluable *History of Greek Philosophy*.

My interest in the Presocratics was first aroused when, as an undergraduate, I attended a course of lectures given by Professor G. E. L. Owen. The views expressed in this book owe a lot to that masterly exposition; and I fear that Professor Owen, should he read my remarks, will find in them many a distorted ghost of his own former opinions. He has my apologies as well as my thanks.

The book was begun and ended at the Chalet des Mélèzes, a living reminder of a lost and better world. An early draft of the first part of the work formed a set of lectures which I gave at Oxford in 1973; but most of the labour was done in Amherst during the Fall of 1973, when I was a visiting professor in Classical Humanities at the University of Massachusetts. I am deeply grateful to the University for the honour of its invitation, and for ensuring that my time there was spent in a pleasant and fruitful fashion; and I must thank the Provost and Fellows of Oriel for granting me sabbatical leave for Michaelmas Term 1973. In Amherst I received valuable help from many hands; in particular, I thank Vere Chappell, John Guiniven, and Gary Matthews, whose criticism—keen, constant, but kindly—brought innumerable improvements to my rude thoughts.

Various parts of the book have been read in various places. An early version of Chapter IV, on Heraclitus, was delivered at Brooklyn College; pieces of Chapter VI, on Pythagoras, formed a paper read at Vassar College; some Eleatic thoughts were aired at the University of Minnesota, and others before the B Club at Cambridge; a part of Chapter XIII, on Zeno, was incorporated into a piece read at the University of Keele. On all those occasions I, at least, profited; and members of my different audiences may expect to see their pillaged suggestions in the following pages. In 1974 I gave a class on Zeno in Oxford, and the discussions there largely moulded my views on that enigmatic figure: I gained greatly from the acute comments of Nicholas Measor and David Sedley.

Work on the Presocratics has occupied me, on and off, for some three years. Thoughout that time I have been aided and encouraged, sometimes inadvertently and often from importunate request, by very many pupils, colleagues, and friends; they will, I hope, accept this book as the tangible reward or punishment for their kindnesses. I am also deeply indebted to Mrs D. Cunninghame and Mrs E. Hinkes, who laboured long hours to produce an elegant typescript from a large and messy manuscript.

Finally, I must thank Ted Honderich, the editor of the series in which this book appears, and David Godwin, of Routledge & Kegan Paul: faced with a typescript far longer than they had anticipated, they reacted with self-control, sympathy, and helpful kindness. In particular, the division of the book into two volumes was their suggestion: the book was written as a unitary whole, and the two volumes should be considered as twin halves of a single work; but each volume has, I think, a certain unity of its own. (The division has occasioned one minor inelegance; for the Bibliography would not split as readily as the text. But that should not cause the reader any serious inconvenience.)

In studying the Presocratic philosophers I have constantly been impressed by the sagacity of Leibniz' judgment: 'these men of old had more worth than we suppose'. If any reader is encouraged by this book to join the Leibnizian party, I shall be well content.

J. B.
Chalet des Mélèzes

Preface to the Revised Edition

The Presocratic Philosophers was conceived and written as a continuous whole: it was the weight and bulk of the typescript, not any lacuna in the narrative, which persuaded the publishers that a division into two volumes would make the work more wieldy. For this revised edition the original form has been reimposed on the obese matter, and the chapters run consecutively from I to XXV. The two Bibliographies of the first edition have been united; a single set of Indexes serves the text.

The Indexes have been redone from scratch. The Bibliography has been slightly expanded. The text itself is fundamentally unchanged: I have corrected a number of typographical mistakes (the proof-reading of the first edition was lamentably sloppy), and I have eliminated one or two startling errors of fact; but I have not attempted to check all the references for accuracy, or to emend the various infelicities of style and substance which friends and reviewers have brought to my attention. The following pages, which the publishers have kindly allowed me, set down a few unsystematic reflections and recantations.

First, let me make four general remarks about the scope and mode of the book. *The Presocratic Philosophers* was never intended to supply a comprehensive account of early Greek thought: there are many aspects of the intellectual lives of the Presocratics which it does not mention, let alone discuss; and the *dramatis personae* of the work were, as I confessed, determined by a convention—lightly introduced and now immovably entrenched—which may give a misleading notion of the philosophical and scientific riches which Plato and his contemporaries inherited at the beginning of the fourth century BC. My aim, then, was modest: I proposed to analyse some of the arguments of some of the early Greek thinkers; and in doing so I hoped to celebrate the characteristic rationality of Greek thought. Recent scholarship has gone out of its way to stress the irrational side of the Greek genius: that even the Greeks had their moments of unreason is not to be denied; but that sad platitude, however engrossing its detailed documentation may be, is surely of far less significance than the happy truth which it balances. For rationality, in a relaxed sense of that term, was the glory and triumph of the Greek mind, and its most valuable gift to posterity. The Greeks stand to the irrational as the French to bad cuisine.

Nor was the book intended to be a scholarly history. Some critics, indeed, have accused me of being anti-historical, and their accusation has some point: I made one or two naughty remarks about history, and I occasionally flirted with anachronistic interpretations of Presocratic views. For all that, the book is a sort of history: it recounts past thoughts, and its heroes are long dead. In speaking slightingly of history I had two specific things in mind—studies of the 'background' (economic, social, political) against which the Presocratics wrote, and studies of the network of 'influences' within which they carried on their researches. For I doubt the pertinence of such background to our understanding of early Greek thought: a few general facts are helpful and a few detailed facts are entertaining; but the chronicles of Elea or the narrative of Melissus' naval exploits do not aid our interpretation of Eleatic metaphysics, and the politics of South Italy have little relevance to Pythagorean philosophizing. I am sceptical, too, of claims to detect intellectual influences among the Presocratics. The little tufts of evidence which bear upon the chronology of those early publications are, as I observed in more than one connection, too few and too scanty to be woven into the sort of elegant tapestry which we customarily embroider in writing the histories of modern philosophy. Much of the historical detail with which scholarship likes to deck out its studies is either merely impertinent or grossly speculative.

My third remark concerns literature. Some of the Presocratics wrote poetry—or at any rate, they versified their thoughts; others were prose stylists. My analysis of the arguments of those thinkers ignored the literary form in which they wrote—indeed, I inclined to dismiss Heraclitus' prosings as so much flummery, and to regard Parmenides' clod-hopping hexameters as evincing a lamentable error of judgment. (Metaphysicians, as I think Carnap said, are musicians without musical ability.) I am not wholly repentant; for I remain to be convinced that art and thought—even in the case of Heraclitus—are inextricably intertwined. But I have certainly shown myself insensitive to some of the finer nuances of certain pieces of Presocratic exposition, and were I writing the book anew I should take a less nonchalant attitude to questions of style and form.

Finally, formalism. I made strenuous efforts to formalize many Presocratic arguments; and not infrequently the devices of modern logic were employed to symbolize their premisses and conclusions. Some readers find, as I myself do, that a judicious use of symbolism can illuminate the structure of an argument; but others are perplexed by the technicality or disgusted by the vulgarity of symbolical transcription, and I was perhaps foolish to provoke their displeasure. However that may be, I made a major blunder in failing to distinguish sharply between formalization and symbolization. By symbolization I mean the replacement of the signs of a natural language (i.e. of Greek or English words) by the symbols of an artificial language. Symbolization produces brevity (for the formulae of logic are as a rule shorter than their natural counterparts), and it has the advantage of rigour (for logical symbols are precisely defined); on the other hand, symbolization can be tedious (for more reasons than one) and it may give a wholly spurious impression of scientific exactitude. But whatever its merits and demerits, symbolization is perfectly dispensable so far as the interpretation of the Presocratics is concerned. Formalization is another matter. Most philosophers set out their arguments informally: formalization consists, first, in distinguishing the different components of an argument—premisses, intermediate steps, conclusions—, and secondly, in articulating the relevant internal structure of those components and exposing the logical features on which the inference depends. (The numbering and indenting of sentences are typographical devices for facilitating the first task; and the second task often requires a pedantic attention to detail and a certain artificiality of style—babu English has its uses.) Formalization does not require symbols: Sextus Empiricus, for example, usually sets out his arguments with an admirable formality; yet he never uses artificial symbols. And formalization, unlike symbolization, seems to me absolutely indispensable for the interpretation and assessment of informal arguments of any complexity: God, no doubt, can immediately perceive the form of an argument through the veil of informal discourse; mortals generally cannot. Most philosophers' arguments are bad arguments; and their informal dress disguises their defects: formalization reveals those faults and flaws—and thereby indicates what, if anything, can be done to repair them.

I turn now to some points of detail.

On p. 57 I advert to the fact that certain Stoics and Christians interested themselves in the thought of Heraclitus. I should also have mentioned the Pyrrhonist Aenesidemus. The precise connection between Aenesidemus and the philosophy of Heraclitus is puzzling and contentious (see, most recently, U. Burkhard, *Die angebliche Heraklit-Nachfolge des skeptikers Aenesidem* (Bonn, 1973)); but it is plain that Aenesidemus devoted some time to the study of Heraclitus. Some of our later sources—notably Sextus—depend upon Aenesidemus, and they no doubt reproduce any distortions which he may have inflicted on Heraclitus' thought.

P. 138: Note that Xenophanes also appears in the Pyrrhonist pedigree at DL, IX.71–3—and earlier in the pedigree claimed by the Sceptical Academy: see Cicero, *Lucullus* v 14. Heraclitus too (see p. 144) figures in both the Academic and the Pyrrhonian line (Plutarch, *adv Col* 1122A; DL, IX.71–3). But it should be said that a glance at some of the other names in those lists—Homer, Archilochus, Euripides—shows that they cannot be taken as sober historical documents.

On p. 145 (cf. p. 297, p. 609 n. 16) I interpret Heraclitus **136** = **B 101** = **15 M** as saying: 'I searched by myself', 'I was an independent inquirer, an autodidact.' That seemed to be how Diogenes' source understood the phrase *edizêsamên emeôuton* ('he studied under no one but searched, as he says, for himself, and he learned everything from himself': IX.5—the text is uncertain but the sense is clear); several ancient authorities, presumably relying on **136**, assert that Heraclitus was self-taught; and a majority of modern scholars have read **136** in this way (see Marcovich [129], 57–8). But that is surely quite mistaken: *edizêsamên emeôuton* cannot mean 'I searched *by* myself', but only 'I searched *for* myself', 'I inquired *into* myself'—Heraclitus is confessing to bouts of introspection, not boasting of periods of solitary study. None of the passages which Marcovich cites as parallel to the former interpretation is comparable; and I find no text in which *dizêmai* + accusative means anything other than 'inquire into'. There is good circumstantial evidence for believing that Heraclitus was, intellectually speaking, a lone wolf—or at least, that he claimed to be; and there is no need to see the influence of **136** behind the ancient reports of his sturdy independence of mind. As for Diogenes' source, he probably got matters right; for the train of thought at DL, IX.5 is this: 'Heraclitus did not adopt views from any teacher; his preferred method of study was introspection, so that all his views came from himself.'

On p. 172 I implicitly ascribe to John Locke the splendid portmanteau word 'alchimerical'; and it is in fact found in the Everyman edition of Locke's *Essay* in the heading to IV v 7. But according to Nidditch's critical edition of the work, Locke wrote 'all . . . chimerical' (there are no variant readings), and I suppose that 'alchimerical' is an invention of the Everyman editor or printer.

On p. 173, and again on pp. 182 and 471, I quote Gorgias' *Concerning What is Not* from the version preserved by Sextus. It is true, as I say on p. 173, that the rival text in the pseudo-Aristotelian *MXG* is 'wretchedly corrupt', so that, in a sense, Sextus' presentation of the argument is superior. But it now seems patently obvious to me that Sextus is not quoting—or pretending to quote—Gorgias' very words: the structure of the arguments, the syntax, and the vocabulary are all thoroughly Sextan. Sextus may preserve the gist of Gorgias' argument (the matter requires further detailed investigation); but he certainly does not reproduce Gorgias' little treatise—and I do not now understand how I (or anyone else) can have thought that he does.

P. 181: Melissus' metaphysics starts from the proposition which I labelled (A): '*O* exists.' I treated the proposition as an axiom—whence the label—and I suggested, on the basis of a passage in the *MXG*, that Melissus did not try to argue for it (p. 184, p. 613 n. 12). But the *MXG* gives only the weakest support to the suggestion, and I now incline to take more seriously the remarks of Simplicius at *in Phys* 103.15–6: Melissus 'begins his treatise thus: "If it is nothing, what can be said about it as being something? . . ."' The long Melissan passage at *in Phys* 103.15–104.15 is certainly paraphrase rather than quotation; but much of the paraphrase can be tested against Melissus' own surviving words, and by that test it proves remarkably accurate. Thus it is permissible to infer that 103.15–6 represents, directly or indirectly, something genuinely Melissan; and in that case we should think that (A) is not an unargued axiom—rather, Melissus offered some sort of argument in favour of the proposition that *O* exists. (See further paragraph 3 of my 'Reply to Professor Mourelatos' in *Philosophical Books* 22, 1981, 78–9.)

On p. 253 I suggest that *metaxu tôn ontôn* in Zeno's *logos* of 'finite and infinite' may mean not 'between (any two) existents' but rather 'in the middle of (each of) the existents'. The suggestion makes excellent philosophical sense, but I now fear that it may be linguistically impossible; at any rate, I have not been able to find any occurrence of *metaxu* + genitive with the sense of 'in the middle of'.

On p. 259 I associate Zeno's paradox of the millet seed with the Sorites puzzle later advanced by Eubulides. The association is, in fact, a commonplace of soritical scholarship; but it is also erroneous—for the millet seed and the Sorites, as Aristotle's ancient commentators knew, are distinct arguments and significantly different in logical form. (I owe this point to David Sedley; see now my 'Medicine,

Experience, Logic', in *Science and Speculation*, ed. J. Barnes, J. Brunschwig, M. F. Burnyeat, and M. Schofield (Cambridge, 1982).) Hence I withdraw what I say about the Sorites on p. 259 and stress the last sentence of p. 260.

On p. 294 I unaccountably forgot to mention the Pythagorean Hiketas: the hint on p. 28 that he may have been one of the first and few ancient thinkers to have grasped the moral of Zeno's Stadium should have been repeated in more glowing form on p. 294.

P. 322: The definitions of homoiomereity in effect turn '. . . is homoiomerous' into a predicate of *properties*; in fact, as the rest of the discussion makes plain, it is *things*—in particular, *stuffs*—to which the predicate is appropriately applied. Definitions (D1) and (D2) should be emended to avoid the mistake; fortunately, the error is self-contained, since those definitions have no important role in my interpretation of Anaxagoras' theory of stuffs.

My discussion of Philolaus in Chapter XVIII now strikes me as highly unsatisfactory, mainly for philological reasons. First of all, Carl Huffmann has persuaded me that I have most probably misread or misinterpreted the texts of Philolaus in certain important places (e.g. the orthodox supplement to sentence [vi] of **279** = **B 2**, which I accepted without question, may well be wrong; the participle *gnôsoumenon*, in **278** = **B 3**, which I construe with most scholars as passive, is most probably active). And in general, the interpretation of the fragments which Huffmann is in the process of producing seems to me superior to my own in many ways. But secondly, I am no longer convinced that the fragments I relied upon are genuine. I claimed to be following Burkert's masterly exposition; but in fact, as Beth Crabb pointed out to me, I reject the argument which Burkert regards as the strongest reason in favour of authenticity; for I do not believe, as Burkert does, that Aristotle's account of fifth-century Pythagoreanism is based upon Philolaus' work. More importantly, as I read the fragments again, I am more impressed than before by their similarities, in style and content, to the many Pythagorean forgeries which are collected in Thesleff [175]. At all events, until Burkert's work is supplemented by a thorough philological investigation of the language of the fragments, I shall remain sceptical—though reluctantly so—of their authenticity.

P. 451: Sextus ascribes the *Sisyphus* fragment to Critias; other sources attribute it (or rather, certain lines from it) to Euripides. Dihle [456 A] has recently argued for Euripidean authorship, and the case for Critias has been restated by Sutton [456 B]. I should have remarked that at lines 19–20 I read *phronôn te kai / prosechôn ta panta*, at 25 *theois enesti*, at 30 *ponêseis* (with the MSS), and at 40 *phobois*. In line 13, '[of the gods]' should be marked as a supplement.

Two small but pervasive points of style may be mentioned. First, the use of 'second', 'third', etc. as adverbs is a foible of the publishers not of the author. Secondly, the slapdash use of inverted commas to distinguish use from mention is due to the author not to the publishers. (I was once taught to believe that a phrase such as 'the term *logos*' was both misleading and incorrect, and that I should write 'the term "*logos*"'. In fact, 'the term *logos*' is perfectly correct (autonymy is a normal feature of English), and it will mislead no sane reader.)

Finally, several readers have justly complained that my discussion of Melissus' metaphysics is very hard to follow: it is difficult to remember, thirty pages on, what theorem (T6) of Melissan metaphysics was; and the exposition cannot be understood without exasperatingly frequent back references. I hope that the bookmark inserted in the present edition may remove that difficulty—and also the similar but minor difficulty in the case of Xenophanes' theology.

In preparing this revision I have incurred some new debts. Timothy Barnes kindly corrected a number of errors of fact in one of the Appendixes; Charles Kahn allowed me to see a draft of his long review of my book for the *Journal of Philosophy*; Alex Mourelatos generously permitted me to scan and to profit from the many *marginalia* in his copy of the first edition; Carl Huffmann and Beth Crabb spent some time in persuading me that I had got Philolaus all wrong; Larry Schrenk and Beth Crabb, despite heavy commitments, jointly undertook the unrewarding task of preparing new Indexes to the book.

The first edition of this book was begun and ended in one of the most pleasant parts of the Old World: it was my good fortune to be able to produce the second edition in one of the most pleasant parts of the New.

J.B.
Austin, Texas
April 1981

Note on Citations

Quotations of and allusions to ancient texts will often carry more than one reference; e.g. '**1**: Diogenes Laertius, I.24 = **11 A 1**'.

A bold arabic numeral accompanies the more important quotations, which are inset from the margin: that numeral documents the position of the text in this book. Thus the quotation labelled '**1**' is the first text of substance that I quote.

The source of every citation is specified: usually the author's name alone is supplied, and further information must be gleaned from Diels–Kranz; fuller details are given for more familiar authors (e.g., Plato and Aristotle), and also in cases where the citation is not printed in Diels–Kranz. Full citations follow the usual canons; and abbreviations of all book titles are explained in Appendix A. (But note here that 'fr.' abbreviates 'fragment'; that titles of the Greek commentaries on Aristotle are abbreviated by prefixing '*in*' to the abbreviated titles of Aristotle's works; that *SVF*, in citations of the Stoics, refers to H. von Arnim's *Stoicorum Veterum Fragmenta*; and that *FGrH*, in citations of certain historians, refers to F. Jacoby's *Fragmente der Griechischer Historiker*.) Thus 'Diogenes Laertius, I.24' refers to Chapter 24 of Book I of Diogenes' only work, the *Lives of the Philosophers*.

Almost all the texts I refer to are printed in the standard source book on early Greek philosophy, *Die Fragmente der Vorsokratiker* by Hermann Diels and Walther Kranz. References to Diels–Kranz, in bold type, cite chapter, section, and item (but the chapter number is omitted wherever it can be divined from the context of the citation). Thus '**11 A 1**' refers to the first item in section **A** of Chapter **11**, 'Thales'. Chapters in Diels–Kranz are usually divided into two sections: section **A** contains *testimonia*; section **B** contains fragments. Sometimes, where no fragments survive, **B** is missing; sometimes a third section, **C**, contains 'imitations'. In the case of Chapter **58**, 'The Pythagorean School', a different principle of division is adopted. Readers should be warned that the **B** sections contain many texts whose status as genuine Presocratic fragments is disputed. (Citations bearing on Heraclitus, Empedocles, Melissus and Zeno sometimes carry an additional bold figure reference: those references are explained in the notes to the chapters in which they are used.)

Finally, where a numeral in plain type is suffixed to a bold type reference, it serves to indicate the line (or occasionally section) of the text in question. Thus '**31 B 115**.9' refers to line 9 of **31 B 115**.

All that is, I fear, somewhat cumbersome; and it makes for unsightliness. But I can discover no more elegant method of citation which is not annoyingly inconvenient.

PROLOGUE

I

The Springs of Reason

(a) *The art of thinking*

Logic is a Greek discovery. The laws of thought were first observed in ancient Greece; and they were first articulated and codified in Aristotle's *Analytics*. Modern logicians surpass Aristotle in the scope of their enquiries and in the technical virtuosity of their style; but for elegance of conception and rigour of thought he is their peer, and in all things their intellectual father.

Aristotle was conscious of his own prowess: commendably immodest, he trumpeted his achievement and solicited the gratitude of posterity. Yet God, as John Locke caustically observed, 'has not been so sparing to Men to make them barely two-legged Creatures, and left it to *Aristotle* to make them Rational'. If Aristotle's predecessors did not study the art of ratiocination, they were expert in its practice; if they were not logicians, they were thinkers of depth and power. Nor indeed was anyone better aware of this than Aristotle himself: Aristotelian man is essentially a reasoner; and Aristotle's writings describe and praise the attainments of those men who first discovered and charted the broad oceans over which the stately galleon of his own philosophy was to sail.

Pre-eminent among those voyagers were Plato and Socrates; but they too had at their disposal a serviceable set of navigational aids. The aids were prepared by a motley band of doctors and poets, scientists and charlatans, on whom their customary title imposes a spurious community. They are the Presocratic philosophers; and their works are the subject of this book. The term 'Presocratic' is stretched a little: some of the thinkers I shall discuss were Socrates' contemporaries rather than his seniors. And the term 'philosopher' is elastic by its very nature: my Presocratics are men of widely differing interests and professions. The storms of time have not been kind to them: their ships are wrecked, a few shattered planks alone surviving. But our meagre evidence shows something of the men: it reveals (to change the metaphor) that they sought out and drank from the springs of reason; and if that original and heady potation at times induced a trembling delirium in their brains, we still owe them an immeasurable debt for their precocious intoxication. Their tipsy gait taught us to walk more steadily; had they not drunk, we should only shamble.

The Presocratic philosophers had one common characteristic of supreme importance: they were rational. And it is their rationality which this book aspires to exhibit and to celebrate. But Presocratic rationality is often misunderstood, and sometimes mistakenly denied. Let me briefly elucidate my assertion that the Presocratics were rational men.

First, that assertion does not imply that the Greeks, as a race, were peculiarly devoted to reason or peculiarly devoid of superstition. Modern scholarship has abundantly illustrated how folly, unreason, and the bonds of superstition were as oppressive in classical Greece as in any other age or land. The average Greek was doubtless as silly as the average Englishman; and the educated men of the sixth and fifth centuries BC were as barbarous and as bigoted as the educated men of today. The Presocratic philosophers were not typical of their fellows: they rose above the vulgar.

Again, it is a simple mistake to think that rationality is the hallmark or the prerogative of the natural sciences. The Presocratics were indeed the first empirical scientists; and in the history books it is the scientific endeavours of the early thinkers which hold pride of place. But reason is omnivorous; it does not pasture exclusively in scientific fields; and the Presocratics did not confine their reasoning powers to a monotonously scientific diet. It is the non-scientific aspects of Presocratic thought with which I am primarily concerned: I shall discuss their metaphysics, not their meteorology.

Third, it is not to be supposed that rational men must resolutely reject the supernatural. Scholars often, and rightly, contrast the naturalistic cosmogonies of the Milesian philosophers with such mythological stories as we find in Hesiod's *Theogony*. Yet the essence of the contrast is sometimes misrepresented: what is significant is not that theology yielded to science or gods to natural forces, but rather that unargued fables were replaced by argued theory, that dogma gave way to reason. Theology and the supernatural may be treated dogmatically or rationally: if the Presocratics reject the blank assertions of piety and poetry, that rejection by no means entails the repudiation of all things divine and superhuman.

Fourth, rational men are not obliged to dream up their ideas for themselves, aloof, autonomous and impervious to influence, classical scholars have, with limited success, investigated the origins and antecedents of Presocratic opinions. Many scholars, having located, or conjectured, the source of an opinion, go on to infer that any argument offered for that opinion is mere rationalization: borrowed beliefs, they suppose, are necessarily unreasoned. The absurdity of that inference is patent: evidently, we may purchase opinions from other men and then advance them for our own. The Presocratics, like all rational men, bought many of their opinions off the peg.

Finally, what is rational is not always right; reasoned beliefs are often false; and reasoning—even good and admirable reasoning—is not invariably clear and cogent. Few Presocratic opinions are true; fewer still are well grounded. For all that, they are, in a mild but significant sense, rational: they are characteristically supported by argument, buttressed by reasons, established upon evidence.

Thus in saying that the Presocratics were rational men I mean no more than this: that the broad and bold theories which they advanced were presented not as *ex cathedra* pronouncements for the faithful to believe and the godless to ignore, but as the conclusions of arguments, as reasoned propositions for reasonable men to contemplate and debate. And in holding that the Presocratics were the fathers of rational thought I hold only that they were the first men self-consciously to subordinate assertion to argument and dogma to logic. Some readers may wonder if such a weak form of rationality is not too common a property to merit admiration: to them I commend the aphorism of Bishop Berkeley: All men have opinions, but few men think.

(b) *Thales on magnets and water*

The originator of natural philosophy, according to Aristotle, was Thales the Milesian (*Met* 983b20 = **11 A 12**). Thales' name is connected with the solar eclipse of 585 BC; he and his native town of Miletus flourished at the beginning of the sixth century. The two theses on which Thales' reputation must rest are not, at first blush, remarkable for their sobriety: 'the magnet has a soul'; 'everything is water'. Yet the first judgment, I shall argue, betrays a keen philosophical eye; the second marks the beginnings of Western science; and both are supported by simple but rational considerations.

I start with the magnet:

> Aristotle and Hippias say that [Thales] gave inanimate things (*ta apsucha*) too a share in soul (*psuchê*), taking his evidence from the magnetic stone and from amber (**1**: Diogenes Laertius, I.24 = **A 1**; cf. Scholiast to Plato, **A 3**).

Aristotle's words have survived:

> It seems, from what they report, that Thales too supposed the *psuchê* to be a sort of motor, given that he said that the magnet has a *psuchê* because it moves iron (**2**: *An* 405a19–21 = **A 22**).

Aristotle does not name his reporter, but it is a plausible conjecture that he alludes to Hippias of Elis, the second authority named by Diogenes. Hippias, a fifth-century Sophist of some distinction, is sometimes hailed as the inventor of the history of ideas; but according to his own account he compiled not a history but a chrestomathy, a collection of wise or ingenious saws, culled from a variety of sources, and woven into 'a new and manifold argument' (**86 B 6**).[1] Thales' magnets and amber evidently caught Hippias' jackdaw eye; but where they lay during the century and a half from Thales to Hippias, we cannot tell.

The argument which Hippias preserved has a pleasing simplicity. Thales adduced two premisses:

(1) If anything has a motor, it has a *psuchê*;

(2) Magnets and pieces of amber have motors;

and he inferred that:

(3) Magnets and pieces of amber have a *psuchê*.

The sceptical will point out that only the conclusion, (3), is unequivocally ascribed to Thales in our sources: premiss (1) is introduced by Aristotle with a cautionary 'it seems', and premiss (2) with the conjunction 'given that'. Perhaps the whole argument was constructed by Aristotle, or by Hippias, and falsely fathered upon Thales?

That melancholy supposition cannot, I think, be disproved; yet I do not find it plausible. Aristotle's 'given that (*eiper*)' most probably means 'since', and thus definitely attributes (2) to Thales; and in any case we can hardly fail to think that Thales rested his paradoxical view upon (2) or some equivalent premiss. And if we give (2) to Thales, it is clear that we may give him (1) to complete the deduction.

What is the sense, and what the cogency, of Thales' argument? The word *psuchê* is commonly translated by 'soul'; and in most contexts this translation is reasonable enough. Here, however, the standard translation masks the charm of the argument, and a heterodox rendering has some justification.

To have a *psuchê* is to be *empsuchos*. *Empsuchos* means 'animate' or 'living': *ta empsucha* and *ta apsucha* jointly exhaust the natural world, being the animate and the inanimate portions of creation. The *psuchê*, then, as Aristotle says, is simply 'that by which we are alive' (*An* 414a12): it is the source or principle of life in animate beings, that part or feature of them (whatever it may be) in virtue of which they are alive.[2] In short, an *empsuchon* is an animate thing; and its *psuchê* is its animator. Instead of 'soul', then, I propose the term 'animator' as a translation of *psuchê*; and I prefer the comic overtones of 'animator' to the theological undertones of 'soul'.

What are the criteria for life? According to Aristotle, 'things are said to be alive on several accounts, and if just one of these belongs to a thing we say that it is alive—viz. understanding, perception, change and rest in place, and again the change brought on by nourishment, and decay and growth' (*An* 413a22–5). More generally, 'the animate seems to differ from the inanimate by two things in particular, motion and perception' (*An* 403b25–7). Aristotle is not putting forward a philosophical thesis here: he is recording, and accepting, a commonplace. Anything that has powers of cognition, of which perception is the most common and the most evident example, is alive; and anything which has the power to alter itself or its environment, of which autonomous locomotion is the most evident example, is likewise alive. If the great marks of animation are the power to perceive and the capacity to locomote or to cause locomotion, then a *psuchê* or animator will be essentially a source of perception, or a perceptor, and a source of motion, or a motor.

Thales' argument now has a superficial plausibility. His first premiss is a platitude: motors—that is to say, self-starting motors—are, on Aristotle's own account, and in ordinary thought, animators or *psuchai*; and anything capable of autonomous locomotion is thereby shown to be animate. His second premiss is a matter of ordinary observation: magnets and pieces of amber are seen to possess the power to cause locomotion in other things and to move themselves. And the conclusion follows: magnets and pieces of amber are animate beings; they may not have the faculty of perception, but for all that they are alive.

Thales' successors ignored his argument. Later scientists felt the force of magnetic attraction, and offered crude mechanistic hypotheses to explain it; but they did not, so far as we know, stop to ponder Thales' curious conclusion.[3] Even Aristotle, who was aware of Thales' argument and who must have seen its power, says nothing directly against it; yet Aristotle hardly believed that magnets were alive.

Aristotle's psychology does, however, contain an implicit answer to Thales; and a short sketch of that answer may bring out the philosophical interest of the magnet.

The magnet, Aristotle would have said, does not initiate locomotion after the fashion of genuinely animate beings. Animate motion is necessarily caused by a 'desire', or *orexis*, on the part of the mover; it is, in a later jargon, preceded by a 'volition' or act of will. But magnets do not have desires or perform acts of will. Thus magnets may move, but they do not move in the manner of living things. To this, Thales has a retort: perhaps magnets do have primitive desires; perhaps their passion for knives and needles, and their indifference to silver churns, evinces a discrimination and a will? And if Aristotle adds that desire implies perception and judgment, Thales will simply say that the discriminatory capacities which magnets, like computers or potato-sorting machines, exhibit are primitive perceptions—and he will have some modern psychologists on his side.

Aristotle distinguishes between 'rational' and 'irrational' powers: if *a* has a rational power to ϕ, then *a* can both ϕ and refrain from ϕing; if *a*'s power to ϕ is irrational, then *a* can ϕ but cannot refrain from ϕing. Animate movers have rational powers: they can withstand temptation, or be bloody-minded. But the magnet is weak-willed and intemperate; if a piece of iron is placed at a suitable distance from it, locomotion commences, and the magnet has no choice in the matter. Magnets are not free: that is why they are not alive.

I do not offer this as the correct rebuttal of Thales' argument; evidently the debate can continue. But enough has, I hope, been done to indicate that Thales' argument is not a naive aberration or a puerile sophism; it raises puzzles of a distinctively philosophical nature. Thales' magnet is the ancient equivalent of the clockwork animals of the eighteenth century and of our modern chess-playing computers: we know that mechanical toys are not alive; and we suspect that the most ingenious computer lacks something that every rabbit possesses. Yet if we attempt to justify those convictions or suspicions, we soon find ourselves lost in the thickets of the philosophy of mind. Vaucanson and Turing are justly celebrated for the challenge they made to lovers of the mind: Thales, I claim, deserves a small bow of recognition.

According to Hippias, Thales did not rest content with (3): he said, more generally, that inanimate things have *psuchai*. It is reasonable to associate this conclusion with the apophthegm 'everything is full of spirits' which, in various forms, is ascribed to Thales (Aristotle, *An*

411a7 = **A 22**; Aëtius, **A 23**; etc.: the same authorities present Thales with the view that the world as a whole has a soul, and Aristotle conjectures that this may have been the source of the apophthegm; but the opposite derivation is more probable). The purport of this generalization of (3) is uncertain: did Thales merely remark that (3) should prepare us for further surprises, that the world is not divided into animate and inanimate as easily as we might think? Should we rather press upon him the assertion that everything is animate, that the common distinction between animate and inanimate objects is illusory? And if we do press this upon him, are we to dismiss it as irresponsible enthusiasm? Or can we ascribe to him the philosophical reflexion that if the common criteria for distinguishing the living from the non-living yield results like (3), then those criteria must be vain creations of the human mind, marking no difference in external reality?

Such questions have no answers: even to pose them may be deemed a sign of speculative lunacy; and I turn hastily to Thales' second and more notorious contribution to rational thought:

> Thales . . . says that [the material principle] is water, and that is why he asserted that the earth rests on water (**3**: Aristotle, *Met* 983b20–2 = **A 12**).

Thus we have two aqueous asseverations:
(4) The material principle of everything is water.
(5) The earth rests on water.
I shall first consider (5).[4] Two chapters of Aristotle's *de Caelo* deal with the position and shape of the earth; and in his historical survey Aristotle adverts again to Thales:

> Some say that [the earth] rests on water. For this is the oldest theory that has been handed down to us, and they say that Thales of Miletus propounded it, supposing that it remains there because it can float, like wood or something else of that sort (**4**: 294a28–31 = **A 14**: again Hippias is probably Aristotle's source).

Here (5) is presented independently of (4) and with an argument of its own.

Some scholars discern a spark of genius in the argument: Thales' quick spirit tackled the grand and remote question of the earth's support by a homely analogy with floating logs; as Newton sat beneath his apple-tree and invented gravity, so Thales sat on a river-bank dreaming of astronomy. Yet Thales' spark is dim: had he amused himself by throwing stones into his river, he might have inferred that whatever the earth floats upon it is not water. The analogy will not do.[5] In any case, Thales' answer recalls Locke's Indian philosopher, who held that the earth rests on the back of an elephant, the elephant on a tortoise, and the tortoise on 'something, he knew not what'. Aristotle puts the point briskly: 'as if the same argument did not apply to the earth and to the water supporting the earth' (*Cael* 294a32–3 = **A 14**). And that, I think, disposes of Thales' claim to genius here.

For all that, Thales' argument has an extrinsic importance. First, its analogy provides the first example of a marked characteristic of Presocratic thought: from Thales onward, analogical illustration and argument are frequent; the analogies are often drawn from humble and unscientific areas, and they are sometimes spun out with some ingenuity. I shall discuss this at more length in a later context (below, pp. 52–6).

Second, Thales offered the first non-mythological answer to a standing problem in Greek science. Aristotle explains the problem with unusual lucidity: 'It would take, I suppose, a somewhat dull mind not to wonder how in the world it can be that a small piece of earth, if released in mid-space (*meteôristhen*), moves and will not stay where it is (and the bigger it is, the faster it moves), while if you were to put the whole earth in mid-space and release it, it would not move; in fact, heavy as it is, it is stable. And yet if you took a moving piece of earth and took the ground from under it before it fell, it would move on and downwards as long as nothing obstructed it. Hence puzzling about this naturally became a philosophical problem for everyone' (*Cael* 294a12–20). Two apparently obvious truths generate the puzzle: first, the earth is clearly at rest; second, the earth is clearly in mid-space. The conjunction of the two is paradoxical, given the observed behaviour of portions of earth.

Thales answered the paradox by denying that the earth is in mid-space; his successors, noticing the infelicity of his proposal, attempted other solutions. Their attempts are sophisticated and of some interest; and they too will be discussed at some length (below, pp. 23–8).

Thales' other watery thesis, (4), poses intricate problems of interpretation. Scholars agree that he cannot have stated (4) as it stands; for it uses the terminology of a later age. Yet (4) encourages the ascription to Thales of some such sentiment as:

(6) Everything is from water (*panta ex hudatos estin*).

It is easy to imagine that Aristotle rendered (6) by (4); and parallels to (6) can be found in the earliest remnants of Presocratic thought.

Was Aristotle's interpretation of (6) correct, and was Thales a 'material monist'? If Aristotle is wrong, what can Thales mean by (6)? I shall return to these questions later. Here, leaving the sense of (6) partly indeterminate, I ask why Thales assented to such a strange hypothesis, and why he should have subscribed to:

(7) There is some single stuff from which everything is,

which is immediately entailed by (6).

Our texts provide no answer to these questions; but it is not hard to excogitate one. (7) offers what is, in a very obvious sense, the simplest hypothesis that will account for the constitution of the world: unity is simpler than plurality; a postulated unity is more fundamental than a plurality. Science always strives for economy and simplicity in explanation; and in adopting (7) Thales was only proving himself an embryonic scientist; he saw that (7) was eminently simple and because of its simplicity he adopted it as a hypothesis.

Given that Thales subscribed to (7), why did he pick on water as his basic stuff, and plump for (6)? Aristotle and Theophrastus supply a set of arguments, which amount to the claim that water is essential in various ways to the existence of living creatures (*Met* 983b22–7 = **A 12**; Simplicius, **A 13**; cf. Aëtius, I.3.1). Now Aristotle's remarks are explicitly conjectural; and Theophrastus joins Thales with Hippo of Rhegium, a fifth-century thinker of little note who later adopted (4) as his own (cf. Hippolytus, **38 A 3**; Alexander, **A 6**; Philoponus, **A 10**): most scholars suppose that the arguments were propounded in a work of Hippo's and projected back onto Thales by the Peripatetics. They may be right: other arguments can be invented (it is usually observed that water, alone of the common constituents of the world, is regularly found in gaseous, solid and liquid states); or we may prefer to suppose that Thales adopted water as a whimsy.[6] But Hippo's reasons are not recondite; nor are they wholly unintelligible reasons, given Thales' psychological views: living creatures are far more prevalent than we ordinarily think; water is evidently necessary for their existence; water is not readily generated from any other stuff; hence water must be a basic constituent of the world. And since, by (7), there is at most one basic constituent of the world, thesis (6) comes tottering in as a conclusion. It does not take a giant intellect to knock holes in that reasoning; but at least there is a piece of reasoning, and not a mere prejudice, to attack.

The two theories which I have just examined show that Thales was no mean thinker. He offers reasoned views on abstract and philosophical subjects, and he merits his traditional place of honour at the head of Western science and philosophy: he was 'the originator of this sort of Philosophy' (Aristotle, *Met* 983b20 =**A 12**; cf. *Cael* 294a29 = **A 14**). *Vixerunt alii ante Agamemnona*:

Theophrastus cautiously supposed that Thales had predecessors whom his own genius eclipsed and hid from the eyes of history (Simplicius, **B 1**). Certainly, Thales was not the first man to think about cosmogony; but what little we know of his predecessors does not contain much that is rational or philosophical in spirit. There is myth, and there is genealogical theogony. Apart from that, a few tantalizingly abstract phrases from the seventh-century Spartan poet Alcman peep coquettishly through the veil of time, exciting the imagination without satisfying the desire.[7] And there is the bizarre figure of Pherecydes of Syros: Aristotle called him a 'mixed' theologian (*Met* 1091b8 = 7 **A** 7), whose work was only partly mythological; and his cosmogony, of which we have substantial fragments, seems in some respects to mediate between Hesiodic myth and Ionian science. But Pherecydes was almost certainly a generation younger than Thales; and in any case his fragments contain nothing of philosophical interest: he is at best a 'literary curiosity'.[8]

In his cosmic speculation, then, Thales had a few uninteresting predecessors. In psychology no one, so far as we know, had preceded him.

It would, of course, be a mistake to infer that Thales was a lonely revolutionary, indulging in abstract ratiocinations remote from the practical concerns of the world. On the contrary, tradition represents him as one of the Seven Sages: early stories depict him as an engineering consultant to the Lydian army (Herodotus, I.170 = **A 6**) and as a national statesman urging Pan-Ionian federation against the Persians (Herodotus, I.75 = **A** 4); and the early record was embellished by a host of later and less trustworthy raconteurs. Most famously, Thales is said to have predicted an eclipse of the sun, which interrupted a battle between the Lydians and the Persians. The story is told by Herodotus (I.74 = **A 5**), but it was known earlier to Xenophanes (**21 B 19**) and to Heraclitus (**22 B 38**). What lies behind the story is uncertain: Thales' prediction cannot have been based on any abstract astronomical theory, and it will not have pretended to any degree of accuracy; probably he had picked up some lore from the East.[9] However that may be, he surely showed some interest in matters astronomical; and Eudemus of Rhodes, who was set to write the Peripatetic history of the exact sciences, duly made him the first astronomer (fr. 144W = Diogenes Laertius, I.23 = **A 1**). Thales also stood at the head of Eudemus' history of geometry, where he was credited with the proof of several abstract theorems.[10] It is no part of my brief to list or assess those ascriptions; and the heated controversy they have aroused will deter all but the most reckless from advancing an amateur opinion. One report, however, will usefully serve to introduce the subject of my next section.

(c) *Tradition and interpretation*

Thales is said to have discovered the theorem which appears as I.26 in Euclid's *Elements*: Triangles *ABC*, *abc* are identical if *AB* = *ab*, angle *A* = angle *a*, and angle *B* = angle *b*.

> Eudemus in his *History of Geometry* ascribes this theorem to Thales; for he says that it was necessary for him to apply it in the method by which they say he proved the distance of ships at sea (**5**: Proclus, **A 20**).[11]

Evidently Eudemus did not find a statement, let alone a proof, of Euclid I.26 in any work of Thales; rather, he found ascribed to Thales a method of calculating the distance of ships from the land; he judged that the method required the application of I.26; he assumed that Thales did apply I.26; and he inferred that Thales had discovered, or even that he had proved, I.26. The weakness of Eudemus' inference is plain enough; and if Thales' geometrical reputation rests wholly on such Peripatetic speculations, we shall be wary of thinking him a geometer at all: birds are not aeronautical engineers.

Eudemus was working in the dark. Aristotle, who relied on the reports of Hippias, had come across no writings of Thales' own (or at any rate none bearing on the subjects which interested him); and it is improbable that Eudemus was any more fortunate than Aristotle.[12] Indeed, there was considerable uncertainty in antiquity over Thales' writings, and a strong tradition supposed that he had written nothing at all (Diogenes Laertius, I.23 = **A 1**).

Such reflections are dispiriting enough in themselves; generalized, they induce a grisly scepticism about our acquaintance with Presocratic thought as a whole. No piece of Presocratic philosophy has survived in its entirety;[13] in most cases we have only a few *disjecta membra*; and those fragments—sentences, mangled phrases, or single words—are as often as not known to us only from the quotations of late sources, who cite them to display their learning or to make a polemical point. We rely, then, on the 'doxography'—on reports, by later authors, of the opinions and arguments of their remote predecessors. For Thales we have no fragments at all; for many later thinkers we are little better off; and even where we possess a page or two of the original, the doxography remains important, both as a source of doctrine not presented in the fragments, and as a means of setting those jewels in a suitable foil.

Then how reliable is the doxography? It is a vast and variegated thing: it stretches in time from the fifth century BC to the fourteenth century AD, and most of the surviving authors of antiquity contribute to it. This tumultuous and many-channelled stream welled in the Lyceum, whence most of its waters derive. The chief source, it seems, was Theophrastus' large study *On the Opinions of the Physicists*; but only a few fragments of that work survive,[14] and we must usually drink from the lower reaches of the stream where the waters are stale and muddy. Moreover, the stream is contaminated. First, many of the later doxographers were not scholars but silly hacks who, by accident or design, regularly mutilated or distorted the Theophrastan material; and in any case they had at their disposal not Theophrastus' original work but some poor epitome and refashioning of it. Second, Theophrastus himself was not a historical purist: imitating his master, Aristotle, whose treatises are regularly prefaced by schematic doxographies, he presents earlier theories in terms of his own philosophy and earlier theorists as lisping Peripatetics.[15] In short, the doxography flows from tainted sources through tainting channels: if it happens to preserve a little pure water, that is a lucky chance.

The doxography is unreliable. Our knowledge of the Presocratics must rest upon their *ipsissima verba*. Few *verba* survive. Hence our knowledge of the Presocratics is exiguous.

I believe that our knowledge of early Greek thought is indeed exiguous: despite the labours of scholarship and imagination, we possess little firm evidence; and it was all so unimaginably different, and so very long ago. Yet we need not plunge to the very depths of sceptical despair: ignorant of most, we know a little. First, Thales is not a typical figure: for most of the major figures in Presocratic thought we do still possess a modest collection of genuine fragments; and it is often plausible to believe that those fragments preserve the most important and most interesting of their philosophical doctrines. Obscurities and uncertainties abound; the fragments hide as much as they reveal; and the doxography is almost always indispensable. For all that (as readers of this book will discover) the fragments form an archipelago of islets in the dark ocean of our ignorance.

Second, the doxography is not utterly despicable. Acute philological scholarship has established the complicated interrelationships of our surviving sources;[16] and we can often reconstruct with some probability the views, if not the words, of Theophrastus himself: science can filter out the impurities which the doxographical stream picked up in the course of its long passage. Nor am I convinced that the Peripatetics were poor, let alone dishonest, historians. They wrote, as we all do, in their own jargon and for their own ends; and they were sometimes slapdash and sometimes inconsistent. But inconsistency is always detectable, and often corrigible; and there is little evidence of widespread carelessness. Thales, indeed, supplies us with a fine example of Peripatetic scholarship: Aristotle himself makes it plain that he is working from second-hand reports, and not from original documents; he indicates, more than once, that his opinions are speculative; and he states with candour that the line of reasoning he ascribes to Thales is conjectural. Moreover, the Aristotelian terminology of his reconstruction will mislead only the most myopic scholar: the Peripatetics do not pretend, and we do not believe, that Thales himself used the phrase 'material principle'; rather, they pretend to express Thales' old thesis in their new terminology.

'But surely,' some will complain, 'such rephrasing of an argument is in itself an unhistorical anachronism; and it is quite enough to condemn an interpretation.' If that complaint is correct, then all attempts to understand the Presocratics are doomed to failure; for understanding requires rephrasing or translation. But the complaint is foolish. Consider, as an elementary example, the connexion between my sentences numbered (1)–(3) above, and Thales' ancient words. It is my contention that sentences (1)–(3) express exactly the same argument that Thales once expressed. The differences between my argument and that of Thales are formal, not substantial; in particular, they reside in three notational devices which I use and Thales did not. First, (1)–(3) set the argument out in deductive form, whereas Thales presented it informally. That device is at worst a harmless pedantry; at best it adds clarity to the articulation of the argument. Second, my argument is mildly formalized: its component propositions are numbered (later arguments will wear the slightly more daring finery of logical symbols). This device, again, is purely clarificatory. Third, (1)–(3) are written in English, not Greek: that device is by far the most dangerous of the three: yet few, I suspect, will insist on keeping the Presocratics concealed in their original tongue.

The Peripatetic approach to the Presocratics is not, in theory, any more reprehensible than the approach adopted in (1)–(3) and common to most modern interpreters of ancient thought. If we are to do more than parrot the fragmentary utterances of the past, we must translate them into a modern idiom. The attempt at translation may, of course, cause disfigurement; but that is a weakness in the translator—translation itself is both intrinsically harmless and philosophically indispensable.

Yet if I defend the doxography against the wilder charges levelled at it, I do not wish to encourage sanguinity. We know remarkably little about the Presocratics. Their texts are frequently obscure in content; and they are usually pigmy in extent. A historian of philosophy who has studied the seventeenth century has difficulties enough; but he possesses a vast mass of moderately intelligible material, and we need not despair of constructing a detailed and well-rounded account of the thought of that period. With the Presocratics nothing like that is true. There are bright patches of detail, and a few dim suggestions of a more general pattern of development; more than that we can never expect. And I cannot refrain from adding the essentially frivolous comment that such a state of affairs is not wholly depressing: in a sea of ignorance the pursuit of truth is more exacting; and darkness adds excitement to the chase.

Enough of such generalities. Later chapters will have occasion to discuss particular instances of doxographical malpractice, and to raise more detailed problems of anachronism in interpretation. The aim of the preceding paragraphs has been to advocate a moderately cheerful scepticism. Our evidence for Presocratic thought is slight and fragmentary; but it is not wholly unreliable. We possess some titbits of knowledge: whether or not they constitute a nourishing and a savoury philosophical meal, the reader's palate must decide; he has, in the theses of Thales, a sort of *hors d'oeuvre*: I hope that his appetite is whetted for the dishes that follow.

EDEN

II

Anaximander on Nature

(a) *Pantological knowledge*

Anaximander was a younger contemporary and a fellow-citizen of Thales; we need not accept the conventional statement that they were teacher and pupil, in order to believe that the younger man knew and was stimulated by his senior's excogitations. Anaximander became 'the first Greek whom we know to have produced a written account *Concerning Nature*' (Themistius, **12 A 7**).[1]

Of that work barely a dozen words have survived; but the doxography enables us to judge its scope and pretensions. It was vast: there was a cosmogony, or account of the original formation of the universe; a history of the earth and the heavenly bodies; an account of the development of living organisms; descriptions of natural phenomena of every sort, and infant studies of astronomy, meteorology and biology; and a geography illustrated by a celebrated *mappa mundi*. Nature, *phusis*, embraces every object of experience and every subject of rational inquiry except the productions of human contrivance; and the Presocratic systems of thought were generally spoken of as accounts *Concerning Nature* (*Peri Phuseôs*). An account concerning nature would begin with cosmogony, and proceed to a description of the celestial universe. It would investigate the development of the earth, of terrestrial life, and of the human animal; it would describe the clouds, the rains, and the winds, the rocky structure of the land, and the salt sea. It would rise from the inorganic to the organic, treating of topics botanical and zoological; it would look at the typology of species and the anatomy of individuals. It would turn to the mind, and study the psychology of sensation and action; and it would ask about the extent and the nature of human knowledge, and about the proper place of man in the natural world. An account *Peri Phuseôs* would, in brief, encompass all science and all philosophy.

Thales, we may imagine, first indicated that vast field of intellectual endeavour. Anaximander was the first to map it out; and his chart, with a few additions and modifications, determined the range and aspirations of almost all subsequent thought. Anaximenes, Xenophanes, and even Heraclitus; Empedocles and Anaxagoras and the Atomists: all worked and wrote in the grand tradition of Anaximander: other men are specialists, their specialism was omniscience.[2]

Even through the thick fog of time which separates us from Anaximander, we can perceive the flashings of 'an intellect of truly amazing grasp and audacity'. The range of his mind was matched by a powerful reasoning capacity and an ingenious imagination. His astronomical system illustrates his intellectual virtuosity: the earth is at the still centre of the turning cosmos; about it lie concentric wheel-rims, one for the stars, one for the moon, one for the sun; the wheel-rims are hollow and filled with fire; and heavenly bodies are holes in those rims, through which shines the enclosed fire (Aëtius, **A 21–2**). Applications of this theory accounted for the various celestial happenings, and it was worked out with a dedicated mixture of mathematics, insight and fantasy.[3]

In this chapter I shall discuss first, Anaximander's 'Darwinism'; second, his account of the stability of the earth; and third, that small fragment of his work which contains the earliest extant words of Western Philosophy. My treatment will not exhibit Anaximander as a systematic thinker; but it will, I hope, show the characteristic virtues and vices of his temperament.

(b) *The origin of species*

> And again, [Anaximander] says that in the beginning men were born from creatures of a different sort, because the other animals quickly manage to feed themselves, but man alone requires a long period of nursing; hence had he been like that in the beginning too, he would never have survived (**6**: pseudo-Plutarch, **A 10**).

Other reports, which do not agree in detail, make men's first parents fish or fish-like creatures who retained their human offspring in their bellies until they were able to fend for themselves (Hippolytus, **A 11**; Plutarch, Censorinus, **A 30**). A further notice indicates that Anaximander's speculations were not confined to his own species:

> Anaximander says that the first animals were born in the moisture, surrounded by prickly barks; and that as they reached maturity they moved out on to the drier parts where their bark split and they survived in a different form (*metabiônai*) for a brief while (**7**: Aëtius, **A 30**).[4]

Thus a theory of human phylogeny was embedded in a broader account of the origins of animal life.

The theory that life began in the wet parts of the earth was accepted by many of Anaximander's successors.[5] It is tempting to connect it with another hypothesis:

> At first, they say, the whole area around the earth was moist, and as it was dried by the sun the part which vaporized made the winds and the turnings of the sun and the moon, while what was left is the sea; that is why they think that the sea is becoming smaller as it dries out, and that in the end it will at some time all be dry (**8**: Aristotle, *Meteqr* 353b6–11 = **A 27**).

Theophrastus ascribes the hypothesis to Anaximander (Alexander, **A 27**). The doxography gives no further details, but a remarkable set of observations ascribed to Xenophanes of Colophon, whose life span overlapped with that of Anaximander, gives grounds for conjecture:

> Xenophanes thinks that a mixing of the earth with the sea is occurring, and that in time it is being dissolved by the moist. He says he has the following proofs: shells are found in the middle of the land and in the mountains, and he says that in Syracuse in the stone quarries there have been found impressions of fish and of seals [?], and on Paros an impression of laurel in the depth of the rock, and in Malta prints of all sea creatures. And he says that this happened some time ago when everything was covered in mud, and that the impression dried in the mud (**9**: Hippolytus, **21 A 33**).[6]

Xenophanes' theory was different from Anaximander's in at least one respect; for he held that the earth was gradually getting wetter, not that it was drying out. But in other ways he may have been imitating his Milesian predecessor. Perhaps Anaximander elaborated a cyclical theory of hydration and dehydration; and perhaps he relied on the sort of fossilized evidence that Xenophanes used—for if he had not heard of the findings in Malta and in Syracuse, Paros at least was near home. And scholars plausibly guess that Anaximander observed and was impressed by the gradual silting of the harbour at Miletus and the general recession of the sea along the Ionian coast.

All that suggests an expansive theory of the origins of life: 'The earth is gradually drying out from an originally water-logged condition. The first living creatures, then, will have been of a fishy variety, to whom a watery environment was congenial. Only later, as the earth dried, will land animals have developed from those aquatic aboriginals. And man, in particular, must have had a peculiar sort of ancestor, given the weak and dependent nature of the human infant.'

On the strength of this theory Anaximander has been hailed as the first Darwinian; and there are grounds for praise: the animal species were not, in Anaximander's view, immutably fixed at their creation; and their development was determined by the nature of their environment. Here we have, in embryo, evolution and the survival of the fittest. Both those 'Darwinian' aspects of Anaximander's theory are found, a century later, in Empedocles. Much of Empedocles' zoogony is strange and disputed (see **31 B 57–62**; Aëtius, **A 72**); but he surely held both that the earliest living creatures were very different from those with which we are familiar, and also that many of those early creatures were, for various reasons, incapable of surviving and perpetuating themselves. The Aristotelian doctrine of the immutability of species later gained a stranglehold on men's minds; and it is only just that we should honour Anaximander and Empedocles for their insight.

Nevertheless, praise should not be lavished with fulsome disregard for accuracy; and the grand theory presented to Anaximander is neither as cohesive nor as evolutionary as I have made it seem. First, our sources do not connect Anaximander's hypothesis of a drying earth with his zoogonical theories; and since, according to Aëtius, the first animals were amphibian and lived at a time when the earth already had dry parts, the physical hypothesis may well have been entirely divorced from the zoogonical theories. Anaximander is perhaps more likely to have been moved to his watery zoogony by the sort of considerations which led Thales to adopt water as a 'first principle' (above, p. 11).

Second, there is no trace of evolution, in the sense of gradual change, in Anaximander's theory. Aëtius implies no more than that the first generation of each species emerged from prickly barks or shells. There is no suggestion that this mode of reproduction occurred more than once; or that the first generation had been preceded by a line of prickly ancestors; or that, once hatched, the first cats and cows, hyenas and horses, differed in any respect from their present descendants. Nor is the speculative origin of mankind evolutionary: it seems probable that the 'fish-like' parents of the first men were similar to the prickly cradles of the other animals, the only difference being that the human barks did not split until their contents were at a relatively advanced stage of development. Censorinus (**A 30**) says that the first men did not emerge 'until puberty'; if his report is accurate, Anaximander's motive is transparent: he wants to ensure that the first generation of men will survive long enough to reproduce and care for a second generation. Anaximander did not envisage a long and gradual alteration in the form and behaviour of animal species in response to their changing environment. He did not ask how the species we know came to have the characteristics we observe in them. His question was simply: How did living creatures first come into being and propagate? And his answer was a genial fantasy.

(c) *The earth at rest*

In the orthodox opinion, the early Ionian astronomers are divided by a deep gulf. On the one side stands the majority, whose accounts, though pretentious in design, are in execution crude and sketchy, offering imprecise and pieeemeal observations on individual problems with no attempt at synthesis or quantification. On the other side stands the lone figure of Anaximander, 'the earliest known type of a mathematical physicist, at any rate outside Babylonia', whose theories rest on a proper scientific methodology 'critical and speculative rather than empirical'.[7] Both sides of this contrast are overdrawn: Anaximander was not quite the purist his admirers imagine, and his colleagues were not as different from him as they have been made to appear. Nevertheless, his astronomy remains an astonishing achievement, and nowhere more so than in his account of the earth's position in the universe.

Anaximander punctured Thales' water-bed: he realized that any solution to the puzzle of the earth's stability needed something stronger than an analogy and deeper than a cushion of water (see above, pp. 9–10). His own answer, which Aristotle expounds and discusses at some length (*Cael* 295b10–296a23 = **A 26**) meets these requirements, and enables him to reconcile the apparently conflicting facts that the earth is at rest and that the earth is in mid-space.

Aristotle's report runs thus:

> There are some who say that it [sc. the earth] stays where it is (*menein*) because of the similarity (*dia tên homoiotêta*); e.g., among the ancients, Anaximander. For what sits in the middle and is similarly related to the extremes has no more reason (*mallon outhen . . . prosêkei*) to go upwards than downwards or sideways;

> but it is impossible for it to make a movement in opposite directions at the same time: so of necessity it stays where it is (**10**: *Cael* 295b10–16 = **A 26**).

Aristotle is echoed in the doxography:

> [Anaximander says that] the earth is in mid-air (*meteôron*), overpowered by nothing, and staying where it is on account of its similar distance from everything (**11**: Hippolytus, **A 11**).[8]

Both Aristotle and Hippolytus speak, in slightly different fashions, of 'similarity': their vague references can be filled out in more than one way, and we have no means of knowing which filling is authentic. The interpretation I offer is speculative; but it fits the words of our reports, and it consists with Anaximander's general cosmology. A *cosmic spoke* is a straight line drawn from the centre of the earth to the boundary of the finite cosmos. A spoke s_1 is *similar* to a spoke s_2 if every point, p_1, n units from the earth along s_1 is qualitatively indistinguishable from the corresponding point, p_2, n units from the earth along s_2. Hippolytus' text suggests that *all* cosmic spokes are similar; Aristotle implies the weaker supposition that for every cosmic spoke there is a similar spoke opposite to it. (Two spokes are 'opposite' if they form an angle of 180° in all planes at the centre of the earth.) In fact, Anaximander needs no more than:

(1) For any cosmic spoke s_i, there is a distinct spoke s_j such that s_j is similar to s_i,

and I shall use (1) as though it were Anaximandrian.

The inference turns, according to Aristotle, on the proposition that the earth does not move because it 'has no more reason' to go in one direction than in another. Implicit in this is the second of the 'two great principles' on which, according to Leibniz, all reasoning is founded: it is 'the Principle of Sufficient Reason, in virtue of which we believe that no fact can be real or existent, and no statement true, unless it has a sufficient reason why it should be thus and not otherwise' (*Monadology*, §32).[9] The Principle can be applied, and Anaximander's argument articulated, in more than one way; I shall present the argument as a *reductio*.

Let us suppose that the earth is moving, i.e., that it is travelling along some cosmic spoke, say s_1; thus:

(2) The earth is moving along s_1.

Anaximander assumes that the motion described in (2) must have some explanation. He is, I suggest, implicitly relying on some such principle as:

(3) If a is F, then for some ϕ, a is F because a is ϕ.

From (2) and (3) he may validly infer:
(4) For some ϕ, the earth moves along s_1 because s_1 is ϕ.
Suppose that the explanatory feature of s_1 is G, then we have:
(5) The earth is moving along s_1 because s_1 is G,
and hence, trivially:
(6) s_1 is G.
Then, by (1) and (6):
(7) Some s_j distinct from s_1 is G.
Suppose, then:
(8) s_2 is G.
At this point, Anaximander needs a further principle, that explanations are 'universalizable'. An appropriate formula here is:
(9) If *a* is *F* because *a* is *G*, then if anything is *G* it is *F*.
Between them, (3) and (9) amount to something like a Principle of Sufficient Reason: (3) asserts that happenings need *some* explanation; (9) indicates how that explanation must be a *sufficient* condition for what it explains.
Now from (5), (8) and (9) there follows:
(10) The earth is moving along s_2.
Since nothing can move in two directions at once, (2) and (10) are incompatible. Hence, by *reductio ad absurdum*, (2) is false: the earth must stay where it is.

Anaximander's argument is clean and ingenious; and it reveals an awareness of certain central features of our notion of explanation. 'Even if we knew nothing else concerning its author, this alone would guarantee him a place among the creators of a rational science of the natural world.'[10] But the argument is hardly convincing. I ignore certain *a priori* objections to premiss (1): the premiss is a scientific hypothesis—a Popperian conjecture—and not an inductive generalization; and if hypothesis is preferable to induction, the status of (1) is a tribute, not an objection, to Anaximander. Moreover, (1) is no isolated hypothesis: it is part of an elaborate description of the heavens (see above, p. 20), which is designed both to save the phenomena and to guarantee cosmic 'similarity'. Nor will it do to object that Anaximander rules out, *sans* argument, any transcendental differences between cosmic spokes. Anaximander is doing astronomy; and astronomy exists as a science only if the gods do not capriciously intervene in the workings of the world. That there is no transcendental, divine, or capricious intervention in natural processes is a presupposition fundamental to the very enterprise of science.

Nonetheless, premiss (1) will not stand. Despite its ingenuity, Anaximander's astronomy does not work: it ensures the 'similarity' required by (1)—though not the stronger 'similarities' implicit in

Aristotle and Hippolytus—but it does not 'save the phenomena'. As an astronomical hypothesis it is falsifiable; and it was immediately seen to be false. Anaximander's argument is scientifically untenable.

Philosophically, there are those who reject the Principle of Sufficient Reason: some attack (3), others attack (9). Opponents of (9) ask why certain features should not simply have an effect on some occasions and not on others: freak weather conditions caused today's typhoon, even though the very same conditions had no devastating effect yesterday. Opponents of (3) may simply point to the occurrence of chance events. More subtle antagonists will ride Buridan's ass: equidistant between two bottles of hay their steed would, were the Principle right, starve to death. In fact, the donkey eats: either there is no explanation for its taking this bottle rather than that, in which case (3) is false; or else the donkey's attraction to this bottle is explained by a feature which that bottle also possesses, in which case (9) is false. This *reductio ad asininum* was anticipated by Aristotle: he compares Anaximander's arguments with 'the argument that a hair which is subject to strong but uniform tension will not break, and that a man who is hungry and thirsty to an extreme but equal degree will abstain alike from food and drink' (*Cael* 295b30–3).

I shall touch on these issues again in later chapters. Here it is enough to remark that the objections to (3) and to (9) are not conclusive against Anaximander; for (3) and (9)—like the prohibition on divine intervention—are, in a certain sense, presuppositions of any scientific astronomy: if either (3) or (9) lapses, then the goal of astronomy itself is unattainable, and we cannot find universal laws explanatory of the celestial phenomena. Any wise man, therefore, will strive to maintain (3) and (9), even if he cannot show them to be true *a priori*; for to abandon them is to abandon the highest ideal of science.

Anaximander's successors are often alleged to have betrayed his memory, retreating to primitive, Thalean, thoughts and quitting the speculative heights to which he had ascended. Thus Xenophanes said that the earth 'reaches downward to infinity' (**21 B 28**; cf. Aristotle, *Cael* 294a21–8 = **A 47**); and Anaximenes had the earth 'riding' on the air (Aëtius, **13 A 20**; cf. **B 2a**). Anaximenes was followed by Anaxagoras and Democritus (Aristotle, *Cael* 294b13–23 = **13 A 20**) and by Diogenes of Apollonia (Scholiast on Basil, **64 A 16a**); and his theory became an orthodoxy, alluded to in poetry and prose, and guyed in comedy ([Hippocrates], Euripides, Aristophanes, **64 C 2**). Empedocles alone offered something similar to Anaximander; but his theory is only half intelligible, and that half is wrong.[11] Anaximander's argument is once ascribed to Parmenides and

Democritus (Aëtius, **28 A 44**); and another source has it that 'Empedocles and Parmenides and almost all the old sages' adopted it (Anatolius, **28 A 44**). But neither of those accounts is trustworthy; and in all probability Anaximander's argument was not taken up again until Plato laid hands on it.[12]

Nevertheless, I do not think that Anaximander's successors were primitive revivalists: he saw what Thales had missed, that the earth may rest in mid-air, *meteôros*, without solid support; and his successors did not relinquish that insight. It is true that in Xenophanes' singular case the earth is *meteôros* only in a Pickwickian sense; but it still differs from Thales' earth in needing no support: an infinitely extended column of earth need and can have nothing holding it up.[13] Of the Anaximeneans, one is expressly said to have held that the earth is *meteôros* (Hippolytus, **59 A 42**); and it is a reasonable conjecture that the others did too. Like Anaximander, they rejected a support for the earth, and sought to reconcile stability and suspension in mid-air; seeing the faults of Anaximander's reconciliation, they offered an account which turned on the observed physical characteristics of the stuff filling celestial space, and not on the conjectural mathematical features of space itself. The earth is physically suspended in air; it is not mathematically suspended by abstract reason.

Of the many pieces of evidence the Anaximeneans adduced for their theory (*Cael* 294b22), only one has survived, and that is not particularly impressive (*Cael* 294b13–21 = **13 A 20**). Nor does the Anaximenean theory provide much philosophical pabulum: compared to Anaximander's argument, it is boring. For all that, Anaximander's successors were not his inferiors; charmed by the elegance of his suggestion, they were sadly conscious of its failure to save the phenomena, and the views they advanced in its stead were intellectually dull but scientifically progressive.

A modern reader will feel a certain impatience with all this misplaced ingenuity. Why, he will ask, did the Presocratics not abandon the hypothesis of a stable earth and so dissolve their whole problem? The answer is that they were too scientific to do so: Anaximander followed Thales in accepting a stable earth; and he was in turn followed by most of the later Presocratics.[14] A few Pythagoreans dared to displace the earth from the centre of the cosmos and let it run around a central fire; but their view was deemed bizarre, and remained unfashionable (see below, p. 383). For once, common sense held the day: when we stand on the earth we have none of the sensations associated with motion; we do not feel the blast of the wind or see the clouds rushing past in regular procession; and the pit of our stomach assures us that all is at rest. As the great Ptolemy observed, 'it is perfectly plain from the phenomena themselves' that the earth is still (*Syntaxis* I.7).

Daily observation confirms the stability of the earth, just as nocturnal observation proves the mobility of the stars. In any case, a moving earth would not solve the Presocratic problem, but merely displace it. The question Thales raised in connexion with the earth would arise again in connexion with the new cosmic centre: *why*, whatever it is, does it remain still in mid-space?

Progress will be made here not by astronomy but by philosophy: the Presocratics needed a closer understanding of the concept of motion before they could improve their scientific hypotheses. Zeno's work laid the foundations for such an understanding (below, pp. 290–4); but even after Zeno there is little evidence of any reflexion on what we mean when we ascribe motion or rest to heavenly bodies. The only text I know of refers to an obscure and probably fourth-century Pythagorean:

> Hicetas of Syracuse, as Theophrastus says, believes that the sky, sun, moon, stars, and in a word all the celestial bodies, are at rest, and that except for the earth nothing at all in the universe moves; and when the earth twists and turns about the axis at great speed, all the effects are just the same as they would be if the earth were at rest and the heavens moved (**12**: Cicero, **50 A 1**).

Hicetas' theory is almost certainly geocentric; his earth revolves on its axis and not about the sun or central fire; and his astronomy is crude and readily refuted. Nonetheless, Hicetas shows some flickering sophistication in his handling of celestial motion; and the Zenonian moral is beginning to be learned.

(d) *Τὸ ἄπειρον*

The first fragment of Greek philosophy is short, dark, and attractive. Besotted scholars see in it the first strivings toward abstract and metaphysical thought: the fragment, they maintain, breaks new ground in the science of theoretical cosmogony; it introduces the potent notion of infinity into Greek speculation; and it allows us to ascribe to Anaximander a sophisticated and superbly rational theory of the primordial principle of the universe.[15]

In this section I shall first set out the famous fragment, together with its doxographical context; then construct an optimistic account of Anaximander's reasonings; and finally criticize that account, reluctantly sprinkling a little cold water on Anaximander's warm reputation. There are very many problems raised by the fragment which I shall not take up.

We owe the fragment to Simplicius, whose text reads as follows (the interpolated numerals are, of course, my own addition):

> Of those who say that [the principle] is one and in motion and unlimited, Anaximander, son of Praxiades, a Milesian who became successor and pupil to Thales, said that [i] the unlimited (*apeiron*) is both principle (*archê*) and element (*stoicheion*) of the things that exist, [ii] being the first to introduce this name of the principle. He says that [iii] it is neither water nor any other of the so-called elements, but some other unlimited nature, from which all the heavens and the worlds in them come about; [iv] and the things from which is the coming into being for the things that exist are also those into which their destruction comes about, in accordance with what must be. [v] For they give justice (*dikê*) and reparation to one another for their offence (*adikia*) in accordance with the ordinance of time—[vi] speaking of them thus in rather poetical terms. And [vii] it is clear that, having observed the change of the four elements into one another, he did not think fit to make any one of these an underlying stuff, but something else apart from these (**13**: **A 9** + **B 1**).

The first principle or element of things, the original and originating mass of the universe, was *apeiros*, unlimited. What limits did it lack? Common sense suggests the boundaries of space and time; and scholarship adds the determination by fixed qualities. Thus we might imagine Anaximander's universal starting-point to be spatially infinite, sempiternal, and qualitatively indeterminate: in the beginning, before the cosmogonic moment, there was a mass of qualityless stuff, unlimited in extent and infinitely old. Why conjecture such a strange start for the familiar world? The doxography suggests a mesh of four arguments.

Argument (*A*) is extracted from sentence [vii] of text **13**. The argument turns on the phenomenon of 'elemental change', and runs as follows:

(1) Each so-called 'elemental' stuff can change into one or more of the other 'elemental' stuffs.

(2) If a stuff S_1 can change into another stuff, S_2, then neither S_1 nor S_2 underlies all change.

(3) If S is the stuff of all things, then S underlies all change.

Hence:

(4) The stuff of all things is not one of the 'elemental' stuffs.

The changes we observe daily are underlain by the 'elements': we observe modifications of earth, air, fire and water. Hence only those elements are candidates for the post of all things; and their candidacy is defeated by argument (*A*). The *Urstoff*, we can only conclude, is indeterminate. What underlies even elemental change can have no qualities of its own; it must be Aristotelian 'prime matter', a 'something we know not what' (cf. *Met* 1069b19 = **59 A 61**).

Argument (*B*) is found anonymously in Aristotle: Aëtius (**A 14**) ascribes it to Anaximander.[16] Aristotle is listing reasons why philosophers have been persuaded of the existence of something actually unlimited:

> Again, because only in this way will generation and destruction not fail—if that from which what comes into being is abstracted is unlimited (**14**: *Phys* 203b18–20 = **A 15**).

Thus:
(5) New things are perpetually being generated.
(6) All generation is the alteration of some pre-existent stuff.
Hence:
(7) There has always existed an infinitely large stock of stuff.

Argument (*C*) forges a link between (*A*) and (*B*); it too comes from Aristotle:

> There are some who make the unlimited body [a stuff distinct from the four 'elements'], and not air or water, in order that the others should not be destroyed by their unlimitedness; for they stand in opposition to one another—e.g., air is cold, water moist, fire hot—and if one of them were unlimited the others would already have been destroyed; but in fact, they say, it [sc. the unlimited body] is something else, from which these [are generated] (**15**: *Phys* 204b22–9 = **A 16**).

Simplicius (**A 17**) refers the argument to Anaximander; it can be expanded as follows:
(8) The *Urstoff* of everything is spatially infinite.
(9) Each of the four elements is opposed to, i.e. tends to destroy, the other three.
(10) If *a* is spatially infinite, and *a* tends to destroy *b*, then for some *n* *a* will destroy *b* within *n* units of time.
(11) For any *n*, the *Urstoff* has existed for more than *n* units of time.
(12) No element has been destroyed.
Hence:
(13) The *Urstoff* is distinct from each of the four elements.

Argument (*C*) thus uses the conclusion of (*B*) to confirm the conclusion of (*A*): it infers qualitative indeterminacy from spatio-temporal infinity.

Finally, *argument* (*D*) shows that any unlimited body must be a principle. Again, the text is the *Physics*:

> It is reasonable that they all make [the unlimited body] a principle. For [viii] it can neither exist to no purpose, nor can it have any other power except as a principle; for everything either is a principle or is from a principle, and the unlimited has no principle—for then it would have a limit. [ix] Again, it is both ungenerable and indestructible, being a sort of principle. For what has come into being necessarily has an end, and there is an end of every destruction. [x] For this reason, as we say, there is no principle of this but this seems to be a principle of the other things and to encompass everything and to govern everything (as those say who do not propose any other causes apart from the unlimited, such as mind or love); and this is the divine; for it is immortal and deathless, as Anaximander and most of the *phusiologoi* say (**16**: 203b4–15 = **A 15**).

Part [x], it is argued, is certainly Anaximandrian; but [viii]–[x] forms an organic whole: hence [viii]–[x] as a whole is Anaximandrian, and we have before us 'a second virtual citation from Anaximander's book, comparable in importance to the famous sentence preserved by Simplicius'.[17] In particular, we can assign to Anaximander the following argument:

(14) Everything is either a principle or derived from a principle.

(15) If *a* is unlimited, *a* has no limit.

(16) If *a* has no limit, *a* is not derived from a principle.

Hence:

(17) If *a* is unlimited, *a* is a principle.

Aristotle here uses 'unlimited' to refer to spatial infinity; we should get a slightly better argument if we took 'unlimited' to refer to sempiternity: any derivative body is temporally posterior to its source; hence no temporally infinite body can be derivative.

A small nest of intertwined reasonings supports Anaximander's unlimited principle, and at the same time elucidates its nature. There is an unargued hypothesis that the processes of generation will never give out: generation requires an infinite source; infinity and the generative function alike require an indeterminate source; and any infinite mass can only be a principle of things. The nest is not tidy but it seems cohesive and strong. Was it built by Anaximander? Or are the materials used in its construction late and synthetic? I take the arguments in turn.

An examination of argument (*A*) demands a nearer look at the passage of Simplicius. Simplicius is quoting Theophrastus, who is quoting Anaximander.

Argument (*A*) comes from sentence [vii]; and though [vi] shows that Simplicius is certainly reporting some of Anaximander's own words, [vii] is beyond the boundary of his quotation. (Indeed, it has been cogently argued that [vii] is Simplicius' own comment on the paragraph [i]–[vi] which he has excerpted from Theophrastus.)[18] Thus argument (*A*) is Anaximandrian only if Simplicius' comment on [i]–[vi] is correct. I am not sure how Simplicius reached his opinion: perhaps he supposed that 'the things that exist' in [iv] must include the elements; and inferred that [iv]–[v] recognize elemental change. He then ascribed to Anaximander the Peripatetic deduction of a non-elemental stuff. To assess his ascription we must analyse [i]–[vi].

Sentence [v] is fairly clearly the 'somewhat poetic' utterance referred to in [vi], and it (or at least most of it) is therefore securely Anaximandrian.[19] What of the earlier sentences? Sentence [ii] has roused passionate debate: did Theophrastus mean to assign the term 'principle' or the term 'unlimited' to Anaximander? It has, I think, been shown that Theophrastus assigned both terms to Anaximander, 'the unlimited' in [ii], and 'principle' in another passage (see Simplicius, *in Phys* 150. 18).[20] In that case, sentence [i] may well be a close paraphrase of something in Anaximander's text. Sentence [iii] is more puzzling: its final clause, containing the curious phrase 'the worlds in [the heavens]', seems archaic to some scholars; but the reference to the 'so-called elements' cannot be Anaximander's. We infer from [iii] that Anaximander said something to the effect that 'the principle is not water, nor earth, nor anything of that familiar sort'. But Diogenes Laertius has a subtly different account:

> Anaximander said that the unlimited is principle and element, not distinguishing it as air or water or anything else (**17**: II.1 = **A 1**: cf. Aëtius, **A 14**).

Did Anaximander positively deny that 'the unlimited' was water or the like? Or did he rather refrain from asserting that it was water or the like? The question is not merely trifling; for the view that Anaximander's principle was qualitatively indeterminate loses in plausibility if he did not positively distinguish it from the elements. Yet I do not see that we can answer the question; indeed, we cannot tell whether Simplicius or Diogenes better represents Theophrastus' judgment.

The doxography conflates sentences [iii] and [iv] (see Cicero, **A 13**;

Aëtius, **A 14**); and some modern scholars concur. But [iii] and [iv] seem to state theses which are perfectly distinct: [iii] deals with the generation of the heavens from 'the unlimited', in a word, with cosmogony; [iv] deals with the generation and destruction of 'the things that exist', with the production of the furniture of the world from its component stuffs or 'opposites' (cf. pseudo-Plutarch, **A 10**).[21] Sentence [iii] deals with the creation of the cosmos; sentence [iv] with the changes that take place within the cosmos.[22]

Sentence [v] connects to [iv] by the particle 'for' (*gar*): what connexion is thereby signalled? The sentiment expressed abstractly in [iv] is ancient and popular:

> Dust to dust and ashes to ashes,
> Into the tomb the Great Queen dashes.

Thus we might suppose that [iv] is, if not a quotation, at least a close paraphrase of Anaximander. And we might ascribe the *gar* to him, thus: 'Natural objects eventually are resolved into the elements from which they sprang (plants rot and form earth and moisture); for no one element perpetually gains at the expense of another—local gains are followed, in time, by compensating losses.' If we connect [iv] and [v] in this way, our interpretation does, I think, support Simplicius' inference in [vii]; at least, it ascribes elemental change to Anaximander. For on this interpretation the generation of natural objects must, characteristically at least, involve an elemental change: only if, say, the production of rain from cloud is construed as an elemental change of air into water will it constitute an 'offence' or encroachment. When clouds yield rain, water gains upon air: to preserve the cosmic balance of stuffs, the rain must at some time turn back into cloud.

The reconstruction is intelligible; but it is not obligatory. Some scholars ascribe [iv] to Theophrastus, and give the connecting particle *gar* to him rather than to Anaximander. The sense of [i]–[vi] is then this: 'Anaximander made "the unlimited" a material principle, i.e. something from which everything comes and into which it is destroyed again (= [i], [ii]). For (a) he *says* that everything comes *from* "the unlimited" (= [iii]); and (b) he accepts the *general* principle that things are destroyed into what they came from (= [iv]), as his own words (= [v]) show'.[23]

This second account of [i]–[vi] is, I think, the more plausible; for it explains the Theophrastan passage as a whole, whereas the ascription of [iv] to Anaximander leaves the connexion between [i]–[iii] and [iv]–[v] inexplicable. As an interpretation of Anaximander it is highly speculative; for [v] does not evidently suggest [iv] as an interpretative gloss. Moreover, it will hardly support Simplicius' inference in [vii]. For all that, it is likely to represent the original sense of Theophrastus' argument.

I return to sentence [vii] and argument (*A*). On any account of [i]–[vi], [vii] is at best an ingenious conjecture, applying a Peripatetic thesis about elemental change to a deeply hidden implication of Anaximander's argument. This is the most favourable construction to be put on [vii]: the most probable construction is that [vii] is a baseless invention. And there is an independent reason for doubting the authenticity of (*A*): premiss (2) is hardly likely to have been embraced by Anaximander. At all events, it was implicitly rejected by his follower Anaximenes, who took air to be the basic stuff of the world and yet was quite happy to let air change into other stuffs.

Perhaps, then, it is argument (*C*) that gives Anaximander's reason for picking 'the unlimited' as his first principle. Premiss (11) is certainly authentic: 'the unlimited' was 'eternal and ageless' or 'immortal and deathless' (Hippolytus, **A 11**; Aristotle, *Phys* 203b14 = **A 15**; cf. **B 2**).[24] Premisses (9) and (12) refer anachronistically to 'the elements'; but the anachronism is trifling, and (9) and (12) together make a plausible reading of sentence [v] of the fragment. Premiss (10) has a Peripatetic ring to it; yet it might, I think, have been advanced, perhaps in a somewhat crude or metaphorical formulation, by Anaximander.

If we are prepared to ascribe (*C*) to Anaximander does that make 'the unlimited' a qualitatively indeterminate 'prime matter'? It is perfectly plain that a mass of 'prime matter' could not constitute a cosmogonical principle. The *Urstoff* was self-subsistent; and any self-subsistent stuff has definite qualities: a piece of stuff, however airy and abstract, cannot be neither ϕ nor non-ϕ for every value of ϕ. Aristotle, it need hardly be said, was well aware of this (cf., e.g., *GC* 329a10).

But if the 'unlimited' was not entirely characterless, what was its character? In several passages Aristotle talks of *phusiologoi* who took as their principle a stuff 'between' (*metaxu*) the other elements; and he probably had Anaximander in mind. According to some scholars, Theophrastus thought that Anaximander's principle was a 'mixture' (*migma*) of all stuffs. These passages are all controversial,[25] but one thing is fairly clear: if the Peripatetics did actually ascribe a *metaxu* or a *migma* theory to Anaximander, they were whistling in the dark. Anaximander's text gave them no light; and I guess that they did not know what Anaximander thought, for the excellent reason that Anaximander himself did not know what to think.

Argument (*C*) assumes, in (8), the spatial infinity of the universe.

That proposition is the conclusion of argument (*B*). The argument is invalid, as Aristotle points out: 'In order that coming to be should not fail, it is not necessary that there should be a sensible body which is actually unlimited. The passing away of one thing may be the coming to be of another, the whole being limited' (*Phys* 208a7–10). This objection is overcome by adding a further premiss to (*B*), viz:

(18) The material supplied by the destruction of existing things cannot be used in the generation of new things.

But it is implausible to ascribe (18) to Anaximander. Sentence [iv] of the fragment, whether or not it is Anaximandrian, is not, strictly speaking, incompatible with (18): [iv] does not imply that the dust produced by destroying a thing is equal in mass to the dust consumed in its generation; and it is not grossly implausible to imagine that the processes of generation and destruction involve a certain wastage of stuff. Sentence [v], however, suggests fairly strongly that Anaximander had some sort of equal balancing in mind; and the probability is that he would have rejected (18).

Argument (*B*) can be repaired without the help of (18); instead of (18) we may add:

(19) The mass of existing things is perpetually increasing.

An adherent of (19) believes that the cosmos is expanding; and there is no direct evidence that any Presocratic held such a belief. But there is a sentence from Anaxagoras which apparently commits him to an expanding universe; and in some respects at least Anaxagoras was a scientific traditionalist.[26] If Anaxagoras embraced (19), perhaps he took it from Anaximander.

It is pertinent to quote here a fragment of Anaximander's pupil, Anaximenes:

> Air is close to the incorporeal; and since we come into being by an effluxion of this, it is necessary for it to be both unlimited and rich, because it never gives out (**18: 13 B 3**).[27]

Anaximenes thus advanced argument (*B*); and he was thereby committed to either (18) or (19). I incline to favour (19), and to take that as some slight evidence for Anaximander's acceptance of (19). Certainly, Anaximenes' adoption of (*B*) makes its ascription to Anaximander more plausible.[28]

What, finally, of argument (*D*)? The end of [x] is Anaximandrian; and many scholars tie the whole of [x] to him. I shall return to this passage later on; here it is enough to say that Aristotle's text in no way implies this wholesale ascription. Moreover, [ix] is, I think, a version of an argument advanced by Melissus (see below, pp. 194–7); and in that case there is no historical unity underlying the logical unity of [viii]–[ix]. Aristotle himself makes this plain enough; for he refers to 'all' the *physiologoi* at the beginning of the passage, and to 'most' of them at the end. We have no reason to ascribe [viii] to Anaximander; [viii]–[ix] is an Aristotelian concoction, prepared from several different Presocratic recipes.

With arguments (*A*) and (*D*) removed, Anaximander's thought about the material principle of things becomes less complicated; yet it remains rational: the principle must be *apeiros*, or spatially infinite, in order to support perpetual generation; and, being *apeiros*, it must be distinct from any of the ordinary cosmic stuffs. Arguments (*B*) and (*C*) together yield a reasoned structure of thought.

It must be admitted, however, that the grounds for ascribing even (*B*) and (*C*) to Anaximander are uncertain; and that uncertainty can easily be aggravated. A powerful chorus of scholars proposes a new etymology for *apeiros*: it is formed not from alpha privative and the root of *peras* ('limit'), but from alpha privative and the stem of *peraô* ('traverse'); and the etymological meaning of the word is thus 'untraversable'.[29] Whether or not this is correct, it is in any case clear that Anaximander could have used *apeiros* of the unimaginably huge: in Homer the sea is *apeirôn*, immense, not infinite. I am inclined to believe that *apeiros* does indeed mean 'unlimited', but that spatio-temporal infinity is not the only criterion of unlimitedness: a mass of stuff may reasonably be called 'unlimited' because of its untraversable vastness, or because its boundaries are indeterminate ('like a fog-bank or the warmth of a fire'), or even because of its qualitative indeterminacy.[30]

Thus the word *apeiros* does not, in itself, show that Anaximander's *Urstoff* was literally infinite. And if it was not, then argument (*B*) loses its point. Some scholars find the source of Anaximander's conception of his *Urstoff* in Hesiod's description of the horrid chasm between earth and Tartarus (*Theogony* 736–43); that chasm is vast, not infinite. Hence *to apeiron* is not 'the Infinite' but 'the Vast'; and its origin is to be found not in cosmogonical ratiocination but in poetical inspiration. In that case, argument (*B*) is probably a rationalization fitted to Anaximander's semi-poetical utterances by a later and more prosaic age.

We might, I suppose, allow that *to apeiron* is only 'the Vast', and that Hesiod inspired Anaximander. For all that, may not arguments (*B*) and (*C*) have been in Anaximander's mind? 'Why must the original mass have been so huge?'—'To support its innumerable offspring.' 'What can its character have been?'—'Vague and obscure, but certainly distinct from the stuffs familiar to us.'

We find ourselves in a desert of ignorance and uncertainty; so, I suspect, did the Peripatetic historians. It is possible that Anaximander set his views down with luminous clarity, and that the monster time devoured his book before the Peripatetics could read its pages; but I doubt it, and I suspect that our uncertainty about Anaximander's meaning reflects an uncertainty and lack of clarity in Anaximander's own mind.

Indeed, I guess that Anaximander's interest in cosmogony has been vastly overestimated, and his achievement consistently mispraised. The partial and fortuitous survival of an obscure utterance has given him an undeserved reputation for metaphysics. That sentence, hinting darkly at a huge primordial *tohu-bohu*, was perhaps supported by a sketchy paragraph of argument; and it was undeniably an impressive exordium to Anaximander's book *Concerning Nature*. But in the context of Anaximander's thought as a whole it had little importance: what mattered was the detailed science that followed: the astronomy, the biology, the geography. Anaximander set natural philosophy on the course it was to follow for many centuries: it is no diminution of his genius to say that his contribution to metaphysical philosophy was of less moment.

III

Science and Speculation

(a) *Material monism*

Anaximenes, the third of the Milesians, is by general consent a poor man's Anaximander: his theories were those of his master. An innovator in detail, he was an imitator in all essentials. And the two main innovations he can be credited with prove him to have lacked the vigour and temerity of Anaximander: he allowed the earth to rest in archaic luxury on a cushion of air; and he smirched the metaphysical purity of Anaximander's unlimited principle by turning it into a mass of gross, material air.

I dissent from that orthodox assessment. First, Anaximenes' two acknowledged innovations are both, I think, improvements on Anaximander's theories. Anaximenes, who evidently studied astronomy with some assiduity,[1] perceived the scientific untenability of Anaximander's argument for the earth's stability, even if he did not question the philosophical adequacy of his version of the Principle of Sufficient Reason. And his own airborne earth is, as I have already argued (above, p. 27), no mere regression to the childish position of Thales. Again, Anaximenes, who wrote in 'simple and economical' language (Diogenes Laertius, II.3 = **13 A 1**), will have seen that Anaximander's 'rather poetical' style disguised a somewhat vague and perfunctory thought as far as the first principles of cosmogony go; and his own theory has the modest merit of replacing Anaximander's indeterminate principle and uncertain cosmogonical operations with a plain, intelligible stuff and a pair of familiar and comprehensible processes.

Second, our evidence, such as it is, suggests that Anaximenes was the more thorough, the more systematic, the more rigorous, and the more scientifically inclined of the two men. Ancient opinion favours this assessment: Theophrastus devoted a monograph to Anaximenes' theories (Diogenes Laertius, V.42); and in the fifth century Anaximenes was taken as the paradigm Milesian.[2]

> Anaximenes said that the principle is unlimited air (**19**: Hippolytus, **A** 7).

Anaximenes, like Thales and Anaximander, was presented in the Peripatetic tradition as a 'material monist', as a thinker who accepted as the fundamental axiom of cosmology:

(1) There is some single stuff which is the material principle of everything.

It is time to keep a promise made on an earlier page and to look more closely at the claims and credentials of 'material monism': was it, as Aristotle thought, the prime Milesian doctrine?

As it stands, (1) is Aristotelian in its mode of expression: 'principle' or *archê* (in non-philosophical Greek, 'beginning' and sometimes 'rule') was indeed used in a philosophical context by Anaximander (see above, p. 32); but it probably did not assume its Aristotelian sense of 'explanatory principle' until much later. 'Matter' or *hulê* (non-philosophically, 'wood') was in all probability an Aristotelian invention. But, as I have already remarked, these linguistic points are of no great significance: Aristotle sometimes uses as a synonym for *hulê* the phrase '*to ex hou*' ('the thing from which': e.g., *Phys* 195a19); and he often expresses the proposition that *X* is *hulê* of *Y* by a sentence of the form '*Y* is from *X*'. Such non-technical expressions were of course available to the Milesians; and it may be conjectured with confidence that the men whom Aristotle takes for monists uttered sentences of the form:

(2) Everything is from *X*.

Finding sentences of the form (2) ascribed to the Milesians, Aristotle interpreted them by way of (1). His interpretation cannot be accepted without ado: (2) may, but need not, express material monism; for '*Y* is from *X*' may express more than one relation between *X* and *Y*. Aristotle was fully aware of the fact: in *Metaphysics* Δ 24 he catalogues several of the ways in which 'being from something (*to ek tinos*) is said' (1023a26; cf. 1092a22–35). Five of these ways can be stated and illustrated as follows: if *Y* is from *X*, then either

(i) *X* is the stuff of which *Y* is made (as a statue is made *from* bronze); or

(ii) *X* is the source from which *Y* comes (as plants grow up *from* the soil); or

(iii) *X* is the agent which generated *Y* (as a child comes *from* his parents); or

(iv) *X* is the event which causes *Y* (as a battle may arise *from* an insult); or

(v) *X* is replaced by *Y* (as day comes '*from*' night, or a tan '*from*' pallor).

Modern commentators add a sixth way: *Y* is from *X* if

(vi) *X* is the stuff from which *Y* was made (as paper is made *from* rags).

(vi) is distinguished from (i) as originative from constitutive stuff. In ordinary English the distinction is sometimes expressed by a contrast between 'from' and 'of'. Thus the paper I write on was made from rags; but I will not say that it is made of rags (for I am not writing on rags). The wine I drink was made from grapes; but I will not say that it is made of grapes (for I am not drinking grapes). Again, the pane I gaze through is made of glass; but I will not say that it was made from glass (for no glazier processed glass so as to turn it into windowstuff). The diamond I cut the pane with is made of carbon; but it was not made from carbon (for no alchemist transmuted carbon into diamond for me).

The question, then, is this: Are we to interpret Milesian utterances of (2) by way of (i), as Aristotle would have it? or rather by way of (ii) or (iii) or (iv) or (v) or (vi)? A scholar who rejects Aristotle's interpretation will suppose that Thales and his successors were engaged in cosmogonical speculation and not in constituent analysis, that they were concerned to discover the original stuff from which the world was put together, and not to divine the underlying materials of its present furnishings. Aristotle believed in an eternal cosmos, rejected cosmogony, and was an exponent of constituent analysis; naturally he read his own interests, and interpretation (i), into the Milesians; and the doxography naturally followed Aristotle. But what is natural may also be wrong; and the Peripatetic version of Milesian monism may be an anachronistic invention, not an historical truth.[3]

That view is supported by two general considerations: first, (1) is wildly implausible in itself, and would hardly have presented itself spontaneously to the Milesian mind; second, (i) was, so to speak, philosophically unnecessary in the days of innocence before Parmenides, and would not have been embraced by the Milesians as an unhappy but inevitable presupposition of cosmogony.

The first consideration I find unconvincing: does interpretation (vi) really give a more 'plausible' thesis than (1)? Is it much more plausible to suppose that everything started from some one stuff than to suppose that everything is ultimately composed of some one stuff?

Both views have the same point of appeal: simplicity. And both face the same difficulty: the amazing diversity of things in the world around us.

The second consideration requires further exposition. Aristotle says that the monists, because they posit a single material principle, 'think that nothing either comes into being or perishes' (*Met* 893b12 = **A 12**); 'they say that so-called simple coming into being is alteration' (*GC* 314a8): change is nothing but an alteration in the properties of some piece of the basic stuff. Now that view of change would only have been resorted to, it is asserted, after Parmenides and his Eleatic followers had argued for the impossibility of generation and destruction. Hence material monism presupposes the cogitations of Elea and cannot have been advanced in Miletus.

The philosophical content of this argument will exercise us later. Here it may be said, first, that the Aristotelian inference is by no means obvious. It assumes a strict, Aristotelian, analysis of generation; and even with that analysis it is only valid on the further assumption that bits of the basic stuff cannot themselves be generated. Aristotle is eliciting a thesis to which, in his view, the Milesians were committed: although he asserts that they 'say' that generation is alteration, he means only that 'it is necessary for them to say' it (*GC* 314a10), that they are committed to it. He does not mean that they expressly asserted it; still less that they stated it from an uncannily prescient desire to pre-empt Parmenidean objections.

Nor, secondly, is there any reason to believe that only Parmenidean worries could provide a motive for monism: a straightforward yearning for simplicity will lead in the same direction and provide explanation enough of any *nisus* towards monism.

Are there, on the other hand, any general considerations that support the Aristotelian interpretation? One line of argument suggests that if the Milesians intended (vi) then they also intended (i); for the distinction between (vi) and (i) seems, in some cases at least, to be illusory. If my table was made *from* wood, then it is made *of* wood. If a cake was made *from* flour, milk and eggs, then it is made *of* flour, milk and eggs. And in general, if *Y* was made from *X*, then it is made of *X*. Aristotle's mode of argument at *Metaphysics* 983b6–27, where he introduces material monism, seems to show both that he accepted the inference himself, and that he ascribed it to the Milesians. Two fragments of Xenophanes, separately transmitted, read as follows:

> Everything which comes into being and grows is earth and water (**20**: **21 B 29**).

For we all come to be from earth and water (**21: B 33**).

It is plausible to conjoin these lines: **B 33** supports **B 29**, and Xenophanes makes an explicit inference from originative to constitutive stuff—from (vi) to (i).

Now if *Y* was made from *X* by a ϕ process, then it is easy to infer that *Y* consists of *X* ϕly processed, and hence that *Y* consists of *X*. But the validity of the inference depends on the nature of the ϕ process: if ϕing involves abstracting, say, the inference is evidently invalid: Bovril is extract of beef, not beef; salt is produced from brine, but is not brine. Aristotle made the point; and he also observed, implicitly, that it is easy to confound valid and invalid versions of the inference (*Top* 127a17). Can we, then, suppose that the Milesians tacitly inferred from 'The cosmos was made from *X*' to 'The cosmos is made of *X*'? The plausibility of the supposition depends, in part at least, on the nature of the cosmogonical process: if the cosmos was constructed like a cake from its ingredients, the supposition has something to be said for it; if the cosmos was extracted like gold from ore, the supposition is implausible. Clearly, the Milesians must be approached individually; and we must ask of each cosmogony whether it suggests an Aristotelian reading.

Thales said:

(3) Everything is made from water.

According to Hippolytus, Thales held that:

> Everything is composed from it [sc. water] as it thickens and again thins out (**22**: *Ref Haer* I.2; cf. Galen, **11 B 3**).

Now if *Y* comes from *X* by 'thickening' or 'thinning', by condensation or rarefaction, then surely *Y* is made of *X*. If ice is condensed water, if it is made from water by a process of condensation, then it is made of water; and in general, if everything is made from water by condensation or rarefaction, then everything is made of water. Thus Hippolytus' report speaks for an Aristotelian interpretation of (3). It has been urged that the Aristotelian interpretation does not fit Thales' account of the earth's stability (**A 12** : above, p. 9); but I see no force in that. Hippolytus' report is, however, weak evidence: it may only be a doxographical conjecture. Prudence leads to a confession of ignorance; we know too little about Thales to judge the sense in which he intended (3).

The case of Anaximander is more complex. His principal claim is:

(4) Everything is from the unlimited.

The cosmogonical process is referred to as a 'separating out' (*ekkrinesthai* : Aristotle, *Phys* 187a20 = **12 A 16**) or a 'separating off' (*apokrinesthai* : Simplicius, **A 9**; pseudo-Plutarch, **A 10**). Pseudo-Plutarch contains the fullest account of Anaximander's cosmogony:

> And he says that something generative of hot and cold was separated off from the eternal thing at the generation of this universe; and a sort of sphere of flame from this formed around the air about the earth, like a bark round a tree; and when this was broken off and shut off in certain circles, the sun and the moon and the stars were formed (**23: A 10**).

Thus first the 'unlimited' principle ('the eternal thing') gives rise to 'something generative'; then this generative stuff or process produces 'the hot' and 'the cold', i.e. the basic materials of the cosmos which are characterizable by means of those 'opposites'; and finally the furniture of the heavens is formed from the basic materials.

The cosmos was thus made from—and probably is made of—the basic materials. But what is the relation between the 'unlimited' principle and the materials? Was 'the unlimited' simply a generating agent, and should (4) be understood in terms of (iii)? But then from what were the basic materials made? Was 'the unlimited' rather the 'reservoir or stock from which all Becoming draws its nourishment',[4] and is (4) to be understood in terms of (ii)? But that suggestion is incoherent unless we assume that (4) is also to be read in terms of (vi), so that the 'unlimited' principle is a mass of *Urstoff* from which (by some entirely unknown operation) the basic materials are produced. The doxography was evidently perplexed: Simplicius, having said that the 'unlimited' is an Aristotelian substrate, adds that Anaximander 'does not produce generation by an alteration in the element, but by a separating off of the opposites' (**A 9**), so that the 'unlimited' is not a substrate after all. The Peripatetics did not know what to make of Anaximander's cosmogony. It is possible that they failed to understand his text, or that they did not possess it in its entirety; but, again, I am more inclined to suppose that their perplexity reflects a vague or incoherent account by Anaximander himself.

With Anaximenes a little light shines through. His principle reads:
(5) Everything is from air,
and the doxography has preserved an account of his cosmogony:

> Anaximenes, son of Eurystratus, a Milesian who became a companion of Anaximander, himself says that the single underlying nature is indeed unlimited, like Anaximander; but he does not make it indeterminate, like him, but determined, calling

> it air. And he says that it differs from one thing to another in rareness and density—rarefied, it becomes fire, condensed, wind, then cloud, still more condensed, water, then earth, then stones—and everything else comes from these things (**24**: Simplicius, **13 A 5**).

The parallel accounts in pseudo-Plutarch (**A 6**) and Hippolytus (**A 7**) show that Simplicius is faithful to Theophrastus here.

Anaximenes' principle is air, present in unlimited quantity; and his cosmogony is achieved by the twin operations of rarefaction and condensation, which in effect amount to the single operation of change in density. Rarefied, air becomes fire; condensed, cloud, water, earth, and so on; and thus are engendered all the stuffs of the familiar world. Anaximenes introduced rarefaction (*manôsis*) and condensation (*puknôsis*) into cosmogony, though those particular terms may not have been his own (cf. **B 1**); and the operations became an orthodox feature of Presocratic science.[5] Certainly, the processes have a cosmogonical significance: the earth we stand upon and the clouds we gaze at were originally formed by the condensation of a vast mass of air. But they also serve to provide a quasi-chemical analysis of the constituents of the present world order. For, as I have argued, the inference from '*Y* was produced from *X* by a ϕ process' to '*Y* is made of *X*' is eminently plausible and natural when the ϕ process is one of condensation or rarefaction; and there is, I think, no cause to doubt that Anaximenes was a material monist in the standard Aristotelian sense.

The Milesians were cosmogonists, concerned to name the originative stuff and state of the world. Yet Anaximenes at least also gave an analysis, in Aristotelian vein, of the present stuff of the world; and he was thus a material monist. With Thales and Anaximander we must rule *non liquet*; and we may hazard it that nothing was clear either in the writings or in the minds of those men. Aristotle boldly offers them a coherent view; but though the Aristotelian interpretation gives them something which they might have said had they said anything clearly, we may prefer to leave their accounts in the dimness which they themselves designed.

(b) *Anaximenes and air*

The doxography reports the first principle and the initial processes of Anaximenes' cosmogony: some sort of motion produces variations in the density of the *Ur*-mass of air, and the basic stuffs of the universe are generated. We also have a quantity of information about Anaximenes' astronomy and meteorology, from which it is clear that the cosmogonical operations also account for many of the phenomena of the present world.

Between these two sets of reports there is a gap. Simplicius' summary notice that 'everything else comes from these things' (**24**) is unrevealing. Is he reporting an 'etc.' in Anaximenes' text, or is he rather abbreviating a wealth of Anaximenean detail? If the latter, did Anaximenes suppose that change in density sufficed to produce all the stuffs that there are, or were supplementary operations called upon? No generative operations other than rarefaction and condensation are ascribed to Anaximenes in our sources; and it is most reasonable to believe that all stuffs were somehow to be generated by the agency of those operations alone.

So far, I have spoken only of the generation of stuffs; and it is a notable feature of Ionian speculation as a whole that its primary concern is with the different materials found in the world. The twin operations of condensation and rarefaction may have seemed sufficient to explain the generation, and the composition, of stuffs such as vapour and rock, wood and flesh; but they are plainly impotent to generate substances, or informed parcels of stuff, such as clouds and pebbles, trees and men. The stuff wood may be compressed air; but trees, even on the crudest analysis, are wood shaped in such and such a way. Flesh and bone may be generable by condensation; but if we want to account for the presence of organic bodies on the earth we need more than lumps of suitable stuffs. In Aristotelian jargon, the Ionian theories touch on the material constitution of things but say nothing about their form. Anaximenes may have thought that he could explain the formal aspect of at least some substances (cf. pseudo-Plutarch, **A 6**: sun, moon, stars); but he appears to have given the question little thought. It was not until the middle of the fifth century that form became a philosophical issue, and then it was tangled in the thickets of Pythagoreanism.

The Pythagoreans associate form with number; and here it might seem that Anaximenes in a sense anticipated them. His cosmogony takes relative density as the one essential feature of stuffs, in terms of which their remaining properties are to be explicated: any stuff is simply air at such and such a density. Now to us density is a quantitative notion, amenable to measurement: thus Anaximenes' physics is fundamentally quantitative, and it adumbrates that principle which comprises 'the very essence of science': 'that quality can be reduced to quantity'.[6] Quantitative sciences allow a mathematical development: seventeenth-century physics advanced precisely because it sloughed off qualities and paraded in its quantitative underskin; and the frailty of modern psychology or economics is due to the false or fantastical quantifications they rely upon.

Was Anaximenes really a precocious quantifier, a Presocratic Boyle? Alas, I suspect he was not. Greek scientists were in general averse to, or incapable of, the application of mathematics to physical processes and phenomena; and there is no evidence that Anaximenes' theory encouraged them to attempt any such application. Nor is there any evidence that Anaximenes himself had any such application in mind: he had no scale and no instrument for measuring density, and for him density was a quantitative notion only in the weakest sense. The scientific appearance of his cosmogonical operations is due to chance, not to insight.

How did Anaximenes attempt to justify or commend his grand theory? We might ask him four questions: (a) why suppose that some single stuff originated and underlies the variety of appearances? (b) why suppose that *Urstoff* to be air? (c) why require an unlimited quantity of air? (d) why generate from air by means of condensation and rarefaction?

To question (a) the only plausible answer is, once more, the compelling attraction of simplicity: the fewer the primitives, the better the system. A single stuff and a single operation (or pair of complementary operations) constitute, from a systematic point of view, the best possible hypothesis. Question (c) is answered in **B 3**, which I have already commented upon (above, p. 35). Fragment **B 2**, which I discuss in a later context (below, p. 55), is sometimes seen as an answer to (b). That leaves (d).

Hippolytus reports that 'the most important factors in generation are opposites—hot and cold' (**A 7**). The two factors recur in a passage of Plutarch:

> As old Anaximenes thought, we should not leave the hot and the cold in the class of substances, but treat them as common properties of matter which supervene on changes. For he says that the compressed and condensed part of matter is cold, and that the thin and loose (that is the very word he uses) is hot; and that hence it is not unreasonably said that a man releases both hot and cold things from his mouth—for his breath is cooled when pressed and condensed by his lips, while if the mouth is relaxed the exhaled breath becomes hot by rareness (**25**: **B 1**).

Only the single word 'loose (*chalaron*)' is a direct quotation from Anaximenes;[7] but Plutarch plainly regards the whole argument in which that word is embedded as Anaximenean, and I am prepared to follow him.[8]

It seems, then, that Anaximenes' cosmogonical speculation began from the familiar paradox that we blow on our hands to warm them and on our porridge to cool it. Observation showed that the hand-warmer huffs with open mouth, while the porridge-cooler whistles through pursed lips; and a further simple observation indicates that the hot air is thinner than the cold: it is palpably less firm against the hand. At this point theory takes over from observation: first, Anaximenes supposes that the thinness of the hot air and the thickness of the cold air are causally connected to their temperature; and he advances the general hypothesis that what temperature a mass of stuff has is determined by its density. Thus changes in temperature are explicable in terms of rarefaction and condensation. Second, Anaximenes generalized his hypothesis further, and suggested that all the properties of a mass of stuff are determined by its density: just as rarefaction can account for the heat of fire, so it can account for its colour and its characteristic motions; just as condensation can account for the coldness of a cloud, so it can account for its opacity and woolly structure. Finally, the theory was applied to a variety of disparate phenomena—astronomical and meteorological—and to that extent confirmed or corroborated.

We need not embrace Anaximenes' conclusions in order to admire his principles and his methodology: observations of a puzzle situation lead him to form explanatory theories of successively greater generality. And the final theory has many of the hallmarks of science: it is highly general; it is devastatingly simple; it explains the original puzzle; and it applies to, and can therefore be tested against, a mass of superficially unconnected phenomena.

(c) *Fairy tales or science?*

Then is Anaximenes a Greek Galileo? And were the early Milesian cosmologists the world's first natural scientists? The question has aroused passion and dispute. At one extreme, there are scholars who think that 'a new thing came into the world with the early Ionian teachers—the thing we call science—and . . . they first pointed the way which Europe has followed ever since'.[9] At the other extreme, it is maintained that the Milesians are properly regarded not as the precursors of science but as the successors of the ancient poet-seers, lay dogmatists concerned to propound a secular *Weltanschauung* and unconcerned to defend it by the tiresomely rational methods of the scientist.[10] Those who prefer a middle path imagine that the Milesians strove towards scientific status but did not quite attain it: 'the *phusiologoi*, despite their eagerness to use the senses for all they were worth, failed not only to use but even to understand the experimental method of modern science'.[11]

The controversy has been muddled by two facts: first, the identity of the disputed terrain is shifting and uncertain; second, the disputants unconsciously bring quite different philosophical presuppositions to their arguments. It is worth indicating at the start some of the things to which all parties assent.

First, none of the Milesian theories is true: the Milesians do not compose a Greek Royal Society; and their Transactions would not make any contribution to the sum of scientific knowledge. They and their successors made and recorded various true observations; but the assembly of those observations into true or well-confirmed theory was a long process which the Milesians scarcely began.

Second, none of the Milesians aspired to the sort of precision we require in a scientific theory: their views are incurably vague; and underlying this vagueness is a complete innocence of the delights of measurement and quantification.[12] Thus Anaximenes, as I have remarked, made no attempt to state what degree of compression turned air into cloud or water, or to formulate an equation correlating density and temperature. As a result, his theories are peculiarly resistant to testing: it is simply not clear in what way they are to be 'applied' to the phenomena, nor, hence, what observations will confirm and what refute them. It might be added that Anaximenes' descriptions of his original puzzle and of his observations are negligent and unrigorous: his theory cannot explain the puzzle, since the puzzle is misdescribed. (The outstanding exception to this generalization about Milesian theorizing is provided by Anaximander's astronomy: that was decked out with precise mathematical hypotheses about the arrangements of the heavenly wheels.)

Third, it will be agreed that the Milesians had certain intellectual aims which are, in a broad sense, characteristic of science: they wanted to describe the phenomenal world; they wanted to explain what the phenomena were and how they were produced; and they aimed at giving an explanation which did not appeal to chance or to stray divinities.

Fourth, the Milesians had some grasp—implicit in their approach if not explicit in their writings—of certain methods of explanation which are also, in a broad sense, characteristic of science: they advanced highly general hypotheses which could (they thought) be applied to and explain the phenomena; they gave reasons for their opinions, however bizarre those opinions might seem; they drew inferences and they suggested analogies or 'models'.

If these points are agreed upon, wherein lies the dispute over the scientific standing of the early Greek thinkers? It is sometimes thought to lie in the question of whether the Milesians adhered to 'the experimental method': crudely put, the Milesians did not indulge in experiments and hence were not scientists.

It is true that, as far as our knowledge extends, the Milesians did not experiment; indeed Greek science as a whole can produce only a handful of experiments, and those are all of a fairly unsophisticated sort.[13] The reasons for this are not hard to guess. Yet I am inclined to think that experimentation is not an essential tool of science, and indeed that in some sciences it is of little or no account. An experiment, after all, is merely the artificial generation of observable phenomena. Experimental observation has certain advantages over observation *au naturel*: the experimenter can isolate the phenomena which interest him, and he can exercise some control over their production. Nevertheless, it is the observable products, and not the manner of their production, which are scientifically significant. In many of the biological sciences (in anatomy, say, or taxonomic botany) experiment has little or no place; in the human sciences (sociology or economics) experiment is not often acceptable; in certain of the physical sciences (astronomy is the prime example) experiment is rarely possible; and in some special sciences (for example, palaeontology) there is no room for experiment at all. The Milesians had a copious abundance of data to explain: 'pioneers, with so many fresh phenomena waiting to be observed, they felt no urge to manufacture more. Having abundance, they saw no need for superabundance.'[14] And in any case, the sciences they showed most interest in are not experimental in any serious sense. Certainly, the devising of a few tests would have enlivened and improved Presocratic science; but the lack of an 'experimental method' does not bar the Presocratics from the halls of science.[15]

Perhaps, then, the Milesians failed because they ignored 'the inductive method': they failed, that is, to live up to Baconian canons of scientific procedure. 'The inductive method' may be interpreted in a procedural or in a logical fashion: it may enjoin either that the garnering of data should precede the formation of theory, or that any formed theory should be supported by a mass of data. Both interpretations have this in common, that they require the scientist to be an ardent collector of particular facts.

The inductive method has fallen on hard times; and few, I imagine, would maintain that an inductive procedure is either essential or even particularly useful to science. Indeed, it is a popular view that the blind collation of data is inimical to the scientific spirit, if not a positively incoherent pursuit. Yet it is reasonable to think that data are not wholly irrelevant to science: a theory which is supported by a vast number of disparate facts is, I suppose, still preferable to a theory which has no support; and whatever our attitude to Bacon, we are unlikely to conclude that the collection of observational data is simply irrelevant to the scientific enterprise.

How do the Milesians fare if they are measured against these standards? We do not know if they attempted to follow an inductive procedure. I have supposed that Anaximenes' theorizing began from his observations of the effects of breath; but that is merely a guess. He might, for all our sources can tell us, have elaborated his theory first and only later come across the porridge puzzle. In any case, Anaximenes' procedure was hardly inductive even if my guess is right: one observation does not make an induction. Then did Anaximenes support his formed theory by amassing a collection of phenomena to which it might be applied? Here the answer is clearly affirmative. The doxography does not allow us to say how large was the *corpus* of Anaximenes' observations, or whether they were the result of personal inspection, or exactly how the observations were supposed to be related to the general theory; and we may well imagine, as I have already said, that neither the observations nor their subsumption under the theory were carried out in a particularly rigorous fashion. Nonetheless, it is beyond reasonable dispute that Anaximenes had a mass of empirical evidence which, he believed, indirectly corroborated his general theory. And that, I submit, is enough to make him as inductively minded as any scientist need be. In general, it seems fair to conclude that 'the alliance between careful observation and bold speculation is not only natural but essential in early Greek thought, the very condition for the creation of science and philosophy in the Greek sense'.[16]

Finally, a third method, the 'critical method', has been judged the especial mark of scientific endeavour. An adherent of the critical method will be most concerned to refute theories, whether his own or others'; he will elicit the particular implications of a general theory and prove them against the facts of observation; he will occupy himself in devising strenuous and varied tests, and he will not rest until he can invent no more hurdles for a theory to stride.

I am not certain that the 'critical method' constitutes a methodology; and I am certain that the 'critical method' is not specifically scientific. Criticism is a feature of rational procedure in every branch of intellectual study; philosophers and historians are not excluded from a form of thought which physicists and geologists may indulge in. Nonetheless, it is obvious enough that a sharp critical acumen and a determination to probe and test hypotheses are intellectual virtues of a high order; and it is apposite to inquire whether the Milesians possessed them.

The common view, I think, is that they did. The history of Presocratic thought is customarily seen in an Hegelian light: thesis and antithesis alternate in dialectical interplay, each new theory springing from the head of its predecessor. Criticism and refutation thus supply the very structure of Presocratic thought, and the 'critical method' is the key to an understanding of the first development of science.

It is, of course, indisputable that the Presocratics knew and were influenced by the views of their predecessors; and the influence was often negative. I have already purveyed the commonplace conjecture that Anaximenes' innovations were devised in response to the inadequacies of Anaximander's theories; and many similar cases will be noted as this book proceeds. Moreover, we have direct evidence of such awareness. Thus Xenophanes referred to Thales (**21 B 19**) and criticized Pythagoras (**B 7**); Heraclitus abused Pythagoras and Xenophanes (**22 B 40**); Hippo and Zeno may have animadverted on Empedocles (Aristotle, *An* 405b2 = **31 A 4**; Suda, **29 A 2**); Diogenes of Apollonia wrote *Against the Natural Scientists* (Simplicius, **64 A 4**); and Democritus attacked Anaxagoras (**68 B 5**) and Protagoras (**68 B 156**). Such references can easily be multiplied; and the Hippocratic treatises offer examples of the substance behind them.

Yet it is one thing to know and to reject one's predecessor's views, another to adopt the critical approach to science and philosophy; criticism, after all, is more than the mere contradicting of an opponent. And it is a remarkable fact that the art of critical or destructive argument scarcely appears in Greek thought before Socrates. The earliest examples I know come in the *Dissoi Logoi*, a treatise on which I shall say more later (below, pp. 517–22). Section 6 of the work discusses the question of whether virtue and wisdom can be taught; the author advances some arguments for a negative answer, points to their weakness, and concludes thus: 'That is my argument—you have beginning and end and middle; and I do not assert that it can be taught—but those proofs do not satisfy me' (**90 A 1**, §6.13; cf. §2.23; §3.15; §5.9). That passage makes, clearly and for the first time, the crucial distinction between rejecting an argument for a conclusion and rejecting the conclusion itself. The art of criticism cannot thrive unless that distinction is grasped.

The critical innocence of the Presocratics appears in two forms. First, there is no Presocratic instance of a philosopher criticizing an *argument*; we might expect the successors and opponents of Parmenides to have investigated the structure of his reasonings and explained where it was weak or defective. Yet no example of such investigation survives: neither Empedocles nor Anaxagoras tells us where and why he thinks Parmenides errs, even though both thought that Parmenides did err. Nor does any philosopher before Aristotle tell us what is wrong with Zeno's paradoxes.

Second, and more surprisingly, we have hardly any instances of philosophers criticizing a *theory*. We may well assume that the successors of Thales thought his water thesis mistaken; yet no text tells us why they thought so, or what counter-examples they offered or imagined. Still less do we find self-criticism. Anaximenes' theory suggests to us any number of critical tests; yet there is no evidence that Anaximenes applied any of them. He may have thought, vaguely enough, that compressed earth becomes harder until it turns to stone; yet he does not seem to have attempted the easy task of compressing air—in a leather wine-skin, say—to see if it turned to cloud or water; and there is no evidence that he ever investigated the implications of his thesis that density and temperature were directly proportional.

Our evidence for the Milesians is slight and fragmentary. It is possible that their writings contained critical inquiries which later authors did not think fit to preserve; it is possible too, that the Milesians regarded criticism as a necessary propaedeutic to construction, but scorned to sully their finished publications with such preliminary observations. At all events, we can scarcely avoid the assumption that the Milesians and their successors sometimes rejected earlier theories, and did so on rational grounds. Yet the evidence lends great plausibility to the thought that the Milesians were more interested in construction than in destruction, and that their energies were too absorbed in the creative task of system building to dwell long on the less sublime business of criticism and refutation.

What do these reflexions suggest? It is, I believe, perverse to deny that the Milesians were scientists—and great scientists at that. Their scientific shortcomings were not methodological: they approached their problems in an admirable fashion; and their failures were due not to lack of understanding but to lack of developed techniques of observation and theory construction. Their methodological failing was general and not specifically scientific: intoxicated by the delights of construction, they did not care to submit their buildings to the rough winds of criticism.

(d) *The use of analogy*

A striking feature of Presocratic thought is its use of analogy.[17] In

Thales' account of the floating of the earth we have come upon the first simple example of this pattern of thought. The most celebrated and elaborate analogies are found in the fragments of Empedocles: one long passage (**31 B 84**) compares the structure of the eye to the structure of a lantern, in order to explain how it is that our eyes 'flash'; a longer and notoriously difficult fragment (**B 100**) accounts for respiration by a detailed comparison with a *clepsydra* or pipette. But examples can be found in every early Greek thinker; and since the scanty doxography on Anaximenes presents us with several interesting analogies, I shall discuss this widespread 'thought pattern' by reference to him.

Historians of ancient thought sometimes treat analogy as an antiquated device; and sometimes they imply that all analogies are logically on a par. Neither of those notions is correct. First, analogy, in one form or another, is a constant—perhaps a psychologically indispensable—accompaniment of scientific thought: the vogue word 'model' is a modern synonym for 'analogy'. Second, an analogy may be invoked for a variety of purposes, only one of which is properly denominated 'argument from analogy'.

Here are seven passages in which Anaximenean analogies appear:

> The soul, being our air, controls us, and breath and air encompass the whole world (**26**: **B 2**).

> The stars move . . . around the earth, just as a turban winds round our head (**27**: Hippolytus, **A 7**).

> And some say that the universe whirls like a mill-stone (**28**: Aëtius, **A 12**).

> Anaximenes says that the stars are fixed in the crystalline in the manner of nails . . . (**29**: Aëtius, **A 14**).[18]

> Anaximenes says that the sun is flat like a leaf (**30**: Aëtius, **A 15**; cf. **B 2a**).

> Anaximenes says the same [about thunder] as him [sc. Anaximander], adding the phenomenon we observe on the sea, which gleams when cut by oars (**31**: Aëtius, **A 17**; cf. **12 A 23**; Aristophanes, *Clouds* 404–7).

> Just as in old buildings certain parts collapse though not struck, when they have more weight than strength; so in the earth as a

whole it comes about that certain parts are loosened by age, and, being loosened, fall and cause the parts above them to tremble. They do this first when they break away (for nothing of any size breaks away without moving what it adheres to). Then, when they have collapsed, they meet something solid and spring back again, like a ball which, when it falls, bounces back and is as often driven back as it is sent up from the ground on a new flight (**32**: Seneca, *nat quaest* 6.10 = Diels-Kranz, I.488.30–5; cf. **A 21**).

These seven examples fall into two, or perhaps three, groups.

First, analogy is often used merely as a rhetorical trope, to add colour and vivacity to a flat description. This is pretty clearly the case in **28**: the phrase 'like a mill-stone' adds nothing new to the verb 'whirls'. Example **27** is obscure; but I assume that it is a joke, designed more to enliven than to illuminate Anaximenes' account of the stars. It is likely that **30** also belongs to this class.

Second, an analogy may be more than entertaining but less than explanatory: we observe that an *F* is *G*, but find the observation somehow puzzling; analogy with more familiar cases of things which are *G* may serve to remove our puzzlement. Example **29** is of this sort: the small stars are evidently fixed somehow to the vault of the sky, yet we may wonder how they can stay up there. The observation of nail-heads fixed in an overhead beam shows that the fixture of the stars need not be paradoxical. Again, in **32** the superficially surprising phenomenon of the earth's quaking without being struck is made intellectually palatable by the observation that old buildings will sometimes tumble without being struck. It may be that **31** is a further example of this type; and **30** too may belong here: the sun can float on air, just as leaves can (cf. **A 20**; above, p. 28).

Analogies of this second type are susceptible to a strong and a weak interpretation. Taken strongly, **29** is supposed to show *how* the stars remain in the sky: they are the upper surface of a long spike which is sunk into the sky and thus holds them in place. So construed, the analogy does indeed aim to be explanatory. Taken weakly, **29** is intended to show only that the stars *can* remain in the sky, and not to offer a suggestion about *how* they are fixed. So construed the analogy has no explanatory pretensions, and Anaximenes might as well have added 'or like flies, or pieces of paper glued to the ceiling'.

The difference between the strong and the weak interpretations is not clear-cut: removal of puzzlement slides insensibly into explanation; and it is usually hard to tell what interpretation an author intends (unless he explicitly offers two or more analogies). For all that, the distinction is important. Some students of computer science attempt to simulate human behaviour and to show how it can be that certain sensory inputs into human organisms elicit certain cognitive or motor responses. Computer simulation may be an enlightening discipline; but it does not claim to show how human organisms work: that a computer can produce the same results from the same materials as I can, does not show that I and the computer work in the same way. Other students of computer science speak of artificial intelligence; they aim not to simulate but to reproduce—and hence to explain—human performances. There are thus two distinct ways in which computers may serve as an analogy or 'model' of the human mind; the second way, evidently, makes far stronger claims than the first.

Finally, analogies may be called upon in argument. Observing first that *a* is *F* and also *G*, and secondly that *b* is *F*, we infer that *b*, too, is *G*. Example **26** is commonly taken in this sense, and is treated as Anaximenes' reason for thinking that air, rather than any other stuff, is the material principle of everything. It is then to be paraphrased as follows: 'We men contain an airy soul; and that air keeps us together, i.e., keeps us alive; the universe as a whole contains air: hence it is air that keeps the universe together, i.e., supplies its underlying stuff.' Air sustains men; so air is probably the *Urstoff* of the universe.

That interpretation of **26** is, I suppose, possible; but it is not demanded by the text (which contains no inferential particle),[19] nor is it a happy interpretation (for the argument it ascribes to Anaximenes is scandalously jejune). Argument by analogy is in effect induction from a single case, and as such it is essentially lacking in probative force; moreover, in the case of **26**, the terms of the analogy are not identical, and the interpretation is obliged to introduce the phrase 'keep together' in order to produce a show of identity. It is preferable to think that **26** contains no argument at all, and *a fortiori* no analogical argument; rather, it presents one of the considerations which may have determined Anaximenes to fix on air as his basic material: if Thales preferred water because water is essential to life, Anaximenes preferred air for the self-same reason. Example **26** does indeed give an answer, or part of an answer, to question (b) of p. 46; for it helps to explain why Anaximenes picked on air as his *Urstoff*. But the answer is not based on analogical argument; and neither in **26** nor elsewhere do we find an argument from analogy in Anaximenes.

Indeed, I do not think there is a single argument from analogy in any of the Presocratics. And that is a happy conclusion: analogies may be scientifically important; they may serve, psychologically, to illuminate a dry exposition or to dispel a puzzlement; and they may be useful, methodologically, in suggesting a synthesis or provoking a generalization. But they have no inferential status: argument 'from analogy' is one of the numerous species of bad argument.

IV

The Natural Philosophy of Heraclitus

(a) *The great account*

When, in his lectures on the history of philosophy, Hegel came to Heraclitus, he was moved to an extravagant effusion: 'Here we see land! There is no proposition of Heraclitus which I have not adopted in my logic.' A prominent opponent of Hegelianism is no less effusive: Heraclitus' fragments, far from adumbrating teutonic dialectics, reveal 'a thinker of unsurpassed power and originality', a Greek Wittgenstein.[1] The truth is that Heraclitus attracts exegetes as an empty jampot wasps; and each new wasp discerns traces of his own favourite flavour.

The existence of such diverse interpretations of Heraclitus' philosophy will sow the seeds of despair in the mind of any honest scholar; and that luxuriant plant receives nourishment from a consideration of the history and nature of Heraclitus' text. We do possess over a hundred fragments from Heraclitus' pen; but many of them have reached us through the labours of two early Christian fathers: Clement of Alexandria saw Heraclitus as a pagan prophet of the Last Judgment; and Hippolytus of Rome made him, for polemical purposes, the spiritual father of Noetus' Monarchian heresy. Moreover, Heraclitus had earned the dubious benefits of popularity even before his Christian renascence; for Cleanthes the Stoic had attempted to give a stamp of authority to the teachings of his master Zeno by deriving them from the ancient doctrines of Heraclitus (Diogenes Laertius, IX. 16 = **22 A 1**).[2]

We see Heraclitus reflected in the distorting glasses of patristic piety and Stoic special pleading. And in their pristine state his doctrines were not easy reading: according to an old fable, 'Euripides gave Socrates a copy of Heraclitus' book and asked him what he thought of it; Socrates replied: "What I understand is good; and I think that what I don't understand is good too—but it would take a Delian diver to get to the bottom of it" (Diogenes Laertius, II.22 = **A 4**).[3] Theophrastus tartly observed that 'from impulsiveness, some of what he wrote was half-completed, and the rest inconsistent' (Diogenes Laertius, IX.6 = **A 1**). Heraclitus the Obscure, the Riddler, the oracular prophet, stands dark and majestic in the early history of philosophy. He set out to imitate 'the king whose is the oracle at Delphi', who, in Heraclitus' own words, 'neither states nor conceals, but gives signs' (**B 93** = **14 M**;[4] cf. Lucian, **C 5**).[5]

Interpretation may thus appear a Herculean task. Yet the filth of the Heraclitean stables has perhaps been exaggerated. First, the textual tradition is not irremediably contaminated: Stoic and Christian accretions are readily recognized and readily removed; and we have enough of Heraclitus' own words to reconstruct his thought without continual reliance on the doxography. Moreover, the obscurity of Heraclitus' writings is customarily misrepresented. He is, like all the Presocratics, given to a vexatious vagueness; he frequently propounds paradoxes; and he has a mild penchant for puns. But puns are harmless and paradox is not always obscure. The fragmentary state of Heraclitus' surviving words often makes his sense opaque; but I do not find his style particularly 'oracular'; he does not present his thoughts in 'riddles' (though he once quotes an old chestnut); and if he sometimes produces similes and analogies, it is gratuitous to suppose that his every remark must be construed unliterally, as the surface sign of an underlying profundity. At all events, I shall proceed on the assumption that Heraclitus usually means what he says. I do not share Nietzsche's view that 'probably no man has ever written as clearly and as lucidly' as Heraclitus; but it will, I hope, emerge that what he says is not always bible black.

We have, moreover, a clear starting point. Fragment **B 1** = **1 M** is twice said to come from the beginning of Heraclitus' book,[6] and we have no good reason to doubt the testimony (Aristotle, *Rhet* 1407b16 = **A 4**; Sextus, **A 16**). The fragment reads:

> And of this account (*logos*) which is the case always men prove to be uncomprehending, both before they hear it and once they have heard it. For although everything comes about in accordance with this account (*logos*), they are like inexperienced men when they experience both the words and the deeds of the sort which I recount by dividing up each thing in accordance with its nature (*phusis*) and saying how it is; but other men do not notice what

> they do when they are awake, just as they are oblivious of things when asleep (**33**).

Aristotle pointed out the syntactical ambiguity of Heraclitus' first sentence, an ambiguity which I imagine to have been deliberate and which is preserved in the translation by the clumsy placing of 'always'; and scholars since Aristotle have devoted much labour and ingenuity to the explication of the fragment. I shall only touch on one exegetical point before stating what I take to be the chief contentions of the passage.

Most scholars have found in '*logos*' a technical term, and they have striven to discover a metaphysical sense for it.[7] Their strivings are vain: a *logos* or 'account' is what a man *legei* or says. We may suppose that our fragment was preceded, in antique fashion, by a title-sentence of the form: 'Heraclitus of Ephesus says (*legei*) thus: . . .'.[8] The noun *logos* picks up, in an ordinary and metaphysically unexciting way, the verb *legei*; it is wasted labour to seek Heraclitus' secret in the sense of *logos*.

It does not, of course, follow from this that Heraclitus had no 'metaphysical' theory to propound, no 'Logos-doctrine', as the commentators have it. On the contrary, **33** makes it clear that his 'account' must include or embody something like a general 'law of nature': 'everything happens' in accordance with the account. Thus Heraclitus' first claim is that he can offer a general account of the world, and that he can do this by explaining what is the *phusis* or essential nature of each thing. Second, he maintains that most men are woefully ignorant of this account: they are 'like the deaf' (**B 34 = 2 M**); they live in a dream world (**B 89 = 24 M**) 'as if they had a private understanding' of how things are (**B 2 = 23 M**).[9] Third, he says that most men do not even know what they are doing or how to act.

Of these three claims this chapter will investigate the first: later chapters will deal with Heraclitus' second claim and the epistemology which underlies it, and with his third claim and the rudimentary ethical theory it suggests. There is, I think, something to be said for the view that this ethical theory was the summit of Heraclitus' thought; but modern discussions inevitably and reasonably spend many more words on the metaphysical foothills.

'Everything happens' in accordance with Heraclitus' account: the account is 'common to everything' (**B 114 = 23 M**; cf. **B 80 = 28 M**); and it is analogous to, or identical with, the single divine law which 'nourishes' all human laws (**B 114**).[10] Alas, we do not possess (and perhaps Heraclitus never gave) a single luminous statement of this law: four muddy fragments contain the nearest we can get to a general account.

> Conjunctions are wholes and non-wholes: what is converging, what is diverging; what is consonant, what is dissonant: from everything one, and from one thing everything (**34**: **B 10** = **25 M**).[11]

> Listening not to me but to my account it is wise to agree that everything is one (**35**: **B 50** = **26 M**).[12]

> They do not understand how what is diverging is converging with itself: there is a back-stretched connexion, as of a bow and of a lyre (**36**: **B 51** = **27 M**).[13]

> One should know that war is common, and justice strife; and that everything comes about in accordance with strife and what must be (**37**: **B 80** = **28 M**).

These four fragments have suggested three abstract theses. First, there is the notorious Theory of Flux: all the furniture of the world is in constant, if imperceptible, change; the cosmos is a battleground, and its pacific façade hides the endless victories and defeats of an interminable internecine strife. Second, there is the Unity of Opposites: behind the coherent surface of things there is a tension of incompatibles; every object, however firm and enduring, is subject to contrary strains, and is constituted by opposing features. Third, there is a doctrine of Monism: in some fashion the diversity of appearances is underpinned or colligated by some single thing or stuff; at bottom, all is one.

Monism appears to be explicitly asserted in **35**, and to be implicit in **34**. The Unity of Opposites has been found in **36**, and also in **34**. Flux allegedly flows from **37**, and perhaps from **36** and **34**. The four fragments, taken alone, are difficult; and all the interpretations I have indicated have been disputed. Nevertheless, I think that all three theses can be ascribed to Heraclitus; and that together they form a metaphysical system.

(b) *Nature's bonfire*

The abstract monism of **35** is given a fiery and substantial nature by other fragments:

> This world neither any god nor man made, but it always was and is and will be, an ever-living fire, kindling in measures and being extinguished in measures (**38: B 30** = **51 M**).

> Everything is an exchange for fire, and fire for everything—as goods for gold, and gold for goods (**39: B 90** = **54 M**).

Fire is the prime stuff of the world. The thesis has a traditional Milesian ring; and on his monism Heraclitus constructed, perhaps not in conscientious detail, a physical science of a standard Milesian type. He also advanced an idiosyncratic theory of man and of the human soul; and the fragments contain the remnants of an unusual theology. Heraclitus attacked the empty polymathy of his predecessors (see below, p. 146); but there is evidence enough that he was a polymath himself; and he takes his place on the board of Ionian scientists—a rebel, perhaps, but not a revolutionary. The details of Heraclitus' science are as controversial as anything in his thought; and I shall not attempt to expound them. Instead, I shall look more generally at the nature and grounds of Heraclitus' monism.

'From everything one, and from one thing everything' (**34**): it is fire, as **38** makes clear, which is the one stuff from which everything comes; and **B 31** = **53 M** elaborates on the bald hypothesis:

> Turnings of fire: first, sea; and of sea, half earth and half burning (*prêstêr*). . . . Sea is dispersed and is measured in the same proportion as there was before (**40**).[14]

Fire turns into water; and water eventually reverts to fire, the proportions remaining constant.

The Stoics, some of whom claimed Heraclitus as their ancestor, subscribed to a doctrine of *ekpurôsis* or cosmic conflagration, according to which the whole universe is periodically consumed by fire to rise again, phoenix-like, from its own ashes (see *SVF* II 596–632). The doxographers ascribe such an *ekpurôsis* to Heraclitus (e.g., Clement, *ad* **B 31**; Simplicius, **A 10**): some scholars accept the ascription, others deny it; and there is large controversy. I incline to agree that Aristotle and the Peripatetics made the ascription; and that nothing in the secondary sources stands against it. Yet **38** says flatly that 'this world . . . always was and is and will be': that is a brusque rejection both of cosmogony and of cosmophthory—'this world (*kosmos*)' did not begin and will not end. And that, as far as I can see, is incompatible with a doctrine of *ekpurôsis*.[15] The doxography, even if Aristotle is its patron, must yield to the evidence of the fragments.

The point is worth stressing: **38** does not merely rule out *ekpurôsis*; it rules out any form of cosmic disintegration, and equally any form of cosmogony. Heraclitus surely knew of the Milesian cosmogonists: why, we may wonder, did he reject their enterprise? and why, for that matter, had the Milesians imagined a beginning to the world, and supposed that one of the tasks of a natural scientist was to supply an account of the world's birth-pangs? Our texts give us no answers. Perhaps the Milesians simply did not entertain the possibility that the present cosmos was sempiternal: their mythological predecessors had fabled a genealogical account of the world's origins, and they conceived it their duty to replace genealogy by science. Every thinker has some unquestioned starting points, and the necessity of cosmogony was perhaps such a starting point for the Milesians.

However that may be, no analogous explanation is available for Heraclitus' case: his rejection of cosmogony was no tacit assumption but a self-conscious piece of polemic; and he must surely have expected a request to explain and justify his innovatory suggestion. He may have preserved a discreet silence (I have already commented upon the curious lack of critical concern among the Presocratics: above, pp. 50–2); but that is an unflattering and an implausible guess. The Atomists, and later Aristotle, rejected cosmogony; but we cannot project Aristotle's highly Aristotelian arguments back on to Heraclitus, and we do not really know how the Atomists argued (below, pp. 430–1). Speculation may invent a variety of reasons to support Heraclitus' stand: I leave the reader to exercise his own fancy here.

The monistic formula, 'Everything is from *X*', can be read cosmogonically. So read, it implies that at some time all things were *X*. That reading, I have just argued, is not possible for Heraclitus; but the formula admits a different interpretation, on which it implies only that everything at some time was *X*. On the first, cosmogonical, reading, at some time everything was *X*; on the second reading, everything was, at some time, *X*. The notation of quantificational logic brings out the distinction clearly. '$(\exists x)\ \phi x$' means 'Something is ϕ' '$(\forall x)\phi x$' means 'Everything is ϕ'. Let the variable x range over physical objects, and let the variable t range over times or instants. Then the cosmogonical interpretation of monism can be expressed by:

(1) $(\exists t)\ (\forall x)\ (x \text{ is } X \text{ at } t)$—'At some time every physical object is *X*'.

And the second reading of monism is given by:

(2) $(\forall x)\ (\exists t)\ (x \text{ is } X \text{ at } t)$—'Every physical object is at some time *X*'.

Here (1) entails (2); but (2) does not entail (1). It seems to me that the analogy Heraclitus draws in **39** fits well with (2) and ill with (1); and that this makes it probable that Heraclitus had (2) fairly clearly in mind.

According to Simplicius,

> Heraclitus . . . made fire the principle, and derives the things that exist from fire by condensation and rarefaction, and resolves them again into fire, taking this as the single underlying nature; for Heraclitus says that everything is an exchange for fire (**41: A 5**).

Fire on this view is the 'material principle' of everything. The view is ubiquitous in the doxography; and it is found in Aristotle (*Met* 984a7 = **18 A** 7).

Simplicius adverts to **39**; and scholars have been quick to point out that the fragment does not require an Aristotelian interpretation. Nor do the two main fragments on fire, **38** and **40**, embody an Aristotelian view; and the assertion in **38** that fire is 'extinguished in measures' has been taken to imply that fire does not, like a substrate, persist through its 'turnings'. Thus in Heraclitus' world things were made from, but are not made of, fire.[16]

Three frail reasons stand against this conclusion. First, Simplicius' reference to condensation and rarefaction supports an Aristotelian interpretation. (But Simplicius may only be reporting a Peripatetic conjecture, or making a conjecture of his own.) Second, 'everything is one' (**35**); and we may say, without abuse of language, that 'everything is fire' only if we mean that everything actually *is*, at bottom, fire. (But Hippolytus, who quotes **35**, suggests a different interpretation of the phrase.) Third, the sort of inference required to reach the Aristotelian view from a thesis like (2) is, as I shall shortly show, characteristically Heraclitean. (But need Heraclitus have made the inference here?) I incline to accept the Aristotelian interpretation; but the evidence is thin, and I put no weight on the matter.

How, then, did Heraclitus argue for his monism? Some scholars would say that this question was misconceived: Heraclitus' statements are oracular, and their production has little to do with argument; 'his conclusions are based on intuition rather than on observation and analysis of data'; or again: 'the content of [Heraclitus'] very general formula seems to have been filled in by a coherent chain of statements linked together not by logical argument but by interlocking ideas and verbal echoes, with an elaborate use of imagery, word-play and enigma'.[17] And those scholars who do perceive argument in Heraclitus regard his chief logical tool as analogy; and they talk of a 'thought pattern' rather than of ratiocination in any inferential sense.[18] Who, in any case, would expect a quick flame from hydropical Heraclitus?

There are certainly analogical statements in Heraclitus; but their number has been overestimated, and where they do occur they seem, to me at least, more a stylistic device than an argumentative mode. Again, there is certainly imagery and word-play in the fragments; but this too is a stylistic embellishment rather than a substitute for logical procedure. The fragments, I think, are consistent with, and indeed positively suggest, the view that Heraclitus, like any good Presocratic, was ready to support his statements by argument and evidence. I hope to make this claim plausible when I turn to Flux and Unity: for Monism the fragments are less helpful.

We might, indeed, imagine (consistently with the hypothesis of a rational Heraclitus) that his monism was an unargued postulate: like the Milesians, Heraclitus saw it as scientifically virtuous to construct his system on the simplest foundations; and like them again, he saw that monism provided the greatest degree of simplicity. Many scholars do not like unargued postulates; and of those, some have taken Heraclitus' monism as an inference from the Unity thesis. Heraclitus, they imagine, offered an *a fortiori* argument: 'If opposites form a unity, then everything forms a unity; hence everything is one.' There is a temptation to see just such an argument in **34**, where the last clauses present Monism, and the first clauses expound the Unity thesis. But the reconstruction is implausible; for the inference it offers Heraclitus is gross: from Unity there is no reasonable path to Monism.

There is, in any case, a better line of reasoning which we can ascribe to Heraclitus. We may suppose, first, that he posited a monistic theory to explain the generation of things; second, that he picked on fire as his fundamental material on the basis of observations of the same vague and general sort which influenced Anaximenes; third, that he understood his fiery monism as a special, cosmic, case of the Theory of Flux; and fourth, that he applied the general argument from Flux to Unity which I shall shortly expound, in order to derive an Aristotelian monism. This reconstruction is wholly speculative: it has the twin merits of ascribing arguments to Heraclitus which we have some reason to think him capable of using, and of placing the three main components of his account of the world in some sort of logical relation to one another.

(c) *All things are a flowing*

Panta rhei, 'Everything flows', is the most familiar of Heraclitus' sayings; yet few modern scholars think he said it, and many think he never had a Theory of Flux at all.[19]

That view is perverse. It is true that the particular phrase '*panta rhei*' first occurs in Simplicius (**40** (c^6) **M**); but the Theory itself is ascribed to Heraclitus by a horde of authorities.[20] Plato is explicit enough:

> Heraclitus, I think, says that everything moves (*panta chôrei*) and nothing rests (**42**: *Cratylus* 402A = **A 6**).

And there is earlier evidence yet: the Hippocratic treatise *de victu* is a silly farrago of ill-digested Presocratic opinions: one particularly Heraclitean chapter of the work, §5, opens with the phrase *chôrei panta*. The treatise probably dates from about 400 BC; and it thus contains a pre-Platonic reference to Heraclitean Flux.[21] The doxography consistently ascribes Flux to Heraclitus; and here, at least, we can trace it beyond the Peripatetic writers.

The doxographers are, I think, supported by the fragments themselves: Heraclitus' remarks on the rule of War and Strife (especially **37**) strongly suggest a dynamic and changing world of the sort envisaged by the Theory of Flux. And several fragments, which I shall shortly consider, offer what are reasonably taken as arguments for, or at least illustrations of, the Theory.

In sum, I think that Flux is Heraclitean; indeed I am disposed to take Plato's *panta chôrei* as an actual quotation from Heraclitus: there is as much reason for accepting this as there is for accepting many of the lines which orthodoxy prints as *ipsissima verba*.[22]

Some of those scholars who accept the Theory as Heraclitean are inclined to see nothing very original in it: the Milesians, after all, had held a similar view. The Milesians, like all observant men before Parmenides, had indeed noticed that things change: the world is patently not a static *tableau*. Yet it is far from a patent truth that *everything* changes, still less that everything *always* changes; and the Milesians, like ordinary men before Heraclitus, seem to have thought that within the changing world there was room for a number of stable and relatively permanent objects: the stars do not change in their courses, and the earth does not move from its place. There is no reason to deny Heraclitus the novelty of generalizing the natural view of a changing world to the more pugnacious thesis that everything changes; whether there was more to his innovation than such a generalization remains to be seen.

Discussion must start from the notorious 'river fragment' which has been associated with the Theory of Flux at least since Plato's time. The *Fragmente der Vorsokratiker* presents us with not one but three quotations:

> On those who step into the same rivers, different and different waters flow (**43: B 12 = 40 M**).
>
> We both step and do not step into the same rivers; we both are and are not (**44: B 49a = 40 (c²) M**).
>
> It is not possible to step into the same river twice (**45: B 91 = 40(C³) M**).

These three passages have sustained a massive commentary.[23] Are all three fragments genuine? Are two genuine and the third a paraphrase? Is one genuine, the other two paraphrases? Are all paraphrases of some single, lost, original? What, if anything, did Heraclitus actually say about rivers? and what did he mean?

Those controversial, and perhaps unanswerable, questions have, I think, acted as a smoke-screen: behind them the chief, and answerable, question has sailed on unheeded. That question is: What doctrine might the river fragments, whatever their original form, suggest, or seem to support? The common core of the fragments is the observation, trite and true, that rivers, on which common parlance and the nomenclature of the geographers impose a permanence and stability, are all the while changing in at least one essential respect: the waters of which they are constituted are never the same from one instant to the next. Plainly, this observation exemplifies, and therefore in some measure supports, the Theory of Flux. The superficial stability of rivers masks a continuous and essential change: things look, but are not, the same. We need not take Heraclitus' river allegorically, as Plato apparently did; but once we have granted Heraclitus a Theory of Flux, it is silly not to take his river to exemplify it. The obvious and the natural message of rivers is this: stability may cover constant change. That message can hardly have been misunderstood by a proponent of Flux.[24]

A less celebrated fragment offers a second piece of evidence:

> The barley drink disintegrates if it is not stirred (**46: B 125 = 31 M**).

Here the moral is less impressively instanced but more easily drawn: cocktails must be shaken or stirred; a glass of stuff whose contents are not continuously changing cannot be a cocktail but will disintegrate into separate layers of barley, honey and wine. Change is essential to the identity and existence of the drink (cf. Themistius, **A 3b**).

A further fragment makes the same point in more general terms:

> Cold things grow warm; warm grows cold; wet grows dry; parched grows moist (**47: B 126 = 42 M**).

A farmer looking at his land will refer to the fields and the soil which he cultivates; his way of thinking and speaking assumes a constancy and stability in nature. Yet momentary reflexion is enough to remind him that the fundamental properties of his farmland, on which its appearance and its powers depend, are changing from day to day and hour to hour. Or again, a man's body is constantly changing its temperature and humidity, as he breathes and digests: the surface stability of the human shape hides a hubbub of operations without which men would soon cease to be.

Fire, like water, evidently flows; and **38** indicates that Heraclitus saw Flux on a cosmic scale: 'This world . . . [is] an ever-living fire, kindling in measures and being extinguished in measures.' Similarly, **40** presumably points to certain familiar but grand meteorological changes: the sea is always losing its substance, parts being drawn up in vapour by the sun, parts being filtered out as silt and adding to the land. Such observable changes indicate that the world as a whole, though apparently divided with some permanence into the great and stable masses of fire, water and earth, is subject to a continuous transformation: even at a cosmic level, reality is essentially changing.

Other fragments can more doubtfully be adduced as pointing to the same conclusion (see, e.g., **B 67 = 77 M**; **B 36 = 66 M**); and one crucial remnant, which I shall discuss in the next section, makes the connexion between Flux and Unity (**B 88 = 41 M**). But the fragments I have already quoted appear to me sufficient to establish a certain rationality to Heraclitus' procedure: the Theory of Flux was no *a priori* intuition or piece of fanciful imagery; it was a general thesis about the nature of reality, founded upon and supported by a series of empirical observations.

The same fragments give us a clearer view of the nature of the Theory, and enable us to scotch two popular interpretations whose intrinsic absurdity may partly account for the reluctance some scholars feel at ascribing the Theory to Heraclitus.

The first interpretation pictures Heraclitus as an early Wittgensteinian who 'visualized the world . . . not as the sum-total of all *things*, but rather as the totality of events, or changes, or facts'. 'Heraclitus' problem' was 'the *problem of change*—the *general* problem: *How is change possible*? How can *a thing* change without losing its identity—in which case it would no longer be *that thing* which has changed?' And Heraclitus' answer was that there are no changing things, but only changes: since nothing changes, the 'problem of change' is dissolved. For 'to Heraclitus the truth is to have grasped the essential being of nature, i.e. to have represented it as implicitly infinite, as process in itself'.[25]

That diverting interpretation does at least take Heraclitus' Theory as a serious philosophical proposition; but it is a fantasy, and a confusion. First, I protest against the widely accepted *dictum* that 'if you want to explain Heraclitus you must first show where his problem lay'.[26] Heraclitus, like his predecessors, did not focus his attention on some one 'problem': he wanted to give a general account of nature or the world. (Moreover, we are in no position to identify any 'problem' he found independently of his 'answers'.) Second, there is no evidence that Heraclitus posed 'the general problem of change': change for him was in particular cases a datum, and in general a theory; it was not a 'problem'. Third, the Theory of Flux does not imply the Wittgensteinian thesis that 'the world is the totality of facts, not of things'. Nor does it imply the different theory that the world is the totality of changes. Rather, it suggests that the world is a mass of things—stuffs and substances—which are subject to constant change. And such a suggestion does not approach, let alone dissolve, the 'general problem of change'.

The second interpretation of the Theory of Flux comes from Plato's *Theaetetus* (179D–183B): it takes the Theory to assert that all things are at every moment changing in every respect. Aristotle gives the following report:

> Again, seeing that the whole of nature is in motion, and that nothing is true of what is changing, they supposed that it is not possible to speak truly of what is changing in absolutely all respects. For from this belief flowered the most extreme opinion of those I have mentioned—that of those who say they 'Heraclitize', and such as was held by Cratylus, who in the end thought one should say nothing and only moved his finger, and reproached Heraclitus for saying that you cannot step into the same river twice—for he himself thought you could not do so even once (**48**: *Met* 1010a7–15 = **65 A 4**).

The surviving evidence on Cratylus the Heraclitean is sparse and puzzling: our two chief sources, the *Metaphysics* and Plato's *Cratylus*, are not easily harmonized; nor, for that matter, are they easily interpreted. I assume that the *Metaphysics* is reliable; and that the main burden of Cratylus' argument is this: 'If the water in the pot is changing temperature, you cannot truly ascribe any temperature to it; if the door is being painted, you cannot truly ascribe a colour to it; and in general, if *a* is changing in respect of some continuum of qualities *S*, then you cannot ascribe any position on *S* to *a*. But everything is always changing in every respect; hence you can say nothing truly about anything.'

The argument assumes the strong version of Flux found in the *Theaetetus*. Plato argues that Flux of that strength is incoherent. To state the theory, it is necessary to refer to subjects of change, to identify objects, or at least areas of space, that are undergoing change; but reference and identification require a certain minimal stability in the object referred to or identified: I cannot refer to *a* unless I can truly assign *some* property to it. The extreme Cratylan theory of Flux thus denies one of its own presuppositions: if the theory is true, it cannot even be stated. Hence it is necessarily false. Cratylus' own argument is an adumbration of Plato's. For, according to Cratylus, Flux implies that nothing can truly be said of any object. Cratylus inferred that one can refer, or point, to objects (if that is why he 'moved his finger') but that one can predicate nothing of them; Plato inferred that one could not even refer to objects, since reference implies predication.

There are interesting hares trembling here for pursuit; but I shall not chase them. For there is no reason at all to ascribe a strong Cratylan Flux to Heraclitus. Cratylus did not sit at Heraclitus' feet, nor did he parrot Heraclitean doctrine: his theory is explicitly presented as a development, not a restatement, of Heraclitean Flux. Cratylus is described as a Heraclitean, and that is intelligible enough: his doctrine, that everything is always flowing in *all* respects, is evidently a child of Heraclitus' doctrine, that everything is always flowing in *some* respects.

(d) *A world of contradictions*

According to Aristotle, 'Heraclitus' account says that everything is and is not' (*Met* 1012a24); at least, this was a view of Heraclitus current in Aristotle's day, even if Aristotle himself, for philosophical reasons, was sometimes reluctant to accept it (cf. *Met* 1005b24–5 = **A 7**). The context of Aristotle's remark allows us to give it a fairly precise interpretation: 'Take anything you like, there is some property which it both has and lacks'; in symbols:

(1) $(\forall x)\ (\exists \phi)\ (\phi x\ \&\ \text{not-}\phi x)$.

Aristotle does not mean that Heraclitus propounded (1) in so many words; and of the fragments only **44** (above, p. 66) explicitly states a case of (1), and that is of dubious authenticity. On the other hand, the fragments do make frequent play with 'opposites' or contrary predicates; and if we jib at (1) we might allow Heraclitus the view that 'opposites belong to the same thing' (Sextus, *Pyrr Hyp* I.210; cf. II.63). Thus, letting 'ϕ'' mark a predicate contrary to 'ϕ' we can state the Heraclitean thesis as follows:

(2a) $(\forall x)\ (\exists \phi)\ (\phi x\ \&\ \phi' x)$.

In Aristotle's view (1) follows at once from (2a) (cf. *Met* 1011b15–22), and that will explain his ascription of (1) to Heraclitus.

Heraclitus did not, of course, say anything quite like (2a): that formula uses the artifices of a later logical notation. Hippolytus, who reports **35**, says that by 'all things are one' Heraclitus meant 'all opposites are one'. If he is right we possess, perhaps, one part of Heraclitus' own formulation of the Unity thesis. In modern notation, that amounts not to (2a) but to:

(2b) $(\forall \phi)\ (\exists x)\ (\phi x\ \&\ \phi' x)$.

We may conclude that the Unity of Opposites is properly expressed by the conjunction of (2a) and (2b): every pair of contraries is somewhere coinstantiated; and every object coinstantiates at least one pair of contraries:

(2) $(\forall \phi)\ (\exists x)\ (\phi x\ \&\ \phi' x)\ \&\ (\forall x)\ (\exists \phi)\ (\phi x\ \&\ \phi' x)$.

Many scholars will object to this interpretation of the Unity of Opposites: it ascribes an anachronistically precise thesis to Heraclitus, and thereby makes his view absurdly and trivially false. I shall say something about the absurdity of Heraclitus' thesis later; here I want to answer the charge of anachronism.

The charge is in effect twofold. First, Heraclitus did not use the categories of formal logic which (2) foists upon him; in particular, the subject-predicate structure of (2) has metaphysical implications which are quite alien to Heraclitus' thought. One part of this criticism is misguided: it is true that (2) states matters with greater precision than any sentence Heraclitus used; but to make a fairly precise statement of a philosopher's loosely expressed thought is not to misrepresent him; rather, it is a necessary preliminary to any adequate interpretation. Another part of the criticism is less clearly erroneous: perhaps (2) is precise in the wrong way? perhaps a different formulation of the Unity Thesis is possible? It is easy to invent other formulations; the only one which has any interest, or any plausibility as an interpretation, is:

(3) $(\forall \phi)\ (\phi = \phi')$.

White is black; heaviness is lightness; and the light is darkness itself: contrary properties are strictly identical with one another.[27]

Now some of Heraclitus' fragments do suggest something like (3);

but others are much more naturally taken to illustrate (2). And those which suggest (3) can be treated, without great strain, as rhetorical essays at (2). Again, (3), together with the harmless assumption that all the opposites are instantiated, entails (2); and on any interpretation what is most puzzling about Heraclitus' thesis is his apparent 'violation of the Law of Contradiction', which is most clearly brought out in (2). Finally, I cannot really believe that Heraclitus subscribed to (3): can anyone have seriously supposed that, say, being wet and being dry was one and the same thing? It is one thing to persuade oneself that one and the same thing is both wet and dry; another to imagine that there is no difference between being wet and being dry.

Thus in answer to the first charge, I say first that the precision of (2) is entirely proper, and indeed necessary; and second, that (2) is probably precise in the right way. Now for the second charge: (2) comes from Aristotle; but Aristotle may have got Heraclitus wrong. In particular, Aristotle may have taken Heraclitus' utterances too literally: by his assertions of 'unity' Heraclitus only means that things 'are "one" . . . in that they all have a common component . . . and because they all connect up with one another *because of* this common structure'.[28] Heraclitus observed that things, even opposites, are connected in far more complex and manifold ways than we incline to imagine; and he expressed this interesting but logically innocuous observation with rhetorical exaggeration. 'All things,' he said, 'are one'; but he meant: 'All things are interconnected'.

Can Heraclitus have meant that? It is small beer; indeed the thesis that 'all things are interconnected' is almost certainly a truism. Heraclitus saw himself as a vendor of novelty and paradox; he can hardly have intended to peddle such dullard truths as that. In any case, there are fragments in which Heraclitus clearly commits himself to instances of (2); and there are explicit statements to the effect that '*X* and *Y* are one'. We can take these as heightened tropes if we choose; but such a choice ignores the obvious sense of Heraclitus' remarks. Moreover, the mild interpretation confuses the grounds of Heraclitus' Unity Thesis with the Thesis itself: it is true, I think, that Heraclitus argues for this Thesis from various observations about 'common structures' and the like. But if the Unity Thesis is supported by such facts, it follows, not that the Thesis is constituted by those facts, but rather that the Thesis is *not* constituted by them.[29]

The Unity Thesis, if it is expressed by (2), is bizarre and outrageous: it will constitute the core of Heraclitus' idiosyncratic 'account' of the way things are. The ancient critics concurred in this judgment: of the thesis that 'everything in the world is by nature pretty well opposite', Philo asked (*quis rer div her*, 43, 214),

> Is it not this which the Greeks say that their great and celebrated Heraclitus set up as the high-point of his philosophy and paraded as a new discovery? (**49**: Diels-Kranz, I.491. 39–42).

What could have impelled Heraclitus to so strange a view? Part of the answer is, I think, given in **B 88** = **41 M**:

> [i] The same thing is living and dead, and what is awake and what sleeps, and young and old; [ii] for these, having changed about, are those; and those, having changed about, these (**50**).

The fragment is textually controversial; and the illustrative examples it adduces are somewhat obscure in themselves—how does youth follow age or life death?[30] But the obscure story offers a plain moral: sentence [i] states three instances of the Unity Thesis and sentence [ii] grounds these instances, as its introductory particle shows, on the Theory of Flux.

Roughly speaking, Heraclitus argues thus: 'Being awake and being asleep succeed one another; therefore, the same things are awake and asleep.' It is plausible to find a similar argument in at least one other fragment:

> Hesiod is a teacher of most men: they are convinced that he knew most things—he who did not know day and night (for they are one) (**51: B 57** = **43 M**: cf. Hesiod, *Theogony* 123).

Thus: 'Night and day are mutually successive; hence the same thing is both night and day'. Text **46**, quoted in illustration of the Theory of Flux, may well have continued by inferring a case of the Unity Thesis; and the wretchedly difficult **B 58** = **46 M** perhaps contained a further argument of this sort.

But do such things deserve the name of argument? They are, at least when soberly expressed, palpably and scandalously invalid. How can Heraclitus have come to accept them? At least three explanations offer themselves. First, the Greeks were, as we are, prone to say that *X* and *Y* form a unity, or 'are one', if they are in some way continuous (*sunechês*). Heraclitus observed the continuity of night and day; he perhaps expressed this by saying to himself that night and day 'are one', and then inferred that night and day are identical. So understood, his argument commits a 'fallacy of equivocation': '. . . are one' means both '. . . form a unity' and '. . . are identical'; and Heraclitus' argument moves silently from the first sense to the second.[31]

Again, the succession of *X* and *Y* can be expressed by '*X* is *ek Y*'; and from '*X* is *ek Y*', in a different sense of '*ek*', the Greeks were often prepared to infer '*X* is *Y*' (see above, p. 42). Perhaps, then, Heraclitus expressed the succession of day and night by means of the phrase 'day is *ek* night'; and then, improperly interpreting '*ek*', inferred the identity of day and night.

The third path of fallacy follows a different route. Flux—the change from one property to its contrary—can be expressed schematically by the following formula:

(4) ϕx at t_1 & $\phi' x$ at t_2.

Heraclitus' inference, then, passes in effect from (4) to:

(5) ϕx & $\phi' x$.

The fallacy lies in dropping the temporal qualifiers, 'at *t* ', or in passing from '*P* at t_i' to '*P*' without qualification. The Aristotelian Greek for '*P* without qualification' is '*P haplôs*'; and in the *Sophistici Elenchi* Aristotle warns against the fallacy of 'dropping the qualification' or of inferring *P haplôs* from some modified version of *P* (166b37–167a20; for an explanation of *haplôs*, see *Top* 115b29–35).

It is not anachronistic to suppose that Heraclitus fell for a fallacy of this sort: Aristotle makes it clear that such fallacies were still rife, and still perplexing, a century and a half after Heraclitus' day.[32] In many cases, of course, qualifiers can be validly dropped: 'Brutus stabbed Caesar' certainly follows from 'Brutus stabbed Caesar with a dagger'; and that may have encouraged a certain insouciance towards adverbial modifiers in general. Moreover, temporal indications are often concealed in ordinary discourse: watching the barber we may chronicle the change in his victim by the successive utterances 'He's hairy', 'He's bald'. Time is marked only by the present tense; and the logic of conjunction may seduce us to the conclusion: 'He's hairy and he's bald'.

That there is an inference in **50**, and that the inference is fallacious, are certainties. It is less clear how the fallacy is to be diagnosed. If I guess that the third diagnosis is Heraclitean, that is because there is some evidence that fallacies of that sort marred other bits of his reasoning. For the Unity of Opposites did not rest simply on inference from the Theory of Flux: it was also supported, as Flux itself was, by a collection of particular cases. And in some at least of these cases the fallacy of the dropped qualification is again visible.

Some twenty fragments in all may plausibly be construed as illustrating the Unity of Opposites. Most of them are controversial; many of them are too vague or too obscure to be worth adducing; and one of the most celebrated is no more than a pun.[33] Of the remainder, one group can be collected about **B 61 = 35 M**:

> Sea is purest and foulest water: for fish it is drinkable and salutary; for men it is undrinkable and lethal (**52**).

There are similar 'relativist' observations in **B 13** = **36 M**, on the pleasures of the pig (cf. Democritus, **68 B 147**); in **B 9** = **37 M**, on the values of the donkey; and in **B 4** = **38 M**, on the eating habits of oxen.

Observations of a generally relativistic type are common enough outside Heraclitus: the Sicilian comedian Epicharmus, who will take the stage in later chapters, provides an example:

> It is no wonder that we talk like this
> and please ourselves, and seem to one another
> to be so fair; for to a dog a bitch
> seems the most fair—and to a bull a cow,
> to an ass an ass, and to a pig a pig (**53: 23 B 5**).

Epicharmus propounded relativism to raise a laugh: Heraclitus' aim is philosophical; for from relativistic observations he could infer cases of the Unity thesis.

In **52** the inference is explicit; it proceeds from:
(6) Seawater is good for fish and bad for men
to:
(7) Seawater is good and bad.
The argument is closely parallel to that from (4) to (5): the omission of two qualifying phrases—'for fish', 'for men'—allows a common truth to yield a paradoxical conclusion. Here at least it is clear that Heraclitus committed the fallacy of the dropped qualification; and it is reasonable to imagine that the collection of propositions of which (7) is my exemplar were all derived by way of that fallacy, and then advanced in support of the Unity Thesis.[34]

Another type of argument lies behind **B 26** = **48 M**. The text of this fragment is hopelessly corrupt; but its shell in all probability reads:

> Man . . . while living touches death . . . and while waking touches sleep (**54**).

The metaphor of touching is susceptible to more than one interpretation. A plausible construe glosses 'touch' by 'resemble'[35] and ascribes to Heraclitus the following argument: 'There is no clear distinction between such opposites as life and death: we cannot say of a sleeping man that he is alive (for he exhibits few of the features of vivacity), nor yet can we say that he is dead (for sleepers and corpses are in many ways distinct). Thus life and death are strictly indistinguishable, and one and the same man is both alive and dead.' This type of argument is surprisingly popular: we are all familiar with the ploy forbidding us to say that *a* is ϕ rather than non-ϕ, on the grounds that there are numerous cases in which we are unwilling or unable to predicate either ϕ or non-ϕ. The argument is silly, and its invalidity is patent once it is stated; yet I think Heraclitus may have fallen for it.

Here, finally, are a few more illustrations of Heraclitean Unity. In **B 60 = 33 M**:

> The road there and back is one and the same (**55**).

Heraclitus observes correctly that we apply the predicates 'going to Thebes' and 'coming from Thebes' to a single subject; and he surely thinks he is providing us with a clear exemplification of (2).[36] **B 103 = 34 M** reads:

> Beginning and end on a circle are common (**56**).

One and the same point is describable both as the first point and as the last point of the circle's circumference. According to **B 59 = 32 M**:

> The path of the carding roller is straight and curved (**57**),

as it rolls over the wool. **B 15 = 50 M** is often read as an attack on popular mystery religions:

> If they did not make a procession to Dionysus and sing a hymn to the organs of shame, they would act most shamefully (**58**).

But I suspect that the phallic hymns are adduced primarily to illustrate the Unity of Opposites: they are reverent (for failure to sing them would be a shameful act); and they are also shameful (for they are paeans to the penis).[37]

The Unity of Opposites thus has twofold support: first, it is inferred from the Theory of Flux and thus has whatever support that Theory lays claim to; second, it rests upon a wide variety of observations, some of them direct instantiations of the Unity thesis, others requiring a small argumentative step to bring out their significance. Even at his most paradoxical, Heraclitus remained a rational thinker: his extraordinary thesis of Unity, no less than his traditional monism, was based on evidence and arguments.

(e) *Sage Heraclitus?*

Empirical observation and bold generalization led Heraclitus to the Theory of Flux: that all things constantly change is a well confirmed scientific hypothesis. Change is between opposites; and the logic of change seemed to draw Heraclitus irresistibly to the Unity of

Opposites: opposites are coinstantiated. Common observation, supported by a further application of the fallacy of the dropped qualification, confirmed the thesis of Unity. The commonplaces of Milesian science gave reason for accepting a Monism: everything was made from, and is made of, one stuff. The continuous cosmic changes provide a grand illustration of Flux; and the inference from Flux to Unity permits the Aristotelian conclusion that fire is the material substrate of the universe.

Of the three interlocking theories which constitute Heraclitus' account of nature, Monism is the least important. The Theory of Flux is a bold development of earlier speculation. The Unity of Opposites is an extraordinary innovation. Monism on the Milesian model is tacked on to these theories to show how Heraclitus can provide any enlightenment which his predecessors could provide, and provide it on a sounder and deeper basis. At all events, it is Flux and Unity which will seem most original and most shocking to modern readers.

And yet both these theories seem idiotic in themselves, and rest upon idiotic arguments; they are not worth a moment's attention from a rational man. Large objections are immediately to hand, and appear to destroy the whole Heraclitean account with ease and finality.

Flux and Unity are open to obvious empirical objections. Some things, no doubt, are in a state of Flux; and some things, perhaps, own perplexingly contrary properties; yet it is evident to the most cursory glance that not all things are in a state of Flux, and that not all things are bound to contrariety: a few careless observations have encouraged Heraclitus to propound a theory which our whole waking life constantly disproves.

Heraclitus anticipated this elementary objection:

> Nature likes to hide itself (**59: B 123 = 8 M**).

> The unevident connexion is stronger than the evident (**60: B 54 = 9 M**).

He illustrated his claim by a little parable:

> Men are deceived with regard to knowledge of what is evident, like Homer who was the wisest of all the Greeks. For he was deceived by some boys who were killing lice and said: 'What we saw and caught, we are leaving behind, what we neither saw nor caught, we are taking with us' (**61: B 56 = 21 M**).

The parable and the Heraclitean claim supply two important glosses on the Theory of Flux and the Unity of Opposites.

First, Heraclitus maintains that scientific truths are not all patent to casual observation: the truth is often hidden, and the fact that common experience suggests stability and coherence rather than flux and contrariety indicates not the falsity of Heraclitus' account but the superficiality of common experience. According to Aristotle, 'some say that it is not the case that some of the things that exist are changing and others not, but that everything always changes although this escapes our perception' (*Phys* 253b9–11). Aristotle does not name Heraclitus; but it seems certain that he had Heraclitus in mind.

The second point embellishes the first. Heraclitus is interested in the 'nature' or *phusis* of things: this emerges both from **59** and also from the various examples of Flux and Unity which have survived; and it was plainly stated at the very beginning of Heraclitus' work: he is concerned to 'divide up each thing in accordance with its nature, and say how it is' (**33**). But what is a thing's 'nature'? According to an ancient doctrine, things—or rather sorts of thing—have a 'real essence'. Locke explains the notion thus: 'By this *real Essence*, I mean, that real constitution of any Thing, which is the foundation of all those Properties, that are combined in, and are constantly found to coexist with the *nominal Essence* [i.e., with the complex *idea* the word stands for]; that particular constitution, which every Thing has within it self, without any relation to any thing without it' (*Essay* III. vi. 6). The real essence of a sort is given by its fundamental constitution, by those features or that structure which explains the remaining properties of items of the sort and without which nothing is an item of that sort.

Real essences have been much derided, but to my mind derision is wrong-headed: one main task of many sciences is to isolate the fundamental structure or features of a thing or stuff (its atomic or its genetic structure) in order to explain its remaining powers and qualities. The theory of real essence is an attempt to describe that scientific enterprise; and Heraclitus' 'nature', I suggest, is an attempt to get at real essence: a thing's 'nature' determines 'how it is'; it is customarily 'hidden' and its discovery requires a penetrating mind; it is 'stronger' than any superficial properties in that it explains and supports those properties.

Heraclitus is thus offering a large scientific theory, comparable to the atomist hypothesis: Flux and Opposition are features in the nature of every sort of thing; they are essential to it and explanatory of its properties. The theory is in principle falsifiable, as atomism is; but it is not refuted by everyday observation, as atomism is not.

This conclusion is, I hope, enough to raise Heraclitus from the ranks of the mystery-mongers and to place him among the great philosopher-scientists; and that is what makes his account the completion and perfection of Milesian science. Flux and the Unity of Opposites are twin horses, bred and nourished on wholesome empirical food, possessed of a deep strength, and harnessed to the old monistic chariot which Heraclitus inherited from his predecessors.

So much for the objection that Heraclitus' theories are empirically absurd. A second objection is this: the theories of Flux and Unity are criminally vague; and the most charitable attitude to real essences hardly raises them to precise hypotheses. I doubt if any precise account will cohere with all the fragments; and to that extent the objection succeeds. Nevertheless, I am inclined to think that the following sketch is both moderately clear and roughly Heraclitean. 'All identifiable things have an identifiable constitutive stuff or amalgam of stuffs: rivers are made of water; fields, of earth; men, of flesh and blood; the universe itself, of earth, water and fire. These stuffs form the 'nature' of what they constitute, in that all the powers and properties of the things—'how the things are'—are determined by their stuffs. Rivers support boats because of the properties of water; the fertility of a field depends on its constitutive earth; the barley-drink revivifies in virtue of its ingredients; men owe the powers and capacities they exhibit to their fleshy make-up. (Ultimately, no doubt, all those properties will be shown to depend upon the intrinsic character of the ultimate constituent of the world, fire.) Observation supports the hypothesis that those constituent stuffs are in a constant flux: they are always changing in one respect or another. And those changes are no chance contingencies. They are essential to the being of all that the stuffs constitute; for those things would cease to exist, and hence to exercise any of their powers, if their natures ceased to change: there is no river if the waters cease to flow; the barley-drink is destroyed as soon as its parts settle; men die when their temperature and humidity becomes constant and they are no longer being nourished; the world itself will fall apart if the cycle of stuffs ever ceases. The changes involved are of different sorts—qualitative, quantitative and locomotive. (No doubt some natures undergo more than one change of more than one sort.) But they all qualify as changes in virtue of one common feature: if a changes between t_1 and t_2, then there is a pair of contrary predicates ϕ and ϕ' such that a is ϕ at t_1 and a is ϕ' at t_2. From this feature of Flux a simple inference leads us to the Unity of Opposites, a thesis which in any case concords happily with experience.'

If such considerations give Heraclitus' theories a somewhat sharper definition, they are only the better prepared to be struck down by the third objection. That objection alleges logical inconsistency: Heraclitus' central contention, the Unity thesis, is inconsistent; it flagrantly violates the Law of Contradiction; hence it is false, necessarily false, and false in a trivial and tedious fashion. It is empty to praise for his scientific insight a thinker whose main and innovatory tenet is a straightforward self-contradiction.

It will not do to admit the charge and try to brazen it out.

Do I contradict myself?
Very well then, I contradict myself.
(I am large, I contain multitudes.)

No one is large enough for that: contradiction implies falsity; and that is that.

It will not do to suggest that 'we need not expect Heraclitus' thought to be by our standards completely logical and self-consistent',[38] and to intimate that by Heraclitean logic the Unity thesis is consistent. The standards of logic are not 'our' standards: they are the eternal standards of truth; and any statement which fails by those standards fails to be true whether its utterer spoke in knowledge or in ignorance of the standard he flouted.

It will not do to observe that Heraclitus never *clearly* violates the Law of Contradiction, and to insinuate that an obscurely stated inconsistency is only a peccadillo. On the contrary, that suggestion adds the vice of obscurity to the sin of inconsistency, and doubles the offence.

It will not do to argue that, as Heraclitus never used the term 'opposites', so he never regarded his thesis as concerned with opposites at all. The 'opposites' Heraclitus adverts to are patently contrary, and patently thought of as such; and the metaphors of war and strife which sound in the fragments are Heraclitus' way of speaking of opposition.

It will not do, finally, to interpret the Unity thesis as saying that *apparent* opposites are not in reality opposed. Some of Heraclitus' examples admittedly adduce properties whose opposition is only apparent; but others adduce plain contraries. And, again, Heraclitus clearly means to shock us: his warfare and strife are not shadows thrown onto the world by the incapacity of the common mind to discern false from true opposition. War and strife—contrariety and opposition—are essential features of reality.

How, then, can we explain Heraclitus' adoption of a self-contradictory thesis? We might begin by asking why Aristotle found his thesis trivially inconsistent. The answer is straightforward: if ϕ and ϕ' are contrary predicates, then '$\phi' x$' entails 'not-ϕx'; the entailment is a necessary (though not a sufficient) condition of contrariety—the logical notion of a contrary predicate is defined by way of the entailment. Given the entailment, 'ϕx & $\phi' x$' immediately and evidently yields the explicit contradiction 'ϕx & not-ϕx', and the absurdity of Heraclitus' view is patent.

Now this logical notion of contrariety was certainly not available to Heraclitus: it is improbable that he even had a word for contrariety as such,[39] let alone excogitated an Aristotelian analysis of the concept. Rather, he was working with a fairly loose, intuitive notion of what 'opposites' were; he would, I imagine, have presented a list, not a definition, if asked to explain himself: wet, dry; up, down; straight, crooked; sweet, sour; hot, cold; male, female; and so on. The list would no doubt be long, and its items would, to our eyes, be logically diverse: some pairs seem logical contraries; some express physically incompatible properties; some are elliptically expressed relations between which no true incompatibility exists.

Heraclitus intended his list to present opposing pairs: each pair was locked in internecine strife, and their harmonious compresence is not a thing to be expected. Yet his list allowed him to see the opposition as, so to speak, a contingent one: some of the pairs in the list plainly do coexist, despite their opposition (they are not genuinely incompatible, as we should say); and that suggests that all the pairs may be found together. Moreover, the lack of an explicit definition of opposition meant that Aristotle's easy inference was never brought to Heraclitus' notice. The examples Heraclitus adduces do not shout incompatibility with a unanimous tongue; the metaphors of war and strife do not lead at once to thoughts of affirmation and contrary negation: with such resources, Heraclitus might well have failed to see the necessary falsity of his position. What is in fact an impossibility had in his eyes the status of a paradox; and the paradoxical is often true.

Some may wonder whether Heraclitus' thesis is properly denominated a Unity of Opposites if he had no clear, Aristotelian, notion of contrariety. There is something in that thought; but it cannot bring Heraclitus an eleventh hour reprieve. For if we refuse to introduce the notion of contrariety into our elucidation of Heraclitus, we leave him without a thesis at all. The Aristotelian notion is simply a precise formulation of the intuitive conception with which Heraclitus was working. Deny him the notion, and he has no thesis to propound; make the notion explicit, and his thesis lapses into inconsistency.

Heraclitus was indubitably a paradoxographer; and his account of the world is fundamentally inconsistent. That, however, does not make him a mystical figure, standing aloof from the young rationalism of Miletus; nor, I submit, does it make him a silly or a shallow philosopher. Evidence and argument are no strangers to the surviving fragments, and their presence places Heraclitus firmly in the Ionian tradition. And he offered a philosophy of science which exhibits an admirable articulation, and foreshadows one of the most influential of Aristotle's doctrines, the doctrine of real essence. A certain conceptual inadequacy doomed his fine system to the fires of contradiction; but that is a fate which more than one great metaphysician has suffered.

V

The Divine Philosophy of Xenophanes

(a) *A wandering minstrel*

Xenophanes of Colophon was a four-square man, remarkable for the breadth of his interests, the depth of his thought, and the length of his life. He was a poet and satirist of note, an erudite and versatile polymath, and a considerable philosopher. The range of his accomplishments, and his unflinching devotion to the gods of reason, make him a paradigm of the Presocratic genius.

His longevity deserves a paragraph. By his own account a nonagenarian (**21 B 8**), he may have achieved a century (Censorinus, A 7). In all probability his life fell within the period from 580 to 470 and thus overlapped with the life-spans of most of the major Presocratic thinkers. He travelled widely; he was a celebrated and controversial figure in his life-time; he was familiar with, and often highly critical of, the thoughts of his predecessors and contemporaries (**B 7**; **B 19**; Diogenes Laertius, IX. 18 = **A 1**; Plutarch, *apud* Proclus, **A 20**); and it can hardly be doubted that his opinions influenced and were influenced by those of his peers. Yet those influences cannot be charted with any certainty, and that for a simple reason: with two uninteresting exceptions (**B 2**; **B 8**), we do not know at what point in his life Xenophanes formulated or made public his views. If his birth and his death can be dated with modest precision, his intellectual biography is a tract of darkness some eighty years across.

What holds of Xenophanes holds of the other Presocratics: they did not usually date their works, and they left behind them no *Nachlass* from which busy scholars might reconstruct their spiritual careers; even where the gross, corporeal chronology of their births and deaths is discoverable, the finer dating of their mental histories remains perfectly unknown.[1] Scholars have combed the surviving fragments for internal evidence of influence and reaction; in a few cases they have produced results commanding general assent; more often the assessment of one scholar nicely balances the contradictory assessment of another. But even where some influence is indubitable, the direction of influence can hardly be discovered in the absence of a detailed external chronology. Thus Xenophanes is often thought to have influenced Parmenides; but the opposite influence is chronologically possible, and has been staunchly maintained. Again, the relation between Parmenides and Heraclitus is as controversial as it is obscure. And later it will emerge that the mutual connexions between the later Eleatics (Zeno and Melissus) and the early neo-Ionians (Empedocles and Anaxagoras) are beyond our grasp.

Any account of Presocratic thought will impose some overall pattern on the material; and at a very high level of abstraction some pattern is indeed discernible. Details, however, escape us; and detail is the stuff of history.

Xenophanes' long life produced a large *oeuvre*. The extent of his enquiries is unquestionable: Heraclitus marked, and scorned, his polymathy (**A 3** = **22 B 40**); and the documents testify to a vast knowledge. There is evidence for a detailed cosmology on the Milesian model (e.g., **B 17–33**; pseudo-Plutarch, **A 32**; Hippolytus, **A 33**);[2] there are social and political comments which might be dignified into a political theory (e.g., **B 2–3**); there is contemporary history (Diogenes Laertius, IX.21 = **A 1**); and there are substantial pieces of a more strictly philosophical nature.

Of this *oeuvre* some forty-odd fragments are all that survives;[3] and the most considerable of these have a literary rather than a philosophical interest. Moreover, the origin of the scientific and philosophical remnants is disputed. Some scholars imagine a fairly formal treatise *Concerning Nature*; others suppose a systematic set of beliefs expressed piecemeal in a variety of poems; the majority view maintains that 'Xenophanes expressed such scientific opinions as he had incidentally in his satires', and had no systematic thoughts to present—that intellectually he was a thing of shreds and patches.[4]

The majority view has no intrinsic merits and is supported by no ancient testimony. Against it there stands the doxography, which recognizes Xenophanes as a well-rounded thinker, and which thrice refers to a work *Concerning Nature*. Furthermore, one fragment (**B 43**, which I shall analyse in a later chapter) appears to have the form of a prologue, or to come from a poem or a passage introducing Xenophanes' philosophical reflexions. In it Xenophanes mentions 'the gods and everything about which I speak': I shall argue later that the phrase refers to theology and natural philosophy; and I believe that **B 34** implies the existence, if not of a poem *Concerning Nature*, at least of a fairly systematic and comprehensive parcel of scientific and philosophical verses. If that is so, then Xenophanes was a professional and self-conscious thinker, and not a poet and satirist whose polemical whims occasionally led him to paddle in philosophical ponds.

As a philosopher, Xenophanes has not received a universally appreciative audience: he is dismissed as unoriginal, 'a poet and rhapsode who has become a figure in the history of Greek philosophy by mistake'.[5] There is, it is true, an ancient error about Xenophanes' philosophical achievement: in the *Sophist* (242DE = **A 29**) Plato, jesting, makes Xenophanes the first Eleatic monist; Aristotle repeated the point (*Met* 986b21 = **A 30**); Theophrastus felt obliged to refer to it; and the doxographers slavishly follow their master (Cicero, **A 34**; pseudo-Galen, **A 35**).[6] The doxographical tradition has no value here; and Xenophanes cannot qualify as a philosopher by pretensions to a monistic ontology. There are, however, other opinions which are securely attributed to Xenophanes on the basis of his own words and which, in my opinion at least, indicate a brilliant, original and sophisticated talent. Those opinions concern epistemology and natural theology. I shall reserve Xenophanes' remarks on the nature and extent of human knowledge for a later chapter; here I deal with his theology.

(b) *Summa theologiae*

At a symposium, Xenophanes says, 'first of all, pious men should hymn the god with decent stories and pure words' (**B 1**, 13–14). It is as a theologian that Xenophanes is most celebrated; for even if it is true, in general, that 'when one reads the Presocratics with an open mind and sensitive ear, one cannot help being struck by the religious note in much of what they say',[7] nevertheless, in the majority of Presocratic writings the note forms part of the harmony: in Xenophanes alone is it thematic.

Xenophanes was, as I have said, an accomplished satirist; and many of his divine *dicta* are negative and polemical in form. Most scholars deny him a systematic theology, and we may readily concede that Xenophanes was no Aquinas, his writings no formal *Summa*. For all that, the various theological sayings which have come down to us can be fitted into a coherent and impressive whole.

I start by listing the divine dogmas whose ascription to Xenophanes is secured by actual fragments of his poems. They are seven in number:

(1) God is motionless.
(2) God is ungenerated.
(3) 'There is one god, greatest among gods and men.'
(4) God is not anthropomorphic.
(5) God thinks and perceives 'as a whole'.
(6) God moves things by the power of his mind.
(7) God is morally perfect.

If we have in (1)–(7) the bones of a theology, is it a natural or a revealed theology? According to Nietzsche, Xenophanes was merely 'a religious mystic'; and modern scholarship concurs: '. . . in Xenophanes we find a new motif, which is the actual source of his theology. It is nothing that rests on logical proof, nor is it really philosophical at all, but springs from an immediate sense of awe at the sublimity of the Divine.' In Xenophanes a 'mystical intuition' replaces the 'pure speculation' of his Ionian predecessors.[8] If that is true, then Xenophanes is the progenitor of that pestilential tribe of theological irrationalists, whose loudest member is Martin Luther and whose recent aspirations to philosophical respectability have been encouraged from the grave by the palsied shade of the late Wittgenstein. Must Xenophanes really incur such profound and posthumous guilt?

There is, I think, no evidence in the fragments to support a mystical or irrational interpretation of Xenophanes' theology: there is no appeal to sublime intuition, no descent to mere enthusiasm. And there is evidence that tells in the opposite direction.

The immobility of God, dogma (1), is thus stated in **B 26**:

> Always he remains in the same state, in no way changing;
> Nor is it fitting for him to go now here now there (**62**).

For the moment I ignore the first line of the couplet. The second line both states and justifies (1); the justification is conveyed by the word 'fitting (*epiprepei*)'. Some scholars take the notion of what is 'fitting' to be an aesthetic one: locomotive gods are not pretty, hence god does not move. It is incredible that any thinker should have advanced such a fatuous piece of reasoning. Fortunately, the word 'fitting' need not be held to a strictly aesthetic sense; it is readily interpreted in a logical fashion: the phrase 'it is not fitting' is Xenophanes' archaic and poetical version of 'it is not logically possible'. It does not 'fit' the essential nature of god, or our concept of what it is to be divine, to imagine that divinities locomote: that is to say, 'God moves' is self-contradictory. That interpretation does not, I think, strain the Greek; and it will turn out to be consonant with the general tenor of Xenophanes' theological reasoning.

The logical aspect of Xenophanes' theology is further exhibited by dogma (2), divine ungenerability.[9] Here the fragments fail us; **B 14** reads:

> Mortals opine that gods are born,
> And have their clothes and voice and form (**63**).

We may safely infer (2) from **63**; but for argument we must apply to the doxography. And in fact we are offered three reasonings.

The first argument is found in Aristotle:

> Xenophanes used to say that 'those who assert that the gods are born are as impious as those who say that they die', for in both cases it follows that the gods at some time fail to exist (**64**: *Rhet* 1399b6–9 = **A 12**).

Gods are essentially sempiternal (cf. Cicero, **A 34**): even in Homer they are 'the gods who always exist' (*theoi aei eontes*: e.g., *Iliad* I. 290). Everyone recognizes that the gods cannot therefore die; yet the theogonies nonchalantly tell of divine births.[10] Xenophanes points out that birth and death are analogous in that each entails a denial of sempiternity: a consistent Homer or a clear-eyed theist will reject divine generation for precisely the same reason for which he rejects divine destruction.

The argument is pointed but not profound: perhaps there is an asymmetry between birth and death; perhaps divine death is ruled out not because it conflicts with sempiternity, but because it implies that something can get the better of the gods and force them out of existence. Thus it is divine power which precludes divine death; and divine power does not similarly preclude divine birth.

That objection is in effect answered by the second and third arguments for (2) which our sources ascribe to Xenophanes. Of the three relevant doxographical reports—in Simplicius, in pseudo-Plutarch, and in the pseudo-Aristotelian treatise *de Melisso, Xenophane, Gorgia* (**A 31; A 32; A 28**)[11]—the fullest is the last:

> And he says that it is impossible, if anything exists, for it to have come into being—stating this in the case of god. For it is necessary that what has come into being should have come into being either from like or from unlike. But neither is possible; for it is not suitable (*prosêkein*) that like should be sired by like rather than sire it (for things that are equal have all their properties the same and in similar fashion as one another); nor that what is unlike

> should come into being from unlike (for if the stronger came into being from the weaker, or the greater from the less, or the better from the worse—or the reverse: the worse from the better—what is would come into being from what is not, which is impossible) (**65**: 977a14–22 = **A 28**).

This report is contaminated by later Eleatic logic; yet that it contains a Xenophanean core is proved not only by certain turns of phrase but also by a striking fragment of Epicharmus.

Epicharmus was a Sicilian playwright, active at the beginning of the fifth century BC. The surviving fragments of his works exhibit an interest, satirical but not superficial, in the philosophical issues of his day; in particular, Epicharmus knew Xenophanes' poems, and parodied them more than once.[12] Fate has preserved a fragment in dialogue form on the birth of the gods; it is evidently a pastiche of Xenophanes:

> —But the gods were always about and never off the scene; and they are always about in the same way and always with the same habits.
> —But Chaos is said to have been first born of the gods.
> —How so? if he didn't have anything from which or to which he could be the first to come?
> —Then nothing came first?
> —No—and nothing second either of the things we're now talking about; but they always existed (**66: 23 B 1**).

In this fragment Epicharmus is tilting at Hesiod (*Theogony* 116–17); but the thought it contains was influential (it drove Epicurus to philosophy: Sextus, *adv Math* X.18); and from it and **65** we can construct two Xenophanean arguments for (2). The nerve of each argument is the claim that a generated god must have something to 'come from'. (I ignore the jocular suggestion in Epicharmus that a generated god must also have something to 'come to'). More generally:

(8) If *a* comes into being, then for some *x a* comes into being from *x*.

I have noted, in another connexion, the ambiguity of the phrase 'from *x*' (above, pp. 39–40). How is it to be glossed in (8)? Epicharmus uses the colourless verb *gignesthai* for 'come into being'; in the *MXG* the word *teknoun*, 'to sire', is employed: it is tempting to suppose that this represents Xenophanes' original thought. If that is so, then 'come into being' in (8) means 'be born'; and (8) states the necessary truth that everything that is born has a parent. But, so construed, (8) supports not (2) but the weaker assertion that gods are not *born*: may not a god come into being without being born? may not divine generation be spontaneous generation? Perhaps Xenophanes would have replied that coming into being cannot be simply inexplicable: a divine generation, like any other, requires a moving cause; and what could a cause of divine generation be but a parent or quasi-parent? Thus divine generation is either divine birth or something logically equivalent to divine birth; and there is no room to drive a wedge between the generation in (8) and the generation in (2).

However that may be, we still have to link (8) to (2). Epicharmus suggests the following supplementary premiss:

(9) If *a* comes into being from *b*, then *b* existed before *a* existed.

That is surely a tautology; and (2) follows from (8) and (9), in conjunction with:

(10) If *a* is a god, then nothing existed before *a* existed.

Now if gods are essentially creative beings, and if nothing exists except as a result of divine creativity, then (10) suggests itself. But the suggestion is hasty: for all that has been said so far, gods may be created, provided that their creators are themselves divine. And the traditional theogonies do, of course, give generated gods divine parents. Thus (10) must be weakened to:

(10*) If *a* is a god, then if *b* exists before *a*, *b* is a god.

I now anticipate myself and call upon Xenophanes' dogma (3), which I shall argue is a statement of monotheism: if there is at most one god, and (10*) is true, then (10) is true too. Thus by tacitly assuming (3), Xenophanes may properly argue from (10), (9), and (8) to (2). That exegesis is undeniably contorted; yet I can see no other way of extracting a decent argument from Epicharmus.

The *MXG* presents a different set of considerations. I shall here draw from the text what I think is its Xenophanean kernel, though I confess that my account has a somewhat arbitrary air. The crucial premiss is:

(11) If *a* comes into being from *b*, then *b* is at least as great as *a*.

What might commend (11) to Xenophanes? There is a general theory of causation which asserts that 'There is as much reality in the cause as in the effect'. We tend to associate the theory with the name of Descartes; but in fact it is much older. Indeed in the next chapter I shall suggest that the Synonymy Principle, as I call it, has a Presocratic origin (below, p. 119); and it is, I think, possible that Xenophanes implicitly rested premiss (11) upon it: if *b* gives greatness to *a*, then *b* must itself possess greatness. But a less general argument suggests itself: if I am able to make a powerful product, then I must surely have as much power as that product possesses; for a product, which owes its power to its producer, can hardly have more power than that producer. Indeed, the power enjoyed by my products is, in a sense, enjoyed by me; for the labour exerted by the products of my labour is itself, at one remove, my labour. The argument will not, and should not, convince the thoughtful reader; but it may suffice to give an air of plausibility to (11).

Now I shall shortly argue that Xenophanes subscribed explicitly to:

(12) If *a* is a god, then *a* is greater than anything else.

From (8), (11) and (12) the conclusion (2) follows deductively.

Thus we have three *a priori* arguments for (2), one from Aristotle, one from Epicharmus, and one from the *MXG*, the two latter arguments using a common premiss. Did Xenophanes use any or all of these arguments? It would be gratuitously sceptical to deny all three arguments to Xenophanes; and since I can see no good reason for singling out any one of them as peculiarly Xenophanean, I conclude that all originate with him.

I turn now to the most notorious, and the most interesting, of Xenophanes' theological tenets: monotheism. The doxographical tradition generally makes Xenophanes a monotheist (e.g., *MXG*, **A 28**; Simplicius, **A 31**; Hippolytus, **A 33**; Cicero, **A 34**; pseudo-Galen, **A 35**; but pseudo-Plutarch, **A 32**, implies polytheism). Most modern scholars have followed the doxographers, finding monotheistic hints in various fragments (especially **B 24–6**), and an explicit assertion in the first line of **B 23**, of which the orthodox translation reads:

> There is one god, greatest among gods and men (**67**).

Some, however, are unhappy with this; and they attack the monotheistic stronghold itself: How, they ask, can **B 23** state monotheism in its first two words (*heis theos*), when the very next phrase ('greatest *among gods*': *en . . . theoisi*) is unequivocally polytheistic? It is customary to answer this by saying that the phrase 'gods and men' is a 'polar expression', and that such expressions may be used in Greek even when one pole, in this case the divine one, is wholly inapposite. Thus, 'greatest among gods and men' means no more than 'greatest of all'; and the phrase carries no polytheistic baggage.[13] But that suggestion leaves Xenophanes with a verse that is inept, to say the least; and if that is the best that can be done for him on the standard translation, then there is much to be said for a different translation.

The Greek has been thought to allow the following version: 'The one greatest god among gods and men is . . .'. This translation turns Xenophanes into a polytheist, and a polytheist of the traditional Homeric type: there is a hierarchy of divinities ruled by a greatest god, as the Homeric Zeus rules, with uncertain sway, the Olympian pantheon.[14] The suggestion restores consistency to the first line of **B 23**: no monotheistic claim opposes the plural *en . . . theoisi*. But consistency is purchased at a high price: the translation is strained (Xenophanes' Greek-speaking admirers and detractors never conceived of it); it flouts the doxography; it is obliged to ignore the monotheistic hints of the other fragments; and it replaces a polemical thesis by a traditional platitude.

Perhaps further reflexion will allow us to keep the orthodox translation without falling into elementary inconsistency. Let us approach the question by asking what argument Xenophanes could have advanced in favour of monotheism. Again, the fragments give no help, and we are forced back upon the doxography. First, the *MXG*:

> And if god is most powerful of all, he [sc. Xenophanes] says that it is suitable (*prosêkein*) for him to be unique. For if there were two or more, he would no longer be most powerful and best of all. For each of the several, being a god, would equally be such. For this is what a god and a god's capacity is—to have power and not to be in someone's power (*kratein alla mê krateisthai*), and to be most powerful of all. Hence, in so far as he is not more powerful, to that extent he is not a god (**68**: 977a24–9 = **A 28**).

Second, Simplicius:

> . . . [Xenophanes] proves that [god] is unique from his being most powerful of all; for if there were several, he says, having power would necessarily belong to them all alike; but god is what is most powerful of all and best (**69: A 31**).

Third, pseudo-Plutarch:

> And about the gods he says that there is no leadership among them; for it is not holy for any of the gods to have a master (*despozesthai*), and none of them stands in need (*epideisthai*) of anything at all (**70: A 32**).

The three reports presumably go back to Theophrastus. A happy chance allows us to trace their argument into the fifth century: in his *Hercules Furens* Euripides has Theseus say:

> But *I* do not believe that the gods love beds
> which right denies them, and that they manacle one another
> I have never credited, nor shall I be persuaded;
> nor that one is by nature master (*despotês*) of another.

For god—if he is genuinely a god—needs (*deitai*)
nothing: these are the wretched tales of poets (71: 1341–6 = C 1).[15]

The last three lines of this passage contain our argument: their context is Xenophanean, and the verbal coincidences between Euripides and pseudo-Plutarch make it probable that the *Hercules* is here paraphrasing a poem of Xenophanes.

The four passages I have just quoted differ in two minor ways and in one major. First, pseudo-Plutarch grounds god's mastery or power on holiness ('for it is not holy'), while Simplicius and the *MXG* make mastery a conceptual requirement of divinity ('but god is . . .'; 'for that is what a god is. . . .'). My prejudice in favour of the latter reading is supported by Euripides ('if he is genuinely a god'[16]). Second, pseudo-Plutarch conjoins divine mastery with divine independence: gods lack nothing; and in Euripides, independence grounds god's mastery. I shall soon return to divine independence; but it is not immediately relevant to the present argument, and the *MXG* and Simplicius have not ignored anything of importance in their presentation of the matter.

The major difference between our reports concerns the premiss expressing divine mastery. In pseudo-Plutarch and in Euripides we find something that can be paraphrased by:

(13) If *a* is a god, then nothing is greater than *a*.

(Note, first, that I treat power and mastery as identical, using the general notion of greatness; and second, that in Euripides' version the consequent of (13) reads: '. . . then no god is greater than *a*'. But since it goes without saying that no non-god can be greater than *a*, (13) can be deployed without qualms.) In Simplicius and the *MXG*, on the other hand, we get not (13) but:

(14) If *a* is a god, then *a* is greater than everything else.

Now (13) and (14) are not equivalent: (14) entails (13), but (13) does not entail (14). Which premiss is to be preferred? The textual evidence inclines us to (13); for Euripides is our earliest and perhaps our most faithful source. (13) does not support monotheism: it is compatible with a plurality of potent divinities, each of which is at least as great as anything else in existence. And since pseudo-Plutarch does not present (13) as part of a monotheistic argument, we might conclude that Simplicius and the *MXG*, misrepresenting Xenophanes' premiss by (14), have falsely fathered on him an argument for a monotheism which he never recognized.

I am not content with that conclusion. If we reject (14), we must accept one of two positions: either Xenophanes asserted monotheism in **B 23**, but did not argue for it by way of (14); or else **B 23** is polytheistic. The latter position imports an inconsistency; for the only polytheism with which (13) is compatible is egalitarian, and the only polytheism with which **B 23** is compatible is hierarchical. The former position has Xenophanes assert a novel creed, come within an ace of arguing for it, and then rest content with (13). For these reasons, I prefer to believe that Xenophanes uttered (14). He may, I suppose, have uttered (13) as well (if pseudo-Plutarch is reporting a distinct argument from that in Simplicius and the *MXG*); but it is easier to believe that pseudo-Plutarch has misrepresented (14) by (13).

From (14) it is easy to infer:

(15) There is at most one god.

And this, together with the premiss that there *are* gods (a premiss to which I shall return) amounts to monotheism.

How, finally, is all that to be reconciled with the first line of **B 23**? In **67** that line was translated: 'There is one god, greatest among gods and men.' It is, I think, not implausible to see here a highly concise epitome of the argument I have just developed; for the line may be paraphrased: 'There is one god, since (by definition) a god is greater than anything else, whether god or man.' The paraphrase seems remote when the line is taken in isolation; but if we imagine **B 23** to have followed an exposition of the argument from (14), then I do not think that the paraphrase imposes an unbearable intellectual strain.

Xenophanes, I conclude, was a monotheist, as the long tradition has it; and he was an *a priori* monotheist: like later Christian theologians, he argued on purely logical grounds that there could not be a plurality of gods.

The next three dogmas, (4), (5) and (6), go together; for we may reasonably take (5) and (6) as partial explanations of (4), which simply says, in general and negative terms, that god is

> not at all like mortals in form or even in thought (**72: B 23**.2).

Some have found an argument for (4) in Xenophanes' assertion that worshippers make their gods in their own image: the dark and hook-nosed Ethiopians, he observes, pray to dark and hook-nosed gods: the gods of the auburn, blue-eyed Thracians are blue-eyed redheads (cf. **B 16**: see below, p. 142). More caustically:

> If cows and horses or lions had hands,
> or could draw with their hands and make the things which men can,
> then horses would draw pictures of gods like horses,
> and cows like cows, and they would make bodies

in just the form which each of them has itself
(**73: B 15**; cf. Aristotle, *Pol* 1252b24–7).

The actual practice of human worshippers and the hypothetical practice of animal statuaries show that ordinary beliefs about the gods are entirely determined by the nature of the believer; hence, Xenophanes implies, those beliefs cannot pretend to the status of knowledge. I shall consider this splendid argument when I turn to Xenophanes' epistemology: here I content myself with the elementary point that **73** and **B 16** do not license a conclusion to (4): if the common belief in the anthropomorphic nature of god does not amount to knowledge, it does not follow that the belief is mistaken, and that the gods in fact are non-anthropomorphic; for the belief, irrational and ill-based though it is, may yet accidentally enshrine the truth.

If we require an argument for (4) we may better look to (5) and (6). Doctrine (5) comes from **B 24**:

He sees as a whole, he thinks as a whole, and he hears as a whole (**74**).[17]

That does not imply, as commentators from Clement onward have asserted, that god is incorporeal, nor even that he perceives without the use of sensory organs; it need mean no more than that any divine organs are, so to speak, spread evenly over the divine body: god is, as Hippolytus says, 'perceptive in all his parts' (**A 33**; cf. *MXG* 977a37 = **A 28**; Simplicius, **A 31**). Why should that be so? It is probable that Xenophanean gods were omniscient: direct evidence is flimsy (see **B 18**; **B 36**; Arius Didymus, **A 24**), but divine omniscience is both traditional (e.g., *Iliad* II.485; *Odyssey* IV. 379, 468), and a plausible corollary of divine mastery.[18] If god is omniscient, his organs of perception can hardly be localized: he needs eyes in the back of his head.

Dogma (6) comes from **B 25**:

Without effort, by the will of his mind he shakes everything (**75**).

We may imagine that Xenophanes moved readily enough to (6) from (1) and the fundamental assertion of god's mastery.

(5) and (6) are enough to prove (4): since god's sensory organs are not localized, he is not like mortals 'in form'; since he can move things 'by the will of his mind', he is not like mortals 'in thought'.

Finally, we have god's moral perfection. That Xenophanes upheld (7) is an inference from **B 11**:

Homer and Hesiod ascribed to the gods everything
that brings shame and reprobation among men—
theft, and adultery, and mutual deception (**76**: cf. **B 12**).

Plainly, Xenophanes is appalled by the brazen assertion of divine peccation; and it is, I think, quite reasonable to infer that he himself was devoted to divine decency. The texts offer no explicit statement of (7); but Simplicius and the *MXG* say that god is essentially 'best'.[19]

Xenophanes' theology is a rational construction, relying on logic and not on mystical intuition: he has earned the title of natural theologian. It remains to be shown that a simple systematic pattern can be discovered in, or imposed upon, his thoughts.

Suppose, with Euripides, that god lacks nothing, or is perfect, and lay this down as an axiom of theology.[20] The axiom first yields the two pivotal theorems found in the *MXG* and Simplicius: god is all powerful, and god is all good. The second pivotal theorem amounts to (7). The first pivotal theorem yields uniqueness (3), ungenerability (2), and the attribute of being creator and sustainer of all things (6). Next, the axiom of perfection implies immutability (as line 1 of **62** perhaps states),[21] and hence motionlessness (1). Thus god's sustaining actions must be effected by the mere exercise of his will. Third, perfection implies omniscience; and this in turn requires a peculiar mode of perception (5). Given (5) and (6), we must deny anthropomorphism and assert (4).

I do not suggest that any Xenophanean poem set out a theology in that systematic fashion (though I am strongly tempted to think that Xenophanes' thoughts were arranged with a moderate degree of clarity and coherence in his mind). I do not suggest that the propositions I have discussed constitute the sum of Xenophanes' theology (I shall shortly mention two other candidates from the doxography). I do not suggest that Xenophanes' theology is a logically coherent system (for I doubt if any natural theology of this sophisticated kind is strictly coherent). But I do suggest that Xenophanes' theology is a remarkable achievement; and that its author managed to attain an astounding level of abstraction and rationality in a field where abstract thought frequently produces only high-sounding vacuity and reason rapidly gives place to ranting.

(c) *Theology and science*

Strictly speaking, Xenophanes' natural theology does not establish monotheism: *a priori* argument leads to the conclusion that there is at most one god; but it does not supply the further proposition that there is at least one god. Why, then, was Xenophanes a theist? On what grounds did he assert that there exist gods? In order to answer this question I shall digress briefly and discuss the evidence for early Ionian theological beliefs.

Aristotle distinguishes the *phusiologoi* who offer argument (*apodeixis*) in support of their opinions from the *theologoi* who simply tell stories or speak *muthikôs* (*Met* 1000a9–20). The decisive innovation of the *phusiologoi* was not that they abandoned the gods and eschewed theology, but that they replaced stories by arguments. Nonetheless, their general cast of mind may well seem not merely rationalistic but also hostile to any form of theism. Science and theology are, after all, natural antagonists: the Darwinian controversy was one unusually violent campaign in an extended war. Poseidon once stirred the sea and Zeus the air; but, taught by science, we no longer expect reference to those divinities in the meteorological forecasts.

> Shall gods be said to thump the clouds
> When clouds are cursed by thunder?
> Be said to weep when weather howls?
> Shall rainbows be their tunics' colours?

Well might Bishop Hermias mutter to himself that 'philosophy took its start from the fall of the angels'.

The antagonism between science and religion was as vivid in the Greek as in the English mind: Aristophanes' Socrates asserts, in the *Clouds*, that 'gods are not currency with us' (247), and he explains at length how physical science has ousted the old divinities from their seat (365–411). In about 430 BC Diopeithes persuaded the liberal democrats of Athens to impeach 'those who disbelieve in things divine or teach doctrines about the heavens (*ta metarsia*)' (Plutarch, *Pericles* 32). Anaxagoras is said to have been caught by this decree (see below, p. 306); and the accusers of Socrates conjoined in their charge atheism and the study of astronomy (Plato, *Apology* 23D). The same conjunction is found in Euripides (fr. 913).

The matter is clearly stated by Plato:

> [Most people] think that those who apply themselves to astronomy and the other arts associated with it become atheists when they see that things can come about by necessity and not by an intelligent will concerning the accomplishment of good things (77: *Laws*, 967A).[22]

Science substitutes natural necessity for divine efficacy: the gods, put out of work, drop out of existence. Hippo, who mined the old Milesian veins in the mid-fifth century, was nicknamed 'the Atheist' 'because he assigned the cause of everything to nothing else beside water' (Philoponus, **38 A 8**; cf. Simplicius, **A 4**; Alexander, **A 9**). A later epigram puts it neatly (**B 2**):

This tomb is Hippo's whom the fates, 'tis said,
Made equal to the immortal gods—he's dead.

Atheism is not an invariable effect of science: on the contrary, Plato argues that a proper appreciation of astronomy leads men to god (*Laws* 886AE), and his argument has Presocratic antecedents (below, p. 99). Again, a naturalistic science may restrict the scope of divine activity without reducing it to nothing. Thus Xenophanes says of the rainbow:

What men call Iris, that too is by nature a cloud,
purple and red and green to see (**78: 21 B 32**).

and he said something similar of at least one other such phenomenon, namely St Elmo's fire 'which some men call the Dioscuri' (Aëtius, **A 39**). In strictness of logic, those sentences do not entail that meteorological occurrences have no spark of divinity in them; but it is plain that by talking of 'what men *call*' Iris or the Dioscuri Xenophanes implies that there is, in reality, nothing divine about those phenomena: rainbows have a purely natural explanation; divine interference is an unnecessary hypothesis. For all that, Xenophanes is no atheist.

Again, though you expel god with a pitchfork, *tamen usque recurret*: if nature or the stuff of the world usurped the function of god, why then nature or the stuff of the world was thereby shown to *be* god. Socrates, having declared an uncompromising atheism at line 247 of the *Clouds*, asserts eighty lines on that his clouds are gods (329); and natural divinities figure frequently in the ensuing scene.

In sum, the advance of science may affect theism in at least three ways: it may seem to abolish the gods entirely, replacing their agency by purely natural operations; it may appear to limit but not to annihilate their realm, taking some phenomena from their control and leaving others within it; and it may give a new twist to our conception of the divine nature, ousting anthropomorphism and introducing a more abstract notion of divinity. In a later chapter I shall return to this theme; here I ask what attitude the Milesians adopted to religion. The answer must rely on a doxography whose evidence is scant and brittle.

According to Diogenes, Thales said that

The universe is alive and full of spirits (79: I. 27 = 11 **A 1**).

But this report derives ultimately from a conjecture of Aristotle's:

> And some say that a soul is mingled in the whole universe—which is perhaps why Thales thought that everything is full of gods (**80**: *An* 411a7 = **A 22**).

If Thales did say that everything is full of gods or spirits, he probably only adverted to his belief in the ubiquity of animation (above, p. 8): there is no good reason to make him a pantheist. Again, according to some, Thales said that 'god is the mind which makes everything from water' (Cicero, **A 23**; cf. Aëtius, **A 23**; pseudo-Galen, 35); according to others, water itself was Thales' god (Hippolytus, *Ref. Haer.* I. 3). Both reports are in all probability late guesses.

The evidence for Anaximander is not much better. A controversial tradition ascribes to him belief in innumerable worlds; and the doxographers make those worlds gods (Cicero; Aëtius, **12 A 17**; pseudo-Galen, 35). The reports are not probative. Text **16** speaks not of the worlds but of Anaximander's principle: 'And this [i.e. the unlimited body] is the divine; for it is immortal and deathless, as Anaximander and most of the *phusiologoi* say' (Aristotle, *Phys* 203b13–5 = **A 15**; above, p. 31). Aristotle does not explicitly say that Anaximander made 'the Unlimited' a divinity. Some scholars ascribe to Anaximander Aristotle's inference from immortality to divinity; others reject the ascription.[23] I see no way of deciding the issue.

Finally, in the case of Anaximenes there are a few weak and disparate reports. Cicero and Aëtius say that Anaximenes called his principle a god (**13 A 10**). Hippolytus' text contains the following absurdity:

> He said that the principle was unlimited air, from which what comes about and what came about and what will be and gods and divine things come to be, and the rest from the offspring of this (**81: A 7**; cf. Augustine, **A 10**).

Hippolytus is garbled; Cicero and Aëtius carry little weight.

It would not require a very ardent scepticism to conclude that the Milesians had no theology at all. If they were not atheists in the sense of positively denying the existence of any gods, at least they were negative atheists: they left no room in their systems for gods, and were not perturbed by the omission. And even if we are disposed to accept the little evidence we have, we shall scarcely imagine that the Milesians were profoundly interested in gods and the divine; at most they said, unemphatically and uninterestedly, that their principles—or some of the things produced therefrom—were gods or godlike.

The case of Heraclitus is quite different. His system was, as I have already argued, scientific in the Milesian manner; and it was also self-consciously deterministic (below, pp. 131–5). Yet Heraclitus had a developed, if idiosyncratic, theology. I shall not expound or examine the material here; for Heraclitus, so far as we know, had nothing of Xenophanes' subtle and complex interest in natural theology. But there are important points of contact both with Xenophanes and with the Milesians: Heraclitus was, probably, a monotheist; his god, like that of Xenophanes, in some fashion or other governed the world; and it is at least possible that this theology was in some sense pantheistic: God and Fire, are, if not identical, at least closely assimilated to one another.

Science and theism are uneasy bedfellows, and the Milesians may have sensed the fact; yet they did lie together, in the thought of Heraclitus and possibly in that of his Milesian models. And they lay together in the mind of Xenophanes. We might expect Xenophanes, the logical theologian, to have said something about the nature of their union. Did he do so?

The doxography adds two further propositions to the seven from which Xenophanes' theology was reconstructed: his god is said to have been spherical (Diogenes Laertius, IX.19 = **21 A 1**; *MXG* 977b1 = **A 28**; Simplicius, **A 31**; Hippolytus, **A 33**; Cicero, **A 34**; Sextus, **A 35**); and he is identified with the universe (Simplicius, **A 31**; Cicero, **A 34**). These reports are generally dismissed as late fabrications; but the dismissal is not indisputable.[24]

The sphericality of god is supposed to be due to an Eleatic interpretation of Xenophanes: his god foreshadowed the 'Eleatic One'; 'the One' was a sphere; hence Xenophanes' god must have been a sphere. A different story can be told. The *MXG* and Simplicius take the fact that god is 'similar in every respect (*homoion hapantêi*)', and infer sphericality from that. A fragment of Timon says that Xenophanes made his god 'equal in all ways (*ison hapantêi*)' (fr. 60 = **A 35**); and there is something to be said for the view that this phrase, like the rest of the fragment, echoes Xenophanes. For Timon was an avid admirer and imitator of Xenophanes; he had access to his poems; and he is unlikely to have been influenced by any disreputable Peripatetic inventor who insinuated *ison hapantêi* into the Xenophanean corpus in order to make his own account of Xenophanes' god seem more authentic. Thus Xenophanes may well have said that god is *ison hapantêi*, 'equal in all ways'; and the only reasonable interpretation of that phrase is the traditional one—his god was a sphere.

The identification of god and the universe derives from Aristotle. Xenophanes, he reports,

> looking at the whole heaven, says that the One is god (**82**: *Met* 986b24 = **A 30**).

A second fragment of Timon makes Xenophanes speak as follows:

> For wherever I turned my mind, everything was reduced to one and the same thing; and everything that exists, however it was twisted, always came to rest in one similar nature (**83**: fr. 59 = **A 35**).

Aristotle may be indulging his imagination; and Timon is writing satire, not history. Yet there is something to be said for the conjecture that Aristotle and Timon each allude to a lost line of Xenophanes; for both reporters, independently of one another, ascribe to him a view for which we find no evidence in the extant fragments. In some lost verses, I suggest, Xenophanes grounded his belief in god on a contemplation of the vast and ordered wonders of the heavens; and Aristotle and Timon each reflect those verses.

If there is anything in these two suggestions, we may add to our picture of Xenophanes the natural theologian: science and astronomical speculation led Xenophanes to god; the starry vastnesses convinced him not of a divinity but of their divinity, and he came to adopt a spherical pantheism. Observing the world in the light of Ionian science, and with a clear and unconventional reasoning power, Xenophanes remained a theist while rejecting the traditional forms of theism. Pure logic moulded his conception of god; science gave his conception substance and matter.

On this view, Xenophanes' thought assumes a sort of unity: science and theology are not dissociated elements in a jackdaw production; rather, science grounds theology, and theology frees science from the shadow of atheistical mechanism. The Milesians may have paid lip-service to the gods, and Heraclitus certainly paid heart-service: Xenophanes used his head; he attempted to construct a new Ionian theology that might be a fitting partner to the new Ionian science. It is clear that Xenophanes failed, and that his pantheism is hardly intelligible or consistent; but his project as a whole, and the execution of many of its parts, are sufficiently remarkable to prove that the initiator of natural theology was by no means its least practitioner.

VI

Pythagoras and the Soul

(a) *Ipse dixit*

The ancient historians of philosophy distinguished between the Ionian and the Italian tradition in Presocratic thought. Something of the early Ionian achievement has been sketched in the preceding chapters; and I turn now to Italy. Although the Italian 'school' was founded by *émigrés* from Ionia, it quickly took on a character of its own: if the Ionians followed up Thales' cosmological speculations, the Italians, I judge, had more sympathy for his inquiry into psychology and the nature of man. But that estimate of the scope of early Italian thought is controversial; and before I look more closely at the Italian doctrines, I must indulge in a brief historical excursus.

The prince of the Italian school was Pythagoras, who flourished in the last quarter of the sixth century, a younger contemporary of Anaximenes.[1] The Pythagorean doxography is of unrivalled richness. We are told more about Pythagoras than about any other Presocratic thinker: and Pythagoras is one of the few Presocratics whose name has become a household—or at least a schoolroom—word.

Pythagoras himself had the wisdom to write nothing.[2] His numerous sectarians, eager to repair his omission, generously ascribed their own views to their master, or even wrote works in his name.[3] Those pious offerings portray an impressive figure: Pythagoras, discoverer and eponym of a celebrated theorem, was a brilliant mathematician; by applying his mathematical knowledge, he made great progress in astronomy and harmonics, those sister sirens who together compose the music of the spheres; and finally, seeing mathematics and number at the bottom of the master sciences, he concocted an elaborate physical and metaphysical system and propounded a formal, arithmological cosmogony.[4] Pythagoras was a Greek Newton; and if his intellectual bonnet hummed at times with an embarrassing swarm of mystico-religious bees, we might reflect that Sir Isaac Newton devoted the best years of his life to the interpretation of the number-symbolism of the book of *Revelations*.

If Greek science began in Miletus, it grew up in Italy under the tutelage of Pythagoras; and it was brought to maturity by Pythagoras' school, whose members, bound in fellowship by custom and ritual, secured the posthumous influence of their master's voice.

What are we to make of this pleasing picture of a Newtonian Pythagoras? It is, alas, mere fantasy: the shears of scholarship soon strip Pythagoras of his philosophical fleece.[5] The evidence for Pythagoras' life and achievements is late. In this he is not extraordinary; but he does suffer from two peculiar disadvantages: first, the survival of Pythagoreanism as a living force, with a strong sense of its own tradition, guaranteed anachronistic ascription of views and discoveries to the founder; second, our sources for the Newtonian Pythagoras are not the careful doxographers of the Lyceum, but later, feebler and more partial men, men of the stamp of Iamblichus and Porphyry.[6]

Scholarly huffing and puffing has blown this chaff from the heap of history; and it has left few grains on the floor. There were two important episodes in the early history of Pythagoreanism. Plato and his followers were to some extent influenced by Pythagorean speculations in science and metaphysics. Their interest led to a syncretism of Platonism and Pythagoreanism, in which a sophisticated Platonic metaphysics was grafted on to a more primitive stock. The syncretic view, which can be traced back to Plato's nephew Speusippus, dominated the later philosophical tradition, and came to be regarded as Pythagoreanism pure and simple. Pythagoras the systematic metaphysician does not antedate Speusippus. We know from Aristotle, who was unimpressed by the Platonizing account, a certain amount about Pythagorean doctrine before it was Platonized.

The other episode occurred about a century earlier: Iamblichus, here drawing on Aristotle, reports the existence of two rival sects of Pythagoreans, the *mathematici* and the *acousmatici*; the schism is tied to the name of Hippasus of Metapontum, and may thus be dated to the middle of the fifth century.[7] The *mathematici*, scientifically-minded Pythagoreans, naturally claimed to be the genuine followers of Pythagoras; and some scholars accept the claim and mark Pythagoras himself as a *mathematicus*. The evidence does not support this view. Pythagoreanism was not a peculiarly scientific sect until the second half of the fifth century: Pythagoras the *mathematicus* is a fiction.

Metaphysical Pythagoreanism is largely a fourth-century product; scientific Pythagoreanism is not found before the fifth century: there remain the *acousmatici*, devotees of the Pythagorean *acousmata* or *sumbola*. The surviving lists of *acousmata* go back in nucleus to the time of Pythagoras himself; they consist of a number of aphorisms (What are the Isles of the Blest?—The Sun and the Moon; What is wisest of all?—Number), and a large mass of rules and prohibitions of a detailed ritualistic nature: the celebrated injunction to abstain from the eating of beans is a typical *acousma*. Some of the *acousmata* are tricked out with reasons; and I shall have something to say about Pythagorean ethics in a later chapter. But by and large there is nothing in the *acousmata* to captivate the philosophic mind.[8]

The Newtonian Pythagoras is thus displaced by a figure more reminiscent of Joseph Smith: a hierophant; something of a charlatan; the leader of a sect, united by prescriptions and taboos—a religious society, not a scientific guild, which dabbled in South Italian politics but did not contribute to the history of Greek philosophy.[9]

If that were all we could say, Pythagoras might justly be banished from the philosophy books. But Joseph Smith is, like Isaac Newton, an exaggeration. The early sources leave no doubt that Pythagoras had intellectual as well as political and religious pretensions: Heraclitus railed at his polymathy (**21 B 40; B 129**); Ion of Chios praised his wisdom (**36 B 4**); to Herodotus he seemed 'not the weakest wise man among the Greeks' (IV.95 = **14 A 2**). The philosophical system later erected in his name was not designed by him; but it does not follow that he had no philosophical ideas: we do not know anything he believed, but we do not know that he did not believe anything.

Our ignorance is not total; one ray of light shines through the clouds, and there is one doctrine, or set of doctrines, that we can ascribe with some confidence to Pythagoras. Aristotle's pupil Dicaearchus gives the following report:

> What [Pythagoras] used to teach his associates, no one can tell with certainty; for they observed no ordinary silence. His most universally celebrated opinons, however, were that the soul is immortal; then that it migrates into other sorts of living creature; and in addition that after certain periods what has happened once happens again, and nothing is absolutely new; and that one should consider all animate things as akin. For Pythagoras seems to

> have been the first to have brought these doctrines into Greece (**84: 14 A 8a**).[10]

The doctrine of metempsychosis,[11] or the transmigration of souls, is on any account characteristic of Pythagoreanism; on Dicaearchus' account, to which I assent, it is the chief constituent of that small body of theory which we are justified in ascribing to Pythagoras. And it is enough, as I shall attempt to show, to secure a place for Pythagoras among the philosophers.

(b) *The progress of the soul*

Dicaearchus wrote two centuries after Pythagoras: what earlier evidence is there for metempsychosis as a Pythagorean doctrine?

Aristotle, a serious student of Pythagoreanism, refers to metempsychosis as a Pythagorean 'myth' (*An* 407b20 = **58 B 39**). Plato more than once advances transmigratory theories; but though we may guess that he was adopting Pythagorean thoughts, he never expressly says that he is.[12] Half a century earlier, Herodotus penned a tantalizing paragraph:

> The Egyptians were also the first to advance the theory that the soul of man is immortal, and that when the body perishes it enters into (*eisduesthai*) another living creature which comes into being at that moment; and when it has gone round all the land animals and all the sea animals and all the birds, it enters again into the body of a man who is coming into being; and this circumambulation goes on for three thousand years. Some of the Greeks adopted this theory—some earlier, some later—as though it were their own; I know their names, but I do not write them down (**85**: II.123 = **14 A 1**).

Herodotus is wrong about the Egyptian origins of metempsychosis; and he is wickedly teasing in concealing the names of its Greek advocates. Yet we can hardly fail to believe that among the 'earlier' thinkers the most celebrated was Pythagoras.[13]

Herodotus' 'later' men will have included Empedocles, who flourished in the earlier part of the fifth century (see below, p. 306); and it is in the fragments of Empedocles' *Katharmoi* or *Purifications* that we find the fullest account of metempsychosis. Empedocles himself says:

> For already have I once been a boy, and a girl,
> and a bush, and a fish that jumps from the sea as it swims (**86: 31 B 117 = 34 Z**).[14]

Empedocles had thus undergone both animal and vegetable incarnations (cf. **B 127** = **16 Z**); and he indicates more than one appearance in human form (**B 146** = **17 Z**). A long fragment tells of a cycle of transmigrations, lasting 30,000 seasons, imposed by Necessity on spirits who 'sully their dear limbs with bloodshed' (**B 115** = **3 Z**). The cycle was by and large woeful (see **B 115–127**); and Empedocles drew the salutary moral that one should avoid bloodshed and stick to a vegetarian diet (**B 135–141**).

It is often asserted that Empedocles ascribes a transmigratory doctrine to Pythagoras; but the fragment in question (**B 129** = **28 Z**) attributes, to an unnamed 'man of extraordinary knowledge', the ability to 'see with ease each and every thing that happens in ten and in twenty human lifetimes': the connexions with transmigration and with Pythagoras are alike dubious.[15] Again, the ancient assertions that Empedocles was himself a Pythagorean are of little worth. The most we can say is that Empedocles' environment was Pythagorean: he came from Acragas in Sicily; and it was in Sicily and South Italy that Pythagoras spent most of his life, and that his doctrines especially flourished. In 476 BC, when Empedocles was a boy, Pindar addressed his second *Olympian* ode to Theron, the ruler of Acragas, and in the poem depicted the delights of transmigration as to an audience familiar with and enamoured of the doctrine.

A final witness takes us back to Pythagoras himself:

> and about [Pythagoras'] having been different men at different times, Xenophanes bears witness in an elegy that begins:
>
> > Now I shall set out another account, and
> > show another way.
>
> and what he says goes like this:
>
> > And once they say he passed a dog that was being whipped;
> > and he took pity on it and uttered this word:
> > 'Stop—don't beat it. For it is the *psuchê* of a friend of mine—
> > I recognized him by his voice (**87**: Diogenes Laertius, VIII. 36 = **21 B** 7).

Xenophanes' story is a jest, not a piece of doxography; but the jest has no point if its butt was not a transmigrationist.[16]

Numerous questions arise about the content of Pythagoras' theory: Do all creatures, or all men, or only a favoured few, undergo transmigration? Are all living things potential recipients of human souls? Is transmigration cyclical? and is there a fixed hierarchy of incarnations? Are there gaps between incarnations? and do these involve some sort of Judgment Day? Is metempsychosis tied to a moral theory, or to a way of life, or to a theology?

To most of those questions we can only conjecture answers; and it is, I think, likely enough that different thinkers held different views. I shall return in a later chapter to the question of the connexion between metempsychosis and morals; for the rest it is enough to say that, whatever their anthropological interest, such peripheral questions have little philosophical bearing. It is the hard centre of the theory which gives it philosophical importance; and that centre consists simply in the contention that, at death, a man's soul may leave his body and animate another.[17]

There is nothing strikingly novel in the view that we somehow survive our earthly deaths; and the view was widespread in Greece from the dawn of history. Nor was there anything new in the supposition that the soul of my grandam might haply inhabit a bird: 'theriomorphism' is a commonplace in Greek mythology. The gods, with tedious frequency, dress themselves in bestial garments; and Circe turned Odysseus' crew to swine.[18] The novelty in Pythagoras' doctrine (if novelty it was[19]) consisted in its conjunction of those two old superstitions: men survive death by virtue of their *psuchê*'s taking on a new form. Survival and transmogrification add up to metempsychosis.

What sort of a *psuchê* does the doctrine of metempsychosis presuppose? I shall advert later to some of the things which the Pythagoreans and Empedocles said, or implied, about the human *psuchê*; here it is only necessary to observe the central fact about metempsychosis: that it proclaims a *personal* survival of bodily death. Pythagoras, in Xenophanes' story, recognized the dog as his friend; Empedocles, on his own account, had himself been a boy, a girl, a bush and a dolphin; when my *psuchê* moves, I move with it, and if my *psuchê* is incarnate in *a*, then I am *a*. Now the transmigration of my liver, or the transplantation of my heart, is of no personal concern to me: my entrails do not constitute myself. If transmigration of the *psuchê* is to do its Pythagorean duty, that can only be because the *psuchê*, unlike the entrails, is intimately connected with the self. John Locke put this very clearly: if soul does not carry self or consciousness, then a man will not be Nestor or Thersites 'though it were never so true, that the same Spirit that informed *Nestor*'s or *Thersites*'s Body, were numerically the same that now informs his. For this would no more make him the same Person with *Nestor*, than if some of the Particles of Matter, that were once a part of *Nestor*, were now a part of this Man, the same immaterial Substance without the same consciousness, no more making the same Person by being united to any Body, than the same Particle of Matter without consciousness united to any Body, makes the same Person' (*Essay* II.

xxvii. 14).

The early history of the notion of *psuchê* is obscure, the texts bearing on it sparse. I do not claim either that Pythagoras had a clearly articulated concept of *psuchê*, or that there was a single and uniform notion of *psuchê* common to the early Greek philosophers. But for all that, the essence of the business is neither dark nor debatable: metempsychosis anchored a personal survival; and the mode of survival was a transmigration of the *psuchê*. Those two facts suffice to show that Pythagoras' *psuchê* was the seat of personality.[20]

Thus the Pythagorean *psuchê* is more than Thales' animator: it is the seat of consciousness and of personality; a man's *psuchê* is whatever makes him the person he is, whatever is responsible for his particular self and personality. Metempsychosis is the doctrine of the transcorporation of the self; and the *psuchê* is the self. It is this which gives Pythagoras' theory a potential philosophical interest; for ever since Locke's discussion of the case of the Prince and the Cobbler, transmigratory fantasies have been a stock element in the discussion of personal identity.

(c) *Metempsychosis, mysticism and logic*

It may be thought fanciful to connect the obscure superstitions of Pythagoras with modern studies on personal identity: 'In Pythagoras' time', it will be said, 'no one knew or cared about the problems of personal identity; and Pythagoras himself was promulgating an eschatological dogma, not propounding a philosophical thesis.' A piece of Epicharmus will refute that sceptical suggestion: a debtor has been hauled to court for failing to pay his creditor; here is his defence:

> DEBTOR. If you like to add a pebble to an odd number—or to an even one if you like—or if you take one away that is there, do you think it is still the same number?
>
> CREDITOR. Of course not.
>
> D. And if you like to add some further length to a yard-measure, or to cut something off from what's already there, will that measure still remain?
>
> C. No.
>
> D. Well, consider men in this way too—for one is growing, one

> declining, and all are changing all the time. And what changes by nature, and never remains in the same state, will be something different from what changed; and by the same argument you and I are different yesterday, and different now, and will be different again—and we are never the same (**88: 23 B 2**).

Thus the defendant in court is not the same person as the borrower of the cash; and it is consequently quite unjust for him to be dunned for money which *he* never borrowed.[21]

This *jeu d'esprit* contains several remarkable features. It discusses personal identity in a legal and moral context; and, as Locke observed, 'person' is primarily 'a Forensick Term appropriating Actions and their Merit' (*Essay* II. xxvii. 26). Second, Epicharmus' debtor clearly takes continuity of consciousness as irrelevant to his case: he is not denying that he has memories of incurring the debt, only that he himself was the man who incurred it. Again, bodily identity is taken as a necessary condition for personal identity: it is the debtor's physical alterations which absolve him from his debt. And finally, the conditions for bodily identity are very strict: any physical change, any increase or decrease in size, disrupts identity.

All that would stand further investigation; but my purpose in quoting Epicharmus is to prove that the problem of personal identity was not alien to Pythagorean critics in the early fifth century. Epicharmus' debtor presents a 'theory' of personal identity that stands at the opposite pole to that implicit in metempsychosis; Epicharmus, if not a Pythagorean himself, was certainly aware of the philosophy preached in his homeland; and I suppose that his play is evidence of a lively debate on matters of personal identity in early Pythagorean circles.

Was the debate a matter of assertion and counter-assertion? or did the Pythagoreans employ argument? Was metempsychosis a rational theory or a religious dogma?

It has been held that 'a doctrine like that of metempsychosis, which transcends normal human ways of knowing, can find a guarantee only in supernatural experience, in the world of the divine or quasi-divine';[22] and the multitude of miraculous stories told of Pythagoras were narrated, according to Aristotle, in an attempt to supply that transcendental guarantee (fr. 191 R[3] = **14 A 7**). But if Pythagoras did display a golden thigh, that would hardly constitute a reason for accepting his doctrine of transmigration. Supernatural experience or an unnatural constitution are not to the point.

It is also false that 'the prophet [of transmigration] must be able to refer to his own example':[23] *any* example will constitute evidence for the thesis; and there is nothing logically superior about Pythagoras' own case. Nonetheless, it is very likely that Pythagoras did refer to his own case; and it is probable that he based his theory on his own experience. Antiquity provides several lists of Pythagoras' incarnations; though they vary in detail they collectively represent an old, and I think an authentic, tradition. Here is the version given by Heraclides Ponticus, a pupil of Plato's who was noted for his interest in the occult (and also for his historical imagination):

> Heraclides Ponticus says that [Pythagoras] says about himself that he was once Aithalides, and was deemed a son of Hermes; and that Hermes told him to choose whatever he wanted except immortality, and so he asked that both alive and dead he should remember what happened. So in his life he remembered everything, and when he died he retained the same memory. Some time later he passed into Euphorbus, and was wounded by Menelaus. (And Euphorbus used to say that he had once been Aithalides, . . .) And when Euphorbus died, his soul passed into Hermotimus. . . . And when Hermotimus died, he became Pyrrhus the Delian diver; and again he remembered everything—how he had been first Aithalides, then Euphorbus, then Hermotimus, then Pyrrhus. And when Pyrrhus died, he became Pythagoras, and remembered everything that has been said (**89**: fr. 89 W = Diogenes Laertius, VIII.4–5 = **14 A 8**).

Pythagoras thus claimed a series of incarnations for himself; and he supported his claim by his *mémoires d'outre-tombe*.

Heraclides' insistence on Pythagoras' memories is no accidental embellishment of his story. The later Pythagoreans were devoted to mnemonics: 'a Pythagorean does not get out of bed before he has recalled the previous day's happenings', and he makes use of a detailed recipe for reminiscence (Iamblichus, **58 D 1**, §165). It is plausible to connect this practice with the theory of metempsychosis: an acute memory will break the bonds of time, and give a Pythagorean vastly increased knowledge, both of the world and also of his own early biography.[24]

Nor, of course, is memory alien to the problems of personal identity; but 'memory' is a term with more than one application, and it is important to single out the appropriate one. Pythagoras is relying on what might be called 'experiential' memory. 'Experiential' memory is typically expressed by way of the formula '*a* remembers ϕing'; and the object of such memory is an experience, and an experience of the rememberer's. I may remember *that* I had a certain experience without having any 'experiential' memory: I remember that I lived in Colyton during 1943, but I cannot remember living there; I remember that I visited the Festival of Britain in 1951, but I remember little or nothing of the visit. I am inclined to think that experiential memory is a fundamental sort of remembering; and that it necessarily involves mental visualizings. (If that is so, then the much-despised empiricist account of memory may be less disreputable than it seems.) But those are obscure and difficult issues; and the present argument is independent of them.

John Locke's account of personal identity is properly expressed in terms of 'experiential' memory; it amounts, I think, to a conjunction of the following two theses:

(M1) If a is the same person as b, and b ϕed at time t and place p, then a can remember ϕing at t p.

(M2) If a can remember ϕing at t p, and b ϕed at t p, then a is the same person as b.

Of these two theses, (M1) seems open to immediate counter-example: the examiner who conscientiously forgets the questions he has set does not lose responsibility for setting them; the criminal may plead amnesia as a mitigating factor, but he cannot advance it as a proof of innocence; and in general we forget many of our past actions without forfeiting our identity with their agent. Locke was well aware that such an objection would be raised against him; and he anticipated it by a characteristically blunt negation (*Essay* II. xxvii. 22). I shall not attempt to say anything in his defence.

(M2), on the other hand, is immediately plausible. Indeed, if we take the notion of place narrowly, so that at most one person can be at p at any given moment, and if we construe 'remember' in a veridical sense, then (M2) is a necessary truth; for if a remembers ϕing, then a ϕed; and if a ϕed and b is the ϕer, then a is identical with b. And it is (M2) which Pythagoras requires. The argument which Heraclides implicitly ascribes to him is simple enough:

(1) Pythagoras remembers being killed by Menelaus at Troy at noon on 1 April 1084 BC.

(2) Euphorbus was killed by Menelaus at Troy at noon on 1 April 1084 BC.

Hence:

(3) Pythagoras is identical with Euphorbus.

The argument is valid; and its validity rests on (M2).

Any Lockean who is committed to (M2) is committed, not of course to Pythagoreanism, but to the possibility of Pythagoreanism. And Locke himself, though he has ironical words for one account of metempsychosis (*Essay* II. xxvii. 6), explicitly allows as much: '*personal Identity* consists . . . in the Identity of *consciousness*, wherein, if *Socrates* and the present Mayor of *Quinborough* agree, they are the same Person' (ibid., 19). According to Locke, we are simply ignorant as to 'whether it has pleased God, that no one such Spirit shall ever be united to any but one such Body' (ibid., 27).

Yet even if Pythagoras' argument is valid, and has the blessing of John Locke, no one, I suppose, will be very impressed by it: premiss (2) we may pass (it is easily replaced by historically more acceptable propositions); but premiss (1) invites challenge: Pythagoras no doubt *says* he remembers being killed—but *does* he? People's memories often play them up; the Trojan War took place a long time ago; and it is, in any case, a touch unusual to remember being killed. Moreover, the Greeks had 'often seen wise men dying in verbal pretence—then, when they come home again, they get the greater honour' (Sophocles, *Electra* 62–4). Perhaps Pythagoras was another of those charlatans?

Pythagoras was well prepared for such appalling scepticism; and he provided an answer to it:

> They say that, while staying at Argos, he saw a shield from the spoils of Troy nailed up, and burst into tears. When the Argives asked him the reason for his emotion, he said that he himself had borne that shield in Troy when he was Euphorbus; they did not believe him, and judged him to be mad, but he said he would find a true sign that this was the case; for on the inside of the shield was written in archaic lettering EUPHORBUS'S. Because of the extraordinary nature of the claim, they all urged him to take down the offering; and the inscription was found on it (**90**: Diodorus, X. 6. 2).

Later Pythagoreans dismissed the story as a vulgarization; and modern scholars agree that it is a confection dreamed up by a fourth-century fabulist. I cannot prove that it is an old tale; yet I hope that it is. For though it may be false, it is certainly *ben trovato*: logically, it is precisely what Pythagoras needs. For of the several ways of defending a disputed memory claim, one is the exhibition of present and indisputable knowledge which can plausibly be derived from the experiences allegedly remembered.

If you show scepticism at my reminiscences of lunching royally in the *Tour d'Argent*, I may describe to you the menu, the decoration and the staff of the restaurant, and show myself capable of recognizing photographs of it. Similarly, but more cogently, by recognizing Euphorbus' shield, Pythagoras exhibited knowledge that could well be explained on the hypothesis that he had indeed fought at Troy. Of course, such facts do not *demonstrate* the truth of memory claims, in the sense that they are logically incompatible with their falsehood. But that is not to the point: the feats provide evidence—more or less good evidence—for the truth of the claims; and evidence is what Pythagoras is asked to supply. If Pythagoras did indeed pick Euphorbus' shield, the Argives will have suspected him of cheating; and if they were convinced that no cheating occurred, they may have shrugged their shoulders and spoken of chance or coincidence. Pythagoras' action does not prove his claim, still less his theory (what action can prove anything?); but it does provide some evidence—and, I suggest, fairly good evidence—for the truth of what he asserts.

That completes the account of metempsychosis. The whole matter is put briefly and neatly in Ovid's *Metamorphoses*; Pythagoras speaks:

> For soules are free from death. Howbeet, they leaving evermore
> Theyr former dwellings, are receyvd and live ageine in new.
> For I myself (ryght well in mynd I beare it too be trew)
> Was in the tyme of Trojan warre *Euphorbus*, *Panthewes* sonne,
> Quyght through whoose hart the deathfull speare of *Menelay* did ronne.
> I late ago in Junos Church at Argos did behold
> And knew the target which I in my left hand there did hold.
> (91: XV. 158–64; trans. Golding)

Metempsychosis is no rough dogma: it is a rational theory, capable of rigorous statement and implying a respectable account of the nature of personal identity; and it was advocated by Pythagoras on solid empirical grounds. We are far from mystery-mongering.

(d) *Selves and bodies*

Epicharmus' debtor still has his appeal: are there not cogent and widely accepted objections to a Lockean account of personal identity? Has it not been shown that bodily identity is a necessary condition of personal identity? And can we not thence infer the impossibility of metempsychosis?

Some philosophers may object to metempsychosis and side with Epicharmus' debtor because they do not feel happy with the prospect of disembodiment: *psuchai*, they suspect, cannot exist apart from a physical body. Now metempsychosis does not, in logic, require disembodiment; and I doubt if the theory was regularly associated with the survival of disembodied *psuchai*.

You might think that metempsychosis involved at least momentary disembodiment, on the strength of the following argument: 'It is a necessary truth that if the *psuchê* which animates *a* at t_1 is the same as the *psuchê* which later animates *b* at t_2, then *a* is the same person as *b*. Suppose, then, that *a* dies at t_3, a moment falling between t_1 and t_2. Well, *b* must have some birthday, t_4, between t_3 and t_2. But t_4 cannot be identical with t_3 (for then the *psuchê* would inhabit two distinct bodies at the same time); nor can t_4 be contiguous with t_3 (for no two instants of time are contiguous). Hence there must be a gap between t_3, and t_4 during which the *psuchê* is disembodied.'[25]

I reject the argument for two reasons: we have no cause to assign a birthday to *b* or to suppose the existence of a birthdate t_4; and even if there is a gap between t_3 and the alleged t_4, we need not suppose that the *psuchê* exists during that gap. (I shall have more to say on the former of these objections when I discuss Zeno: below, pp. 270–1).

The argument from birthdays fails; and I can think of no other feature of metempsychosis that might appear to commit Pythagoras to disembodiment. Nor does anything commit him to dualism: he need not suppose that bodies are made of 'matter' and *psuchai* of that completely different substance, 'spirit'. Metempsychosis is transcorporation of the *psuchê*: that implies nothing about the status of the *psuchê*'s constituent stuff.

If I am right so far, the philosophical opponent of transmigration must do more than deny the hypothesis of an immaterial, spiritual substance; and more than reject the possibility of disembodied persons. He must, in effect, maintain that the *psuchê* and the body are identical; for only if *a*'s *psuchê* actually is *a*'s body does metempsychosis become impossible; only if I am the person I am by virtue of having the body I have, can I be prevented, by logic, from changing bodies.

I know of only one serious *a priori* argument which purports to prove the identity of *psuchê* and body. It is the duplication argument, and it runs like this.

Suppose that, on the day after Pythagoras made his startling identification of Euphorbus' shield, Xenophanes visited Argos. On being told the hot news of Pythagoras' identity, he claimed that not Pythagoras but he was Euphorbus: *he* could remember being killed by Menelaus; and what is more, *he* could pick out the shield to prove it. And suppose further that Xenophanes successfully picked out Euphorbus' shield, and indeed succeeded in duplicating *every* feat that Pythagoras had performed. There are now two candidates for identity with Euphorbus: each can marshal exactly the same facts in his favour as the other can; yet both cannot be Euphorbus, for then they would be identical with one another, and one candidate not two. Hence to identify either with Euphorbus is strictly unreasonable. And since anyone with Pythagorean pretensions must always be prepared to face a rival Xenophanes, it can never be reasonable to accept any Pythagorean claim. The theory of metempsychosis is consequently vain.

The duplication argument is impressive; but it has its chinks. First, observe that it does not yield the conclusion that neither Pythagoras nor Xenophanes is Euphorbus: it concludes only that we can have no reason for preferring either candidate to the other. If that conclusion is correct, it indicates that the doctrine of metempsychosis is in a certain sense empty; but it does not show that Pythagoras was wrong.

Second, notice that the argument applies in all cases of 'experiential' memory. I remember sitting in seat K 5 of the Playhouse last night; and if you care to doubt my word I can produce, perhaps, a ticket stub and a sworn affidavit from a *soi-disant* occupant of seat K 6. Now it is perfectly possible that a *Doppelgänger* should appear and claim that *he* remembers occupying seat K 5; and that he should produce a ticket stub as informative as mine, and a sworn statement from an alleged neighbour. Moreover, any further efforts I may make to support my claim will immediately be imitated by my *Doppelgänger*. Thus there are two rival claimants to one seat: neither of us produces any evidence not immediately matched by the other; and though it does not follow that neither of us occupied the seat, it does follow that for you to believe one of us rather than the other is strictly unreasonable.

I and my *Doppelgänger* are in all relevant respects analogous to Pythagoras and Xenophanes: *any* memory claim can be disputed; *any* evidence can be matched; *any* reminiscent raconteur may find his duplicate, reminiscing with equal plausibility and recounting with equal sincerity. Duplication is not restricted to metempsychotic memories: it applies impartially to all.

But what does the possibility of duplication prove? If my *Doppelgänger* actually arrives and mimics my claims in that monstrous way, then you will be right to credit neither of us. Similarly, if Xenophanes had actually turned up at Argos and mimicked Pythagoras, the Argives would have done well to retreat into a bewildered scepticism. But it does not follow from this that the mere possibility of such a *Doppelgänger* is evidence against my claim to have sat in seat K 5, or that the mere possibility of Xenophanes' appearance is evidence against Pythagoras. Schematically, the case looks like this: a set of propositions, P_1, counts as reasonable evidence for a claim C_1; and a rival set, P_2, counts as reasonable evidence for an incompatible claim, C_2. P_1 and P_2 are logically compossible. If both

P_1 and P_2 are known to be true, then it is unreasonable both to believe C_1 and to believe C_2. But it is absurd to infer that if P_1 is known to be true, then it is unreasonable to believe C_1 because P_2 is compatible with P_1.

These considerations evidently need deeper probing; but they seem to me enough to throw doubt upon the strength of the duplication argument, at least as a refutation of the possibility of metempsychosis. C. S. Peirce once asserted that 'Pythagoras was certainly a wonderful man. We have no right, at all, to say that supernal powers had not put a physical mark upon him as extraordinary as his personality'; indeed, we have for this 'far stronger testimony than we have for the resurrection of Jesus'. Peirce was speaking of Pythagoras' golden thigh; but his remarks apply equally to Pythagoras' incarnations. Peirce's credulity is charming; and his comparison is apt: if we reject Pythagoras' claim, it must be on the same grounds that we reject the miraculous stories of the early Christians. The materialist enemies of John Locke cannot shoot Pythagoras down with *a priori* arrows; if their failure leaves us with a disagreeable feeling, we may hope that the notorious shafts of Hume will drop him along with other miracle-mongers. But however that may be, it seems to me that the doctrine of metempsychosis does indeed have 'a rigour and a speculative power that is the mark . . . of a bold and original thinker'.[26]

(e) *Intimations of immortality*

According to Dicaearchus, Pythagoras taught the immortality of the *psuchê* (above, text **84**).[27] Metempsychosis does not in itself entail immortality: a feline *psuchê* enjoys nine transmigrations but no more. And we may ask how Pythagoras and his followers justified their immortal pretensions. We may ask; but we receive no answer. And other Presocratic psychologies are no more informative. According to Diogenes,

> Some say—among them Choirilus the poet—that [Thales] was also the first to hold that *psuchai* are immortal (**92**: I. 24 = **11 A 1**; cf. Suda, **A 2**);

but the report does not inspire much confidence, and no trace of an argument survives. Heraclitus may have subscribed to the doctrine of immortality; but again, no argument, and no clear assertion, survives. And other early thinkers did not greatly bother their heads about their *psuchai*.

There is one bright exception to that generalization. Alcmeon of

Croton, an eminent physician and an amateur of philosophy, both believed in and argued for psychic immortality; and his argument so impressed Plato that he adopted it for his own.

Alcmeon probably worked at the beginning of the fifth century, a younger contemporary of Pythagoras. According to Diogenes, 'most of what he says concerns medicine, but he sometimes treats of natural philosophy' (VIII. 83 = **24 A 1**). His philosophical interests included astronomy (e.g., Aëtius, **A 4**); and he offered some metaphysical reflexions which seemed vaguely Pythagorean in tone to Aristotle (*Met* 986a27–34 = **A 3**). He also touched upon epistemological matters (see below, pp. 136, 149). But his main interest appears to have lain in what may loosely be called the philosophy of man—and in particular, in human psychology. It is here that his argument for the immortality of the *psuchê* belongs.

We know the argument by report, not by quotation; but before turning to the reports it will be well to quote one of the few fragments of Alcmeon's own writings:

> Men perish for this reason, that they cannot attach the beginning to the end (**93: B 2**).

There have been many attempts to elucidate this enigmatic apophthegm, but none is particularly satisfactory.[28] Whatever the fragment may mean, it shows that Alcmeon made a distinction between a man and his *psuchê*. Men are mortal, perishing things; but *psuchai*, as the argument we are to examine pretends, are immortal and deathless. Now it is tempting to argue thus: 'If men are mortal and Socrates is a man, then Socrates is mortal. But men, according to **B 2**, perish; so Socrates will perish, and the immortality of his *psuchê* will not secure his own survival. Alcmeon and the Pythagoreans part company: for Alcmeon, psychic immortality is not personal immortality; my soul may go marching on, but I shall not.' To avoid that conclusion we must divorce the notions of *man* and *person*, and maintain, with Locke, that the term 'man' connotes a being of a certain form and physical constitution: to be a man is to be an animal of a determinate type. Persons, then, are not necessarily men: Socrates may cease to be a man without ceasing to be. Plato probably took Alcmeon to be arguing for personal immortality; for when he adopts Alcmeon's reasoning, he does so in the conviction that it supports a doctrine of individual immortality. Again, the Pythagorean doctrine of metempsychosis, with which Alcmeon was indubitably acquainted, closely associated psychic and personal survival, and thus implicitly distinguished between persons and men. Finally, the Lockean distinction between person and man, which some modern philosophers find outlandish and absurd, was familiar to every Greek schoolboy: when Odysseus' companions were turned into swine by Circe they ceased to be men, but did not lose their personal identity. Circe did not kill Odysseus' crew: she transmogrified them.

I thus suppose that according to Alcmeon men die but people do not: the survival of the *psuchê* does not guarantee 'human' survival; but it does hold out the promise of personal survival. Alcmeon's argument may indeed have been intended to give philosophical respectability and rational support to the plain assertions of the Pythagoreans.

I turn to Alcmeon's argument. There are five reports to be mentioned. First, Aristotle:

> Alcmeon . . . says that [the *psuchê*] is immortal because it is like the immortals; and that this holds of it in virtue of the fact that it is always moving. For all divine things are always moving continuously—moon, sun, the stars, and the whole heavens (**94**: *An* 405a29–b1 = **A 12**).

Second, a fragment of Boethus:

> Looking at this [sc. the similarity of our *psuchê* to god], the philosopher from Croton said that, being immortal, it actually shuns by nature every form of rest, like the divine bodies (**95**: Eusebius, *PE* XI. 28. 9).

Third, Diogenes:

> He says that the *psuchê* is immortal, and that it moves continuously like the sun (**96**: VIII. 83 = **A 1**).

Fourth, Aëtius:

> Alcmeon supposes [the *psuchê*] to be a substance self-moved in eternal motion, and for that reason immortal and similar to the divine things (**97**: **A 12**).

The fifth text does not name Alcmeon; it is the section of the *Phaedrus* in which Plato transcribes and adapts Alcmeon's argument. I quote the beginning and the end of the passage:

> Every *psuchê* is immortal. For what is ever-moving is immortal. And what moves something else and is moved by something else, having a respite from movement has a respite from life; thus only that which moves itself, in so far as it does not abandon itself, never stops moving. . . . Every body whose movement comes from

> without is inanimate (*apsuchos*) and every body whose movement comes from within is animate (*empsuchos*), this being the nature of an animator (*psuchê*). And if this is so, and if what moves itself is nothing other than an animator, then from necessity animators will be both ungenerated and immortal (98: *Phaedrus* 245C–246A).

Plato's text is disputed at crucial points;[29] and the structure of his argument is controversial: he appears to have grafted Alcmeon's reasoning onto a distinct set of considerations (they appear in the passage I have omitted), and the grafting is uncharacteristically crude. Moreover, we cannot be sure how far Plato is embellishing Alcmeon, and how far he is simply following him.[30] We must, therefore, rely primarily on Aristotle and the doxographers for the reconstruction of Alcmeon's argument.

Those reports ascribe three propositions to Alcmeon:

(1) *Psuchai* are always moving.

(2) *Psuchai* are like the divine heavenly bodies.

(3) *Psuchai* are immortal.

Diogenes lets the three propositions stand without any clear inferential linking. Boethus appears to present an argument from (3) to (1). Aristotle and Aëtius, more plausibly, make an argument from (1) to (3).

According to Aristotle, Alcmeon inferred (2) from (1), and (3) from (2). His argument is thus a hideously feeble analogy: *psuchai* are like the heavenly bodies in one respect—they move continuously; hence they are like the heavenly bodies in another respect—they are immortal. As well infer that *psuchai* are flat discs—for the sun is so shaped (Aëtius, **A 4**).

According to Aëtius, Alcmeon inferred (2) from (1), and also inferred (3) from (1). (3) does not require the analogical mediation of (2): it follows directly from (1). Plato supports Aëtius here; and I am inclined to accept his report. Alcmeon, I suppose, originally said something like this: 'Animators, like the divine denizens of the heavens, move continuously; hence, like those divinities, they are immortal.' Aristotle misread the illustrative comparison with the heavenly bodies as an analogical premiss; but Aëtius preserves the true deductive character of the argument. To make the argument fully explicit we need to add a further premiss:

(4) Anything that always moves is immortal.

From (1) and (4), (3) follows.

Premiss (4) is a necessary truth. According to Aëtius, Alcmeon's *psuchai* were 'self-moving';[31] and 'self-motion' occurs in Plato's version of the argument. Some scholars opine that the introduction of that notion into the argument was the work of Plato; but there is no reason to deny the notion to Alcmeon: the belief that living things—men, animals, and heavenly bodies—are 'self-moving', in the sense that they move without being impelled from outside, is not a deeply philosophical opinion. Since anything that has the power to cause motion is alive (above, p. 7), any self-mover is alive. Hence anything that is moving itself at *t* is alive at *t*; and anything in continuous self-motion is eternally alive. And to assert that is to assert (4).

There is more difficulty in premiss (1): in what way can *psuchai* move? Why should we suppose that they *do* move? And why should we agree that they *always* move?

There is a temptation to connect the animator's motion with its cognitive function: it might be suggested, in a Cartesian vein, that animators cogitate, and that cogitation is a species of 'motion', in a relaxed sense of that term. Then Alcmeon's premiss that *psuchai* always move will parallel the notorious Cartesian thesis that the soul always thinks.

The suggestion is attractive; but I fear we must be content with a far cruder account of psychic locomotion. In one of the more bizarre portions of that most bizarre work, the *Timaeus*, Plato explains how the minor gods in their creation of men 'imitated the shape of the universe, which is round, and confined the two divine revolutions in a spherical body, which we now call the head, and which is the most divine part of us and rules over everything in us' (44D). The 'two divine revolutions' are the whirling circles of the Same and the Other, which constitute our *psuchê*. The human skull is thus an orrery, representing the heavens; and the soul, revolving within it, mimics the revolutions of the heavenly bodies. That strange conception is full of obscurities which I am happy to ignore; it is enough to say that so many of its features are reminiscent of Alcmeon that the whole theory, in outline at least, may plausibly be ascribed to him. In the *Timaeus*, as in the *Phaedrus*, Plato draws on Alcmeon. As far as premiss (1) of Alcmeon's argument is concerned, the moral is this: the movements of the *psuchê* are, quite literally, locomotions—circular revolutions in the space of the skull.

Why should Alcmeon have felt drawn by so strange an hypothesis? According to Aristotle, 'some say that an animator is first and foremost what gives motion. And, believing that what is not itself in motion cannot move anything else, they supposed the animator to be something moving' (*An* 403b28–31). What moves other things must itself move; hence the animator, being a motor, is in motion. The argument did not appeal to Aristotle; but it is, I think, a particular application of the Synonymy Principle of causation (above p. 88); and that principle can be found in Aristotle's own works. 'Causation is by synonyms': who breeds fat oxen must himself be fat. The fire warms me only if it is itself warm; ice cools gin because ice itself is cold; this ink, which is black, renders this paper black; sweet-smelling lavender makes the sheets smell sweet. In general: if *a* brings it about that *b* is ϕ, then *a* is ϕ.

The principle is supported by numerous examples; and it helps to explain the occult property of causality: causes produce changes in the objects they effect by transferring or imparting something to those objects; when the fire makes me warm, it bestows heat upon me; and the lavender, we say, gives the sheets their sweetness. Now since I cannot give you what I do not myself possess, causes must themselves be endowed with the properties they impart. This emerges plainly from a passage in which Descartes employs a particular instance of the principle: 'Now it is manifest by the natural light that there must be at least as much reality in the efficient and total cause as in its effect. For, pray, whence can the effect derive its reality if not from its cause? And in what way can this cause communicate this reality to it, unless it possesses it itself?' (*Meditation* III).

If some examples commend the principle, many more stand against it; and it is not difficult to see that the principle both is false in itself and conveys a misleading notion of the causal process. Berkeley was characteristically abrupt: 'Nihil dat quod non habet or the effect is contained in y[e] Cause is an axiom I do not Understand or believe to be true' (*Philosophical Commentaries* A § 780). And indeed it is easier to show the inadequacy of the principle than to explain its popularity and longevity.

The origin of the principle is, I think, unknown: it is found, as I have said, in Aristotle, and it is traceable in Plato's *Phaedo*; I do not doubt that it is Presocratic, and I see no reason to question Aristotle's implication that it lay behind Alcmeon's argument for the immortality of the *psuchê*: a *psuchê* causes locomotion; therefore it must itself move.

If animators must move, why need they be moving continuously? Why is sporadic or temporary motion not sufficient? After all, the bodies they move do not move continuously or for ever. The *Phaedrus* suggests alternative answers to this question. First, Plato observes that 'that which moves itself, in so far as it does not abandon itself, never stops moving' (245C). The point is obscure to me; perhaps Plato means this: 'Self-movers are autonomous agents, whose movement is not dependent upon external forces; consequently the moved thing, being always attached to—since it is identical with—an autonomous motor, will always move.' That is an uncompelling argument: the heavenly motions in my head may, I suppose, be autonomous in the sense that no external mover causes my cerebral motor to move; but it does not follow that my *psuchê* is entirely indifferent to the outside world, or that my psychic revolutions will survive a sharp crack on the skull.

A passage from the end of Plato's argument suggests a different type of explanation for the eternity of psychic motion. It is, Plato says, 'the nature of an animator' to move the body; 'what moves itself is nothing other than an animator'; so that 'from necessity' animators are immortal. These phrases hint at the following argument: 'An animator is, by definition, a motor; motors, of necessity, themselves move. Hence of necessity animators move. Hence an animator cannot at any time not be moving. Hence animators are always moving.' Psychic motion, in short, is a matter of logical necessity; and evidently what happens of necessity happens always.

Alcmeon's argument for the immortality of the *psuchê* can now be set out fairly explictly. It runs, I suggest, thus: 'I am animate, and hence, trivially, contain an animator. My animator is, by definition, a motor; for it is, *inter alia*, whatever is the source of my various locomotive efforts. The analysis of causation shows that of necessity motors move. Thus my animator moves of necessity; and hence it moves always and continuously. Now anything in autonomous movement is alive, so that anything always in motion is always alive, and thus immortal. *Ergo*, my animator is immortal.'

That is a complex and a sophisticated argument. Indeed, in certain respects it bears comparison with St Anselm's notorious Ontological Argument: both proofs start from a definition, and both end with an eternal existent. Both proofs are unsound; and Alcmeon's is both less perplexing and less philosophically fecund than Anselm's. But I shall leave criticism of Alcmeon to the reader, and end this chapter on a note of mild commendation: I do not know of any argument for the immortality of the soul one half so clever as Alcmeon's, the very first argument in the field.

VII

The Moral Law

(a) *First steps in ethics*

One of the more delicious prerogatives of the philosopher is that of telling other people where their duties and obligations lie, and what they ought to do. Ethics is a traditional branch of philosophy; and, with the exception of a few modern heretics, all professors of ethics have been primarily concerned to discover the rules of right and wrong, and to disseminate their discoveries. Of course, not every preacher is a philosopher; and if philosophers have a pre-eminent claim to our attention when they choose to moralize that is in large part because they do not, professionally at least, offer piecemeal and dogmatic injunctions, but are prepared to provide some general prescriptions for conduct which are systematic, rational, and analytic. The natural tendency of the human mind to proffer advice and instruction might lead us to expect that ethics was a subject of interest to the earliest Presocratic philosophers. Their historical circumstances, and their known practical bent, support that expectation. A potent drive to ethical reflexion has always been given by observation of the radical differences in moral outlook from country to country and from age to age. Such observation was made by quick-minded Greek travellers of the sixth century; and if Xenophanes was moved by his acquaintance with different religious beliefs to advance a rational theology, surely acquaintance with different moral beliefs would move him and his peers to investigate the grounds of morality?

Again, the Presocratics did not live as anchorites or academics, far from the madding crowd's ignoble strife. On the contrary, they strove. Plutarch, defending philosophy against the charge of irrelevant other-worldliness, lists and applauds the political cares and achievements of its practitioners. Even Parmenides, that most abstract of intellects, took sufficient time off from metaphysics to 'arrange his own country by excellent laws, so that the citizens still make their officials swear each year to abide by the laws of Parmenides' (Plutarch, *adv Col* 1126A = **28 A 12**). The Seven Sages—those early Greek heroes distinguished by their capacity for political wisdom and brisk aphorism—included Thales in their number; and the tales of Thales' practical prowess are not unique: stories of a similar nature and content are told, not incredibly, of most of the Presocratics.

Nonetheless, ethics was not a central interest for the majority of the early philosophers: the Milesians offered no moral philosophy at all. Xenophanes evinces various ethical sentiments: his strictures on Homeric theology imply a conventional morality (**21 B 11–12**); he has some caustic remarks about the degenerate and effeminate dress of his contemporaries (**B 3**); and he makes a pleasingly heterodox assessment of the relative worth of philosophers and Olympic victors (**B 2**). Yet there is nothing particularly philosophical about those opinions. As a moralist, Xenophanes works in the tradition of the didactic poets of old Greece: Hesiod, Theognis, Solon.

I do not know why the early Presocratics were largely silent about ethics: they will hardly have thought it a subject too serious or too slight for philosophizing. Perhaps they said nothing for the reason, as rare as it is commendable, that they had nothing to say. However that may be, the silence was broken only by two men, Heraclitus and Empedocles. Their views are not vastly impressive; yet they have a fascination, if only because they represent the first tottering steps ever taken in the still tottering subject of ethics.

(b) *Eating people is wrong*

Whether or not Empedocles was a Pythagorean, the moral views which he vociferously advocates plainly rest upon those elements in his philosophy which are most Pythagorean in their nature. The question arises whether he is not a mouthpiece for an earlier Pythagorean ethics.

We possess a long account of Pythagorean views on ethics, politics and education; the account is, in a loose sense, systematic; and it is also in most respects sensible, wise and humane (**58 D**). But its author is the fourth-century philosopher Aristoxenus; and there is no reason to treat it as a document bearing on Presocratic Pythagoreanism. The Pythagorean *sumbola*, on the other hand, are in nucleus early; but they do not pretend to systematic organization or philosophical backing. Some of the rules and rituals are indeed tricked out with reasons; but those reasons, like the allegorical interpretations which sometimes accompany them, are evidently embellishments, designed by later devotees whom the primitive taboos of the early Pythagoreans offended and embarrassed. Pythagorean ethics, so far as we know, first became a philosophical morality in the hands of Empedocles. For all that, it is, I think, appropriate to discuss Empedocles' ethical views out of their chronological context; for they depend on the Pythagorean eschatology I have already sketched, and they do not (so far as I can see) make use of any later philosophical contentions.

Aristotle remarks that 'there is, as everyone divines, by nature a common standard of justice and injustice, even if men have made no society and no contract with one another' (*Rhet* 1373b6); by way of illustration he quotes some celebrated lines from Sophocles' *Antigone*, and a couplet from Empedocles. The couplet runs thus:

> But that which is lawful for all stretches endlessly through the broad
> aether and through the vast brightness (**99: 31 B 135 = 22 Z**).

Evidently, as Aristotle implies, Empedocles wanted to contrast a law of morality, universal and absolute, with those temporal and changing laws which vary from state to state: the couplet implies a staunch rejection of moral relativism.

And, taken in isolation, the couplet might appear to indicate a fairly comprehensive system of morality. But if we hope to find in Empedocles a wide-ranging and absolute code of conduct, that hope is soon dashed: Aristotle says that **99** is concerned with 'not killing living creatures'; and the surviving fragments of Empedocles' ethics bear him out. We are enjoined to abstain from 'harsh-sounding bloodshed' (**B 136 = 29 Z**), and in particular to avoid sacrifice (**B 137 = 31 Z**); moreover, we must not eat meat (**B 138 = 33 Z**); nor, for that matter, beans or bay leaves (**B 140 = 36 Z**). And that, so far as the fragments go, is that: Empedocles' universal law amounts to a prohibition on bloodshed, and a modified vegetarianism.[1] The high intimations of **99** are not borne out: no one will maintain that Empedocles' ethics supplies answers to more than a minuscule proportion of our moral questions.

For all that, Empedocles' injunctions were both revolutionary and rational. Acragas was 'a rich town and a devout town'. Animal sacrifice was a normal part of Greek religious practice, and the streets of Acragas 'must have resounded with the shrieks of dying animals, its air reeking with the stench of blood and burning carcases'.[2] To advocate bloodless liturgy in such circumstances will have seemed both impious and absurd.

Why, then, did Empedocles dare to be so shocking? The answer starts from his theory of metempsychosis, and his conception of the long series of incarnations to which people were necessarily bound. The descent from a divine to a terrestrial life begins, indeed, by bloodshed:

When any one defiles his dear limbs with bloodshed
—one of the spirits who have been allotted a long-lasting life—
he is to wander thrice ten thousand seasons away from the blessed ones . . . (**100: B 115. 3– = 3Z**).[3]

Bloodshed, the cause of our woeful sojourn on earth, is evidently an unwise operation; yet if murderous spirits were imprudent, it does not follow that murderous men are immoral. Why, we may still ask, should we now abstain from the delights of the butcher's knife?

A further fragment from the *Katharmoi* reads as follows:

The father lifts up his own son in a different shape
and, praying, slaughters him, in his great madness, as he cries piteously
beseeching his sacrificer; but he, deaf to his pleas,
slaughters, and prepares in his halls an evil feast.
Just so does son take father, and children mother:
they tear out their life and devour their dear flesh (**101: B 137 = 31 Z**).[4]

The sheep you slaughter and eat was once a man. Once, perhaps, your son or your father: patricide and filicide are evidently wrong; to avoid them you must avoid all bloodshed. And to avoid dining off your late relatives you must avoid eating meat or any of those select members of the vegetable kingdom which may receive once-human souls. The doctrine of transmigration, in short, shows that killing animals is killing people, and that eating animals is eating people; and eating people is wrong.

The ancient doxographers all agree that metempsychosis thus grounded Empedoclean ethics. Theophrastus and Xenocrates applauded the moral inference; and modern scholars concur: 'the self-evident corollary of the doctrine of metempsychosis would have to be complete vegetarianism'.[5] The inference from metempsychosis to vegetarianism is far from self-evident to me; but that, I fear, is because I can see nothing very reprehensible in eating people: *chacun à son gout*. The inference from metempsychosis to the prohibition on killing animals is a different matter; and there Empedocles seems, at first blush, to be on firmer ground. Killing animals is killing people, and killing people gratuitously (as in sacrifice), or for our own enjoyment (as in butchery), is surely a morally objectionable practice.

101, it must be admitted, does not itself prove that Empedocles found it objectionable to kill a person as such: the fragment suggests that the wickedness in killing animals derives from the danger of killing a close relative; and it is consistent with this to suppose that if you could be sure that a sheep was no kinsman of yours, you might with propriety wield the knife. **B 136**, however, appears to state a more general thesis:

> Will you not cease from harsh-sounding bloodshed? Do you not see that you are slaughtering one another in the thoughtlessness of your mind? (**102: B 136 = 29 Z**).

The commentators tacitly suppose that **101** merely gives a peculiarly dramatic instance of **102**, in order to underscore the horror of animal sacrifice. And they are surely right.

Nonetheless, it is not clear why Empedocles should have found killing people objectionable. There was, I am told, an early sect of Christians who took the promise of Heaven seriously and threw themselves off cliff-tops to expedite their journey to Paradise. If death marks not the cessation of life but rather the transformation to a different vital form, death will often be a boon for the victim; and a metempsychotic killer might well reason that the slaughter of a sheep was a deed of moral worth, in that it removed a person from the tedium of ovine existence and accelerated his return to the divine status from which his psychic peregrinations began. I cannot see why Empedocles should have disapproved of that humane practice.

However that may be, such Empedoclean concerns may seem entirely remote from us. It is true that in Oxford, as in Acragas, we daily consume monstrous quantities of flesh; and in our academies, as in the Acragantine temples, the blood runs freely on the sacrificial altars: the modern scientist, like the Sicilian seer, kills in the hope of gaining knowledge. Yet we do not believe in metempsychosis; and Empedocles' fulminations may therefore leave us unmoved.

That is a hasty conclusion. Late authorities ascribe to the Pythagoreans a doctrine of the kinship of all living creatures; Sextus, in his introduction to **102**, speaks of a relationship (*koinônia*) which we have 'not only to one another and to the gods, but also to brute creatures' (*adv Math* VII. 127); and it is on that relationship that he grounds Empedocles' prohibition on killing. If animal souls are identical with human souls, then, trivially, animals and humans are psychically akin. And since it is not the physical form or constitution of a man, but rather some feature of his psychic make-up, which makes killing people wrong, what is wrong for men is by the same token wrong for animals.

Modern defenders of the rights of animals are, I think, essentially Empedoclean in their stance. In their view, the orthodox morality which condones vivisection and animal experimentation and fails even to discern a moral issue in the eating of meat, is a form of 'speciesism'; and speciesism, if less imprudent than racism, is no less obnoxious: any argument against racism is, *mutatis mutandis*, an argument against speciesism; and the pragmatic question '"Is a vegetarian diet nutritionally adequate?" resembles the slave-owner's claim that he and the whole economy of the South would be ruined without slave labour'.[6]

Psychologically, we are all Aristotelians: we do not believe, with Empedocles, in the formal identity of all souls. But the opponents of speciesism will happily accept this; for Aristotelianism assigns to men and animals alike the faculty of sentience, and it is the possession of sentience (more particularly, of the capacity to suffer) which gives men a title to moral consideration. We cannot adopt one moral rule for human killing and another for animal slaughter; for the feature which makes human killing morally wrong is common to all animal life. Jeremy Bentham put it best: 'The French have already discovered that the blackness of the skin is no reason why a human being should be abandoned without redress to the caprice of a tormentor. It may come one day to be recognized, that the number of legs, the villosity of the skin, or the termination of the *os sacrum*, are reasons equally insufficient for abandoning a sensitive being to the same fate. What else is it that should trace the insuperable line? Is it the faculty of reason, or, perhaps, the faculty of discourse? But a full-grown horse or dog is beyond comparison a more rational, as well as a more conversable animal, than an infant of a day, or a week, or even a month, old. But suppose the case were otherwise, what would it avail? The question is not, Can they *reason*? nor, Can they *talk*? but, Can they *suffer*?' (*Introduction to the Principles of Morals and Legislation*, ch. XVII, n.)

Metaphysically, Bentham and Empedocles are poles apart; morally, Bentham (unlike some of his modern disciples) never indulged in the wholesale and passionate condemnations which flowed from Empedocles' Sicilian pen. Yet for all that, the comparison I have just marked is not far-fetched: both Empedocles and Bentham find a psychic element common to man and beast; both Empedocles and Bentham rest a moral doctrine on that common element. The appeal which the two men make to us is, at bottom, the same; and it is, I think, an appeal to which many of us assent in our hearts. But we lie in our teeth.

(c) *Heraclitus and the laws of God*

We generally treat Heraclitus as a metaphysician, not as a moralist. Diodotus, a Stoic teacher of Cicero, held the opposite view: Heraclitus' book, he argued, 'is not about nature, but about government, and the remarks about nature have an illustrative function' (Diogenes Laertius, IX.15 = **22 A 1**).[7] Diodotus is hardly right; yet he errs in the right direction: there is evidence enough that Heraclitus was a moralist as well as a metaphysician, and that he attempted to found an idiosyncratic ethical code upon his idiosyncratic metaphysical system.

The surviving fragments contain several utterances which are, or probably imply, specific moral judgments; and many of these can be loosely attached to features of Heraclitus' non-moral views. Thus his austere and apparently monotheistic theology accounts for **B 5b = 86 M**:

> They pray to these statues, as though a man were to chat with his house (**103**).[8]

The metaphysical thesis that strife is essential to existence comports with **B 53 = 29 M**:

> War is father of all, king of all; and it has shown some as gods, some as men; it has made some slaves, some free (**104**).

(The fragment is usually and plausibly read as an approval of things martial.) Again, Heraclitus' psychological and eschatological views, obscure though they are,[9] evidently lie behind such judgments as **B 25 = 97 M**:

> Greater deaths receive greater shares (**105**),

or **B 96 = 76 M**:

> Corpses are more to be thrown out than dung (**106**).[10]

Some of Heraclitus' *dicta* are trite, some are shocking; some are plain, others dark; but none, I think, has any great intrinsic interest.

Behind those detailed judgments, and doubtless in some sense supporting them, there lie a few remarks of a more general and systematic nature; and it is these which I shall consider. It is best to approach them obliquely.

The doxographers made Heraclitus a determinist in the Stoic mould: he says that 'everything happens according to fate (*heimarmenê*), and that this is the same as necessity (*anankê*)' (Aëtius, **A 8**). The report presumably derives from **37** (**B 80 = 28 M**), which asserts that 'everything comes about in accordance with strife and what must be'.[11] Since, according to **33** (**B 1 = 1 M**) 'everything comes about in accordance with [Heraclitus'] account', his account or *logos* expresses a law under which all events are subsumed: bound by law, the world and everything in it is governed by necessity.

Necessity is orderly. Heraclitus more than once points to the regularity of things: the world itself is a *kosmos* or ordered arrangement (**38: B 30 = 51 M**); fire, the basic constituent of everything, is exchanged for things as gold is exchanged for goods (**39: B 90 = 54 M**), and the exchange rate was fixed in certain 'measures' or *metra* (**38, 40: B 31 = 53 M**); celestially, the sun has its 'measures' which it will not overstep (**B 94 = 52 M**); and the coming and going of human generations is marked by a numerically specifiable periodicity.[12] Order and regularity permeate the harmonious Heraclitean universe.

Universal regularity suggests a universal regulator:

> The thunderbolt steers everything (**107: B 64 = 79 M**).

> The one wise thing has the knowledge by which everything is steered in all ways (**108: B 41 = 85 M**).

There is a single divine law (*nomos*) which 'controls as much as it wishes' (**B 114 = 23 M**). The world is governed by God; and if

> Time is a child, playing, moving its pawns—the kingdom is a child's (**109: B 52 = 93 M**),

then perhaps that government is a divine whimsy, and we are little chessmen, pushed about on the board of the universe at the pleasure of a god.[13] As flies to wanton boys are we to the gods: they kill us for their sport.

Heraclitus' theology, and his view on the relation between god and the world, are matters of profound scholarly controversy; and the account which I have just sketched is far from universally accepted. But its central feature, that the events in the world are all governed by law, is, I think, beyond serious dispute; and it is that feature on which the rest of my argument turns.

There is a vulgar and perennial confusion induced by the equivocity of the English word 'law'. In the language of science, a law is a general description of natural phenomena; scientific laws state how things are, or perhaps how, by a kind of 'natural necessity', things must be. Such laws cannot be broken or violated: if Kepler's 'laws' of planetary motion ascribe a certain orbit to Neptune, and Neptune is observed to stray from that orbit, it is not Neptune but

Kepler who is at fault. Kepler's laws are not broken but falsified, they are shown to be inadequate descriptions of the celestial phenomena; they are not laws of nature after all. In the language of legislation, which moralists and politicians professionally pillage, a law is a general prescription for human behaviour; legislative laws state how things are to be or how they ought to be. Such laws cannot be falsified: if Dracon's laws lay down that Athenians are not to abstract one another's purses, and Cleonymus steals my purse, then it is not Dracon but Cleonymus who is at fault; Dracon's laws are not falsified but violated. They are shown, perhaps, to be inadequately policed; they are not shown to be invalid, or to be no laws at all.

The distinction between the descriptive laws of the scientist and the prescriptive laws of the legislator is obvious enough; yet it is blurred or ignored with tedious frequency. Moral laws are construed as accounts of what must be; scientific laws are read as injunctions to natural phenomena.

The English word 'law' is closely paralleled in this unfortunate respect by the Greek word *nomos*.[14] '*Nomos*' has a long history, and it is applied in many contexts; only two of those applications are of moment here. First, a *nomos* may be a custom or a regularity: if all *A*'s are *B*, or if *A*'s are, as a general rule, *B*, then it may be said to be a *nomos* that *A*'s are *B*. Second, a *nomos* may be a law or a rule: if *A*'s are enjoined or urged to be *B*, by implicit rule or explicit ordinance, then it may be said to be a *nomos* for *A*'s to be *B*. These two distinct applications are neatly confused in a passage from Hesiod's *Works and Days*:

> The son of Cronos ordained this *nomos* for men:
> that while fish and beasts and winged birds
> eat one another (for there is no justice among them),
> to men he gave justice, which is by far the best—
> for if anyone is prepared to say just things from knowledge, to him
> far-seeing Zeus gives riches;
> but whoever in bearing witness willingly swears an oath
> and lies, and violating justice does an evil deed,
> he leaves behind him a feeble offspring—
> and the offspring left behind by the faithful man is better
> (**110**: 276–85).

Zeus' *nomos* for brutes is that they eat one another; his *nomos* for men is that they should deal justly with one another. The animal *nomos* is a law of nature; the human *nomos* is a law of morality. The word *nomos* occurs but once; its changing application is shown not only by the sense of what Hesiod says, but also by his fluttering syntax.

In English, 'justice' does not have the same ambivalence as 'law'. We do not speak of the 'justice' of nature in the way we speak of the laws of nature; 'justice' remains a purely prescriptive term. The Greek word '*dikê*' is often correctly translated as 'justice'; but '*dikê*' is also used outside prescriptive contexts: '*dikê*' may mark the way things are as well as the way things ought to be. In that respect, '*dikê*' and '*nomos*' run parallel courses.

I do not know whether or not we should say that '*nomos*' and '*dikê*' are ambiguous terms, each having at least two distinct senses; so far as I know, no ancient text distinguishes descriptive from prescriptive senses of the words, and it may be that in the notions of *nomos* and *dikê* description and prescription are merely confused. What is clear is that both prescriptions and descriptions are expressed by the words *nomos* and *dikê*.[15] I shall shortly exhibit a Heraclitean example; and I am inclined to believe that this feature of the Greek language played a part in forming one of the most obvious and familiar features of early Greek science: 'The early Greek notion of justice'—and of law—'lends itself with seductive ease to application far beyond the bounds of politics and morals'.[16] The first thinker to be seduced was Anaximander: 'The things from which is the coming into being for the things that exist are also those into which their destruction come about, in accordance with what must be;[17] for they give justice and reparation to one another for their offence, in accordance with the ordinance of time' (**13**). The primary principle of nature is formulated, appropriately enough, in terms of natural necessity: things come about 'in accordance with what must be'; they happen as they are bound to happen. But Anaximander then explains that grand fact in terms of crime and punishment, of offence and reparation, of transgression and justice. The language of prescription improperly replaces the language of description, and the lawyer invades the province of the scientist.

Heraclitus echoes Anaximander: 'one should know that war is common, and justice strife; and that everything comes about in accordance with strife and what must be' (**37: B 80 = 28 M**). Characteristically, Heraclitus corrects Anaximander: where Anaximander sees in the 'strife' of things an offence which must be corrected, Heraclitus sees justice in this very strife; but the fundamental insight of the two men is the same: natural phenomena are bound by law and are subject to a cosmic justice. A striking fragment illustrates Heraclitus' general thesis:

> The sun will not overstep its measures; otherwise the Furies, ministers of justice, will find it out (**111: B 94 = 52 M**).

The natural laws of celestial motion are backed by sanctions: why else would the sun consent to its tedious diurnal round? Keplerian descriptions are confused with Draconian prescriptions; what is and what ought to be are confounded.[18]

To ascribe such a gross confusion to Heraclitus may seem at best uncharitable: '**37**, after all, glosses "justice" by "what must be"; and **111**, with its Homeric echo (*Iliad* XIX. 418), may be no more than a colourful metaphor. Cosmic justice is a figure of speech, not a theory; a piece of harmless rhetoric, not a logical confusion.' Charity is always tempting; but it rarely comports with the harsh facts of history: let us consider the two main theses in Heraclitus' moral theory.

Christianity has hardened us to the absurd; and there are, I believe, those who can contemplate with serenity the assertion that we live in a *nonpareil* world.

> All Nature is but Art, unknown to thee;
> All Chance, Direction, which thou canst not see;
> All Discord, Harmony, not understood;
> All partial Evil, Universal good;
> And, spite of Pride, in erring Reason's spite,
> One truth is clear, 'Whatever IS, is RIGHT'.

Since God is both all-good and all-potent, the natural theologians, those metaphysical estate agents, must market the world as a desirable residence. Their contemptible claims have won the approbation of numerous great men; and their professions were not wholly unknown in the ancient world. In a later chapter I shall consider some late-fifth-century assaults on theodicy: here I limit attention to Heraclitus.

For Heraclitus was a Presocratic Pangloss. He says clearly enough that whatever is is right:

> To god everything is fine and good and just; but men have taken some things to be unjust and others to be just (**112: B 102 = 91 M**).

This fragment does not illustrate Heraclitus' thesis of the Unity of Opposites; it does not, as some scholars think, urge that 'just and unjust are one and the same'. On the contrary, it avers that nothing is unjust: despite ordinary human judgments, everything that happens is, in God's eyes and hence in reality, a just and good happening. After all, if 'everything happens in accordance with strife' and 'justice is strife', it is an easy inference that all events are just, and that our world is a perfect world.

Why did Heraclitus espouse that belief? Consider the following pair of syllogisms: 'Everything happens in accordance with *nomos* (*logos*); what happens in accordance with *nomos* happens justly: *ergo*, everything happens justly.' 'Everything occurs *kata dikên*; what occurs *kata dikên* occurs justly: *ergo*, everything occurs justly.' Both arguments are valid; in each the first premiss is Heraclitean, and the second premiss seems tautological. Yet the arguments are evidently unsound: they trade on the confusion between prescriptive *nomos* and descriptive *nomos*, between prescriptive *dikê* and descriptive *dikê*. The first premiss in each argument uses its keyword descriptively, asserting the regularity of cosmic phenomena. The second premiss in each argument is true and tautological only if its keyword is taken prescriptively. Both arguments are examples of the 'fallacy of equivocation'. I do not suggest that Heraclitus consciously advanced those arguments; I do incline to believe that the confusions which they brazenly exhibit helped to ease Heraclitus into his absurd position.

I turn finally to the second main thesis of Heraclitean ethics. Fragments **B 114** and **B 2** are plausibly conjoined to read as follows:

> Those who speak with sense (*xun nôi*) must put their strength in what is common (*xunôi*) to all, as a city in law—and much more strongly. For all human laws are nourished by one, the divine [law]; for it controls as much as it wishes, and it is sufficient for all, and is left over.
>
> For that reason one should follow what is common (*xunôi*); yet though the account is common, most men live as though they had a private understanding (**113: B 114 + B 2 = 23 M**).[19]

The importance of law was clear in Heraclitus' mind:

> The people should fight for their law as for their city-wall (**114: B 44 = 103 M**).

Those terrestrial laws are nourished by the one divine law, which is the content of Heraclitus' 'account'; consequently, men should pay heed to that great law, follow it, and obey its ordinances.

Heraclitus' argument in **113** is obscure; for it relies on an uncertain metaphor. He is, I take it, arguing to the conclusion that we should act in accordance with the common *logos*; and his premiss is the content of **114**, that we should obey our political laws. His argument is *a fortiori*: our human laws are 'nourished' by the divine law; if we should follow them, plainly we should follow it.

The metaphor of nourishment is difficult; and it is not explained by the statement that the divine law 'controls, is sufficient and is left over'. I offer the following tentative exegesis: 'Human *nomoi* owe what validity they have to the divine *nomos*: since that *nomos* governs everything, the human *nomoi* are valid only in so far as they coincide with, or translate into particular terms, the divine injunction; hence if human *nomoi* are to command obedience, that can only be in so far as they mirror the divine law; and since, by **114**, human *nomoi* are valuable, the divine *nomos* is to be followed.'

However that may be, the main burden of **113** is plain enough. Like Empedocles, Heraclitus contrasts human laws with an overarching injunction; like Empedocles, he enjoins assent to that universal ordinance. But whereas Empedocles' great law relates only to one aspect of life, Heraclitus' law is all-embracing. We must regulate our lives in accordance with the general account which describes the total workings of nature and the world; and those particular regulations which Heraclitus saw fit to emphasize are simply some of the possible specifications of the ultimate moral injunction to 'follow what is common'. If anyone doubts the wisdom of 'following what is common', let him remember the Furies who await an aberrant sun; for

> How might anyone escape the notice of that which never sets? (**115: B 16 = 81 M**).

> Justice will catch up with the fabricators and purveyors of lies (**116: B 28a = 19 M**);

> There awaits men when they die what they do not expect or imagine (**117: B 27 = 74 M**).[20]

Thus:

> It is wisdom to speak the truth and to act knowingly in accordance with nature (**118: B 112 = 23 (f) M**).

The sentence is a paraphrase, not a quotation; but it summarizes Heraclitus' doctrine well enough. The Stoics adopted and developed the view: like Heraclitus, they were determinists; and like Heraclitus, they stated the ultimate moral injunction as *oikeiôsis*: Zeno of Citium 'said that the end is to live in agreement with nature (*homologoumenôs têi phusei*), which is to live virtuously' (Diogenes Laertius, VII. 87 = *SVF* I. 179). Similar views have been enunciated more recently.

John Stuart Mill opined that 'the fundamental problem of the social sciences is to find the law according to which any state of society produces the state which succeeds it and takes its place'; and by the aid of such a science 'we may hereafter succeed not only in looking far forward into the future history of the human race, but in determining whatever artificial means may be used, and to what extent, to accelerate the natural progress in so far as it is beneficial, to compensate for whatever may be its inherent inconveniences or disadvantages, and to guard against the dangers or accidents to which our species is exposed from the necessary incidents of its progression' (*System of Logic* VI. 10). Here the *bourgeois* Mill borrows from the aristocratic Heraclitus, and lends to Karl Marx.

Holders of such a Heraclitean position have three theses to maintain: first, that every event, and consequently every human action, occurs in accordance with some universal law or set of laws; second, that men ought, therefore, to give destiny a helping hand and accommodate their actions to the demands of the universal legislature; and third, that those law-breakers and malingerers, who are inevitably to be found, will suffer discomforts, either terrestrial or eschatological, for their temerarious disobedience. As you will act, so you should act—and if you don't God help you.

The position is patently muddled; and it is frequently denounced as ridiculously and irretrievably confused. It contains a grand inanity and a simple inconsistency.

The inanity is the conjunction of the first and second theses: 'if all men *will* act in accordance with the universal law, then it is fatuous to urge them that they *ought* to act in accordance with it. If they will act so, then they will act so whether urged or not; and moral injunction is a futile form of language.'

The ramifications of that line of argument are multitudinous and familiar; and I cannot here be more than dogmatic: the fact that all men will act in accordance with the universal law does not make Heraclitus' injunction pointless. His utterance of the injunction in **113** will, of course, itself be determined by the universal law; yet it may for all that form a link in the causal chain—or one of the causal chains—which shackle future actions to the past. Heraclitus' injunction may have causal efficacy in a deterministic world: had he (*per impossibile*) not so enjoined, men would not so have acted. His injunction is neither fatuous nor futile. Indeed, he may comfort himself with the thought that he is after all playing a bit part in the universal comedy; and the comfort will only dissolve when he reflects that the comforting thought is itself determined by the universal law, a line written into the script of a play whose actors are forbidden to *ad lib*.

The inconsistency of the Heraclitean position resides in its first and third theses. Here the matter is simple: the first thesis says that everyone *does* act by the law; the third implies that some men do *not*. And that is the simplest form of contradiction one can hope to find, even in a Presocratic text.

The contradiction emerges from a strict reading of certain fragments; in particular, it requires us to take the word 'everything' in **33** and again in **37** in the strongest possible sense. Perhaps that is unjust: 'everything', after all, is regularly used hyperbolically or loosely; and in any case, the larger context of its Heraclitean use is lost to us. Thus Heraclitus might be extricated from inconsistency, and in more than one way. 'Everything' might be restricted to inanimate phenomena: the world of heartless, witless nature runs according to the universal law, by necessity; we do not—but since we cannot fly to Venus or to Mercury we are well advised to accommodate our acts to that law. Or again, 'everything' might be interpreted weakly, implying a general but not a strictly universal law: there is a *nomos*, a general rule or regularity; but it allows exceptions—if we are prudent, we shall conform to it rather than taste the delusory joys of unconventionality.

We do not possess enough remnants of Heraclitus' book to know if either of those suggestions fits his thought; other suggestions are possible. Yet if we take the surviving fragments at their face value—a reasonable procedure, in all conscience—we shall return, reluctantly, to the conclusion that Heraclitus admitted human renegades to a cosmically determined world. And we are also obliged to credit Heraclitus with the crude command 'There is a universal law—obey it', wherein descriptive and prescriptive laws are confused. Thus Heraclitus initiated two perennial confusions in philosophical ethics: if it takes a great philosopher to originate a great error, Heraclitus has a double grandeur.

VIII

The Principles of Human Knowledge

(a) *The origins of scepticism*

The sceptical philosophers of Hellenistic Greece held that no one at all could know anything at all; and with commendable consistency they proceeded to deny that they themselves knew even that distressing fact. Their splendid doctrine, or antidoctrine, had, they believed, been adumbrated in the epistemological reflexions of the early Presocratics; for although scepticism had not flourished until the late fifth century, Parmenides' predecessors had reflected, at least casually, on epistemological matters, and some of them had emitted pronouncements of a sceptical tone. And that, after all, is hardly surprising: the first philosophers had propounded theories of unprecedented scope and presumption. Their utterances must have aroused wonder and amazement; and wonder, as Aristotle observes, is the father of thought. Having wondered that the Milesians knew so much, men might wonder how they knew so much; and having wondered how, it was but a short step to wondering whether they knew quite everything that they professed:

> all ignorance toboggans into know
> and trudges up to ignorance again.

The uphill trudge is the natural successor to the heady slide.

At all events, the early Presocratics did, I believe, invent epistemology or the science of knowledge; and they brought a form of scepticism to birth. We may start from Alcmeon of Croton. According to Diogenes Laertius, Alcmeon's treatise *Concerning Nature* opened as follows:

> Alcmeon of Croton, son of Peirithous, said this to Brotinus and to Leon and to Bathyllus: concerning things unseen the gods possess clear understanding (*saphêneia*); but in so far as men may guess [. . . I say as follows . . .] (**119: 24 B1**).

The text of the fragment is controversial:[1] on any account **119** is sceptical in tone; but different versions give radically different sorts of scepticism.

With the text I adopt, Alcmeon is no Pyrrhonian; he does not absolutely deny the possibility of knowledge and the rationality of belief. First, he ascribes knowledge, even of 'things unseen', to the gods; only men are deprived of knowledge: it is the human candle whose illuminatory powers are feeble. Second, it is only 'things unseen' which escape human knowledge: what we see, Alcmeon implies, we can indeed know. Alcmeon is thus closer to the urbane scepticism of Locke than to the hyperbolical doubt of Pyrrho and his followers. And that, perhaps, is to the good; for while Pyrrho's views are ostentatiously incredible, Lockean scepticism is both plausible enough to be persuasive and sufficiently removed from our unreflective thoughts to be disconcerting.

Lockean scepticism was endemic in the Greek mind. Its *locus classicus* is in the second book of the Iliad, where the poet seeks help from the Muses:

> for you
> Are goddesses, are present here, are wise, and all things know,
> We only trust the voice of fame, know nothing. . . .

There are numerous imitations and parallels;[2] and the melancholy sentiment is of a piece with that 'modest assessment of the importance of mankind in the universe'[3] which is characteristic of early Greek writings. Such effusions express a mournful emotion rather than enunciate a philosophical belief; and we might be tempted to regard Alcmeon's sceptical proem as no more than a bow to a Greek convention: a decent modesty is expected of a man who is about to describe the history and nature of the universe. But Alcmeon has philosophical as well as poetical predecessors; and it is to them that I now turn.

Xenophanes, according to pseudo-Plutarch, 'says that the senses are false, and together with them he also delivers a general attack on reason itself' (**21 A 32**). Sotion, more briefly, makes him 'the first to say that everything is unknowable' (Diogenes Laertius, IX. 20 = **A 1**). Timon, who was of a sceptical turn of mind, evidently found a kindred spirit in Xenophanes; for his poetical dialogues on the history of philosophy are feigned to have occurred between himself and his predecessor (Diogenes Laertius, IX. 111). Sextus places Xenophanes at the head of the sceptical sect (*Pyrrh Hyp* II. 18; *adv Math* VII. 48–52).[4]

Four of the surviving fragments of Xenophanes' poems bear on epistemological matters; and the longest of them, amounting to no more than four lines, was certainly the chief and perhaps the sole source of his sceptical reputation. It runs thus:

> And the clear truth (*to saphes*) no man has seen nor will anyone
> know, about the gods and concerning everything of which I speak.
> For even if he should actually manage to say something that is the case,
> nevertheless he himself does not know. But for all there is belief
> (**120: B 34**).[5]

The lines are prefatory in character; and I accept the suggestion that they come from an exordium to Xenophanes' philosophical *oeuvre* (see above, p. 83). Antiquity read **120** in a sceptical fashion: by modern scholars the sense of the fragment is hotly disputed.

First, it has been argued on philological grounds that **120** has nothing whatever to do with scepticism. Xenophanes, the argument goes, asserts not that no one *knows*, but that no man has *seen*, the truth about the gods; and the phrase which I have translated 'nor will anyone know' (*oude tis estai eidôs*) is more properly rendered by 'nor will anyone see'—for the verb *eidenai*, of which *eidôs* is the participle, is originally a verb of perception. **120** does not, then, advocate scepticism: it states that on certain subjects *perceptual* knowledge is unattainable, thereby implying that a non-perceptual form of knowledge is appropriate there, a perceptual form elsewhere. **120** classifies knowledge, it does not attack knowledge; and Xenophanes the sceptic slopes off into the populous limbo of historical fantasy.

The argument has, I think, now been conclusively refuted. Careful research does indeed show that, etymologically, *eidenai* is a perceptual verb; but further extensive researches have incontrovertibly shown that even in Homer the verb bears the general sense of 'know', and that this sense was normal by Xenophanes' time: in Xenophanes, as in classical texts, *eidenai* simply means 'know'.[6] Moreover, *eidôs* in line 2 contrasts with *dokos* in line 4; and since *dokos* can only mean 'belief', *eidôs* will naturally be translated by means of the verb 'to know'. Thus, **120** does after all enunciate some sort of sceptical thesis: it asserts that no man has known or will know certain things.

Second, we may ask whether Xenophanes' scepticism is, like Alcmeon's, a thesis about the capacities of human cognition. That question is easily answered. **120** talks explicitly of men; **B 18** and **B 36**, which I shall shortly quote, imply that the gods have knowledge which men lack; and Arius Didymus explicitly says that, according to Xenophanes, 'god knows the truth, but for all there is belief' (**A 24**): the second clause comes from **120**; and it is a happy suggestion that the first clause, which is metrical, is also a quotation from Xenophanes.[7]

Third, what is the scope of Xenophanes' scepticism? Is he denying all knowledge to men, or only certain areas of knowledge? **120** specifies the scope by the phrase 'about the gods and concerning everything of which I speak'. If, as I believe, **120** prefaced a scientific poem in the Milesian tradition, then Xenophanes means to say that knowledge about things divine and knowledge about natural science lie beyond our human grasp.

That interpretation is confirmed by a passage from a justly celebrated treatise in the Hippocratic *corpus*: the treatise is *On Ancient Medicine*, and it was probably composed towards the end of the fifth century. Alcmeon specified the scope of his scepticism by the phrase 'the things unseen (*ta athêêta*)'; the Hippocratic treatise takes up Alcmeon's notion, if not his phrase, to pillory those pretentious disciplines which deal with 'what is invisible and puzzled over (*ta aphanea te kai aporeomena*)'. The pretentious scientists are men who study 'the things in the air (*ta meteôra*) and the things underground'. Those words pick out the main areas of early scientific interest;[8] and an attack on the students of *ta aphanea* is an attack on the pretensions of Ionian science. The stars are visible, and the rocky substance of the earth is not unseen; for all that, the early scientists could be said to apply their minds to *ta aphanea* and *ta athêêta* inasmuch as their astronomical and geological theories advanced far beyond the bounds of perception.

On Ancient Medicine criticizes its scientific opponents in the following terms:

> If one should state and declare how these things are, it would be clear neither to the speaker himself nor to his hearers whether they were true or not; for there is nothing by referring to which one can know the clear truth (*to saphes*) (**121**: §1).

The connexions between this passage and **120** are close; I think they are too close to be coincidental, and I suggest that in *Ancient Medicine* we find an early and favourable exegesis of Xenophanes' fragment. Thus in **120** Xenophanes advocated a limited, and not a general scepticism: it is theology and natural science, not knowledge in general, that must elude our human grasp.[9]

Three further fragments bear on the question. **B 18** reads thus:

> Not from the beginning did the gods show everything to mortals; but in time by inquiring they find things out better (**122**).

The fragment is complemented by **B 36**:

> Whatever they have revealed to mortals to be seen . . . (**123**).

122 shows that 'they' in **123** refers to the gods; and **123** in turn indicates that **122** should be glossed as follows: 'The gods did not reveal everything to men at once; but their few revelations, aided by patient inquiry, will lead to progress.' It is a plausible inference from the two fragments that Xenophanes does allow some knowledge to men: patient inquiry will increase the small stock of god-given knowledge. Finally, **B 35**:

> Let these things be believed (*dedoxasthô*) as being similar to what is true (**124**).

Belief and verisimilitude, not knowledge and truth, mark the goal of man's cognitive journey. The reference of 'these things' is determined by **120**: as **120** formed part of a prologue to Xenophanes' *oeuvre*, so **124** comes from its epilogue; and as the scepticism of **120** is limited to theology and science, so too is the injunction of **124**.

The conclusion, that Xenophanes advocated a limited and not a general scepticism, is again confirmed by *Ancient Medicine*. Immediately after his echo of **120**, the author announces that in the art of medicine knowledge is not only attainable, but has, to some extent, been attained; and that, he says, was achieved 'by inquiring for a long time' (§2). That surely is an echo of **122**; indeed, it is possible that Xenophanes himself mentioned medicine as a potential field for knowledge and progress; and it is probable that doctor Alcmeon did so.

Xenophanes did not merely assert a scepticism; he argued for it. The second couplet of **120** begins with an inferential particle:

> For (*gar*) even if he should actually manage to say something that is the case,
> nevertheless he himself does not know.

The reference to saying is, I take it, insignificant: and the antecedent of the couplet glosses as: 'even if *a* truly believes that *P* . . .'. Pretty clearly, Xenophanes is implying that knowledge consists of true belief and something more; the implication was developed in Plato's

Theaetetus; and it has stood as a central problem in modern epistemology. Knowledge is more than true belief; but what must be added to true belief to attain knowledge? and how can the addition be secured?

Xenophanes' answer to those questions has been sought in **120**. Sextus glosses the consequent of the second couplet as follows: '. . . *a* does not know that *a* truly believes that *P*'.[10] So construed, **120** argues thus: '*a* does not know that *P*; for even if *a* truly believes that *P*, he cannot know that he does'. The principle behind the argument is:

(1) If *a* knows that *P*, then *a* knows that *a* truly believes that *P*.

The principle has some initial attractions: it suggests, on the one hand, a thesis about knowing that one knows that has been much canvassed in recent philosophical literature, and on the other hand, it hints at the danger of an infinite regress of the type Plato was so concerned to avoid.

A closer inspection proves (1) less attractive. If '*a* knows that *a* truly believes that *P*' is equivalent to '*a* knows that *a* believes that *P* and *a* knows that *P* is true', then (1) is equivalent to:

(2) If *a* knows that *P*, then *a* knows that *a* believes that *P* and *a* knows that *P* is true;

and (2) is equivalent to:

(3) If *a* knows that *P*, then *a* knows that *a* believes that *P*.

Now even if (3) is true, as on some interpretations of 'know' perhaps it is, it is not a proposition with any seriously sceptical implications. In the context of Xenophanes' argument, it implies that the additional element required to turn true belief into knowledge is the knowledge that you hold the belief in question. And such knowledge is surely not peculiarly elusive: of all things, our own beliefs are most accessible to us.

In short, Sextus' interpretation imputes the following argument to Xenophanes: 'we cannot aspire to knowledge of theology and science, for such knowledge presupposes knowledge of our own beliefs'. Such an argument is feeble, and I therefore incline to reject the Sextan interpretation. For a simpler interpretation is possible: the consequent of the couplet reads simply '*a* does not know that *P*'; and **120** argues thus: 'you cannot know that *P* for though you may attain true belief, that is not knowledge'. The argument turns on the fact that knowledge is not just true belief. It immediately raises the question of why the additional component in knowledge, whatever it may be, is so hard to come by; but it does not answer the question or even identify the extra component. For that we must look beyond the confines of **120**, and reconsider some of the fragments of Xenophanes' theology.

The gods are commonly supposed to be anthropomorphic (**63: B 14**), yet a little imagination will indicate that cows and horses, had they the wit to conceive of gods at all, would make them theriomorphic (**73: B 15**); and observation shows that:

> Each group of men paints the shape of the gods in a fashion similar to themselves—as Xenophanes says, the Ethiopians draw them dark and snub-nosed, the Thracians red-haired and blue-eyed (**125**: Clement, **B 16**).[11]

With these fragments we should compare **B 38**;

> If god had not made golden honey, men would say that figs are much sweeter (**126**).

There is, I think, an epistemological moral here: our beliefs—or many of them—are explicable in terms of our circumstances; they do not, therefore, amount to knowledge.

Let me expand upon that. A Thracian believes that the gods are red-haired. His belief is explicable in a way which has no connexion with the actual nature of the gods: because the Thracian is himself red-haired, he believes the gods to be red-heads too. The causal hypothesis is supported by the findings of comparative anthropology; for everywhere men's gods are themselves writ large. The hypothesis does not show the Thracian's belief to be false; but it does show it to fall short of knowledge. Again, an Athenian nurtured on honey from Hymettus holds that figs are only moderately sweet. His belief is explicable in a way which has no connexion with the intrinsic nature of the figs: because the Athenian has had a taste of honey, he believes figs to be mildly sweet. The causal hypothesis is supported by the findings of comparative sociology; for men's gustatory judgments vary according to their gustatory experience. The hypothesis does not show the Athenian's belief to be false; but it does show it to fall short of knowledge. And in general, for a very large and important class of beliefs, if *a* believes that *P*, then there is some causal hypothesis, quite unconnected with the content of his belief, which explains why he believes that *P*. 'For all there is belief': some lucky men may 'actually manage to say something that is the case'; but for all that, 'the clear truth no man has seen, nor will anyone know'.

It is important to see what Xenophanes is not saying here. First, he is not commenting on the disreputable origins of most of our beliefs: many of my beliefs about Roman history were first fixed in my mind by the novels of Robert Graves and Peter Green; yet for all that, some at least of my beliefs have been turned into knowledge. Thin opinions, illicitly imbibed, may later be transformed by an intellectual digestion into red-blooded knowledge. Xenophanes does not deny that. Second, Xenophanes is not objecting to causal explanations of knowledge as such. My present belief that Caesar was murdered on the Ides of March is, I suppose, causally explicable by reference to my avid reading and memorizing of the accounts of his death in various ancient texts. It does not follow—nor does Xenophanes imply that it does—that my belief falls short of knowledge.

Rather, Xenophanes' point is that many of my beliefs are explicable by a causal hypothesis which has no direct connexion with the content of those beliefs. I believe that *P*, and *P* is true: yet there is a causal chain explaining my belief which was neither originated nor at any stage supplemented by the fact that *P*. And that is why my belief is not knowledge.

Xenophanes' thesis requires a more careful statement and a lengthier consideration than I can give it here. I am confident, however, that the philosophical part of it is true: *if* my belief that *P* was caused by events having no suitable connexion with the fact that *P*, then I do not know that *P*. The non-philosophical part of Xenophanes' thesis, that very many of our beliefs do have defective causal antecedents of that sort, cannot be assessed in general terms: to test it, we must take believers and their beliefs piecemeal. I shall, however, indulge myself to the extent of offering an unsupported judgment that here too Xenophanes is probably right.

Men's beliefs do not amount to knowledge because they have unsatisfactory causes. The conclusion suggests that true belief will amount to knowledge if its causal antecedents are reputable. The extant fragments give no clue to Xenophanes' canons of respectability, if indeed he ever formulated any. He implies, if my interpretation is correct, that in some areas at least knowledge is attainable by men; and it is therefore reasonable to ask what features of those favoured areas make them open to human cognition, and to require of Xenophanes, if not a general account of causal respectability, at least an indication of certain cases in which the causal chain leading to belief has the strength and direction to turn that belief into an item of knowledge.

(b) *The foundations of empirical knowledge*

The key is again to be found in *Ancient Medicine*:

> You will find no measure or number or balance by referring to which you will know with certainty—except perception (**127**: § 9).

An elaboration of that blunt assertion will produce an empiricist theory of knowledge. The first attempt to sketch such a theory is to be found in the writings of the early Presocratics.

Heraclitus certainly had the makings of a cynic; and some see him as a sceptic. He denounces the claims to knowledge made by his great predecessors, Hesiod, Hecataeus, Pythagoras, and even Xenophanes;[12] and he regularly rails at the folly of mankind:

> Most men do not understand what they meet with, nor when they learn do they gain knowledge—but they seem to themselves to do so (**128:22 B 17 = 3 M**).

> What understanding or intelligence have they got? They put their faith in folk-singers, and they use the multitude as a teacher, not knowing that 'the many are bad and few are good' (**129: B 104 = 101 M**).[13]

Again, there are several fragments of a relativist bent, reminiscent of Xenophanes' comment on the sweetness of honey:

> Disease made health sweet; famine, satiety; exhaustion, rest (**130: B 111 = 44 M**).

> A man is held foolish by a spirit, as a child is by a man (**131: B 79 = 92 M**).

And several fragments suggest scepticism more directly:

> Nature likes to hide itself (**59: B 123 = 8 M**).

> Human character has no insights (*gnômai*), divine character does (**132: B 78 = 90 M**).

If you seek knowledge, you will be like gold-diggers who 'dig over much earth and find little' (**B 22 = 10 M**); and if you had the temerity to study psychology,

> you would not find in your journey the limits of the *psuchê*, even if you travelled the whole road—so deep is its account (*logos*) (**133: B 45 = 67 M**).

A narrow inspection, however, does not support that interpretation of Heraclitus: the scornful attacks on other men's pretensions and on the ignorance of the multitude do not suggest scepticism but the reverse; for the attacker claims a superiority. The relativistic fragments served a metaphysical rather than an epistemological purpose (see above, p. 74). The sceptical fragments, with the exception of **132**, are designed only to stress the important platitude that knowledge is not easily won; and **132** may carry a moral rather than an epistemological message.

Certain optimistic philosophers have embraced a doctrine of Manifest Truth. According to Spinoza: 'Truth at once reveals itself and also what is false, because truth is made clear through truth—that is, through itself—and through it also is falsity made clear; but falsity is never revealed and made manifest through itself. Hence anyone who is in possession of the truth cannot doubt that he possesses it, while one who is sunk in falsity or in error can well suppose that he has got at the truth' (*Short Treatise on God, Man and his Well-Being*, ch. 15).[14] That curious and confused view would certainly have been rejected by Heraclitus: truth does not 'reveal itself'—it lies hidden at the bottom of the well, and only an accomplished workman will have skill enough to draw it up. To say that is to be a realist, not a sceptic.

A difficult fragment has indeed been read as an explicit rejection of Xenophanean scepticism:

> For the most trustworthy man (*ho dokimôtatos*) knows how to guard one from what seems to be the case (*ta dokeonta*). And indeed justice will catch up with the inventors and purveyors of lies (**134: B 28 = 20 M + 19 M**—see above, p. 133).

According to Xenophanes, we must be content with belief (*dokos*); according to Heraclitus, a clever man (*dokimôtatos*) can preserve us from *dokeonta* and lead us to genuine knowledge.[15] Whether or not that is the right reading of **134**, its import is undeniably Heraclitean.

The path to preservation requires a sturdy independence: we must not behave like 'children of parents', accepting what we are told on the mere authority of the teller (**B 74 = 89 M**); and if

> Eyes are more certain witnesses than ears (**135: B 101a = 6 M**),

that is partly because our ears bring us hearsay evidence and are responsible to a greater extent than our eyes for the inculcation of second-hand opinions. We are not to accept things even on the authority of Heraclitus himself: we must listen not to him but to what he says (**35: B 50 = 26 M**); and his *logos* is to be accepted for its intrinsic merits, not on the say-so of its first discoverer. Diogenes says of Heraclitus that 'he studied at no one's feet, but he says that he searched for himself and learned everything by himself' (IX. 5 = **A 1**). A knower must be able to say, with Heraclitus,

> I searched for myself (**136: B 101 = 15 M**).[16]

The fragments indicate that Heraclitus was true to his own prescription: 'he learned at the feet of no philosopher but was educated by nature and by industry' (Suda, **A 1a**).

It is to this context, I suspect, that two celebrated fragments on 'polymathy', or the learning of many things, belong. The fragments read thus:

> Polymathy does not teach understanding (*nous*)—otherwise it would have taught Hesiod and Pythagoras, and again Xenophanes and Hecataeus (**137: B 40 = 16 M**).

> Pythagoras, son of Mnesarchus, practised inquiry most of all men, and excerpting those writings he claimed for himself wisdom—polymathy, malpractice (**138: B 129 = 17 M**).[17]

A vulgar Baconianism holds that science advances by first amassing countless pieces of particular information and then inferring a universal law: understanding, on this view, is the product of polymathy; and it is tempting to regard Heraclitus' dismissal of polymathy as a deliciously modern protest against a precocious form of Baconianism.

I doubt that interpretation. It seems to me that it is the second and not the first half of the word 'polymathy' which arouses Heraclitus' scorn. Pythagoras' fault is not that he learned a lot, but that he stole his thoughts from others: he claimed wisdom, when he had indulged only in malpractice and polymathy. *Manthanein* means 'to learn', and in particular 'to learn from another'; and polymaths are men who have acquired a large stock of opinions from other men. Learning and discovery are opposed.[18] Learners have not 'sought for themselves'; and it is for that reason that, however much they may have learned, they cannot lay claim to understanding or knowledge. John Locke urged that testimony, or the word of other men, could support a probable opinion but could never sustain knowledge. Keats expressed the same view in another terminology:

> knowledge dwells
> In heads replete with thoughts of other men;
> Wisdom in minds attentive to their own.

Heraclitus, I suggest, is the originator of that epistemological tradition.

And like Locke, Heraclitus was an empiricist; indeed, our evidence suggests that he was not only an empiricist but a sensationalist: knowledge must be built on experience, and specifically on sense-experience.

> The things we learn of by sight and hearing, those do I prefer (**139: B 55 = 5 M**).[19]

> If all things became smoke, the nostrils would discern them (**140: B 7 = 78 M**).

In our familiar world, eyes and ears give the basis for knowledge; and even in a radically different world the appropriate senses would be our only ultimate guide. An ill-attested fragment says that according to Heraclitus the sun has 'the breadth of a human foot' (**B 3 = 57 M**). Some scholars take this to make the banal assertion that the sun looks about a foot across; others find in it a metaphorical expression of some psychological theory.[20] But if the fragment is not a mere forgery, we must take it to mean what it says: it is a crude piece of astronomy, and it evinces a strict and severe sensationalism. Our eyes tell how big the sun is; and they are the best witnesses we could have.[21]

A further fragment remarks that

> We must be knowers of very many things (**141: B 35 = 7 M**).

There is, of course, no incompatibility between that prescription and Heraclitus' rejection of 'polymathy';[22] and **141** immediately suggests the second stage in the classical empiricist recipe for attaining knowledge: the senses give us particular information; frequent and diverse inquiry amasses an organized quantity of such information; it only remains to transmute that mass of dross into the gold of knowledge.

How is the transmutation to occur? Some scholars find a hint in **B 107 = 13 M**:

> Bad witnesses for men are the eyes and ears of those who have barbarous *psuchai* (**142**).

Sextus, who reports the fragment, takes it to 'refute perception' (**A 16**); but he misconstrues the Greek. The fragment should rather be compared with **128** ('Most men do not understand what they meet with . . .') and with **61: B 56 = 21 M** ('Men are deceived with regard to knowledge of what is evident . . .'): the truth is not manifest; only a practised eye will discern what is presented to it; the senses need direction by a mind that is not 'barbarous'.

Can we press the notion of a 'barbarous mind' into epistemological service? The Greeks used the word '*barbaros*' to denominate, rudely, foreigners. Etymologically it is connected with the idea of twittering or babbling: *barbaroi* are men who cannot talk intelligibly. (I do not know if *barbaros* means 'foreign' or 'non-Greek'; the lexicons offer both translations as if they were synonymous.) It is usually, and plausibly, supposed that 'barbarous minds' belong to men with some sort of linguistic deficiency; yet what deficiency can Heraclitus have in mind in **142**?

Heraclitus is hardly advancing the chauvinist thesis that non-Greek speakers cannot attain knowledge; nor is he anticipating those delightful Frenchmen of the seventeenth century who held that the ancient tongues were peculiarly appropriate to the expression of scientific and metaphysical truth. Again, Heraclitus is hardly expressing the insight that scientific knowledge is available only to men who can speak a language; for **142** tilts against the ignorant masses and Heraclitus will hardly have supposed that the majority of his contemporaries were literally incapable of speech.

Some scholars connect **142** with Heraclitus' alleged interest in the subtle metaphysical implications of some linguistic turns; and they suggest that the fragment means that 'your senses will deceive you if you do not have an accurate understanding of your own language'[23]—such understanding being the key to the Heraclitean thesis of the Unity of Opposites. But Heraclitus' main 'metaphysical' tenets derive not from a consideration of language but from a contemplation of the evidence of the senses. Heraclitus, as I read him, was not *un homme entre les choses et les mots*: he had, no doubt, a lively interest in language, and a keen nose for a pun; but language and a deep study of linguistic modes did not guide him in his philosophical endeavours, and he has no reason to require linguistic study from others.

I incline, therefore, to a more metaphorical reading of '*barbaros*' in **142**: barbarous *psuchai* are ignorant, uncomprehending *psuchai*; they are characteristic of men who have no intellectual grasp of things, men who, in a neighbouring metaphor, cannot read the great Book of Nature. For 'the phenomena of Nature', as Berkeley quaintly observed, 'form not only a magnificent spectacle, but also a most coherent, entertaining, and instructive Discourse. . . . This Language or Discourse is studied with different attention, and interpreted with different degrees of skill. But so far as men have studied and remarked its rules, and can interpret aright, so far they may be said to be knowing in nature. A beast is like a man who hears a strange tongue but understands nothing' (*Siris* §254).

It is a pleasant metaphor; but it is a metaphor. And it is not clear what literal point lies behind it. Perhaps Heraclitus is merely insisting on the need for attentive and selective observation: in order to see that the road to Thebes is the road from Thebes, that the course of the carding-roller is straight and crooked, that the river is constantly changing its waters, and all the other detailed facts which are scientifically significant, no ordinary or casual inspection is sufficient; unless you are well-acquainted with the ways of nature, her secrets and their significance will elude you. No doubt that is true and important; but it does not answer the question of how our many observations are to be turned into universal knowledge. The remaining fragments of Heraclitus' book do not shed any further light on the question: either Heraclitus ignored it, or fate has deprived us of his answer.

Another source supplements that deficiency. In the *Phaedo* Socrates recounts his early infatuation with natural philosophy; one of the questions that entranced him concerned the nature of thought:

> And is it blood with which we think? or air? or fire? Or is it none of these, but does the brain rather supply the senses of hearing and seeing and smelling, and memory and belief come from them, and then, when memory and belief come to rest, in this way knowledge comes about? (**143**: 96B = **24 A 11**).

Socrates is referring to Presocratic theories: Empedocles has us think with blood; Anaximenes, and Diogenes of Apollonia, with air; Heraclitus with fire. Who, then, propounded the more complicated theory which Socrates mentions after these brief accounts? and what exactly does that theory state?

According to Theophrastus, Alcmeon says that

> Man differs from the other animals because he alone has understanding (*sunesis*), while the others perceive but do not understand (**144**: *Sens* §25 = **24 A 5**).

Alcmeon was singular among Presocratics in making such a sharp distinction between perceiving and understanding, sensation and knowledge; and the author of Socrates' theory made just such a distinction. Again, Alcmeon gave a detailed physiological account of perception. In it he argued that 'all the senses are in some way connected to the brain' (Theophrastus, *Sens* §26 = **A 5**). The theory in the *Phaedo* contains precisely that thesis. Those two facts make it plausible to ascribe Socrates' theory to Alcmeon. Plato, as we know, was acquainted with Alcmeon's work, and apparently fond of it; it is no surprise that a theory of Alcmeon's should be accorded some little pre-eminence in the short intellectual biography of Socrates.[24]

What, precisely, was Alcmeon's theory? It is the first statement of a view familiar to us from Aristotle's *Metaphysics* (A1) and *Posterior Analytics* (B19); and those passages are the twin origins of modern empiricism. The theory presupposes that full-blooded 'scientific' knowledge is expressible in universal propositions of the form 'Every *F* is *G*'. And it offers a causal explanation of how such knowledge is possible: I perceive an *F* which is *G*; opine that this *F* is *G*; and store that opinion in my memory. As time passes, I perceive many more *F*s which are *G*; and store many more opinions in my memory. At this stage, according to Aristotle, I have 'experience' or *empeiria*, but not yet knowledge. Knowledge comes about when these various memories 'come to rest' (*êremein: Phaedo* 96B; *APst* 100a6) and somehow coalesce into a universal proposition. In the *Metaphysics* Aristotle illustrates his theory, in tacit tribute to Alcmeon, by a medical example: I observe that hellebore helps Socrates when he is feverish, and that it helps Callias when he is feverish, and so on in many cases, until those multitudinous particular opinions, collected in my memory, unite into the knowledge that all feverish men are helped by hellebore.

Universal knowledge is thus possible. If I believe that all *F*s are *G* then my belief amounts to knowledge, provided that it was acquired in the way the theory specifies; and a careful attention will ensure that, in some cases at least, the proper path to acquisition is narrowly followed. I suppose that this theory was roughed out by Heraclitus in answer to Xenophanean scepticism; and that it was first formulated in something like its Aristotelian guise by Alcmeon.

How successful was the theory? Xenophanes, if my interpretation is right, required beliefs to have a respectable causal ancestry if they were to amount to knowledge; Heraclitus and Alcmeon attempted to specify an ancestry which could command respect. If their specification were accepted, then we could say that some at least of Heraclitus' major claims were preserved from Xenophanean criticism; for his major thesis—the elements of his *logos*—were, I argued earlier, intended to have their basis in perception.

Yet Alcmeon and the Hippocratic author, empiricists both, still maintained a Xenophanean scepticism. They must have felt, for reasons which we cannot now divine, that Heraclitus' bold theories simply outflew his modest epistemology. They played Locke to Heraclitus' Boyle: empiricism was the only hope for scientific endeavour; yet it did not permit those profound searchings into the very nature of things which Heraclitus desired to justify. I doubt if this critical attitude to Heraclitus is wholly correct; but to discuss its credentials would be both tedious and speculative. In any case, such considerations may well seem petty. Later philosophers would question this early empiricism in a far more severe fashion. The theory has us pass from a host of particular opinions to a universal belief; but that inductive move, as a later age insisted, is of dubious validity; and an empiricism which ignores sceptical doubts about perception and induction is a weak theory. But it would be absurd to disparage Alcmeon for ignoring problems which no one had yet raised, and to deny him the signal credit of sketching out the first rough draft of an empiricist epistemology.

THE SERPENT

IX

Parmenides and the Objects of Inquiry

(a) *Parmenides' journey*

Parmenides of Elea marks a turning-point in the history of philosophy: his investigations, supported and supplemented by those of his two followers, seemed to reveal deep logical flaws in the very foundations of earlier thought. Science, it appeared, was marred by subtle but profound contradictions; and the great enterprise undertaken by the Milesians, by Xenophanes and by Heraclitus, lacked all pith and moment. The age of innocence was ended, and when science was taken up again by the fifth-century philosophers, their first and most arduous task was to defend their discipline against the arguments of Elea. If their defence was often frail and unconvincing, and if it was Plato who first fully appreciated the strength and complexity of Parmenides' position, it remains true that Parmenides' influence on later Presocratic thought was all-pervasive. Historically, Parmenides is a giant figure; what is more, he introduced into Presocratic thought a number of issues belonging to the very heart of philosophy.

Parmenides' thoughts were divulged in a single hexameter poem (Diogenes Laertius, I.16 = **28 A 13**) which survived intact to the time of Simplicius (**A 21**). Observing that copies of the poem were scarce, Simplicius transcribed extensive extracts; and thanks to his efforts we possess some 150 lines of the work, including two substantial passages. It is hard to excuse Parmenides' choice of verse as a medium for his philosophy. The exigencies of metre and poetical style regularly produce an almost impenetrable obscurity; and the difficulty of understanding his thought is not lightened by any literary joy: the case presents no adjunct to the Muse's diadem.[1]

The poem began with a long allegorical prologue, the interpretation of which is for the most part of little philosophical importance. Its last four lines, however, call for comment; for they present one of the strangest features of Parmenides' work. The prologue is a speech to the poet from the goddess who leads him on his intellectual journey and describes his philosophy to him and to us. At the end of her speech she promises thus:

> And you must ascertain everything—
> both the unmoving heart of well-rounded truth,
> and the opinions of mortals in which there is no true trust (*pistis*).
> But nevertheless you will learn these too (**145: B 1**.28–31).[2]

The words are echoed near the end of the long central fragment:

> Here I stop the trustworthy (*pistos*) account and the thought
> about truth; henceforth learn mortal opinions,
> listening to the deceitful arrangement of my words (**146: B 8**.50–2).

The goddess has two stories to tell: the truth, and mortal opinions. And Parmenides' poem, after its exordium, falls into two corresponding parts, the first recounting the Way of Truth, and the second the Way of Opinion.

The Way of Opinion is paved with falsity: 'there is no true trust' along it, and its description is 'deceitful'. It could hardly be stated more plainly that the Way of Opinion is a Way of Falsity. Many scholars have found themselves incapable of believing that one half of Parmenides' work should have been devoted to the propagation of untruths; and they have accordingly advanced the palliative thesis that the Way of Opinion is a way of plausibility or verisimilitude or probability, and not exactly a way of falsehood. That conciliatory effort has origins in antiquity; and the dispute between its proponents and those sterner scholars who see no Truth in Opinion, is ancient (Plutarch, **A 34**; cf. Simplicius, **A 34**; *in Phys* 38.24–8). Yet Parmenides' own words decide the contest: he says unequivocally that the Way of Opinion is a path of falsehood and deceit; he says nothing of any probabilities lying on the road; and we are bound to take him at his word. Nor, after all, is it unusual for a philosopher to describe, at length, views with which he vehemently disagrees.

Moreover, the goddess tells us why she troubles to chart the Way of Opinion:

> I tell you all this appropriate arrangement
> in order that no thought of mortals may ever drive past you
> (**147: B 8**.60–1).

The metaphor of 'driving past (*parelaunein*)' is not transparent. Some gloss it by 'outstrip', or the like, and explain that knowledge of the Way of Opinion will enable Parmenides to hold his own in argument with any old-fashioned cosmologists he may meet. A better gloss, perhaps, is 'get the better of' or 'convince': the goddess, by describing the Way of Opinion and thereby indicating its flaws, will ensure that Parmenides does not succumb to its meretricious temptations. However that may be, the Way of Opinion does not express Parmenides' own convictions. Only a few fragments of that Way survive: it seems to have paraded a full scale account of natural philosophy in the Ionian tradition; but the details are controversial and for the most part unexciting.[3] In a later chapter I shall discuss one fragment from the Way of Opinion (below, p. 486); here I ignore that primrose path and struggle instead up the steep and rugged road of well-rounded Truth.

(b) *At the crossroads*

Before leading him up the Way of Truth, the goddess instructs Parmenides about the nature of the different ways that face the neophyte philosopher; and she provides him with a proof that the Way of Truth is alone passable. He not only should follow that Way—he must follow it; for no other way leads anywhere. The goddess's exposition and argument are difficult. I shall begin by setting out the relevant texts: if my English translation is in places barely intelligible, that is partly because Parmenides' Greek is desperately hard to understand.

> Come then, I will tell you (and you must spread the story when you have heard it)
> what are the only roads of inquiry for thinking of:
> one, both that it is and that it is not for not being,
> is the path of Persuasion (for Truth accompanies it);
> the other, both that it is not and that it is necessary for it not to be
> —*that*, I tell you, is a track beyond all tidings.
> For neither would you recognize that which is not (for it is not accomplishable),
> nor mention it. (**148: B 2**).

> The same thing is both for thinking of and for being (**149: B 3**).[4]

> What is for saying and for thinking of must be;[5] for it is for being,
> but nothing is not: those things I bid you hold in mind;
> for from this first road of inquiry I restrain you.
> And then from that one, along which mortals, knowing nothing,
> wander, two-headed; for helplessness in their
> breasts directs a wandering mind; and they are carried about
> deaf alike and blind, gawping, creatures of no judgment,
> by whom both to be and not be are thought the same
> and not the same; and the path of all is backward turning (**150: B 6**).

> For never will this be proved, that things that are not are.
> But do you restrain your thought from this road of inquiry (**151: B 7.** 1–2).

(Note that my translations of **149** and **150**.1 are not universally accepted. **150**. 8–9 is also controversial: see below, p. 168.)

Let us begin with **148**: what are 'the only roads of inquiry'? and what does the goddess mean when she says that they 'are for thinking of'?

The phrase 'are . . . for thinking of' (line 2) renders '*esti noêsai*'. The verb '*noein*', of which '*noêsai*' is the aorist infinitive, plays a central role in Parmenides' subsequent argument, where it is standardly translated as 'think of' or 'conceive'. Some scholars, however, prefer the very different translation 'know', and thereby change the whole character of Parmenidean thought.[6] I think that the standard translation makes better sense of Parmenides' argument; and I doubt if the heterodox translation is linguistically correct. It is true that in certain celebrated Platonic and Aristotelian passages, the noun '*nous*' is used to denote the highest of cognitive faculties; and there are passages in those philosophers, and in earlier writers, where 'intuit', 'grasp', or even 'know' is a plausible translation of '*noein*'. But against those occurrences (which are fairly uncommon and usually highflown) we can set a host of passages where '*noein*' simply means 'think (of)': '*noein*' is the ordinary Greek verb for 'think (of)', and 'think (of)' is usually its proper English equivalent. Moreover, the linguistic context in which the verb occurs in Parmenides favours (indeed, to my mind requires) the translation 'think (of)'. For '*noein*' is thrice conjoined with a verb of saying: with '*legein*' at **150**.1; and with '*phasthai*' twice in **B 8**.8 (cf. '*anônumon*' at **B 8**.17). '*Legein*' and '*phasthai*' mean 'say', not 'say truly' or 'say successfully' (the Greek for which is '*alêtheuein*'); and the contexts of their occurrence imply that 'say' and '*noein*' share at least one important logical feature: they both stand in the same relation to 'being'. In this respect it is 'think that *P*' and 'think of *X*', rather than 'know that *P*' and 'know *X*', which parallel 'say that *P*' and 'mention *X*'; and that fact, I think, establishes the traditional translation of '*noein*'.

So much for the meaning of '*noêsai*'. All, however, is not yet plain; for the syntax of '*esti noêsai*' is disputed. Phrases of the form *esti* + infinitive recur later in the poem, and their presence is indicated in my translation by phrases of the rebarbative form 'is (are) for ϕing'. The usage, which is not uncommon in Greek, has connexions with the 'potential' use of '*esti*'. (*Esti* with infinitive often means 'it is possible to . . .'. In that case '*esti*' is 'impersonal', whereas in our locution it always has a subject, explicit or implicit.) Indeed, it seems to me reasonable to gloss '*a* is for ϕing' either by '*a* can ϕ' or by '*a* can be ϕed'—the context will determine whether active or passive is appropriate. Thus in **148**.2 'are for thinking of' means 'can be thought of'.[7] Observe that the gloss differs from its original in one important feature. The grammatical form of the phrase '*a* is for ϕing' may seduce us into making a fallacious deduction: from '*a* is for ϕing' it is easy to infer '*a* is'. The grammatical form of the gloss does not provide the same temptation. The point may assume significance later.

Then what roads of enquiry can be thought of? **148** mentions two roads: Road (A) is described in line 3, and proved by line 4 to be the Way of Truth; Road (B) is the 'track beyond all tidings', delineated in line 5. **150**. 3–4 also mentions two roads: Road (C), described in lines 4–9, is that 'along which mortals . . . wander', and it is therefore the Way of Opinion. The 'first road' of line 3 also has pitfalls (for the goddess 'restrains' Parmenides from it); and it cannot therefore be identical with Road (A), the Way of Truth. Now lines 1–2 contain the end of an argument concerned with this 'first road'; and, as I shall show, it is plausible to find the beginning of the argument in **148**. 7–8, which starts to recount the horrors of the 'track beyond all tidings'. If that is so, then the 'first road' of **150** is identical with Road (B); and in consequence Road (B), the 'track beyond all tidings', is not the Way of Opinion.

148 and **150** show Parmenides at a crossroads, faced by three possible paths of inquiry: (A) the Way of Truth; (B) the 'track beyond all tidings' and (C) the Way of Opinion.[8] The first duty of the goddess is to characterize those three roads in a logically perspicuous fashion. Road (A) maintains 'both that it is (*esti*) and that it is not for not being' (**148**. 3);[9] Road (B) maintains 'both that it is not and that it is necessary for it not to be' (**148**. 5); Road (C) is not explicitly described in comparable terms, but must have maintained 'both that it is and that it is not' (cf. **150**. 8).

The three roads are thus distinguished by means of the word '*esti*', 'it is'. Both the sense of the verb and the identity of its subject are matters of high controversy. Since they are also vital to any interpretation of Parmenides' argument, we cannot burke the issue. I begin by asking what is the sense of the verb '*einai*' as Parmenides uses it here. The classification of the different 'senses', or 'uses', of the verb '*einai*' is a delicate task, abounding in linguistic and philosophical difficulties;[10] and my remarks will be crude and superficial. Nevertheless, something must be said.

We can distinguish between a complete and an incomplete use of '*einai*': sometimes a sentence of the form '*X esti*' expresses a complete proposition; sometimes '*esti*' occurs in sentences of the form '*X esti Y*' (or the form '*X esti*' is elliptical for '*X esti Y*'). In its complete use, '*einai*' sometimes has an existential sense '*ho theos esti*' is the Greek for 'god exists'; '*ouk esti kentauros*' means 'Centaurs do not exist'. In its incomplete use, '*einai*' often serves as a copula, and the use is called predicative: '*Sôkratês esti sophos*' is Greek for 'Socrates is wise'; '*hoi leontes ouk eisin hêmeroi*' means 'Lions are not tame'. Many scholars think that Parmenides' original sin was a confusion, or fusion, of the existential with the predicative '*einai*'; and they believe that the characterization of the three roads in **148** catches Parmenides *in flagrante delicto*. If we ask what sense '*esti*' has in line 3, the answer is disappointing: '*esti*' attempts, hopelessly, to combine the two senses of 'exists' and 'is *Y*'.[11]

Now I do not wish to maintain that Parmenides was conscious of the distinction between an existential and a predicative use of '*einai*'; credit for bringing that distinction to philosophical consciousness is usually given to Plato. But I do reject the claim that **148** fuses or confuses the two uses of the verb. I see no reason to impute such a confusion to the characterization of the three roads; for I see no trace of a predicative 'is' in that characterization. The point can be simply supported: Road (B) rules out '*X* is not'; if we read 'is' predicatively, we must suppose Parmenides to be abjuring all negative predications. to be spurning all sentences of the form '*X* is not *F*'. Such a high-handed dismissal of negation is absurd; it is suggested by nothing in Parmenides' poem; and it is adequately outlawed by such lines as **B 8**.22, which show Parmenides happy to accept formulae of the form '*X* is not *F*'.[12] '*Esti*', in the passages we are concerned with, is not a copula.

Then is '*esti*' existential? Aristotle distinguishes what has been called a 'veridical' use of '*esti*'; '*X esti*', in this use, is complete, and '*esti*' means '. . . is the case' or '. . . is true'. If Socrates asserts that cobblers are good at making shoes, his interlocutor may reply '*Esti tauta*', 'Those things are' or 'That's true'. It has been suggested that Parmenides' complete '*esti*' is veridical, not existential.

That suggestion can be accommodated, I think, to **148** and **150**; but the accommodation is not easy, nor (as far as I can see) does it have any philosophical merit. In any event, the suggestion breaks on the rocks of **B 8**: in that fragment, Parmenides sets himself to infer a number of properties of *X* from the premiss that *X esti*. None of those properties consists with the veridical reading of '*esti*': the very first inference is that *X* is ungenerated; and if it is not, strictly speaking, impossible to take '*X*' in '*X* is ungenerated' to stand for the sort of propositional entity of which veridical '*esti*' is predicable, it is grossly implausible to do so, and the implausibility mounts to giant proportions as the inferences of **B 8** proceed. Since the inferences in **B 8** are tied to the '*esti*' of **148** and **150**, the veridical reading of '*esti*' in those fragments can only be maintained at the cost of ascribing to Parmenides a confusion between veridical and non-veridical '*einai*'. And I see no reason for making that derogatory ascription.[13]

Existential '*einai*' remains. The obvious and the orthodox interpretation of '*esti*' in **148** and **150** is existential; and that interpretation is felicitous: it does not perform the impossible task of presenting Parmenides with a set of doctrines which are true, but it does give Parmenides a metaphysical outlook which is intelligible, coherent and peculiarly plausible. I shall continue to translate Parmenides' '*einai*' by 'be'; but I shall paraphrase it by 'exist'.

Road (A) thus says that 'it exists', *esti*. Scholars have naturally raised the question of what exists: what is Parmenides talking about? what is the logical subject of '*esti*'? Some have denied the appropriateness of the question, urging that we need no more ask after the subject of '*esti*' than we do after '*huei*', 'it is raining'. I find that suggestion perfectly incomprehensible.[14] Nevertheless, the spirit behind it is sound: '*esti*' need not have a logical subject. For in general, we can make sense of a sentence of the form 'it ϕs' in either of two ways: first, we may find a determinate reference for 'it', so that 'it ϕs' is understood as '*a* ϕs'. ('How is your motor car?'—'It's working again'.) Here we do look for a logical subject and we expect to find it, explicit or implicit, in the immediate context. Second, 'it ϕs' may be the consequent of a conditional or a relative sentence: 'If you buy a machine, look after it'; 'Whatever machine you buy, something will go wrong with it'. In ordinary discourse, the antecedent is often not expressed: 'What will you do if you catch a fish?—Eat it'. Here there is no question of finding a logical subject for the predicate 'ϕs': 'it' does not name or refer to any particular individual.

One standard view gives '*esti*' in **148**.3 a logical subject: that subject is 'Being'; and Road (A) asserts, bluntly, that Being exists. I am at a loss to understand that assertion; what in the world can be meant by 'Being exists'? Nevertheless, behind abstract Being there lurks a more concrete candidate for the post of logical subject: '*to eon*', 'what is'. Should we gloss '*esti*' as 'what is, is'?[15]

Phrases of the form 'what ϕs' do not always serve as logical subjects: 'what ϕs' may mean 'whatever ϕs' ('What's done cannot be undone'); and then 'what ϕs ψs' means 'for any x: if x ϕs, x ψs'. Thus we might gloss Parmenides' '*esti*' by 'what is, is', and yet deny that 'what is' is a logical subject; for we might explain the phrase by 'what*ever* is, is'. Road (A), on that view, maintains that whatever exists exists and cannot not exist. It has been objected to that interpretation that Parmenides attempts to prove that Road (A) is right, and Roads (B) and (C) mistaken; but that the interpretation makes (A) tautologous, and hence in no need of proof, and (B) and (C) contradictory, and hence in no need of disproof. But the objection is doubly mistaken: first, tautologies can, and sometimes should, be proved; and contradictions can, and sometimes should, be disproved. Second, Road (A) does not turn out tautologous; since it is far from a tautology that what exists *cannot not exist*.

'What ϕs' may mean 'the thing that ϕs', and serve as a logical subject. Thus '*to eon*' may mean 'the thing which exists'. Then Road (A) maintains that the thing that exists—'the One' or 'the Whole' or 'Nature'—exists and cannot not exist. It has been objected to that interpretation that Parmenides proceeds in **B 8** to prove that the subject of his poem is One; and that he can hardly have intended to prove the tautology that 'the One is one'. Again, the objection is weak: first, Parmenides may have tried to prove a tautology; second, it is far from clear that Parmenides ever does try to prove that the subject of his poem is One; and thirdly, it is not clear that it is tautologous to say that 'the Whole' or 'Nature' or 'Reality' is one.

Nevertheless, I do not believe that '*to eon*', on either interpretation, is a likely supplement to Parmenides' '*esti*'. The reason is simple: nothing in the context of **148** could reasonably suggest to even the most careful reader that by 'it is' Parmenides meant 'what is, is'. The term 'what is' does not appear in **B 1** or in **148**; and it is not the sort of term a reader would naturally supply for himself.[16]

A close investigation of the context of **148** has supplemented '*esti*' in a different way: instead of 'what is', supply 'what can be thought of' or 'what can be known'. Road (A) then says that 'what can be thought of exists'; and 'Parmenides' real starting-point is . . . the possibility of rational discourse' or of thought.[17] My objection to that suggestion is a weaker version of my objection to '*to eon*': nothing in the introductory context of **148** suggests such a supplement for '*esti*' at line 3; reflexion on the subsequent argument may indeed lead us to 'what can be thought of', but it will also lead us to berate Parmenides for a gratuitously roundabout and allusive way of expressing himself; for the most careful reader, on this view, will only understand the crucial lines of **148** after he has read a quantity of later verses.

Nonetheless, the philosophical advantages of the interpretation are considerable; and we may well be loth to abandon the spectacle of a Parmenides who investigates, in Kantian fashion, the implications of rationality. We can retain the advantages and avoid the objection by modifying the interpretation slightly. I suggest the following paraphrase for lines 1–3: 'I will tell you . . . the different conceivable ways of inquiring into something—the first assumes that it exists and cannot not exist . . .' In the paraphrase, 'it' has an explicit antecedent, and 'inquiring into' has an explicit object: viz. the word 'something'. In the Greek text there is no explicit subject for '*esti*' and no explicit object of '*dizêsios*' ('inquiry'). Subject and object must both be supplied, and nothing is easier than to make this double task one: the implicit object of '*dizêsios*' is the implicit subject of '*esti*'. 'Of the ways of inquiring [about any given object], the first assumes that [the object, whatever it may be] exists.'

Thus Road (A) says that *whatever we inquire into* exists, and cannot not exist: Parmenides' starting-point is the possibility, not exactly of rational thought, but of scientific research. The immediate context of **148**, and the general atmosphere of **B 1**, make that an intelligible way of understanding the goddess's roads; the argument about the relative merits of the three roads is, as we shall see, thoroughly consonant with the interpretation; and we find Parmenides, in a historically appropriate fashion, investigating the logical foundations of the programme of the early Greek philosophers.

If the '*esti*' of **148** is now explained, the characterization of the three roads is still not completely clear: two uncertainties remain. First, are the objects of inquiry to be specified by singular or by general terms? does road (A) say that if anyone studies things of a given sort (stars, winds, horses) then there must exist things of that sort? or does it say that if anyone studies any individual object (the sun, Boreas, Pegasus) then that object must exist? Philosophers' attitudes to Parmenides' argument may differ according to which alternative we choose; but nothing in the poem indicates that Parmenides saw two alternatives here, and had he done so he might, I think, have decided to embrace their conjunction.

Second, how are we to interpret the modal operators in the second half of lines 3 and 5? Road (A) maintains that what is inquired into 'is not for not being' or 'cannot not be'; Road (B) holds of what is inquired into that 'it is necessary for it not to be'. Road (A) states that objects of inquiry necessarily exist, Road (B) that they necessarily do not exist; does 'necessarily' here mark *necessitas consequentis* or *necessitas consequentiae*? does Road (A) state:

(1) If a thing is studied, it has the property of necessary existence, or rather:

(2) It is necessarily true that anything studied exists?

I cannot tell if Parmenides' Greek favours either (1) or (2); and I suppose that Parmenides did not see that two distinct propositions were on view: confusion between *necessitas consequentis* and *necessitas consequentiae* is distressingly common.

Let me now try to characterize Roads (A) and (B) a little more formally: I use '$\Box$ P' to abbreviate 'necessarily P'. Each Road has four possible formulations:

(A1) $(\forall x)$ (if x is studied, $\Box x$ exists).
(A2) $(\forall \phi)$ (if ϕs are studied, $\Box$ there exist ϕs).
(A3) $\Box$ $(\forall x)$ (if x is studied, x exists).
(A4) $\Box$ $(\forall \phi)$ (if ϕs are studied, there exist ϕs).
(B1) $(\forall x)$ (if x is studied, $\Box$ x does not exist).
(B2) $(\forall \phi)$ (if ϕs are studied, $\Box$ there exist no ϕs).
(B3) $\Box$ $(\forall x)$ (if x is studied, x does not exist).
(B4) $\Box$ $(\forall \phi)$ (if ϕs are studied, there exist no ϕs).

If we ignore the distinction between 'x exists' and 'there exist ϕs', we may limit ourselves to two versions of Roads (A) and (B); how, then, are we to formulate road (C), the Way of Opinion?

There are three aids to formulation: Road (C) is the road of ordinary mortals; it is expressible, vaguely enough, by the phrase 'it is and it is not'; and the triad of (A), (B) and (C) includes all the conceivable paths of thought. The first version of (A) and (B) gives:

I (Ai) $(\forall X)$ (if X is studied, $\Box$ X exists).
(Bi) $(\forall X)$ (if X is studied, $\Box$ X does not exist).

For (C) we might perhaps imagine:

(Ci1) $(\forall X)$ (if X is studied, $\Box$ X exists & $\Box$ X does not exist).

or else:

(Ci2) $(\exists X)$ (X is studied & $\Box$ X exists) &
$(\exists X)$ (X is studied & $\Box$ X does not exist).

If the triad of roads is to be genuinely exhaustive, we need rather:

(Ci3) $(\exists X)$ (X is studied & not-$\Box$ X exists)
& $(\exists X)$ (X is studied & $\Box$ X exists).

The second version of (A) and (B) yields:

II (Aii) $\Box(\forall X)$ (if X is studied, X exists).
(Bii) $\Box(\forall X)$ (if X is studied, X does not exist).

And then for Road (C) we may offer:

(Cii1) $\Box(\forall X)$ (if X is studied, X exists & X does not exist).
(Cii2) $\Box(\exists X)$ (X is studied & X exists) &
$(\exists X)$ (X is studied & X does not exist)
(Cii3) $\Diamond(\exists X)$ (X is studied & X does not exist)
$\Diamond(\exists X)$ (X is studied & X exists).

(In (Cii3), '$\Diamond$' abbreviates 'possibly'.)

I state these possibilities neither to bemuse the reader nor to exhibit my own virtuosity: their statement is a necessary preliminary to any examination of Parmenides' metaphysics; and if we are to treat his argument with the respect it deserves, we must be prepared to analyse its components with a rigour that Parmenides himself was not equipped to supply. I turn now to the argument itself.

(c) *The paths of ignorance*

The argument against Road (B) begins in **148**. 6–8. Line 8 is a half line, and so is **149**: the two halves make a metrical and a rational whole, and I assume that **149** is in fact continuous with **148**. Finally, **150**. 1–2 completes the case against the track beyond all tidings.

Let us take a student, *a*, and an object of study, *O*; and suppose that *a* is studying *O*. Now first, Parmenides observes, 'neither would you recognize that which is not . . . nor mention it'; i.e.

(1) $(\forall X)$ (if X does not exist, then no one can recognize X and no one can mention X).

From (1) we infer:

(2) If *O* does not exist, then *a* cannot recognize *O*, and *a* cannot mention *O*.

But why should we credit (1)? It is not, after all, a particularly plausible thesis on the face of it. **149** comes next in our text; and it amounts to: 'Whatever can be thought of can exist, and vice versa'; i.e.

(3) $(\forall X)$ (X can be thought of if and only if X can exist).

Now (3) yields:

(4) If *a* can think of *O*, then *O* can exist.

But (4) does not offer us any immediate help.[18]

Let us, then, try **150**. 1–2. 'What is for saying and for thinking of must be': a plausible translation is:

(5) $\square$ (∀X) (if *X* can be mentioned or *X* can be thought of, then *X* exists).

Now (5) gives:

(6) If *a* can mention *O* or *a* can think of *O*, then *O* exists.

Let us ascribe another premiss to Parmenides, viz:

(7) (∀X) (if *X* can be recognized, *X* can be thought of)

and let us infer from (7) to:

(8) If *a* can recognize *O*, then *a* can think of *O*.

Now we have an argument for (2); for (6) and (8) together entail (2).

So far, (3) has done no work, and (5) is unsupported. **150**.1 continues: 'for it is for being'; i.e., 'for what is for saying and for thinking is for being', or:

(9) (∀X) (if *X* can be mentioned or *X* can be thought of, then *X* can exist)

whence:

(10) If *a* can mention *O*, *O* can exist.

There remains the first clause of **150**.2, 'but nothing is not'. That means, of course, 'But nothing is not for being', i.e., 'nothing cannot exist'. Now 'nothing (*mêden*)' is used as a synonym for '*to mê on*', 'what is not' (cf. **B 8**.10); so that we have:

(11) (∀X) (if *X* does not exist, *X* cannot exist);

whence:

(12) If *O* does not exist, *O* cannot exist.

Proposition (3) can now be put to use; for (4), (10) and (12) together entail (6).

Let us now suppose that Road (B) is the one *a* chooses to follow in his inquiry; whether we pick (Bi) or (Bii) we can infer:

(13) If *a* studies *O*, *O* does not exist.

Now it is evidently true that students must be able to say what they are studying, or at least to recognize the objects of their inquiries; i.e.

(14) (∀X) (if *X* is studied, then *X* can be mentioned or *X* can be recognized).

Hence:

(15) If *a* studies *O*, then *a* can mention *O* or *a* can recognize *O*.

But if *a* studies *O*, we can now infer, from (6), (15) and (13), that *O* exists and *O* does not exist. But that is impossible; hence if *a* is a student, (13) is false; and, in general, no student can proceed along Road (B). And that completes Parmenides' argument: Road (B) is indeed a track beyond all tidings.

My reconstruction has been laborious; and it may be of use if I state more briefly the train of argument it ascribes to Parmenides. First, premiss (9) [= **150**.1] gives (10), and premiss (3) [= **149**] gives (4). Then premiss (11) [= **150**.2] gives (12); and (4), (10) and (12) together yield (6) [cf. **150**.1]. A new premiss, (7), gives (8); and (6) and (8) entail (2). A further new premiss, (14), gives (15). Assume that there are students, and that they follow Road (B). Then via (13), we meet with an explicit contradiction. And that licenses the rejection of our assumption.

The argument is, I claim, subtle and ingenious. (I offer a symbolized version in the Appendix to this chapter.) I suppose that it convinced Parmenides of the pointlessness of Road (B). Yet as it stands, in naked rigour, it shows at least one ugly blemish: premiss (11) is false, and obviously false. Not all nonentities are *impossibilia*: many things might, but do not, exist. So obvious and so offensive a flaw may be thought to show that the argument I have constructed cannot have been propounded by a thinker of Parmenides' calibre. But to say that is to ignore the seductive powers which certain falsehoods may have when they are stated informally in ordinary English or in ordinary Greek. Premiss (11) is conveyed by some such sentence as 'what doesn't exist can't exist'; and that sentence is an 'untruism'; that is to say, it is an ambiguous sentence expressing, on one interpretation, a trivial truth and on another, a substantial falsity. 'Nothing is not for being', or 'What doesn't exist can't exist', may mean either:

(16) It is not possible that what does not exist exists;

or else:

(17) If a thing does not exist, then it is not possible for it to exist.

Either:

(16a) □ (if *a* does not exist, *a* does not exist),

or

(17a) If *a* does not exist, □ (*a* does not exist).

If Parmenides' sentence is interpreted as (16) it is true; but it does not yield (11). If it is interpreted as (17) it yields (11); but it is false. Parmenides, I suggest, was blind to the ambiguity of the sentence he used: he supposed that he could, as it were, take advantage in one and the same proposition, both of the truth of (16) and of the logical implications of (17). Parmenides' philosophy rests, if I am right, on an untruism; it is some slight consolation that his was by no means the last system to be built on such a sandy foundation.

I turn now to Road (C). Scholars have given **150** a quantity of attention; for some have found in it evidence that Parmenides was attacking Heraclitus. The evidence is weak—an alleged verbal echo or two—and since Road (C) is the Way of Opinion, which most mortals tread, Heraclitus is at best one of its travellers and not a lone rambler. If Parmenides has Heraclitus in mind at all (which I doubt), it is only as a particularly striking representative of all that is bad in mortal opinions.[19]

However that may be, my present interest centres on the reasons for Parmenides' rejection of (C) rather than on the protagonists of the rejected view; and **151** provides a better starting-point than **150**.

'For never will this be proved—that things that are not are'. No doubt; but what is that to the travellers on Road (C)? A very simple argument suggests itself: (C) is committed to the view that at least some objects of inquiry do not, or may not, exist. Suppose that *O* is such an object: then by **151**.1, since *O* does not exist, it will never be shown that *O* does exist; but the argument against Road (B) showed precisely that *O*, if it is an object of inquiry, does exist. Thus Road (C) leads to contradiction and must be abandoned.

In short, Road (C) leads nowhere for the same reasons that (B) leads nowhere; and the argument against (B) applies immediately to (C). That does not imply, as some scholars have feared, that (B) and (C) somehow fail to be genuine alternatives: if a mine wrecks two bridges at once, it does not follow that the bridges only offered one way across the river. And anyone who has argued against (B) in the Parmenidean mode will hardly fail to see that his argument can be deployed against (C).

What, then, of **150**? Most of the fragment is abuse; yet the last three lines appear to offer an argument against Road (C) which is distinct from the one I have just extracted from **151**.1–2. In **150**.7 Parmenides asserts that men wander about 'deaf alike and blind, gawping, creatures of no judgment'; and in line 9 he concludes that 'the path of all is backward turning (*palintropos*)'.[20] To say that a man's path turns backward is presumably to say that he contradicts himself; and we should expect to find in line 8 something which is, or directly implies, a contradiction. Our expectations are not disappointed: line 8 brims with contradictory-looking phrases. The problem is to determine which of them Parmenides meant to saddle mortals with: we need not suppose that, in Parmenides' view, ordinary men are given to uttering explicit contradictions; he means only that men are committed to contradictions. But committed to what contradictions? and why?

The Greek of line 8 has been deemed to allow at least three translations:

(i) 'By whom both to be and not to be are thought to be the same and not the same';

(ii) 'By whom it is thought both to be and not to be both the same and not the same';

(iii) 'By whom it is thought both to be and not to be, both to be the same and not to be the same'.

Translation (i) ascribes to mortals the compound contradiction:

(18) (Being = not-being) & (Being $\neq$ not-being).
But (18) is a strange proposition; and I cannot concoct any line of reasoning that plausibly produces it from mortal opinions.

Translation (ii) has often suggested a simple interpretation: according to ordinary folk, many things change and yet retain their identity; thus, in an obvious sense, men are committed to the view that things are and are not the same (hence, equivalently, that they are and are not not the same). Translation (iii) may well be construed in a similar fashion: by allowing generation and destruction, mortals commit themselves to propositions of the form '*a* is and *a* is not'; by allowing alteration, they commit themselves to '*a* is the same and *a* is not the same'.

Grammar, I think, favours (iii) over (ii);[21] and (iii), on this interpretation, offers a thicker sense. But a weighty argument tells against (ii) and the interpretation of (iii) in terms of change: the interpreters will have it that Parmenides finds contradiction in men's ordinary talk of change. Now fragment **B 8** contains a long and intricate argument against the possibility of change and generation; and that argument rests upon the foundation of Road (A). Are we to suppose that in his attack on Road (C), in a fragment which only prepares the ground for the major deductions of **B 8**, Parmenides can have anticipated, without apology, the main and most striking conclusion of those deductions? Parmenides was not so cack-handed a fellow: the abolition of change is the business of **B 8**, and it cannot have been presupposed in **150**.

Translation (iii) does not have to be interpreted in terms of generation and change. I quote a sentence from the *Dissoi Logoi* (see below, p. 517):

> And the same things exist and do not exist; for the things that exist here do not exist in Libya, and those in Libya do not exist in Cyprus; and the same goes for everything else. Thus things both exist and do not exist (**152:90A5**, §5).

Ask a man in Libya if there exist any lions, and he will give you a fearful affirmative; ask the same man in the peaceful streets of Athens 'Are there any lions?'—he will answer 'By the dog, no'. Conjoin the replies, each of which seems ordinary and respectable, and the result is contradiction: 'There are and there are not lions'. Again, it is the same things that are and are not; for it is lions which are said to be, and lions which are said not to be. But evidently the lions which *are*, the Libyan lions, are beasts of a far tougher character than those Athenian animals which do not exist. Lions, in sum, 'are and are not, are the same and not the same'.

That interpretation of line 8 seems to me the least implausible. But the reasoning it ascribes to Parmenides will stand no weight; and it is fortunate that Parmenides need set no weight on it. For, as I have argued, in rejecting Road (B), Parmenides has said quite enough to reject Road (C) too: Road (A) alone is left for intellectual travellers.

Parmenides draws a moral from his rejections of Road (C):

> Do not let much-experienced habit force you along this road,
> to let run an aimless eye and an echoing ear
> and a tongue; but judge by argument (*logôi*) the much-
> contending refutation uttered by me (**153: B** 7. 3–6).

I shall return later to the attack on sense-perception allegedly contained in these lines (below, p. 297). Here I wish to point out the positive part of Parmenides' moral: we are to judge his 'refutation' of Road (C) by 'argument' and not by appealing to experience. The request is as sound as it is simple: no amount of assertion, however well grounded on sensory evidence, can show where Parmenides' reasoning fails; if we want to refute Parmenides, we must attack argument with argument, *logos* with *logos*.

This sane request was ignored by most of Parmenides' successors. I have already remarked upon the fact that the Presocratics rarely gave any critical examination of the arguments whose conclusions they opposed (above pp. 50–2). That failure is nowhere more evident than in the reaction to Parmenides: later thinkers knew that his conclusions were unacceptable; but they could not, or would not, say where his arguments broke down. Parmenides saw where his opponents' task lay better than they did themselves. And in attempting to analyse Parmenides' argument, and to show where it goes wrong, I have done no more than follow Parmenides' own advice.

Parmenides' attack on Road (B) fails, and with it his attack on Road (C); consequently, he fails to show that Road (A) is the only traversable road. Can we perhaps come to Parmenides' support and offer him more powerful weapons from our own logical arsenal? We might attempt to save him at any of three points. First, we might attempt to support proposition (5) of his argument: what can be mentioned or thought of exists. Of modern philosophers, only Berkeley would dare to defend Parmenides here; for Berkeley held that whatever is thought of exists. I quote his notorious argument: 'But say you, surely there is nothing easier than to imagine trees, for instance, in a park, or books existing in a closet, and nobody by to perceive them. I answer, you may so, there is no difficulty in it: but what is all this, I beseech you, more than framing in your mind certain ideas which you call *books* and *trees*, and at the same time omitting to frame the idea of any one that may perceive them? *but do not you yourself perceive or think of them all the while*? this therefore is nothing to the purpose; it only shows you have the power of imagining or forming ideas in your mind; but it does not show that you can conceive it possible the objects of your thought may exist without the mind: to make out this, *it is necessary that you can conceive them existing unconceived or unthought of, which is a manifest repugnancy*' (*Principles of Human Knowledge*, § 23). Berkeley's argument is in direct line of descent from Parmenides. It is fallacious (though the fallacy is interestingly elusive); and Berkeley's Parmenidean conclusion will not stand. 'For Scylla and Chimaera, and many non-entities, are', as the Sophist Gorgias said, 'thought upon' (**82 B 3**, § 80). We do think of unicorns and centaurs, of Zeus and Jehovah, of phlogiston and the luminiferous ether; and such objects do not exist. Existential questions can be sensibly entertained; I can wonder whether Homer existed or whether there really ever were any dodos. And the fact that such questions can be posed is sufficient to show that non-entities can be thought upon.

If proposition (5) is indefensible, perhaps we can take a stand on (1), and agree that anything that can be recognized or mentioned must exist? Surprisingly many philosophers will defend Parmenides at that point: perhaps we can think of non-entities; but we certainly cannot mention them or discourse about them. If I am to mention an object, then I must be able to predicate things of it, to identify it, to refer to it; but we cannot ascribe properties to non-entities; we cannot identify the non-existent; we cannot refer to things which are not there for referring—what is for speaking of, must be.

That popular argument is, I think, mistaken; but it requires more consideration than I can give it here.[22] We do, in our unphilosophical moments, imagine that we can talk about non-entities: mythographers refer felicitously to Scylla and Chimaera; scientists will talk dismissively about phlogiston; and literary critics will write you a book about Hamlet at the drop of a hat. And if it is allowed that we can *think* of non-entities, surely it must follow that we can *identify* and *refer to* non-entities? In order to think about Pegasus, I must somehow pick out that mythical beast for myself; and if I can pick him out, mentally, for myself, why can I not pick him out, linguistically, for you? I do not pretend that talking about the non-existent is easily analysed; but it is easily done. And that is enough to dispose of Parmenides' proposition (1).

If we can salvage none of Parmenides' argument, may we save his conclusion, that Road (A) is the only traversable path? that objects of enquiry, at least, must exist? Again, many philosophers, allowing thought of and reference to the non-existent, might finally agree that the non-existent cannot be the object of scientific research: 'a thing must exist if we are to study it or institute inquiries concerning its nature and properties'.[23] Aristotle, in whose view science started from the *ousia* or essence of things, held that only entities have an essence, so that scientific inquiry is restricted to the things that really exist. According to Locke, 'real' knowledge must bear upon real objects; otherwise it is vain and alchimerical (*Essay* IV.iv). And if Locke argues not that knowledge of non-entities is impossible but only that it is fatuous and footling, nevertheless it is not hard to find a stricter, Parmenidean thesis below the surface of his text: zoologists study horses, not unicorns; chemists study oxygen, not phlogiston; historians study Shakespeare, not Hamlet.

But surely mythologists study unicorns, not horses; historians of science study phlogiston before oxygen; and literary men may inquire into the character of Hamlet rather than of Shakespeare? A tough-minded Parmenidean may argue that mythologists are really investigating not the nature of non-existent beasts but the beliefs of once-existent men, and that literary critics inquire into the intentions of Shakespeare and not the character of his fictions; and he might further suppose that historians really study the present traces of past ages and not those ages themselves. The argument deserves lengthy development; but in the end it is, I think, unconvincing. Nor can it account for the efforts of the paradigmatic inquirers; for natural scientists regularly study idealized entities: the objects of their theories are not the rough and ready physical bodies of our mundane world, but ideal approximations to them; they study frictionless surfaces, not ordinary tables or desks; they talk of an isolated system, not of a piece of our messy world. Physics is the most unreal of sciences.

We can and do think of things that do not exist; we can and do talk of things that do not exist; we can and do study things that do not exist. Such thoughts, such discourses, and such studies are not always fatuous. Parmenides has given us no good reason to reject those ordinary opinions; and in consequence his metaphysics is based upon a falsehood and defended by a specious argument. But for all that, Parmenides' views on the objects of inquiry are not merely antique exhibits in the roomy museum of philosophical follies: the arguments he adduces, though unsound, are ingenious and admirable; their conclusion, though false, has a strange plausibility and attractiveness. Many eminent philosophers have struck Parmenidean attitudes, and have done so for essentially Parmenidean reasons.

(d) *Gorgias on what is not*

Gorgias of Leontini 'in his book entitled *Concerning What Is Not or Concerning Nature* establishes three points—first, that nothing exists; second, that even if anything exists, it is inapprehensible to mankind; third, that even if it is apprehensible, at all events it is incommunicable and inexpressible to a neighbour' (Sextus, *adv Math* VII.65 = **82 B 3**). Gorgias was active in the last third of the fifth century; he was, at least primarily, a rhetorician; but his bizarre tract *Concerning What Is Not* has close connexions with Eleatic philosophy, and those connexions win it a place in a book on Presocratic argument.[24]

Some scholars make Gorgias a profound thinker, a nihilist and a sceptic; others treat *What Is Not* as a serious and witty *reductio* of Eleatic metaphysics; others again take it for a rhetorical *tour de force* or a sophisticated joke. A similar problem arises in connexion with Gorgias' *Helen*, which I discuss in a later chapter (below, pp. 523–30). I do not know what Gorgias intended me to think of his two pamphlets; nor do I lament that ignorance. Whatever Gorgias may have thought, his writings contain matters of some interest, and I shall take his writings (if not their author) seriously.

We do not possess the original text of *What Is Not*; instead, we have two paraphrases, one by Sextus (*adv Math* VII.66–86 = **82 B 3**) and the other in the *MXG* (979a10–980b22). I shall follow Sextus' account both because the text of the *MXG* is wretchedly corrupt and because Sextus' presentation and argument are, in my view, regularly superior to those of the *MXG*.[25]

Here I quote without comment the second part of Gorgias' treatise. The first and the third parts will be found on later pages (below, pp. 182, 471). Passages in square brackets are Sextan comments; and Sextus' paragraph numbers are included for ease of reference.

> (77) [It must next be shown that even if anything exists it is unknowable (*agnôston*) and unthinkable (*anepinoêton*) by mankind.] If what is thought of (*ta phronoumena*) [says Gorgias] is not existent, then what exists is not thought of. [And that is reasonable; for just as, if being white belongs to what is thought of, then being thought of belongs to what is white, so if not being existent belongs to what is thought of, of necessity not being thought of will belong to what exists. (78) Hence 'If what is thought of is not existent, then what exists is not thought of' is sound and preserves validity.] But what is thought of [for we must take this first] is not existent, as we shall establish. What exists,

therefore, is not thought of. Now that what is thought of is not existent is evident; (79) for if what is thought of is existent, then everything that is thought of exists—and that in the way in which one thinks of them. But that is not sensible. For it is not the case that if anyone thinks of a man flying or chariots running over the sea, a man thereby flies or chariots run over the sea. Hence it is not the case that what is thought of is existent.

(80) In addition, if what is thought of exists, what does not exist will not be thought of. For opposites belong to opposites, and what does not exist is opposite to what exists. And for this reason if being thought of belongs to what exists, then not being thought of will certainly belong to what does not exist. But this is absurd; for Scylla and Chimaera and many non-existent things are thought of. What exists, therefore, is not thought of.

(81) And just as what is seen is called visible because it is seen, and what is audible audible because it is heard, and we do not reject the visible because it is not heard or the audible because it is not seen (for each must be judged by its own sense and not by another), so too what is thought of will exist even if it is not seen by sight or heard by hearing, because it is grasped by its proper criterion. (82) If, then, someone thinks that chariots run over the sea, even if he does not see them, he must believe that chariots running over the sea exist. But this is absurd. What exists, therefore, is not thought of and apprehended (**154**).

Appendix: *A formalization of Parmenides' argument*

'$M\alpha\beta$' abbreviates 'α mentions β'; '$T\alpha\beta$', 'α thinks of β'; '$R\alpha\beta$', 'α recognizes β';'$S\alpha\beta$', 'α studies β'; '$E\alpha$', 'α exists'. Numerals in square brackets pair lines of the formalization with the steps in the informal presentation of section (c).

1	(1)	$(\forall x)(\forall y)(Sxy \rightarrow \sim Ey)$	A [(Bii)]
2	(2)	$(\exists x)(\exists y)Sxy$	A
3	(3)	$(\exists y)Say$	A
4	(4)	Sab	A
5	(5)	$(\forall y)(((\exists x)\Diamond Mxy \vee (\exists x)\Diamond Txy) \rightarrow \Diamond Ey)$	A [(9)]
6	(6)	$(\forall x)(\forall y)(\Diamond Txy \leftrightarrow \Diamond Ey)$	A [(3)]
7	(7)	$(\forall y)(\sim Ey \rightarrow \sim\Diamond Ey)$	A [(11)]
8	(8)	$(\forall x)(\forall y)(\Diamond Rxy \rightarrow \Diamond Txy)$	A [(7)]
9	(9)	$(\forall x)(\forall y)(Sxy \rightarrow (\Diamond Mxy \vee \Diamond Rxy))$	A [(14)]
1	(10)	$Sab \rightarrow \sim Eb$	1,UE [(13)]

1, 4	(11)	$\sim Eb$	4, 10, MPP
9	(12)	$Sab \rightarrow (\Diamond Mab \vee \Diamond Rab)$	9, UE [(15)]
4, 9	(13)	$\Diamond Mab \vee \Diamond Rab$	4, 12, MPP
8	(14)	$\Diamond Rab \rightarrow \Diamond Tab$	8, UE [(8)]
4, 8, 9	(15)	$\Diamond Mab \vee \Diamond Tab$	13, 14 T
5	(16)	$((\exists x) \Diamond Mxb \vee (\exists x) \Diamond Txb) \rightarrow \Diamond Eb$	5, UE
6	(17)	$\Diamond Tab \leftrightarrow \Diamond Eb$	6, UE [cf. (4)]
18	(18)	$\Diamond Mab$	A
18	(19)	$(\exists x) \Diamond Mxb$	18, EI
5, 18	(20)	$\Diamond Eb$	16, 19, T
21	(21)	$\Diamond Tab$	A
6, 21	(22)	$\Diamond Eb$	17, 21, T
4, 5, 6, 8, 9	(23)	$\Diamond Eb$	15, 18, 20, 21, 22, v E
7	(24)	$\sim Eb \rightarrow \sim\Diamond Eb$	7, UE
4, 5, 6, 7, 8, 9	(25)	Eb	23, 24, MTT
1, 4, 5, 6, 7, 8, 9	(26)	$Eb \& \sim Eb$	25, 11 & I
4, 5, 6, 7, 8, 9	(27)	$\sim(\forall x)(\forall y)(Sxy \rightarrow \sim Ey)$	1, 26 RAA
2, 5, 6, 7, 8, 9	(28)	$\sim(\forall x)(\forall y)(Sxy \rightarrow \sim Ey)$	3, 4, 27 EE; 2, 3, 27 EE

The argument is, I think, formally valid. ('T' stands for 'tautology'; the other rules are standard.) It is not elegant; but I blame its lack of beauty on Parmenides.

X

Being and Becoming

(a) *Parmenidean metaphysics*

According to Aristotle, metaphysics or 'first philosophy' is the study of 'being *qua* being'. The Aristotelian metaphysician, in other words, attempts to discover, to elucidate and to analyse the properties which must belong to every existent thing as such. And Aristotle's notion of metaphysics, in a somewhat relaxed and sophisticated form, is still the modern notion. The first full-blooded metaphysician was Parmenides; and the first systematic metaphysics was the Eleatic philosophy. We have two accounts, both almost complete, of Eleatic metaphysics. The first is contained in fragment **B 8** of Parmenides, the second occupies the several fragments of Melissus; the two accounts differ in important detail, but their overall structure and their general intellectual *nisus* are one and the same; and it is, I think, helpful as well as convenient to consider them side by side.

Having argued that every object of inquiry must exist, Parmenides proceeds to consider the properties that objects of inquiry, as existent, must possess—the properties of beings *qua* being. Parmenides' consideration is strictly deductive: 'he agreed to nothing if it did not seem necessary, while his predecessors used to make assertions without demonstration' (Eudemus, fr. 43W = **28 A 28**). The point has often been repeated; and it is borne out by the fragments of Parmenides' poem. **B 8** is an intricate and concise argumentation, continuous in form and some fifty lines long. Simplicius, who preserves the fragment for us, implies that it contains the whole of Parmenides' metaphysics (cf. **A 21**); and its self-contained form corroborates the implication.[1] Thus we have, in these few compact lines, a complete deductive metaphysics.

On the strength of **B 8** Parmenides has been hailed as the founder of logic. The title is not wholly apposite, for Parmenides does not theorize about logic, and he was not the first thinker to propound deductive arguments; but it happily underlines the fact that in **B 8** we have a deduction far more complex and far more self-conscious than anything the Presocratics have yet offered us. Melissus' argument is as complicated as his master's, and Zeno's paradoxes are as sophisticated as anything in Parmenides; but Melissus is essentially a derivative thinker, and Zeno does not show the logical stamina of Parmenides. We meet nothing comparable to **B 8** until the middle dialogues of Plato.

Further subtlety is sometimes sought. In **B 5** the goddess announces:

> It is indifferent to me
> whence I begin; for I shall come back there again (**155**).

The announcement has been attached to **B 8** and given a logical sense: the order of the 'signposts' along the Way of Truth is indifferent; we may begin at any one of them and proceed to deduce all the others. In other words, the various properties of existents are all mutually implicative: truth is indeed 'well-rounded' (**B 1**. 29). I do not think that this interpretation of **155** can be ruled out; and it is possible to invent arguments, similar to those of **B 8**, which would support the thesis it ascribes to Parmenides. But as it stands **B 8** does not attempt to establish the mutual implication of all the 'signposts'; and **155** is certainly capable of different interpretations. Whether Parmenides' metaphysics contains the subtlety of circularity may be left an open question.[2]

A different subtlety has recently been found in **B 8**: 'to repeat that memorable image of Wittgenstein, Parmenides' argument is a ladder to be climbed up and thrown away. Such arguments are not, [to] put it picturesquely, horizontal deductions; if they parade as deductions they are patently self-defeating.'[3] Parmenides' arguments certainly do parade as deductions: the language of **B 8** leaves no doubt about that. Whether and in what sense they are self-defeating are questions which must wait upon a detailed examination of their successive steps. Here I consider only the suggestion that the deductive parade is somehow a sham: the arguments are not really deductive and self-defeating; they are something else—not deductions at all, or at least not 'horizontal' deductions.

I find myself unable to understand the suggestion. The adjective 'horizontal' is no doubt picturesque; but the picture tells no story: I do not know what a non-horizontal deduction might be. Equally, the notion that Parmenides' argument might not be deductive at all escapes me: how can there be an argumentative sequence that is not, or is not equivalent to, a deductive train? Parmenides' arguments are hardly inductive or analogical. Thus I shall ignore the finer niceties of logic which have been read into **B 8**, and treat it as an ordinary deduction. Such a conventional treatment is in any case quite hard enough.

Here, first, is a translation of the whole of **B 8**. The fragment contains textual problems, to some of which I shall later advert; and its obscurities are deliberately left dark by my fairly literal rendering. For all that, some of the character of the piece may come across.

A single story of a road
is left—that it is. And on it are signs
very many in number—that, being, it is ungenerated and undestroyed,
whole, of one kind and motionless, and balanced.
Nor was it ever, nor will it be; since now it is, all together,
one, continuous. For what generation will you inquire out for it?
How, whence, did it grow? Neither from what is not will I allow
you to say or think; for it is not sayable nor thinkable
that it is not. And what *need* would have aroused it
later or sooner, starting from nothing, to come into being?
In this way it is necessary either for it to be altogether or not.
Nor ever from what is will the strength of trust allow
it to become something apart from itself. For that reason neither to come into being
nor to perish has justice allowed it, relaxing her chains;
but she holds it. And judgment about these things lies in this:
it is or it is not. And it has been judged, as is necessary,
to leave the one [road] unthought and unnamed (for it is not a true
road) and to take the other, whereby it is, actually to be real.
And how might what is be then? And how might it have come into being?
For if it came into being, it is not, nor if it is about to be at some time
Thus coming into being is extinguished, and destruction is unheard of.
Nor is it divided, since it is all alike
And neither more here (which would prevent it from holding together)
nor less, but it is all full of what is.
Hence it is continuous; for what is neighbours what is.

And motionless in the limits of great chains
it is, beginningless, endless; since coming into being and destruction
have wandered far away and true trust has driven them off.
And the same, remaining in the same state, it lies in itself
and thus firmly remains there. For a strong necessity
holds it in chains of a limit which fences it about,
because it is not right for what is to be incomplete;
for it is not lacking—otherwise it would want everything.
And the same thing are to think and a thought that it is.
For not without what is, on which what has been expressed depends,
will you find thinking; for nothing is or will be
other than what is—since *that* has Fate fettered
to be whole and motionless. Hence all things are a name
which mortals have laid down, trusting them to be true—
to come into being and to perish, to be and not,
and to change place and to alter bright colour.
And since there is a furthest limit, it is complete
from all directions, like the bulk of a well-rounded ball,
equally balanced from the centre in all directions. For neither any more
nor any weaker can it be here or here.
For neither is there anything that is not, which might stop it from reaching
its like; nor is there anything that is, so that there might be of what is
here more and there less—since it is all inviolable.
Hence, equal from all directions, it meets the limits alike.
Here I cease the trustworthy account and thought
about the truth . . . (**156**).

The logical articulation of the fragment is, I think, less clear than is sometimes claimed. And a preliminary statement of my view of its structure may not come amiss: support for this statement must wait upon detailed discussion.

The fragment begins with a prospectus, listing the 'signs' along the Way of Truth; in other words, summarily stating the properties of being *qua* being which **156** is to demonstrate.[4] The prospectus occupies lines 3–4. Line 3 gives a pair of properties, ungenerability and imperishability: they are argued for in lines 5–21. The beginning of line 4 presents a textual *crux*: I follow the modern orthodoxy, and read *oulon mounogenes te*.[5] *Oulon* ('whole') is taken up in lines

22–5. I incline to associate *mounogenes* closely with *atremes* ('motionless'), and I suppose that 'monogeneity' and immobility are jointly advocated in lines 26–33. At the end of line 4 the manuscripts, with trivial exceptions, read *êd' ateleston* ('and incomplete'). I agree with those scholars who find that reading incompatible with what is said in lines 32 and 42. Of the several conjectures, I have hesitatingly preferred *êd' atalanton*.[6] And I suppose that this last announcement in the prospectus is answered in lines 42–9. Lines 34–41 remain: I cannot associate them with anything in the prospectus; and I have sympathy with the proposal to place them after line 49, and to read them as a sort of summary of the Way of Truth. The plausibility of that suggestion may be assessed later on.

(b) *Melissus' metaphysics*

Melissus of Samos presents a melancholy aspect in the official portrait: his one book *Concerning Nature or What Is* (Simplicius, **30 A 4**) is no more than a cheap edition of Parmenides' poem, full of misprints and misunderstandings, to be purchased only by the intellectually impoverished. Aristotle initiated that *damnatio memoriae*: Melissus was 'a trifle crude' (*Met* 985b26 = **A 7**), his reasoning 'uncouth' (*Phys* 186a9 = **A 7**). Aristotle's magisterial judgment was elaborated by the author of *MXG* (**A 5**) and generally parroted by the later Peripatetics (**A 10a R**).[7] An amateur philosopher (and an amateur admiral), Melissus has a certain historical and personal interest; yet his fragments will hardly divert or detain us if we can listen to his master's voice.

Aristotle's judgment should be contested. Melissus was not despised by Plato (*Theaetetus*, 183E = **A 7a R**); and there is some evidence that he was for a time regarded as the authoritative spokesman of Eleatic thought.[8] His plain prose has an admirable lucidity, and a certain naive charm: it abandons the tortuous expression of Parmenides, but retains the conscientious intricacy of his logical argumentation. The Eleatic system is stated with strength, and also with clarity. Nor is Melissus wholly derivative: if one of his aims was the exposition and defence of the Parmenidean position, at several points he deliberately rejects his inheritance and advances views entirely his own. Perhaps he is a trifle crude; certainly he cannot be held innocent of logical blunders. (What philosopher can?) But his fragments are, to my mind, as interesting as those of Parmenides, and equally deserving of sympathetic study.

The ten surviving fragments are all preserved by Simplicius; with perhaps two exceptions they form part of a systematic deduction parallel to Parmenides' Way of Truth. The fragments themselves are sufficient to establish the general outline of Melissus' progress; and corroboration is available from the running paraphrases in the *MXG* (**A 5**), in Simplicius (*ad* **B 1–7**), and in Philoponus (**A 10a R**). Here, then, is a sketch of Melissus' system.

If we can think and talk about any object *O*, then it is axiomatic that

(A) *O* exists.

Melissus lays down (A) and then asks what follows from it;[9] he argues first, in **B 1**, that:

(T1) *O* is ungenerated,

and then infers from (T1), in **B 1** and **B 2** that:

(T2) *O* is eternal,

or in other words (**B 2**, **B 4**) that:

(T3) *O* is temporally unlimited.

An analogous argument (**B 3**, **B 4**) yields:

(T4) *O* is spatially unlimited.

From (T4) we are next to infer (**B 5**, **B 6**) that:

(T5) *O* is unique.

It seems certain (cf. **B** 7.1) that Melissus proceeded from (T5) to:

(T6) *O* is homogeneous.

The long fragment, or pair of fragments, **B** 7, passes from (T6) to:

(T7) *O* does not alter,

and hence to:

(T8) *O* is not destroyed,

(T9) *O* does not grow,

(T10) *O* is not rearranged,

(T11) *O* does not suffer pain,

and:

(T12) *O* does not suffer anguish.

Next,[10] Melissus proceeds to:

(T13) *O* is not empty,

and hence to:

(T14) *O* is full.

And from (T14) he infers both:

(T15) *O* does not move,

and:

(T16) *O* is not dense or rare.

Finally **B 10** infers from (T15) to:

(T17) *O* is not divided up.

That, so far as we know, is the end of Melissus' metaphysics. Two fragments remain: **B 8** contains an interesting argument against the validity of sense-perception, which came from, or perhaps formed, a polemical appendix to Melissus' work; and **B 9** is a controversial remark about incorporeality. I shall deal separately with these two fragments (below, pp. 298, 227).

As a coda to this section I quote the first part of Gorgias on *What is Not*. The passage is not an exposition of Eleatic metaphysics and does not stand in any sense as a parallel to **B 8** of Parmenides or the fragments of Melissus; but I shall on occasion refer to it, and it is pertinent and strange enough to warrant transcription. Again, I follow Sextus' version (above, p. 173).

> (66) [That nothing exists, he argues in this fashion:] If something exists, either what exists exists or what does not exist exists or both what exists and what does not exist exist. But what exists does not exist, as I will establish, nor does what does not exist, as I will show, nor do both what exists and what does not exist, as I will teach. It is not the case, therefore, that something exists.
> (67) Now that which does not exist does not exist. For if what does not exist exists, at the same time it will exist and it will not exist—in so far as it is conceived of as not existing, it will not exist; in so far as, not existing, it exists,[11] it will again exist. But it is utterly absurd that anything should at the same time both exist and not exist. What does not exist, therefore, does not exist. Again, if what does not exist exists, what exists will not exist; for these are contrary to one another, and if existence holds of what does not exist, non-existence will hold of what exists. But it is not the case that what exists does not exist; nor, then, will what does not exist exist.
> (68) But neither does what exists exist. For if what exists exists, it is either eternal or generated or at the same time eternal and generated; but it is neither eternal nor generated, nor both, as we shall prove; what exists, therefore, does not exist. If what exists is eternal (for we must begin here), it does not have any beginning.
> (69) For everything that comes into being has a beginning, but what is eternal, being ungenerated, has no beginning. But not having a beginning, it is unlimited. And if it is unlimited, it is nowhere. For if it is anywhere, that in which it is is different from it, and thus what is, being contained by something, will no longer be unlimited; for the container is greater than the contained, but nothing is greater than what is unlimited; so that what is unlimited will not be anywhere. (70) Nor is it surrounded by itself. For then that in which it is and that which is in it will be the same, and what exists will become two, place and body (for that in which

it is is place and that which is in it is body). But that is absurd. Nor, then, is what exists in itself. Hence if what exists is eternal, it is unlimited and if it is unlimited, it is nowhere; and if it is nowhere, it does not exist. Hence if what exists is eternal, it is not existent at all. (71) But neither can what exists be generated. For if it was generated, it was generated either from an existent or from a non-existent. But it was not generated from an existent; for if it is existent, it was not generated but already exists. Nor from a non-existent; for what does not exist cannot generate anything because, of necessity, that which generates anything must partake in subsistence. What exists, therefore, is not generated. (72) And by the same token it is not both together, eternal and generated at the same time. For these are destructive of one another, and if what exists is eternal it was not generated; and if it was generated, it is not eternal. Thus if what exists is neither eternal nor generated nor both together, what exists will not exist.

(73) Again, if it exists, it is either one or many. But it is neither one nor many, as will be established; what exists, therefore, does not exist. If it is one, it is either a quantity or continuous or a magnitude or a body. But whichever of these it is, it is not one—but if it is a quantity it will be divided; if continuous, it will be split; and similarly if it is conceived as a magnitude it will not be indivisible; and if it is a body, it will be threefold, for it will have length and breadth and depth. But it is absurd to say that what exists is none of these; what exists, therefore, is not one. (74) Nor is it many. For if it is not one, it will not be many. For the many too are taken away with it. That neither what exists nor what does not exist exists is clear from these considerations.

(75) That both together—what exists and what does not exist—do not exist is easy to argue for. If what does not exist exists and what exists exists, what does not exist will be the same as what exists, as far as existence goes; and because of that, neither of them exists. For that what does not exist does not exist is agreed; and what exists has been proved to be the same as this; it too, then, will not exist. (76) But if what exists is the same as what does not exist, it is not possible for both to exist. For if both do, they are not the same; and if they are the same, not both do. From which it follows that nothing exists. For if neither what exists nor what does not exist nor both exist, and if nothing apart from these is conceived of, then nothing exists (**157**).

(c) *On generation and destruction*

Melissus' fragment **B 1** stood at or near the beginning of his book: I doubt that he offered a preliminary paragraph justifying axiom (A), that *O* exists;[12] rather, he assumes the success of Parmenides' attack on the two false roads of inquiry, or else he is uninterested in any alternative hypothesis to (A). **B 1** contains only the briefest argument for (T1), the theorem of ungenerability:

> Whatever is[13] always was and always will be. For if it came into being, it is necessary that it was nothing before coming into being; now if it was nothing, in no way might anything come into being from nothing (**158**).

The *MXG* (975a3 = **A 5**) pertinently asks why we should accept Melissus' brusque assertion that 'nothing comes from nothing'. Melissus has no explicit answer; but it is evident that here too he is relying on Parmenidean precedent. And indeed, in Melissus' presentation of Eleatic philosophy, (T1) has little intrinsic importance: it is only adduced in the course of an argument for (T2)—(T5).

In order to grasp the Eleatic attack on generation, therefore, we must undertake the arduous task of elucidating the opening argument in Parmenides' deduction. It will emerge, however, that Melissus is not wholly useless: there are two features of **B 1** which throw light on Parmenides' argument and confirm two otherwise controversial items of interpretation.[14]

I turn, then, to Parmenides, **156**, lines 5–21. I leave lines 5–6a aside for the moment, and begin with the questions of 6b–7a: 'For what generation will you inquire out for it? How, whence, did it grow?' Some scholars distinguish between the question of generation and the question of growth;[15] but I find nothing in the subsequent lines that reflects such a distinction, and I take 'grow' as a picturesque synonym for 'come into being'. On the other hand, 'how' and 'whence' do not appear to be synonymous: we appear we have two questions: How could *O* have come into being? Whence did *O* come into being?

Most commentators focus their attention on the latter question; and they find that Parmenides argues his case by way of a dilemma: 'Suppose that *O* comes into being from *O′*; i.e., that *O′* generates *O*. Then either *O′* is non-existent or *O* is existent. But *O′* cannot be non-existent (lines 7b–11); nor can it be existent (lines 12–13a). Hence *O* cannot come into being at all.'

That interpretation seems to me to be mistaken on two counts. (It also requires an emendation in line 12; but I do not cite that as an objection; for, on different grounds, I accept the change of text.)[16]

First, I do not find a dilemmatic argument in Parmenides' poem; nor do I find one in Melissus, who summarily repeats Parmenides' argument against generation; nor yet in Empedocles, who makes self-conscious use of the same argument. Both of Parmenides' followers assert simply that *O* cannot come into being from what is not; they do not add 'or from what is'.[17] Second, I dislike the importation of generators into Parmenides' argument; for that importation burdens him with a patent *non sequitur*: having urged that *O* is not generated by *O'* he is made to conclude that *O* does not come into being at all. The interpretation has him use the tacit, undefended, and unevident premiss that whatever comes into being is *brought* into being by something. An interpretation which does not insinuate that premiss is preferable.

Let us take a closer look at Parmenides' phrase 'from what is not' (*ek mê eontos*). Phrases of the form 'from X' (*ek* X) take more than one paraphrase: I have already listed several different 'senses' of 'from' in connexion with Milesian monism. One such 'sense' (sense (v) of p. 40) has us gloss '*Y* comes into being from *X*' by: 'What was formerly *X* is now *Y*'. The stock Aristotelian example is 'the musical comes into being from the unmusical' (*Phys* 190a23), i.e. 'what was unmusical is now musical'. The hypothesis which Parmenides rejects is: 'What is comes into being from what is not'. I suggest that we interpret that hypothesis thus: 'Something that was non-existent is now existent'. Nothing speaks against that interpretation; and two texts speak for it. First, in **158** Melissus says that 'if it came into being, it is necessary that it was nothing (*mêden*) before coming into being'. That is Melissus' version of the hypothesis that 'what is came into being from what is not' (for *mêden* is synonymous with *to mê on*: above, p. 166); and he plainly understands the hypothesis as I have interpreted it. Second, Empedocles' account of Parmenides' argument presupposes the same interpretation: in **31 B 11** he berates those who 'expect that what formerly is not comes into being'; and he explains that 'it is impossible to come into being from what in no way exists' (**B 12**). Melissus and Empedocles interpret '*O* comes into being from what is not' as '*O*, which formerly did not exist, now exists'; and their interpretation is authoritative.

The generative dilemma disappears from Parmenides' text. In its place, we find the following taut argument: 'If *O* exists, then *O* cannot have come into being. For if *O* comes into being at *t*, then prior to *t* *O* did not exist. But, by the argument in **148–150** against Road (B), it is impossible for *O* not to exist.'

Is that a good argument? There are at least three objections to it.

First: 'Parmenides says in lines 8b–9a that "it is not sayable nor thinkable that it is not"; and that is taken as a reference to the rejection of Road (B). But in **148–150** Parmenides only urged that if *O* does not exist, you cannot think of *O*; he did not urge that you cannot think that *O* does not exist.' The objection is not fatal; if I can think *that* *O* is something or other, then presumably I can think of *O*; hence if I cannot think of *O* I cannot think that *O* does not exist.

The second objection follows immediately: 'Parmenides says that it is unthinkable that *O* does not exist; he needs the premiss that it is *impossible* that *O* should not exist. How can he bridge the gap between inconceivability and impossibility?' Parmenides himself makes no attempt to bridge the gap. He is content to observe that the judgment '*O* does not exist' cannot be true. If it makes sense, it is false; and if it makes no sense, it is of course neither true nor false. And perhaps this is all that he needs; for an opponent cannot intelligibly say that although the *judgment* that *O* does not exist cannot be true, nevertheless *O* may not exist: such a retort is simply contradictory. The opponent might reply that some facts are ineffable and unjudgeable; but again Parmenides has an answer: If there are unjudgeable facts, *O*'s non-existence cannot be among them; for if it were a fact that *O* does not exist, then the judgment that *O* does not exist would be true. If we drive a wedge between facts and judgments, then the facts must be utterly unspecifiable: the opponent wants, impossibly, a fact that is *both* specifiable *and* unjudgeable.

The third objection is more severe. The Parmenidean connexion between thought and existence, as I have presented it so far, has not carried any explicit reference to time. Yet in the context of a discussion on generation such reference must be made; and the result of making it surely yields:

(1) $(\forall t)$ (if at t a thinks that *O* exists, then *O* exists at t).

Now the suggestion that *O* comes into being 'from what does not exist' amounts to:

(2) *O* exists at t and at some t' prior to t *O* did not exist.

But no contradiction can be won from (1) and (2): the first conjunct of (2) guarantees the thinkability of *O*; and that seems enough to sustain the thought that *O* did not exist. The time of the thought and the time of *O*'s putative non-existence are different: Parmenides has at most shown the absurdity of '*O* does not exist'; he has not yet shown any absurdity in '*O* did not exist'. And (2) requires only the latter judgment.

Now Parmenides might counter that argument by appealing to a general and plausible thesis about the relation between truth and time, viz:

(3) $(\forall t)$ $(\forall t')$ (if at t a truly says that [P at t'], then if at t' a says that [P at t'] he speaks truly).

What is now truly said to have happened yesterday could yesterday have been truly said to be happening then. Hence if at t I can truly say that O did not exist at t', at t' I might truly have said 'O does not now exist'. But, by (1), I cannot truly say at t' 'O does not now exist'; hence at t I cannot truly say 'O did not exist at t''.

Of course, anyone who accepts both (1) and (3) will be obliged to infer that no true propositions at all can be made about beings whose existence has temporal limits. That conclusion may seem absurd, yet it is not a conclusion to make an Eleatic shudder; and I am inclined to think that Parmenides' argument in lines 6–9 has considerable force. If I reject it, that is because I have already rejected (1). I suspect, indeed, that some who are sceptical of (1) will still feel some force in Parmenides' first argument against generation; I shall return briefly to this point at the end of my discussion of lines 5–21.

The next argument occupies lines 9b–10: it takes up the question of *how* O might come into being 'starting from nothing'. (*Tou mêdenos* again means *tou mê eontos*.) '. . . what *need* would have aroused it later or sooner . . .?' The phrase *husteron ê prosthen* is sometimes translated 'later rather than sooner', or 'at one time rather than at another'. Thus Parmenides is applying the Principle of Sufficient Reason, and his argument runs as follows:

(4) If O does not exist during a period T, then for any two points t, t' in T, O has a property P at t if and only if it has P at t'.

(5) If O comes into existence at t, then for some P, O comes into existence at t because O has P at t.

Suppose, then:

(6) O comes into existence at t_1.

Then:

(7) O comes into existence at t_1 because O has P at t_1.

Hence:

(8) O has P at t_1,

and so, by (4):

(9) O has P at t_2.

But from (9) and (7) we can infer:

(10) O comes into existence at t_2.

And that is incompatible with (6).

The Principle of Sufficient Reason operates at step (5) and at step (10): (5) is an application of the requirement that all happenings have *some* explanation; and the inference from (9) and (7) to (10) assumes that the explanation must be *sufficient* for what it explains. Compare Anaximander's argument about the stability of the earth (above, pp. 23–6).

There is a fairly obvious weakness here: (4) is, at best, true only if *P* is restricted to non-relational properties of *O*; yet it is precisely in terms of its relational properties that we would hope to explain the generation of *O*: *O* may not change intrinsically during *T*; but at t_1 something may hold of it which does not hold of it at t_2—the demiurge may have determined upon t_1 as the appropriate time to create *O*.

That may encourage us to seek a simpler argument in the text; and scholars have doubted the propriety of ascribing (4)—(10) to Parmenides, both on linguistic and on historical grounds.[18] If we revert to the earlier translation, 'later *or* sooner', and gloss that by 'at any particular time', we need only ascribe to Parmenides the blunt assertion that if *O* does not exist prior to *t*, then there is no reason why *O* should come into existence at *t*, or at any other time. Unfortunately, that simple argument is open to a simple version of the objection to the sophisticated argument: why ever should we suppose that an intelligent agent might not pick upon *t* as the time for exercising his creative powers on *O*?

The objection raises interesting issues; but I think that Parmenides would be unmoved by it. For his line of thought is, I suspect, simpler than is usually supposed: if *O* does not exist at *t*, then nothing can 'rouse' it into existence, for it is not there to be 'roused'. And if we soften 'rousing' into creating we are no better off: *a* cannot create *O* at *t* unless he can think of *O* at *t*. And since, *ex hypothesi, O* does not exist at *t*, then by (1) *a* cannot think of *O*. Thus construed, Parmenides' second argument has as much force as his first.

The two arguments are summarized in line 11; but the line is puzzling. '*Pampan*' ('altogether') must bear a temporal sense; and '*houtôs*' ('in this way') should mean something like 'as far as the considerations so far broached take us'. Thus I gloss the line as follows: 'As far as generation goes, *O* either exists at all times or not at any'.[19] The case against generation is now concluded: unless we can make out a case for the destructibility of what exists, we must allow its sempiternity.

We therefore expect an argument against destruction; and line 14 implies that the expectation has been satisfied. But lines 12–13 are desperately difficult: they contain a textual *crux*, and two ambiguities.

I have translated an emended version of line 12: the manuscripts read '*ek mê eontos*': 'Nor from what is not will the strength of trust allow *gignesthai ti par' auto*'. In the last phrase, '*ti*' may be either subject or complement of '*gignesthai*', and '*auto*' may refer either to 'what is' or to 'what is not'. Thus the manuscript text yields four readings: (i) 'From what is not, it is not possible for anything to come into being apart from what is'; (ii) 'From what is not, it is not possible for anything to come into being apart from what is not'; (iii) 'From what is not, it is not possible for it to become anything apart from what is'; (iv) 'From what is not, it is not possible for it to become anything apart from what is not'.

None of (i)—(iv) is satisfactory: (iii) and (iv) make no decent sense at all; (i) is impotent as an argument against generation and cannot constitute an argument against destruction. If we construe 'from' in the generator sense, then we can conjure an argument out of (ii): 'If O' does not exist and O' generates O, then O does not exist; hence if O exists and is generated from O', it is not the case that O' does not exist.' But I doubt if that argument is Parmenidean: first, the very notion of the generation of non-entities is remote from Parmenides' thought; second, (ii) interprets 'from' in the fashion which raises problems for the rest of lines 5–21; and third, (ii) has no bearing upon destruction.

Several scholars, for different reasons, have emended '*ek mê eontos*' in line 12 to '*ek tou eontos*' or some equivalent phrase.[20] With that text '*auto*' can only pick up 'what is'; and there are thus just two readings: (v) 'From what is, it is not possible for anything to come into being apart from what is'; (vi) 'From what is, it is not possible for it to become anything apart from what is'.

Reading (v) yields the gloss: 'If O exists, and O generates O', then $O = O'$'. There is an argument against generation here if we add the plausible premiss that a thing cannot generate itself: 'If O exists and generates something, it generates itself; but nothing generates itself; hence nothing can be generated from what exists'. But I find it hard to impute that argument to Parmenides: the thesis that existent generators could only generate themselves is bizarre, and can hardly stand unsupported in the text; nor does that reading yield an argument against destruction.

I therefore turn to reading (vi); and my translation is designed to fit that reading. Given (vi), the word 'from' has the same sense as I have given it earlier; and Parmenides offers us an implicit argument against destruction. I paraphrase: 'Nor from a state of existence can O become something other than what is'; i.e., O cannot change from existing to not existing, O cannot be destroyed. That offers a statement, not an argument. Yet it is obvious what argument we are to supply: if O is destroyed at t, then O exists before t and O does not exist after *t*. But 'it is not sayable nor thinkable that it is not.' The objections and replies that I rehearsed in connexion with lines 6–9 will bear equally on lines 12–13; I shall not march them out again. It is worth saying, however, that those philosophers who sympathize with lines 6–9 are unlikely to extend their sympathy to 12–13: Parmenides sees an exact symmetry between generation and destruction, past and future: the neo-Parmenideans feel an important asymmetry here. That feeling will be discussed later.

We can now conclude that either *O* exists 'altogether'—is sempiternal, or else it exists not at all. And lines 13b–18, relaxing the tight stays of Parmenides' argument, remind us that the second alternative is already ruled out; for we are travelling along the Way of Truth.

(d) *Being and time*

By now, then, 'coming into being is extinguished and destruction is unheard of'; but before he states that conclusion Parmenides interposes two more lines of argument. Line 19 offers two theses, in the form of rhetorical questions; and line 20 offers two supporting reasons. Theses and reasons are arranged chiastically.[21]

The second reason is unambiguously expressed: 'it is not, . . . if it is about to be at some time'; i.e.:

(1) If *O* is going to exist in the future, *O* does not exist.

The first thesis is crabbed: 'how might what is be then?' We can extract an intelligible thought if we read 'then' (*epeita*) as 'in the future'; thus:

(2) If *O* exists, *O* will not exist in the future.

For (2) actually follows from (1); hence (1) may reasonably be advanced in support of (2). And Parmenides plainly means us to infer that *O* will not exist in the future.

The first reason reads: 'if it came into being, it is not'; i.e.:

(3) If *O* came into existence, *O* does not exist.

And the second thesis, correspondingly, should run:

(4) If *O* exists, *O* did not come into existence.

That, at least, is the natural construe; but it suffers from a severe disability; for the deliberately symmetrical form of Parmenides' verse turns out to mask an asymmetrical content: (1) talks about future being, (3) about past *becoming*. There are two ways of restoring symmetry. Some interpret '*genoito*' and '*egento*' in lines 19–20 as though they were past tenses of '*einai*': 'And how could it *have existed*? For if it *existed*, it is not'. Then (3) denies past existence to what is, just as (1) denies future existence to it. Alternatively, '*epeita peloi*' and '*mellei*' may be twisted to refer to future becoming: 'How might what is *come to be* in the future? . . . nor if it is going *to come to be*'. Then (1) denies future becoming to what is, just as (3) denies past becoming to it.

Neither of those suggestions fits the Greek easily; and neither fits the context peculiarly well: on the first reading we have a pair of thoughts which are inappropriate harbingers of the conclusion at line 21. On the second reading, we have a further otiose attack on generation. Moreover, on neither interpretation does Parmenides have a pellucid argument. On the second reading, the case against future generation is sound: if *O* is to come into existence at *t*, *O* does not now exist. But the case against past generation cannot be stated in a parallel fashion: from '*O* came into existence at *t*' it does not follow that *O* does not exist now; in order to extract that conclusion we must pad the argument with Parmenidean premisses drawn from earlier parts of the attack on generation: 'if *O* came into existence at *t*, then before *t* *O* did not exist; and if *O* ever failed to exist, *O* always fails to exist'.

On the first reading, we cannot find a sound argument either for (1) or for (3). The first reading does, however, suggest a plausible explanation of why Parmenides should have thought (1) and (3) true. There is a distinction between what a man implies in stating something, and what his statement implies. Very roughly, in saying that *P* I imply that *Q* if it would be odd or unconventional or misleading for me, in those circumstances, to say that *P*, if I also believed that not-*Q*. *P* implies *Q* if it is impossible for *P* to be true and *Q* false. If you ask me how many hours a day I work, and I say 'At least four', I imply that I do not regularly work for ten hours a day; but my statement does not imply that. Similarly, if I say '*a* is going to be *F*' or '*a* was *F*', then I imply that (at least as far as I know) *a* is not yet, or no longer, *F*; but what I say does not have those implications. Now it is easy to confuse the implications of what I say with the implications of my saying it; and I suggest that Parmenides may have fallen into just such a confusion here: observing, correctly, that anyone who says '*O* was' or '*O* will be' implies that *O* is not now, he mistakenly inferred that '*O* was' and '*O* will be' both imply '*O* is not', and hence concluded that *O* was not and *O* will not be.

On the whole, then, I incline to the interpretation of lines 19–20 which has them deny past and future existence to what now exists. Evidently, that interpretation raises severe difficulties of a logical and of a structural nature: how can Parmenides argue against the generation of what exists and yet hold that what exists did not exist in the past? Why does he interpolate lines 19–20 before his conclusion, in line 21, about generation and destruction? Before facing up to those difficulties, I shall attempt to elucidate lines 5–6a of **156**:

> Nor was it ever, nor will it be; since now it is, all together,
> one, continuous.

Textually the lines are far from certain; but, for once, the variant readings offer no serious variation in sense. I begin with three preliminary points. First, we should not take 5–6a as part of Parmenides' prospectus; for the lines overtly contain an argument. Second, we may not divorce 5–6a from 6b–21; for an explanatory particle unites them. Third, the three phrases *homou pan, hen* and *suneches* ('all together, one, continuous') are synonymous, or at least mutually explicatory. To say that *O* is 'one' is to say that it is a unity, and a prime way of being unitary is being continuous (cf. Aristotle, *Met* 1015b36–1016a3). Continuity here is temporal: *O* is continuous if there are no temporal gaps in its career. And to say that *O* is 'all together' is only to say that it is 'altogether' (line 11): there are no temporal periods which do not contain it.[22] Thus the conclusion expressed in line 5a is derived from a premiss asserting that *O* is temporally continuous; and that premiss, it seems, is in turn to be derived from the argument in lines 6b–21 that I have already analysed.

What conclusion does line 5a state? At least four interpretations are on the market. (a) Some say that line 5a merely denies generation and destruction, in a rhetorically elevated style; and that view has tidiness in its favour, for it leaves lines 5–21 with a single subject. Tidiness, however, is outweighed by two considerations: line 5a purports to offer a deduction from the ungenerability of what is, and not merely to assert its ungenerability; and only the wildest rhetorical fancy will read line 5 as expressing the same sentiment as lines 3 and 21.[23] (b) Others say that line 5a states the omnitemporality of what exists; and that view comports well with lines 6b–21; for if *O* is ungenerable and indestructible, it exists for ever. But I am unable to see how an assertion that *O* did not and will not exist can amount to an expression of the omnitemporality of *O*. (c) Third, it is said that line 5a sets *O* outside the boundaries of time: *O* is a timeless entity in the sense that no temporally tagged predications hold good of it. That interpretation sees Parmenides through Platonic eyes, and reads into line 5a an adumbration of the doctrine advanced in the *Timaeus* (37D–38A). There are attractions in the view; but again there is strong textual evidence against it: line 5 expressly says that *O* 'now is' (*nun estin*), and that is flatly incompatible with the thesis of atemporality. (d) Finally, it has been supposed that *O* exists in time and endures through time, but that all times are eternally present in a changeless now. Such a notion has had theological and poetical adherents; thus God, according to Plutarch, 'exists in no time, but in the changeless and timeless *aiôn* . . . being one, he has filled eternity in a single now' (*de E apud Delphos* 393AB). But that notion is hopelessly confused: there is no sense in the suggestion that time past and time future are all one in time present, that all moments are eternally present; for the idea of a plurality of times implies a past or a future distinct from the present. I am loth to ascribe such a vile thought to Parmenides.

What, then, does line 5a say? The message seems to be simple enough: '*O* exists now' is true; '*O* exists at *t*' is false whenever *t* is distinct from now, either past or future. Is that message coherently supported by lines 5b–6a? Is it coherent in itself? Does it cohere with the views expounded in lines 6b–21?

It is tempting to find a sophisticated and powerful argument in 5b–6a.[24] Parmenides may be thought to rely tacitly upon Leibniz' principle of the Identity of Indiscernibles, applied to temporal instants: 'Two instants in *O*'s career are distinct only if they are "discernible": only if something is true of *O* at one instant and not true of it at another. But *O* never changes in any respect—it is "all together" or alike in all respects—and so nothing could be true of it at any instant in its career which was not true of it at every instant. Hence there are no distinct instants in *O*'s career; and we cannot sensibly say of it that it was or that it will be.' That construction is attractive but misconceived. Parmenides does indeed argue that *O* cannot change in any respect at all; but his argument is not presented until lines 26–33. Thus the conclusion stated in line 5a is supposed to depend on an argument which is not advanced for another twenty lines. The gap is considerable, and nothing in the text of lines 26–33 invites us to think back to line 5a.

Let us take another look at the sweep of argument in lines 6–21. Consider the diagram:

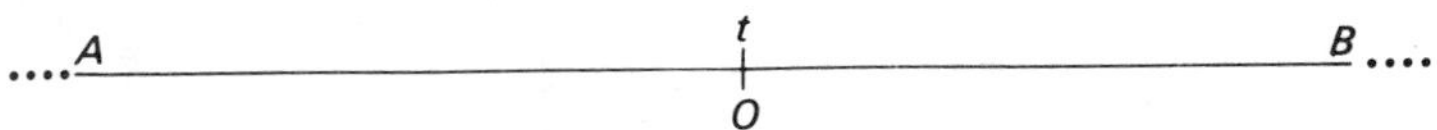

Here *t* is the present moment on the time-line *AB*. We know that *O* exists at *t*. Now the arguments of 6b–18, ruling out generation and destruction, show that *O* exists 'altogether'; in other words, that there is no point on *AB* at which *O* does not exist. And the argument in 19–20 shows that *O* does not exist at any point on *AB* except at point *t*. Those conclusions are not inconsistent: together they entail that every point on *AB* is identical with *t*. Not only is there no time like the present—there is no time but the present. *O*'s existence is not a beautiful atoll in the empty sea of eternity: there are no points in time not embellished by *O*, because time itself embraces no more than a point. Thus *O* is 'all together, one, continuous': it occupies every point of time at once; for time has only one point. The present moment's all its lot.

Is that view coherent? It is often believed that 'there is no time without change'. Take any two instants t_1 and t_2: if the state of the universe at t_1 is the same as its state at t_2, and if there is no instant t_3 between t_1 and t_2 such that the state of the universe at t_3 is different from its state at t_1, then $t_1 = t_2$. The Parmenidean universe is entirely changeless; consequently, if time implies change, that universe is punctual. *O*, and anything else there may be, exists only at *t*. I do not wish to defend that view of time here. I mention it only to indicate that the thesis I ascribe to Parmenides is not simply absurd; a later context will give an opportunity to return to the question.

Is that view of 5–6a consistent with the rest of Parmenides' philosophy? The punctual existence of *O* is not announced in the prospectus; it is not stated in line 21; it is not used to infer any of the other properties of *O*: it is, superficially at least, contradicted by lines 29–30, which appear to speak of a stable and enduring entity. Such facts will lead different readers to different conclusions. I incline to infer that Parmenides did not have a firm grasp of the inordinately slippery fish he held in his hand. Others may say that Parmenides simply contradicts himself; or that he changed his mind (perhaps incorporating lines 5–6 into a second edition of his poem); or that he never contradicted his punctual thesis but merely did not care to use it. Still others will infer that my interpretation of lines 5–21 is mistaken. Anyone who has given more than three minutes thought to those lines will recognize them as terrain in which true trust is impossible: the conclusion I offer here is not a thing I advocate; it is rather the view I am least often inclined to reject.

(e) *Eternity*

The first fragment of Melissus introduced my discussion of Parmenides' thoughts on generation. It is time to return to Melissus and to consider the second thesis of his philosophy: that *O* is eternal. With (T2)–(T4) Melissus leaves the safety of Parmenides' shadow, and strides forward on his own; at precisely this point, according to Aristotle, he walks into the quicksands of fallacy. First, here is the text of **B 2**:

> Again, [i] since it did not come into being but it is, it always was and always will be, and it has no beginning and no end but is unlimited.[25] For [ii] if it had come into being, it would have had a beginning (for [iii] it would have begun coming into being at some time) and [ii^a] an end (for [iii^a] it would have ended coming into being at some time). But [iv] since it did not begin or end, it always was and always will be and it has no beginning or end; for [v] it is not accomplishable that what is not altogether is always (**159**).

As its first sentence shows, **159** intends to prove (T2) and (T3) on the basis of (T1): ungenerability grounds eternity and temporal infinity. (Propositions (T2) and (T3) are, I take it, equivalent; at all events, Melissus makes no attempt to distinguish between them.)

In presenting the argument of **159** I shall abbreviate '*O* always was and always will be, and has no beginning and no end but is unlimited' to '*O* is ϕ'. Thus, as sentence [i] shows, **159** is to prove:

(1) *O* is ϕ,

and to prove it by *modus ponens* from:

(2) If *O* is ungenerated, then *O* is ϕ.

Thus the burden of **159** is the establishment of (2).

(2) is derived from two propositions:

(3) If *O* is generated, then *O* has a beginning and *O* has an end.

(4) If *O* did not begin and did not end, then *O* is ϕ,

Proposition (3) is expressed in [ii] and [ii^a]; and it is supported in [iii] and [iii^a], which state:

(5) If *O* is generated, then *O* at some time began to be generated and *O* at some time ceased being generated.

Proposition (4) is expressed in [iv] and supported in [v] by:

(6) It is not possible that *O* is not altogether and *O* is always.

Each step in Melissus' argument is questionable. First, let us look at the inference from (6) to (4). The chief problem here is the obscurity of (6). Perhaps we should explain Melissus' phrase 'it is altogether (*pan*)' by Parmenides' phrase 'it is altogether (*pampan*)' (**156**. 11): *pampan* required a temporal explanation in Parmenides, and a temporal explanation of Melissus' *pan* will at least fit (6) into the context of **159**; moreover, it will make (6) a tautological truth.[26] Now it is possible to construe (4) as a tautology; and that construe is, I think, the one Melissus requires. Consequently, (4) follows trivially from (6).

Second, there is the inference from (5) to (3). The text in sentences [iii] and [iii^a] is uncertain: the canonical reading is not '*ginomenon*' (which I translate) but '*genomenon*'. That reading requires the following translation: '[ii] . . . had a beginning (for [iii], having come into being, it would have begun at some time) and [ii[a]] an end (for [iii[a]], having come into being, it would have ended at some time)'. But on that translation [iii] and [iii[a]] merely restate [ii] and [ii[a]]: they add nothing. The reading '*ginomenon*' is in any case better attested; and it gives an argument to Melissus. Unfortunately, the argument is feeble. Proposition (5) is indeed true: if *O* underwent a process of generation, then that process had a beginning and also had an ending. But (5) will yield (3) only by means of:

(7) If *O* began or ceased being generated, then *O* began or ceased.

Now the consequent of (7) must be read as '*O* began or ceased *to exist*'; and it is plain that (7) is false. We may imagine that Melissus gave his tacit assent to (7); for it involves just that move of 'dequalification' which we saw reason to ascribe to Heraclitus and which, on Aristotle's testimony, was a frequent and pervasive fallacy (above, p. 73). Certainly, Melissus' argument for (3) is fallacious; and it is hard to dream up any more plausible defence of (3).

What, finally, of the inference from (3) and (4) to (2)? Schematically, Melissus moves from propositions of the form:

(A) If *P* then *Q*,

and:

(B) If not-*Q*, then *R*,

to one of the form:

(C) If not-*P*, then *R*.

And that argument pattern is invalid. I suppose that Melissus took 'If *P* then not-*Q*' and 'If not-*P* then *Q*' to be equivalent: it is easy to see how that equivalence will license the move from (A) and (B) to (C). (In finding that false equivalence behind the argument of **159**, I am, I think, agreeing with Aristotle, who accused Melissus of using illicit conversions on conditional propositions.[27]) Those who are schooled in formal logic, and acquainted with the complexities of the conditional, may despise Melissus for committing so gross a blunder. But the logic of conditionals is remarkably difficult to apprehend; in particular, it is easy to reason that if *P* implies not-*Q*, then not-*P* cannot also imply not-*Q* and so must imply *Q*. Plato and Aristotle were aware of the pitfalls surrounding conditional propositions; but they did not escape them all. Centuries later, Aulus Gellius delighted to find the Melissan fallacy committed by Pliny, 'the most learned man of his age' (IX.xvi). And if the modern logician is censorious of Melissus, let him reflect upon his own tiro entanglement with the logic of *if* and *then*.

Melissus' (T2) is not a Parmenidean thesis, if my interpretation of Parmenides as a punctualist is correct. Eleatic entities are ungenerable and incorruptible—that much is shared by Parmenides and Melissus. But while Parmenides' beings have no temporal duration, Melissan beings are sempiternal. The difference of view seems immense; but it reduces to a disagreement over the relation between time and change. Melissus' entities, like Parmenides', are immutable. Melissus, however, thought (tacitly, no doubt) that an immutable world might sensibly be said to endure; Parmenides implicitly denied that. Both philosophers agree that for any instant *t*, *O* exists at *t*. Parmenides believes and Melissus does not believe that all instants are identical.

(f) *The logic of becoming*

The theory that all genuine entities are sempiternal has had a remarkable popularity in the history of philosophy: it is a Platonic doctrine; it appears in Aristotle in the view that form and matter cannot be created or destroyed; the seventeenth-century rationalists held that substances are sempiternal; today we vaguely talk of the Conservation of Matter, and imply a belief that the basic stuff of the world has an Eleatic stability. I shall have a little to say about that theory in a later chapter; I end this chapter with a few notes on generation.

Most philosophers would agree that neither Parmenides nor Melissus proved the impossibility of generation; but many, I guess, will think that a finger plunged into the Eleatic pie will pull out a sweet philosophical plum.

Consider the logic of generation. 'If *O* comes into being at time *t*, then before *t* *O* does not exist, and after *t* *O* exists'. Generation, it seems, is a species of change or alteration. To put it roughly, *O* alters at *t* if and only if for some property *P*, before *t* *O* lacks *P* and after *t* *O* has *P*. Let *P* be existence; then the formula I have just used to express generation is only trivially different from one expressing a type of alteration. Aristotle is aware of this, or something like it: in *Physics* A 7–9 he first offers an analysis of 'absolute becoming' or generation which makes it a special case of alteration; and then he states that only in that way are Eleatic doubts about generation surmountable. Aquinas, reporting the Aristotelian position, puts it succinctly: *Omne fieri est mutari*, all becoming is changing (*Summa Theologiae* Ia, q.45, 2).

Aquinas did not like it: it follows, he says, that 'creation is a changing; but every changing depends on a subject [i.e., is the alteration of some pre-existing subject matter]. . . . Therefore it is impossible for anything to come into being from nothing by God's action.' Now the first chapter of *Genesis* proves that argument to be unsound; for God created the world *ex nihilo*. The Aristotelians, attending only to the present world, observed no sublunary creation and felt no misgivings about the thesis that becoming is changing. Aquinas agreed with their sublunary observations, but he accused them of ignoring the cosmic and original act of creation.

But Aquinas does not think that Aristotle is simply in error; he has a subtler thing to say: 'Creation is not a changing, except only in respect of our way of understanding. In creation, by which the whole substance of things is produced, you cannot find some one thing which is differently qualified now and before—except only in respect of our understanding, since some object is understood first not to have existed at all, and afterwards to exist' (ibid., *ad* 2). We cannot understand generation unless we think in terms of an object's changing from non-existent to existent; but our thought fails, in an important way, to correspond to the facts.

There is surely truth in this: creating a table is not like painting a table red. When it is painted, my pre-existent and complete table loses one property and acquires another: what was green is now red. When it is made or constructed, the table does not undergo any comparable process; for there is no table there to undergo any process: there is no table off-stage, leaving the green room of non-being to wait in the wings of becoming for its cue to pirouette onto the boards of reality. The metaphysics of creation and generation is not like that: becoming is not altering. And a precisely analogous argument goes for destruction: when I die, I do not alter—I cease to be: I do not lose one and assume another property—there ceases to be any property-bearer at all.

That argument is impressionistic. To delineate it more precisely would require a digression both long and unwarranted; for even though the argument raises interesting problems about generation, they are not, I think, Eleatic problems. According to Elea (if I may state things crudely) the formula '*O* did not exist and now *O* exists' is untrue—and that is why generation is impossible. According to Aquinas, the formula is potentially misleading; but for all that it may be true. And indeed, it is surely consistent, and plausible, to maintain on the one hand that Socrates' birth is not a process undergone by Socrates in the way in which his growing pale is; and on the other hand that part of what we mean when we say that Socrates was born in 470 BC is that before 470 Socrates did not exist, whereas after 470 he did exist.

Thus I leave Aquinas and turn to two modern dogmas with an Eleatic flavour. The first dogma is contained in the slogan 'Existence is not a Predicate'. If '*O* comes into being' entails '*O* did not exist and now O exists', then generation is indeed impossible. For in 'O did not exist and now O exists', 'exist' is used as a predicate of O: since existence is not a predicate, that formula is ill-formed; hence 'O comes into being' cannot say anything true. The argument has an Eleatic conclusion; but it out-Herods Herod: it eliminates 'O does not exist', but it also eliminates the Eleatic axiom 'O exists'. The Eleatics are going to get no help from the dogma that existence is not a predicate; and I therefore leave the dogma, observing only that it commits its holders to an Eleatic denial of generation—and that it is perfectly false.

The second dogma relates to issues I have discussed in the previous chapter. It connects thought with existence, holding that if I am to judge that O has P, then I must be able to refer to O, but that I cannot, at any instant t, refer to O unless O exists at t or existed prior to t. It follows that no sentence of the form 'O will come into being' can express a true judgment. For if I judge that O will come into being, O must already exist or have existed; and so my judgment is false.

That view is Eleatic, but not full-bloodedly so; for it countenances an asymmetry between past and future. Assume the dogma true and consider this diagram.

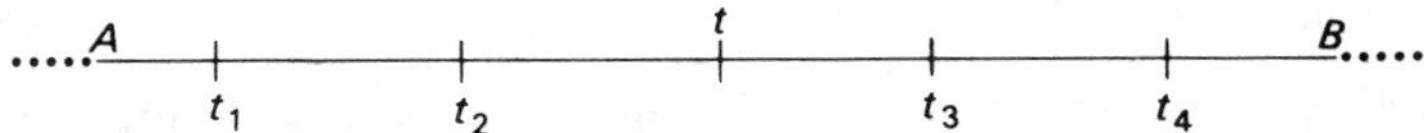

Take the following judgments, all made at t: (i) 'O came into being'; (ii) 'O will come into being'; (iii) 'O was destroyed'; (iv) 'O will be destroyed.' Suppose, first, that O in fact lasts from t_1 to t_2: then (i) and (iii) are true; (ii) and (iv) are false. Next, suppose that O in fact lasts from t_2 to t_3: then (i) and (iv) are true; (ii) and (iii) are false. Suppose, finally, that O in fact lasts from t_3 to t_4: then (i), (ii), (iii) and (iv) are all false. Thus (ii) alone is inevitably false; each of (i), (iii) and (iv)—which the Eleatics renounce along with (ii)—can be true.

The second dogma is thus Eleatic, but only to a low degree. In any event, the dogma seems to me to be false: I can, I think, judge that O has P even if O does not yet exist; I can judge that the Smiths' second child will be male, or that the Cup Final will be won by Arsenal. It is a difficult question to determine precisely under what conditions I can judge that O has P; and a question I shall not presume to broach here. But I end the chapter by saying, confidently, that neither the existence nor the pre-existence of O is a necessary condition for making judgments about O.

XI

Stability and Change

(a) *The limits of the world*

Following Melissus' account rather than that of Parmenides, I turn next to (T4), the theorem that *O* is spatially infinite. The Melissan texts read thus:

> But just as it is always, so it must always be unlimited (*apeiron*) in magnitude too (**160: B 3**).

> Nothing having both a beginning and an end is either eternal or unlimited (**161: B 4**).

I construe 'unlimited in magnitude' in **160**, and 'unlimited' in **161**, as 'spatially infinite'. The arguments against this orthodox position are unconvincing.

Some commentators suppose that Melissus infers (T4) from (T3), spatial from temporal infinity; and they point out the folly of the inference.[1] But **160** implies not that (T4) is inferred from (T3) but that the argument for (T4) is parallel to that for (T3); and **161** corroborates the implication. Thus I suppose that Melissus hoped to deploy the argument of **159** for a second time, concluding to (T4). And presumably the central proposition in his argument will therefore have run:

(1) If *O* is generated, then *O* at some place began to be generated and *O* at some place ceased to be generated;

and (1) will have been used to ground:

(2) If *O* is generated, then *O* has a spatial beginning and a spatial end.

The general thought behind (1) seems to be this: if *O* undergoes a process of generation, then *O* must come into existence in stages, and so there must be a first piece of *O* to be generated and also a last piece; and thus *O* cannot be spatially infinite. There are at least three flaws in that argument. First, why suppose (1) to be true? Why may not *O* spring fully-formed from Zeus' head? Second, (1) does not entail (2): suppose that *O* is generated in instalments, and that *A* is the first and *Z* the last piece of *O* to be generated; still, it does not follow that *A* and *Z* are on the edges of *O* or that *O* has edges at all. Third, (2) does not entail (T4): in inferring (T4) from (2) Melissus again confuses 'if *P*, then not-*Q*' with 'if not-*P*, then *Q*'. The Melissan fallacy is committed again.

Some scholars, appalled by the febrile appearance of this argument, have ascribed a different piece of reasoning to Melissus. Speaking of the Eleatic philosophy, Aristotle reports thus:

> They say that the whole is one and unmoved, and some that it is unlimited; for the limit would limit it against the void (**162**: *GC* 325a15–16 = **A8**).

Scholars say that 'some' refers to Melissus; and that Aristotle's argument here is the genuine Melissan attack on spatial finitude.[2]

I doubt it. First, **162** cannot represent the argument alluded to in **161**: if **162** is a Melissan argument for (T4), then Melissus had two arguments for (T4). Second, the argument in **162** rests on (T13) or something like it: the denial of the void. Now from (T13) we can only infer (T4) if we use (T5), the uniqueness theorem; and (T5), as we shall shortly see, is deduced from (T4). If **162** were Melissan, it would represent a simple circularity: its argument is as frail as that of **161**. Third, Aristotle does not mention Melissus by name in **162**; the passage, which is designed to explain the philosophical ambience of the birth of atomism, reads to me more like an Aristotelian *pot-pourri* than a piece of serious-minded historical doxography. The relation between **162** and Melissus is similar to that between **16** and Anaximander (see above, p. 35): the passage contains thoughts on an Eleatic theme, not reports of Eleatic pronouncements.

162 does not help (T4); and **161** remains impotent. Yet (T4) is an important theorem of Melissan metaphysics, and we might properly look to support it from the poem of Parmenides. What, then, did Parmenides have to say on the subject? The question is highly controversial. It rests on the interpretation of **156**. 42–9, to which I now turn.

The traditional and natural reading of those lines has Parmenides argue that what exists is finite and spherical; and if that reading is correct, then far from supporting (T4), Parmenides is committed to its negation. Aristotle observed that 'we should think that Parmenides spoke better than Melissus; for the latter calls what is infinite a whole, while the former says that the whole is limited, "equally balanced from the middle"' (*Phys* 207a15–17 = **28 A 27**; cf. Aëtius, **30 A 9**). The contrast between a finitist Parmenides and an infinitist Melissus is thus ancient; and a unanimous tradition repeats it. There is, however, a rival reading of lines 42–9; and on that reading Parmenides anticipates Melissus and argues for (T4). The reading requires attention; but first I shall expound a version of the traditional view.

The logical structure of lines 42–9 is fairly clear: a central core of argument in 44b–48 is preceded and followed by a statement of the thesis to be proved.[3] Let us look first at the central core.

The argument is supposed to establish the proposition stated in lines 44b–45: '. . . neither any more nor any weaker can it be here or here'. I take that Delphic utterance to announce the 'existential homogeneity' of *O* in space. By that revolting phrase I mean something like this:

(3) Every subvolume v_i of the volume of space determined by the boundaries of *O* contains some existent part, O_i, of *O*.

There cannot, in short, be any spatial gaps or holes in *O*. (3) is supported by two considerations. The first, lines 46–47a, is moderately clear, though the text of line 46 is uncertain: 'neither is there anything that is not, which might stop it from reaching its like'; i.e., if you start from some point in *O* you cannot come across any non-existent bit of *O* which will block your progress to 'its like', i.e., to another existent bit of *O*. You cannot do so for the simple reason that there can be no non-existent bits of *O*. The second consideration occupies lines 47b–48: 'nor is there anything that is, so that there might be of what is here more and there less—since it is all inviolable'. Conceivably Parmenides is saying that no part of *O* can be 'more' or 'less' existent than any other. That is true; for there is no sense at all in the notion of one part of a thing being 'more existent' than another (even if we can, in other contexts, graft some Platonic sense onto the odd notion of 'being more real'). But it is hard to see how Parmenides' assertion that 'it is all inviolable (*asulon*)' supports that.[4] Nor is it clear how the truth is related to (3).

From (3) we are to infer that '. . . equal from all directions, it meets the limits alike' (line 49). But (3) says nothing about spatial 'equality'; and it makes no mention of 'limits'. The second omission is explicable; for line 42a has already asserted that 'there is a furthest limit', and that is intended as a premiss for the argument of 42–9. Thus 42–9 first state that *O* has limits, and then establish (3); and from those two propositions they infer that *O*, 'like the bulk of a well-rounded ball', 'meets the limits alike'. In short, *O* is bounded (line 42); and *O* is spatially homogeneous (lines 44–5): therefore *O* is a sphere (line 49).

Parmenidean entities, unlike Melissan entities, are finite in extent; and they are spherical. That conclusion accords with a long-standing tradition.[5] Some scholars assert that Parmenidean spheres are geometrical, not physical entities; and they find in the contrast between the Way of Truth and the Way of Opinion an adumbration of the distinction between the abstract realm of pure mathematical entities and the mundane world of nature. But that assertion goes far beyond the evidence of the fragments.

The traditional interpretation of lines 42–9 has come under heavy fire.[6] I shall mention five objections to it. 'According to the traditional interpretation, the argument uses as a premiss the thesis that *O* has spatial boundaries; but nothing in **156** entitles Parmenides to that thesis. Rather, "limit" in line 42 must be taken in a metaphorical sense: it refers to the "invariancy" of *O* which (3) then articulates.' I cannot believe that: the language of lines 42 and 49 is resolutely spatial; and it is hard to take it all as a metaphor for invariancy. Parmenides has already argued that *O* is motionless, and his argument refers to 'limits' (lines 30–1). He assumed, I guess, that if *O* is motionless, then *O* must remain within fixed spatial limits. The assumption is highly plausible; and it is true provided that *O* is finite in magnitude.

'The move from (3) to "*O* is equal from all directions" is evidently invalid: Parmenides could not have meant to make it; and "equal from all directions" is only a metaphor.' I sympathize with the objection; but the remedy the objector proposes is less acceptable than the ill he seeks to cure. Parmenides, on any account, is not at his best in these lines. I suppose he thinks that if *O* is internally homogeneous it must have, so to speak, an externally homogeneous façade ; and in that case it must be a regular solid, if not necessarily a sphere.

'The prospectus in lines 3–4 does not mention sphericity.' Line 4, on the common reading, does however say that *O* is 'complete'; and that is naturally connected with *tetelesmenon* in line 42, and hence with sphericity. On my reading, 'balanced', the prospectus picks out the feature with which most of lines 42–9 are occupied. The relation between prospectus and text is not tidy on that reading; but it is no worse than that between the prospectus and lines 5–21.

'The argument used to reject any internal gaps in *O* will equally show the impossibility of anything beyond *O*, and hence will show that *O* is infinite. (Moreover, the importation into (3) of reference to *parts* of *O* is textually unwarranted: instead of (3) we require some proposition which eliminates external as well as internal non-entity).' Again, I have only a weak reply: (3) is not the only interpretation of the text, but it is a plausible one; and Parmenides' argument, even if it could show the lack of any non-entity beyond *O*, does nothing to disprove the suggestion that *O* is surrounded and close-packed by other entities, and hence nothing to establish the infinitude of *O*.[7]

'Parmenides must surely have asked himself the question: What lies outside the Sphere? And he must have hit upon the celebrated dilemma of Archytas:

> Archytas, according to Eudemus, put the argument thus: 'Standing at the edge (e.g. at the heaven of the fixed stars), could I extend my hand or my cane outside it or not?' That I could not extend it is absurd; but if I do extend it, then what is outside will be either body or space (**163**: Eudemus, fr. 65W = **47 A 24**).

Anticipating Archytas, Parmenides cannot have believed in a finite spherical existent'. I answer: first, why should Parmenides have anticipated Archytas' subtle thought? Second, if he did, why should he have anticipated Archytas' dubious answer to his dilemma? Third, if the subject of Parmenides' deduction is not the Universe but any object of inquiry, then Archytas' argument is simply irrelevant.

It is certainly not the case that Parmenides clearly and explicitly argued for an infinite existent. Indeed, had such an argument been in his mind, he could hardly have found worse terms in which to expound it than those he uses in lines 42–9; for almost every reader of those lines has taken them to argue in precisely the opposite sense. On the other hand, if lines 42–9 do argue that any existent must be a finite sphere, they do so in an obscure and unsatisfying fashion. I conclude lamely: first, lines 42–9 contain no good or interesting argument; second, they are probably intended in the sense a long tradition ascribes to them. On any account, Melissus represents an advance over Parmenides here.

(b) *The Eleatic One*

The most celebrated of Eleatic doctrines is that of monism; and it is also the most shocking. After all,

> It is patent to the eye that cannot face the sun
> The smug philosophers lie who say the world is one.

But then those philosophers will retort, smugly but philosophically enough, that the eye is a bad purveyor of fact; and that pure reason bears out their solitary view. At all events, such is the retort that an almost unanimous tradition has ascribed to Parmenides, to Melissus, and to Zeno. From Plato onwards, students of philosophy have talked, in capitals, of the Eleatic One.

The Milesians, of course, were monists. But their 'material' monism was a milk-and-water affair compared to the heady Eleatic potion. Eleatic monism, or 'real' monism as I shall call it, does not say that everything is made of some single stuff; it says that there exists just one single thing: one reality, one entity. And that Melissus held and argued for such a strange thesis is indubitable.

Here is the relevant text:

> If it were [unlimited] it would be one; for if it were two, they could not be unlimited, but they would have limits against one another (**164: B 6**).[8]

Eudemus objected to the argument: 'Why is it one? Not because several things will somehow be limited against one another; for past time is thought to be unlimited, though it is limited against the present' (fr. 41 W = Simplicius, *ad* **B 5**; cf. *MXG* 976a31 = **A 5**). Convinced by Eudemus' argument, some scholars have saved Melissus by insisting that his 'real object was . . . to prove its infinity from its unity'.[9] But that scholarly suggestion gratuitously rearranges the train of Melissus' thought; and Eudemus' objection is in fact an irrelevancy. By (T3) and (T4) O has no temporal and no spatial boundaries. To infer monism from that we need only the weak auxiliary premiss that if O and O' have exactly the same spatio-temporal co-ordinates, then $O = O'$. Thus take any two entities, O and O': by (T3) and (T4) both O and O' are eternal and infinite; hence a spatial point p falls within O at t if and only if it falls within O' at t. Hence, by the auxiliary premiss, $O = O'$. The argument is valid: Melissus escapes Eudemus' objection because O is limitless in *all* directions, unlike past time which is 'limited' by the present.

Melissus' argument for monism is, I think, correct. What of Parmenides? If my tentative conclusions about lines 42–9 are right, he cannot have anticipated Melissus' argument for (T5), for he did not accept (T4). And in any event, there is no trace in the fragments or in the doxography of the Melissan argument. Then did Parmenides argue for monism? And if so, how?

There is doxographical testimony enough that Parmenides was a real monist; yet the fragments themselves, though they preserve the whole of the Way of Truth, offer very little that even appears to bear upon the matter. I shall avoid what would be a long and negative discussion, and concentrate on the only part of the Way which can reasonably be imagined to state or argue for a monistic thesis.

The lines are **156**. 34–41. According to Aristotle:

> Believing that what is not is nothing apart from what is, of necessity he [sc. Parmenides] thinks that what is is one and there is nothing else (**165**: *Met* 986b29 = **28 A 24**; cf. 1001a32).

Aristotle's remark is duly repeated by Theophrastus, Eudemus, and the doxography (see Simplicius, **A 28**). Its source, I think, is **156**. 36b–37a: 'for nothing is or will be other than what is'. If that is so, Aristotle does not report an argument for monism independent of anything in **156**, but he does give a monistic interpretation of two difficult lines.

The first thing to observe is that lines 36b–37a occur in the middle of an argument; they give neither the premiss nor the conclusion of the section. If they are intended as Parmenides' main statement of monism, they are placed in a strangely inconspicuous position. Second, note that the text of line 36b is corrupt. I have translated the generally accepted emendation; but I have no confidence in it, and I am strongly inclined to think that we do not even know what words Parmenides used at this critical point in his argument.

Still, the general drift of lines 34–41 is perhaps clear enough: 'Whatever exists is whole and motionless (line 38); hence nothing exists apart from what is (lines 36b–37a); hence there can be no thought apart from what is (line 35); hence thinking and thinking that something exists are the same (line 34); hence mortal language, which continually implies that things do not exist, cannot convey thoughts but is mere verbiage (lines 39–41).'

The premiss of the argument derives from lines 22–5 and 26–33, which attempt to prove that what is is continuous and motionless. How does that support the inference that 'nothing is or will be other than what is'? The thought, I take it, is this: what now exists is continuous—hence there is no room for there to be anything now apart from what now exists; and what now exists is motionless—hence there is no way in which present conditions might change and allow the insinuation of something other than what now exists.

The rest of the argument can be reconstructed on that base. For, given that the only things there are or ever will be are presently existing things, 'not without what is . . . will you find thinking'.[10] If anyone thinks, he thinks of something; everything now exists: hence if anyone thinks, he thinks of something now existing. That deals with line 35. Next, line 34: sense and syntax are hotly disputed; and only the argumentative context can provide a solution to the disputes: whatever it means, line 34 must be a plausible intermediary between 35 and 39–41. If line 34 is translated as I have translated it, viz. 'And the same thing are to think and a thought that it is', then a reasonable thesis can be extracted from it. 'The same thing' must be read loosely: Parmenides is not asserting the absurd proposition that the *only* thinkable items have the form '*O* exists'; nor need he be asserting that every thought has, as one of its explicit components, some item of that form. A charitable construction will allow him the more modest claim that any thinkable item carries an implicit rider of the form '*O* exists'. Thus construed, line 34 is plausible inference from line 35; and from line 34 we can infer the contents of 39–41; for if every thought implies '*O* exists', then those mortal utterances which imply the contradictory—'*O* does not exist'—cannot be deemed to carry coherent thoughts at all; they are 'a name', mere verbiage, unbacked by any intelligible content.[11]

Lines 34–41 do not introduce any new matter into the Way of Truth; and if those scholars who see them as a mere summary of what has already been said are not exactly right, the kernel of their claim is acceptable. If 34–41 import nothing new, they do not import the novel thesis of monism. And in fact my reconstruction gives no plausibility to the suggestion that monism is asserted or argued for in lines 36b–37a. The Peripatetic interpretation could only occur to scholars desperate to find monism in Parmenides, and prepared to gaze myopically at half a dozen words, taken out of their context. The lines say that nothing does or will exist apart from what now exists: quite evidently that does not state or imply any monistic thesis. It is worth repeating that the vital lines are corrupt; but I see no possibility of introducing a monistic sentiment by emendation—monism is simply irrelevant to the context.

Was Parmenides a monist? The surviving fragments do not make him one. Since we are fairly confident of possessing the whole of the Way of Truth, I incline to believe that Parmenides' poem was not monistic. And since we hear nothing of any Parmenidean doctrine not included in the Way of Truth, I suspect that Parmenides was not a monist. At all events, as far as our evidence goes, real monism was an invention of Melissus.

(c) *Homogeneity*

After arguing for monism, Melissus turned to homogeneity. The fragments fail us here, but their loss can be made good: **B 7** asserts and twice employs the homogeneity of the unique Melissan entity; and it implies that the homogeneity thesis (T6) was inferred from

(T5). That implication is confirmed both by Simplicius' paraphrase and by the *MXG*. In the *MXG* the argument runs as follows:

> And being one, it is in all respects homogeneous (*homoion*); for if it were heterogeneous (*anhomoion*), being several things it would no longer be one but many (**166**: 974a 12–14 = **A 5**).

I suppose that *homoion* means 'qualitatively uniform';[12] and I take it that (T6) can be written as:

(1) If O_1 and O_2 are parts of O, then O_1 and O_2 are qualitatively identical.

Melissus' argument is a *reductio*. Suppose (1) false, i.e.:

(2) For some P, O_1 has P and O_2 does not have P.

Then by Leibniz' law:

(3) $O_1 \neq O_2$.

Since any part of an existent object must itself exist, (3) implies that more than one thing exists. And that, by (T5), is impossible.

You may scoff at that: surely O may be unique and yet have differentiated parts; for 'O is unique' only makes sense if it is taken as elliptical for some proposition of the form 'O is the unique f'. Number, as Frege showed us, is parasitical upon concepts: 'O is one', 'O and O' are two', are nonsense if strictly construed; we are always obliged to ask 'One what?', 'Two what?' But if O is the unique f, that in no way rules out (3); for O_1 and O_2 may be a pair of gs. Moreover, if 'O is unique' makes no sense, we may well ask what happens to Melissus' monism. It appears that (T5) is senseless: real monism, far from being a thesis provable inside the Eleatic system, is an unthinkable confusion.

The generous reader will run to Melissus' aid: O, after all, is not completely uncharacterized—it is, essentially, existent. Real monism says not that O is unique, but that O is the unique entity; indeed (to anticipate some future revelations) we may take (T5) to say that O is the unique physical object. (3) will then assert that O_1 and O_2 are distinct entities or physical objects; and that will not consist with (T5). Melissus springs the Fregean trap.

Here we might call on Aristotle to support Frege. Aristotle insists that all counting presupposes some determinate unit (that is essentially Frege's point); and he adds that the unit must be 'indivisible'. What he means is this: if we are to count fs, then no part of an f may itself be an f; fs must be indivisible *into* fs. Thus we can count horses, for parts of horses are not horses; but we cannot count horse-parts, for parts of horse-parts are horse-parts. We can count hands, but we cannot count lumps of flesh; we can count tables and chairs, mice and men; but we cannot count physical objects, or things, or entities.

That view of Aristotle's is, I think, true. You cannot count 'homoiomerous' things because in their case there is no determinate answer to the question: How many *f*s are there? and there is no unique way of counting *f*s. If I point to the sea and ask how many bits of water you observe, my question has no answer; the sea is divisible into arbitrarily many bits: there are *n* gallons, *m* thimblesful, *k* barrels—but there is no number of bits. Similarly, you cannot say how many parts of the body there are, or how many lumps of flesh make up a mouse. (Convention does allow us to give sense to some questions of this sort: there is, in equestrian circles, a fixed number of 'points of the horse'; and if you show me five oranges and ask me how many orange things I see, you expect the answer 'five'. But that does not defeat the Aristotelian claim.)

Thus if the Fregean objection shows that real monism cannot be expressed by the formula '*O* is unique', the Aristotelian objection rules out '*O* is the unique entity or physical object'.

There is no appropriate *f* which will allow Melissus to state his thesis as '*O* is the unique *f*'. Candidate terms that escape the Aristotelian objection are too specific to be interesting: it is a boring falsehood that there is at most one horse, a boring truth that there is at most one phoenix. Instead, Melissus might try something like:

(4) For every *f*: *O* is the unique *f*,

where *f* is restricted to terms of the appropriate countable sort. But (4) will not do; for it implies the absurdity that for every *f*, *O* is an *f*. Nor will an existentially quantified analogue to (4) fare any better. A more complicated formula is required:

(5) For some *f*: *O* is the unique *f* and everything that exists is the same *f* as *O*.

Is (5) strong enough to state monism? Might there not be one or more *g*s in addition to the unique *f*? Suppose that *O* is the unique *f*, and that *O′* is a *g*. Then by (5) *O′* is an *f*, and the same *f* as *O*. But then *O* is surely a *g*, and the same *g* as *O′*? That argument may be sound; but it is controversial. In any case, it is needlessly sophisticated; for by (T3) and (T4), *O′* and *O* share the same spatio-temporal co-ordinates; in such circumstances, I do not see how we could have any reason to say that *O* is the same *f* as *O′* but a different *g*, given that *O′* is a *g*.

Then let (5) stand as the revised and fortified version of monism. Can we argue from (5) to any form of (T6)? Does monism entail homogeneity? Suppose that (2) holds; then (3) follows, and O_1 is not the same *f* as O_2. But by (5) O_1 is the same *f* as *O*, and so is O_2. Hence

O_1 is the same f as O_2: the *reductio* goes through, and (T6) is established.

The trouble with Melissus' argument is strength, not weakness: it threatens to prove far too much. For the *reductio*, it seems, will work against the supposition that O has homogeneous parts as well as against the assumption of heterogeneity. It is partition, not heterogeneity, into which the argument fastens its teeth: we need only suppose that O_1 and O_2 are distinct parts of O to generate the contradiction. Then is the one Melissan entity partless, though infinite? At this point a notorious fragment clamours for consideration: since, however, a full discussion of that fragment, **B 9**, must wait on an account of **B** 7, I shall add a touch of suspense to the Melissan saga and postpone further probing of parts and partlessness until a later section.

(d) *Wholeness*

What of Parmenides? He asserts that what is is *homoion* (it is 'all alike': **156**. 22); and it is usually supposed that he was the first mover of (T6): homogeneity, like monism, is normally ascribed to the grand originator of Eleaticism. If Parmenides advanced (T6) then he did so either in lines 22–5 or else in the formally similar passage at lines 44–8. I have already offered some thoughts on the latter passage; and unless I am very much mistaken, there is no whiff of (T6) there: 'existential homogeneity', as I called it, by no means implies qualitative homogeneity. What then of lines 22–5?

The word 'whole' does not occur in 22–5; but it is scarcely to be doubted that 'continuous' (*suneches*) in line 25 answers to 'whole' (*oulon*) in the prospectus, line 4. What sort of 'wholeness' or 'continuity' Parmenides has in mind is less easy to settle. The orthodox view has Parmenides arguing for the spatial continuity of what is: O cannot be discontinuous, in the way in which a pack of cards or the United States of America is discontinuous; all its parts must be in spatial contact with one another. The language of the lines has been thought to impose that interpretation; and the lines do contain terms whose primary sense is spatial. But spatial terms are readily used with a temporal reference; and I do not think that Parmenides' language suffices in itself to rule out a temporal interpretation: O is certainly continuous in a temporal sense (unlike, say, a symphony that may have gaps between its movements) and temporal wholeness may be the message of 22–5. To decide on the sense of Parmenides' conclusion we must look first at the course of his argument. I quote the lines again:

Nor is it divided, since it is all alike
and neither more here (which would prevent it from holding together)
nor less, but it is all full of what is.
Hence it is continuous; for what is neighbours what is.

The orthodox punctuation puts a heavy stop at the end of line 22, giving three separate tracts of argument: line 22, lines 23–4, line 25. In line 22 we then have the unsupported premiss that 'it is all alike'. Thus isolated, the phrase must be taken in the Melissan sense: 'it is qualitatively homogeneous'. But its presence is jarring: nothing in the earlier part of **156** suggests it, and we are left to suppose that Parmenides brazenly helps himself to a premiss to which he has no possible claim. But the orthodox punctuation is not sacrosanct: instead of a stop at the end of line 22, let us place a comma or indeed no punctuation mark at all;[13] 22b still expresses a premiss of Parmenides' argument, but that obscure expression is expanded and explained in lines 23–4. So construed, the structure of the section is this: *probandum* (22a); premiss (22b–24); restatement of conclusion (25a); intermediate step (25b). The logic is clear; and there is some hope that from 22b–24 we shall be able to drag out a proposition to which Parmenides is entitled. That, at any rate, is the supposition on which my translation and the following exegesis depend.

In 22a the *probandum* says: 'Nor is it *diaireton*'. Translators usually render this 'divisible'; and many scholars talk of 'theoretical indivisibility': *O* is not just undivided, it is not, even in theory, divisible into parts. But *diaireton* in 22a must be understood by way of *suneches* in 25a; for 'it is *suneches*' restates the conclusion of these four brief lines. And *suneches* ('continuous') does not imply indivisibility: the Mediterranean is *suneches*, but it is theoretically divided in atlases, and a cunning engineer might divide it physically by a causeway. In 22–5 Parmenides commits himself only to the view that *O* contains no gaps, not to the stronger view that gaps cannot be made in it, and still less to the very strong view that it does not admit of 'division in thought'.

The premiss for this conclusion is that 'it is all alike'; and the sense of that phrase is given by the gloss: '. . . neither more here . . . nor less'. The commentators think here, as they think at lines 44–5, of 'degrees of being': existence is not spread unevenly over *O*, like the butter on my morning slice of toast. But I cannot see how an uneven spread of existence would prevent it from holding together (*sunechesthai*, i.e., being *suneches*)—the butter on my toast is uneven but continuous. And I guess that Parmenides has a simpler thought in mind: 'If you take any two stretches of *O*, you will not find more existence in one than in the other. It is "all full of what is", "what is neighbours what is": at every point in every stretch of *O*, *O* exists; and thus *O* is indeed without gaps, continuous, undivided.'

Are the 'stretches' of *O* spatial or temporal? There is one strong argument against the spatial orthodoxy: lines 44–9 attempt to establish the spatial continuity of Parmenidean entities, and a brief but complete anticipation of that argument in 22–5 would be pointless, to say the least. On the other side, four short lines drawing an evident corollary of the denial of generation and destruction are apposite and intelligible: if *O* cannot be generated or destroyed (lines 5–21), then clearly it cannot have temporal gaps; the corollary is easily and appropriately drawn in lines 22–5.

There is an objection to the heterodox temporal interpretation: if Parmenides' entities are punctual, then how could he refer in 22–5 to temporal stretches in their careers? How can 'what is neighbour what is' in time, if whatever is is only now? Why did Parmenides not simply say: 'It is not temporally divisible, because it exists only now, and "now" is logically indivisible'? We might, I suppose, read my references to 'stretches' in *O*'s career in a counterfactual way: 'if there *were* two temporal stretches in *O*'s career, neither *could* "contain more existence" than the other'; and we might conjecture that Parmenides chose this way of demonstrating *O*'s temporal continuity because he preferred to rest his argument on the fundamental and well understood notion of ungenerability rather than on its slippery partner, punctuality. After all, lines 22–5 *do* establish temporal continuity, given lines 5–21: the objection we are considering is merely that they do not do that in the most economical and telling fashion. But any reader who refrains from believing that explanation has my sympathy; and I readily concede that my interpretations of 5–21 and 22–5 do not unite in whole-hearted amity. If, for all that, I stick by them, it is because alternative interpretations seem to me to be still less congruous: again, I do not think that Parmenides—the first student of metaphysics—has fully grasped the implications of his own thoughts.

Lines 22–5 do not, I conclude, either argue for or state (T6); and I infer that Melissus was the first to maintain the thesis of homogeneity. For all that **156** says, Parmenidean entities may be qualitatively variegated.

As an appendix to this section, here is a further fragment of Parmenides:

> Regard alike firmly in your mind things absent, things present;
> for you will not cut off what is from holding to what is,
> neither scattering everywhere in every way through the world,
> nor gathering together (**167: 28 B 4**).

This is an utterly baffling quotation: its first line is, in the Greek, multiply ambiguous;[14] its position in Parmenides' poem defies determination.

The first line seems to envisage a plural world; and that has led some scholars to place **167** in the Way of Opinion. I do not accept the inference; but the conclusion is tempting. Simplicius, after all, implies that **156** represents the whole of the Way of Truth, and **156** cannot accommodate **167**. On the other hand, the content of **167**—to put the matter vaguely—smacks of Truth; and it has been cleverly suggested that **167** formed a tailpiece to the Way of Opinion: 'So much for the Way of Opinion: do not be misled along it, but "regard alike . . ."'.[15] If that suggestion is correct, what sense does **167** have?

The argument runs thus: '(i) What is can neither scatter nor coalesce; hence (ii) what is always holds to what is; hence (iii) you should regard absent and present alike.' Now (i) follows from the motionlessness of what is; Parmenides has argued for that in lines 26–33, and we may reasonably be expected to apply the moral in **167**, Next, (ii) will follow from (i) on the supposition that at the present 'what is holds to what is'; and that supposition can be found either in line 25 (on a spatial reading of 22–5) or else in lines 42–9. This reading of (ii) has consequences for (iii): 'present' and 'absent' must refer to spatially present and absent parts of *O*, not to temporal presence or absence, and not to a plurality of individuals. For the inference from (ii) to (iii) must run: 'Since there can never be spatial gaps in *O*, you may safely treat present and absent bits of *O* alike'. And the underlying thought is merely this: no bits of *O* are non-existent; so you will run no danger of pseudo-thought by thinking of any bit of *O*, however remote.

167 on this interpretation is not peculiarly interesting or novel; but novelty is not wanted at the end of a poem. It is worth pointing out that my reading of **167** to some extent confirms my remarks about divisibility in line 22: **167** allows that *O* has parts that are at least notionally distinct; it denies that those parts may become physically separated from one another.

(e) *Change and decay*

It was the Eleatic denial of change and motion which most troubled the philosophical and scientific world of the fifth century: generation and destruction the later scientists felt they could dispense with; sempiternity, too, could be accommodated to their designs, and monism was not perhaps felt as a very serious or persuasive thesis. But without change, and without locomotion, science was at a stand; and we shall see, in the later attempts to escape from the logical clutches of Elea, that the rehabilitation of locomotion, and with it of change, was the central and vital issue.

On this topic Parmenides, again, is dismally obscure; and I shall not look at his remarks on change and motion until I have examined Melissus' relatively clear and intelligible contribution. The theses in question are (T7)—(T12); they occupy the first part of **30 B 7**. That long fragment reads thus:

> [i] In this way, then, it is eternal and infinite and one and all homogeneous. And [ii] it will not perish,[16] nor become greater, nor be rearranged, nor suffer pain, nor suffer anguish. For [iii] if it underwent any of these, it would no longer be one. For [iv] if it alters (*heteroioutai*), it is necessary that what is is not homogeneous, but that what was earlier perishes and what is not comes into being. Again, [v] if it were to become different (*heteroion*) by a single hair in ten thousand years, it will all perish in the whole of time.
>
> But [vi] neither is it accomplishable that it be rearranged (*metakosmêthênai*); for [vii] the arrangement (*kosmos*) which was earlier is not destroyed, nor is that which does not exist generated. And [viii] since nothing is added or destroyed or alters, how might anything that is be rearranged?[17] For [ix] if it were to become different in any respect, it would thereby be rearranged. Nor [x] does it suffer pain. For [xi] it would not be altogether if it were in pain; for [xii] a thing in pain could not be always. [xiii] Nor does it have equal power with what is healthy. [xiv] Nor would it be homogeneous if it were in pain; for [xv] it would be in pain in virtue of something's passing from it or being added to it, and it would no longer be homogeneous. [xvi] Nor could what is healthy be in pain; for [xvii] what is would perish,[18] and what is not would come into being. [xviii] And about anguish there is the same argument as for being in pain.
>
> Nor [xix] is it empty (*keneon*) in any respect; for [xx] what is empty is nothing, and it will not be nothing. Nor [xxi] does it move; for [xxii] it has no way to retreat, but it is full. For [xxiii] if it

were empty, it would retreat into what was empty; but not being empty, it has not any way where it may retreat. And [xxiv] it will not be dense and rare. For [xxv] it is not accomplishable that what is rare is as full as what is dense, but what is rare thereby becomes emptier than what is dense. And [xxvi] one must make this distinction between what is full and what is not full: if it yields at all or receives, it is not full; and if it neither yields nor receives, it is full. [xxvii] Now it is necessary for it to be full, if it is not empty; and if it is full, it does not move (**168**).

Sentence [i] restates, without further argument, (T2), (T4), (T5) and (T6). Sentences [vii]–[xviii] are curiously convoluted, and I shall not attempt to unravel all their complexities.[19] Sentence [ii] asserts (T8)–(T12). [iii] supports this by observing that the negation of any of (T8)–(T12) entails the negation of (T5); and [iv] supports *this* by claiming that the negation of (T7) entails the negation of (T6). Thus: (T5) gives (T6); (T6) gives (T7); and (T7) gives each of (T8)–(T12). Monism gives homogeneity; homogeneity gives unalterability; and unalterability rules out destruction, growth, rearrangement, pain, and anguish.

I have already discussed the first of those inferences; and I suppose that a suitably generous understanding of 'alter' (*heteroiousthai*) will validate the third. The second inference may surprise: why, after all, should *O* not change from one homogeneous state to another? from being wholly red, say, to being wholly blue? Provided that the change occurred uniformly there would be no instant at which *O* was not homogeneous. But that reflection misses the full force of Melissus' argument for homogeneity: O_1 and O_2 were taken as 'parts' of *O*; but 'part' is not to be construed in a narrowly spatial sense: any spatio-temporal chunk of *O* will count as a 'part'. (If *O* is three-dimensional, then 'parts' of *O* are given by five co-ordinates, three spatial and two temporal.) As far as I can see, that gloss on 'part' does not affect Melissus' argument for (T6); and it renders immediately valid his inference from (T6) to unalterability (T7).

Sentence [iv] contains, however, a hint at a different argument for (T7). The hint lies in the phrase: 'what was earlier perishes, and what is not comes into being'. It is taken up again in [vii]; and it is important because it allows (T7) to by-pass (T5) and (T6), and to rest upon (T1) alone. Thus the denial of change need not depend upon monism. I turn, therefore, to [vii], remarking incidentally that sentence [v] is unintelligible to me.[20]

The sentence restricts itself to (T10), the denial of rearrangement;[21] and the full significance of (T10) will become clear at a later stage.

The argument of [vii] turns on the following principle:

(1) If *O* is rearranged at *t*, then at *t* *O*'s earlier arrangement is destroyed and *O*'s later arrangement comes into being.

Hence, since nothing can be destroyed or come into being, (T10) is established. As it stands, the argument makes use of (T8), the denial of destruction; and since (T8), in Melissus, is only established by way of (T5), (T10) is still, strictly speaking, dependent upon monism. But that dependence is easily broken. Replace (1) by:

(2) If *O* is rearranged at *t*, then at *t* *O*'s later arrangement comes into being.

To get (T10) from (2) only (T1) is required: in brief, ungenerability rules out rearrangement.

The argument can be generalized: if *O* changes colour at *t*, then at *t* *O*'s new colour comes into being; if *O* changes size at *t*, then at *t* *O*'s new size comes into being. Generally:

(3) For any *F*: if *O* becomes *F* at *t*, then *O*'s *F*ness comes into being at *t*.

Proposition (2) is a special case of (3); the phrase 'what is not comes into being' in [iv] points to a second case of (3); and in [xvii] there is something very close to a general statement of (3). Thus I do not hesitate to infer that some general principle such as (3) was in Melissus' mind.

The strength of (3) is great. In effect, (3) reduces all change to generation: every sentence of the form '*O* becomes *F*' implies some sentence of the form '*O*′ comes into being'. But no sentence of the form '*O*′ comes into being' can express a truth; hence no sentence of the form '*O* becomes *F*' can express a truth—since generation is extinguished, change cannot light our scientific path. And (3) is surely true: what does '*O*'s *F*ness comes into being' mean if it does not mean '*O* becomes *F*'? Unless we rule out phrases like '*O*'s *F*ness' as ill-formed—a desperate and unconvincing stratagem—we are bound to concede that (3) is true.

Melissus has forged a powerful argument: from (T1) he can validly infer (T7), by way of (3); and (3) is true. If generation goes, then so does change of every sort. The value of his argument was never appreciated by Melissus' successors: they attempted to hold on to (T1) while rejecting (T7); yet they say nothing of (3). Aristotle, who despised Melissus and prided himself on his overthrow of the Eleatic arguments, nowhere faces up to (3). I do not wish to suggest that Melissus' argument is impregnable; but at this stage I leave it in control of the field—it deserves to enjoy at least a temporary victory.

The next sentences of **168** are curiosities. They attempt to establish that *O* is free from pain and free from anguish: (T11) and (T12). It is hard to believe that Melissus would have invented those strange theses off his own bat; yet scholars have unearthed no suitable opponent against whom they may have been enunciated. Again, what moral are (T11) and (T12) intended to suggest? Is Melissus denying the sensitivity of *O*, and implicitly rejecting an animate or divine being? For 'he used to say that one should say nothing about the gods; for there is no knowledge of them' (Diogenes Laertius, IX.24 = **A 1**). Or is he rather affirming the sensitivity of *O*, and hence implicitly its bliss and divinity? For according to other sources he made 'the One' a god (Aëtius, Olympiodorus, **A 13**). Or are (T11) and (T12) jokes?

(T11) is argued for in sentences [xi]–[xvii]. The structure of the passage is not clear to me. [xi]–[xii], I take it, rule out the possibility that *O* is permanently in pain: if *O* were in pain throughout its career, it would not 'be altogether' (*pan*: see p. 195), i.e., it would not exist for ever. I suppose that some fairly crude thought lies behind the argument: perhaps it is that pain weakens the sufferer, and in time will therefore destroy him. Sentences [xvi]–[xvii] rule out the possibility that *O* is sometimes in pain: *O* cannot pass from a healthy to a painful state; for *O* cannot change at all. Proposition (3) lies behind the argument. [xiv]–[xv] seem to have a more general scope: Melissus' point is that '*O* is in pain' implies '*O* is altering', for pain consists in the addition to or subtraction from the substance of the sufferer. There is presumably some sort of physiological theory behind this. Finally, sentence [xiii] is puzzling. Conceivably, it argues against the suggestion that *O* is both in pain and healthy, all the time, but in different parts of itself. Pain and health, Melissus avers, could not coexist in harmonious equilibrium as that suggestion requires; physiology, again, must be in the offing.

The argument in the first half of **168** is not set out with perfect grace; and parts of the paragraph are given over to Christmas-cracker philosophizing. That may explain the neglect of **168** in modern discussions of the Eleatic stand on change. At the risk of tedium, let me briefly restate the case: of all the Eleatic theses, (T7) and its companions are the most important; and of all the Eleatic theses, (T7) has the strongest support; for through the garish curtains of **168** there appears a fairy godmother of an argument: a touch of (3), and (T1) is magicked into (T7).

(f) *The void*

The remainder of **168** is concerned with local motion or change in place. In these paragraphs Melissus offers an argument which I think is original to him. The argument proved to be one of the most controversial in the history of philosophy, and indeed of physics. For the next two millennia every student of motion was obliged to take account of it; and the critics and defenders of Melissus' opinion are roughly equal both in numbers and in gravity. The logical articulation of the passage is given in [xxvii]: from (T13), absence of void, we get (T14), 'fullness'; and from (T14) there follows the denial of motion, (T15). The sentences about 'dense and rare', constituting (T16), muddy the waters of the argument.

We start, then, with 'the void'. Sentences [xix]–[xx] are standardly translated as follows: 'Nor is anything empty; for what is empty is nothing; so nothing will not be'. The particle 'so' (*oun*) is logical nonsense; the grammar of the third sentence strongly suggests the Polypheman fallacy of construing 'nothing' as a singular term (Odysseus tricked Polyphemus by giving his name as 'No one': the blinded Polyphemus then bellowed to his friends, 'No one has hurt me'); and the first sentence fits uneasily into the run of Eleatic theses, all of which have the form '*O* is *F*'. My translation[22] avoids all three difficulties, and yields the following argument:

(1) *O* is not nothing [sc. in any respect].

(2) What is empty is nothing.

Hence:

(T13) *O* is not empty [sc. in any respect].

Since 'nothing' is here, as often, used as a synonym of 'non-existent', (1) restates the Melissan axiom (A), with the tacit rider 'in any respect'. But (2) is a new and not a universally accepted proposition. That an object cannot have non-existent parts—be non-existent in some respect—seems evident enough; but does it follow that an object cannot have *vacuous* or empty parts? After all, a vacuum is an essential part of a vacuum flask. Part of the space occupied by my flask is empty; hence a part of my flask is vacuous—my flask is 'empty in some respect'.

That is a bad argument; and Melissus is right. His entity, *O*, is an occupant of space, an extended body. Let the volume of space *O* occupies be *Vo*. Now, trivially, every part of a volume of space occupied by an object is occupied by a part of that object. Suppose, then, that *O* is empty in some respect. That is to say, suppose that some part of *Vo* is not occupied by any body at all. Then that part is not occupied by any part of *O*. And hence *Vo* is not the volume occupied by *O*. But by hypothesis *Vo* is the volume occupied by *O*. The vacuum in my flask is not a part of my flask any more than the water in a bucket is a part of the bucket.

I conclude for Melissus. Moreover, from (T13) we can quickly infer the complete absence of void from the world. By (T4), *O* is infinitely extended, or occupies every region of space; by (T13) no part of *O* is vacant: hence no part of space is vacant, and 'the void does not exist'. This strong thesis is, of course, essential to Melissus' argument against motion; and that, I suspect, is why sentence [xix] receives the translation it ordinarily gets. But the strong thesis is easily and obviously inferred, given the translation which I have adopted.

In [xxvii] Melissus indicates that (T15) follows from (T13) by way of (T14); and that, as we shall see, is not a casual hint. In [xxi]–[xxiii], however, (T14) is ignored; and the canonical Eleatic argument against motion, in its standard presentation, derives (T15) directly from (T13). For the moment I shall follow this tradition, postponing discussion of (T14) to the following section.

The argument for (T15) is sublimely simple: 'not being empty, it has not any way where it may retreat';[23] *O*, or parts of *O*, can move only if they have room for manoeuvre, and a full universe leaves no room at all. Locomotion is change of place, the transition from one locale to another. If an object moves, then it comes to occupy a new place; and that new place, prior to receiving its occupant, must be empty. Thus the general principle licensing the inference from (T13) to (T15) is something of the following sort:

(3) If *O* comes to occupy place *p* at time *t*, then immediately prior to *t p* is empty.

The principle has considerable plausibility; and Melissus may have taken it for self-evident: if *p* is occupied up to *t*, then *O* cannot get into it; for two things cannot occupy the same place at the same time. To make any headway, *O*'s nose must be pointed at a vacuum: the parts of a rigid, close-packed, body do not and cannot move; for they leave no vacancies about them into which they can insert themselves.

Evidently, there are answers to that argument; and Melissus cannot be granted (3), or (T15), without more ado. Some at least of his successors exercised their ingenuities over (3) and proposed alternatives to it which apparently permit locomotion inside a *plenum*. I shall look at those proposals in their later historical setting and I shall not anticipate them here: for the extent of this chapter, let Melissus hold the field; his argument will shortly be reinforced by Zeno.

Before I turn to Parmenides' thoughts on motion and change, let me get Melissus' (T17) out of the way: *O* is not divided up. Fragment **B 10** reads:

> If what is has been divided (*diêirêtai*), it moves; but moving it would not be (**169**).[24]

The fragment infers from (T15) some denial of division. Simplicius (*ad* **B 10**) thinks that 'it has been divided' means 'it is divisible'; but the Greek will hardly bear that construction. Comparison with **167** suggests a different gloss: 'Since it cannot move, it cannot be split up into bits'. The argument is correct, and we may expect Melissus to have assented to it; but the past tense, 'it *has been* divided', is not explicable. A third suggestion wonders if '*O* has been divided' is supposed to entail that some parts of *O* are not in contact with one another. Then those parts are separated by a void; so *O* is in some respect empty, and 'if it were empty, it would retreat into what was empty'. I incline to think this the most probable interpretation of **169**; but I cannot say why Melissus should have decided to argue for (T17). However that may be, **169** introduces us to no new items of Melissan philosophy.

In **156**. 26–33 Parmenides attempts to show that what exists is *akinêton*, motionless:

And motionless in the limits of great chains
it is, beginningless, endless; since coming into being and destruction
have wandered far away, and true trust has driven them off.
And the same, remaining in the same state, it lies in itself
and thus firmly remains there. For a strong necessity
holds it in chains of a limit which fences it about,
because it is not right for what is to be incomplete;
for it is not lacking—otherwise it would want everything.

Lines 26–8 mean: 'since *O* cannot come into being or be destroyed, it is *akinêton*'. '*Kinêsis*' in philosophical Greek regularly carries wider connotations than 'motion' in English: it covers any form of change—alteration and change of size as well as locomotion. Line 41, which refers to locomotion and alteration as empty 'names', implies that Parmenides has rejected both locomotion and alteration; and the only passage where he might think to have done that is lines 26–33. Thus *akinêton* in line 26 rejects all forms of change. Lines 29–30a confirm that conclusion; for the words 'the same' contain a rejection of alteration; and 'firmly remains there' deny locomotion. ('remaining in the same state (*en tautôi*)' may refer either to alteration or to locomotion (see p. 322, n. 21). 'it lies in itself' presumably means 'it stays in the one place it occupies'.) I believe, too, that the prospectus prepares us for this combined treatment of alteration and locomotion: 'of one kind and motionless (*mounogenes te kai atremes*)' means 'unalterable and immobile'. *Akinêton* in line 26 thus denies both change and locomotion.

Being immobile, what is remains 'in the limits of great chains'. Modern scholars take 'limits' and 'chains' in lines 26 and 31 in a metaphorical sense: Parmenides has logical chains in mind; '*O* is motionless in the limits of chains' means simply 'as a matter of necessity, *O* is motionless'. That is hard to believe: first, the phrase 'strong necessity' (line 30) gives, non-metaphorically, the sense of *a priori* immobility. Second, the literal sense of 'limits' is wholly appropriate: if *O* is immobile, what more natural than to infer that it stays forever within the spatial limits given by its original position? The point is not wholly niggling: as we have already seen, an important issue in the interpretation of lines 42–9 turns on the reading of the word 'limit' (above, p. 203).

One final point before advancing to the argument of the lines: if *O* has a purely punctual existence, how can it be said to 'remain' in limits? Remaining implies endurance; and *O* has no duration. The question is essentially the same as one raised earlier in connexion with **167** (above, p. 212). And again there are two answers: first, it is easy to suggest that Parmenides had not got the hang of his own punctuality thesis, and failed to see that although it does imply immobility, it is incompatible with an enduring immobility or 'remaining'. Second, we might gloss 'it remains at *p*' by 'For all *t*, if *O* exists at *t*, then at *t* *O* is at *p*'; and thus, at the price of a certain sophisticated artificiality, punctuality and 'remaining' are formally reconciled. I do not offer this second answer as an account of what Parmenides 'really thought'; I offer it to show that the objection to his using the verb 'remain' (*menein*) is a quibble.

Lines 26–33 contain two distinct arguments. The first occupies 26–28; it consists in the simple formula: 'No generation or destruction, so no *kinêsis*'. There is more than one way of expanding that into an argument, and I cannot see any internal evidence that points clearly in any particular direction. I surmise that Melissus' main argument against change, expressed in **168**, was intended as an elucidation of these brief lines; I do not intend to improve upon Melissus—though if he was offering his own argument to Parmenides he was a charitable man.

The second argument occupies lines 30b–33. Some scholars see no argument against motion here: they translate *houneken* ('because') in line 32 by 'wherefore' and find a self-contained piece of argumentation in lines 32–3.[25] I cannot understand 'wherefore' here; and in any case 'because' is linguistically preferable as a translation of *houneken*. With that translation Parmenides presents us with an argument for motionlessness starting from the premiss:

(4) If *O* is lacking, *O* wants everything.

Hence he infers:
(5) *O* is not lacking;
whence:
(6) *O* is not incomplete,
and so to '*O* is motionless'.

I find the argument baffling; and the text of line 33, from which the premiss (4) is drawn, is uncertainly transmitted and of uncertain sense.[26] Some scholars discover Melissus' canonical argument, supposing that Parmenides infers immobility from the lack of a void. The key to their interpretation is the construe of (5) as 'no space is not occupied by *O*', i.e., 'there is no vacuum'. (4) then means 'if there were a vacuum, *O* would occupy no space at all'; and the premiss which allows us to infer (5) from (4) is the proposition that *O* is a space occupier. It is hard to believe all that: it requires great faith to find any statement about vacuums in (5);[27] and why ever should Parmenides offer us (4)? What, again, is the function of (6)? Had Parmenides wanted to give the Melissan argument, he had the linguistic means at his disposal; I cannot believe that he would have disguised his intentions as thoroughly as this interpretation supposes.

I suspect that the argument has an element of teleology in it: 'If *O* moves—*kineitai* in the broadest sense—that could only be because *O* had not achieved some end or goal (was 'incomplete'); and that would only be true if *O* lacked something. But if it lacked anything it would lack everything. (Why? Perhaps the Principle of Sufficient Reason lurks behind the text: all of *O*'s properties are on a par—if it lacked a property P_1, then it would lack P_2 and P_3 and everything else.) But that is an absurd supposition, for it would make *O* into a propertyless non-thing.' That interpretation is perhaps preferable to the Melissan one; yet it hardly presents Parmenides with a decent argument, and I do not believe I know what he is saying in lines 32–3.

Once again, Melissus seems to me to be Parmenides' superior: in **156**. 26–33 little is clear and nothing is explicit and detailed; if those lines were all that Elea could muster in support of its case against *kinêsis*, then that case would not deserve a hearing. Melissus, on the contrary, presents reasonably lucid and relatively detailed arguments; and from his fragments it is possible to construct, without any special pleading and with surprisingly little polishing or pruning, two very respectable arguments, one against alteration and one against locomotion.

(g) *Corporeal being*

Matter, according to Descartes, is three-dimensional extension and nothing more. To see this, 'we have only to attend to our idea of some body, e.g., a stone, and remove from it whatever we know is not entailed by the very nature of body'. We 'remove' in this way hardness, colour, weight and temperature, and, in conclusion 'we may now observe that absolutely no element of our idea remains, except extension in length, breadth and depth'. Matter is thus identified with space, and the identification allows Descartes to reject the possibility of a vacuum: the notion of empty space, bodiless body, is a trivial contradiction.[28]

The Cartesian view might well have appealed to Melissus; but it was a heterodox view and there seemed to be overwhelming objections to it: how can Descartes distinguish between a geometrical 'solid' and a physical 'solid'? between a stereometrical sphere and a rubber ball? between an area of space and that area's occupants? He cannot, yet he must: geometrical bodies have no causal powers; geometry is a static subject, yet even if geometrical objects moved, they would not effect motion in one another—they have not the body to do so. A world of moving geometrical objects is like a world of images on a cinema screen: thin, unsubstantial, powerless, immaterial.

Three-dimensionality is perhaps necessary to materiality; but it is not sufficient. What more is needed? The classical answer is: Solidity, or impenetrability. And the *locus classicus* for that answer is in Locke's *Essay*: 'This of all other, seems the *Idea* most intimately connected with, and essential to Body, so as no where else to be found or imagin'd, but only in matter: and though our Senses take no notice of it, but in masses of matter, of a bulk sufficient to cause a Sensation in us; Yet the Mind, having once got this *Idea* from such grosser sensible Bodies, traces it farther; and considers it, as well as Figure, in the minutest Particle of Matter, that can exist; and finds it inseparably inherent in Body, where-ever, or however modified. This is the *Idea* belongs to Body, whereby we conceive it *to fill space*. The *Idea* of which filling of space, is, That where we imagine any space taken up by a solid Substance, we conceive it so to possess it, that it excludes all other solid Substances; and, will for ever hinder any two other Bodies, that move towards one another in a strait Line, from coming to touch one another, unless it removes from between them in a Line, not parallel to that which they move in' (II.iv.1–2). Solidity, impenetrability, resistance: physical objects, or 'bodies', do not merely have spatial location; they fill or occupy space. And if *O* fills a volume of space *V*, then *O* excludes from *V* any other physical object *O′*, so that no two things can be in the same place at the same time (cf. *Essay* II. xxvii.1). Thus by filling *V* and excluding *O′* from it, *O* 'resists' *O′* and is 'impenetrable' to it.

The Atomists grasped this notion clearly enough: atoms, they said, are solid (*stereos*), massy (*nastos*), full (*plêrês*)—they are space occupants in the strong Lockean sense (see below, p. 345). The atomists took their view from Melissus; for in (T14) he expresses for the first time the thesis that substance is solid: '*O* is full (*pleôn*)' means '*O* is a space filler' or '*O* is solid'.

At first sight, Melissus' explanation of 'fullness' in sentence [xxvi] of **168** does not suggest that gloss. More homely and familiar thoughts come to mind: a diamond, say, which neither 'yields' to pressure nor 'receives' other stuffs is 'full'; a squash ball, a wine bottle, and a loofah are not 'full'—the ball yields to the racquet, though it does not 'receive'; the bottle accepts the wine, though it does not 'yield'; the loofah both yields to the fingers and receives the bathwater. But on that account 'fullness' is an unhappy hybrid notion, compounded from hardness and non-porosity. (Locke carefully distinguishes solidity from hardness: *Essay* II.iv.4.) And in any case, the account cannot be correct. What is not full is, according to Melissus, empty, i.e. partially vacuous; and Melissus cannot have supposed that a rubber ball, an empty bottle and a dry loofah all contain vacuums. The bottle will 'receive'; but the 'received' wine displaces air, not a vacuum. The loofah will squash; but when squashed the water drips out of it.

A different account is required; and Lockean solidity is the only plausible alternative: when Melissus says that *O* is 'full', he means that it 'fills space'; when he says that *O* 'does not yield', he means that it has 'resistance'; when he says that *O* does not 'receive', he means that it is 'impenetrable'. The concept of solidity, delineated here with astonishing clarity and accuracy, was one of Melissus' most influential and valuable bequests.

Did he bequeath a truth or a falsity? Leibniz observed, correctly, that shadows and rays of light may interpenetrate (*Nouveaux Essais*, II.xxvii.1), and the same holds for smells and for sounds.[29] But such things are not primary substances, or physical objects. Again, a human body and a collection of cells will occupy the same place at the same time; yet they are distinguishable physical objects. But here the cells constitute the body; and evidently the Melissan principle does not rule out the interpenetration of a body and the sum of its parts or the sum of its physical constituents.

A third potential counter-example is more interesting. Science—

that unimpeachable and incomprehensible god—assures us that macroscopic physical objects are made up of a myriad atoms whirling about in a void: physical objects are not, in fact, solid; they are perforated and channelled by vacuous space. Perhaps, then, a certain correspondence and symmetry in the atomic sub-structure of physical objects might allow two bodies to interpenetrate; as an electric plug fits into a socket, so two electric plugs might fit into one another were their atoms and vacant interstices suitably arranged. Does this show that physical bodies are not essentially solid? or should we rather dissociate solidity from impenetrability so that physical objects are necessarily solid, but not necessarily impenetrable? Or is it not better still to infer that macroscopic objects are not in fact physical bodies, though they appear so to the untutored eye? The only genuinely physical objects in the world are the ultimate corpuscles of matter, microscopic objects which contain no vacancies. This third suggestion was made by the ancient Atomists; and I find it the least offensive of the three solutions. Necessarily, physical objects are solid and impenetrable; but it is a question for science to answer whether any of the macroscopic objects we daily observe are in actual fact physical objects.

However that may be, such atomist worries would not have moved Melissus; for he has already argued implicitly that atomism is false: substances contain no vacancies. From his denial of emptiness Melissus moves immediately to an assertion of fullness: 'it is necessary for it to be full if it is not empty' (sentence [xxvii]). (T14) is inferred at once from (T13): what has no vacancies is solid or impenetrable; what is in no respect empty is full—the inference seems trivial enough.

Yet is it sound? Leibniz, for one, doubted it: 'We see, for example, two shadows or rays of light which interpenetrate, and we might invent for ourselves an imaginary world wherein bodies would act in the same way' (*Nouveaux Essais* II. xxvii.1). Such an invention does not greatly tax the imagination: we are all familiar in childhood with men who walk through walls. But the imagination is a bad judge of the impossible: if we cannot, like the White Queen, believe five impossible things before breakfast, we can surely imagine them; and Leibniz' point is not that interpenetration is imaginable but that it is logically possible. Suppose we discover a new metal, and make a pair of billiard balls from it; the balls are hard and seem solid, they do not fall through the cloth of the table or disappear into the side cushions. Place ball *a* on one side cushion at point *A*, and cue it to the opposite cushion at *A′*; place *b* on the end cushion at *B*, and cue it to the opposite cushion at *B′*. The lines *AA′* and *BB′* intersect; call the point of intersection *C*. Now replace *a* at *A* and *b* at *B*. Strike *a* and *b* in such a way that each, if unimpeded, would reach *C* at the same time, *t*. Ordinary balls would clash and be diverted from their paths; but *a* and *b*, to the amazement of the spectators, continue through *C* to *A′* and *B′*. At *t*, then, *a* and *b* were in exactly the same place, *C*; at *t a* and *b* interpenetrated.

The case is imaginable: is it logically possible? I cannot show that it is; but equally I know of no argument that it is not. And the additional specification, that *a* and *b* are not 'empty in any respect', does not enable me to concoct an argument. I suppose that stories should count as logically innocent until they are proved guilty; and I therefore take the case of the curious billiard balls as setting up a *prima facie* refutation of Melissus' move from (T13) to (T14).

The matter is not indifferent to Melissus. For, contrary to the tradition which I have so far followed, Melissus' denial of motion in (T15) requires (T14) and not merely (T13): a body, *a*, may move into a location *p* even if *p* is already occupied by some other non-empty body *b*, provided that *b*, though not empty at all, is not impenetrable. Space may be, as it were, overfull: at no time is any volume of space unoccupied; but various volumes of space have several distinct occupants. Unless Melissus can establish (T14), in the strong sense of impenetrability, he cannot reach (T15). I shall, as I promised, consider objections to Melissus' argument against motion in a later chapter; but those objections are distinct from the one I have just canvassed. Nor are they otiose; for even if it is granted that (T14) does not follow logically from (T13), it may still be conceded to Melissus that if (T13) is true, then, as a matter of contingent fact, so is (T14).

From (T13) Melissus infers (T16): *O* is not 'dense or rare'. He means, of course, that *O* does not exhibit different degrees of density in its several parts. He clearly states that if *O* is rarer than *O′*, then *O* must contain more void than *O′*; and given that, his inference holds. As far as I can see, it is not a logical truth that rare bodies contain more vacancy than dense bodies; and I do not know whether or not it is a scientific truth. At any rate, Melissus does not succeed in proving (T16). He might have done better to derive it from (T6); for homogeneity presumably excludes variation in density no less than in any other property. But (T16) is not a very interesting thesis, and I shall say no more about it.[30]

Whatever the value of Melissus' arguments in the latter part of **168**, they leave one point in no doubt: Melissus' entity, *O*, is a solid, physical body; it is 'full', a material occupant of space; and it is impenetrable, refusing to countenance any co-occupants.[31]

That conclusion was denied by Simplicius, who thought he could disprove it out of Melissus' own mouth:

> And that he wants it to be incorporeal (*asômatos*) is shown by his saying: 'If, then, it were, it must be one; and being one, it must not have body' (**170: B 9**).

Elsewhere Simplicius continues his quotation:

> And being one, it must not have body (*sôma*). But if it had mass (*pachos*), it would have parts, and it would no longer be one (**171**).[32]

It is worth setting the argument out explicitly. From:
(1) *X* is one,
Melissus infers:
(2) *X* has no parts.
Then to:
(3) *X* has no mass,
and finally to:
(4) *X* has no body.
It is only natural to identify *X* with *O*: then (1) is (T5); the move from (1) to (2) mirrors that from (T5) to (T6); and (4) implies that *O* is unextended—a geometrical point, perhaps.

That conclusion conflicts flatly with (T4); and those scholars, beginning with Simplicius, who consequently deny (T4) to Melissus fly in the face of the evidence.[33] Other scholars observe that (4) does not in fact require a purely punctual existence for *X*: *X* might be an infinitely extended geometrical solid. That conclusion fares no better: it conflicts flatly with (T14): *O* is physical, not geometrical.[34]

A bold answer to these difficulties rejects the identification of *X* with *O*: Simplicius wrongly took **171** to be about the Eleatic entity; in fact the fragment came from the polemical portion of Melissus' book and constitutes part of an attack upon the pluralist opponents of Elea. That there was such a portion to Melissus' work is made probable by **B 8**, which I examine in a later chapter; and **171** readily yields an argument of Zenonian stamp: 'Suppose that there are many *X*'s. Then each must be a unity; hence it can have no parts; hence it cannot be corporeal.'

There are two powerful objections to that bold answer. First, it goes against Simplicius' express assertion that **171** is about 'the One'. But Simplicius' assertion is made in order to prove a contentious point; and, as his treatment of **160** and **161** shows, he is not at his best in dealing with Melissus. Moreover, the *MXG* implies, against Simplicius, that Melissus did not say that 'the One' is incorporeal.[35]

Second, even if **171** appeared in a polemical context, Melissus must surely have realized how close it stood to some of his positive remarks: how could he have argued for the incorporeality of pluralist units without seeing that the same argument applied to his own Eleatic entity? Perhaps he thought that the argument did not apply to his entity *O*. After all, if *X* is identified with *O*, then the argument from (2) to (3) is dismal: from the fact that *O* is partless, in the sense of homogeneous, it does not even seem to follow that *O* is incorporeal or unextended. On the other hand, if *X* is a pluralist unit, the inference can be given a passable complexion: Melissus doubtless held that the items in a plurality must be separated from one another (cf. Aristotle, *GC* 325a5; *Phys* 213b22); perhaps he maintained that any such free-floating item must, if it were divisible, in the course of time come to be divided and so cease to be a unity: pluralist units, being inherently liable to split, must be mere partless points if they are to be unitary; such reasoning does not apply to the Eleatic One.

I do not find the suggestion delicious. But it is less unpalatable than its rivals; for unless **171** is read as a piece of polemic, Melissus is left with a downright contradiction; and unless the polemic is read in the fashion I suggest, it will not yield any remotely reasonable argument.

I end this section by observing that **171**, as a polemical fragment, sheds no light on the question of the divisibility of *O*. **169**, as I have already observed, talks of being divided, not of being divisible. What, then, of the puzzle raised by Melissus' argument for (T6)? Did he go on to say that *O* is not even theoretically divisible, on the grounds that if you could notionally distinguish two parts of *O* (say in terms of co-ordinates based on an arbitrarily chosen point of origin in *O*) then there would exist at least three things, *O* and its two parts? There is no evidence that Melissus did make this move; nor is there any reason why he should have done: physically distinct or physically distinguishable parts of *O* are doubtless existent individuals, and such parts must therefore be denied by a monist. But the same does not obviously hold for notionally distinguishable parts. Aristotle would have assigned to such parts only 'potential' existence; and Melissus, I suggest, might (had he ever contemplated the question) have allowed notional divisibility to *O* on the grounds that such divisibility offends neither against uniqueness nor against homogeneity.

(h) *The philosophy of Elea*

Parmenides' Way of Truth is short, and the cluster of truths, or alleged truths, along it is small. What exists is ungenerated and without destruction; it forms a continuous whole in time and space; it is changeless and does not move. Probably it has a purely instantaneous existence; probably it is a finite sphere. Melissus adds little: what exists is full, it does not have degrees of density, it is homogeneous—those theses Parmenides might have accepted. Melissus also holds, in contradiction to Parmenides, that what is is spatially infinite and temporally eternal; and he maintains a real monism, where Parmenides was prudently silent.

The Eleatic system is brief, but powerful in its implications: those few properties which Eleatic beings have are, it seems, sufficient to bar them from the field of scientific investigation, and hence to leave the scientist with nothing but his own fantasies to contemplate: in a completely stable world the laws of physics will be trivial or dull.

That is not to say that the Eleatics leave absolutely nothing to science. It is often supposed that the Way of Truth, and Melissus' amended route, are both intended to be complete, that there is nothing to be said about the world which Parmenides and Melissus have not said. There is no warrant at all for that supposition in the case of Melissus, whose fragments nowhere pretend to completeness. Parmenides' goddess does indeed offer to tell him 'everything' (**28 B** 1.28) and his mares escort him 'as far as desire may reach' (**B 1**.1); but it is implausible to read those unsystematic remarks as an explicit claim to metaphysical completeness.[36]

I am inclined to think that the Eleatic system is, in theory at least, extendable: further metaphysical research might add further essential properties of *to on*. (It is a plausible conjecture that Parmenides discovered the punctuality of *O* after he had ordered the rest of his deduction: surely he would wish to leave open the way to further discoveries?) Moreover, I see nothing that positively excludes the scientific and experimental discovery of contingent properties of existents. One example must suffice: *O*, according to **156**. 41, cannot 'alter bright colour'. I infer that *O* has a 'bright colour', or perhaps a wash of different bright colours. Now **156** does not, and perhaps metaphysics cannot, infer the colour or colours of *O*; here, perhaps, is a little opening for scientific endeavour; and other openings, of a similar unexciting kind, are readily imagined.

It may be that this possibility is ruled out by Melissus: in **30 B 8** (below, p. 298), he lists as potential items in a plural universe 'earth and water and air and fire and iron and gold and living and dead and black and white and the other things which men say are real'. If 'black and white' are *not* real, as **B 8** implies, then perhaps *O* is neither black nor white nor any other colour: *O* has just those properties deducible from the fact that it exists; it has no contingent properties. I doubt the inference. Melissus' list divides into four groups of incompatibles; the reason is clear: if black *and* white are both real, then, since they are contraries, there must exist at least *two* things, contrary to monism. It does not follow that both black and white are unreal: Melissus could consistently allow that *O* was, say, black, and maintain the falsity of pluralism. He need not object to there being some one thing which is both gold and yellow: that does not infringe on the claims of monism; he need only object to there being both gold and iron, both yellow and grey. **B 8** is a polemical fragment, and Melissus is less explicit in certain parts of it than we might like. Nonetheless, I incline to think that he, like Parmenides, leaves open a narrow and fairly tedious path to the scientist.

I do not press these final remarks: Parmenides and Melissus were certainly not engaged in a conscious effort to point out the path of legitimate science; and it is absurd to praise them as the founding fathers of theoretical physics.[37] Indeed, had they observed the loopholes I have just indicated, they might, I suppose, have hastily closed them up: metaphysics will countenance no scientific tax-dodgers. My point is a gentle one: taken strictly, the surviving words of Parmenides and Melissus do not warrant the assertion that their Eleatic systems were intended to exhaust the whole well of human intellectual achievement. They could happily have encouraged further metaphysical speculation; they might not have frowned too severely upon a little elementary scientific research.

XII

Zeno: Paradox and Plurality

(a) *The Eleatic Palamedes*

According to Coleridge, 'the few remains of Zeno the Eleatic, his paradoxes against the reality of motion, are mere identical propositions spun out into a sort of whimsical conundrums'. Depreciatory judgments of that character excited a splendid retort from Russell: 'In this capricious world, nothing is more capricious than posthumous fame. One of the most notable victims of posterity's lack of judgment is the Eleatic Zeno. Having invented four arguments, all immeasurably subtle and profound, the grossness of subsequent philosophers pronounced him to be a mere ingenious juggler, and his arguments to be one and all sophisms.'[1]

Philosophers have been driven to repentance by Russell's lashes. Zeno now stands as the most celebrated of Presocratic thinkers; and his paradoxes are again vivacious philosophical issues. Yet of Zeno himself our knowledge is exiguous: the surviving fragments count barely two hundred words; the doxography is slight and repetitious; and the structure and impetus of Zeno's thought remain dark and controversial.

We know surprisingly little of Zeno's life and history;[2] and most of our information comes from the celebrated but suspect story in Plato's *Parmenides*. The passage is worth quoting at length; Pythodorus is describing the visit of Parmenides and Zeno to Athens:

> . . . They came to Athens, as he said, at the great Panathenaea: the former was, at the time of his visit, about 65 years old, very white with age, but well favoured. Zeno was nearly 40 years of age, tall and fair to look upon: in the days of his youth he was reported to have been beloved by Parmenides. He said that they lodged

with Pythodorus in the Ceramicus, outside the wall, whither Socrates, then a very young man, came to see them, and many others with him: they wanted to hear the writings of Zeno, which had been brought to Athens for the first time on the occasion of their visit. These Zeno himself read to them in the absence of Parmenides, and had very nearly finished when Pythodorus entered, and with him Parmenides and Aristoteles who was afterwards one of the Thirty, and heard the little that remained of the dialogue. Pythodorus had heard Zeno repeat them before.

When the recitation was completed, Socrates requested that the first thesis of the first argument might be read over again, and this having been done, he said: What is your meaning, Zeno? Do you maintain that if entities are many, they must be both like and unlike, and that this is impossible, for neither can the like be unlike, nor the unlike like—is that your position?

Just so, said Zeno.

And if the unlike cannot be like, or the like unlike, then according to you, entities could not be many; for this would involve an impossibility. In all that you say have you any other purpose except to disprove the existence of the many? and is not each division of your treatise intended to furnish a separate proof of this, there being in all as many proofs of the non-existence of the many as you have composed arguments? Is that your meaning or have I misunderstood you?

No, said Zeno; you have correctly understood my general purpose.

I see, Parmenides, said Socrates, that Zeno would like to be not only one with you in friendship but your second self in his writings too: he puts what you say in another way, and would fain make believe that he is telling us something which is new. For you, in your poems, say The All is one, and of this you adduce excellent proofs; and he on the other hand says there is no many: and on behalf of this he offers overwhelming evidence. You affirm unity, he denies plurality. And so you deceive the world into believing that you are saying different things when really you are saying much the same. This is a strain of art beyond the reach of most of us.

Yes, Socrates, said Zeno. But although you are as keen as a Spartan hound in pursuing the track, you do not fully apprehend the true motive of the composition, which is not really such an artificial work as you imagine; for what you speak of was an accident; there was no pretence of a great purpose: nor any serious intention of deceiving the world. The truth is that these writings of mine were meant to protect the arguments of Parmenides against those who make fun of him and seek to show the many ridiculous and contradictory results which they suppose to follow from the affirmation of the one. My answer is addressed to the partisans of the many, whose attack I return with interest by retorting upon them that their hypothesis of the existence of many, if carried out, appears to be still more ridiculous than the hypothesis of the existence of one. Zeal for my master led me to write the book in the days of my youth, but someone stole the copy: and therefore I had no choice whether it should be published or not: the motive, however, of writing was not the ambition of an elder man, but the pugnacity of a young one. This you do not seem to see, Socrates; though in other respects, as I was saying, your notion is a very just one.

I understand, said Socrates, and quite accept your account (**172:** 127A–128E, trans. Jowett).

The details of the story, and the chronology implicit in it, are not my concern. What matters is the central core of Plato's account, which most scholars accept as historical truth. According to that core, Zeno in his youth, incensed by the ignorant attacks on his master's monism, wrote a collection of arguments designed to reduce pluralism to absurdity and so to defend monism. The story thus ascribes a plan, an aim and a method to Zeno; let us take them in turn.

Zeno's tract contained many arguments (127E). Proclus, in his commentary on the *Parmenides*, says that there were forty *logoi* in all (**29 A 15**; so too Elias, **A 15**); and there is no reason to reject his testimony. All those *logoi* attacked the hypothesis of pluralism: of the eight Zenonian arguments that we possess, two certainly were numbered among those forty. The standing of the four paradoxes on motion is uncertain: they can be pressed into a suitable form for membership of the forty; but Elias (**A 15**) says that in addition to the forty *logoi* there were five arguments against motion.[3] Moreover, it is clear from Aristotle's account that the paradoxes of motion were customarily treated as a special unity; and that may reflect a special origin. For the rest, antiquity supplies four Zenonian book-titles;[4] but they do not enable us to say anything about the original format of Zeno's publications.

Some scholars are not content with the information that Zeno's tract contained forty *logoi*: they attempt to discern a grand architectonic structure uniting several of the *logoi* into a complex and sophisticated argument against pluralism. Thus Zeno is bent on attacking pluralism: if the world is divisible into parts, then it is finitely or infinitely divisible; if finitely divisible, then its parts are separated by other bodies or by gaps (which **B 3** rules out), or else they abut one another (which the Arrow rules out); if infinitely divisible, then either the division is completable (which **B 2** rules out) or it is not (which the Dichotomy and the Achilles rule out). By a happy chance, the *logoi* we possess form a single integrated construction.[5]

Such architectonic interpretations have a certain attraction. But closer inspection reveals gaps and botches in the building: if Zeno did build thus, he was not a particularly skilful builder. Moreover, those interpretations are wholly products of the scholarly fancy. There is not a jot of evidence in any ancient text that Zeno's *logoi* ever formed such an integrated and interdependent whole; no ancient author knows anything of Zeno the logical master-builder. On the contrary, there is some evidence against the interpretation; for Plato asserts that each *logos* itself constituted a proof against pluralism. And if the fragments and reports of Zeno's arguments have been supposed to suggest an overall structure, that supposition is, in my view, quite illusory; and my discussion of the paradoxes will give no hint of a systematic interdependence among Zeno's different arguments.

So much for the plan of Zeno's arguments. Their aim, according to the *Parmenides*, was to defend Parmenides against those who were attempting to make fun of him (128C). Modern scholars have tried to identify those anonymous mockers, but without success. Many have invoked the Pythagoreans: a curious philosophy, called 'unit-point-atomism', has been ascribed to the sect; the philosophy has been judged a consciously anti-Parmenidean invention; and Zeno's arguments have then been interpreted as a rejection of the philosophy and hence as a defence of Parmenides. But that account is the merest fantasy: 'unit-point-atomism', if it existed, would not constitute a peculiarly incisive and mocking rejection of Parmenides; it is pluralistic, but so is every non-Eleatic theory. And in any case, the doctrine never existed: there is no direct evidence for it; and in order to infer its existence from Zeno's paradoxes we must subject those arguments to a gratuitously tortuous interpretation. For many years scholars have campaigned for and against a Pythagorean opposition to Parmenides; by now the campaign should be over.[6]

Did Zeno defend Parmenides against philosophical attack from some other quarter? I doubt it. Plato implies that the attacks on Parmenides were satirical rather than philosophical, and the Eleatic position is an obvious target for satire and ridicule. We can be sure that Parmenides, like all later metaphysicians of any originality, was an object of popular mirth: where his doctrines were known—or half-known—they will have been jeered at. It is to such receptions, and not to philosophical opposition, that Plato refers.[7]

Was it Zeno's aim to defend Parmenides against mockery? I am inclined to doubt Plato's suggestion that it was. First, I doubt that Parmenides was a monist at all. Second, even in the *Parmenides* Zeno does not claim to have been defending monism in any straightforward way. He asserts that the defence of monism which Socrates has read into his *logoi* was only incidental; his aim was to show that pluralism suffers 'still greater absurdities' than monism. That is hardly the language of an ardent monist. Third, even if pluralism *is* absurd, monism is not thereby defended; Plato is wrong in saying that a proof of monism and a refutation of pluralism come to the same thing. Zeno's pupil Gorgias was well aware of that: he was, notionally at least, a nihilist.[8] Fourth, more than one of Zeno's arguments seem to bear with equal force against pluralism and against monism. I shall note these cases as I discuss the paradoxes; here I observe that they make it hard to envisage Zeno as a self-conscious monist.

Those considerations seem to be supported by a strand in the doxographical tradition. The thesis that Zeno attacked 'the One' is discussed, and rejected, by Simplicius (*in Phys* 97.9–99.31; 138.3–139.23); and it originated with Eudemus.[9] Unfortunately, Eudemus offered only weak support for his opinion, citing an anecdote and preparing a collage of three Zenonian arguments. The arguments, as Simplicius observes, are taken from Zeno's *logoi* against pluralism, and I shall consider them later; whatever their force, they do not reveal Zeno as a formal opponent of monism. The anecdote runs like this:

> They say that Zeno used to say that if someone would tell him what on earth the one (*to hen*) is, he would be able to talk about the things that exist (**173:** Eudemus, fr. 37aW = **A 16** = **L 5**).[10]

Nothing can be based on this second-hand story: '*to hen*' may, I suppose, mean 'the [Eleatic] One', and Zeno may have meant to cast doubt on its credentials; but '*to hen*' may equally mean 'a unit', and refer to the units that construct the pluralist world.[11] Eudemus' evidence does not establish that Zeno overtly attacked monism; but the four preceding considerations do at least show that he was not greatly concerned to defend it.

I turn to the question of Zeno's logical method. In the *Parmenides* (127E), Socrates gets Zeno to agree that each of his arguments is intended to have the form of a *reductio ad impossibile*; and later writers dutifully expound them in that form (cf. Proclus, **A 15**). Aristotle called Zeno the father of 'dialectic', and 'dialectic' may mean 'logic'. Modern scholars often regard Zeno as the first self-conscious logician, or at least as the inventor of argument by *reductio*.[12]

A pinch of sceptical snuff will clear the mind. Zeno was not the first thinker to use *reductio*, nor was he the first logician to reflect upon *reductio*; others had argued reductively before Zeno, and no one studied logic before Aristotle. Moreover, it is improbable that Zeno himself used reductive arguments. Indeed Plato almost says as much; for he represents Socrates as extracting from Zeno the realization that his arguments are reductive and not as finding a reductive form in the *logoi* themselves. Socrates is bringing to fictional consciousness what was at best latent in historical reality. Zeno's surviving fragments contain no *reductio*: he takes an hypothesis and infers an absurdity from it; but he never makes the characteristic move of *reductio*, the inference to the falsity of the hypothesis. He argues 'If *P*, then *Q*', where *Q* states some absurdity; but he does not explicitly infer the falsity of *P*. In other words, he does not use *reductio ad absurdum* as a technique for disproof.

In the *Parmenides* Zeno presents himself, or at least his juvenile self,[13] as an eristic debater, a sophist out to impress an audience; and in the *Phaedrus* he is called an *antilogikos* or logic-chopper.[14] I do not suggest that Zeno was a charlatan, a purveyor of arguments which he knew to be fallacious; nor do I mean that he had no philosophical interest in Eleaticism. But I do suggest that Zeno was not a systematic Eleatic solemnly defending Parmenides against philosophical attack by a profound and interconnected set of reductive argumentations. Many men had mocked Parmenides: Zeno mocked the mockers. His *logoi* were designed to reveal the inanities and ineptitudes inherent in the ordinary belief in a plural world; he wanted to startle, to amaze, to disconcert. He did not have the serious metaphysical purpose of supporting an Eleatic monism; and he did not adopt a ponderous logical precision in his method.

That conclusion has some slight importance. Many modern interpreters of Zeno have argued that such and such an account of a paradox is wrong because it attributes a silly fallacy to a profound mind. Zeno was not profound: he was clever. Some profundities did fall from his pen; but so too did some trifling fallacies. And that is what we should expect from an eristic disputant. If we meet a deep argument, we may rejoice; if we are dazzled by a superficial glitter, we are not bound to search for a nugget of philosophical gold. Fair metal and base, in roughly equal proportions, make the Zenonian alloy.

(b) *Large and small*

It is appropriate to begin with those of Zeno's surviving arguments which specifically attack pluralism. They account for all that we possess of Zeno's own words; they were certainly a part of his collection of *logoi*; and some of the issues they raise underlie the subtler paradoxes of motion.

The hypothesis under attack, pluralism, simply says that 'there exist many things'. I shall abbreviate this to *P*. It is, I take it, a moderately clear and unambiguous hypothesis. If Zeno is out to show the absurdity of pluralism, we may expect his attacks on *P* to conclude to propositions of the form:

(Z*) If *P*, then *Q* and not-*Q*.

That is equivalent to:

(Z) If *P*, then *Q*; and if *P*, then not-*Q*,

and the surviving evidence shows that, in some cases at least, Zeno did set himself to demonstrate a conjunctive proposition of the form (Z); and his procedure was the obvious one of arguing independently for each conjunct of the conjunction.[15]

According to the *Phaedrus*, Zeno made 'the same things seem like and unlike, and one and many, and at rest and in motion' (261D = **A 13**). To those three pairs of opposites we may add at least two others: large and small (**B 1–2**), and finite and infinite (**B 3**). Such pairs can all readily be accommodated to the schema (Z). Doubtless there were more pairs; but it is hardly likely that the forty arguments used forty distinct pairs of opposites.[16]

The first *logos* in Zeno's treatise used the pair 'like and unlike' (**172**: *Parm* 127D-E). Zeno's first conclusion, then, will have been:

(Z1) (a) If *P*, then everything is alike, and (b) if *P*, then everything is unlike.

We do not know how Zeno argued for (Z1), nor what he meant by 'everything is alike'.[17] The word for 'alike' is '*homoios*'. Perhaps: 'If *a* and *b* are distinct existents, then they are similar (*homoios*) in so far as each exists—hence they are alike; and they are dissimilar (*anhomoios*) in so far as each is different from the other—hence they are unlike.' Or perhaps rather: 'If *a* and *b* are distinct existents, then as existent each will be homogeneous (*homoios*)—hence they are alike; and yet being distinct, they are heterogeneous and hence unlike'.

Neither argument has any power; for neither conclusion is more than an apparent absurdity: the consequents of (Z1) do not together amount to anything of the damning form '*Q* and not-*Q*'. The first argument is sound and harmless; the second, even if it were sound, would cause no pluralist any loss of sleep. For all that, it is worth starting with (Z1), for two reasons. First, it may finally kill the desire to find a subtle argument behind Zeno's every *dictum*. Second, it exhibits an interesting feature of Zeno's technique: *P* contains the two notions of *existence* and of *plurality*. In (Z1), conjunct (Z1a) makes use of the notion of *existence* in *P*, and conjunct (Z1b) turns to that of *plurality*. *P* is absurd (Zeno urges) because it conjoins two notions with contradictory implications.

I turn now to the *logos* of 'large and small'; we know that it preceded the *logos* of 'finite and infinite' (Simplicius, *in Phys* 140.34), but we do not know its absolute position among the forty *logoi*. For this *logos* we possess some of Zeno's own words. Simplicius, who preserves them, quotes them in the course of a piece of commentatorial controversy; and it is necessary to reconstruct the original argument from two passages in Simplicius' text. Since scholars have not agreed on the reconstruction, I shall begin by displaying the two passages.[18]

In the first passage, Simplicius is concerned to refute the opinion of Alexander and Eudemus that Zeno 'rejected the One':

> In the treatise of his which contains many arguments, he proves in each one that anyone who asserts that there exist many things is committed to asserting opposites. One of these is an argument in which he proves that [i] if there exist many things, they are both large and small—large so as to be unlimited in magnitude, small so as to have no magnitude. Now in this he proves that [ii] what has neither magnitude, nor mass, nor bulk, would not even exist. '[iii] For', he says, 'if it were attached to something else that exists, it would not make it larger; [iv] for if it is of no magnitude but is attached, that thing cannot increase at all in magnitude. [v] And in this way what is attached will thereby be nothing. [vi] And if, when it is detached, the other thing is no smaller, and, when it is attached again, it will not grow, it is clear that what is attached is nothing, and likewise what is detached.' And Zeno says this not in order to reject the One, but [vii] to show that each of the many things has a magnitude—and an unlimited one at that (for there is always something in front of what is taken, because of the unlimited division). [viii] And he proves this having first proved that each of the many things has no magnitude from the fact that

each is the same as itself and one (**174**: *in Phys* 139.5–19; cf. **B 2** = **9 L**).[19]

In the second passage, which is part of the same long note on *Physics* 187a1, Simplicius is arguing against Porphyry's view that the 'dichotomy' argument to which Aristotle refers belongs to Parmenides rather than to Zeno:

> And why should we waste words when [the argument] is actually produced in Zeno's own treatise? For in proving that if there exist many things the same things are unlimited and limited Zeno writes in these words: [ix] 'If there exist many things, it is necessary that they be as many as they are and neither more than themselves nor less. But if they are as many as they are, they will be limited. If there exist many things, the things that exist are unlimited. For there are always other things in the middle of the things that exist, and again others in the middle of those. And thus the things that exist are unlimited.' And in this way he proved their numerical unlimitedness from the dichotomy. Their quantitative unlimitedness [he proved] earlier by the same method of argument. [x] For having proved beforehand that if what exists had no magnitude it would not even exist, he continues: '[xi] and if there exist [many things], it is necessary for each to have a certain magnitude and mass, [xii] and for the one part of it to be separate from the other. [xiii] And the same argument holds of what protrudes; for that too will have a magnitude, and some part of it will protrude. [xiv] Now it is all one to say this of one case and to say it of every case; for no such part of it will be last, nor will there not be another part related to another.[20] [xv] Thus if there exist many things, it is necessary for them to be both small and large—so small that they have no magnitude, so large that they are unlimited' (**175**: *in Phys* 140.27–141.8: cf. **B 3** = **11 L**; **B 1** = **10 L**).

Sentence [ix] (= **B 3**) contains the *logos* of 'finite and infinite'; since it appeared in Zeno's treatise after the 'large and small', I shall postpone discussion of it. Sentence [x] shows that the argument in [xi]–[xiv] was preceded by the argument in [iii]–[vi]; and sentences [vii] and [viii] show that the argument in [xi]–[xiv] was preceded by the argument briefly retailed in [viii]. Simplicius does not state explicitly that the argument of [viii] preceded that of [iii]–[vi]; but the content of the two arguments, and the form of Zeno's antinomy, make that precedence clear.

[i] and [xv] give the conclusion of the *logos* of 'large and small'; it is striking:

(Z2) (a) If P, then everything has no magnitude, and (b) if P, then everything has infinite magnitude.

Given (Z2a), Zeno need only argue that everything has some positive magnitude; given (Z2b) he might rest content with a proof that everything has a finite magnitude: to urge both (Z2a) and (Z2b) is logically excessive; and Zeno's urging is a *tour de force*.

Zeno's argument for (Z2a) is given in sentence [viii]; the argument for (Z2b) is stated in [xi]–[xiv], and it is prepared for in [iii]–[vi]. These latter sentences argue for the lemma:

(L) If a exists, then a has a positive magnitude.

Thus from Simplicius' text we can reconstruct the following account of Zeno's *logos*:

(Z2a) = [viii];
lemma (L) = [iii]–[vi],
whence (Z2b) = [xi]–[xiv]:
hence (Z2) = [xv].

I shall accordingly discuss the *logos* in the order (Z2a); (L); (Z2b).[21]

(c) *Existence*

(Z2a) need not detain us long. Zeno appears to have moved from 'a is self-identical and one' to 'a is without magnitude'. Scholars mediate the move by 'a is partless', and refer to Melissus, **171**, and to Plato's *Parmenides*, 137CD.[22] I have already commented briefly on this argument (above p. 227). I am not sure that it was Zeno's (it makes no use of the premiss of self-identity); but I have no alternative to offer. It may be observed that the hypothesis, P, plays no part in the derivation of (Z2a); as we shall see, P is similarly inactive in the derivation of (Z2b): the antinomy works impartially against P and against monism.

What of the argument for (L)? Some scholars feel that it prevaricates upon the word 'nothing'[23] but I do not share the feeling, and I shall ignore Zeno's use of the word in [v] and [vi]. The logical articulation of [iii]–[vi] is not wholly clear: if we use '$a + b$' to mean 'the result of attaching a to b'; and 'mag: a' for 'the magnitude of a', then [iii], I think, expresses the following proposition:

(1) If mag: $a = 0$, then if b exists and a is attached to b then mag: $a + b$ = mag: b.

As far as I can see, [iv] merely repeats [iii]. As for [v], that states:

(2) If, if b exists and a is attached to b, then mag: $a + b$ = mag: b, then a does not exist.

[vi] repeats the matter of [v] and adds to it a parallel clause about 'detachment'. I assume that [vi], which Aristotle calls 'Zeno's axiom' (*Met* 1001b7 = **A 21**), is an improved or completed version of [v]; a similarly improved version of [iii] is needed, if any inference is to be made from [vi]. (1) and (2) immediately yield:

(3) If mag: a = 0, a does not exist.

If we make the harmless assumption that nothing can have a negative magnitude, then (3) yields (L).

Is (2), Zeno's unimproved axiom, true? The words '*prosgignesthai*' and '*apogignesthai*', which I translate 'be attached to' and 'be detached from', are standardly rendered by 'be added to' and 'be subtracted from'. That rendering gives encouragement to those who see a geometrical base to Zeno's paradox and construe (L) as a theorem about geometrical points;[24] but it is mistaken: Zeno is thinking of the collocation and dislocation of physical objects; and '$a + b$' denotes the complex object formed by juxtaposing, intermixing, fusing or otherwise uniting the two objects a and b. The term 'magnitude' in (2) is generally taken to mean 'size' or 'volume'. It is apparent, then, that (2) is not a logical truth; indeed, it turns out to be a contingent falsehood. It plainly presupposes that, in general, mag: $a + b$ = mag: a + mag: b; but that presupposition, as every schoolboy knows, is false: a pint of alcohol mixed with a pint of water does not yield a quart of liquor. Moreover, (2) itself, I am told, is false: one of the peculiarities of the stuff zeolite is that, when added to water, it does not increase the volume of the water: mag: $z + w$ = mag: w.

Zeno might attempt to escape from this objection in either of two ways. First, he might abandon the physical interpretation of 'attachment' and tell us that it is, after all, a mathematical operation that he has in mind. Alternatively, he might prefer to have 'magnitude' understood as 'mass'. (According to Simplicius, he uses *megethos, pachos*, and *onkos* indiscriminately.) On both readings, the presupposition that mag: $a + b$ = mag: a + mag: b turns out true: on the first reading, it is a tautology; on the second, a primitive version of the Law of Conservation of Matter.

Yet neither of those defences will save Zeno. (2) carries a second, more general, presupposition, namely that if a is attached to b then a must be the sort of thing to have a magnitude—a volume or a mass, Surely, though, I can 'attach' my shadow to a wall, or 'attach' a picture to a cinema screen: shadows and pictures occupy no volume and have no mass; the shadowy wall and the coloured screen have precisely the same magnitude as the sunlit wall and the vacant screen;

yet for all that cast shadows and projected pictures exist. And that appears to refute (2).

Aristotle anticipated and answered this objection: Zeno advances his axiom

> clearly assuming that what exists is a magnitude—and if a magnitude, corporeal (*sômatikon*); for that is what exists in all ways [i.e. is three-dimensional] (**176**: *Met* 1001b9 = **A 21**).

(2) holds only if *a* and *b* are three-dimensional physical objects: I objected to (2) by citing cases in which *a* is a two-dimensional object; Aristotle suggests the simple retort: 'restrict *a* and *b* to three-dimensional objects'. It makes no odds whether we say that (2) is false but open to simple emendation; or rather that (2) is true when properly understood. The important fact is simply this: (2) is true if *a* and *b* are three-dimensional. And Zeno is surely entitled to that hypothesis: any pluralist will be proclaiming a world populated by fairly ordinary middle-sized objects; and it is such a pluralism that Zeno is out to attack. The commentators say as much in connexion with a later *logos*.

If (2) is true, so is (1); and thus Zeno has his conclusion. Moreover his conclusion need not decide between the two interpretations of 'magnitude'; for three-dimensional physical objects—bodies, for short—have both volume and mass. But victory is won at a price; and the price is triviality. The lemma (L), which reads like a strong ontological thesis, asserting that only things with magnitude can exist, turns out on examination to state no more than the analytic truth that all existent bodies occupy space and have a positive mass. From (L) nothing follows about the ontological status of shadows, of numbers, of points, of abstract entities—or of anything else.

The triviality of (L) may prove unimportant; what matters is whether it can function in the main argument for (Z2b). Yet it is, in a sense, distressing: the argumentative apparatus in [iii]–[vi] seems singularly pointless if (L) is as trifling as I claim; and some may still think that Zeno has stronger meat to cook. I can only say that no stronger conclusion will emerge from [iii]–[vi]; that there is no positive harm in impressing the truth of (L) by what is, after all, a sound argument; and that the interest of (L) lies in any case in its application to (Z2b), an application to which I now turn.

(d) *Infinite division*

The argument in [xi]–[xiv] is peculiarly difficult to grasp; and my presentation will, I fear, be both laborious and unconfident. First, let me offer a somewhat more precise version of its component sentences.

Sentence [xi] says that 'if there exist many things, it is necessary for each to have a certain magnitude and mass'; that, I assume, amounts to:

(1) If there exist objects $a_1, a_2, \ldots, a_n$, then for each i, mag: $a_i > 0$.

That is simply an application of the lemma (L). Sentence [xii] reads: '. . . and for the one part of it to be separate from (*apechein*) the other'; i.e.:

(2) If a_i exists, then there exist distinct parts of a_i, b_i and c_i.

I assume that the word *apechein* connotes nothing stronger than distinctness: that assumption is all that Zeno needs. Sentence [xiii]—'And the same argument holds of what protrudes'—applies (1) and (2) to one of the parts of a_i, say b_i. (I see no special significance in Zeno's label, 'what protrudes'.) And [xiv] asserts that (1) and (2) can be applied again to the parts of b_i, to the parts of the parts of b_i, and so on.

All that seems innocuous enough: how on earth are we to extract from it the lethal poison of (Z2b)? How can we generate, or seem to generate, infinitely large elephants from the little mice that play before us?

The rough answer to this question is not difficult to discover. By (2), every existent object contains infinitely many existent parts; and by (1) each of those parts has a positive magnitude. Now the magnitude of any object is equal to the sum of the magnitudes of its parts; and since any object has infinitely many parts, its magnitude is equal to the sum of the magnitudes of that infinity of parts. But the sum of infinitely many positive magnitudes is infinite; hence the magnitude of any object is infinite.

That, I think, is an uncontroversial expansion of Zeno's argument. The only premiss it requires which is not found in the Greek text is the thesis that the sum of an infinite set of magnitudes is infinite; and all scholars agree that some such thesis must be ascribed to Zeno. But the argument is still imprecise and impressionistic. I shall now attempt a more rigorous presentation. The ferociously technical aspect of what follows is, I believe, indispensable: if an argument is worth stating, it is worth stating precisely; and I cannot find a less unattractive route to precision than the one I follow here.

First, I need the notion of a *Zeno-set* or *Z-set*. Roughly speaking, a *Z-set* of an object *a* is any collection of all its parts: four legs and a top are a Z-set of the table I write upon; a few hundred pages, a spine, and two boards are a Z-set of the book you are reading; take a motor-mower engine to bits and beside you on the lawn you will have, if you are fortunate, a Z-set of the engine. Formally:

(D) $\{x_1, x_2. \ldots, x_n\}$ is a Z-set of y if and only if (a) every x_i is a proper part of y, (b) no x_i is a part of any other x_i, and (c) no part of y is not a part of the sum of all the x_is.

In place of Zeno's premiss (1) we can employ the simpler:

(3) If a exists, then mag: $a > 0$.

And in place of (2) we must use the more complex:

(4) If mag: $a > 0$, then there is a Z-set of a, $\{x_1, x_2, \ldots\}$, such that for every i mag: $x_i > 0$.

A further premiss is now required:

(5) If $\{x_{11}, x_{12}, \ldots\}$ is a Z-set of x_1, and $\{x_{21}, x_{22}, \ldots\}$ is a Z-set of x_2, and ... and $\{x_{n1}, x_{n2} \ldots\}$ is a Z-set of x_n, and $\{x_1, x_2, \ldots x_n\}$ is a Z-set of a, then $\{x_{11}, x_{12}, \ldots x_{21}, x_{22}, \ldots, \ldots x_{n1}, x_{n2} \ldots\}$ is a Z-set of a.

That is formidable in appearance; but it only expresses, in formal dress, the mundane truth that any object is made up of the parts of its parts.

From (3)–(5) I infer:

(6) If a exists, then for any n there is a Z-set of a, $\{x_1, x_2, \ldots, x_m\}$, such that $m > n$,

For suppose that the most numerous Z-set of a is k, or $\{x_1, x_2, \ldots, x_k\}$. Then mag: $x_k > 0$, and hence there is a Z-set of x_k, say $\{x_{k1}, x_{k2}, \ldots, x_{kj}\}$. But then there will be a Z-set of a $\{x_1, x_2, \ldots, x_{k-1}, x_{k1}, x_{k2}, \ldots, x_{kj}\}$; and that will be more numerous than k. Hence k is not the most numerous Z-set of a.

In effect, (6) says that a is infinitely divisible, or contains infinitely many parts. A further premiss, of self-evident truth, is now needed:

(7) If $\{x_1, x_2, \ldots x_n, \ldots\}$ is a Z-set of a, then mag: a = mag: x_1 + mag: x_2 + ... + mag: x_n + ...

I use the sign S^n_m to name the set $\{x_n, x_{n+1}, \ldots, x_m\}$; and '$\infty$' for infinity. By (6), then, there is a Z-set of a S^1_∞; and hence, by (7):

(8) If a exists, then mag: a = mag: S^1_∞.

Finally, we need a premiss concerning the summing of infinite sets, viz:

(9) If for every x_i in S^1_∞ mag: $x_i > 0$, then mag: $S^1_\infty = \infty$.

It is now a simple inference to:

(10) If a exists, mag: $a = \infty$.

And (10) is equivalent to (Z2b).

Evidently, the argument is unsound; and it has found no serious defenders. Yet its opponents are in disarray, and there is no agreement on just where the flaws—or the chief flaws—are to be found. In the next section I shall discuss five objections against Zeno.

(e) *The toils of infinity*

First, and most obviously, Zeno's opponents may deny (2) or (4): it is simply not true that every part of *a* has parts; it is simply not true that partition may continue *ad infinitum*. Physical bodies have minimal parts; and, being composed of a finite number of finite parts, they are felicitously finite in magnitude. In **174** and **175** Zeno is speaking of physical bodies: there is no reason to believe what he says in (2) and good reason to disbelieve it.[25]

That atomistic answer has left most Zenonians unmoved. No doubt Zeno is talking of the physical parts of physical bodies; but he need not be construed as talking of physical operations of division or splitting. Behind the physical façade of proposition (2) there lies a mathematical substance; and (2) rests not upon false or dubious physical theory but on a truth of stereometry: every geometrical solid s has a Z-set $\{s_1, s_2, \ldots\}$ all of whose members are geometrical solids; and since the magnitude of a physical body is determined by the volume of the geometrical solid which its spatial co-ordinates describe, if the volume is infinitely large, so too is the magnitude.

Some Greek thinkers were moved by that argument to posit indivisible geometrical magnitudes: just as physical division stops somewhere, so, they supposed, geometrical division has a terminus. Xenocrates, a pupil of Plato's, 'gave in to this argument about the dichotomy and accepted that everything divisible is many . . . for he said that there are atomic lines of which it is no longer true that they are many' (fr. 44 H = Simplicius, *in Phys* 138.10–6). Doubtless Xenocrates also postulated indivisible geometrical solids.[26] If a stereometrical atomism thus backs up physical atomism, premiss (2) may still be rejected.

Ancient critics observed, truly enough, that geometrical atomism emasculated their geometry (cf. Xenocrates, fr. 43 H); and they opined that Zeno's argument was bought off at suicidal expense. Modern critics need not at once concur; for they can propose a subtler version of the atomic objection: physical atomism, they allow, is irrelevant to Zeno's argument; and Euclidean solids are infinitely divisible. But between physical bodies and geometrical solids lies space. Zeno presupposes that space is infinitely divisible or continuous; i.e., he tacitly assumes that the geometry of space is, in that respect at least, Euclidean. But that assumption is unwarranted; indeed, the moral to be drawn from Zeno's paradoxes is precisely this: that space (and time) are not continuous.[27] Physical bodies have smallest physically separable parts; but that is no serious objection to Zeno. Euclidean geometry allows infinite division to its solids; but that is no help to Zeno. Physical bodies occupy space; and in maintaining that bodies are infinitely divisible, Zeno is maintaining that space is infinitely divisible, that space has no minimal *quanta*. If we care to reject that assumption, we do not fall foul of geometry: we merely imply that the geometry of space is non-continuous. And we may reject premiss (2).

That sophisticated atomism is a tempting hare; but I shall not indulge in pursuit. For it seems to me that none of the arguments in favour of spatial atomism, and none of the arguments against spatial atomism, is cogent; and I incline to regard the question of the structure of space as an empirical one—to be settled, no doubt, by the abstract theorizings of the physicist rather than by microscopic inspection of pieces of space. If that is right, then we may say at least that Zeno's proposition (2) is not a truth of logic; but for all that, (2) may be true: it may be a truth of physical theory. And of course, almost all physicists hold that it *is* true. Further speculation on this topic would be idle: let us grant Zeno (2) and (4).

The second objection to Zeno's argument attacks proposition (9), his 'hidden premiss': '(9) proposes a principle for summing infinite series which is simply false; Zeno's arithmetic was naive, and a sophisticated mathematician will immediately refute his paradox. Z-sets of a are created by dichotomy: the first operation yields $\{b_1, b_2\}$, where mag: b_i = $^1/_2$ mag: a; the second operation yields $\{b_1, c_1, c_2\}$, where mag: c_i = $^1/_2$ mag: b_i. And so on. Thus the magnitude of the infinite Z-set $\{b_1, c_1, d_1, \ldots\}$ is equal to $^1/_2$ mag: a + $^1/_4$ mag: a + $^1/_8$ mag: a + ... The infinite series to be summed is:

(S) $^1/_2 + {}^1/_4 + {}^1/_8 + \ldots$

Evidently, the sum of S does not exceed 1; and arithmeticians now make it 1 by definition. Zeno's infinite series is convergent; and the sum of a convergent series is finite. The principle enunciated in (9) is falsified by the very series Zeno means to apply it to: Zeno's hidden premiss was accepted by most ancient thinkers, with the honourable exception of Aristotle; but it is tediously false.'[28]

That objection is horribly confused; rather than anatomize its imperfections I shall show that it is undisturbing to any competent Zenonian. The text of **B 1** does, I think, lend plausibility to the claim that Zeno imagined his Z-sets as being generated in the way I have just described; but not all ancient commentators understood the generation in that light. Thus Porphyry restates the argument as follows:

> If it is divisible, he[29] says, let it be divided in half, and then each of the parts in half. And if this happens in every case, it is clear, he says, that either there will remain some smallest, atomic magnitudes, infinite in number, and the whole will consist of smallest magnitudes infinite in number [sc. and so will be infinitely large], or else it will vanish and be dissolved into nothing and will consist of nothing. And both alternatives are absurd. . . . (**175**: Simplicius, *in Phys* 139, 27–32).

Porphyry's argument was known to Aristotle (see *GC* 316a14–34; 325a8–12). Some scholars suppose it to be a Zenonian argument, related to but not identical with the argument of **B 1**; but Porphyry and Simplicius both treat it as a version of **B 1**, and I am inclined to take it as an ancient modification or interpretation of our argument.

The important point in Porphyry is this: the dichotomy does not yield Z-sets the magnitudes of whose members form a convergent series; the partitions are 'through and through'. Each part of a is divided, and every division produces a set whose members are equal in magnitude. Thus the second Z-set of a will not be $\{b_1, c_1, c_2\}$ but rather $\{c_1, c_2, c_3, c_4\}$, where each c_i has the same magnitude as each of its fellows. Let us define a Z*-set as a Z-set all of whose members are equal in magnitude; and let us replace premiss (4) by:

(4*) If mag: $a > 0$, then there is a Z*-set of a, $\{x_1, x_2, \ldots\}$ such that for every i mag: $x_i > 0$.

Premisses (5) and (7) must be correspondingly emended (the emendation of (7) is trifling, that of (5) more complicated); and the argument will proceed felicitously to (8). To reach (10), we need not (9) but:

(9*) If S^1_∞ is a Z*-set and for every i in S^1_∞ mag: $x_i > 0$, then mag: $S^1_\infty = \infty$

Unlike (9), (9*) is true; for the sum of an infinite series whose members each have the same finite magnitude is indeed, and evidently, infinite. I suppose that those later Greeks who adopted the 'hidden premiss' were in fact embracing (9*), on the tacit assumption that the elements to be summed were all of equal magnitude. I doubt if Zeno himself made that assumption; but it is enough that the assumption is readily superadded to his argument, and that the superaddition destroys the arithmetical objection.[30]

The third objection has Aristotelian roots. According to an Aristotelian *dictum*, the infinite exists only potentially: potentially, bodies may be divided infinitely often; actually, such a division is impossible. Infinite division cannot be actualized; the dichotomizing always comes to a finite stop; partition *ad infinitum* cannot be completed. Now Zeno's argument implies at (4) that infinite division is completable; and it is just there that Zeno goes astray.

Such an objection is worth pondering in connexion with the paradoxes of motion; but here it is readily dismissed. The premisses of the *logos* on 'large and small' contain no reference, explicit or implicit, to any process of dividing: Zeno is not enjoining us to cut, carve or chop up *a*; nor is he asking us to divide *a* 'in thought'. Like Leibniz, he holds that 'each portion of matter is not only infinitely divisible . . . but is also actually subdivided without end, each part into further parts' (*Monadology*, §65); but he does not say that every body *has been*, or *could be*, divided into parts—he asserts that it *has* parts. He is talking of a characteristic or state of bodies, not of an operation upon bodies. Since Zeno says nothing about dividing, he says nothing about dividing *ad infinitum*; and reflexions on the possibility of completed divisions are not germane to his argument.

Potentiality, too, is only a toy sword; it is not clear what application that notion has in the context of Zeno's argument. Aristotle applies his *dictum* to infinite processes and not to an infinity of parts; the *dictum* is, in Aristotle at least, a mere ukase; and in any event appropriate injections of the term 'potentially' into Zeno's argument would leave it with its force unimpaired.

The fourth objection comes from Thomas Hobbes. Hobbes had Zeno's Achilles in mind; but the considerations which led him to reject the Achilles as a 'sophistical caption' apply equally to our present argument. Hobbes accuses Zeno of mishandling the concept of infinity: 'The force of that famous argument of Zeno . . . consisted in this proposition, *whatsoever may be divided into parts, infinite in number, the same is infinite*: which he, without doubt, thought to be true, yet nevertheless is false. For to be divided into infinite parts is nothing but to be divided into as many parts as any man will. But it is not necessary that a line should have parts infinite in number, or be infinite, because I can divide and subdivide it as often as I please: for how many parts so ever I make, yet their number is finite' (*De Corpore* V.13).

Hobbes appears to vacillate between two objections. On the one hand, he seems to deny that *a* in fact has infinitely many parts; it has as many parts 'as you please', but your pleasure stops short of infinity. If that is his real intention, then he is, in effect, denying the validity of the move from (6) and (7) to (8): the introduction of the sign '∞' in (8) is illegitimate. But Hobbes does not explain *why* this is illegitimate, simply asserting that Zeno argues sophistically.

On the other hand, Hobbes appears to allow that *a* can be divided into infinitely many parts, but to draw the teeth of his admission by claiming that 'infinitely many' here simply means 'as many as you please'. If that is his real intention, then in effect he allows Zeno to proceed as far as (8) but no further; for on Hobbes's understanding of 'infinite', premiss (9*) is no more true than (9): the sum of as many finite parts as you like need not be infinite. Now Zeno must certainly allow that, given Hobbes's equation of infinity and the *ad lib*, premiss (9*) is false; but he is under no obligation to accept the Hobbesian equation. And indeed, that equation is false: there are infinitely many natural numbers; but that is not to say that there are as many numbers as you like; however many you like, there are more (indeed, infinitely many more).

Hobbes, I think, did not grasp the flaw in Zeno's argument; but his fingers came close to it, and he saw where the argument must be attacked, namely in its handling of the concept of *infinity*. My fifth and final objection to Zeno owes much to Hobbism; and I preface my remarks with a few elementary reflexions upon the notion of infinity.

It is peculiarly tempting to suppose that the phrase 'infinitely many' stands, so to speak, at the very end of the natural number series. If we start counting from 1, the numbers get bigger and bigger, until we pass from the large to the monstrously large, and from the monstrously to the incredibly large—and eventually, if only we went on for ever, we should reach the infinitely large. Thus 'There are infinitely many *F*s' may seem to have the same logical structure as 'There are seventeen *F*s'; and '*a* can be divided infinitely many times' is, so to speak, the last member of a series which starts, modestly, with '*a* can be divided once'.

That is all wrong: 'infinitely many' does not function like 'seventeen'; it does not specify a number of *F*s or a fixed set of divisions. 'Infinitely many' is, on that score, more like 'as many . . . as you like' or 'more . . . than you could imagine'. Those latter phrases are not indefinite numerical adjectives like 'many' or 'a lot of'; but nor are they definite in the sense of specifying some particular number. 'Have as many chestnuts as you like' does not mean 'Have lots of chestnuts', nor 'Have *n* chestnuts' (for some determinate *n*); rather, it means something like: 'For any *n*, if you want *n* chestnuts, have *n* chestnuts'.

In a not wholly dissimilar fashion, 'infinitely many' is neither an indefinite modifier, like 'hundreds of', nor a specifying modifier, like 'seventeen'. To that extent Hobbes was right. But he erred when he went further and defined 'infinitely many' as 'as many as you please': the infinite contains as much as you please—and then more; it is inexhaustible, its contents are never used up. To say that a set contains infinitely many members is to say that, however many of its members you have picked out or enumerated, there are still more to count; more precisely, it is to say that for any positive integer n the set contains more than n members. Thus as a first definition of infinity I offer:

(Di) S contains infinitely many members if and only if for every n S contains more than n members.

Now the paradigm of an infinite set is the set of natural numbers or positive integers, {1, 2, 3, ... }. However many natural numbers you have taken, more remain; for if you have abstracted k numbers, at least $k + 1$, the successor to k, remains to be abstracted. Pretty clearly, we might use that fact to give a second definition of infinity, viz:

(Dii) S contains infinitely many members if and only if S contains as many members as there are positive integers.

Definition (Di) is not technical; definition (Dii) leaves the infinity of the positive integers unaccounted for; a better definition is sought for. And one can be found (thanks mainly to the work of the German mathematician Dedekind) by way of the notion of a *one-to-one correlation*. Take any two sets of things, S and S': a relation, R, will set up a one-to-one correlation between S and S' if it pairs each member of S with exactly one member of S' and each member of S' with exactly one member of S. Consider a monogamous society, and let S be the set of husbands and S' the set of wives. Then the relation of *being married to* sets up a one-to-one correlation between husbands and wives; for each husband is married to exactly one wife, and every wife has exactly one husband married to her. Again, let S be the set of even positive integers, {2, 4, 6, . . .}, and S' the set of positive integers, {1, 2, 3, . . .}. Then the relation of *being double* sets up a one-to one correlation between S and S'; for every even positive integer is the double of exactly one positive integer, and every positive integer has exactly one even positive integer that is its double.

The new definition of infinity also requires the notion of a *proper subset*. That is readily explained: S is a proper subset of S' if and only if every member of S is a member of S' and not every member of S' is a member of S. Thus the set of husbands is a proper subset of the set of married people; for all husbands are married, but not all married people are husbands. And the set of even positive integers is a proper subset of the set of positive integers; for every even positive integer is a positive integer, but not every positive integer is even.

Now we can offer:

(Diii) S has infinitely many members if and only if there is a proper subset of S, S', and a relation R, such that R sets up a one-to-one correlation between S and S'.

Clearly, the set of natural numbers is infinite by (Diii); for the relation *double of* will set up a one-to-one correlation between the set of even integers and that set. Hence any set which is infinite by (Di) or (Dii) is infinite by (Diii).

Is any set that is infinite by (Diii) also infinite by (Di) and (Dii)? Suppose that S is infinite by (Diii) but not by (Dii). Then S contains fewer members than there are natural numbers. (I disregard, as irrelevant to Presocratic concerns, the higher infinities or the 'transfinite' numbers.) Hence for some k, S contains exactly k members; hence every subset of S contains less than k members; hence no subset of S can be correlated one-to-one with S; hence S is not, after all, infinite by (Diii). Any set infinite by (Diii) is infinite by (Dii), and by (Di); and since (Diii) is precise and explanatory, it is preferable to (Di) and (Dii) as a definition of infinity.

What is all that to Zeno? It helps us to show that Zeno's argument breaks down at the move from (6) and (7) to (8)—or rather, at the move from (6*) and (7*) to (8). I attempted to ease that move by suggesting that 'by (6) . . . there is a Z-set of a S^1_∞', i.e. a Z-set containing infinitely many members. Let us make that into an explicit inference from (6*), thus:

(11*) If a exists, then there is a Z*-set $\{x_1, x_2 \ldots\}$ of a containing infinitely many x_is.

From (7*) and (11*), (8) is validly inferred; but without (11*) Zeno has no way of attaining (8); his argument turns on there being a Z*-set with infinite members.

Yet Zeno has no title to (11*). (11*) does not follow from (6*), nor from any other Zenonian premiss. (6*) does indeed show that a possesses infinitely many Z*-sets: the Z*-sets of a can be placed in one-one correspondence with the natural numbers; and Zeno's 'dichotomy' shows how that is so. But each Z*-set contains finitely many members. Thus let the Z*-sets be generated by successive dichotomies. Then the first Z*-set contains 2 members, the second 4, and so on: in general, the nth Z*-set contains 2^n members; and for every n, 2^n is finite. There are infinitely many Z*-sets of a. That is to say, for any integer n, there are more than n Z*-sets of a; the Z*-sets of a are as numerous as the integers; certain relations (e.g., *having twice as many members as*) set up a one-to-one correlation between proper subsets of the set of Z*-sets of a (e.g., the set of Z*-sets whose members are multiples of 4) and the set of Z*-sets itself. There are infinitely many Z*-sets of a. But the number of elements in any

Z*-set is finite: for any Z*-set S, there is a natural number k such that there are just k members of S.

It does not follow that no set of parts of a has infinitely many members; indeed, the fact that there are infinitely many Z*-sets of a suggests a way of constructing just such a set. A super-Z-set of $a\{x_1, x_2, \ldots\}$ takes x_1 from the first Z*-set of a; x_2 from the second Z*-set of a, where x_2 has no part in common with x_1; x_3 from the third Z*-set, having no part in common either with x_1 or with x_2; and so on. Clearly, super-Z-sets will have infinitely many members, since each super-Z-set of a has as many members as there are Z*-sets of a. Equally clearly, super-Z-sets are not Z*-sets; for the members of a super-Z-set are not all equal in magnitude. On the contrary, the magnitudes of members of any super-Z-set form a convergent series: $1/2$, $1/4$, $1/8$ . . . Thus if Zeno were to retreat from Z*-sets to super-Z-sets the traditional arithmetical objection would hold: the sum of the magnitudes of the elements of a super-Z-set is not infinite.

But if Zeno remains with ordinary Z*-sets, his paradox disappears. What follows from his argument about the magnitude of a? Nothing of any interest. By (7) and the principle that if m and n are finite, $m + n$ is finite, we can infer that mag: a is finite. If the Z*-sets are the products of dichotomy, then the magnitude of an element of the nth Z*-set of a will be equal to mag: $a/2^n$. Since the nth Z*-set of a has 2^n members, we may conclude, by (7*), that mag: $a = 2^n \dfrac{\text{mag: } a}{2^n}$ And that is an unexciting conclusion to Zeno's *logos*.

(f) *The totality of things*

I turn now to the *logos* of 'finite and infinite', which is contained in sentence [ix] of **175**. The *logos* concludes to the following antinomy:

(Z3) (a) If P, then there are finitely many existents, and (b) if P, then there are infinitely many existents.

The argument for (Z3a) is short: 'it is necessary that they be as many as they are . . . But if they are as many as they are, they will be limited'. I paraphrase: 'If there are many As, then there is some true proposition of the form: "There are as many As as Bs". Hence there is an answer to the question: "How many As are there?" Hence there is some true proposition of the form "There are n As", where n is a natural number.'

The argument has been called 'beautiful in its simplicity',[31] but it is merely *simpliste*. Zeno's final move supposes that a set S is finite if there is a set S' such that every member of S can be paired uniquely with a member of S' and vice versa; in other words, if we can set up a one-to-one correlation between S and S'. But as we have seen, that is not so: the set of even integers can be correlated one-to-one with the set of integers, though both sets are infinite. Zeno's argument is at once destroyed. Indeed, I find the 'proof' an uninstructive sophism.

The argument for (Z3b) is puzzling: 'There are always other things in the middle of the things that exist (*metaxu tôn ontôn*)'. Zeno is usually taken to mean that *between* any two existents there is always a third. And if Simplicius is reporting Zeno in unabbreviated form, that assertion stood bare of argument. Now between any two points on a line, there is indeed a third; and some scholars take Zeno to be speaking of geometrical points, and thus give his argument a happy gloss. Unfortunately, Zeno's text does not encourage that interpretation. Others suppose the following train of reasoning: 'If *a* and *b* were contiguous, they would be one object, not two. Hence they must be separated; and since, by Eleatic argument, there cannot be an empty space between them, they must be separated by a third object.' According to Aristotle, the Pythagoreans said that 'the void divides nature, the void being a sort of separation and dividing of contiguous things' (*Phys* 213b22–7 = **58 B 30**). Perhaps Zeno was implicitly rejecting their view? But that interpretation too requires us to read a great deal into a very plain text.

Perhaps '*metaxu tôn ontôn*' means not 'between the things that exist' but rather 'in the middle of any existent'. Then 'there are always other things *metaxu tôn ontôn*' means:

(1) For any x, if x exists there exists something distinct from and in the middle of x.

Now Zeno might surely have argued for (1) by appealing to an argument entirely analogous to that in **B 1**: if *a* exists, then *a* has some positive magnitude; and if *a* has a positive magnitude, then *a* is divisible into three parts, two 'outside' parts and a 'middle'. Simplicius, I think, took Zeno's argument in this way; at least, I can think of no other reason why he should have thought that the argument used the 'dichotomy'. The interpretation is linguistically permissible; and it gives Zeno the conclusion he requires without calling upon any extraneous Eleatic attitudes. Philosophically, of course, this reading of the *logos* of finite and infinite supplies no food for thought that has not already been digested in considering **B 1**.

(g) *One and many*

The fourth *logos* is the 'one and many'. Plato mentions it, and we have no reason to doubt that Zeno argued for:

(Z4) (a) If *P*, then everything is one, and (b) if *P*, then everything is many.

Zeno's own words have not survived; nor has any explicit doxographical account of the *logos*. But we can, I think, reconstruct at least part of Zeno's argument on the basis of some remarks of Simplicius and Philoponus.[32] The remarks go back to Eudemus, who gives the closest approximation to (Z4) that we possess:

> Zeno, the friend of Parmenides, tried to prove that it is not possible for what exists to be many because [i] nothing among the things that exist is one, and [ii] the many are a quantity of ones (*plêthos henadôn*)[33] (**178**: fr. 37aW = **A 21**).

Here [i], I take it, derives from (Z4b), [ii] from (Z4a).[34]

For (Z4b) we may again call upon Eudemus. Having retailed the anecdote of Zeno and the One (above, p. 235), he continues:

> He was puzzled, as it seems, by the fact that each of the perceptible things is called many both by way of predication (*katêgorikôs*)[35] and by partition, while the point cannot even be posited as one (for what neither increases when added nor diminishes when subtracted he thought not to be an existent). . . . But if points are of that character, and each of us is said to be many things (e.g., white, musical, etc.) and similarly with a stone (for each one can be infinitely split), how will there be any one? (**179**: fr. 37aW = Simplicius, *in Phys* 97.13–21; cf. **A 21**).

Eudemus' argument runs as follows: 'If there are many things, each is either [a] a perceptible object or [b] a point. If [b], then the object has no existence, and *a fortiori* is not "one" thing. If [a] then [i] the object is infinitely divisible and so is "many" not one; and [ii] the object, having many predicates true of it, is "many" not one.'

Eudemus' reconstruction is his own: he is not pretending to report an argument of Zeno's, but to discover why he should have been puzzled by 'the One'. But Eudemus bases himself firmly on Zenonian soil: [b] comes from **B 2**, and [a] [i] repeats the familiar move of **B 1**. [a] [ii] is a novelty to us; but I think we are entitled to trust Eudemus and to regard it too as Zenonian; and I suppose that it constituted Zeno's argument for (Z4b).[36]

The argument rests on the truism that everything has more than one property: Socrates is both pale and snub-nosed; Socrates possesses the property of pallor and also the distinct property of snub-nosedness. In general:

(1) $(\forall x)(\exists P).(\exists Q)$ (*P* is distinct from *Q*, and *x* has *P*, and *x* has *Q*).

How did Zeno infer from (1) that 'everything is many'?

Most of the commentators suppose that he indulged in a naive and archaic confusion: muddling together predication and identity, Zeno managed to construe 'Socrates has pallor' as though it were 'Socrates is pallor'; and he thus read (1) as though it were:

(2) $(\forall x)$ $(\exists P)$ $(\exists Q)$ (P is distinct from Q, and $x = P$ and $x = Q$).

Given (2) we can see how 'everything is many'; for everything is identical with at least two distinct things.

The confusion which encourages us to move from (1) to (2) was not unknown to the Greeks. According to Aristotle, in order to avoid the paradox of 'one and many' 'some did away with "is" (e.g., Lycophron), and others emended the language, saying that the man (not is pale but) has paled, and (not is walking but) walks' (*Phys* 185b27–30 = **83 A 2**). Aristotle reports a diagnosis and a prophylactic. The diagnosis has it that our confusion between identity and predication is brought about by the word 'is': if we take 'Socrates is the Chairman' to assert an identity between Socrates and the Chairman, we may be seduced into taking 'Socrates is pale' to assert an identity between Socrates and pallor. The prophylactic is simple: abolish 'is'; instead of 'Socrates is pale' write 'Socrates pale' or 'Socrates has paled'.

The 'paradox' which worried Lycophron and the others seems trifling to us; but it clearly seemed serious to Zeno's contemporaries, and we may well imagine that (Z4b) trades upon it. (Note that Eudemus reported Zeno's argument in his *Physics*: Eudemus' *Physics* corresponds closely to Aristotle's, and the Eudemian fragment happens to answer to *Phys* 185b27–30.) For all that, I am not entirely happy in ascribing (2) to Zeno: (2) is contradictory in itself (for if $x = P$ and $x = Q$, then $P = Q$), and therefore not an ideal component in an antinomy. At all events, it is worth casting about for an alternative interpretation.

Let us return to Eudemus. According to him, 'Plato thought that "is" [sc. in "Socrates is pale"] does not signify what it does in the case of man, but that just as "is thoughtful" signifies to think and "is seated" to sit, so it is in the other cases too, even if there are no ready-made names for them' (fr. 37aW = Simplicius, *in Phys* 97.25–8). Plato's answer to a puzzle of predication distinguished, in effect, between the 'is' of essential and the 'is' of accidental predication. If that answer was appropriate, then it suggests a paradox about essence, rather than one about identity: '[a] Each thing is just one thing, i.e., has a unique essence. [b] If a has P, then having P is what a is; i.e., is the essence of a. Hence, by (1), each thing has more than one essence or is many.' If that Platonic puzzle seems anachronistic, let me double the offence by adverting to a peculiarly Aristotelian concern: the unity of definition. Thus: '[a] Each thing is a unity. [b] If *a* has *P* and *Q*, and having *P* does not involve having *Q*, nor vice versa, then *a* is a diversity; hence by (1), *a* is a diversity or "many".'[37]

These three diagnoses of Zeno's problem, the traditional one, the Platonic, the Aristotelian, are all unsatisfactory in one way or another; and it may be that no precise interpretation is possible. In his paradox of 'one and many', Zeno raised, in a vague and indeterminate fashion, several issues that were to excite and perplex his successors; he himself merely saw, or imagined, a conflict between 'being one' and 'being many', which properties all objects surely possess. It was left to Zeno's successors to distinguish particular knots in that tangled skein, and to pose plain puzzles to the adherents of pluralism. But note, again, that pluralism is not peculiarly vulnerable to this antinomy: Zeno's arguments, however they are elucidated, work whether *a* is a member of a numerous plurality or the sole inhabitant of the world: the 'one and many' is an antinomy of being, not a paradox of plurality.

(h) *The paradox of place*

I shall end the chapter by looking at two minor arguments which seem only loosely connected with the main theme of Zeno's *logoi*. These arguments are the paradox of place, and the paradox of the millet seed.

The paradox of place is twice adverted to by Aristotle (*Phys* 209a23; 210b22 = **A 24** = **13–14 L**), and it is discussed by Aristotle's commentators. Zeno's actual words do not survive; but an argument in Simplicius (*in Phys* 563.1–33) persuades me that the closest approximation to authenticity is achieved by Philoponus:

> For if everything that exists is somewhere, he used to say, and place too is something, then place too will be somewhere. Hence place will be in a place; and so *ad infinitum* (**180**: Philoponus, *in Phys* 510.4–6 = **16 L**; cf. Simplicius, *in Phys* 534.6–15).[38]

Zeno's immediate conclusion was, presumably, that there is no such thing as place. Conceivably, he then inferred that existent things are not in any place, and aimed to construct an antinomy:

(Z5) (a) If *P*, then everything is somewhere; and (b) if *P*, then everything is nowhere.

Here (Z5b) is the ultimate conclusion of the paradox of place; and

(Z5a) will have been inferred along the lines of **B 2**: if *a* exists, it has magnitude; if it has magnitude, it is spatially extended; hence it is 'somewhere'.[39] (Note again that in (Z5) the pluralist hypothesis is idle.)

The kernel of Zeno's argument is his assertion that everything that exists is 'somewhere' or occupies some place:

(1) If *a* exists, then for some *x a* occupies *x*.

The second premiss, that 'place too is something', may be construed as:

(2) If *a* occupies *b*, then *b* exists.

From (1) and (2) Zeno hopes to generate an infinite regress of places. Let us make the innocuous assumption that the relation of *occupation* is irreflexive, asymmetrical, and transitive; i.e., that:

(3) Nothing occupies itself.

(4) If *a* occupies *b*, *b* does not occupy *a*.

(5) If *a* occupies *b* and *b* occupies *c*, then *a* occupies *c*.

Now it is easy to prove from (1)—(5) that any existent body occupies infinitely many distinct places:

(6) If *a* exists, then for any *n* there are more than *n* distinct places occupied by *a*.

According to Zeno, (6) is absurd; hence (Z5b).

Is (6) absurd? Well, how can places be distinct other than by having distinct boundaries? And how can one and the same object, *a*, have more than one set of boundaries?

If (6) is unacceptable, does Zeno's argument for it fail? The ancient critics attack (1). According to Aristotle, the term 'occupy' is ambiguous: everything must indeed be 'in' something, but not all ways of being 'in' a thing are cases of occupying a *place*. Heat, say, is 'in' a body; but the body is a substrate, not a place, for heat (*Phys* 210b22–30). Thus (1) does not state any one truth because it does not state any one thing at all; and if it is made explicit that occupation in (1) is a matter of being in a place, then (1) is false, as Eudemus says: 'now if [Zeno] assumes that what exists is in a place, his assumption is incorrect; for neither health nor courage nor ten thousand other things would be said to be in a place' (fr. 78 W = **A 24**).[40]

I am, I confess, inclined to side with Zeno here, and to support some version of (1): if existents need not occupy places, then they exist in so far as they are related to some place holder, and they exist only in a derivative sense. But it is unnecessary to develop that line of thought here; for (1) is easily repaired against the Aristotelian attack. Zeno need only restrict *a* and *b* in (1) and (2) to things of a sort capable of being located in space; for surely anything that *can* occupy a place exists only so long as it actually *does* occupy a place. Premiss

(1) then asserts, uncontroversially, that any potential occupant of space does, if it exists, actually occupy a place.

Premiss (1) is true. Is (2) false? If (2) is true, then places are themselves capable of being located. It might be said that an object *a* occupies a place *p* if and only if the co-ordinates defining *p* determine the surfaces of *a*; and since places do not have surfaces, they are not locatable in space. But that is pedantry; why should we not say that a place *p* occupies a place *p'* if and only if the co-ordinates of *p'* determine the co-ordinates of *p*? In general, *a* occupies *b* if and only if the determining co-ordinates of *a* are the same as those of *b*. Necessarily, places have places: (2) is necessarily true. But the truth of (2) is bought at a price. For on that account of occupation, (3) and (4) are both false: occupation is neither irreflexive nor asymmetrical; for places are their own locations. As Newton put it: 'Times and spaces are, as it were, the places as well of themselves as of all other things'.

I do not insist on the Newtonian answer; for nothing, I think, hangs upon it. Some will accept Zeno's (1) and (2), rejecting (3) and (4). Others may prefer a weaker notion of existence, and deny (1); yet others will contrive reasonable grounds for rejecting (2). Zeno's argument certainly fails: it is interesting to observe that it fails even if we grant Zeno both of his explicit premisses.

(i) *The millet seed*

The paradox of the millet seed is reported by Simplicius:

> In this way [Aristotle] solves the problem which Zeno the Eleatic set for Protagoras the Sophist. 'Tell me, Protagoras,' he said, 'does a single millet seed make a sound when it falls? Or the ten thousandth part of a seed?' Protagoras said that it didn't. 'What about a bushel of millet seed', he said, 'does that make a sound when it falls, or not?' He said that the bushel did make a sound. 'Well', said Zeno, 'isn't there a ratio between the bushel and the single seed, or the ten-thousandth part of a single seed?' He agreed. 'Well then,' said Zeno, 'won't the sounds too stand in the same ratios to one another? For as the sounders are, so are the sounds. And if that's so, then if the bushel makes a sound, the single seed and the ten-thousandth part of a seed will make a sound too' (**181: A 29 = 38 L**).

Simplicius is reporting a later dramatization of the paradox; but Aristotle's testimony ensures that the argument itself is genuinely Zenonian (*Phys* 250a19 = **A 29 = 37 L**).

The argument is sometimes supposed to be an attack on

sense-perception: reason proves the millet seed to make a sound, even though our ears detect none. Archytas later asserted, conceivably with Zeno's millet seed in mind, that 'many sounds are not apprehensible by creatures of our nature, some because of the weakness of the blow [which produces them], others . . .' (**47 B 1**). The millet seed might, I suppose, illustrate a problem in the philosophy of perception; yet interest in such problems is not Eleatic. Nor will the millet seed argue for an Eleatic scepticism: at most it might persuade us of the uncontroversial fact that many things elude our perception even though they are intrinsically perceptible.

Imagine that one of Zeno's forty *logoi* aimed to prove:

(Z6) (a) If *P*, then each existent makes a sound, and (b) if *P*, then each existent is mute.

The millet seed argues for (Z6a); and we might easily concoct an inverted version of the same argument to support (Z6b). The suggestion is purely speculative and not worth developing; but the millet seed itself warrants another page.

The Megarian philosophers of the early fourth century, who are often spoken of as the successors to the Eleatic school, invented a series of logical puzzles. Two of them, the heap (*sôreitês*) and the bald man (*phalakros*) are near cousins to the millet seed. One grain of sand is not a heap, and the addition of one grain cannot turn what is not a heap into a heap; a man with a full head of hair is not bald, and the extraction of a single hair cannot make what is not bald bald: hence there are no heaps, and no bald men. The puzzles are jocular but the point they make is serious. They seem to provide counter-examples to the powerful logical tool of mathematical induction. The general formula for such an induction is this: Take an ordered sequence $\langle a_1, a_2, \ldots, a_n, \ldots \rangle$; if a_1, is *F*, and if, if a_n is *F* then a_{n+1} is *F*, then every a_i is *F*. The millet seed and the Megarian puzzles can be formulated as mathematical inductions: the a_is are bags of millet seed, each a_i containing exactly *i* seeds; and for '*F*' read 'makes no audible sound on falling to the ground'. The conclusion, that every a_i is *F*, states the absurdity that no amount of millet seed makes a noise on falling.

It is often said that puzzles of this sort essentially use 'vague' concepts; and the moral is drawn that precise logical manoeuvres, such as mathematical induction, do not work for vague concepts. We might accept that and still worry about the Megarian puzzles: first, have they not shown a decisive logical flaw in such common notions as those of 'a heap' and of 'baldness'? And second, how are we to define the conditions a concept must satisfy if it is to be amenable to precise logical deployment?

Consideration of the millet seed thus opens some fairly large questions about the connexion between formal logic and ordinary language. Yet I am not sure that Zeno's paradox depends for its solution on an answer to those questions. After all, the predicate 'makes an audible sound' is not particularly vague: either I can hear the seed or I cannot; there is no halfway house between hearing and not hearing, in the way in which there seems to be between being bald and not being bald. Aristotle offers an answer to Zeno which in no way turns on the notion of vagueness: in effect, he challenges Zeno's implicit claim that if a_n makes no sound, then a_{n+1} makes no sound (cf. *Phys* 250a9–28). There is, for each of us, a threshold of audibility: the addition of a single seed to a parcel of millet may indeed make all the difference between audibility and inaudibility—even though that seed, falling alone, is not audible. Zeno, according to Aristotle, supposes that if n grains make a sound of volume V, that can only be because each grain makes a sound of volume V/n. And that assumption, which is not a logical but an empirical proposition, is false. Aristotle's diagnosis of Zeno's error, and his answer to Zeno's puzzle, seem to me to be correct.

XIII

Zeno: Paradox and Progression

(a) *Sprightly running*

Zeno's four arguments against motion are known to us from Aristotle's discussion of them in *Physics* Z. The Greek commentators on Aristotle for once fail us: they do not reproduce any of Zeno's own words, and with one trivial exception they provide us with no information we cannot glean from Aristotle's text. The paradoxes were famous in antiquity, and they influenced philosophers other than Aristotle: it is odd, as well as unfortunate, that our knowledge of them is virtually confined to the brief and polemical reports in the *Physics*.[1]

Z 9 contains Aristotle's main discussion: the section begins thus:

> There are four arguments of Zeno's about motion which provide difficulties for their solvers—first, the one about a thing's not moving because what is travelling must arrive at the half-way point before the end (we have discussed this earlier) . . . (**182**: *Phys* 239b9–14 = **A 25** = **19 L**).

I shall refer to this first paradox as the Dichotomy; it is also called the Stadium, but I reserve that title for the fourth paradox.[2]

Aristotle's earlier discussion of the Dichotomy appears in Z 2:

> That is why Zeno's argument assumes a falsehood—that one cannot pass through an unlimited number of things or touch an unlimited number of things individually in a limited time. For both length and time—and, in general, whatever is continuous—are called unlimited in two ways: either by division or as to their extremes. Now one cannot touch things unlimited in respect of quantity in a limited time, but one can so touch things

> unlimited by division—for the time itself is unlimited in this way. Hence it is in an unlimited and not in a limited time that, as it turns out, one traverses the unlimited, and one touches the unlimited things in unlimited and not in limited times (**183**: *Phys* 233a21–31 = **A 25** = **19 L**).

From this critical appraisal, and the half-line of description in Z 9, we must reconstruct the Dichotomy.

Suppose that in a finite period of time *T*, a body *b* traverses a finite distance *AB*. Then at some instant within *T b* will 'touch' a_1, the mid-point of *AB*; and at some later instant, again within *T*, *b* will 'touch' a_2, the mid-point between a_1 and *B*; and so on: in general, for any a_i there is a point a_j, mid-way between a_i and *B*, which *b* will 'touch' at some instant within *T*. Thus within *T b* will 'touch' infinitely many points along *AB*; but that is impossible: hence *b* cannot traverse *AB* in *T*. And, in general, locomotion is impossible.

The exposition requires three preliminary comments. First, it interprets the Dichotomy in terms of a division which may be drawn thus:

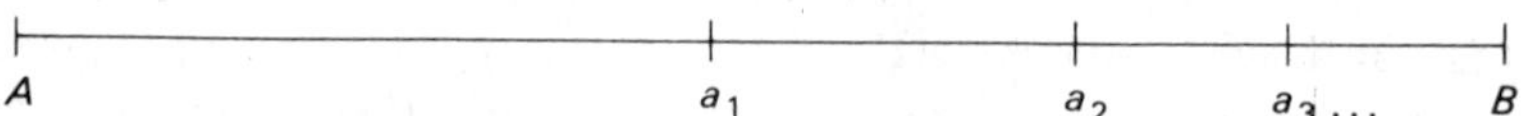

Aristotle's commentators prefer a different diagram:

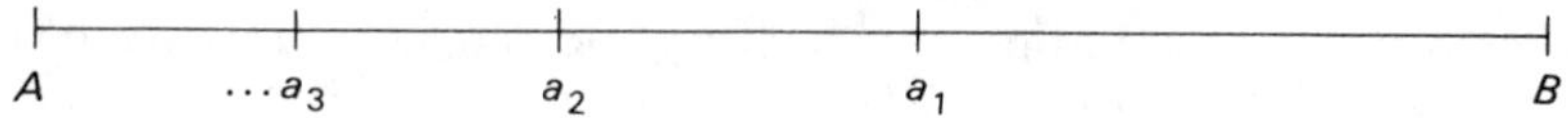

Thus: 'Before reaching *B*, *b* must touch the midpoint a_1 of *AB*; and before reaching a_1, *b* must touch the midpoint a_2 of Aa_1 . . .'. Aristotle, I think, had the first diagram in mind;[3] and I rest on his authority. But it is to be observed that there is no interesting logical difference between the two ways of expounding the paradox. Many commentators suppose that, with the first diagram, Zeno attempts to show that no moving body can ever *complete* its journey: it can never take the last step to *B*, since there *is* no last step. With the second diagram, they say, Zeno shows, more strikingly, that no body can ever *start* its journey: it can never take its first step, since there *is* no first step to take. But that distinction is unimportant: with either diagram, Zeno means to show that no body can traverse a finite distance in a finite time—in other words, that no body can move. The first diagram does not allow travellers to begin but not end their journeys; for every journey begun is *eo ipso* a journey ended.

Second, we may wonder what is meant by 'touch' (*haptesthai*) in Aristotle's exposition, and why Zeno should think that moving bodies must 'touch' points in their travel. Some sources compare 'touching' to counting: *b*, they say, can no more 'touch' each a_i inside *AB* than he can count each a_i as he passes it; and some scholars have supposed that Zeno's original traveller went on a mental rather than a physical journey: *b* cannot run through *AB* in his mind, for he cannot, so to speak, give his mind in turn to each of the points in *AB*. 'Touching', on this view, is a sort of mental stopping: the physical runner 'touches' a_i in so far as, on passing a_i, he stops mentally and says to himself: 'This is a_i'.[4]

That interpretation is surely not Zenonian: Aristotle explicitly distinguishes between Zeno's paradox and the argument which requires the traveller to count the halfway points on his journey (*Phys* 263a6–11); and it is clear that the counting version was a vulgarization of Zeno's argument. 'Touching' in Zeno is what it sounds like: physical contact. Let us idealize the example: suppose *b* to be a perfect cube travelling along the straight path *AB*; and represent each a_i by a line across *AB* parallel to the front edge of *b*. Then *b* touches a_i if and only if a_i lies on the same plane as the front surface of *b*. Clearly, then, if *b* is to traverse *AB*, it must, in this sense, touch successively every a_i inside *AB*.

Third, we must be on our guard against the wiles of infinitude: in the paradox of 'large and small' Zeno falsely claimed an infinite regress; here does Zeno really show that *b* has infinitely many a_is to touch? It is easy to show that he does: the successive a_is are constructed by dichotomy: if $AB = 1$, then $Aa_1 = {}^1/_2$, $a_1a_2 = {}^1/_4$, $a_2a_3 = {}^1/_8$, and in general $a_na_{n+1} = \frac{1}{2^{n+1}}$. Thus the a_is can be put in one-one correspondence with the powers of 2; hence they can be put in one-one correspondence with the natural numbers, and they are infinitely numerous.

Were he to travel from *A* to *B*, *b* would perform infinitely many tasks: there are infinitely many a_is between *A* and *B*, each of which *b* must touch; there are infinitely many distinct propositions of the form '*b* touches a_i', and if *b* reaches *B* every one of these propositions has been made true. Thus Zeno thinks to establish:

(1) If anything moves, it performs infinitely many tasks.

Since he holds it to be a truism that:

(2) Nothing can perform infinitely many tasks,

he concludes that nothing moves. Unless we are to follow Zeno into his immobile world, we must reject either (1) or (2). Philosophical controversy has settled about (2); but I shall begin my discussion with a few thoughts on (1).

Some philosophers reject (1): in running from *A* to *B*, they say, *b* does not have to undertake, successively, infinitely many tasks; his run from A to B is not composed of an infinite sequence of progressively shorter runs. He performs one run, takes a hundred strides, feels fifty heart-beats, and so on; but he does not do or undergo an infinity of anything.

As an exercise in pure pedantry there is something to be said for that objection; for it is indeed mildly odd to call each of b's successive moves to the next a_i a 'run' or a 'task'. Yet the point is merely verbal: Zeno himself does not use the terminology; and if b need not perform infinitely many tasks, that does not show that he has not got infinitely many a_is to touch, infinitely many points to pass, infinitely many subsections of AB to traverse. The claim that b's operations are not 'tasks', or are only 'tasks' in a Pickwickian sense, is boring.[5]

Proponents of the boring claim sometimes mean to deny (1) outright; but sometimes they offer a slightly subtler suggestion: b's move from A to B, they suggest, is a *single* run, a *century* of paces, *half a century* of heart-beats, etc. To get from A to B requires the performance of many *finite* sets of tasks. Now, they continue, we can *describe* b's journey in terms of an infinite succession of tasks; but that does not show (1) to be true: the performances required of a locomotor can indeed be described in terms of infinity, but for all that they are finite performances.

I set down this view because I have frequently heard it; but I dismiss it shortly: if any piece of locomotion can be truly described as the successive performance of an infinity of operations, then (1) is true. There are no two ways about it: either the description does not apply, or else it does apply and (1) is true; you cannot allow the description and brush aside the infinity it imports.

A more interesting objection to (1) can be formulated: (1) is true only if space is continuous or infinitely divisible; for it rests upon the assumption that any stretch of space, AB, contains infinitely many spatial points, a_i. That assumption, which I adverted to in the previous chapter (above, pp. 245–6), is not examined in our ancient texts; and those philosophers who do examine it usually accept it on insufficient grounds, tacitly supposing that a continuous geometry is applicable to physical space (and to time). Any full-scale examination of Zeno's paradoxes would be obliged to discuss the geometry of space: for reasons I gave earlier, I shall not enter upon such a discussion here.

(b) *Infinity again*

There have been numerous and diverse attempts to deal with premiss (2); the most convenient approach begins by asking wherein the impossibility of infinite performances is judged to lie: what is it about infinite performance in general, or the infinite performance of *b* in particular, that involves an impossibility? I shall mention seven lines of argument.

First: '*b* cannot run through infinitely many points; for that would mean that he traversed an infinite distance'. Many philosophers have faulted Zeno in the Dichotomy, as in the *logos* of 'large and small', for bad arithmetic.[6]. Let *AB* measure 1 mile; then in order to reach *B*, *b* must traverse $1/2 + 1/4 + 1/8 + 1/16 + \ldots$ miles. Now the sum of that series does not exceed 1 mile; but Zeno, it is alleged, supposed it to be infinitely great, and for that reason upheld (2).

If that was Zeno's reason for asserting (2), it was a tediously bad reason. And I am not confident that Zeno can be excused: if in the *logos* of 'large and small' he supposed the sum of $1/2 + 1/4 + 1/8 + \ldots$ to be infinitely great, then he may well have made the same supposition in the Dichotomy. But whatever Zeno may have argued, others have found (2) plausible despite a degree of mathematical expertise; and we cannot dismiss the Dichotomy on the grounds that Zeno misreasoned for (2).

Aristotle's criticism of the Dichotomy in *Physics* Z 2 suggests a second way of defending (2): 'Locomotion must take a finite period of time: *b* gets from *A* to *B* in *T*; but in order to touch infinitely many a_is, *b* requires an infinite span of time.' Thus (2) is true because we are all hemmed in by the finitude of our lives.

Aristotle's reply is apt: just as *AB*, though finite in extent, contains infinitely many points, a_i; so *T*, though finite in duration, contains infinitely many instants, t_i. Each a_i in *AB* can be uniquely paired with a t_i in *T*. Similarly, every spatial sub-interval a_ia_j of *AB* can be uniquely paired with a temporal sub-interval t_it_j of *T*. If space is infinitely divisible, so too is time; and thus in his run from *A* to *B*, *b* will never be short of time; there are as many instants available for touchings as there are points to be touched.

Aristotle assumes that time, like space, is continuous. And Zeno might be defended by denying that assumption: space is continuous, but time is not; unlike space, time consists of a succession of discrete *minima*. Time is granular, space is smooth: the parallelism between the two dimensions is broken, and with it Aristotle's objection. One of Aristotle's successors, Strato of Lampsacus, apparently held this view; and it has its modern supporters. I content myself with asserting that it is based on a bad lot of arguments, and that its acceptance involves a host of difficulties.[7]

In any event, that strange view is not the only way of defending Zeno: the second defence of (2) fails; but (2) does not fall with it: (2)

has been upheld by men who are convinced of the continuous nature of time. Aristotle himself came to see that:

> But this solution [sc. that of Z 2] is adequate with regard to the questioner (for he asked whether one could traverse or count unlimited things in a limited time), but it is not adequate with regard to the facts and the truth; for if someone were to forget about the length and about asking whether one can traverse unlimited things in a limited time, and were to make this enquiry of the time itself (for the time has unlimited divisions), this solution is no longer adequate (**184**: *Phys* 263a15–22).

The observation that time as well as space is infinitely divisible only raises the further question of how we can endure through a finite stretch of time, if every such stretch contains limitless parts. Instead of one infinity to traverse, we have two: if *AB* is impenetrable, *T* is unendurable.

Aristotle is right: no Zenonian will be greatly moved by the solution of *Physics* Z 2. Aristotle himself suggests that we ignore *AB* and consider progress through *T* by itself; Zeno, I suspect, would have preferred to consider *AB* alone, without reference to *T*. Indeed, I am inclined to think that the reference to a finite time *T* did not occur in Zeno's original paradox: Zeno considered it impossible to touch infinitely many points; the impossibility is contained in the infinity of points, and factors of time are impertinent. Time is not, and need not be, mentioned in (2).[8]

After recanting his remarks in *Physics* Z 2, Aristotle essays a second solution to the Dichotomy; and his second solution suggests a third reason for upholding (2). Thus: 'If *b* is to touch infinitely many a_is, then an infinity of points must actually exist on *AB*; but there cannot *actually* be infinitely many existent points in a finite space.' That argument for (2) is of little intrinsic interest; but Aristotle's second solution to the Dichotomy warrants a moment's attention.

Here is the text:

> Hence we must say when asked if it is possible to traverse unlimited things—either in time or in distance—that in a way it is, and in a way it isn't: if they exist actually, it is not possible; if potentially, it is. For someone moving continuously traverses unlimited things incidentally, not absolutely; for it is incidental to the line to be unlimitedly many halves, but its essence and its being are different (**185**: *Phys* 263b3–9).

That is an obscure paragraph. I take Aristotle to mean that *b* may touch infinitely many a_is provided that the a_is do not all actually exist. Thus (2) would be true if touching a_i involved the actual existence of a_i; but in fact, the a_is need only exist potentially, and that they may do.

All that, I think, has little effect on any honest Zenonian: Aristotle simply asserts that b can touch the infinitely many a_is, provided that he touches them 'incidentally' and they exist 'potentially'. The Aristotelian jargon only partially disguises the fact that Aristotle is offering a denial of, and not an argument against, premiss (2).

But there is something of interest here: a sufficient condition for the 'actual' existence of a_i is b's stopping at a_i. According to Aristotle, b can touch the a_is as long as he does not stop at them, and hence actualize them. The keyword here is 'continuously (*sunechôs*)': b is safe, Aristotle opines, if he runs smoothly, leaving the infinite a_is in their state of innocent potentiality. Tolstoy agreed: referring to the Achilles, which raises the same puzzle as the Dichotomy, he wrote: 'The ancients regarded this as an unanswerable dilemma; its absurdity lies in the fact that the progress of Achilles is calculated on units with stoppage between, while it is in fact continuous' (*War and Peace*, bk 12, ch. XXII).

Consider a runner c who, like b, is set to traverse AB. c is allowed $2T$ for his performance; and he determines to produce a staccato run. Thus in $\frac{1}{2}T$ he runs from A to a_1; then he rests for $\frac{1}{2}T$ at a_1. In the next $\frac{1}{4}T$ he runs to a_2, and then rests for $\frac{1}{4}T$ at a_2. In general, he takes, like b, $T/2^n$ to traverse the interval $a_{n-1}\,a_n$; but, unlike b, he rests for $T/2^n$ at each a_n.

Aristotle will allow b to reach B, but will deny c his goal; for c's rest periods involve the impossible actualization of the infinitely numerous a_is. And, of course, though we meet b every day, we do not come across staccato runners like c. Much modern discussion of the Dichotomy has in fact focussed on staccato performances; and a central problem has been to determine the truth of (2) if the performances are discrete or staccato in the way in which c's is. We might, I think, intelligibly uphold (2) for c while rejecting it for b. Yet if that view seems reasonable, we have as yet no reason for accepting it. Aristotle's talk about actualized points is unconvincing; and no other argument yet allows us to distinguish between b and c in respect of (2). 'Intuition'—the kind name for untutored prejudice—favours b's chances above c's; but intuition is a fool's guide in this as in every other branch of philosophy.

Aristotle's double discussion of the Dichotomy is meritorious but not conclusive; and I turn now to the fourth of the seven reasons for maintaining premiss (2). It is comfortably simple: 'Infinite sequences of tasks have, by definition, no last member; and it is, trivially, impossible to complete a series of operations none of which is the last operation.'

Both premisses in this argument are false. The sequence actually employed in the Dichotomy does indeed lack a last member; but Zeno could easily have provided a sequence with both a last and a first member, as the following diagram shows:

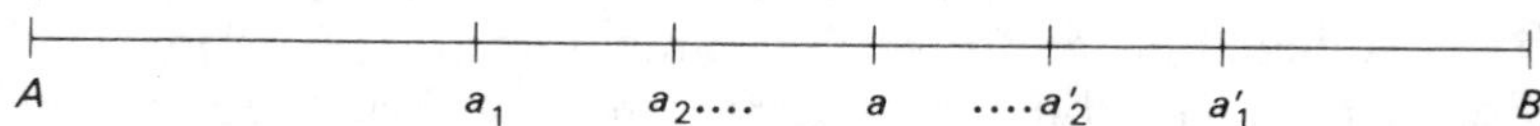

If *b* is to traverse *AB*, he must touch each of the infinitely many points $a_1, a_2, \ldots, a, \ldots a'_1, a'_2$. His first step is from *A* to a_1; his last is from a'_1 to *B*.

As for the second premiss, it owes the little plausibility it has to an equivocation: you might, I suppose, say that the 'completion' of a series of tasks is simply the performance of the last member of the series; I complete the crossword in entering the last light, I complete the book in writing the ultimate sentence. And in *that* sense of 'complete' (if it is really a sense at all), sequences with no last member cannot be completed. But the obvious sense of 'complete' does not yield that consequence: if *S* is the set of tasks $\{x_1, x_2, \ldots x_n, \ldots\}$, then *b* has completed *S* if and only if *b* has performed every x_i. To complete a set of tasks is to perform all the tasks, not to perform a *last* task. From '*b* has performed every x_i' we cannot infer '*b* performed one x_i after all the other x_is': even if *S* is finite, it need contain no last member; *b* may perform two, or three, or all of the x_is at the same time.

That simple reflexion may still some disquiet about the propriety of speaking of 'completing' an infinite sequence of operations; but it will leave some readers unsatisfied. Surely, they will feel, even if you do not need to perform a *last* task in *S* in order to complete your performance, yet you cannot *complete* *S* without coming to an end of your tasks; and your tasks, being infinite, have no end. Thus (2) is true; and its truth follows from the nature of completion: infinite tasks cannot, logically, be completed.

But that, too, is a bad argument; and it, too, trades on an equivocation. Someone who said '*b* cannot come to an end of his tasks' might mean:

(3) $(\forall t)$ $(\forall n)$ (if at *t* *b* has performed exactly *n* x_is, then there is an x_j that *b* has not performed by *t*).

He might, alternatively, mean:

(4) $(\forall t)$ $(\exists j)$ (*b* has not by *t* performed x_j).

Now Zeno's premiss (2) is equivalent to (4); and if *S* is infinite it is easy to demonstrate the truth of (3). But (3) and (4) are not equivalent; nor does (3) entail (4). By adding a further premiss:

(5) $(\forall t)$ $(\exists n)$ (by t b has performed exactly n x_is)

it is possible to deduce (4) from (3); but to assert (5) is precisely to deny that b can perform an infinite number of tasks—and that is the very proposition at issue. In short, to say that you can never get to the end of an infinite sequence either crudely reasserts that you cannot perform infinitely many tasks, or else observes (truly but irrelevantly) that whatever finite number of tasks you have performed, more yet remain; neither assertion has any tendency to prove the truth of (2).

The next reason for supporting (2) turns on the notion of progress: 'If I perform a sequence of tasks, my performance is marked by a certain type of progress. I gradually tick off the tasks to be done, reducing their number until eventually all are finished and behind me. But if S is infinite, I can make no progress of that sort; for however many x_is I have performed, I still have exactly as many x_is left to perform: however many a_is b has touched, he still has exactly as many a_is left to touch. Performance depends on progress; infinitude mocks progress: (2), then, is true.'

The second premiss of this argument is true: if b has touched n a_is, he still has infinitely many a_is to go. In general, if S has infinitely many members, and S' is a finite subset of S, then $S-S'$ has as many members as S. (The series $\langle n, n + 1, n + 2, \ldots \rangle$, where n is any natural number, can be put in one-one correspondence with the natural numbers.)

What of the first premiss? I confess I see little force in it. It decrees that progress in the performance of a sequence of tasks must consist in the performance of a successively larger fraction of those tasks. If that decree is accepted, then many performances will exhibit no progress. If I design to break every window in the quadrangle, I need not throw successive stones and do my job piecemeal; a single bomb, suitably placed, will blow in all the windows at once. And in any case, it is unnecessary to accept the decree. I may surely make progress in my plan to defenestrate the quadrangle, even if the actual blowing in of the windows occurs all at an instant: my progress might well be measured by the length of time still to elapse before my object is attained. Similarly, we may say (if we wish) that b is progressing in his task of touching all the a_is, on the grounds that the time at which his task will be completed is getting nearer. In short, performance does not evidently require progress; and the notion of progress is in any case readily accommodated to apply to the performance of infinite tasks.

The sixth consideration advanced in support of (2) is more complex and more interesting. It invites us to consider the state of affairs that would hold were an infinite series of tasks to be successfully performed. Imagine a reading-lamp with a push-button switch for turning it on and off. The lamp is always either on or off; if it is on, a push of the switch turns it off; if it is off, a similar depression illuminates it. Take the lamp and depress its switch infinitely many times (first at noon, say; then at 12.30; then at 12.45 . . .). Now consider its state after the switchings are completed, at 1.00 p.m. Disregard any technological or physical obstacles which you may have met with and ask simply whether the lamp is on or off at 1.00 p.m. It cannot be on; for every time you switched it on you immediately switched it off again. It cannot be off; for every time you switched it off you immediately switched it on again. So it is neither on nor off. But by hypothesis it is always either on or off. The supposition of infinite switchings thus leads to an overt contradiction: premiss (2)—in a particular case at least—is established.[9]

That ingenious argument raises many questions; I shall not consider them in their generality, but instead construct a parallel argument for the Zenonian runner, and consider the credentials of that. 'Zeno's runner, *b*, has to complete the infinite set of tasks consisting of touching a_1, touching a_2, ... Suppose that *b* manages to complete his tasks: where is he at the moment of completion? Not, alas, at *B*; for *B* is not a member of the set of a_is, and each task which *b* performs brings him to an a_i. Nor beyond *B*; for no a_i is situated beyond *B*. Nor, thirdly, is he short of *B*, between *A* and *B*; for suppose he is at *C*, between *A* and *B*; then there are a_is (infinitely many of them) between *C* and *B*, and he has not after all completed his tasks. But clearly, after the completion of the tasks *b* must be either at *B* or beyond *B* or short of *B*. Hence he cannot complete his tasks.'

The argument sounds plausible; but its conclusion is invalidly drawn. More formally stated, the argument puts up for *reductio* the hypothesis that *b* completes his infinite tasks at some time *t*; and it does indeed reduce that hypothesis to absurdity, by showing that there is no consistent description of *b*'s state at *t*. Hence we may conclude that there is no time at which *b* completes *S*. But from that we cannot infer that *b* does not complete *S*: he may complete *S* without there being any time which is the time of his completion, the last instant of his performance.

That contention may sound paradoxical; but in fact it only applies to the completion of *S* a general truth about the completion of any task or set of tasks. This general truth, which has nothing to do with the problems of infinity, was first grasped by Aristotle.[10] Take any change; i.e., suppose that at t a changes from being ϕ to being non-ϕ, thus:

Consider the point of change, t. If t is the last point in *a*'s ϕness and also the first point in *a*'s non-ϕness, then a is ϕ at t and a is non-ϕ at t. But that is impossible. Hence, in general, there can be no point that is both the first point of *a*'s non-ϕness and the last point of *a*'s ϕness. Suppose, then, that t is the first point of *a*'s non-ϕness. Suppose there is a point t' prior to t which is the last point of *a*'s ϕness. Since time is continuous, there are points t_1, t_2, . . . between t' and t (in fact there are infinitely many such points). At t_1 a is not ϕ, for t_1 is later than t'; and at t_1 a is not non-ϕ, for t_1 is prior to t. But that is impossible. Hence, in general, if there is a first point of *a*'s non-ϕness there is no last point of *a*'s ϕness. An exactly analogous argument shows that if there is a last point of *a*'s ϕness there is no first point of *a*'s non-ϕness.

The application to Zeno is plain. There is a first point of *b*'s having completed the tasks in *S*–viz. the point at which he touches *B*. Hence there is no last point at which he completes the tasks in *S*; i.e., there is no last instant of his performance. That is no paradox: it simply brings out a general feature of all change: change can occur without there being a last moment of the unchanged state.

Thus the illustration of the lamp does show something about the logic of infinity; but it does not show that (2) is true. And I turn to the seventh and final argument for (2). The situation in which a performer of infinitely many tasks finds himself can be represented as a progress along an asymptotic curve:

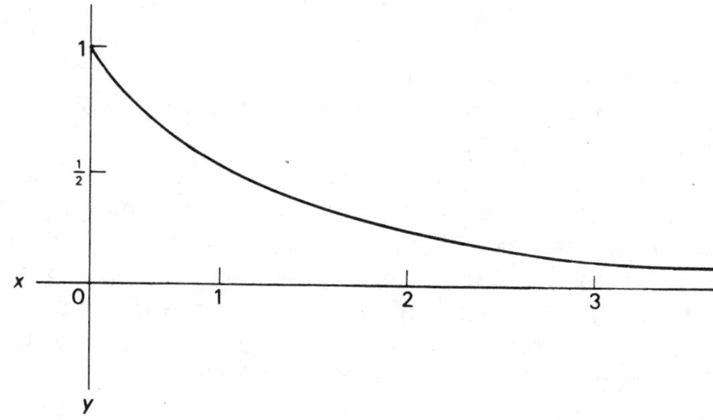

In the Zenonian case, the curve plots *b*'s distance from *B*, the *x*-axis representing that distance, the *y*-axis marking off the a_is. The curve constantly approaches 0 but never reaches it. In general, progress *via* an infinite sequence of operations can be represented by an asymptotic line on a graph; and the discontinuity or gap between the line and the *y*-axis provides a puzzle; for it appears to mark a gap in the causal nexus of events. The runner's progress through the a_is is surely causally connected to his arrival at *B*; yet there is an unbridgeable gap between his arrival at the successive a_is and his arrival at *B*.

Thus, first, there is always a physical gap between *b*'s position at the end of any run to an a_i and his goal. How can causation send its spark across that spatial chasm? Second, there is no event among the touchings of the a_is which may be linked to the arrival at *B*; for any causal chain would bind the arrival to the *last* touching, and there is no last touching. How can a causal chain hold firm when there is no link locked to its last link? Third, consider the period *T* during which *b* travels from *A* to *B*. There is no last instant of *b*'s travelling, and hence no last instant in *T*. Let *t* be the first instant after *T*: given the details of *b*'s progress we can say for any instant *within* *T* exactly where *b* will be: at t_i he will be at a_i. Yet we cannot in the same way predict where *b* will be at *t*. (Reconsider the lamp: the plan to switch it on at 12.30, off at 12.45, and so on enables us to predict the lamp's state at any time *between* 12.00 and 1.00; it does not license a prediction for 1.00.) How can a causal law cover that hole in the path of predictability?

Thus we have a seventh reason for upholding (2): 'If (2) were false, the great chains of causation would snap'.[11]

The argument deserves a longer presentation than I can give it here. I content myself with three summary observations. First, the argument does not show the truth of (2); at most it shows that (2) is true in a Laplacean world, where every event is causally determined by its predecessors; and no one has yet shown that our familiar world is Laplacean. Perhaps there are causal hiatuses; many philosophers and scientists hold that there are.

Second, the argument is stated too grossly. In the case of *some* infinite performances there seems no difficulty in formulating causal laws that 'bridge the gap'. The Zenonian runner provides such an example: given that he starts from *A* and proceeds at uniform speed through all the a_is, we can predict that he will be at *B* at a given time after his departure from *A*. The fact that the a_is are infinite and the distinct fact that no a_i is contiguous to *B* have no bearing on the question: causal 'chains'—a poor metaphor at the best of times—do not have to link events to their immediate neighbours; they can bind events together even if immediate neighbours are lacking.

Third, it is by no means clear that in *any* infinite performances there will or must be causal 'gaps'. Causal laws are empirical hypotheses; as far as I can see, nothing in the description of the infinite switchings of the lamp, or in any other infinite performance, rules out any causal hypothesis. Switch the lamp off at t_1, on at t_2; and so on. Is the state of the lamp at t predictable? Is it causally determined by its earlier states? Those questions cannot be answered *a priori*. Suppose that numerous experiments of such switchings were carried out, and that in all of them the lamp was found to be on at B; then we should have reason to favour the causal hypothesis that the lamp's state, after infinite switchings of the sort described, was *on*. Of course, a different result might be obtained: we might always find the lamp *off*; or there might be a random selection of *offs* and *ons*. Of course, we do not know, now, what the state at B would be. Of course, we shall never be able to conduct any such tests as those I have imagined. But those points are irrelevant: the seventh argument purports to show that only (2) will shield us from a world of random happenings. That is not so; and the notion of causation does not, I think, help us to ground our desire to believe (2).

I believe (2) to be false: of the many arguments designed to support (2), all are wanting in one or more particulars. But I cannot show that (2) is false; indeed, the reason why Zeno's Dichotomy is so fascinating an argument is to be sought in (2): men want to believe (2); they cannot believe that we possess infinite powers; and they keep producing ever more ingenious arguments in favour of Zeno. For all that, until a new batch of arguments comes forward I shall continue to reject Zeno's conclusion by rejecting (2).

(c) *Achilles and the tortoise*

The second paradox in Aristotle's list is the Achilles:

> Second is the one called Achilles. This says that the slow will never be caught in running by the fastest. For the pursuer must first get to where the pursued started from, so that it is necessary that the slower should always be some distance ahead (**186**: *Phys* 239b14–8 = **A 26** = **26 L**).

Take a racecourse, AB, of indefinitely great length. Let Achilles be placed at A; let the tortoise—as we have come to know his opponent—be placed at any point C between A and B; and at t let Achilles and the tortoise each begin to move towards B. (The paradox says—and need say—nothing about their relative speeds, about the absolute speed of either, or about the uniformity of either's progress.) Suppose that Achilles does catch up with the tortoise; i.e., that there is some point P on AB such that at some time t' after t both Achilles and the tortoise are at P. Since the tortoise has been moving towards B, P is between C and B, thus:

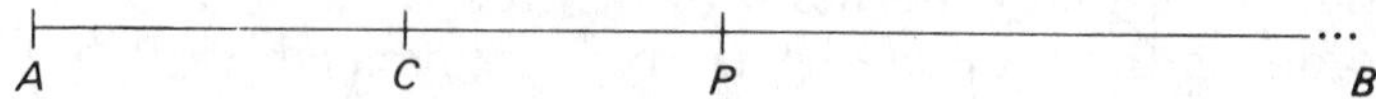

It follows that 'the pursuer must first get to where the pursued started from'; i.e., that at some time between t and t' Achilles is at C. Now when Achilles is at C, the tortoise is at some point, C_1, between C and B; but clearly Achilles must reach C_1 before t'; and when he is at C_1, the tortoise is already ahead, at C_2, between C_1 and B. And in general, if Achilles is at C_i, the tortoise is already at C_{i+1}, one step ahead of him. Thus 'it is necessary that the slower should always be some distance ahead', and Achilles can never catch the tortoise.

According to Aristotle, the Achilles paradox is merely a twopenny coloured version of the Dichotomy. Achilles is dramatized (*tetragôdoumenos*), but at bottom 'this argument is the same as the Dichotomy (only differing in that the added magnitude is not divided in half) . . . so that it necessarily has the same solution' (*Phys* 239b18–20; 25–6). Most modern scholars disagree with Aristotle; at all events, the Achilles is regularly discussed at length and in its own right, whereas the Dichotomy is regularly ignored. (Most of the arguments about infinite performances which I have examined under the rubric of the Dichotomy were originally advanced in connexion with the Achilles.) And at first sight, things do seem to go against Aristotle: according to the Dichotomy, Achilles can never reach the tortoise's starting position; according to the Achilles, even if he could do so, he could never catch the tortoise; in the Dichotomy, the race has a fixed finishing post, which can never be reached; in the Achilles, the finishing post itself is perpetually receding. Achilles, it seems, has double the toil and trouble of his undramatic counterpart in the Dichotomy. He cannot move; and if, *per impossibile*, he could, he would never reach his goal.

Nevertheless, a closer inspection of the Achilles vindicates Aristotle's judgment: the paradox, if not identical with the Dichotomy, is no more than the Dichotomy with an unharmonious coda.

The last step of the argument is invalid. From:

(1) For every i, if Achilles is at C_i, then the tortoise is at C_{i+1},

Zeno invites us, in effect, to infer:

(2) For every point p on AB, if Achilles is at p, the tortoise is at some point p' between p and B.

Now (1) is true; and Zeno's argument shows it to be true. And (2) does imply that Achilles never catches the tortoise. But (2) does not follow from (1). (2) could be inferred from the conjunction of (1) and:

(3) For every point p on AB, there is an i such that C_i is between p and B.

But clearly (3) is not available to Zeno. Every C_i is, by construction, between C and the hypothetical meeting point P; for C_i is simply the point on AB where the tortoise is at the time when Achilles is at C_{i-1}. Thus on the twin assumptions that the tortoise never ceases to move and that Achilles' speed is finite, for *no* i does $C_i = C_{i-1}$. But if C_i = P, then $C_i = C_{i-1}$; hence for no i does C_i = P. Evidently, no C_i is between P and B. Hence every C_i is between C and P. It follows that Achilles and the tortoise never meet at any C_i, as (1) says. But that conclusion is now seen to be the merest triviality: the two runners will never meet at any point before their first meeting point. From this, nothing like (2) follows; from the fact that they do not meet before they meet, we can scarcely infer that they never meet.

Aristotle saw all that very clearly: 'when [the tortoise] is ahead, he is not caught; but nevertheless he is caught if you grant that one can traverse a limited distance' (*Phys* 239b27–9). According to Aristotle, (1) is true but trivial. How, then, can we get any paradox out of the Achilles? Only, Aristotle implies, by denying that Achilles can traverse the finite distance AP. And how might Zeno propel us towards such a denial? Only, Aristotle implies, by adducing the considerations that he advanced in the Dichotomy. Thus (1) brings out, in a clear enough fashion, the fact that before Achilles reaches the tortoise he must touch infinitely many points; and it is easy to see from (1) that however close to the tortoise Achilles may be—however many C_is he may have successively touched—he still has infinitely many C_is still to touch before he reaches P. And such infinite performances are, Zeno invites us to suppose, impossible.

That manoeuvre reduces the Achilles to the Dichotomy; and any objections to the argumentation in the latter paradox will apply immediately to the former. I do not deny that the Achilles is both clever and elegant; but I agree with Aristotle that it raises no philosophical difficulties which its more prosaic predecessor has not already flushed out.

(d) *The arrow*

The third paradox of motion does break new ground. It is the Arrow. Aristotle's brief description and curt dismissal read thus:

> Third is the one we have just mentioned—that the travelling arrow is at rest. This comes about from assuming that time is composed of 'nows' (*ta nun*); for if that is not granted, there will be no deduction (**187**: *Phys* 239b30–3 = **A 27** = **28 L**).

Aristotle refers back to the opening of Z 9, where the transmitted text reads as follows:

> Zeno misargues; for if, he says, everything always rests or moves whenever it is against what is equal (*kata to ison*), and what is travelling is always in the now (*en tôi nun*), the travelling arrow is motionless (**188**: 239b5–7 = **A 27** = **29 L**).

After that brief report there is the same dismissal as at 239b30–3.

Two further, non-Aristotelian, texts may be adduced. Epiphanius gives the following report:

> He [sc. Zeno] also argues thus: what is moving moves either in the place in which it is or in the place in which it is not. And it moves neither in the place in which it is nor in that in which it is not. Therefore nothing moves (**189**: *adversus haereticos* III.11 = **18 L**).

The second text, from Diogenes, repeats the argument in an abbreviated form (IX.72 = **B 4** = **17 L**). Some scholars think that this dilemma is an independent Zenonian argument, the fifth paradox of motion; others, judging it feeble in itself, attach it to the Arrow: 'Either the arrow moves in the place where it is, or it moves in the place where it is not; evidently it cannot move in the place where it is not; by the Aristotelian argument it cannot move in the place where it is: hence it cannot move.' That reconstruction may possibly be right; but it has no ancient warrant. Moreover, the sources who ascribe the dilemma to Zeno are not unimpeachable; and elsewhere the dilemma is associated with the name of Diodorus Cronos.[12] I incline to the sceptical view that a later dilemma has been anachronistically fathered on Zeno. However that may be, I do not think that the dilemma is very exciting; and I shall confine my discussion to Aristotle's text.

That text is hard enough, in all conscience. It offers Zeno two premisses:

(1) If a is 'against what is equal' at t, then either a rests at t or a is moving at t.

(2) If *a* is moving at *t*, then *a* is 'in the now' at *t*.
From these propositions we are invited to conclude that:
(3) If *a* is moving at *t*, *a* is not moving at *t*.
And hence:
(4) *a* is not moving at *t*.
(I have replaced Aristotle's word 'travelling' (*pheromenon*) by 'moving' in (1) and (3); the terms are synonymous.)

The inference from (3) to (4) is valid; and it is worth noting that Zeno uses a subtle theorem of propositional logic later known as the *Lex Clavia*: if if *P* then not-*P*, then not-*P*. (The companion law, the *Consequentia Mirabilis*—if if not-*P* then *P*, then *P*—was used in a celebrated context by Aristotle.) The move from (3) to (4) is, however, the only uncontroversial element in the paradox: all scholars recognize the obscurity in (1) and (2) and the difficulty in moving from them to (3); and many philosophers deny that (4) is sufficient to establish Zeno's desired conclusion, that nothing moves. I shall first deal with (1) and (2).

(1) and (2) will not yield (3). Instead of (1) and (2) we might well expect:
(5) If *a* is 'against what is equal' at *t*, then *a* rests at *t*.
(6) If *a* is moving at *t*, then *a* is 'against what is equal' at *t*.
If we add the further premiss:
(7) If *a* rests at *t*, then *a* is not moving at *t*,
we can validly infer (3). Premiss (7), which may well seem a thoroughly trifling proposition, is easy enough to supply; but (5) and (6), neither of which follows from (1) and (2), surely need explicit statement. Scholars have accordingly emended the text of the *Physics* so as to produce (5) and (6).

The simplest means of producing (5) is the excision of the words 'or moves' (*ê kineitai*) from 239b6; then (1) vanishes from the argument and is replaced by an explicit statement of (5). (6) might be derived from (2) in conjunction with:
(8) If *a* is 'in the now' at *t*, then *a* is 'against what is equal' at *t*.
It is possible to introduce (8) into Aristotle's text; but it is perhaps preferable to treat (8) as a suppressed premiss. Zeno states (2) and expects us to infer (6) by way of (8).[13]

Thus I suggest that Aristotle's text originally presented (5) and (2) explicitly, and expressly inferred (3) from those two premisses. And I suggest that Zeno's original argument started from (5), (2) and (8); that it first inferred (6) from (2) and (8); that it then inferred (3) from (5), (6) and (7); and that it finally inferred (4) from (3), concluding that nothing moves. The textual suggestions are, I think, of no great importance: what matters is that Zeno intended us to reach (3), and hence (4), from (5) and (6).

What, then, is the precise sense of Zeno's premisses? In particular, how are we to understand the two odd phrases 'in the now' and 'against what is equal'? 'The now (*to nun*)' is Aristotle's standard term for an instant of time; but it makes no sense to say, baldly, '*a* is at *t*', where *t* names some instant: I may be in a place, but I cannot simply be 'at a time'. We might construe 'is (*esti*)' strongly, as 'exists'; or, better, we might take it as a verb-variable, so that '*a* is in the now' means '*a* ϕs at *t*'—for some suitable verb ϕ and some definite instant *t*. (Aristotle says '*in* the now (*en tôi nun*)'; I say '*at t*': some philosophers find a significant difference here; but I think that 'at' is simply the appropriate English translation of '*en*'.)

The commentators all gloss 'is against what is equal' by 'occupies an equal space'; and the gloss is surely correct. Most of them add that 'an equal space' is elliptical for 'a space equal to its volume'; so that '*a* is against what is equal' becomes '*a* occupies a space equal to its own volume:

No Creature loves an empty space;
Their Bodies measure out their Place.

I accept that explanation: nothing else will give Zeno an argument of any plausibility.[14]

Thus interpreted, are Zeno's premisses true? Premiss (2) has become:

(2*) If *a* is moving at *t*, then there is some instant *t'* such that at *t a* is ϕing at *t'*.

And that is a tautology. The suppressed premiss (8) reads:

(8*) If there is some instant *t'* such that at *t a* is ϕing at *t'*, then at *t a* occupies a space equal to its own volume.

That is a peculiar observation; and I cannot divine why Zeno should have propounded it. Indeed, the very notion of being 'in the now' seems only to add an unnecessary complication to Zeno's argument; for (6), which has now become:

(6*) If *a* is moving at *t*, then at *t a* occupies a space equal to its own volume,

can be justified on far less mysterious grounds: it is a necessary truth that everything always occupies a space exactly equal to its own volume; i.e., that for any object *x* and time *t*, the volume of space occupied by *x* at *t* is equal to the volume of *x* at *t*. For what is the volume of an object if not the amount of space it occupies? But then whether or not *a* is moving at *t*, *a* is 'against what is equal' at *t*; hence (6) is necessarily true.

What, then, of premiss (5)? If that is true, then Zeno has reached (4) and we are potentially in trouble. (5) now reads:

(5*) If *a* occupies at *t* a space equal to its own volume, then *a* rests at *t*.

Some philosophers hold that (5*) is not even coherent, let alone true. According to Aristotle, 'at an instant, it is not possible for anything to be either in motion or at rest' (*Phys* 239bl; cf. 234a32). Rest is a matter of endurance: things rest *for a period* of time; they cannot intelligibly be said to rest *at a point* in time. Aristotle has a multitude of followers. The question is usually discussed in connexion with Zeno's conclusion, (4); and I shall follow the custom. For at step (5) Zeno is easily and trivially defended; we need only replace (5*) by:

(5^+) If *a* occupies at *t* a space equal to its own volume, then it is not the case that *a* is moving at *t*.

Indeed, (5^+) not only evades the captious objection about rest; it also enables Zeno to dispense with the additional premiss (7): (5^+) and (6*) together entail (3) with no more ado.

Those many thinkers who agree with Aristotle that 'at an instant, nothing moves' are obliged to accept (5^+). And (6*) is certainly true. Since (5^+) and (6*) entail (3), it seems that Zeno is vindicated: the moving arrow does not move.

(e) *Movement in a moment*

Russell, for one, happily assents to (4): Zeno, he says, did prove that 'we live in an unchanging world, and that the arrow, at every moment of its flight, is truly at rest. The only point where Zeno probably erred was in inferring (if he did infer) that, because there is no change, the world must be in the same state at one time as at another.' In short, (4), far from being a monstrous paradox, is 'a very plain statement of a very elementary fact'. But (4) does not entail the absence of motion. Rather, it enables us to see more clearly the real nature of motion: 'People used to think that when a thing changes, it must be in a state of change, and that when a thing moves, it is in a state of motion. This is now known to be a mistake. When a body moves, all that can be said is that it is in one place at one time and in another at another.'[15]

Russell's views are not entirely plain. I take it that he is saying three things about the inference from (4) to the denial of motion—strictly speaking, about the inference from:

(9) $(\forall t)$ (if *t* is in *T*, then *a* is not moving at *t*),

to:

(10) *a* does not move during *T*.

Russell says *first* that the inference is invalid; *second*, that a correct understanding of the concept of motion will reveal its invalidity; and *third*, that Zeno may well not have made or intended the inference. I find Russell's view bizarre; on all three counts his reaction to the Arrow is mistaken. I take the points in reverse order.

First, then, all the ancient commentators treat the Arrow as part of Zeno's general attack upon motion. They plainly regard (4) as the penultimate step leading to a negation of motion: I see no reason to dispute their view; and I suppose that Zeno ended his argument by explicitly saying 'the arrow does not move'—indeed it is natural to construe Aristotle's words at 239b7 in precisely that way.

Second, let us consider Russell's account of motion. Russell naughtily describes it as a 'static' account; it can, I think, be formulated as follows:

(D1) a moves during T if and only if for every pair of distinct instants t_1 and t_2 in T there is an instant t_3 between t_1 and t_2 and a pair of distinct places p_1 and p_3 such as a is at p_1 at t_1 and a is at p_3 at t_3.

That looks needlessly complicated. In fact its complexities are necessary, and must be multiplied (as the ancients realized) if we are to say of spinning tops that they move. Zeno in (4) talks of motion at an instant; does (D1) show such talk to be odd? does it show the inference from (9) to (10) to be invalid? Motion at an instant is easily defined:

(D2) a is moving at t if and only if for some T t is within T and a moves during T.

Given (D2), (9) immediately implies (10): if (D1) and (D2) offer a correct account of motion, they do not thereby reveal the invalidity of the Zenonian inference. Quite the contrary. (I do not mean to imply that Zeno himself had in mind a Russellian account of motion. Nor do I think that there are just two ways of envisaging motion: the one given in (D1–2), and the one rightly rejected by Russell according to which motion is an intrinsic quality of the moving object, in much the way that triangularity is an intrinsic quality of a triangular object. My point is only that Zeno has nothing to fear from (D1).)

Finally, is the inference from (9) and (10), or from (4) to Zeno's immobile conclusion, valid? It seems to me gratuitously paradoxical to deny its validity: if the inference is invalid then we must, in Bergson's celebrated phrase, accept 'the absurd proposition that movement is made of immobilities'.[16] Every period of motion will consist of an infinite sequence of motionless states. Ordinary usage accustoms us to talk of 'motion at an instant': I can say that the car was travelling at 34 m.p.h. at the moment when the bus hit it; or that at 9.10 this morning I was cycling into College. And ordinary usage sanctions inferences of the relevant sort between statements of 'motion at an instant' and statements of enduring motion: if I claim to have been cycling between 9.05 and 9.15 I cannot consistently deny that I was cycling at 9.10; if the car moved steadily at 34 m.p.h. until it hit the bus, then it was moving at 34 m.p.h. when it hit the bus. Indeed, it is, I think, a general truth that if *a* ϕ s during *T*, then *a* is ϕing at every instant *t* in *T*; and the acceptability of that proposition in no way depends on restricting the range of 'ϕ' to static verbs.

Why should any philosopher go against that natural mode of speech and argument? It cannot be said that the notion of 'motion at an instant' makes no sense; clearly it does make perfectly ordinary sense, and a sense that can be lucidly articulated in some such definition as (D2). Are there, then, hidden inconsistencies in the definition, or any that may replace it?

Some have argued as follows: 'All motion has duration, and it always makes sense to ask, of a moving object, how long it has moved for; consequently, the notion of instantaneous motion is logically contradictory; and thus motion at an instant is impossible.'[17] It is true that all motion involves duration: if *a* moves, then there is some period *T* such that *a* moves during *T*. And it does follow from this that instantaneous motion is a logical impossibility: 'a ϕs instantaneously' means, I take it, that for some *t a* ϕs at *t* and for no *T* does *a* ϕ during *T*. In that sense some things, e.g., dying or learning—may or may not be instantaneous; and some things, of which change and all its species are the most conspicuous examples, are necessarily not instantaneous. But that does not show that the argument I have just considered is sound; for its final step involves a gross confusion: it is one thing to reject instantaneous motion, another to reject motion 'at an instant'. To believe that motion at an instant is possible is to believe that '*a* moves at *t*' is consistent; to believe that instantaneous motion is impossible is to believe that '*a* moves at *t* and for no *T* does *a* move during *T*' is inconsistent. Plainly, those two beliefs are compatible: I uphold motion 'at an instant'; but I also believe that if *a* moves then for some *T a* moves during *T*, and thus I reject instantaneous motion.

Aristotle provides a different argument against motion at an instant: 'That nothing moves at an instant is evident thus: if it did, a thing could move both quicker and slower. Let *N* be an instant, and let the faster thing have moved the distance *AB* at *N* (*en autôi*). Now at the same instant (*en tôi autôi*) the slower thing will have moved a shorter distance, say *AC*. But since the slower has moved through *AC* in the whole instant, the faster will have moved [through *AC*] in a shorter time than this—so that the instant will have been divided. But that is impossible—hence it is not possible to move at an instant' (*Phys* 234a23–31).

There are two related errors in this argument. The first is more evident in the translation than in the Greek: it consists in treating the term 'instant (*nun*)' as though it connoted a period of time, as though it were the last member of the set of terms that includes 'year', 'day', 'hour', 'minute', 'second'. In English we do sometimes talk of things happening 'in an instant', and the same idiom is, I suppose, possible in Greek. But when we say 'in an instant' we are using the term 'instant' loosely, as a synonym for 'split second'. Aristotle misses this point; and his argument depends on his construing '*en tôi nun*' as though it were logically on a par with '*en miai hôrai*' ('in an hour').

The second, allied, error, is harder to exhibit clearly. It lies in Aristotle's supposition that 'the faster thing has moved the distance *AB en autôi*'. Behind that supposition lies the truism that if a has moved at all, then there is some distance through which a has moved. But from that truth Aristotle falsely infers that if a moved at t, then there is some distance through which a moved at t, say the distance AB. Now he might properly have inferred that there is some distance through which a was moving at t: at t a was moving from A to B if t falls within a period of constant motion T and if during T a moved from A to B. But from 'a was moving from A to B at t' we cannot infer 'a moved from A to B at t'. Indeed, we cannot, in general, infer 'a ϕed at t' from 'a was ϕing at t' (as, in another context, Aristotle in effect recognizes). I was eating breakfast at 8.45, but I did not eat breakfast at 8.45; I was reading a book at 10.30, but I did not read a book at 10.30. In general, if 'a ϕs' entails 'for some T, a ϕs during T', then 'a is ϕing at t' does not entail 'a ϕs at t'.

Thus Aristotle's argument against motion 'at an instant' fails. And I know of no other, more compelling, argument.

I end this section by considering Aristotle's objection to the Arrow: he says simply that 'time is not composed of indivisible nows' (239b8). I take it that he means to ascribe the following argument to Zeno:

(11) $(\forall t)$(if t is in T, a is not moving at t).

(12) T is composed of the set of instants it contains.

Hence:

(13) a does not move during T.

Here (11) represents (4), and (13) is a version of Zeno's wholesale rejection of locomotion. And Aristotle objects that (12) is false.

I have two comments. First, we might disagree with Aristotle about

(12) and yet agree with him that the argument from (11) to (13) is unsound. For the pattern of inference represented by (11)–(13) is invalid: it is a case of the 'fallacy of composition', the fallacy of arguing from 'All the parts of *X* are *F*' to '*X* is *F*'. (All the molecules that make up this glass of beer are tasteless, so the beer is tasteless.) Second, I see no reason to ascribe Aristotle's argument to Zeno: Zeno infers (13) directly from (11). There is no need to invoke (12); and hence no occasion to charge Zeno with a fallacy of composition.

(f) *The arrow blunted*

If I am right, we cannot allow Zeno to reach proposition (4) without giving him his conclusion that motion is impossible. Since (6*) is true, we must reject (5⁺); and indeed (5⁺) seems to me to be clearly false: objects do, at every instant in their temporal careers, occupy a space exactly equal to their volume at that instant. And they do so even if they are in motion throughout their temporal careers. Why should anyone find that puzzling?

Some might argue as follows: 'If we think of the arrow as occupying a given position for a time of zero duration, it will be obvious enough that it cannot be moving *then*: it will have no time in which to move.'[18] That is a bad argument: *a* needs time to move from *A* to *B*; but *a* needs no time *to be moving* from *A* to *B*. The arrow is moving at *t*; it does not follow, as I have already said, that the arrow *moves* through some distance at *t*. If that argument lies behind (5⁺), then (5⁺) is not established.

But the argument makes no essential reference to the space which *a* occupies at *t*; and I suspect that a different consideration operated on Zeno's mind. I suspect that he argued as follows: 'If at *t a* occupies a space no greater than itself, then *a* has no room in which to move. Moving involves the transition from one place to another, and hence occupancy of more than one place. But at *t a* occupies just one place, viz. the place marked out by its own boundary.' That argument too is bad; and the grounds of its badness have already been presented: if *a* moves, then there are two points, *A* and *B*, such that *a* moves from *A* to *B*; and if *a* is moving at *t*, there are points *A* and *B* such that at *t a* is moving from *A* to *B*. But it does not follow that if *a* is moving at *t*, then there are points *A* and *B* such that at *t a* moves from *A* to *B*. Similarly if I smoke my pipe, there is a plug of tobacco which I consume in the process; and if I am smoking a pipe at *t*, then there is a plug of tobacco which I am consuming at *t*. But it does not follow—and it is not true—that if I am smoking a pipe at *t*, then there is a plug of tobacco which I consume at *t*.

It is perhaps worth setting out in one paragraph the various facts about motion which I have tried to express and to deploy. First, motion requires duration: '*a* moves' entails 'For some period *T*, *a* moves during *T*'. Second, motion requires extension: '*a* moves' entails 'For some distance *AB*, *a* moves from *A* to *B*.' Third, motion 'at an instant' requires durational motion: '*a* is moving at *t*' entails 'For some period *T*, *a* moves during *T*'. Fourth, motion 'at an instant' requires motion through a space: '*a* is moving at *t*' entails 'For some distance *AB*, *a* moves from *A* to *B*'. Fifth, motion 'at an instant' does *not* require instantaneous motion: '*a* is moving at *t*' does not entail 'For no period *T*, *a* moves during *T*'. Sixth, motion 'at an instant' does *not* require instantaneous transition: '*a* is moving at *t*' does not entail 'For some distance *AB*, *a* moves from *A* to *B* at *t*'. There is evidently much more to be said about the logic of motion than that. But I believe that the six facts I have just listed are sufficient to show that the customary answers to Zeno's Arrow are mistaken. Zeno's argument is valid; but it relies on a false premiss.

There remains the possibility of an eleventh hour reprieve: so far I have taken Aristotle's phrase 'the now' to denote an instant; and one of my complaints has been against the misconstrual of instants as small periods of time. Now some scholars suppose that Zeno's argument should in fact be conducted entirely in terms of periods of time, and not at all in terms of instants. I do not think that Aristotle's text encourages such a supposition; and I do not believe that we can seriously hope to recover a genuinely Zenonian argument behind a distorted Aristotelian presentation. Nonetheless, it is clearly desirable to see what difference might be made to the penetrative powers of the Arrow if it is freed from the notion of movement 'at an instant'.

In the new version proposition (5) is replaced by:

(14) If *a* occupies during *T* a space equal to its own volume, then *a* is at rest during *T*.

As it stands, (14) seems plausible, or at least more plausible than (5). But in fact it is ambiguous. Its plausible sense is more explicitly given by:

(14a) If there is a place *p* equal to the volume of *a* such that at every instant *t* in *T* *a* occupies *p*, then *a* is at rest during *T*.

Indeed, (14a) is not only plausible: it is evidently true. Clearly, however, (14a) and (6) do not together entail (4). To secure the entailment, (6) too must be replaced by a proposition talking about periods of time. The proposition required is:

(15) If *a* is moving during *T*, then there is a place *p* equal to the volume of *a* such that at every instant *t* in *T* *a* occupies *p*.

And just as (14a) is evidently true, so (15) is evidently false.

If (14) is read as (14a), the Arrow has no penetration. The alternative reading of (14) is:

(14b) If at every instant t in T there is a place p such that a occupies p at t, then a is at rest during T.

A suitable replacement can be found for (6) which, together with (14b), entails (4). And that replacement will be true. But now (14b) turns out to be false; for the antecedent of (14b) is compatible with there being distinct places p_1, p_2 . . . which a occupies at distinct instants t_1, t_2 . . . in T; and occupancy of distinct places during T is incompatible with rest during T. Thus if (14) is interpreted as (14b) the Arrow gets no further. And I conclude that the proposal to read Zeno's paradox in terms of periods of time rather than in terms of instants has no philosophical merit. Not only does it fail to give Zeno a better argument; it also fails to raise any interesting philosophical puzzles.

Let me end my discussion of the Arrow with two negatively polemical remarks. It is usually supposed that Zeno's paradox carries with it some philosophical theory about the nature of time; and Zeno's commentators regularly adduce rival theories in the course of their reflexions upon it. My discussion has shown the falsity of that common supposition; for in expounding and criticizing the Arrow I have neither explicitly nor implicitly invoked any theory of time. In particular, I have not accused Zeno of treating time as being 'composed of instants'; nor have I ascribed to him the view that time is made up of 'atomic minimal parts'; nor have I made him assume that motion proceeds cinematographically. The paradox, as we should expect and desire, is innocent of any such theories: it presupposes only the two harmless and common notions that there are instants, as well as periods, of time; and that things move, if at all, at instants.

Many scholars find an architectonic structure uniting Zeno's four surviving paradoxes of motion: the paradoxes form a dilemmatic attack upon movement, the Dichotomy and the Achilles supposing that time and space are infinitely divisible, the Arrow and the Stadium supposing that there are indivisible spatial and temporal *quanta*. My account of the Arrow seems to me to have revealed the falsity of that neat fantasy.

(g) *The stadium*

The fourth and final paradox is the Stadium:

> [i] The fourth is the one about equal bodies which move alongside equal bodies in the stadium from opposite directions—the ones from the end of the stadium, the others from the middle—at equal speeds, in which he thinks it follows that half the time is equal to its double. [ii] The misargument consists in requiring that [a body travelling] at an equal speed travels for an equal time past a moving body and a body of the same magnitude at rest. That is false. [iii] E.g., let the stationary equal bodies be *AA*; let *BB* be those starting from the middle of the *A*s (equal in number and in magnitude to them); and let *CC* be those starting from the end (equal in number and in magnitude to them, and equal in speed to the *B*s). [iv] Now it follows that the first *B* and the first *C* are at the end at the same time, as they are moving past one another. [v] And it follows that the *C* has passed all the *A*s, and the *B* half; [vi] so that the time is half, [vii] for each of the two is alongside each for an equal time. [viii] And at the same time it follows that the first *B* has passed all the *C*s. [ix] For at the same time the first *B* and the first *C* will be at opposite ends, [x] being an equal time alongside each of the *B*s as alongside each of the *A*s, as he says, [xi] because both are an equal time alongside the *A*s. [xii] This is the argument, and it rests on the stated falsity (**190**: *Phys.* 239b33–240a18 = **A 28** = **35 L**).

The outline of that argument is clear enough. We have three equinumerous groups of bodies in a stadium, and the bodies are all equal in size. How many bodies each group possesses is not stated: the number is immaterial to the argument; and I shall take the simplest case, that in which each group contains just two bodies.[19] Aristotle does not say that the members of each group are contiguous and arranged in a row (like the carriages of a railway train); but the argument plainly requires that assumption. One row of bodies, the *A*s, is stationary. The *B*s and the *C*s move; and I shall refer to the leading *B* and the leading *C* as B_1 and C_1.

Aristotle gives, in [i] and [iii], a description of the stadium before the *B*s and *C*s begin their movements. I shall call this the *starting position*. Then [iv]–[x] list three things that 'follow' once the moving bodies have left the starting position. Let us call the starting time t_1; then at some later point, t_2, the bodies will be in what I shall call the *crucial position*. And if we consider what has happened during T, the interval between t_1 and t_2, we shall (according to Zeno), be faced with paradoxical or contradictory results. The problems of interpretation are thus three: first, to determine the starting position, at t_1; second, to determine the crucial position, at t_2; third, to discover what paradox is supposed to arise from our consideration of *T*, and how it is supposed to arise. The problems cannot be tackled separately; but it helps, I think, to begin by looking at the second of the three things that allegedly 'follow'.

That second result is stated in [v]–[vii], which describe, or partially describe, the state of the stadium at the crucial time, t_2. The description contains a vagueness; but I shall simply assume that the phrases 'the *B*' and 'the *C*' in sentence [v] denote the *first B* and the *first C*. Thus sentence [v] asserts that at t_2 the first *C* has passed all the *A*s and the first *B* has passed half the *A*s; C_1 has passed two *A*s, B_1 has passed one *A*. Given that the *C*s and the *B*s are proceeding at the same speed, we can infer that at some time prior to t_2—call it, for the moment, t_x—the stadium looked like this:

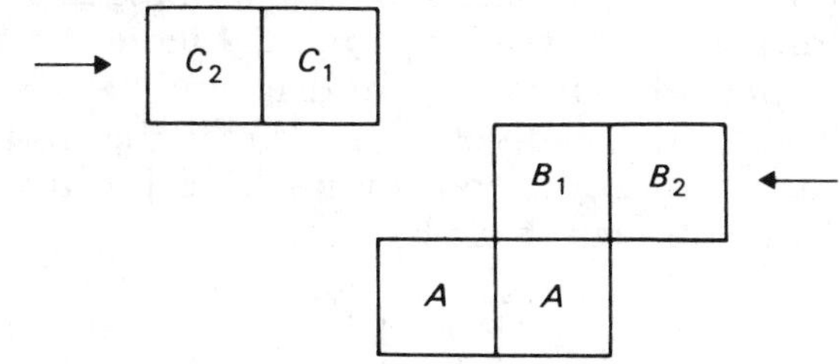

fig. 1

As far as t_2 goes, each of the following two diagrams seems to be consistent with the words of Aristotle's description:

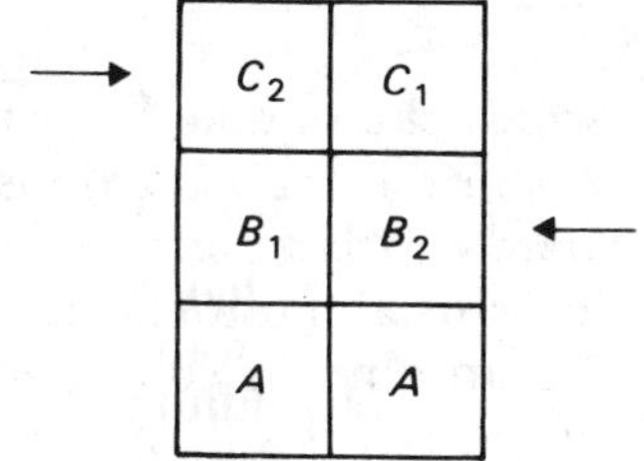

fig 2.1

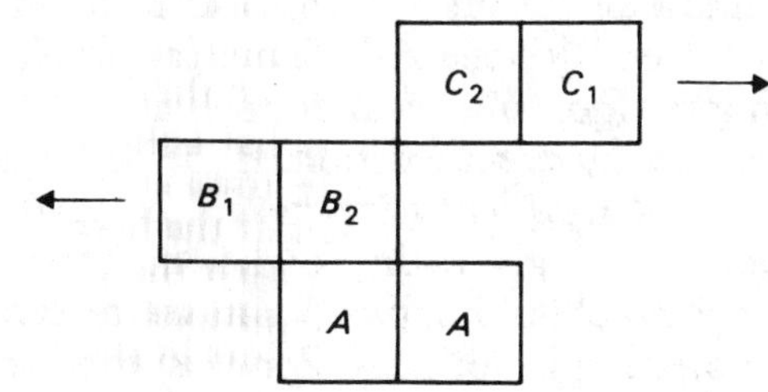

fig 2.2

Now Zeno infers in [vi] that 'the time is half'. The obvious expansion of this reads: 'the time taken by B_1 to get from its *fig. 1* position to its new position is half that taken by C_1 to get from its *fig. 1* position to its new position'. And Zeno's argument for that, in [vii], glosses as follows: 'In the interval between *fig. 1* and the new position, B_1 has passed half as many *A*s as C_1 has; and both B_1 and C_1 are travelling at the same speed.' That reasoning allows us to fix on *fig. 2.1* as the correct diagram for t_2.

Let us now glance briefly at the *first* result, stated in [iv]. I assume that the time of this result is the same as the time of the second result, i.e. t_2. The run of the text favours the assumption; and if we introduce a further time I see no way of reconstructing any argument. At t_2, then, B_1 and C_1 are 'at the end'. That phrase is wholly opaque. Four glosses at least are possible; and three of those glosses produce a plurality of diagrams. But given that *fig. 2.1* represents the stadium at t_2, we can limit the choice to two diagrams. (a) If 'at the end' means 'at the [opposite] end[s of the *A*s]', then the diagram must be *fig. 2.1* itself. (b) If 'at the end' means '[each] at the end [of the other's row]', the diagram must be:

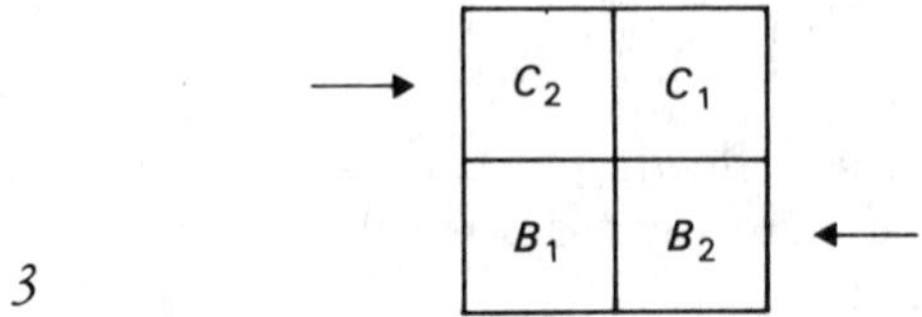

fig. 3

One manuscript has a reading which shows that *fig. 3* represents an ancient interpretation; and since we do not want the second result merely to repeat the first, we should clearly plump for (b) and *fig. 3*.

We have thus identified the 'crucial position' as the position diagrammed in *fig. 2.1*, and it is an obvious conjecture that *fig. 1* represents the starting position at t_1. Can that conjecture be supported from the text?

Aristotle describes the starting position twice, in [i] and in [iii]. The latter sentence adds something to the former: it specifies that the *B*s start 'from the middle of the *A*s'. In *fig. 1* they do; and the *C*s similarly start 'from the end [of the *A*s]'. That confirms that *fig. 1* represents the starting position of the three rows at t_1.

There is an objection to my reconstruction. If the bodies start in the position depicted in *fig. 1* they will never reach the position of *fig. 2.1*; it is logically impossible, given the conditions Zeno stipulates, that both *fig. 1* and *fig. 2.1* should depict points in the careers of the *B*s and *C*s. But that objection is not fatal: Zeno, after all, is trying to find contradictions in the concept of motion; and we should not necessarily be dismayed to find that his paradoxes represent as achieved what in reality and logic is impossible. The question, then, is not: Can *fig. 1* yield *fig. 2.1*? It is: Can Zeno have thought, or have made it seem plausible to think, that *fig. 1* yields *fig. 2.1*? And we might attempt to answer that question by looking at the *third* result, sentences [viii]–[xi].

Textually, that too is uncertain. In [viii], at 240a13, where I translate 'the first *B*', most manuscripts read '*ta B*', 'the *B*s'. Given that reading, we should have 'at the same time'—i.e. at t_2—the following position:

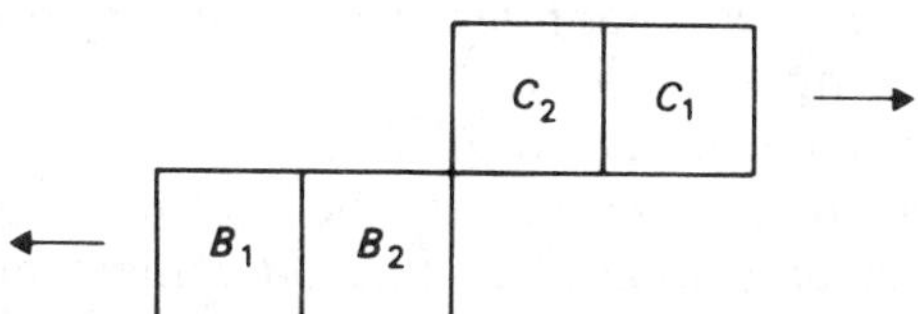

fig. 4

Now *fig. 4*, though a part of *fig. 2.2.*, is not reconcilable with *fig. 2.1*. Nor can I find any plausible argument which makes use of *fig. 4*. Consequently, the majority reading must be rejected; and we must read either '*to B* (the *B*)' or '*to prôton B* (the first *B*)'.[20]

We now have an argument designed to show that the third result actually occurs: i.e., that:

(1) At t_2 B_1 has passed both C_1 and C_2.

The text presents three sentences: sentence [ix] gives:

(2) At t_2 B_1 is against C_2 and C_1 is against B_2.

Sentence [x] gives:

(3) C_1 is alongside each *B* for the same length of time that it is alongside each *A*.

Sentence [xi] gives:

(4) The *B*s and the *C*s spend an equal time alongside each *A*.

Each of these three sentences allegedly supports its predecessor. Can anything be made of the argument?

Proposition (2) re-expresses the first result; and (1) follows easily enough from it and the initial description of the stadium. Proposition (4) is true, given the equal speed of the *C*s and the *B*s. Zeno, I suppose, argued thus: 'If, as (4) says, B_1 spends *n* time units against an *A*, and C_1 spends *n* time units against an *A*, then plainly B_1 spends *n* time units against C_1. Thus (3) is established.[21] And since by t_2 C_1 has been alongside *two A*s, it must—by (3)—have been alongside two *B*s as well. Hence (2). Finally, given the starting conditions, we may deduce (1).'

Let me now try to restate Zeno's whole argument in briefer and more perspicuous fashion. Suppose that at t_1 the *A*s, *B*s and *C*s are arranged as in *fig. 1*; and let the *B*s and *C*s move as specified. Let t_2 be the time at which C_1 has passed every *A*. Now C_1 has passed two *A*s and hence two *B*s; therefore *fig. 2.1* represents the position at t_2. C_1 and B_1 each take n units of time to pass a body. Hence *T*, the period from t_1 to t_2, is $2n$ units long. But in T B_1 has passed only one *A*. Hence $T = n$. Hence $T = {}^1/_2T$.[22]

The argument is not sound; but no version of the Stadium will yield a sound argument. It is not elegant; but Aristotle's text does not suggest an argument with the elegance of the Achilles. I am inclined to think that this reconstruction is as close to Zeno as anything we can now produce; and I have expounded it at some length because it goes against the prevailing orthodoxy.

Different interpretations fall into two classes. First, there are those which agree that *fig. 1* represents the starting position.[23] Such interpretations are only minor variants on mine; and they do not require special discussion. Second, there are those which abandon *fig. 1* and adopt as a starting position:

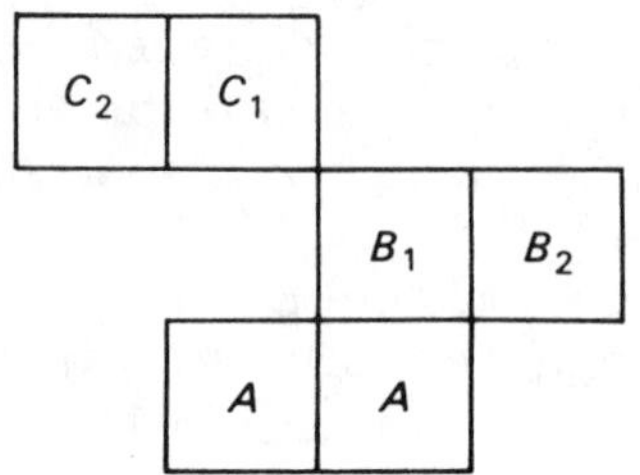

fig. 5

From *fig. 5* the position of *fig. 2.1* is easily reached; and in that lies the advantage of *fig. 5* over *fig. 1*. For my part, as I have already intimated, I do not think that the advantage is very great. And on the other side, adoption of *fig. 5* requires two changes in the text of **190**, one of which is most implausible.[24] But I shall not pursue the question further: philosophically speaking, it matters little whether we choose *fig. 1* or *fig. 5*.

(h) *A most ingenious paradox?*

Thus far I have concentrated on textual *minutiae* and little problems of interpretation; and it may well be wondered whether such attention is worth the paper it consumes. Aristotle dismisses Zeno's argument curtly enough: Zeno, he says, wrongly assumes that the *C*s will take as long to pass a moving *B* as they will to pass a stationary *A*. To most scholars the criticism seems both apt and conclusive: the paradox of the Stadium is philologically the most complicated of Zeno's four arguments; philosophically it is the simplest and the least interesting—correct a childish mistake and all is in motion again. As Eudemus long ago saw, the puzzle is 'very silly, because the misargument is obvious' (fr. 106W = **A 28**).

Moved by those considerations, yet convinced of Zeno's logical acumen, some scholars have inferred that Aristotle has misrepresented Zeno. Zeno's argument, they say, in fact assumed that the *A*s, *B*s and *C*s were *minimal* bodies, indivisible atoms of stuff. And it further assumed that the time taken for a *B* or a *C* to pass a stationary *A* was a *minimal* period of time, an indivisible temporal *quantum*. Given those two assumptions, the Stadium becomes a sound and a significant argument; for in effect it shows that absurd results follow from such an atomic attitude to matter and time. The Stadium, in short, is an early essay in the logic of the continuum.[25]

I do not deny the philosophical interest of that sophisticated version of the Stadium paradox; but it was not Zeno's. There is no evidence that anyone prior to Zeno had entertained the atomistic theory he is imagined to be attacking; and there is no reason why he should himself have invented such a theory simply to knock it down. The sophisticated Stadium has no historical support. Nor is the train of reasoning which introduced it very compelling. It is simply false that Zeno was a brilliant logician who would never have committed an elementary error—I have already discussed more than one argument indubitably Zenonian and of less subtlety than the Aristotelian Stadium. Indeed, a stronger case can be put: the Aristotelian Stadium, as it stands, is not immensely impressive; but it points to a crucial feature in the concept of locomotion. In short, the Aristotelian Stadium is philosophically important, and not 'very silly'.

I offer the following argument as a refurbished account of the Stadium. 'Our concept of motion is intimately connected with the two continua of space and time. The concept is linked logically to those two notions in a variety of ways; two of the most important are mirrored in these two implications:

(1) If a moves past a sequence of n Fs and each F is k units long, then a moves nk units.

(2) If a moves for a period of T units at a constant speed of j u.p.u., and covers m units in that time, then $T = m/j$ units.

Now consider *fig. 5* and *fig. 2.1*. Substitute B_1 for a in (1) and (2): it is easy to show, by two applications of (1) and (2), that T, the period from t_1 to t_2, is equal to $\frac{1}{2}T$. For the passage of B_1 past the single A gives $T = 1k/j$. And the passage of B_1 past the two Cs gives $T = 2k/j$.

Thus the concept of motion implies (1) and (2); and (1) and (2) lead to contradiction. Hence the concept of motion is incoherent. Hence nothing can move.'

Such a reconstruction has two points in its favour. First, it relates the Stadium to Zeno's general attack on motion; most accounts do not explain the connexion between the fourth paradox of motion and Zeno's overall aim. Second, it provides an interesting argument against motion. For I am inclined to think that both (1) and (2) would have commended themselves to Zeno's contemporaries, and do commend themselves to us in our unthinking moments. Our conception of locomotion is such that (1) and (2) seem to be implicit in it; yet (1) and (2) lead to unacceptable results. Zeno infers, I suggest, that the concept of motion is inconsistent; we may prefer to say that men who subscribe to (1) and (2) confusedly grasp the consistent concept of motion. The mode of expression is immaterial: if we are to move in the Stadium we must articulate a concept of motion which does not give rise to (1) and (2).

Aristotle's answer to Zeno may now seem as unsatisfactory as in reality it is: according to Aristotle, Zeno ignores the fact that the *A*s are stationary and the *B*s moving. The criticism is not profound: where, we may ask, does Aristotle's objection fit into the argument based on (1) and (2)? How would he reject those twin principles? What notion of movement would he supply which avoids (1) and (2)? I do not say that those questions are unanswerable; I do say that they are unanswered, and that that fact makes Aristotle's reply to Zeno inadequate.

An adequate reply to Zeno, and an adequate account of motion, would focus on the truth that motion is a relational thing: '. . . it doth not appear to me that there can be any motion other than *relative*: so that to conceive motion, there must be conceived two bodies, whereof the distance or position in regard to each other is varied. Hence if there was only one body in being, it could not possibly be moved. This seems evident, in that the idea I have of motion doth necessarily include relation' (Berkeley, *Principles of Human Knowledge*, § 112).

Motion, in brief, is relative not absolute. That slogan may mislead; and it is worth stating clearly two things that it does not imply. First, it does not imply the incoherence of 'absolute' motion in Newton's sense: Newtonian 'absolute' motion is merely a privileged form of relative motion; for according to Newton a body is in 'absolute' motion if it is changing position relative to absolute space. (It is a further question whether anything can be made of absolute space.) Second, the rejection of 'absolute' motion does not require a wholesale change in our everyday language of movement. For though we do regularly speak as though motion were absolute, it is fairly simple to translate such talk into talk of motion relative to our human inertial frame, the earth: 'he's moving' can regularly be taken as elliptical for 'he's changing position relative to (some point on) the earth's surface'. (Regularly, but not, of course, always: in the enclosed world of an aeroplane or a ship we naturally take the enclosing vehicle as our reference frame; and Christmas cracker puzzles, such as the conundrum of the man running round the monkey, remind us that all is not plain sailing here.)

To say that motion is relative is to say no more than this: '*a* moves' only makes sense if it is taken as elliptical for some two-place predication of the form '*a* changes position relative to *b*'. '*a* moves' is comparable to '*a* leads' or '*a* follows'; leading and following are relational notions, even though we often and intelligibly use the verbs without explicitly mentioning a *relatum*: and just as '*a* leads' is elliptical for '*a* leads *b*', so is '*a* moves' elliptical for '*a* moves *vis-à-vis* *b*'. There is, of course, nothing unusual in having such elliptical, absolute-seeming, uses for essentially relational verbs; in the case of 'move', however, there is a peculiar danger of taking the absolute-seeming use at face value, and inventing an absolute quality of motion to serve as *denotatum* for the absolute verb. (I suspect that this connects with the old Aristotelian view that motion is immediately perceptible, a 'simple idea': if we can simply *see* that a thing is in motion, surely motion is an intrinsic quality and not a relation?)

What bearing has the relativity of motion on the Stadium? It allows us to retain the essence of implications (1) and (2) while rejecting their cruel accidents. Thus, to take the case of (1), we shall have:

(1*) If *a* moves past a sequence of *n* *F*s and each *F* is *k* units long, then relative to those *F*s *a* moves *nk* units.

The plausibility of (1) carries over to (1*) and (1*) contains the truth which (1) strove in vain to express. Moreover (1*) has no hard consequences, once we realize that there is no contradiction between '*a* moves *n* units relative to *b*' and '*a* moves *m* units relative to *c*' (where $b \neq c$ and $n \neq m$). For I may move relative to one thing while resting relative to another—there are a thousand everyday examples of that.

I do not claim that only a relative concept of motion will answer Zeno's argument; but that such a concept is both correct in itself and sufficient to answer Zeno seems clear enough. If Zeno's Stadium encourages us to clarify our conception of motion in that way, then that, I submit, is enough to make an honest argument of it. Zeno, of course, did not intend his Stadium to refute 'absolute' motion and elicit a relativized concept; and indeed he does not seem to have stirred any of his successors to develop such a sanitary notion. For all that, the Stadium does show, in a pointed and pregnant way, the need for a subtler concept of locomotion than we are apt at first sight to formulate. And that turns the paradox of the Stadium, in its plain Aristotelian form, into an argument of some significance.

(i) *Two last remarks*

I end my long consideration of Zeno's paradoxes with two general comments.

First, what, we may wonder, is the connexion between the four paradoxes on motion and the Platonic schema into which I attempted to fit the paradoxes of plurality? We may always suppose that the arguments about motion, which Aristotle treats as a unitary group and which according to Elias constituted an independent Zenonian volume, were in their original form a separate publication. We might indeed conjecture that they were worked out later in Zeno's life, the fruits of his intellectual maturity.

On the other hand, Plato names 'at rest and moving' as one of the set of opposites which Zeno proved to hold of 'the many' (*Phaedrus* 261D = **A 13**). Thus one case of the Platonic scheme will be:

(Z7) (a) If *P*, then everything moves, and (b) if *P*, then nothing moves.

Here (Z7a) will have required no special argument: evidently, the 'many things' which the pluralists admit do, all of them, move. And it is not vastly implausible to see the four paradoxes of motion as intended to support (Z7b). In that case, the paradoxes will, originally, have appeared in Zeno's juvenile book, alongside the other arguments I have dissected; and some later editor will have assembled them in a little treatise of their own, preserving their philosophical content while divesting them of their original polemical form.

Second, what general portrait of Zeno emerges from these two chapters? My discussion has, I think, confirmed the view I sketched on an earlier page (above, p. 236). Zeno 'put forward no view of his own but puzzled further about' Eleatic issues (pseudo-Plutarch, **A 23**). Zeno was no original philosopher; he is not a member of the long line of thinkers stretching from Thales to Melissus, men of vast learning, wide pretensions, profound insights. Rather, he puzzled: negative, destructive, polemical, Zeno was the first of the 'Sophists'. His aims were critical, not constructive; his methods subtle not solid.

Yet from his Sophist's quiver he drew a few darts of brilliance and acuity; and those darts have made him a prince of philosophers *malgré lui*.

XIV

The Ports of Knowledge Closed

(a) *Parmenides on sense and reason*

'Antisthenes the Cynic, unable to answer [Zeno's arguments against motion], got up and walked, deeming a proof by action more potent than any logical confutation' (Elias, **29 A 15**). Zeno's paradoxical conclusions disagree outrageously with what we like to call 'common sense'; and if common sense has no part to play in the serious dramas of science, in philosophy it often assumes a leading role. Moreover, in its antagonism to Elea, common sense has a powerful ally: perception. We perceive, everyday, the falsity of Eleatic metaphysics and Zenonian immobility; and our common sense is trustworthy just because it is securely backed by those quotidian perceptions.

The Eleatics, naturally enough, became enrolled in the sceptical army: in the crude words of Aëtius, 'Parmenides says that the senses are false' (**28 A 49**). Sextus, our chief quarry for ancient scepticism, numbers Parmenides among his tribe (*adv Math* VII. 114); and Timon, the sceptical satirist, praised Parmenides, 'who turned his thoughts from the delusion of fantasy' (fr. 44 = **A 1**). Aristotle sums it up: the Eleatics 'pass over perception and disregard it, thinking that one should follow reason. . . . In the light of their arguments this seems to follow; in the light of the facts it is near to madness to hold such opinions' (*GC* 325a13–18 = **A 25**).

No Eleatic could be unaware of the way in which his conclusions disregard the data of perception; and we might expect some little argument from Elea to excuse or justify its high-handed treatment of the chief instrument of Ionian science. Epistemology, after all, was in existence, a young discipline but not an infant; and if Parmenides had a sceptical predecessor in Xenophanes, he had an opponent in

Heraclitus. A philosopher of the fifth century could not simply shrug off his epistemological commitments.

In fact we find little in the Eleatic fragments; and the little we find is probably all there ever was. Nothing suggests that Zeno wrote in an epistemological vein; for Melissus we possess one substantial fragment, but no hint that his work contained anything further of that sort; and for Parmenides we have a few brief lines.

In support of his claim that Parmenides 'makes it clear that one should not attend to the senses but to reason', Sextus quotes text **153**; and Diogenes quotes the same lines in the same connexion (IX. 22 = **A 1**). Plainly, the later tradition knew no other sceptical utterances from Parmenides. (The quatrain on thought, **B 16**, is irrelevant here: it will be considered in chapter XXII.) I transcribe **153** again (see above, p. 170):

> Do not let much-experienced habit force you along this road,
> to let run an aimless eye and an echoing ear
> and a tongue; but judge by argument (*logôi*) the much-contending refutation uttered by me.

The lines do not argue for scepticism: they enjoin, they do not reason. But many scholars find in them a wholesale rejection of sense-perception. I think that the lines say both more and less than that.

First, the lines mention the tongue; and the tongue is the organ of speech as well as of taste. I agree with those scholars who attend to the former function and suppose that Parmenides has in mind not gustatory illusions (never a very rich source of sceptical argument) but rather the perils inherent in ordinary language. The empty words of mortals, which Parmenides lists at **156**. 40–1, habitually trip off our tongue; and if we let them do so, they will lure us, like a fatal *ignis fatuus*, along the marshy path of Opinion.[1] It seems probable that the 'echoing ear' is to be understood in the same fashion. Parmenides is not thinking of auditory illusions; he is warning us against listening to the foolish words of other mortals which perennially seduce us from the narrow path of Truth. Compare Heraclitus' advice to disregard other men's flowers and 'seek for ourselves' (above, p. 145). If I am right, then two of the three organs mentioned in **153** feature not as instruments of disreputable sense-experience but as channels for the subtle and semi-conscious insinuation of mortal opinion. The lines in **153** do more than warn against the errors of the senses.

Second, **153** does less than utter a general warning against perception. The lines occur in a specific context and their moral has a specific point: it is not that the senses are in general to be distrusted;

it is that the senses are not to be used against Parmenides' 'much-contending refutation'. Parmenides' request, as I have already remarked, is entirely just: when we turn to the backgammon board, we may find it impossible to believe that the Way of Truth is the way to metaphysical bliss; but that is no disproof of Parmenides' contentions. If we are to reject Parmenides' conclusion, then we must match reason with reason: we must show where his argument goes wrong.

In sum, **153** has very little to do with scepticism. Parmenides is saying no more than this: 'If you think my argument wrong, then *prove* it wrong; don't fall back into the lazy habits of common sense.' I do not deny that Parmenides was an enemy of the senses and that he 'hurled the senses out of truth' (pseudo-Plutarch, **A 22**). But that enmity is left implicit in Parmenides' poem: we have no formal argument for scepticism in the text, and no explicit statement of scepticism. Parmenides made no contribution to the history of Pyrrhonism.

(b) *Melissus on perception*

The case is otherwise with Melissus. Fragment **30 B 8** is long, but it merits a complete translation:

> [i] Now this argument is the greatest sign that there is only one thing; but there are the following signs too.
>
> [ii] If there were many things, they would have to be such as I say the one thing is. For if there is earth and water and air and fire and iron and gold and living and dead and black and white and the other things which men say are real—if there are these things, and we see and hear correctly, then each of them must be such as it first seemed to us, and must not change or become different (*heteroion*), but each thing must always be just as it is.
>
> [iii] But now we are saying that we see and hear and grasp (*sunienai*) correctly; but what is hot seems to us to become cold, and what is cold hot, and what is hard soft, and what is soft hard, and living creatures seem to die and to come into being from what is not alive, and all these seem to alter (*heteroiousthai*), and what was and is now seem to be in no way homogeneous; but the iron which is hard seems to be rubbed away by the finger . . .,[2] and so do gold and stone and everything else that seems to be strong, {Hence it follows that we neither see nor know what is the case[3]} and earth and stone seem to come into being from water.
>
> [iv] Now these things are not in agreement with one another. For although we say that the many things both are eternal and

have forms and strength, they all seem to us to alter and to change from the state in which they are at any time seen.

[v] It is clear, then, that we do not see correctly, and that those many things do not correctly seem to be. For they would not change if they were real, but they would be just as each seemed to be; for nothing is greater than what is real. But if they change, what is has perished and what is not has come into being. Now in this way if there were many things they would have to be such as the one thing is (**191**).

As paragraph [i] explicitly states, the burden of **191** is to provide additional support for monism: the 'argument' to which [i] refers is presumably that of **164**; whether **191** contains all the additional 'signs' that Melissus promises is unknown. Aristocles, who quotes part of [ii] and [iii], says that Melissus 'wants to show that none of the phenomena and things we see exists in reality' (**A 14**); and Simplicius introduces **191** to illustrate Melissus' attitude to sense-perception. And those ancient critics were at least half correct; for one of the things Melissus attempts to do in **191** is to argue that 'we do not see correctly'.

The argument is in *reductio* form. Paragraph [ii] sets out the hypothesis to be reduced; it is in fact the conjunction of:

(1a) There exists several things, a_1, a_2, . . . a_n,

and

(1b) Our senses are veridical.

Melissus' illustrations for (1a) sound strange to modern ears; but they doubtless reflect the various pluralisms, lay and professional, that Melissus met with in his philosophical conversations.[4] The conjunct (1b) is usually stated for the cases of sight and hearing; but I assume that Melissus has the general case in mind, and I believe that by '*sunienai* (grasp)' in [iii] he means 'perceive'.

Paragraph [ii] also begins the *reductio*: asserting, reasonably, that each member of the plurality in (1a) would have to have the properties which the Eleatic deduction has shown to be essential to all existents, Melissus infers in particular that:

(2) No a_i ever changes.

He also argues, with needless ingenuity, that:

(3) If a_i seems ϕ at t, then a_i is always ϕ.

Paragraph [iii] looks more seriously at (1b): any number of changes seem to take place; the hardest things are rubbed away, and the most different things emerge from one another. Our senses tell us that everything changes; hence, by (1b), we get to:

(4) Every a_i constantly changes.

(The word 'constantly' is not in Melissus' text; but it is, I think, implicit in the last phrase of paragraph [iv].)

The argument is now over; for, as [iv] points out, (2) and (4) 'are not in agreement with one another'. Thus [v] concludes to the negations of (1a) and (1b): 'we do not see correctly, and . . . those many things do not correctly seem to be'.[5] The remainder of [v] merely repeats the assertion made in [ii], that from (1a) an Eleatic can properly derive (2) and (3): if the many things are *real*, then the predicates of Eleatic metaphysics must hold of them.

What are the merits of this ingenious piece of reasoning? First, it is worth noting that, despite [i], it does not purport to be entirely independent of Eleatic metaphysics; on the contrary, the move from (1a) to (2) explicitly applies familiar Eleatic properties to a putatively plural world. Such an application might seem wholly trivial: apply monism itself, and (1a) leads at once to a contradiction. But that would be unbearably jejune; and Melissus does not intend it. In his move to (2) he applies (T 7), the thesis that what exists does not alter. Now (T 7) was indeed inferred from (T 5), the thesis of monism; but it was also inferred directly from (T 1), the thesis that what exists cannot be generated (above, p. 215), and paragraph [v] serves the important function of indicating that it is that second inference that Melissus means to call upon. In short, Melissus argues that any pluralist must accept at least (T 1), and hence (T 7); and that then pluralism collapses. The 'neo-Ionians', to whom the next several chapters are devoted, did, some of them, attempt to hold both (T 1) and pluralism.

Aristocles introduces his quotation of [ii]–[iii] with a scathing criticism:

> Now this is most absurd: showing by argument that [the senses] are useless, in fact they continually rely heavily upon them—Melissus, who wants to show that none of the phenomena and the things we see exists in reality, proves it by means of the phenomena themselves.

Having quoted Melissus' own words he proceeds:

> When he says this, and much more in the same vein, one might well ask him: 'Is it not by perception that you know that what is now hot later becomes cold?'—and similarly in the other cases. For as I said, he will be found to be doing away with and refuting the senses by means of a peculiar trust in them (**192: A 14**).

Aristocles here initiates a longstanding objection to scepticism of the senses: in order to construct their arguments, the sceptics have to start from the data of perception; so based, their arguments are bound to be self-refuting. Melissus relies heavily on the senses; for he sets down (1b) as a premiss, and construes it in the strongest way possible, as saying that every sense report is true. Having said that, he proceeds to infer the falsity of all sense reports. What could be more absurd?

The charge of self-refutation may stand against some sceptics, but it has no hold on Melissus. Aristocles has misread Melissus' argument: Melissus does not assert that (1b) is true—he presents it as a hypothesis which he will show to be false. Nor does he assert that (2) is true; for (2) depends upon (1b). The only fact about the senses to which Melissus does commit himself is this: that, according to our senses, things change. To believe that is not to show 'a peculiar trust' in the senses.

Aristocles' charge of self-refutation fails, but there is a sound point in his criticism. Melissus construes (1b) in a strong fashion; and no self-respecting partisan of the senses would maintain that every sense report is true. In fact, Melissus does not need the strong construe of (1b); without it he will get neither (3) nor (4)—but he does not really use (3), and he does not require (4). To discover a contradiction he need only establish the contradictory of (2), which is not (4) but:

(5) Some a_is sometimes change.

However weak we care to make (1b), it will surely remain powerful enough to give (5): the man who pretends to place some trust in his senses and yet believes that the world is an unchanging place can hardly be taken seriously. Partisans of the senses must not believe everything their favourites tell them; but their partisanship is empty if they deny such propositions as (5).

A more tolerable objection remains: 'Melissus' handling of the *reductio* is poor: the conjunction of (2) and (5) is certainly a contradiction; but Melissus cannot infer that both (1a) and (1b) are false: at most he can infer the negation of their conjunction, "Not both (1a) and (1b)".' That objection is sound; and it makes a fatal breach in Melissus' argument as he states it. But it is possible to repair the wall and restore the argument.

Since he cannot retain both (1a) and (1b), Melissus' opponent has two positions open to him: he may abandon (1a) and hold to (1b); or he may maintain (1a) and give up (1b). The first of those positions is quickly demolished by an argument closely parallel to that of **191**: if our senses are veridical, then we live in a plural world. Just as any serious advocate of (1b), however weakly he construes it, must admit the truth of (5), so any serious advocate of (1b) must allow that the world exhibits diversity and is not a monolithic whole. It is absurd to support the senses and be a monist. Melissus' opponent must therefore retreat to the second position; and that too must be abandoned if Melissus can prove:

(6) If there exist several things, $a_1, a_2, \ldots a_n$, then our senses are veridical.

Now Melissus will certainly have reflected that it is only sense perception which suggests a plural world: reason, as the Eleatic deduction shows, leads inexorably to monism. That reflexion will not yield (6) but it will yield:

(7) If there is reason to believe that there exist several objects, $a_1, a_2, \ldots a_n$, then our senses are veridical.

I imagine that even pluralists who deny Melissus' rational path to monism will be prepared to accept (7). In itself (7) does not suffice to demolish the second position; but it does show that any occupant of that position is committed to:

(8) There exist several things and there is no reason to believe that there exist several things.

Propositions of the same form as (8)—'*P* and there is no reason to believe that *P*'—are not self-contradictory; but anyone who holds to (8) is thereby acting irrationally, in one clear sense of that term. Many philosophers will maintain that some irrationalities of that sort are acceptable: there are some things we may or even must believe in the absence of reasons; but even if that is true, it seems unlikely that (8) can be numbered among such favoured propositions. I conclude that in (8) Melissus has a final answer to his opponent: the argument of **191** cannot be rationally defeated. Of course, Melissus has not proved scepticism; he has argued that, given the fundamental thesis of Eleatic metaphysics, (T 1), scepticism can be securely established by way of (T 7). The argument is not general: it is tied to Eleatic theory; but it is, for all that, ingenious and powerful.

PARADISE REGAINED

XV

The Ionian Revival

(a) *A few depressing facts*

If the Eleatics are right, scientists may as well give up their activities: *a priori* ratiocination reveals that the phenomena which science attempts to understand and explain are figments of our deceptive senses; the scientist has little or nothing to investigate—let him turn to poetry or to gardening.

Fortunately few Greeks reasoned in that way; and some of the brightest gems of Greek philosophical science were polished in the generation after Parmenides. Empedocles, Anaxagoras, Philolaus, Leucippus, Democritus, Diogenes of Apollonia, all pursued the old Ionian ideal of *historia* despite the pressure of the Eleatic *logos*. And these neo-Ionian systems contain much of interest and much of permanent influence. How far they were genuine answers to the Eleatic metaphysics, and how far they were obstinate attempts to follow an out-moded profession, are questions which I shall later discuss. First, I shall offer a brief and preliminary survey of the main neo-Ionian systems which will, I hope, indicate the connexions between these men and their early models, show the respects in which their new systems must lead to conflict with Elea, and uncover the novelties of thought and argument by which they hoped to win that conflict.

This section, however, will concern itself primarily with a few issues of chronology. I begin with Anaxagoras: his dates are remarkably well attested, and we know he lived from 500 to 428 BC (Diogenes Laertius, II.7 = **59 A 1**); between his birth in Clazomenae and his death in Lampsacus he enjoyed a thirty-year sojourn in Athens, during which time he is said to have 'taught' Pericles and Euripides (e.g., Diogenes Laertius, II.10; 12 = A 1) and to have been condemned on a charge of impiety brought against him by Pericles' political opponents (e.g., Diogenes Laertius, II.12 = **A 1**). The dates of that sojourn are uncertain: the period from 463–433 seems not improbable.[1] A charming though doubtless apocryphal story has it that as he lay dying the rulers of Lampsacus asked him how he would like to be commemorated, 'and he said that every year the children should be allowed a holiday in the month of his death' (Diogenes Laertius, II.14 = **A 1**).

The dates of our other philosophers are less certain. Empedocles was 'not much younger' than Anaxagoras, according to Theophrastus (Simplicius, **31 A 7**) and he died at the age of sixty, according to Aristotle (fr. 71 R[3] = **A 1**). A perplexingly ambiguous phrase in the *Metaphysics* (984a11) says that Anaxagoras was *tois ergois husteros* than Empedocles: I agree with those scholars who give *husteros* its literal sense of 'later', and I suppose that Empedocles wrote before Anaxagoras.[2] If the question is controversial, it is also unimportant; for I see no evidence of any interaction between the two philosophers.

Of Philolaus' life and dates we know little. A passage in Plato's *Phaedo* (61 E) and a scholiast's note upon it (**44 A 1 a**) suggest that as a young man Philolaus, a Pythagorean, escaped the persecutions of his sect and left South Italy in about 450 BC to reside in Thebes. He appears to have lived on into the fourth century. A working career spanning the years 450 to 400 will not be wildly inaccurate.[3]

The Atomists, Leucippus and Democritus, are shadowy figures: 'I came to Athens,' Democritus allegedly said, 'and no one knew me' (**68 B 116**); and Epicurus, who is said to have studied under Leucippus, is also reported to have denied that Leucippus ever existed (Diogenes Laertius, X.13 = **67 A 2**). A strong tradition says that Leucippus was a 'pupil' of Zeno (Diogenes Laertius, IX.30 = **A 1**; Clement, **A 4**; etc.); and a late report makes him, interestingly, a student of Melissus (Tzetzes, **A 5**). Simplicius observed that

> Leucippus the Eleatic or Milesian—for both titles are given him[4]—having shared in the philosophy of Parmenides, did not follow the path of Parmenides and Xenophanes about what exists but, it seems, quite the opposite path (**193: A 8**; cf. Epiphanius, **A 33**).

Democritus came from Abdera; and he was a 'companion' or 'pupil' of Leucippus (Diogenes Laertius, IX.34 = **68 A 1**; Suda, **A 2**; etc.). He is also said to have 'heard' Anaxagoras (ibid.). By his own account he was a young man in Anaxagoras' old age, perhaps forty years his junior (Diogenes Laertius, IX.34, 41 = **A 1**); and that puts his birth in 460 BC. His major work, the *Mikros Diakosmos* or *Little World-Order*, was published, so he said, 730 years after the capture of Troy (Diogenes Laertius, IX.41 = **A 1**). Alas, we do not know to what year Democritus dated the fall of Troy; but if we think of the period of 440–400 as his working life we shall not be far wrong.[5]

Those sparse, dry facts are of little intrinsic interest; I mention them in the hope of throwing light on the relations between the Eleatics and their neo-Ionian opponents. But hope is illusory. Parmenides' work, we may be sure, antedated all these neo-Ionian inquiries; but the relationships between Melissus and the neo-Ionians, and between Zeno and the neo-Ionians, which are of much greater interest, must remain dark. Melissus' dates are unknown; and we can say little better for Zeno. Did any of the neo-Ionians know and study Melissus' prose system of Eleatic metaphysics? Did any of them puzzle over Zeno's paradoxes? The chronological data I have listed are far too scanty to encourage an answer to those questions: the dates we have are compatible with several competing answers. Nor will internal evidence help us: it is, of course, frequently appealed to, but in contradictory senses. Thus some scholars find evidence in the fragments that Empedocles knew and attempted to answer Melissus' views on motion; others are equally certain that Melissus attacks Empedocles' doctrine of the four roots. Again, many scholars find in Anaxagoras a clear knowledge of Zeno's views of infinite divisibility; but others see, if anything, an opposite influence.

The moral is negative: we cannot hope to chart in any detail the course of fifth-century philosophical thought. We may speak generally of 'answers to the Eleatic challenge'; and one or two particular connexions between neo-Ionian fragments and the verses of Parmenides can be discerned. Beyond that, all is speculation. When we study the history of seventeenth-century thought, our philosophical and our historical appetites are whetted and satisfied together; we consider, say, Locke's attack on innate ideas, and Leibniz' defence. As philosophers, we are keen to decide whether the Leibnizian defence breaks Locke's attack; and as historians we can enter the fray with dates and personalities, for we know that Leibniz' *Nouveaux Essais* were written as a commentary upon Locke's *Essay*. The intellectual excitement of the fifth century BC must have been no less intense than that of the seventeenth AD, and the cut and thrust of debate was doubtless as violent and as personal in Greece as it was later in enlightened Europe: when Greek meets Greek, then comes the tug of war. But we cannot recover and relive those Olympian games; and if the handbooks on ancient philosophy make us think we can, they are deceptive. We must reconcile ourselves to ignorance of the historical wars and be content to investigate the abstract battles of ideas. The prospect is sad, but not appalling: men are less permanent than thought.

(b) *Empedocles' cosmic cycle*

This section is purely expository. I shall state what I take to have been the Empedoclean world-view; and I shall briefly sketch the basic positions of Anaxagoras, of Philolaus, and of the Atomists. I shall have little more to say about Empedocles' cosmology, which is philosophically unrewarding; but some of my remarks on Empedoclean psychology in a later chapter will refer back to his 'cosmic cycle'. Anaxagoras, Philolaus and the Atomists will receive detailed treatment later on; and Diogenes of Apollonia will get a chapter to himself.

Everything connected with Empedocles' cosmology is now controversial: there is what may be called the traditional view of his theory, which I shall expound and which I believe to be in all essentials true; and there are various heterodoxies, recently advocated with great scholarly power and ingenuity. I shall not enter into any of these issues; and the reader should be warned that my exposition here is more than usually one-sided.

The main text is **31 B 17**.1–13[6] (most of its contents are repeated, sometimes verbatim, in **B 26** and **B 35**):

> I shall tell a double tale; for at one time they[7] increased to be one thing alone
> from being many; and then again they grew apart to be many from being one.
> And two-fold is the generation of mortal things, two-fold their disappearance;
> for the one[8] the collocation of everything both brings to birth and destroys,
> and the other is nourished and flies apart[9] as they again grow apart.
> And they never cease from continuous interchange,
> now by Love all coming together into one,
> now again each carried apart by the enmity of Strife.
> [Thus in so far as they have learned to become one from being many][10]
> and as the one grows apart they become many,
> thus far do they come into being and there is no stable life for them;

but in so far as they never cease from continuous interchange,
thus far do they exist forever, changeless in the cycle (**194**).

The fragment has as its subject the four elemental stuffs or, as Empedocles call them, 'roots (*rhizômata*)': earth, air, fire, water (cf. **B 6**; **B 21**.3–8). According to Aristotle, fire had a place of special importance in Empedocles' system (*GC* 330b20; *Met* 985b1 = **A 36–7**; cf. Hippolytus, **A 31**); but that is not apparent from the fragments. Nor need we pay any heed to the doxographical assertion that the roots had an atomic or corpuscular substructure (e.g., Aëtius, **A 43**).[11] The roots are eternal (cf. **B 7**); they are obliquely characterized in **B 21** and given divine appellations in **B 6**.[12]

The roots are involved in a never-ending cycle of change (**194**. 6; 12–3; cf., e.g., Aristotle, *Phys* 187a24 = **A 46**). One part of the cycle is dominated by the agency of Love (**194**. 7), during which the elements gradually commingle into one mass; another part is dominated by Strife (**194**.8), during which the elements gradually separate out into four distinct masses. The ontological status and the causal functions of these two cosmic powers will be discussed in a later chapter. When Love is supreme, a homogeneous Sphere is formed in which all the roots promiscuously interpenetrate (**B 27**; **B 28**; cf., e.g., Philoponus, **A 41**; Simplicius, **A 52**); and the Sphere is at rest for a period of time.[13] Then the force of Strife grows again; the Sphere breaks up (cf. Eudemus, fr. 110 W; Aristotle, *Met* 1092b6); and the elements eventually become completely separated. It appears that this state, when Strife is totally dominant, is instantaneous.

As the four roots 'run through one another, they become different in aspect' (**B 21**. 13), and their interminglings form the cosmos and everything in it:

For from these comes everything that was and is and will be—
trees sprang up, and men and women,
and beasts and birds and water-dwelling fish,
and long-lived gods who are first in honour (**195**: **B 21**. 9–12).

The creative process is described in a pleasant analogy:

As when painters decorate offerings—
men well trained in their craft by skill—
they grasp the many-coloured pigments in their hands,
mixing in harmony more of some and less of others,
and from these they make forms resembling all things,
creating trees, and men and women,
and beasts and birds and water-dwelling fish
and long-lived gods who are first in honour

> —so let not your mind be conquered by the falsehood that from anywhere else
> is the spring of all the myriad mortal things that are plain to see;
> but know this clearly, hearing the tale from a god. (**196: B 23**; cf. Galen, **A 34**).

From a few primary colours painters make an imitation world: in the same way, the mixing of the four elements produces the natural world, one proportion making bone (**B 96**), one blood (**B 98**), others other stuffs (Aëtius, **A 78**; Simplicius, *ad* **B 96**).

The natural world and its production were described in detail in Empedocles' poem *Concerning Nature*: there was a cosmogony, an astronomy, a meteorology; a zoogony; a biology and a botany; remarks on embryology and anatomy, on physiology and psychology—in short, a detailed and often novel natural science in the grand Ionian tradition.

The cosmic cycle rolls on endlessly; a partial map of it may have looked like this:

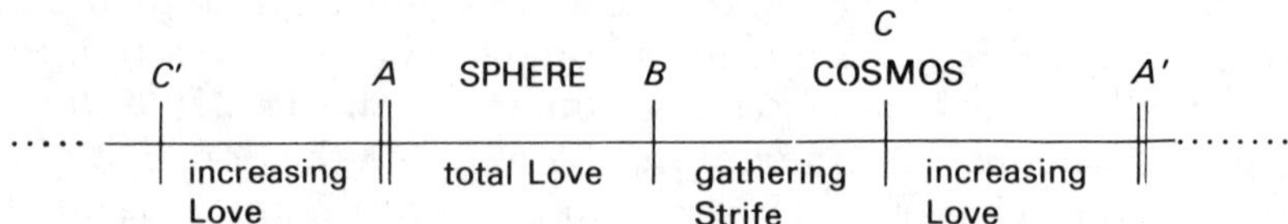

AA′ represents one complete cycle: identical cycles are repeated infinitely often. *AB* = *BA′*: during *AB*, for just half the cycle, the elements are homogeneously commingled into the Sphere. At *B* the hold of Love is relaxed: Strife gradually regains its powers, separating the elements until, at *C*, they lie completely distinct, arranged about one another in concentric hollow spheres. Then Love increases again, until the Sphere is reformed at *A′*. *C*, the point of total Strife, is midway between *B* and *A′*.

BC and *CA′* are mirror images of one another: take any point *P* on *BC* and construct *P′* on *CA* such that *PC* = *CP′*; then the state of the world at *P* is qualitatively indistinguishable from its state at *P′*. We live in *BC* the period of increasing strife (Aristotle, *GC* 334a5 = **A 42**): our world is doomed to destruction; but after that destruction another world will be created, a perfect reflexion of our own. And before and after these twin worlds there have been and will be infinitely many others.

Empedocles' system may have had less order and symmetry than I have ascribed to it; for my account has idealized in some places and ignored serious controversy in others. But few would deny the cosmic cycle a subtle aesthetic fascination; and Empedocles' poetical style—grand, formulaic, repetitive, hierophantic—adds to that seductive power.[14] Poetry and reason do not always cohabit; and Empedocles has frequently been held to have lost in ratiocinative capacity what he gained in poetical talent. Thus according to Aristotle, 'anyone who says this should not simply state it—he should also give the explanation of it, and not posit it or lay down some unreasoned axiom but bring either an induction or a demonstration' (*Phys* 252a22–5; cf. *GC* 333b22–6). A modern scholar has generalized Aristotle's criticism: 'Imaginative vividness took hold of [Empedocles] with more persuasiveness than did logical consistency, and he inevitably baffles minds not constituted like his own. The important thing in understanding him is to stop thinking at the right moment'.[15]

That criticism is harsh, but not wholly unfair: certainly, we shall look in vain for any argument in favour of Empedocles' cycle; it is a construction of great 'imaginative vividness', but it lacks all rational support. I do not say that it is inconsistent, only that it was, so far as we can now tell, unreasoned. And what holds of the general scheme holds of many of its particular parts: we look in vain for argument, either inductive or deductive. Thus Empedocles confidently gives us a recipe for making bone: it is patent that he never tested his own recipe—a poor intellectual cook. Or again, he says much about the activity of Love and Strife; yet he nowhere explains why Love and Strife are the two active principles in the cosmos, or why they do what they are alleged to do.

But it would be wrong to dismiss Empedocles as a mere fantastic, a writer of versified science fiction. There are fragments which contrive to be both descriptive and illuminating, genuine contributions to natural science; the two long similes about the structure of the eye (**B 84**) and about the nature of respiration (**B 100**) are only the most extended examples of that. And there are one or two fragments containing philosophical argument. These philosophical fragments, which I shall quote below, are Eleatic in tone and content: though Empedocles never mentions Parmenides, the many echoes of Eleatic verse in his poem prove that he knew his great predecessor's work;[16] and since Empedocles' cycle is patently un-Eleatic, it is hard to avoid the conclusion that he was consciously striving to answer the Eleatic challenge and to restore Ionian science to its high intellectual place.

So much for Empedocles. Let me now describe in barest outline the other major neo-Ionian systems.

Anaxagoras' cosmology differs considerably from Empedocles'; but in Elea the differences would have seemed trifling. Anaxagoras' world begins in an undifferentiated mass of stuffs, comparable to

Empedocles' Sphere. An active principle, Mind, then stirs the mass into rotatory motion; and that rotation produces our world, the different stuffs in the primordial mass commingling and separating in different amounts and proportions. Like Empedocles, Anaxagoras raised a full Ionian science on these foundations; the doxography preserves much of the detail, even though we have almost nothing of it in Anaxagoras' own words. Anaxagoras' cosmogony ends with the creation: his variegated world did not finally break apart into its elements; nor did the original mass ever reform; nor, consequently, did Anaxagoras follow Empedocles in postulating an infinite sequence of worlds.[17]

Anaxagoras' system is less strange than Empedocles'; and it was expounded in plain prose. Moreover, it was in a strong sense a rational structure: the fragments contain a quantity of argument; and it is clear that Anaxagoras was not content to state, but strove to prove. Much of that argument will be investigated in the next chapter. Finally, observe that in Anaxagoras no less than in Empedocles there are clear traces of Eleatic influence.

Philolaus was a Pythagorean; and some will object to my calling him 'neo-Ionian'. My excuse is simply this: he offered a cosmogony and an astronomy, as all good Ionian scientists did; and he paid some attention to Eleatic arguments, as all good neo-Ionians had to. His system was sensibly different from those of Anaxagoras and Empedocles in all other respects: Philolaus has cosmic 'principles', two in number, but they have curiously abstract and immaterial names. From the union of those principles our world was somehow formed and made intelligible; and the union was carried out under the auspices of Harmony, a force eminently comparable to Empedocles' Love (which indeed is sometimes called Harmonia: e.g., **31 B 27**). That brief sketch will hardly inspire excited anticipation; but I hold out the promise that Philolaus' cosmogony will prove stimulating.

The Atomists 'say that the full and the empty are elements, calling the one "being" and the other "not being"' (Aristotle, *Met* 985b5 = **67 A 6**). Apart from 'the full and the empty', atoms and the void, there is nothing. The atoms, which differ from one another in shape and size, move perpetually through the infinite void. The movement occurs by necessity (**67 B 2**); and in its course the atoms knock against, and sometimes adhere to, one another. Sometimes those adhesions increase in size and complexity; and our own universe is the result of a vast set of such atomic collisions. Not merely the formation of the world but everything else is ultimately explicable in terms of atomic structure: macroscopic qualities and relations rest upon microscopic form and arrangement; macroscopic changes are but the phenomenal results of microscopic motions.

With the Atomists' adoption of 'the void', and their assertion that 'what is not is', we meet the most far-reaching challenge to the Eleatic philosophy that the Presocratics produced; with the Atomists' thoroughgoing corpuscularianism, and their self-conscious and systematic development of its implications, we meet the most impressive achievement of Presocratic science. The Atomists are often regarded as the *élite* of the Presocratics; of all the early thinkers their thought was nearest to our own—and hence, of course, most rational.

Here, then, are the neo-Ionian systems. That they clash, obviously and fundamentally, with the doctrines of Elea, is a plain fact. And it is plain too that, to some extent at least, their proponents were conscious of the clash.

(c) *Four blind alleys*

The success of the neo-Ionian attack on Elea cannot be judged until its nature has been determined; and since there are several popular misconceptions of the nature of the attack, I begin by mentioning four routes along which the neo-Ionians did not march.

First, it is frequently said that Empedocles' Sphere or *Sphairos* corresponds to the ball or *sphaira* to which Parmenides likened 'what is'. Parmenides 'One' is spherical, homogeneous, and motionless: Empedocles' *Sphairos* is also homogeneous and motionless. After describing the 'One', Parmenides gives an account of the plural, changing world of Mortal Opinion: from the *Sphairos* Empedocles generates the plural, changing world of natural science. Empedocles, in brief, replaces the logical relation between the Way of Truth and the Way of Opinion by a chronological relation between the time of the Sphere and the time of the Cosmos; and thus he 'perpetuates Parmenides' insight, while reconciling it with common sense'.[18]

There are literary links between Parmenides' *sphaira* and Empedocles' *Sphairos*; and perhaps psychologically Empedocles was influenced by Parmenides here. But it is perfectly plain that the Sphere in no way 'perpetuates Parmenides' insight', nor does it marry Eleaticism with science. Even if Parmenides was a spherical monist he would have scorned the *Sphairos*: the *Sphairos* generates the natural world; the *Sphairos* is no more real than the plural world it produces; the *Sphairos* is not sempiternal; nor is it changeless—it lasts for a fixed period of time and then gradually breaks up into the world we know. A silly person might attempt to reconcile Zeno and Antisthenes by urging that for half of his time in the stadium the runner really is at rest, and that for the other half he moves. Such a reconciliation is ludicrous. No less ludicrous is the suggestion that Empedocles' stable *Sphairos* 'reconciles' Parmenidean metaphysics with Ionian science. I do not believe that Empedocles could have imagined anything so foolish.

The *Sphairos* is irrelevant to the neo-Ionian answer to Parmenides. I suppose that no one will suggest that Anaxagoras' primordial mass, or Philolaus' originative elements, or the little bodies of the Atomists, have any conciliatory tendencies.

Second, it is often observed that the neo-Ionians were, so to speak, axiomatic pluralists: they made it an initial posit that there is a plurality of things or stuffs. Thus Empedocles lays it down that there are four originative and ungenerated 'roots'; Anaxagoras has an indefinite variety of stuffs in his primordial mixture; Philolaus starts from a pair of principles; the atomists begin with an irreducible infinity of bodies. Parmenides, it is then said, observed the old Ionian systems, and found an impossibility in the suggestion that their single primordial stuff should give rise to a plural world. And against Parmenides the neo-Ionians reasoned thus: 'Parmenides was right in denying that a plurality could ever be derived from an ultimate unity; but what if there was no ultimate unity, but a plurality of primary entities which had always existed?'[19] Parmenides, in short, rejects the move from one to many; the neo-Ionians concur, but they counter the argument by presenting cosmogony as a move from many to many: a derived manifold is possible, for all that Parmenides has said, provided only that it derives from a primitive manifold.

It would be tedious to set out all the confusions and inaccuracies in that account of the central feature of Presocratic philosophy; and the account can be rejected by a quick and easy observation. Parmenides objects, not to the generation of a manifold from a unity, but to generation *tout court*. He does not argue, specifically, that nothing can be derived from a unity; he argues, quite generally, that nothing can be derived at all. The account I have just reported ascribes the grossest *ignoratio elenchi* to Empedocles and his fellows; I see no reason to suppose that they had misunderstood Parmenides' message in so crude a fashion. Indeed, on that point at least they were fully aware of the force of the Eleatic argument.

The word '*homoios*' signposts the third alley. Empedocles' roots are 'always utterly homogeneous' (**31 B** 17.35); for 'all these are fitting to their own parts' (**B 22**.1). Any parcel of a given elemental stuff has all and only those qualities possessed by any other parcel. In a similar way, Anaxagorean stuffs are 'homoiomerous': the precise sense of that controversial appellation will be investigated later (see below, pp. 320–2); here it is enough to say that homoiomereity imparts some measure of homogeneous stability to Anaxagoras' world.

The Eleatics argued that the world was *homoios*, homogeneous. The neo-Ionians accepted the argument, but to a limited extent: the elemental stuffs of the world, they admitted, are *homoia*; but that admission is consistent with change and decay. Plainly, that constitutes no answer to Elea: just as the postulation of a temporary Sphere does not reunite science with the Eleatic ban on change, so the admission of homogeneous elements does not unite scientific truth with the assertion that the whole universe is homogeneous. I do not think that Anaxagoras and Empedocles can have seriously supposed that their references to homogeneity constituted an answer to Elea; and I turn to the fourth and final alley.

It is drawn only on the map of Empedocles' thought. In **194**.9–13 (= **B 26**.8–12) Empedocles explains how, in one respect, things 'come into being and there is no stable life for them', while in another respect 'they exist forever, changeless in the cycle'. The language is reminiscent of Parmenides; and we may suspect that Empedocles is offering an answer to Elea. Roughly, Empedocles' position is this: *within* any cosmic cycle there is constant change—birth and decay, alteration and locomotion; but viewed from a higher vantage point the cosmos exhibits an eternal fixity—there is nothing new in the world; each event has occurred already infinitely many times, and will recur infinitely often. There is local change but global stability; for the local changes occur in accordance with unalterable global laws. Thus the Empedoclean universe is, at a global level, Eleatic: its laws do not change; its grand cycles are forever fixed. But that Eleatic stability can be reconciled with the changes observed by the scientist; for the stability itself governs and accounts for those changes.

Now as an answer to Parmenides, that is plainly futile: if Parmenides is right, there is no possibility of change, either at a global or at a local level. Eleatic arguments work, if they work at all, across the board; and if we suppose that Empedocles failed to see that fact, we accuse him of a wretched blindness: as well say that astronomy can be harmonized with Zenonian immobility by the reflexion that the stars always return to their starting points. And in fact, **194**.9–13 is not to be construed as an answer to Elea at all: rather, it makes, in somewhat picturesque language, a perfectly sane and sober point. Empedocles is saying, in effect, that the choppings and changings of the phenomenal world do not remove that world from the domain of rational science, whose first postulate is the existence of some system and stability in the phenomena; for the choppings and changings, though they may seem careless or random, are in fact the manifestations of eternal regularities; behind the phenomena lie stable and strong laws. That is not an original thought in Empedocles, although in **194** it has an idiosyncratically Empedoclean twist; but it is a comprehensible and a true thought—and a thought that has no bearing on the problems raised for science by Eleatic metaphysics.

(d) *Five through roads*

If those four alleys are blind, where are we to go? There are, I think, five main lines of contact between the Eleatics and the neo-Ionians; together they constitute the framework within which the new scientists tried to pursue their craft without falling foul of old Parmenides. First, the neo-Ionians agree with the first theorem of Eleatic metaphysics: generation, the absolute coming into being of real entities, is an impossibility. But, second, they hold that the alteration (in some sense) of existing entities is a possibility; and, third, they believe that locomotion is also possible. Then, fourth, they supply a 'moving cause' which will explain and account for the changes that the world contains; and finally, they reinstate, in a guarded fashion, the methodology of empirical observation. Generation goes, but locomotion stays; locomotion is causally explicable, and in turn will account for alteration; and perception, the first instrument of science, will reveal what locomotions and what alterations take place.

Scientifically speaking, the final point is crucial: in order to return to the rich pastures of Ionian science, the neo-Ionians were obliged to rescue the senses as instruments of discovery and signposts to truth. The complex and ingenious hypotheses of Empedocles, of Anaxagoras, of Philolaus, and of the Atomists are designed to organize and to explain 'the phenomena'; such hypotheses are chimerical if the phenomena have no objective status but remain, as they are in Elea, dreams and delusions of the human fantasy; and the phenomena can only be granted a decent scientific status if our senses, by which the phenomena are apprehended, have some claim to be regarded as dispensers of truth.

Philosophically, the third point is crucial: locomotion must be saved at all costs; for it was, as we shall see, primarily by their defence of the possibility of locomotion that the neo-Ionians hoped to rehabilitate the world of science. Generation and destruction, they believed, could, with some important reservations, be left in the Eleatic hell of nonentity; and they were surprisingly nonchalant in their attitude towards alteration. But on locomotion they were adamant: *pace* Elea, things can move; and they do move. In that way science gains a toehold in reality, and it can again dare to ascend the lofty cliffs of truth.

Such, I believe, is the essential doctrine of the neo-Ionian counter-reformation. Different thinkers developed it in different ways, and it is their differences which, being intrinsically fascinating, are generally held up for inspection and admiration. Yet it is important to grasp in a general and abstract way the common *nisus* that guided their diverse efforts to escape from the narrow and blinkering tenets of Elea. That *nisus* had nothing to do with the desire to balance periods of change against periods of stability, nor with the hope of securing phenomenal pluralities on the basis of elemental multiplicity. It had everything to do with the possibility of locomotion.

In the next three chapters I shall look into the different systems proposed by the neo-Ionians. The discussion will lead away from the common core of neo-Ionian doctrine. But the core must not be forgotten; and I shall take occasion later to examine it in more detail and to assess its power to defend Ionia against Elea.

XVI

Anaxagoras and the Nature of Stuffs

(a) *Outlines of Anaxagoreanism*

Anaxagoras' book was available at the *bouquineries* in the Athenian agora (Plato, *Apology* 26E = **59 A 35**). Some infer that it was 'read and understood without much difficulty';[1] if that is so, times have changed: of all the Presocratics Anaxagoras is the most difficult. Thanks to Simplicius, we possess substantial portions of the first part of Anaxagoras' work *Concerning Nature*;[2] and there is a rich doxography. But Anaxagoras' views are of considerable complexity, his arguments subtle in conception; and his thought is often (or so I at least find) of a peculiarly elusive character.

I shall begin by offering a crude statement of what I take to be Anaxagoras' fundamental tenets about the nature of the physical world. I shall first set them down, and then quote the several fragments in which I claim to find them expressed. The fundamental tenets are three:

(A) In the beginning, everything was mixed together.
(B) There is no smallest portion of anything.
(C) Now, everything is mixed together.

(Note that 'mind (*nous*)' is not included in 'everything' here: I shall leave *nous* out of the discussion in this chapter; it is readily separated from Anaxagoras' physical theories, and separation makes for easier exposition.) I find these three theses in the following fragments:

> All things were together [= A], unlimited both in quantity[3] and in smallness; for the small too was unlimited [= B]. And since all things were together [= A], nothing was clear by reason of the smallness. For air and aether contained[4] everything, both being unlimited. For these are the greatest items present in all things, both in quantity and in magnitude (**197: B 1**).

For neither of the small is there the least [= B], but there is always a less (for what is cannot not be)—but of the great too there is always a greater, and it is equal in quantity to the small.
And in relation to itself each is both great and small (**198: B 3**).

These things being thus, it is necessary to suppose that there are many things of every sort in everything that is conjoined [= C], and seeds of all things having various aspects and colours and tastes (**199: B 4a**).[5]

And men were compounded, and the other animals that have a soul (*psuchê*). And these men possess inhabited cities and cultivated fields, as we do; and they have a sun and a moon and the rest, as we have; and the earth grows for them many and various things, the most beneficial of which they gather into their dwellings and use. This, then, have I said about the separation—that it would have been separated not only by us but elsewhere too (**200: B 4b**).

Before these things were separated off, since everything was together [= A], not even any colour was clear; for this was prevented by the commingling of all things [= A]—of the wet and the dry and the hot and the cold and the bright and the dark, there being much earth present and seeds unlimited in quantity and not like one another. For of the other things none is like any other. And these things being thus, it is necessary to suppose that all things are present in everything [= C] (**201: B 4c**).

And since too there are equal portions of the great and the small in quantity, for this reason too everything is in everything [= C]; nor can they exist separately, but everything shares a portion of everything [= C]. Since the least cannot be [= B], things cannot be separated nor come to be by themselves, but as in the beginning [= A], so now too everything is together [= C]. And in all things there are many even of the things that are separating off, equal in quantity in the greater and in the smaller (**202: B 6**).

The things in the one cosmos have not been separated from one another [= C], nor have they been cut off by an axe—neither the hot from the cold nor the cold from the hot (**203: B 8**).

In everything there is present a portion of everything [= C], except mind; and in some things mind too is present (**204: B 11**).

These are the central fragments bearing on Anaxagoras' theory of physical nature. Thesis (B) is stated clearly enough; in the various statements of (A) and (C) I assume a synonymy among 'everything is *together*', 'everything *is* (*present*) *in* everything' and 'everything *has a portion of* everything'. My first task is exegetical: what does Anaxagoras mean by 'things'? The question is, surprisingly, difficult and controversial; and it calls for a section to itself.

(b) *The nature of things*

'All things were together': *homou panta chrêmata ên*. With those words Anaxagoras began his book (Simplicius, *ad* **B 1**). The Greek word '*chrêma* (thing)' gives nothing away; and in any case Anaxagoras sometimes simply uses the pronoun 'everything, (*panta*)'. The delicious suggestion that by 'all things' Anaxagoras meant literally 'all things' is, alas, untenable: 'all things are in all things' will then imply that Anaxagoras is in my typewriter and Clazomenae in its keys; and those idiocies were evidently no part of Anaxagorean physics.

We might start by considering Anaxagoras' examples of 'things'. They are: air, fire (**197**); wet, dry, hot, cold, bright, dark, earth (**201**); hair, flesh (**B 10**); thin, thick (**B 12**); cloud, water, stone (**B 16**). The doxographers add such things as: gold, blood, lead (Simplicius, **A 41**); white, black, sweet (Aristotle, *Phys* 187b5 = **A 52**). We do not, of course, know whether these latter examples actually occurred in Anaxagoras' text.

Do the examples suggest any generic determination for the notion of a 'thing'? Two suggestions have been widely canvassed. First, it is suggested that the Anaxagorean things are in fact the opposites: hot and cold, light and dark, wet and dry, and so on. Where we ordinarily speak of something's being hot, philosophically-minded men may say that a thing has the property of heat or hotness, or that heat or hotness or 'the hot' resides or inheres in the thing. And it is those properties which Anaxagoras had in mind when he talked about 'all things'. Such at least is the suggestion. But it is palpably false: hair and flesh, water and stone, are not properties or 'opposites'; but they are used by Anaxagoras himself in illustration of his theory. A modified version of the suggestion has it that if X is in Y, then X, but not Y, is an 'opposite'. That version fares no better: earth, according to **202**, is 'in' things; and in any case, the formula 'everything is in everything' shows that if X is in Y then Y is in X. Specific talk of the opposites may profitably be dropped from the discussion of Anaxagoras' theory of nature.

The second suggestion, far more complicated and influential, goes back at least to Aristotle:

> But Anaxagoras says the opposite [to Empedocles]; for [he makes] the homoiomeries elements (I mean, e.g., flesh and bone and each of those things), and air and fire mixtures of these and of all the other seeds; for both of these are put together from all the invisible homoiomeries (**205**: *Cael* 302a31–b3 = **A 43**).

The passage raises several questions: I want first to single out the 'homoiomeries' for attention; and I shall consider the simple suggestion, implicit in Aristotle and repeated *ad nauseam* by the doxographers, that Anaxagoras' things are in fact homoiomeries.

Aristotle explains the term 'homoiomerous' in another passage:

> For he [sc. Anaxagoras] posits the homoiomeries as elements—e.g., bone and flesh and marrow and the other things whose parts are synonymous (**206**: *GC* 314a18 = **A 46**).

Thus an *F* is homoiomerous if the parts of *F* are themselves synonymous with the whole, i.e. if they are *F*: flesh is homoiomerous because parts of a lump of flesh are themselves flesh; hands are not homoiomerous, because parts of hands are not hands.[6]

It is not clear precisely what Aristotle means to ascribe to Anaxagoras. Most generously, we might imagine him to offer Anaxagoras the *term* 'homoiomerous', so that some lost part of Anaxagoras' book will have said: 'By "thing" I mean homoiomerous thing'. But there is no special reason to interpret Aristotle so strictly; and it seems, on linguistic grounds, improbable that Anaxagoras would have coined a word like '*homoiomerês*'.[7] Most pinchingly, we might imagine that Anaxagoras gave no general description at all of his things: Aristotle read through his examples, saw that they were all what *he* would call homoiomeries, and hastily concluded that Anaxagoras meant to include all and only homoiomeries under his umbrella of things. There is a slight difficulty with this view: Anaxagoras' examples include opposites or properties, and Aristotle more than once uses that fact in criticism of Anaxagoras' theory (*GC* 327b21; *Phys* 188a6 = **A 52**; *Met* 989b3 = **A 61**). Now properties are not homoiomerous in Aristotle's mind; and it is therefore a trifle hard to suppose that Aristotle eyed Anaxagoras' examples and judged them all to be homoiomeries. The difficulty is not great; but it is enough to give some plausibility to a third way of understanding Aristotle's ascription: Anaxagoras, we may suppose, did give some general characterization of his things, and that characterization seemed to Aristotle to fit his own notion of a homoiomery. Indeed, there is no reason why Anaxagoras should not have said something like this: 'All things—I mean air and fire and flesh and blood and everything where the part is like the whole . . .'

Thus the notion of a homoiomery may point in a genuinely Anaxagorean direction; but the value of the pointer is modest. For the notion itself is neither as clear nor as precise as it appears to be. How are we to define homoiomereity? A first attempt might read:

(D1) A property *P* is homoiomerous if and only if if *a* has *P* then some part of *a* has *P*.

That is too weak: it will allow benches and buildings, swarms and schools, to be homoiomeries; and it is plain that they should not be included in the class. A stronger definition is:

(D2) A property *P* is homoiomerous if and only if if *a* has *P* then every part of *a* has *P*.

Now that, I suspect, does answer to Aristotle's thought; but for us it is far too strong: it makes all Aristotle's paradigmatic homoiomeries anhomoiomerous; for it is not the case that *every* part of a piece of flesh is itself flesh, since the atomic parts of ordinary stuffs do not share their properties.

(D2) can be emended—adding the word 'macroscopic' before 'part' might do. But it is better to abandon (D2) and to ask, more laxly, what sort of thing Aristotelian homoiomeries are supposed to be. The answer is plain: homoiomeries are *stuffs*; homoiomeries relate to substances as matter to formed individuals; the homoiomeries are the material of which substances are composed (e.g., Aristotle, *Meteor* 389b27; *GA* 715a11).

Thus I propose that we read Anaxagorean 'things' as stuffs; and I claim that the proposal is fundamentally Aristotelian.[8] What of the obvious objection, that 'the hot', 'the cold', 'the wet' and so on are not stuffs?[9] Here again I side with Aristotle: according to him, Anaxagoras mistakenly treats properties, like 'the hot', as substances; the criticism seems to me to be just, for the fragments reveal Anaxagoras doing exactly that. Moreover, Anaxagoras was not the only early thinker to substantialize qualities; on the contrary, such substantiation was, notoriously, a common feature of Greek thought (for a nice example see [Hippocrates], *nat hom* 3). In short, the occurrence of the opposites among the examples of Anaxagorean things shows not that those things are not stuffs but that Anaxagoras misidentified the opposites as stuffs.

I have not provided much argument for the suggestion that Anaxagoras, like his Ionian predecessors, has an ontology of stuffs. The proof of the suggestion must come in my exposition of his arguments.

(c) *The seeds of the world*

Before turning to those arguments there are some preliminary questions to be raised about Anaxagoras' third tenet, that everything is now mixed together or that 'everything has a portion of everything'. That tenet can now be expressed as follows:

(C*) For any pair of stuffs, *S*, *S′*: in every piece of *S* there is now a portion of *S′*.

In what sense can a portion of *S′* be in a piece of *S*? The obvious suggestion is that the lump of *S* contains, scattered through its volume, particles of *S′*; those particles will be invisible to gross observation (for *S* does not wear the aspect of *S′*), and they will be multitudinous, or even infinite (for they permeate every part of *S*). Such a particulate view of matter is traditionally ascribed to Anaxagoras; and it seems to make sense. The ascription is supported by four props.

The first prop is the word 'seed (*sperma*)'. Aristotle talks of the homoiomeries 'and all the other seeds' (*Cael* 302b2 = **A 43**); and the word *sperma* is Anaxagorean: 'seeds of all things' 'seeds unlimited in quantity' are present in the primordial mass (**199**; **201**).[10] It is easy to imagine that 'seeds' of *S* are (minimal) particles of *S*: the original mass contains everything inasmuch as little seed-particles of every stuff are suspended in it like pollen in the summer air.

That is a tempting interpretation, but not an obligatory one. *Sperma*, in Greek, is as much a biological as a botanical term: where the word 'seed' suggests particles to us, the word *sperma* would not have done so to a Greek. The language of seeds does not imply a particulate theory of stuffs; and to say that *X* contains seeds of *Y* need mean no more than that *Y* may grow from *X*.[11]

The second prop for particles is the word 'unlimited'. According to Aristotle, Anaxagoras 'says that the principles (*archai*) are unlimited (*apeiroi*)' (*Met* 984a13 = **A 43**; cf. *Phys* 187a25 = **A 52**); Theophrastus repeated the assertion, with reservations (Simplicius, **A 41**); and it is a doxographical commonplace. Must not these 'unlimited principles' be an infinite set of minimal particles or atoms?

No. Aristotle, as his context shows, is thinking not of an infinity of particles, but of an infinity of kinds of stuff. Moreover, we almost certainly possess, in **197**, the words that Aristotle is here interpreting: 'All things were . . . unlimited both in quantity (*plêthos*) and in smallness'. The sentence plainly does not refer to an infinity of corpuscles, and Aristotle rightly did not so construe it; rather, he took Anaxagoras to mean that there was an unlimited quantity of kinds of thing: earth, air, stone, flesh, bone, blood, etc. Aristotle's negative point is correct; but his positive interpretation is not. By 'S is unlimited in smallness' Anaxagoras means: 'For any n and m, where $m < n$, if there is a portion of S of magnitude n units, then there is a portion of S of magnitude m units.' Thus if S is 'unlimited in smallness' it follows that the *portions* of S are unlimited in number; for if two portions have a different magnitude, they cannot be identical. And that, I suggest, is precisely what Anaxagoras means by 'S is unlimited in quantity': for any n and m, where $m > n$, if there are n portions of S, then there are m portions of S (see below, pp. 33–7). That doctrine does not commit Anaxagoras to infinitely numerous discrete atoms of S; it does not commit him to an Aristotelian infinity of stuffs;[12] it does not commit him to the view that some portion of S is infinite in size—for S's infinitely numerous portions may all be happily nested inside one another.

Third, consider Anaxagoras' language when he talks of the composition of things and stuffs: things are 'commingled' (*summignusthai*: **B 17**) or 'conjoined' (*sunkrinesthai*: **199**) or 'compounded' (*sumpêgnusthai*: **200**; **B 16**). Those words surely suggest the amassing of discrete particles of stuff. Similarly, Anaxagoras uses 'separate off' (*apokrinesthai*: **B 2**; **201**; etc.) and 'separate out' (*diakrinesthai*: **B 5**; **B 12**; etc.) to denominate the discrimination of sensible stuffs from the rough primordial mass; and such terms suggest an effluxion of particles.

Against that I have little to say but Boo: commingling and separating do not suggest to me the confluence or effluence of particles.[13]

The fourth prop for the view that Anaxagorean stuffs are particulate in structure is the strongest. The doxographers, who follow Aristotle in stressing the imperceptibility of Anaxagorean stuffs in the original world-mass, also follow Aristotle in explaining that imperceptibility in terms of the smallness of the stuff-particles. Stuffs, in the neat and anachronistic phrase of Aëtius, are composed of 'intellectually contemplatable parts (*moria logôi theôrêta*)' (**A 46**).[14] We can imagine, but we cannot perceive, the fine particulate structure of chalk and cheese.

Here too we need not rely on doxographical interpretation: we have, again in **197**, the original words in which Aristotle and his followers replied:

> And since all things were together, nothing was clear by reason of the smallness. For air and aether contained everything, both being unlimited. For these are the greatest items present in all things, both in quantity and in magnitude.

'Nothing was clear by reason of the smallness.' It is natural to explain the word 'smallness' by way of its first occurrence in **197**: there it indicated small *portions* of stuff; here, accordingly, it is naturally taken in the same way, and the Aristotelian interpretation seems to be confirmed. But a portion of *S* is not a part of *S*; and portions, however small, need not be conceived of as particles. Moreover, we can find a better interpretation for the sentence 'nothing was clear by reason of the smallness'.

Consider the word 'greatest' in the last sentence of the fragment. Anaxagoras' point here is fairly straightforward: if we look about the world today we see that two stuffs, air and aether, are vastly more extensive than any others; consequently, Anaxagoras invites us to infer, air and aether must, in the original mixture, have 'contained' or dominated everything else. The 'greatness' of air and aether lies in the fact that the total amount of air and aether in the world is greater than that of any other stuff. Similarly, the 'smallness' of, say, gold, consists not in its being divided into minute particles but rather in the simple fact that there is very little gold in the world.

In the original mixture the proportion of gold or flesh was so small that it made no perceptible difference, as a glass of wine thrown into the sea makes no perceptible difference to the brine. (That, of course, is why the original mass has no colour (**201**): air and aether, themselves colourless, are large enough to absorb the colours of all the other stuffs commingled with them. A glass of Burgundy will not make the green one red.)

I conclude that we have no binding reason for ascribing to Anaxagoras a particulate theory of matter. Moreover, there is one excellent reason for denying him such a theory.[15] If *every* piece of *S* contains a particle of *S′*, and if every piece of a piece of *S* is a piece of *S*, then every piece of *S* is wholly composed of particles of *S′*—which is absurd. The inference is easy enough to grasp; and even if Anaxagoras had no notion of it (which I doubt), we must deny him particles if we are to give him a theory of matter consistent with his tenet (C*). Anaxagorean stuffs contain portions of all other stuffs; but those portions are not located at one or more points within the parent lump—they are mingled smoothly and regularly throughout its body. Any stuff contains every stuff; but the contained stuffs are not present by virtue of a mechanical juxtaposition of particles; they are present as the items in a chemical union.[16] Every cloud contains a little silver; but the silver is not spread out as a lining: there is no part of the cloud which is pure, or even impure, silver.

A rough analogy may help. Artists may make a patch of their canvas seem green in either of two ways. First, and unusually, they may adopt a *pointilliste* technique, setting minute dots of blue next to minute dots of yellow: from a distance the effect is green; from close up we see adjacent spots of blue and yellow. Alternatively, they may mix masses of blue and yellow on their palette and apply the mixture to the canvas: the effect from a distance is green; and however closely we look at it, the effect is still green. No part of the canvas, however small, is painted blue; and no part yellow. For all that, the green on the canvas 'contains' blue and yellow; they are its constituents, and some chemical technique might, for all I know, be capable of 'extracting' some of the yellow from the artist's green. Atomists are physical *pointillistes*: their world is made up of microscopical dots, individually indistinguishable to the eye. Anaxagoras was a painter of the traditional type: his world is made of stuffs mixed through and through, its components as invisible to the microscope as to the naked eye.

That conclusion allows us to solve a little puzzle in Anaxagorean scholarship. Anaxagoras' theory of matter, it is said, 'rests on two propositions which seem flatly to contradict one another. One is the principle of homoiomereity: a natural substance such as a piece of gold consists solely of parts which are like the whole and like one another—every one of them gold and nothing else. The other is: "There is a portion of everything in everything".'[17] That criticism misinterprets the principle of homoiomereity: the principle says, not that every part of a lump of gold is 'gold and nothing else', but that every part of a lump of gold has the same material constitution as the lump itself. If 'everything is in everything', then the lump of gold contains a portion of every other stuff. Hence every part of that lump contains a portion of every other stuff. Is there a contradiction, flat or curvaceous, here? Not, I think, if Anaxagorean stuffs are non-particulate. The view is certainly strange; but I see no logical inconsistency in it. In short, given a non-particulate theory of matter, Anaxagoras may safely maintain both (C*) and a principle of homoiomereity.

(d) *Elements and compounds*

Green is a compound colour; blue and yellow are simple or elemental. Are the stuffs in (C*) limited to elemental stuffs? Does Anaxagoras distinguish between elements and non-elemental stuffs? The doxography is clear enough: the homoiomeries are standardly called 'elements' (*stoicheia*: e.g., *Cael* 302a32 = **A 43**) or 'principles' (*archai*: e.g., *Met* 984a13 = **A 43**). If that does not quite suffice to distinguish elemental from non-elemental *stuffs*, two texts take that further step: the *de Caelo* asserts that 'air and fire' are not elements but 'mixtures of the homoiomeries' (302b1 = **A 43**); and elsewhere Aristotle says that 'they [sc. the Anaxagoreans] [say] that these [i.e. the homoiomeries] are simple and elements, and that earth and fire and water and air are compounds' (*GC* 314a24 = **A 46**). The former passage, as its context makes clear, is relying on **197**. **197** does give a special status to air and aether (which Aristotle interprets as fire); but it surely does not imply that air and aether are compounds and not elemental. The second Aristotelian passage is, I suspect, no better based: Aristotle carelessly assumes that what, in his opinion, holds of two of the Empedoclean roots must hold for all four. At all events, I can find no fragment which clearly supports Aristotle's view, or makes any distinction between elemental and non-elemental stuffs.[18]

'But surely Anaxagoras must have realized that some stuffs are compounds of others: that bronze is made from copper and tin; that wine is a mixture of water, sugar, alcohol, and so on. Then why need his original mass contain bronze *in addition to* copper and tin, wine *in addition to* water, sugar and so on? At best such additions are otiose; at worst they are confused. In general, then, the original mass will contain only those stuffs which science shows not to be compounds of other stuffs.'

But what does that suggestion really amount to? If the original mass contains a portion of green then it contains, *eo ipso*, portions of yellow and of blue; and equally, if it contains a portion of yellow and a portion of blue, it contains a portion of green.[19] It is easy to deny that; but the denial rests on an unconscious adherence to a particulate theory of stuffs: we imagine, wrongly, that the blue and the yellow must, as it were, be located in determinate parts of the mass and that they will produce green only if their locations happen to be related in one out of innumerable possible ways. But blue and yellow are not located in any such fashion; they are smoothly mixed throughout the mass of stuff. What more could possibly be required for us to say that the mass contains green? Does the mass contain green *in addition to* blue and yellow? It contains yellow and it contains blue and it contains green; and that is that. I conclude that Anaxagoras' theory takes no stand on the question of elements: it has no peculiar resistance to them; and it provides no special place for them. The contrast between element and compound is of secondary interest to the theory.[20]

But is that theory coherent? It is sometimes argued that theorem (C*) implies that there are no 'pure' stuffs and hence that we cannot intelligibly talk of such stuffs, let alone say that they occur in different proportions in different places. Anaxagoras' theory is self-stultifying: it is a theory about stuffs; but its main tenet is inconsistent with the existence of stuffs.[21]

I shall approach that argument obliquely. The end of **B 12** reads thus:

> And there are many portions of many things; but nothing is altogether separating off or separating out, one from another, except mind. And all mind is homogeneous (*homoios*), both the greater and the smaller. But nothing else is homogeneous,[22] but each single thing is and was most clearly those things of which most are present in it (**207**; cf. **301**).

The last sentence is adequately glossed by Aristotle: 'Things seem different and are given different names from one another on the basis of what especially preponderates in quantity in the mixing of the unlimited [stuffs]. For there is no whole which is purely white or black or sweet or flesh or bone; but the nature of the thing seems to be that of which it contains the most' (*Phys* 187b2–7 = **A 52**). Simplicius puts it bluntly: 'that is gold in which there is much gold, though many things are in it' (**A 41**; cf. Lucretius, **A 44**); and we have already come across an Anaxagorean illustration of the point in **197**: the original mixture, since it contains more air and aether than anything else, is, or wears the aspect of, air and aether. Dig up a spadeful of stuff from your back garden: you can be sure that it will not be a spade of any pure stuff; it will contain countless impurities of every sort. But you are, for all that, warranted in calling it earth; and you may properly surmise that it contains a dominant proportion of earth—which accounts for its earthy aspect.

Here the charge of incoherence shows its teeth: 'How can you know that the dominant stuff in your spadeful is earth? How can you even speak sensibly of "earth"? It will not do to define earth by way of **207**, saying that *a* is earth if and only if *a* is a lump of stuff in which earth predominates. Such a definition is vainly circular. And if we evade the circle by putting subscripts to the term "earth"—"*a* is $earth_1$ if and only if *a* is a lump of stuff in which $earth_2$ predominates"—then "$earth_2$" remains unexplained. If $earth_2$ is elemental, it cannot be explained in terms of any components; and since, by (C*), $earth_2$ is never present in the world, we cannot learn the meaning of $earth_2$ by "ostensive definition". In short, "earth", or "$earth_2$" if you prefer, is a bogus term: it has no use in science.'

That argument constitutes a serious challenge to Anaxagoras, whether or not we ascribe to him a distinction between '$earth_1$' and '$earth_2$'. Moreover, it poses, I think, a more general difficulty: every schoolboy chemist learns that all the sample elements he uses in the laboratory are impure; no process will guarantee the removal of every impurity from a bottle of stuff. Now the chemist needs and uses the notion of (pure) hydrogen. Yet he lives in an impure world, and he experiments on impure samples of hydrogen. How can Anaxagoras and the modern chemist speak intelligibly of earth or of hydrogen? How can Anaxagoras seriously say that most of the stuff on my spade is earth? How can the chemist determine that most of the stuff in the test-tube is hydrogen?

A part of the answer to those questions runs, I think, like this. We begin by observing, crudely, that different lumps of stuff have different qualities: two buckets of stuff look and smell and feel and taste different; they act and behave differently; and we give them different names—'sand', say, and 'sea'. Evidently, the buckets do not contain pure samples of sand and sea; for we can see plainly that the sea is sandy, and we can feel the wetness of the sand. For all that, we can distinguish sand from sea, and begin some quasi-scientific tests. Various observations and experiments will associate one set of properties with buckets of sand and another set, largely non-overlapping, with buckets of sea. And we may now define the 'scientific' notion of 'pure' sand as 'the stuff—whatever its structure may be—that supports *those* properties'; and sea as 'the stuff—whatever its structure may be—that supports *those* properties'. Such definitions are dangerous and indeterminate: they are dangerous because they suppose that some single structure is common to all our buckets of sand; and closer, microscopic, observation might falsify that supposition (whales and dolphins are not, after all, fish; mercury is a metal). They are indeterminate because the batch of properties they assemble and refer to may well change in the course of time and further investigation. For all that, definitions of such a type do allow us to get a grip on the notion of a 'pure' substance, even though all our buckets of sand and sea are impure.

Do those definitions import new senses for our stuff names? or do they make old senses more precise? Does 'water' have two senses, one of which is explicable by the chemist in terms of H and O, the other of which is explained by pointing to rivers and seas? And does Anaxagoras mean to suggest that stuff names like 'earth' are ambiguous between '$earth_1$' and '$earth_2$'? I see no hint of ambiguity in Anaxagoras;[23] I see no good reason to suppose an ambiguity in English; and I find nothing of interest in the question.

However that may be, as science advances our investigatory techniques are improved. Let us leave the seaside and enter the laboratory. We have a jar of gas which we know is predominantly oxygen. The next question is: can we discover *how much* oxygen the jar contains? How can we determine the *degree* of impurity in the gas if we can never extract *all* the impurities? Now our techniques will have developed a process of separating H from a predominantly O mixture, and another process of extracting O from a predominantly H mixture. Take a jar of predominantly O gas: by the first process, extract *n* units of predominantly H gas, leaving *m* units of predominantly O gas. Now apply the second process to the *n* units and the first to the *m* units; and so on. Applications of those processes will always provide results; for though we may purify our H we can never produce pure H—you cannot cut H off from O with an axe. Yet it is not hard to see that the continued applications of the two processes will enable us to give ever closer approximations to the proportion of H to O in the original jar. No doubt

> of the things that are separating off one does not know the quantity either by reason or in fact (**208: B** 7)—

but one can make an indefinitely close approximation to knowledge.[24]

My argument here has been, I fear, somewhat jejune: to consider the issue at full length would call for a chapter on its own. Yet the issue is important enough: if the objection I have been considering is correct, then Anaxagoras' physical theory (and with it modern chemistry) is blown up. I do not think the objection has any such explosive powers.

(e) *Inherent powers*

Some of the difficulties in (C*) have now been aired; and I turn to the connexion between that tenet and the other parts of Anaxagoras' system. I begin by asking why Anaxagoras put forward his first tenet, that 'in the beginning, everything was in everything'. That tenet can be expressed by:

(A*) For any pair of stuffs *S*, *S′*: in every piece of *S* there originally was a portion of *S′*.

Discussion may start from a passage in Aristotle:

> They [the Anaxagoreans] say that everything was mixed in everything because they saw everything coming to be from everything (**209**: *Phys* 187b1 = **A 52**).

Simplicius gives a somewhat breathless gloss:

> Seeing, then, everything coming to be from everything, if not immediately at least serially (*kata taxin*)—for air comes from fire,

and water from air, and earth from water, and stone from earth, and fire again from stone; and though the same food, e.g., bread, is applied, many different things come into being, flesh bones veins muscles hair nails—and perhaps wings and horns—even though like is increased by like: for these reasons he supposed that in the food—in water, if that is what trees feed on—there is wood and bark and fruit; and that is why he said that everything was mixed in everything, and that coming to be comes about by virtue of a separating out (**210: A 45**).

No extant text of Anaxagoras contains precisely that argument, and it has been supposed a Peripatetic rationalization.[25] But I am inclined to go along with Aristotle's interpretation; for the alternative is baffled silence, an unendurable fate. Nor do the fragments bear no relation to the Peripatetic argument. **B 16** reads as follows:

From those things as they separate off is compounded earth; for from clouds water separates off, and from water earth, and from earth stones are compounded by the cold, and these are further distant from water (**211**).[26]

The fragment reveals an interest in what Simplicius calls 'serial' generation: A come from B serially if A comes from C_1 and C_1 comes from C_2 and . . . and C_{n-1} comes from C_n and C_n comes from B. An anecdote in Diogenes runs as follows: 'they say that when someone asked him if the mountains in Lampsacus would ever be sea, he said: "If time doesn't give out"' (Diogenes Laertius, II.10 = **A 1**).

But such remarks are Presocratic commonplaces. The Peripatetic argument requires us to ascribe to Anaxagoras the thesis that 'everything comes from everything'. By 'everything' is meant 'every stuff'; and I take 'S comes from S'' to mean 'from any quantity of S' a quantity of S is extractable'. Thus 'Water comes from cloud' means: 'From any bit of cloud you can extract a drop or two of water'; 'Flesh comes from bread' means: 'From any lump of bread you can extract a piece of flesh'; 'Fire comes from flint' means: 'From any flint stone you can extract a spark of fire'. Then to say that 'everything comes from everything' is to assert:

(1) For any pair of stuffs S, S': from any piece of S there is extractable a piece of S'.

On the Peripatetic interpretation, proposition (1) is the logical foundation-stone of Anaxagorean physics, more fundamental even than the three tenets, (A)—(C), which I set out at the start of this chapter. (The proposition uses the word 'extract' in a highly general sense, to cover all cases in which one stuff is wrung from another.

What particular process of extraction is appropriate in any given case is a matter for experiment: thus ice is extracted from water by refrigeration (cf. **211**); flesh from bread by digestion; salt from brine by evaporation; cheese from milk by compression; fire from stone by concussion; and so on.)

Why should Anaxagoras have embraced (1)? According to Aristotle, on the basis of empirical evidence: he 'saw' that 'everything comes from everything'. **211** suggests that a part of that evidence derived from the stock-in-trade of the old Ionian scientists: the familiar meteorological processes provide clear and repeated evidence for the serial generation of the main world-masses from one another. Biology provides another area of observation: Simplicius, in **210**, refers to the phenomena of nutrition; and the reference is repeated (e.g., Lucretius, **A 44**; Aëtius, **A 46**). A further testimony points to the allied phenomena of reproduction, where from a seed there develops an embryo with its complement of flesh and bones and hair (**B 10**, see below). There are close connexions between Anaxagoras and the fifth-century doctors;[27] and there is biological terminology in the fragments: it is tempting to conclude that the study of biology and medicine led Anaxagoras to his philosophical position. That conclusion is conjectural, and I suspect that it is exaggerated. But it is plausible to suppose that Anaxagoras was as impressed by biological as by meteorological changes: if flesh and blood and bone may come from bread and milk and cheese, then surely anything may come from anything?

Proposition (1), then, may stand as an Anaxagorean hypothesis. Like the cosmological hypotheses of the Milesians, it is strong and simple; and it is supported by a mass of empirical evidence. It has a further dialectical advantage: it stands in the strongest possible contrast to the stability of Elea. If (1) can be defended against Eleatic attack, then any weaker hypothesis, which further experiment may put in the place of (1), need fear nothing from that quarter.[28]

In order to proceed from proposition (1) to tenet (A*), the thesis that 'everything was in everything', we need a further premiss. The premiss is suggested by the following passage:

> For in the same seed he says there is hair and nails and veins and arteries and muscles and bones, and they are invisible because of the smallness of their parts but as they grow they are gradually separated out. 'For how', he says, 'might hair come to be from what is not hair and flesh from what is not flesh?' (**212**: Scholiast on Gregory, **B 10**).

The passage comes from a late scholiast; but the scholiast seems to be familiar with the doxographical tradition, and I assume that the substance of the passage is Anaxagorean, even if the final question is not (as many scholars think) an original quotation.[29]

'Hair cannot come from what is not hair.' The principle suggested by that thought is:

(2) For any pair of stuffs, S, S': if S' comes from S, then $S = S'$.

But (2) is absurd; and Anaxagoras surely has in mind a less extravagant principle, namely:

(3) For any stuff S' and object x: if S' comes from x, then S' was in x.

Hair cannot come from 'what is not hair', i.e. from what does not *contain* hair.

Is principle (3) borrowed from Elea? or is it an empirical observation? or is it, in intention at least, a truism? If I take an egg out of the egg-box, the egg was in the box; if I draw milk from a cow, the cow contained the milk; and in general, if Y comes *out* of X, then Y was *in* X. The sentiment is prehistoric: 'deriving his fire . . . commonly from the friction of wood or bamboo, primitive man naturally concluded that fire is somehow stored up in all trees, or at all events in those trees from the wood of which he usually extracted it.'[30] When the iron-master extracts metal from ore, he does not need Parmenides to tell him that the metal does not spring into being; he knows that it was there all along. When the milk-maid extracts butter from her milk, she has not previously *observed* the butter in the unchurned milk. Principle (3), I suggest, was not forced upon Anaxagoras by Elea; nor did he propose it on the basis of empirical research: rather, it seemed to him to be a self-evident truth.

Principle (3) needs careful statement. It is easy to read it as:

(4) For any stuff S' and object x: if a piece of S' is extracted from x, then x contained a piece of S'.

But Anaxagoras does not want to hold that x contained a *piece* of S'; for that wrongly suggests that extraction is a matter of isolating some part of x; and if x is a piece of S, every part of x is a piece of S and no part a piece of S'. We need to hold clearly in mind a distinction which has underlain most of this chapter: the distinction between pieces and portions.[31] x contains a *piece* of S' only if some physical part of x is a piece of S'; but x may contain a *portion* of S' even if no part of x is a piece of S'. The *pointilliste*'s green patch contains blue pieces and yellow pieces; the orthodox or Anaxagorean green patch contains blue portions and yellow portions, but no blue or yellow pieces.

The principle Anaxagoras needs is this:

(5) For any stuff S' and object x: if a piece of S' is extracted from x, then x contained a portion of S'.

And (5) can be defended in the same way as (3): if I extract a pound of salt from a tub of brine, then the brine contained salt; if I get a thimble of water from a cactus plant, the cactus contained water. And if you can't get blood from a stone, that is because (in un-Anaxagorean physics) stones do not contain blood. I propose that we grant Anaxagoras (5), and that we take it not as a piece of Eleatic metaphysics, nor as an inductive generalization, but as a safe truism.

We must make (5) a little more precise by introducing a reference to time, thus:

(5*) For any stuff S', object x, and time t: if a piece of S' is extracted from x at t, then prior to t x contains a portion of S'.

From (5*) it is reasonable to infer:

(6*) For any stuff S', object x, and time t: if it is possible to extract a piece of S' from x at t, then x contains a portion of S' at t.

The principle behind the inference is this: if, given that X is extracted from Y, Y contained X, then if X is extractable from Y, Y contains X; if what is extracted from Y was contained in Y, then what is extractable from Y is contained in Y.

Sentence (1), like sentence (5), requires to be made more precise, thus:

(1*) For any stuffs S and S', object x, and time t: if x is a piece of S, then it is possible to extract a piece of S' from x at t.

Now (1*) and (6*) entail:

(7) For any stuffs S and S', object x, and time t: if x is a piece of S, then x contains a portion of S' at t.

Finally, we make two trivial deductions from (7), viz:

(8) For any stuffs S and S', and object x: if x is a piece of S, then x contained a portion of S' at the time when the cosmogony began.

(9) For any stuffs S and S', and object x: if x is a piece of S, then x now contains a portion of S'.

Now (8) is, of course, nothing more than tenet (A*); and (9) is tenet (C*). Thus from the two Anaxagorean principles, (1) and (5), we have successfully inferred two of the basic tenets of Anaxagorean physics. If 'everything comes from everything', and if 'what comes from a thing must have been in it', then 'everything was originally in everything', and 'everything is now in everything'.

So far so good. But the two formulations of (A) and (C), viz. (8) and (9), immediately suggest a potentially embarrassing question: (8) seems to ascribe to the original mass exactly the same constitution that (9) ascribes to the present world. Does not that lead at once to an

Eleatic universe, stable and changeless? How is any sort of 'extraction' possible, given the fundamental similarity holding between the world past and the world present? How can Anaxagoras allow a cosmogony? How can change and variation take place in the world we know?

I shall return to these questions. First, however, I want to look at the second of Anaxagoras' three tenets: what does (B) amount to? and how is it related to (A) and to (C)?

(f) *Anaxagoras and infinity*

That second tenet has it that 'there is no smallest portion of anything'. The tenet is advanced in **198** and **202**. I begin with **198**:

> [i] For neither of the small is there the least, but there is always a less (for [ii] what is cannot not be)—but [iii] of the great too there is always a greater, and [iv] it is equal in quantity to the small. And [v] in relation to itself each is both great and small.

Sentence [i] states tenet (B); I paraphrase this (for reasons which will become clearer later) as follows: 'However small an object may be, there is no smallest portion of S contained in it.' The reference to the object's smallness is, I take it, a literary rather than a logical device; thus the tenet reads, formally:

(B*) For any stuff S and object x: if x contains a portion of S, S^b, then there is a portion S^c contained in x such that $S^c < S^b$.

It is easy to see that (B*) entails that if there are any portions of S in an object, there are infinitely many such portions. And there is every reason to think that Anaxagoras saw the implication: when **197** asserts that 'all things were together, unlimited both in quantity and in smallness', we may suppose (as I have already suggested) that the unlimited quantity of portions of stuffs as well as their unlimited smallness is inferred from thesis (B*). Anaxagoras, I think, 'shows an understanding of the meaning of infinity which no Greek before him had attained'—not even Zeno, if Zeno indeed came before him.[32]

But how did Anaxagoras acquire that understanding? And why did he adhere to thesis (B*)? A tempting suggestion has him derive (B*) directly from (C*). Take any piece of S, say a. By (C*), a contains a portion of S'. Extract that portion, or part of it, and call the resulting piece of S' b. By (C*) b contains a portion of S: extract that, too, and call the new piece of S c. Plainly, $c < a$; equally plainly, successive applications of (C*) will yield an infinite sequence of pieces of S, each smaller than its predecessor. Since the extracted pieces of S all come from *a*, we may safely conclude that *a* contained no smallest portion of *S*.

198 does not contain that argument; instead, it offers the parenthetical reflexion, [ii]: 'what is cannot not be'. That has foxed the commentators. Some refer, loosely and unconvincingly, to Zeno's argument in **175** = **29 B 3**.[33] Others offer Anaxagoras arguments of ludicrous implausibility: 'If one presupposes that there is a smallest, one must assume that that which is less than the smallest does not exist, and consequently that there is a void.' Others again have Anaxagoras equivocate: 'If the division of something into smaller and smaller pieces could ever come to an end, this would mean that there was nothing further to divide; i.e., by cutting up an existing thing one would have reduced it to non-existence.'[34] (After such a division there is 'nothing further to divide', i.e. no magnitudes left which are divisible; it does not, of course, follow that the only thing left to divide is nothing—so that the dividing has somehow produced nothing or a nonentity.)

Can anything better be done for sentence [ii]? Suppose that *a* contains *c*; then, plainly, *c* exists. Now let *a* be the smallest portion of *S*. Then by the argument I have already rehearsed, *c* is smaller than *a*; but if *a* is the smallest portion of *S*, *c* cannot exist. Hence *c* exists and *c* does not exist—but 'what is cannot not be'. On that view, sentence [ii] does not introduce the notion of division: it does not say 'what is cannot *become* non-existent'. It is not making an Eleatic point at all, but stating the simple truism that what exists cannot also not exist.[35] The parenthesis, in short, is a reminder that a *reductio* argument is readily constructed for (B*).

I continue the discussion of **198**. Sentence [iii] is usually taken to state either that there is an infinitely large amount of every stuff in the world (which is absurd and contradicts **197**), or that the total world stuff is infinite in extent (which is implied by **197** but is wholly irrelevant to **198** and thesis (B*)). Comparison with (B*) suggests rather the following interpretation:[36]

(1) For any stuff *S* and object *x*: if *x* contains a portion of *S*, S^b, then there is a portion S^c contained in *x* such that $S^c > S^b$,

In short: there is no largest portion of *S* in any given piece of stuff.

How might Anaxagoras have argued for (1)? Let S^b be the largest portion of *S* in *a*. Extract S^b from *a*, and call the remainder of *a* *c*. By (C*), *c* contains a portion of *S*, S^c. Now the compound portion $S^c + S^b$ was contained in *a* and is greater than S^b. Hence S^b is not the largest portion of *S* in *a*. We can, of course, say that *a* contains no portion of *S* of magnitude greater than *n* (if *n* is the magnitude of *a* itself); but then there is no portion of *S* equal to *n*. However much *S* you extract from *a*, there is always a little left; however large a portion of *S* you have discovered in *a*, it is possible to enlarge it.

The argument for (1) is parallel to my argument for (B*), just as (1) itself is parallel to (B*). And the language of **198** leads us to expect such a parallelism. Moreover, we can now ascribe an easy sense to sentence [iv], '. . . it is equal in quantity to the small'. Of the many interpretations of that phrase,[37] one has all the advantages: 'there are as many large portions of *S* in *a* as there are small portions'. Let *X* count as a 'large' portion if $X \geqslant {}^3/_4a$; and let *X* count as a 'small' portion if $X \leqslant {}^1/_4a$. Then, as Anaxagoras has in effect already shown, *a* contains infinitely many large and infinitely many small portions of *S*. The large and the small portions can be matched one to one: they are, as Anaxagoras says, 'equal in quantity'. Here again, Anaxagoras shows a sophisticated grasp of the method of 'counting' infinite sets.[38]

The final sentence of **198** is no less vexing than its predecessors. A popular reading of [v] again connects 198 with Zeno. Anaxagoras is alleged to mean something like this: 'Considered in itself, *a* is great—for it contains infinitely many parts or ingredients, each of them having some finite size; but, again, *a* is small—for each of its component parts is infinitesimally small.' That is a very silly argument; and it hardly 'answers Zeno': it is silly in that neither leg contains a decent inference; and to think that '*a* is great and small' is an *answer* to Zeno is grotesque—it is a mere parroting of Zeno. We do better to follow Simplicius and read 'each (*hekaston*)' not as 'each piece of stuff' but as 'each stuff'. The sentence then merely says that there are both large and small portions of any stuff; and that unexciting fact follows from what has gone before.

202 is closely related to **198**:

> And [i] since too there are equal portions of the great and the small in quantity, for this reason too [ii] everything is in everything; [iii] nor can they exist separately (*chôris*), but [iv] everything shares a portion of everything. [v] Since the least cannot be, [vi] things cannot[39] be separated (*chôristhênai*) [vii] nor come to be by themselves (*eph 'heautou*); but [viii] as in the beginning, [ix] so too now everything is together. [x] And in all things there are many even[40] of the things that are separating off, equal in quantity in the greater and in the smaller.

The burden of **202** is the proof of [ix]; and [ix] states the third thesis, (C*), of Anaxagorean physics. The argument proceeds from (A*) via (B*) to (C*): the word 'too' in [i] marks the argument as a secondary proof; and (C*) has, of course, already been argued for.

The further proof is offered, I suggest, in order to make it quite certain that you cannot have (A*) and reject (C*); you cannot suppose that an originally commingled world is now entirely separated out. Such an argument, from past commingling to present commingling, is adverted to again in **201**; and it lies behind the statement in **203** that stuffs today 'have not been separated from one another, nor have they been cut off by an axe'.

How, in detail, does the argument run? I assume that [ii], [iii], [iv] and [ix] express, in different words, the same proposition: thesis (C*); and I assume that [vi] and [vii] are equivalent to one another. Thus **202** in effect consists of three implications: the first infers [ii] from [i]; the second infers [vi] from [v]; the third infers [ii] from [viii]. (Sentence [x], as I understand it, simply presents a special case of [ii]: 'even if *S* is separating off from other stuffs, still some portion of *S* will remain in every piece of every other stuff'.) The three implications can be moulded into a single argument: 'Given [viii], i.e. (A*), we can infer [v] and hence [i], by the argument of **198**. But from [v] or [i] it follows that [vi]; and [viii] and [vi] yield [ii].' In words: 'Since everything was originally mixed, there are no smallest portions of any stuff. Hence, no stuff can become entirely separate from all other stuffs; hence no stuff can—now or ever—be separate from all other stuffs.'

That interpretation makes a number of disputable assumptions; and it is by no means wholly satisfactory: in particular, it leaves sentence [i] with no serious work to do; for [v] is all that Anaxagoras needs. But it does have two advantages: it gives Anaxagoras a coherent-looking argument; and it ties **202** closely to **198**.

Of the three constituent implications of the argument, the first has already been discussed in connexion with **198**; and the third is an evident truth: if things *were* once *F*, and if nothing can *become* non-*F*, then things still *are F*. What, then, of the second implication? Why, if there is no smallest portion of *S*, should it be thought to follow that no object can consist of nothing but *S*? Anaxagoras implies that 'the very act of separation presupposes a smallest that can be separated'[41]; but why does he think that? Perhaps he imagines that the only way to assemble a piece of pure *S* would be to conglomerate a number of microscopical pieces of pure *S*; and those microscopical pieces could only have their purity guaranteed if they were minimal *quanta* of stuff, if they were simply too small to contain any impurities. That is a feeble argument; but I can find no better way of understanding Anaxagoras here.

My suggestions about how the main principles of Anaxagorean physics interlock have been a trifle complicated; and I shall end this section with a brief summary. Thus: amazed at the variety of material interchanges. Anaxagoras posits the hypothesis that any stuff can be extracted (by some method and through some intermediaries) from any other. The hypothesis leads to the conclusion that every stuff contains every other; and that, in turn, yields tenet (A), that 'originally all things were together', and tenet (C), that even now all things are together. Further reflexion shows, first, that matter cannot be particulate in structure; and, second, that there can be no smallest portion of any stuff, (B). Finally, the structure of the proof is strengthened by a cross-argument deriving (C) from (A) and (B).

(g) *The vortex*

At the beginning of the world, everything was in everything; now, everything is still in everything. How, then, have things changed? In what does cosmogony consist? How, indeed, can cosmogony, or any other less massive process, take place at all? If *a* is a piece of *S*, then *a* and every part of *a* is predominantly composed of *S*; no clipping or cutting, however ingenious, can scissor off a bit of *S′* from *a*. And if originally the world-mass, and all its parts, are pieces of air, how can it be that the world-mass now presents so various an appearance?

Anaxagorean cosmogony cannot consist of an *apokrisis*, or separating off, in the crude and simple sense of a cutting or chopping off of parts of the *Urstoff*: such operations will produce no differentiation. But Anaxagorean 'extraction' is not (despite the contrary hint in **203**) a 'chopping off'. Miners may hack coal or gold from the rock-face; but in Anaxagorean physics extraction is a different operation: earth 'separates off' from the *Ur*-mass of air and aether as cheese separates off from milk, or butter from cream. The churn produces cheese or butter; but it does not do so by picking bits of cheese and butter from the milky liquid. Extraction is, to put it roughly and anachronistically, a chemical and not a mechanical operation: just as every piece of stuff is a chemical union and not a mechanical juxtaposition, so every change in stuffs is a chemical reaction and not a mechanical locomotion.

What is extraction? And how can it occur? No *general* account of extraction can be offered: different stuffs are extracted by different operations, and the discovery and description of such operations is an empirical, not a philosophical, chore. Thus straining will produce salt from brine; squeezing will produce water from cheese; boiling will produce jam from raspberries; and the technical sciences of biology and chemistry will gradually uncover a host of further and subtler extractive operations by which blood is produced from bread, hair from beer, nitrogen from air, copper from copper sulphate, and so on. The details are unimportant; it is the general point that matters: the general way to get a piece of S' is to start from a piece of S and extract the portion of S' which it contains. Philosophically, that is all that happens: we do not generate a new stuff, but only bring into perceptible form some portion of a pre-existent stuff; and how that operation is to be performed is not to be determined by *a priori* argument.

Yet Anaxagoras was a scientist as well as a philosopher; and he did offer some explication of extraction, though his explication remains, necessarily and properly, at a high level of generality. Part of Anaxagoras' vocabulary for 'extraction' I have already mentioned: *apokrinesthai*, *diakrinesthai, summignusthai*, etc. Here I stress the locomotive element in such terms, and set them alongside three other overtly locomotive words which Anaxagoras uses in a cosmogonical context: cosmogony begins when the *Ur*-mass is 'moved' (*kinein*: **B 13**); its characteristic form of locomotion is 'revolution' (*perichôrêsis*: **B 12**, etc.); and as a result of the revolution or vortex certain stuffs 'come together' (*sunchôrein*: **B 15**).[42] Science, Anaxagoras implies, can be saved if locomotion is possible: give the scientist a set of stuffs and the power to move their masses, and he will build on these slight foundations the mass of the physical world. It is worth underlining the economy, the power, the sophistication, and the relative coherence of Anaxagoras' position. As an answer to Elea, it is far from despicable: how successful it is will be discussed in a later chapter; I end this chapter with two minor questions.

First, is Anaxagoras' account of 'extraction' scientifically adequate? Can Anaxagoras really explain the phenomena of change in terms of the impoverished vocabulary and the non-particulate physics he allows himself? I suppose that the answer is: No. Certainly, Anaxagoras' Abderite successors gave a firmly negative answer to it. But the question is surely an empirical one: the world might, logically, be as Anaxagoras describes it.

The second question is this: why does Anaxagoras suppose that the primordial *Ur*-mass was an undifferentiated mixture of stuffs, wearing the external appearance of 'air and aether'? Nothing in the fragments suggests any answer to that question; and it cannot have been motivated by Eleatic worries. Here, I think, Anaxagoras is most clearly connected with his Milesian ancestry: those old Milesians offered as the simplest cosmogonical hypothesis a material monism and a uniform *Ur*-state. Anaxagoras abandons material monism; but he holds onto the second limb of the hypothesis: present differences are best explained by way of a primordial uniformity. Assume that there was a cosmogony; and that cosmogonical change had a clear point of origin. What, then, is the simplest assumption about the state of the world-stuffs at that original point? Surely, uniformity. In making these assumptions Anaxagoras proves himself a follower of the Milesians: he was attempting to salvage as many planks as possible of the old Ionian galleon from the wreck it suffered in the Eleatic tempest.[43]

XVII

The Corpuscularian Hypothesis

(a) *The origins of atomism*

'Leucippus of Abdera, a pupil of Zeno, first excogitated the discovery of the atoms' (pseudo-Galen, **67 A 5**). The attribution seems to be correct: Anaxagoras and Empedocles did not have particulate theories of matter; and Democritus, the great name in ancient atomism, was Leucippus' pupil. Leucippus is naturally praised: we are all atomists now; and we are both obliged and delighted to pay homage to the first inventor of that subtle truth.

A famous paragraph in Newton's *Opticks* states succinctly enough the elements of modern atomism: 'All these things being consider'd, it seems probable to me, that God in the Beginning form'd Matter in solid, massy, hard, impenetrable, movable Particles, of such Sizes and Figures, and in such Proportion to Space, as most conduced to the End for which he form'd them; and that these primitive Particles being Solids, are incomparably harder than any porous Bodies compounded of them; even so very hard, as never to wear or break in pieces; no ordinary Power being able to divide what God himself made one in the first Creation. While the Particles continue entire, they may compose bodies of one and the same Nature and Texture in all Ages; But should they wear away, or break in pieces, the Nature of Things depending on them, would be changed.' Those minute rondures, swimming in space, form the stuff of the world: the solid, coloured table I write on, no less than the thin invisible air I breathe, is constructed out of small and colourless corpuscles; the world at close quarters looks like the night sky—a few dots of stuff, scattered sporadically through an empty vastness. Such is modern corpuscularianism.

Against that Newtonian paragraph let us set Aristotle's description of ancient atomism. The account comes from his lost monograph on Democritus, a fragment of which Simplicius preserves:

> Democritus holds that the nature of what is eternal consists of little substances, unlimited in quantity; and to these he subjoins something else—space, unlimited in magnitude. He calls space by the names 'the void', 'nothing', 'the unlimited'; and he calls each of the substances 'things', 'massy' and 'being'. He thinks that the substances are so small that they escape our perception. There belong to them every kind of shape and every kind of form and differences in magnitude. Now from these, as from elements, he generates and combines the visible and perceptible masses.
> And they battle and are carried about in the void on account of their dissimilarity and the other differences aforesaid, and in their courses they hit upon one another and bind together with a binding that makes them touch and be next to one another but does not generate any genuinely single nature whatever out of them; for it is absolutely silly to think that two or more things could ever become one. The reason why the substances stay together with one another up to a point, he finds in the overlappings and interlockings of the bodies; for some of them are scalene, some hooked, some hollow, some convex—and they have innumerable other differences. Thus he thinks that they hold on to one another and stay together for a time, until some stronger necessity comes upon them from their surrounding, shakes them about, and scatters them apart (**213**: fr. 208 = **68 A 37**).

The connexions between Democritus and Newton are evident; and it would be absurd to deny the link between ancient and modern atomism: conceptually, there are narrow ties; historically, an unbroken (if curiously circuitous) line reaches from Leucippus to Rutherford.

Modern atomism is a scientific theory, based upon and confirmed by a mass of experimental data: if the layman does not have those data at his fingertips, the textbooks will refer him to such things as chemical isomerism and Brownian motion. We are tempted, therefore, to welcome Leucippus and Democritus as the founders of modern science.

But there is, alas, no such thing as 'modern science', and the theory I have called 'modern atomism' is a myth: Newton states only one of several very different theories which have been propounded in the last four centuries and which have claimed the name of atomism. There is no unitary atomic theory, invented by Leucippus and successively refined by later scientists; rather, there is a group of theories, loosely connected, all owing something to Leucippus but each differing in vital ways from its companions. Moreover, Newtonian atomism, if I understand aright, is *passé*; and according to the physicist Heisenberg, 'concerning the structure of matter, Plato has come much nearer to the truth than Leucippus or Democritus, in spite of the enormous success of the concept of the atom in modern science'; for 'these smallest units of matter are not physical objects in the ordinary sense; they are forms, ideas which can be expressed unambiguously only in mathematical language'.[1]

Second, by stressing the scientific and empirical aspect of modern atomic theories, we give a false show of virtue to their ancient ancestors: Leucippus and Democritus had not observed Brownian motion; they were largely ignorant of chemistry; they did not rest their atomism on a host of special observations. Their theory was indeed a scientific one, in the old Ionian fashion; it was not a myth, nor an abstract philosophy. But its foundations, unlike the foundations of modern atomisms, were solidly philosophical: if we treat Leucippus as a Presocratic Dalton we shall miss the characteristic touches to his theory.

In short, a naively panegyrical attitude to ancient atomism distorts both the subject and its history. In this chapter I shall gaze at Leucippus and Democritus through antique blinkers: if they restrict the scope of my vision, they may enhance its accuracy.

The first thing to do is to forget the word 'atomism': the Abderite theory[2] was undeniably atomistic; but to label it atomism gives, I think, a misleading prominence to the notion of atomicity or indivisibility. The fragments of Democritus do indeed use the adjective '*atomos* (uncuttable)', in the neuter phrase '*ta atoma* (sc. *sômata*)', 'the uncuttable [bodies]' (**68 B 9**; **B 125**); and the doxography uses '*hê atomos* (sc. *ousia*)', 'the uncuttable [being]' (**68 B 141**; cf. **B 167**; Plutarch, **A 57**). But alongside that overtly atomic vocabulary stand other terms: Democritus is said to have referred to the atoms by the word '*phusis*' (**68 B 168**)[3]; Aristotle, an opponent of atomism who devoted much attention to the views of Leucippus and Democritus, regularly uses the words '*to plêres* (the full)' and '*to stereon* (the solid)' to designate the Atomists' material principle (cf. especially *Met* 985b4–22 = **67 A 6**); and in his monograph on Democritus, he says that Democritus calls each of the substances [*ousiai*, i.e. the atoms] 'thing (*den*)', and 'massy (*naston*)' and 'being (*on*)' (**213**).

That last report implies that *den, naston* and *on* were Democritus' preferred ways of referring to his substances; and I see no reason to doubt the implication. Indeed, it is tempting to suppose that the term *on* ('being') gives the starting point of Abderite theorizing: the fundamental designation of the Atomists' substances was, trivially enough, *onta*. Abdera, like Elea, embarked upon an inquiry into *onta* and their attributes: the discipline at Abdera was the study of *onta*, of beings *qua* being. Atomism, in its ancient form, begins with metaphysics.

And Abdera follows Elea in thesis as well as in discipline. The first property of Abderite *onta* is solidity: whatever is is *naston*, *stereon*, *plêres*. The thesis is starkly Melissan (above, pp. 223–8). The Abderites may indeed have adopted a Melissan style of argumentation for the principle that *onta* are solid; but our sources ascribe neither that argument nor any other to the Atomists, and it may be that they took solidity as a self-evident property of substances: beings, in the primary sense, are plainly bodies;[4] and bodies are plainly solid.

Solid, the Abderites' substances are also eternal, *aïdion* (**213**); they are ungenerable (cf. Plutarch, **68 A 57**) and indestructible (Dionysius, **A 43**). The thesis is Eleatic, and the doxographers duly offer Democritus the old Eleatic argument, 'nothing comes into being from what is not or is destroyed into what is not' (Diogenes Laertius, IX. 44 = **68 A 1**); Plutarch indeed ascribes the pseudo-Parmenidean dilemma to him (**68 A 57**). But that argument is not easily embraced by a man who happily concedes the being of 'what is not';[5] and 'Leucippus thought he had arguments which, by stating what was in agreement with the senses, would not do away with generation or destruction' (Aristotle, *GC* 325a23–5 = **67 A 7**). Leucippus wanted to preserve generation and destruction, in some cases at least; he cannot therefore have indulged in the Eleatic argument, and he must have found an argument against the generation and destruction of atoms which would not do away with generation and destruction as such.

Aristotle presents a different argument:

> As for time, with one exception [i.e. Plato] everyone is clearly in agreement; for they say that it is ungenerated. And in this way Democritus proves that it is impossible for everything to have been generated—for time is ungenerated (**214**: *Phys* 251b14–17 = **68 A 71**).

Simplicius says that Democritus took the ungenerability of time as self-evident (**68 A 71**); but what did that self-evident axiom prove? Did Democritus merely and trivially urge that since time is ungenerated, then at least one thing, viz. time, is ungenerated? or did he, more interestingly, urge that some substances at least must be ungenerated, since at any moment in time there must exist some substances, 'empty' time being an absurdity? The interesting argument is, alas, invalid; and in any case, neither the trivial nor the interesting version will show that all substances are ungenerated.

In the absence of a satisfying tradition we are tempted to invent; and an argument for substantial eternity can be cooked up: I shall postpone the concoction for a few pages.

Solid and eternal, Abderite substances are also immutable:

> The atoms do not suffer (*paschein*) or change, by reason of their solidity (**215**: Plutarch, **68 A** 57);

they are 'impassive (*apathês*) because of their being massy and having no share in the void' (**217**: Simplicius, 67 **A** 14).[6] 'Impassivity' is unalterability: a body is *apathês* if any features it ever has it always has. Impassivity, again, is an Eleatic property; but the Abderites did not use an Eleatic argument to establish it. Instead they argued that solidity rules out mutability. Why should that be so? Why may a solid body not change its colour or its temperature? Why cannot an atom grow wet or become smooth? The questions require a detour.

(b) *Atoms characterized*

I turn now to the property *par excellence*, the eponymous property, of Abderite substances: atomicity. Atoms are indivisible, uncuttable, unsplittable; they are the ultimate and unanalysable bits out of which the material world is constructed. That Abderite property is no more an Abderite invention than solidity, ungenerability or immutability: Eleatic entities, whether Parmenidean or Melissan, do not divide. It is not easy to disentangle what the Eleatics said about division; but it is clear enough that the first atoms came from Elea.[7]

If the atomic thesis is Eleatic, the arguments by which Leucippus and Democritus supported it were fresh. I begin with a perforated quotation from Simplicius; the holes will be made good later:

> Those who rejected unlimited cutting, on the grounds that we cannot cut without limit and thus gain evidence for the incompletability of the cutting, said that bodies consist of indivisibles and are divided into indivisibles—except that Leucippus and Democritus think that not only their impassivity, but also their smallness . . . explains why the primary bodies are not divided, whereas Epicurus . . . says that they are atoms because of their impassivity (**216: 67 A 13**).

In another passage Simplicius says of Leucippus, Democritus and Epicurus that

> they thought that [the principles] are atomic and indivisible and impassive because of their being massy and having no share in the void; for they said that division comes about by virtue of the void in bodies (**217**: **67 A 14**).

In the same mood, Dionysius says of Epicurus and Democritus that 'both say they are atoms, and are called so, because of their indissoluble solidity' (**68 A 43**).

These passages appear to contain four distinct arguments: (A) We cannot cut bodies infinitely often (**216**); (B) the primary bodies are impassive (**216**); (C) the primary bodies are solid (**217**; **68 A 43**); (D) the primary bodies are small (**216**). All four arguments are explicitly ascribed both to Leucippus and to Democritus;[8] and there is no reason why they should not have advanced more than one argument in favour of indivisibility.

I begin with argument (D), which according to Simplicius was not adopted by Epicurus. Epicurean atoms were all very small—indeed imperceptibly so (*ad Hdt* §§55–6), and the same is regularly said of Democritus' substances: according to Aristotle, 'he thinks that the substances are so small that they escape our perception' (**213**); But there are three curious passages to the contrary: according to Diogenes,

> the atoms are unlimited in magnitude and quantity (**218**: IX. 44 = **68 A 1**):

and the most plausible gloss of that text gives Democritus atoms of every size. Again, Dionysius contrasts Epicurus with Democritus on precisely this issue:

> They differ to the extent that the one [sc. Epicurus] thought that they are all very small and for that reason imperceptible, while Democritus held that some atoms were actually very large (**219**: **68 A 43**).

Finally, Aëtius avers that in Democritus' view

> it is possible for there to be an atom the size of the universe (**220**: **68 A 47**).

Epicurus attacks the view that 'every size exists among the atoms';

for were it true, then 'some atoms would be bound to reach us and be visible—but that is not seen to happen, nor can we conceive how an atom might become visible' (*ad Hdt* §§55–6). It is natural to suppose that Epicurus is attacking a real target; and Democritus is the obvious candidate.[9] On that assumption Epicurus' text yields a nicer message: if Democritus both allowed that some atoms could be visible and also denied that we ever perceive any, that would account for Epicurus' two objections: that visible atoms are simply inconceivable, and that if there could be such things they would be sure to have come to our notice.

Suppose, then, that Democritus said something like this: 'The primary bodies are not essentially small: as far as logic goes, there may be atoms of a cosmic size. As far as science goes, there must be a variety of atomic sizes. As far as experience goes, it seems that all the primary bodies in our part of the universe are too small to be perceived.' That view is self-consistent; and it accommodates, more or less, all the superficially irreconcilable evidence we possess. It carries an important consequence: smallness is at best a contingent property of the primary bodies; it is not a feature of *onta qua onta* that they are imperceptible. Simple observation suggests that all macroscopic objects, even the most durable, can be smashed, split, broken, crushed or whittled away in the course of all-devouring time. Since the primary bodies are unsplittable, and macroscopic things split and dissolve, the primary bodies are microscopic. The argument is healthy; and it is *a posteriori*.

What of argument (D)? Democritus may have said something like this: 'The primary bodies are in fact very small; so small, indeed, that they defeat the finest blade of the sharpest knife; and hence they are indivisible.' The argument is naive: we are not impressed by the hypothetical suggestion that if Democritus cannot get his pocket-knife into an atom, atoms cannot be split. And if, as I imagined, Democritus argued that atoms must be small because they are unsplittable, he can hardly also urge their atomicity on the grounds of their minuscule size.

Argument (B) is curious. It occurs only in **216**, where Simplicius ascribes it to Epicurus, as well as to the Abderites. Now Epicurus' surviving argument for indivisibility goes thus: 'These are atomic and changeless . . . being full in their nature, not having any way or means by which they will be dissolved' (*ad Hdt* §§41). The passage presents argument (C); and it explains the reports of Dionysius in **68 A 43** and of Simplicius in **217**. It puts impassivity on a par with indivisibility; and that seems to be its proper place: how then, can impassivity ground indivisibility? Argument (B) is found only in **216** and it is intrinsically implausible: I wonder if Simplicius is not using '*apatheia*' loosely here; perhaps it denotes solidity and 'argument (B)' is merely a ghost of argument (C). At all events, if that suggestion is rejected, then in **216** Simplicius ascribes to Epicurus as his sole argument for indivisibility a train of reasoning found nowhere else; and he ignores a genuinely Epicurean argument which elsewhere he shows himself perfectly familiar with.

Argument (C) rests on the firm Abderite thesis of solidity: atoms are indivisible because they are solid, i.e. because they contain no void; and solidity precludes division because division must occur 'in virtue of the void'. I take it that we have here a physical, not a metaphysical, hypothesis: in order to split an object we must be able to get a knife between its parts and prise them away from one another; but in a solid body there is no vacant gap, however narrow, into which the knife-blade might be inserted. We can only cut along the dotted line; and solid bodies offer no vacancies or dots. Solidity does not logically imply indivisibility; but the physical process of division requires a porous body to work upon.

An objection arises: take two atoms and juxtapose them so that there is no void in the interstices between them; then by the argument I have just offered they cannot be parted; yet on atomist principles any two atoms may be conjoined and parted. I guess that Leucippus anticipated that reflexion: Aristotle says that Leucippan atoms may 'touch', *haptesthai* (*GC* 325a33 = **67 A 7**); Philoponus offers the following gloss:

> Democritus does not use the word 'touch' strictly when he says that atoms touch one another; . . . but he talked of touch when the atoms are near one another and not far away—for they are in any event separated by void (**221: 67 A 7**—the same view is ascribed to Leucippus, ibid.)

Between any two atoms there is always a void; hence they can never conjointly form a solid molecule, and they can always be separated (cf. Alexander, **68 A 64**).

In the same passage of the *GC* Aristotle reports that:

> From what is truly one, a plurality (*plêthos*) could never come about, nor one from what are truly plural; but that is impossible (**222**: 325a35–6 = **67 A 7**; cf. **213**; *Cael* 303a6).

The second part of the doctrine will prove important later; here my concern is with its first part: 'no plurality from a unity'.

It is possible that Aristotle is merely elaborating upon argument (C): units are solid; hence they cannot be split; hence they cannot yield a plurality. But the *Metaphysics* suggests a more sophisticated view:

> If a substance is a unit, it cannot consist of inherent substances in this way, as[10] Democritus rightly says; for he says that it is impossible for one thing to come from two or two from one (for he makes the atomic magnitudes his substances) (**223**: 1039a7–11 = **68 A 42**).

The argument is this: 'Democritus' bodies are substances; substances are units, i.e. not aggregates; hence no substance can split into two or more substances; hence no Democritean body can split'. That genuine substances cannot be aggregates is a Democritean view, and it has had many adherents (see below, p. 445). Yet if a substance cannot *be* an aggregate, may it not *become* one? why cannot a unit split up and become a plurality? Aristotle's text suggests that if *b* and *c* 'come from' *a* at *t*, then prior to *t* they must have conjointly constituted *a*, so that *a* consisted of 'inherent substances' and was an aggregate. Why should that be so? Well, neither *b* nor *c* can be identical with *a*; since each is, by hypothesis, a part of *a*. But in that case either *a* ceases to exist at *t* (which is impossible, since substances are eternal), or else *a* was all along the aggregate of *b* and *c* (and hence not a primary substance). In short, substances are unitary and eternal; hence they cannot split.

That account provides a philosophical argument for indivisibility; and one of some power. If I hesitate to put it alongside (A)—(D) and ascribe it to Democritus himself, that is because no source outside the *Metaphysics* knows it. Probably, it is a genial Aristotelian development of Democritean views; but it is, at worst, a development fully in the spirit of atomism.

I have left argument (A) to last; it too appears only once in our sources, and perhaps it is an invention by Simplicius. It is, however, worth a brief exposition. If I read it aright, it goes thus: 'We cannot actually divide any body into infinitely many parts; hence we can never have reason to believe that bodies are infinitely divisible; hence we should believe that bodies are not infinitely divisible.' We cannot have evidence for the falsity of atomism: we therefore have reason to believe it true.

The principle behind the argument is this: if we cannot have evidence that not-*P*, we should believe that *P*. In a weaker form (if we do not have evidence that not-*P*, we should believe that *P*) the principle has supported any number of bad arguments. Why the principle is popular I do not care to guess; that it is false is evident: if I have no evidence for not-*P*, I may also have no evidence for *P*; and in most cases it is irrational to believe that *P* without having evidence for *P*. Moreover, the application of the bad principle to atomism requires the use of a second bad principle. For in asserting that because we can never actually cut up a body infinitely often, we can have no evidence for infinite divisibility, the Atomists appear to assume that we have no evidence that *P* is true unless we possess knowledge that entails *P*. And that is absurd.

Thus argument (A) is both ill-attested and disreputable. Yet it has two points of mild interest. First, it is the earliest example of a perennially seductive mode of argumentation. Second, it introduces a different problem from those dealt with by arguments (C)—(D): they argue that substances are indivisible; it argues that there are indivisible substances. It is one thing to show that no substance can be divided, another to prove that there exist indivisible substances. The former task is futile unless the latter has been successfully undertaken (what scientist cares for a proof that unicorns have only one horn?); and, if we disregard argument (A), the Atomists have not yet attempted the latter task. The question will arise again.

It is fair to say, I think, that solidity supplies the chief argument for the eponymous atomicity of Abderite substances. Atomicity is not inferred *a priori* from solidity: the inference rests upon a physical thesis about the nature of splitting. Impassivity or immutability also depend on solidity. I suggest that here again we must supply a physical hypothesis as the link in the logical chain: alteration was deemed by the atomists to involve either the splitting or the combining of atoms; a cubic atom, say, could only become spherical if bits were chipped off or added to it (or both); an atom could only grow or diminish by the addition or the loss of bits of stuff. (And those, as we shall see, are the only intrinsic changes an atom could possibly undergo.) But a solid atom cannot have bits chipped from it; and an atom with bits conjoined to it will never constitute a solid body. That may, I suppose, be Aristotle's meaning when he says:

> It is necessary to say that each of the indivisibles is impassive, for it cannot 'suffer' except through the void (**224**: *GC* 326a1–3).

It is tempting to find a similar connexion between solidity and ungenerability (cf. Plutarch, **68 A 57**). The generation of macroscopic objects, according to the Atomists, consists merely in the rearrangement of particles at the microscopic level. Did they reject microscopic or atomic generation on the basis of a similar thesis? An atom *a* could only be generated in virtue of some rearrangement of sub-atomic particles; but such a mode of generation is impossible: were *a* compounded from sub-atomic fragments, it would not be solid; and were there sub-atomic parts, they could only have been produced by the shattering of an atom. Since atoms are solid, they cannot have been put together; and such a putting together is the only sort of generation not evidently outlawed by Eleatic logic.

My discussion has rambled; and it may be convenient to provide a summary before advancing any further. The Atomists asked themselves what were the properties of *onta qua onta*; and (as I have surreptitiously presupposed) they were concerned with *onta* of the primary sort, with *ousiai* or substances.

Every substance, they argued, was *unitary* (not an aggregate) and *solid*. What is solid is, by a physical necessity, *indivisible* or atomic; and what is unitary is indivisible by logical necessity. What is solid is, again by physical necessity, *eternal* (or ungenerable and indestructible); and also *immutable* or impassive. Primary substances are bodies, solid and unitary; they are physically indivisible, they endure for ever; and they are subject to no change. That, I think, constitutes the basic account of the Abderite theory. We may now proceed to its further elaboration.

(c) *Fractured atoms?*

Atoms, though indivisible, may have parts: we may not be able, physically, to split an atom; but we can, theoretically, divide it into notional parts: 'the half nearer to *b*', 'the part with the point on', and so on. And if we take a large Democritean atom we may even be able to measure it, to mark it into parts, to draw a design upon it; the only thing we cannot do is cut it along our marks or carve it to the drawn design. The doxographers say nothing about the notional parts of Abderite atoms; but both Alexander (*in Met* 36. 25–7) and Simplicius (*in Phys* 82. 1–3) mention them casually.

Epicurus said more about sub-atomic particles (*ad Hdt* §§58–9). His views are controversial;[11] but an orthodox interpretation runs thus: every atom is theoretically, but not of course physically, divisible; but just as physical splitting eventually reaches atoms or physical indivisibles, so too theoretical division ultimately reaches *minima* or theoretical indivisibles; and an atom is thus composed of a finite set of theoretically indivisible *minima*, conjoined by a physically indissoluble bond. Epicurus is a second-hand thinker; and it is proper to wonder if his theory was not taken from Democritus, along with the other trappings of atomism. Alexander implies that it was:

> [Leucippus and Democritus] do not say whence the weight in the

> atoms comes; for the partless items (*ta amerê*) conceptually present in (*epinooumena*) the atoms and parts of them are, they say, weightless: but how could weight come about from weightless components? (**225**: *in Met* 36.25–7).

I shall return to the issue of weight in a later section. Here I am concerned only with Alexander's assertion that the Abderite atoms have conceptually distinguishable parts which are themselves conceptually partless. That is precisely Epicurus' view.

Few scholars believe Alexander, imagining that he is, carelessly or deliberately, projecting back onto the Abderites a theory he found in Epicurus. And it is observed that Aristotle nowhere distinguishes between atomic and sub-atomic indivisibles in his many discussions of Abdera, even though in one or two passages (e.g., *Cael* 303a21) he could hardly have failed to mention the distinction had he known it. Arguments *e silentio Aristotelis* are not conclusive; and Democritus may, I suppose, have advanced the Epicurean theory in an inconspicuous or informal fashion; but I doubt it, and I shall proceed on the assumption that Alexander's report is in error.[12]

A somewhat subtler suggestion now presents itself. Suppose that Democritus had held his substances to be both physically and theoretically indivisible; then Epicurus is still a follower, but not a slavish adherent: he retains both varieties of indivisibility in his theory, but attaches them to different objects. Where Democritus asserted that atoms were both physically and theoretically indivisible, Epicurus maintained that atoms were physically indivisible, their minimal parts theoretically indivisible. Democritus does not allow sub-atomic particles, notionally distinguishable within the atom: his atoms have no parts at all—neither by the axe nor by the mind can you splinter them.

Are Democritean atoms theoretically indivisible? Some scholars think that they are, arguing thus: 'The Abderites were concerned, *inter alia*, to answer Zeno's dichotomy arguments; only theoretically indivisible atoms will give them an answer. Hence they ought to have embraced theoretical indivisibility. Moreover, several ancient texts in fact support the attribution of theoretical indivisibility to the Abderite atoms.' I shall first set this argument out in more detail, exhibiting the texts on which it is based, and then offer some critical comments.

At *Physics* 187a1 Aristotle reports thus:

> Some surrendered to both arguments—to the one concluding that everything is one (if being signifies one thing) by saying that what

> is not is; to the one from the dichotomy, by positing indivisible magnitudes (**226**).

Plainly 'some' refers to the Atomists;[13] for only the Atomists *both* said that 'what is not is' *and* posited 'indivisible magnitudes'. It is the second move that we are concerned with here: Aristotle represents atomism as an answer to Zeno's dichotomy argument.

The brief notice in the *Physics* is expanded in the *de Generatione*:

> One can see from this too the great difference between those who study scientifically (*phusikôs*) and those who study dialectically (*logikôs*). For on the question of atomic magnitudes, some [i.e. the Platonists] say that the triangle itself will be many [sc. if there are no atomic magnitudes], but Democritus would seem to have been persuaded by appropriate and scientific arguments. What we mean will become clear as we proceed (**227**: *GC* 316a10–14).

There follows an involved argument, of Zenonian flavour, which I have already mentioned (above, p. 247). I summarize it as follows: 'Suppose a magnitude is infinitely divisible, and that such a division is possible. Carry it out: what are you left with? Not a magnitude; for then you have not carried out the division. Not nothing; for bodies are not compounded of nothing. Not points; for points cannot constitute a magnitude. It won't do to suppose that the process of dividing produced some quantity of sawdust; for the same questions apply to that. Nor can you say that the division separates qualities from underlying points or contacts' (*GC* 316a15–b19 = **68 A 48b**). Aristotle then offers to 'restate' the puzzles (316b20–8), and concludes with the following paragraph:

> But that it divides into magnitudes that are separable and always smaller and apart and separated, is evident. Now if you divide part by part the breaking will not be unlimited, nor can it be divided at every point at the same time (for that is not possible), but only to a certain point. Necessarily, then, invisible atomic magnitudes inhere in it, particularly if generation and destruction is to come about by dissociation and association. This, then, is the argument that seems to necessitate the existence of atomic magnitudes (**228**: *GC* 316b28–317a2).

The *GC* expands the brief aside of the *Physics*: Zenonian anxiety causes the spots of atomism.

Four passages, or groups of passages, support the inference drawn from the *GC*. First, in a passage I mangled earlier, Simplicius says:

> . . . except that Leucippus and Democritus think that not only their impassivity but also their smallness and their partlessness explains why the primary bodies are not divided, whereas Epicurus later does not regard them as partless but says that they are atoms because of their impassivity (**229: 67 A 13**—cf. **216**).

By 'partlessness (*to ameres*)' Simplicius clearly intends theoretical indivisibility;[14] otherwise the contrast with Epicurus is nonsensical.

Second, a scholiast on Euclid X.1 reports:

> That there is no smallest magnitude, as the Democriteans say, is proved by this theorem, that it is possible to take a magnitude less than any given magnitude (**230: 68 A 48a**).

The report is iterated by Simplicius (*in Cael* 202.27–31).

Third, the passage in the *de Caelo* on which Simplicius thus comments illustrates the catastrophic results of a small initial error:

> E.g. if someone were to say that there is a smallest magnitude; for he, by introducing a smallest, overthrows the greatest part of mathematics (**231**: 271a9–11).

The same accusation is levelled later against Leucippus and Democritus:

> Again, it is necessary that those who talk of atomic bodies clash with the mathematical sciences, and do away with many reputable opinions and data of perception, about which we have spoken in our remarks on time and motion (**232**: 303a20–4).[15]

Atomism clashes with mathematics only if atoms are theoretically or mathematically indivisible.

Finally, there is a strange passage in Plutarch usually supposed to quote Democritus' own words:

> If a cone is cut by its base in a plane, what should one think of the surfaces of the segments—are they equal or unequal? For if they are unequal, they will make the cone uneven, with a lot of step-like corrugations and roughnesses; and if they are equal, the segments will be equal and the cone will evidently have suffered the fate of a cylinder, being constructed from equal and not unequal circles—which is utterly absurd (**233: B 155**).

The fragment connects with a further passage in the *de Caelo* (307a17 = **B 155a**) which appears to ascribe to Democritus the view that a sphere has angles, i.e. is a polyhedron. Why should a cone be corrugated and a sphere polyhedral? The only explanation is that geometrical solids are composed of theoretically indivisible parts.

So much for the texts on which theoretical indivisibility is founded. Before examining them it will be prudent to ask just what thesis they are supposed to maintain: what does it mean to say that atoms are 'theoretically' indivisible?

First, the thesis might be that atoms are *conceptually* indivisible: we cannot conceive or think of anything smaller than an atom. Conception is treated as a form of imagining; and the thesis amounts to saying that there is a lower limit to our powers of imagination: just as there is a threshold to our physical eye, so there is a threshold to our inner eye. Some things are too small to be seen; others would be too small to be imagined or conceived. That, if I understand him, is Epicurus' notion of theoretical indivisibility (*ad Hdt* §§58–9); and it was revived by Hume. It is a wretched muddle; for it confounds thinking or conceiving with the forming of mental images; and it supposes that to imagine a small object is to form a small image. But I shall not attempt to tease out all the horrible confusions it contains.

Second, the thesis might mean that atoms are *geometrically* indivisible: the volume occupied by an atom has no mathematically distinguishable parts; there is no quantity designated by such phrases as 'half the volume of an atom', 'two thirds the volume of an atom', and so on. 'But surely,' it is said, 'Democritean atoms are magnitudes, *megethê*, and not points (like the atoms of Boscovich); but all magnitudes (in Euclidean geometry at least) are divisible: hence those atoms are not geometrically indivisible— Democritus was "too good a mathematician" to maintain any such view.'[16] But we know that Plato and Xenocrates both entertained a theory of geometrically indivisible magnitudes (above, p. 245), and we may not deny on *a priori* grounds that Democritus anticipated them. There is no *geometrical* error in abandoning the continuous space of Euclidean thought and substituting a granular space; and the theory that atoms are geometrically indivisible is the theory that the geometry of space is granular, that space is made up of minimal volumes.

Finally, the thesis of theoretical indivisibility might mean that atoms are *logically* indivisible: the notion of a sub-atomic body is self-contradictory. There is a trivial sense in which atoms are logically indivisible; for 'atomic' *means* 'indivisible', so that '*a* is an atom and *a* is divisible' is a simple contradiction. But that trivial thesis is not what the supporters of 'theoretical' indivisibility have in mind; for it states only that, as a matter of logic, physically atomic bodies are physically indivisible. Rather, supporters of 'theoretical' indivisibility maintain, on this interpretation, that if *a* is an atom, then it is logically impossible to divide *a*. And that thesis is not a trivial truth: it asserts that atomicity is an essential trait of atoms, much as being even (say) is an essential trait of the number 2.

Theoretical indivisibility is not a unitary thing: which sort of indivisibility, if any, is suggested by the texts I have referred to?

233 is, I think, entirely inconclusive. It presents a dilemma, and the dilemma is based on the supposition of an atomist geometry. 'Take a cone of *n* atomic lengths from base to apex, and divide it into *n* segments. Consider the top surface of segment *i*, and the bottom surface of segment *i* + 1: if the former is greater than the latter, the cone will be corrugated or stepped, like a ziggurat; if the two surfaces are of the same area, the solid will be cylindrical.' Such a reconstruction makes sense of **233** and provides a genuine dilemma. And we may safely infer that Democritus had envisaged the possibility of a non-continuous geometry. Some scholars think that Democritus accepted the first horn of the dilemma: cones are indeed ziggurats; and they infer that Democritus embraced geometrical *minima*. Others think that the dilemma was intended rather as a *reductio ad absurdum* of the notion of such *minima*. We cannot tell: each interpretation is plausible, neither can be favoured.[17]

B 155a is more to the point: if a sphere has angles, then surely that can only be because its surface is composed of minimal planes. But apparently Democritus said not that a sphere 'has angles' but that it 'is an angle (*gônia*)'; and Simplicius offers the following explanation:

> The spherical whole is an angle (*gônia*); for if what is bent (*sunkekammenon*) is an angle, and a sphere is bent at every point on its surface (*kath' holên heautên*), then it is reasonably called a whole angle (*holê gônia*) (**234: B 155a**).

Geometers who talk of 'straight angles'—angles of 180°—do not suppose that straight lines are really bent: Democritus' phrase 'whole angle' need not imply that spheres are really polyhedrons.[18]

Next I turn to *de Caelo* 303a21 and the clash between atomism and mathematics. Surely, the physical indivisibility of atoms cannot pose any problems for mathematics; if there is a clash, it can only be caused by a mathematical indivisibility? The answer is not as simple as it seems; for the question at issue is not whether physical indivisibility conflicts with mathematics, but rather whether Aristotle would have deemed such a conflict to exist. And I think that he would have done: in the *Physics* he argues that since the universe is finite in extent, there are no infinite magnitudes for the geometers to reason about (207b15–21); and he excuses himself by saying that the geometers can get by if they are allowed to divide an object at any point (207b27–34). Geometry, for Aristotle, is essentially an applied science: it talks about lines and planes in the physical world, idealizing them, but for all that treating of them and not of objects of a more aetherial nature. Geometers assume that their subject matter is continuous or divisible at any point; but their subject matter, in Aristotle's view, is the physical world; consequently, the geometers will be at odds with any theory of *physical* indivisibles. If that is so, the *de Caelo* does not provide evidence that Democritean atoms are theoretically indivisible: Aristotle's criticism of atomism, given his own views on the nature of geometry, is compatible with the assumption that he ascribed only physical indivisibility to the Atomists.[19]

Simplicius, *in Cael* 202.27–31, and the scholiast on Euclid depend on the *de Caelo*; and their statements give no independent evidence for mathematical atomism. In **229**, on the other hand, Simplicius is not simply drawing on Aristotle; and there he must be using 'partless (*amerês*)' in the sense of 'theoretically indivisible'. Now Simplicius' ascription of 'partlessness' to the atoms is singular; and I am inclined to think that it is an inference of Simplicius' own.[20] '*Amerês*', I suggest, is Simplicius' gloss on '*smikros* (small)': wanting to explain the inference from smallness to indivisibility; believing (on the basis of the *de Caelo*) that the Atomists' corpuscles were geometrical *minima*; and observing that, unlike Epicurus, the two founders of atomism did not say anything about the 'parts' of their atoms, he understandably inferred that '*smikros*' in their argument connoted theoretical indivisibility. We need not accept Simplicius' inference; and **229** drops from the controversy.

All depends, then, on the Aristotelian view that Atomism grew from a reflexion upon, or a surrender to, Zeno's dichotomy argument. How much of the long argument, or set of arguments, in the *GC* we can safely ascribe to Democritus I do not know: Aristotle speaks tentatively—'Democritus would appear to have been persuaded'—and the passage which I summarized is certainly Aristotle's in form even if it is not so in substance.[21] In any case, I do not see that the argument says anything about 'theoretical' divisibility: Aristotle praises Democritus for arguing *phusikôs*, and that should mean something like 'with a close eye on the relevant scientific facts'—facts, presumably, about physical division. The argument is expressly designed to refute the hypothesis that 'a body is divisible throughout, and that is possible' (316a16): I take that to mean 'bodies are physically divisible through and through, and you can actually effect the division'; for the curious *addendum* 'and that is possible' is otiose unless we read it as meaning 'and you can actually effect the division'. Moreover, the argument speaks of actually dividing a 'body or magnitude', and it refers, only half-jestingly, to the possibility that the process of division may generate a sort of sawdust. All that, and the very language of the argument, suggest a physical and not a notional division. In sum, as I read the passage from the *GC*, it has Democritus reply to the Zenonian argument by positing physically indivisible atoms.

We are left with *Physics* 187a1. Can a physical atomism be represented as a surrender to Zeno's dichotomy? Plainly, if we develop the argument of **29 B 1–2**, we can produce a position which cannot be answered or evaded by positing a physical atomism; certainly, no one who is gripped by the hideous claws of Zeno's logic will think highly of a scientist who simply shrugs his shoulders and says, 'Well, then, I suppose matter is composed of physically indivisible atoms'. But for all that, we can, I think, make sense of Democritus' 'surrender to the dichotomy' without introducing notionally indivisible particles—and that in either of two ways. First we might suppose that Democritus read Zeno's Dichotomy and took it at its face value, as an argument about physical division; had he done so, he would have been justified, if intellectually unadventurous, in asserting physical atomism and getting on with his scientific work. For as Zeno states it, the paradox is adequately solved by physical atomism (see above, p. 245). It is only when we reflect upon that solution, and attempt to reconstruct the paradox in its face, that we develop an argument impervious to physical atomism. And there is no reason to ascribe such reflexion to Democritus. Second, and more easily, we may construe *Physics* 187a1 in the light of the argument in the *GC*: when Aristotle says that Democritus gave in to 'the argument from the dichotomy' he need not have any precise Zenonian argument in mind; the term 'dichotomy' was certainly used later to refer to any argument of that Zenonian type—any argument turning on considerations of infinite divisibility —and it seems to me most probable that the argument to which, in Aristotle's opinion, Democritus 'surrendered' was none other than the quasi-Zenonian concoction in the *GC*. Thus if the *GC* does not drive us to mathematical atomism neither does the *Physics*.

I conclude that the evidence does not oblige us to make the Atomists' corpuscles theoretically indivisible; the verdict must be *non liquet*. But the investigation of theoretical indivisibility is not wholly negative in its results: I do not want to claim that Aristotle's account in the *GC* has no historical value; on the contrary, I suppose that it gives us the answer to the outstanding question of atomism: Why imagine that there are any physical *minima* in the material world?

Leucippus and Democritus, reflecting in a vaguely Zenonian fashion on physical division, urged that unless macroscopic bodies were ultimately composed of indivisible corpuscles, the material world would fall apart into insubstantial points or bare nothings. When asked to explain what feature of these hypothetical corpuscles could account for their indivisibility and prevent their dissolution, they produced a plausible physical answer: substances are solid, and what is solid cannot be divided. The dichotomy argument assures us that there *are* indivisible corpuscles; further considerations, which I have already rehearsed, explain *why* those corpuscles are indivisible.

Unfortunately, the Atomists mishandle the dichotomy argument. I shall not expose their errors; for my remarks on Zeno have implicitly indicated them. But it is worth noting one fallacy in their reasoning: consideration of what would happen if everything were actually divided through and through leads them to infer that:
(1) It cannot be the case that everything has been divided.
From (1) they conclude to atomism, or:
(2) There are some things which cannot be divided.
From a proposition of the form '$\sim \Diamond (\forall x) \phi x$' they infer the corresponding proposition of the form '$(\exists x) \sim \Diamond \phi x$'. The invalidity of the inference, which is hidden in the dowdy garb of ordinary language, shows up clearly when it is more formally dressed. Zenonian considerations will only lead to atomism by way of a fallacy.

(d) *Bodies without number*

There are infinitely many atoms. Simplicius has an interesting report:

> Thus they reasonably promised that, if their principles were unlimited, they would account for all affections and substances and explain under what agency and how anything comes into being; and for that reason they say that only for those who make the elements unlimited does everything turn out in accordance with reason (**235: 68 A 38**).

Observe the character of that argument: only if the atoms are infinite can the phenomena be explained; only an infinity of principles can account for the variety and vacillations we observe among macroscopic substances and their affections. The attitude evinced in such an argument is resolutely un-Eleatic; to Melissus, the phenomena required no explanation: reason, by dictating a rigid monism, revealed the plural world of sense-perception as a false imagining of the jaded mind. In the north of Greece they had a robuster sense of reality: the things we see and touch cannot be mere fictions; monism must be mistaken, and the plural phenomena require an explanation.

Yet Simplicius' argument will not do as it stands: perhaps an infinity of atoms is sufficient to explain the diversity of phenomena. But is it necessary? Or can any other arguments lead us to postulate an infinity? In fact three further lines of thought have been discerned. First, the Atomists believed that there was an infinite variety of atomic shapes; and that belief immediately entails an infinity of atoms. I shall return shortly to the question of atomic shapes: here I note only that the easy inference from shape to quantity is nowhere ascribed to the Atomists in our sources.

Second, Simplicius says that

> [Leucippus] hypothesized unlimitedly many eternally moving elements—the atoms—and the unlimited quantity of the shapes among them because nothing is rather such than such, and as he observed unremitting generation and change in existent things (**236**: **67 A 8**).

Did the observation of 'unremitting generation and change' ground the numerical infinity of the atoms? and does Simplicius ascribe to Leucippus the argument elsewhere ascribed to Anaximander (see above, p. 30) that eternal generation requires an infinite fund of matter or material particles? I do not think so: as I read Simplicius' text, the observation of 'unremitting generation and change' was adduced to establish the eternal motion of the atoms rather than their numerical infinity.

The third argument infers the infinity of the atoms from the infinity of the space in which they swim. Before examining it, therefore, we might well ask why space should be deemed infinite. Our texts contain no direct answer to that question; but a celebrated argument has been adduced to fill the evidential gap.

> Archytas, according to Eudemus, put the argument thus: 'Standing at the edge (e.g. at the heaven of the fixed stars), could I extend my hand or my cane outside it or not?' That I could not extend it is absurd; but if I do extend it, then what is outside will be either body or space (**163**: Eudemus, fr. 65 W = **47 A 24**).

Lucretius took over Archytas' argument (I. 968–983); hence Epicurus used it: and if Epicurus, why not Democritus?[22]

The Archytan dilemma presupposes that every finite extension has edges; for Archytas imagines himself at the edge of the universe. That presupposition links the dilemma to an argument which Aristotle cities as the fourth of five alleged proofs of the existence of the infinite:

> Again, what is finite is always bounded by something; so that necessarily there is no boundary, if it is always necessary for one thing to be bounded against another (**237**: *Phys* 203b20–2).

That argument too was accepted by Epicurus (*ad Hdt* §41); and it too may have originated with Democritus.[23]

Aristotle answers the argument by distinguishing between 'being bounded (*peperanthai*)' and 'touching (*haptesthai*)': what touches, he asserts, must indeed touch something else; but what is bounded need not be bounded by anything else (*Phys* 208a11–14). The answer is perplexing, and Epicurus was rightly unimpressed by it; yet for all that, Aristotle was unwittingly correct. We are all familiar with two-dimensional extensions that are finite and yet have no edges—'finite and unbounded', in the jargon of the geometers. The surface of a football is a mundane example of such an apparently paradoxical thing. Why, then, should there not be three-dimensional extensions that are finite and unbounded? finite, in that they contain no straight lines of infinite length; unbounded, in that they have no edges. If I understand the doctrine that space-time is 'curved', it implies that our familiar space has precisely those properties.

The Epicurean argument fails; and with it goes Archytas' dilemma; for the presupposition of that dilemma proves unsatisfactory: it is not true that every finite extension has edges. Yet would the dilemma work if its presupposition were true? I do not think so; for I do not see why it is 'absurd' to suppose that I simply could not extend my hand were I in Archytas' situation. Lucretius suggests that if I cannot extend my hand, then there must be something in the way, preventing the extension; but there may be something behind me (a gravitational field, say), holding me back. 'But even if you cannot, physically, extend your hand, still it is logically possible to do so.' Perhaps; but to say that it is logically possible for me to extend my hand two feet in front of me is not to say that there is a *place* two feet in front of me. And Archytas' argument is designed to show that there must be a space (occupied or unoccupied) in front of me.

So much for infinite space. How is it connected with the infinity of the atoms? Plainly, if there are infinitely many atoms, each of a minimum size, space must be infinite if it is to contain them; but if space is infinite, why must it have infinite denizens? Epicurus argued that 'if the void were infinite and the bodies finite, the bodies would not stay anywhere but would be carried about, scattered through the infinite void' (*ad Hdt* §42).[24] In short, a finite number of atoms would be dotted about in an infinite space, and no cosmogonical collisions would ever occur. But why should a finite number of atoms not simply chance to congregate in one corner of infinite space? The answer is, I think, implicit in Aristotle's *Physics*:

> If the region outside the heavens is unlimited, so too, it seems, are body and the worlds; for why should it be here rather than here in the void? Hence mass is, if anywhere, everywhere (**238**: *Phys* 203b25–8).

Aristotle's ancient commentators ascribed this argument to Democritus, and modern scholars accept their judgment;[25] for the argument relies on the *Ou Mallon* Principle, and the principle is known to be Democritean. 'There is no reason for there to be atoms in one place rather than in another; but there are atoms in certain parts of the universe. Hence atoms are scattered throughout the universe.' And we may, if we please, concoct a similar piece of reasoning for Epicurus: 'There would be no reason for a finite group of atoms to congregate in one place rather than in another. But they could not congregate everywhere; hence they would not congregate at all.'

That Democritus did hope to establish the infinity of atoms from the infinity of space by way of the *Ou Mallon* Principle is, I suppose, undeniable. I shall examine the Principle in a later chapter: here it is only necessary to say that the Democritean argument does not succeed.

(e) *Infinite variety*

There are infinitely many atoms, each solid, indivisible, immutable, eternal. How, then, does one atom differ from another? What further characteristics, by which they might be differentiated, do atoms possess? I have already mentioned size: atoms, being bodies, have a magnitude or size; and they differ in size from one another. Perhaps they exhibit an infinite variety of size; perhaps some are gigantic. At any event, even those authors who hold that all atoms are small, allow that they come in different sizes (e.g., **213**).

Having magnitude, the atoms also have shape, or (in the technical terminology of Abdera) *rhusmos* (e.g., *Met* 985b16 = **67 A 6**); and atomic shapes differ: 'There belong to them every kind of shape and every kind of form . . . some are scalene, some hooked, some hollow, some convex—and they have innumerable other differences' (**213**: cf., e.g., Cicero, **67 A 11**). The differences are numberless: atomic shapes are infinitely varied.

Two arguments for the infinity of atomic shapes have survived. The first is transmitted by Aristotle:

> Since they [sc. Leucippus and Democritus] thought that the truth was in appearances, and the appearances were contrary and unlimited, they made the [atomic] shapes unlimited (**239**: *GC* 315b8 = **67 A 9**).

The argument is echoed, with an important nuance, by Epicurus: 'It is not possible that so many varieties should come about from the same comprehended (*perieilêmmenôn*) [atomic] shapes. And in each shaping, the similar atoms are unlimited without qualification; but in their differences they are not unlimited without qualification but only incomprehensible (*aperilêptoi*)' (*ad Hdt* §42). To explain the varied phenomena you require a multiplicity of atomic shapes, but not an infinity. The shapes are incomprehensibly, but finitely, many; they have a determinate number, even though we shall never determine it.

It is tempting to read Epicurus' view back into Leucippus: a literal infinity of atomic shapes is theoretically overgenerous; and our texts perhaps allow us to take the terms 'numberless' and 'unlimited' in a relaxed sense. But the Epicurean argument for the finitude of shapes may not have been available to the Atomists: 'the principles of things vary in a finite number of shapes. If that were not so, some seeds would thereby have to be of infinite bodily magnitude' (Lucretius, II. 479–82). This, presumably, was the argument which Epicurus used to show that atomic shapes were finite; and, as Lucretius explicitly recognizes (II. 485), it hangs on the assumption of 'minimal parts': only if there are theoretically indivisible magnitudes will infinite shapes imply infinite sizes.[26] That assumption (as I have argued) cannot be shown to have been Abderite; nor, therefore, can we ascribe Lucretius' argument to the early Atomists.

Let us allow, then, that the Atomists posited an infinite variety of atomic shapes. The argument given in **239** for that hypothesis is a thunderingly bad one: if there are, literally, infinitely many differences in the phenomena, that at most requires that there are infinitely many different atomic structures underlying the phenomena. It does not require that the atomic *shapes* be infinitely various; indeed, it does not require that there be more than one atomic shape. How could the Atomists have failed to see that?

Now Simplicius offers a different reflexion: Leucippus 'hypothesized unlimitedly many eternally moving elements—the atoms—and the unlimited quantity of the shapes among them, because nothing is rather such than such . . .' (**236: 67 A 8**). The *Ou Mallon*

Principle is here applied to atomic shapes: there are, mathematically speaking, infinitely many possible shapes; there is no reason why there should be atoms of shape *S* rather than atoms of shape *S′*; hence there are atoms of every shape. I shall look at the argument again when I discuss the Principle it incorporates. The argument is, I suspect, the official Abderite argument for an infinity of atomic shapes; and I am tempted to suppose that **239** does not contain an Abderite *argument* at all: having argued for infinity by the *Ou Mallon* Principle, the Atomists observed that an infinity of atomic shapes would amply explain the phenomenal infinity of the macroscopic world. Their observation was later misconstrued as an independent argument for infinity of shapes.

(f) *Atomic weight and motion*

Solid magnitudes will have a mass or weight (*baros*); and since the atoms differ in size, they will vary in mass. There is ample evidence that this was explicitly stated by the Atomists:

> Democritus says that each of the indivisibles is heavier in accordance with its excess [in size] (**240**: *GC* 326a9 = **68 A 60**).

> The Democriteans, and later Epicurus, say that the atoms . . . have weight (**241**: Simplicius, **68 A 61**).

> Democritus distinguishes heavy and light by magnitude (**242**: Theophrastus, *Sens* §61 = **68 A 135**).

Other equally grave witnesses can be called. Against them there is a single voice: Aëtius twice reports that

> Democritus says that the primary bodies . . . have no weight (**243**: **68 A 47**).

These testimonies have aroused great controversy; orthodoxy now lies with Aëtius—the atoms do not have weight, at least not 'absolute' weight.[27] But I think it is evident that Aristotle and Theophrastus are preferable to Aëtius, who is confused by the whole question; and the thesis that atoms have weight or mass is an obvious corollary of the central tenets of atomism.

Mass goes with motion; and

> Leucippus says that . . . [the atoms] are infinite and always moving and that generation and change are continuous (**244**: Hippolytus, **67 A 10**);

according to Democritus, the atoms 'battle and are carried about in the void on account of their dissimilarity and the other differences aforesaid' (Aristotle, **213**). Aristotle once compares the atoms to the motes we see in a sunbeam (*An* 404a3 = **67 A 28**); the image is developed at length by Lucretius in his account of the precosmic motion of the Epicurean atoms:

> For observe closely when the light of the sun
> is poured by the intruding rays through the darkness of the house:
> you will see many tiny bodies mingling in many ways through the empty space
> in the very light of the rays,
> and as though in eternal combat waging wars and battles,
> striving in companies and never giving pause,
> harried by constant meetings and partings.
> So you can guess from this what it is like when the principles of things
> are tossed about for ever in the vast void (**245**: II. 114–22).

Lactantius (*de ira* X. 9) ascribes the image to Leucippus: it was plainly a commonplace in atomist thought, and it is reasonably ascribed to the founder of the school. The atoms are shapes as gay and numberless as the motes that people the sunbeams.

If Leucippus gave an image, Democritus perhaps contributed a technical term:

> They . . . said that, moving by virtue of the weight in them, they move through the void which yields and does not resist them;[28] for they say that they *peripalaisesthai* (**246**: Simplicius, **68 A 58**).

Editors emend *peripalaisesthai* to *peripalassesthai*; they then restore the verb, or the noun *peripalaxis*, in other Democritean contexts; and they proclaim that *peripalaxis* is the technical term for atomic motions. Alas, most of the restorations are probably unjustified; and the meaning of *peripalaxis* is itself a matter of dispute (the standard translation is 'vibration'). The whole issue is unenlightening.[29]

However that may be, we have a moderately clear picture of atomic movement: in any area of space, numerous particles are dancing aimlessly, in various directions and at various speeds, sometimes colliding, sometimes moving unimpeded. What determines their different motions? Our sources give three answers: first, the atoms move 'by virtue of the weight in them' (Simplicius, **246**). That is repeated by several authorities (e.g., Hermias, **67 A 17**; Simplicius, **68 A 61**); and it appears to have roused objections from Epicurus (*ad Hdt* § 61 = **68 A 61**). Aristotle, on the other hand, refers to 'dissimilarity and the other differences' in order to explain atomic motion (**213**), and he marks shape as an important determinant of motion (*An* 404a4 = **67 A 28**). Third, the doxographers speak of 'blows':

> Democritus says that by nature the atoms are motionless, and that they move by blows (**247**: Simplicius, **68 A 47**).

> Democritus says that the primary bodies . . . have no weight but move in the unlimited [void] by counter-striking (*allêlotupian*) (**248**: Aëtius, **68 A 47**).

> [Leucippus and Democritus] say that the atoms move by counter-striking, i.e. by hitting one another (**249**: Alexander, **67 A 6**; cf. Aëtius, **68 A 66**).

The commentators find difficulty here. Some distinguish two phases in atomic movement: the first occurs *before* the atoms have struck one another, and is free motion through space; the second occurs *after* a 'counter-striking' and is compelled motion. But there is no textual evidence for a period in which the atoms roamed freely, untouched by their fellow occupants of space; and if the atoms have been moving for all eternity, it is hard to imagine why there should ever have been such a period.

Nor do our sources provide any genuine difficulty. Aëtius' denial of weight to the atoms may be dismissed (above, p. 365); the remaining testimony gives a coherent picture: in themselves, atoms are indeed motionless; that is to say, they would not be moving had they not collided with other atoms and so been jolted into motion. ('How, then, did the atomic motion ever *begin*?' That is a tale for a later chapter.) But if collision is the propellant cause of motion, the speed and direction of an atom's travel is determined by its weight and its shape—more precisely, by the weight, shape, and anterior motions of the colliding bodies. Throw a stone at a cat, and its rebounding path will be determined by its own weight, shape, and anterior motion, and by the corresponding properties of the cat: the stone rebounds because of its 'counter-striking' the cat; the trajectory of its rebound is determined by weight and shape. No doubt it is wrong to construct the dynamics of atomic motion from observations of macroscopic motion through air; and Epicurus' account of atomic motion differs radically from the account I have ascribed to Democritus. For all that, the early atomist account is rational, coherent, and sane: if it is wrong in fact, at least it was intelligently constructed.

(g) *Atomic indifference*

> They say that there are these three differences: shape, order and position. For they assert that existents [*to on*, i.e. the atoms] differ only in *rhusmos* and *diathigê* and *tropê*; of these, *rhusmos* is shape, *diathigê* order, and *tropê* position. For *A* differs from *N* in shape; *AN* differs from *NA* in order; and *N* differs from *Z* in position (**250**: Aristotle, *Met* 985b13–19 = **67 A 6**).[30]

Elsewhere Aristotle uses a similar analogy: in explanation of how the rearrangement of a group of atoms can produce radically different macroscopic results, he says that 'tragedy and comedy are put together from the same letters' (*GC* 315b15 = **67 A 9**). Scholars infer, with some plausibility, that the alphabetical analogy was employed by the Atomists themselves (cf. **68 B 18b–20**).

Aristotle's three differences make a clumsy triad. First, they are not the only, nor even the only important, differences among atoms: atoms also differ in size, in weight, and in velocity. Second, difference in *diathigê* and *tropê* is a relation among groups of atoms and not among individual bodies; that is evident in the case of *diathigê* and only slightly less so for *tropê*—the letter *N* has, in itself, no *tropê* in space. I suspect that Leucippus or Democritus saw that the letter analogy would neatly illustrate *rhusmos, diathigê* and *tropê*, and, pleased by the discovery, overlooked its minor awkwardnesses. However that may be, it is plain that *diathigê* and *tropê* are characteristics of groups of atoms and not of individual corpuscles.

The doxographers several times say that atoms are *apoioi* (Plutarch, **68 A 57**; Aëtius, **68 A 124**; **125**). *Apoios* usually means 'qualityless' (*a* + *poiotês*), but it can mean 'inactive', 'inert' (*a* + *poiein*). Most of the ancient sources take it in its former sense: Galen says that the atoms are all 'small bodies, without qualities' (**68 A 49**); Plutarch gives as an illustration of *apoios* 'colourless' (**68 A 57**). Then, uneasy with the bland assertion that atoms are unqualified, our sources explain that this means 'without *sensible* qualities' (cf. Aëtius, **68 A 124**; Sextus, **68 A 59**; *Pyrr Hyp* III. 33; and see Epicurus, *ad Hdt* §54).

A passage from Aristotle seems to take the other road, implying that atoms are *apoioi* in the sense of impotent:

> It is necessary to say that each of the indivisibles is both impassive (*apathes*) . . . and productive of no affection (*pathos*)—for it can be neither hard nor cold (**251**: *GC* 326a1–3).

Atoms are impassive and inactive, equally incapable of receiving and of giving affection. Some scholars construe inactivity here as the inability to affect other atoms: inactivity then follows immediately from impassivity; for if atoms cannot be changed, then no atom can change any atom. That is a part of the story (cf. 326a11); but Aristotle means to assert not merely that atoms cannot affect other atoms, but that they cannot be 'hard or cold' or anything else—in short, he wants to assert that they are *apoia* in the sense of 'lacking (sensible) qualities'. And his argument is not hard to distil. It relies upon the Principle of Synonymy (above, pp. 88, 119); if *a* is active, *a* can bring it about that *b* is *F*; but if *a* can bring it about that *b* is *F* (where *F* is a sensible quality), then *a* is *F*. In short, Aristotle means to say, in the concise and somewhat ill-humoured passage at 326a1–24, that atoms lack sensible qualities and, consequently, active powers.

If atoms lack sensible qualities, they cannot differ one from another in respect of sensible qualities. Aristotle takes the point in the same crotchety passage of the *GC*: he asks: 'again, do all those solids [i.e. the atoms] have one nature, or do they differ one from another—as it might be, some being fiery, others earthen in mass?' (326a29–31). And he answers:

> They say that they have a single nature—as it might be, each being a separate bit of gold (**252**: *Cael* 275b31 = **67 A 19**; cf. *GC* 326a17).[31]

Dalton, who is often hailed as the founder of modern atomism, disagreed: his atoms are diverse; they are indivisible particles of different chemical stuffs. Daltonian atomism is familiar from schoolboy chemistry, where we may incautiously take such a formula as 'H_2O' to indicate the amalgam of two atoms of hydrogen with one of oxygen. Atoms of hydrogen have those powers or sensible qualities which characterize the gas hydrogen; and that fact distinguishes them from atoms of oxygen, of chlorine, of iron, and of all the other chemical elements. This chemical atomism, as I may call it, may be contrasted with a physical atomism, according to which the chemical differences between oxygen and hydrogen do not exist at the corpuscular level: there are not atoms of oxygen and atoms of hydrogen, any more than there are atoms of sugar or atoms of soap. Atoms are bits of stuff, having all the characteristics of matter and none of the characteristics specific to any particular type of matter. 'Body, common to everything, is the principle of everything, differing in its parts by size and shape' (*Phys* 203a34–b2 = **68 A 41**). Davy championed physical atomism and the unity of matter; Dalton, chemical atomism and the irreducible diversity of matter: the unitarian view, which had served in an Aristotelian guise as the foundation of alchemical hopes, in the end triumphed.

Democritus is no Daltonian; but his atoms are not, strictly speaking, 'indifferent' or *adiaphoroi*: they differ intrinsically in shape and size, and as a consequence in weight and motion. In a pure physical atomism, each atom would be precisely similar to every other; there would be one atomic shape and one atomic size; macroscopic diversities would be explained solely in terms of differences in atomic structures and not in terms of differences among the components of those structures.

(h) *The status of sensible qualities*

Atoms are not coloured; they have no taste and no smell. Did the Atomists simply deny the reality of sensible qualities? Did they offer any account of the qualities of macroscopic bodies? Did they really mean to assert that atoms lack *all* sensible qualities?

It is clear that the doxographers are speaking loosely when they say that the atoms have no sensible qualities: shape, size and motion are, after all, sensible qualities; and if the atoms are too small for their qualities to be discerned, that does not deprive those qualities of their sensible nature. Moreover, it appears that the atoms had a further and indubitably sensible property: temperature. Aristotle is scathing here: 'Yet it is absurd just to ascribe heat to round shapes' (326a3–5); 'No atoms have any sensible qualities—except that round atoms are hot' (cf. *Cael* 303a12–14 = **67 A 15**). Theophrastus expands the point: it is absurd, he says, for Democritus

> to make intrinsic natures of heavy and light and hard and soft . . . but to make hot and cold and the rest relative to sensation—and that though he says frequently that the shape of the hot is spherical (**253**: *Sens* §68 = **68 A 135**).

On the one hand, heat is treated alongside other sensible qualities and so should not belong to the individual atoms (cf. **B 9; B 117**); on the other hand, heat is associated with spherical atoms, because spherical atoms move most easily (Aristotle, *An* 404a7 = **67 A 28**), and easy movers cut and burn (*Cael* 303b32).

The criticism does not apply to Leucippus, who offered a different account of heat (Simplicius, **67 A 14**). Perhaps the criticism is in any case inapposite; perhaps the Atomists never intended to distinguish between sensible and non-sensible qualities and to deny their atoms the former; perhaps they had some other criterion for determining whether or not a quality was of a type to be possessed by an atom.

Here I introduce one of the most celebrated of Democritean sayings. It is transmitted to us in several forms; and indeed it may have been stated in different forms by Democritus himself. I quote Plutarch's version; for although his text is corrupt, his version is the fullest and the best:

> By convention (*nomôi*) is colour, and by convention sweet, and by convention [every] combination (*sunkrisin*), [but in reality (*eteêi*) the void and atoms] (**254**: *adv Col* 1110 E).[32]

Democritus means to draw an ontological distinction between 'atoms and void' on the one hand, and certain other things on the other; and he intends to assign 'atoms and void' a superior ontological rank to those other things. So much is clear: the rest, I think, is more puzzling than is usually allowed.

In all our sources other than Plutarch, the list of 'conventional' items is a list of qualities (hot, cold, bitter, sweet, colour); and Diogenes Laertius says simply that 'qualities (*poiotêtes*) are by convention' (IX.45 = **A 1**). Diogenes is speaking loosely: I assume that we may add to the *eteêi* side of the great divide a list of atomic qualities: shape, size, weight, motion. And I assume too that the distinction between 'conventional' and 'real' qualities gives the criterion for atomic qualities: a quality is non-atomic if it is 'conventional', if it exists *nomôi*. There is no explicit suggestion that *nomôi* qualities are sensible qualities; and the thesis that atoms lack sensible qualities has already been judged erroneous. What, then, is it for a quality to be 'conventional'? (A 'combination' (*sunkrisis*) is not a quality: I return to that word in a later context, below, pp. 141–5.)

The seventeenth-century corpuscularians made much of a distinction between 'primary' and 'secondary' qualities. The classic exposition of the distinction is found in Locke's *Essay*, in a chapter where Locke, as he admits, is more than usually indebted to the scientists, and in particular to Boyle. Locke introduces the distinction as follows: 'Qualities thus considered in Bodies are, First such as are utterly inseparable from the Body, in what estate soever it be; such as in all the alterations and changes it suffers, all the force can be used upon it, it constantly keeps; and such as Sense constantly finds in every particle of Matter, which has bulk enough to be perceived, and the Mind finds inseparable from every particle of Matter, though less than to make itself singly be perceived by our Senses. . . . These I call *original* or *primary Qualities* of Body' (*Essay* II. viii. 9).

Notice first, that Locke does not talk of primary qualities *simpliciter*, but of primary qualities of body (elsewhere he mentions the primary qualities of spiritual substances (II. xxi. 73; xxii. 17–18)—and he might consistently have singled out primary qualities of any kind of thing); second, that the distinction between primary and secondary qualities is not logically tied to a particulate or atomist theory of matter; and third, that primary qualities 'of body' are properties of pieces of stuff and not of stuff *simpliciter*.

Thus we may say, generally:

(D1) *Q* is a primary quality of *F*'s if and only if necessarily any *F* has *Q*;

and, particularly:

(D2) *Q* is a primary quality of bodies if and only if necessarily every body has *Q*.

Primary qualities, in short, are essential properties (cf. II. iv. 1).

Secondary qualities are introduced as follows: '2*dly*, Such *Qualities*, which in truth are nothing in the Objects themselves, but Powers to produce various Sensations in us by their *primary Qualities*, *i.e.* by the Bulk, Figure, Texture and Motion of their insensible parts, as Colours, Sounds, Tastes, *etc.* These I call *secondary Qualities*' (*Essay* II. viii. 10). Locke is trying to say too much at once; let me be rudely dogmatic and say what I think Locke should have said. First, he wants a definition of 'secondary quality'; and he needs:

(D1*) *Q** is a secondary quality of *F*s if and only if some *F*s have *Q** and *Q** is not a primary quality of *F*s.

Second, he wants to advance a number of theses about the secondary qualities of bodies; these include the following: secondary qualities are not 'real'; they are powers; they are relational; they are mind-dependent; and their presence in objects is explicable in terms of the primary qualities of their component corpuscles.

The last point requires a little elaboration. Consider, first, the property of being cubic. That, clearly, is a secondary quality of bodies; but it stands in a special relationship to the primary quality of figure or shape: *being cubic* is, in a convenient jargon, a determinate of the determinable property *being shaped*. Call qualities which are thus determinates of primary qualities 'proper' qualities. Then Locke's thesis is this: corpuscles, or atoms, have no properties apart from primary qualities and proper qualities of body; macroscopic bodies have secondary qualities, but those qualities are all explicable by way of the primary and proper qualities of the corpuscles which constitute the macroscopic bodies.

It is often suggested that Democritus' distinction between *nomôi* and *eteêi* qualities is the first version of the distinction between primary and secondary qualities: *eteêi* means 'real' or 'primary'; and if *nomôi* does not exactly mean 'secondary', nevertheless *nomôi* qualities are secondary qualities. That view is clearly mistaken (sphericality, say, is a secondary quality, but it is not *nomôi*); but it is on the right road. In its place I suggest the following thesis:

(D3) *Q* is *eteêi* if and only if *Q* is either a primary or a proper quality of bodies.

I do not mean that the Atomists explicitly embraced (D3)—there is no trace of any such defintion in the doxography; but I think that (D3) is the thesis which best explains the atomist attitude to atoms and qualities.

The list of atomic properties—duration, solidity, mobility, mass, shape, size—is close enough to the Lockean list of primary qualities. And it is not implausible to imagine that Democritus ascribed these qualities to atoms just because he thought them essential to bodies.

Moreover, the Atomists thought that the secondary qualities of macroscopic objects are explicable in terms of the properties of their atomic constituents.

> The elements are qualityless, . . . and the compounds from them are coloured by the order and shape and position [of the atoms] (**255**: Aëtius, **68 A 125**).

> White and black, he says, are rough and smooth; and he reduces the savours to the [atomic] shapes (**256**: Aristotle, *Sens* 442b11 = **68 A 126**).

A long passage in Theophrastus' *de Sensu* is devoted to Democritus and it contains numerous Democritean accounts of the sensible qualities; I quote a short (and controversial) passage:

> Sour taste comes from shapes that are large and multi-angular and have very little roundness; for these, when they enter the body, clog and blind the veins and prevent their flowing—that is why the bowels too come to a stand. Bitter taste comes from small, smooth, rounded shapes whose periphery does have joints; that it why it is viscous and adhesive. Saline taste comes from large shapes which are not rounded or scalene but angular and many-jointed (he means by scalene those which interlock and combine with one another)—large, because the saltiness stays on the surface (for if they were small and struck by those surrounding them they would mingle with the universe); not rounded, because what is saline is rough and what is rounded is smooth; not scalene, because it does not interlock—that is why it is friable (**257**: §66 = **68 A 135**).[33]

In that account of gustatory qualities, and throughout Theophrastus' report, it is the shapes of individual atoms which account for macroscopic qualities. Shape is far more important in the atomism of Democritus (who significantly called his corpuscles *ideai* or 'shapes') than in modern atomism, where it is the interrelations and relative locomotions of the constituent atoms which are primarily responsible for macroscopic phenomena. But fundamentally Democritus and Locke are at one: atomic qualities underlie and explain macroscopic qualities.

Why suppose that atoms have no secondary qualities? First, the atoms, being physical bodies, are logically bound to possess a certain set of properties: solidity, size, shape, etc. Then let us hypothesize that those are *all* the properties they possess, and attempt to explain the phenomena in terms of them. The hypothesis is maximally economical: if it is successful in explaining the phenomena, then we shall certainly have no reason to ascribe any secondary qualities to atoms, and hence should not do so. Moreover, it may well be that an analysis of secondary qualities will show that some or all of them could not in fact belong to atoms. Suppose that elasticity is explained in terms of density, i.e. in terms of a certain distribution of atoms and void in an atomic conglomerate; then clearly no single atom can be elastic. Suppose that sourness is explained in terms of the effect of a mass of corpuscles on the gustatory organs; then clearly no single corpuscle can be sour.

The most perplexing part of Locke's account of secondary qualities is his assertion that they are not real: did the Atomists adumbrate that part of the account too? and can we make any sense of it? 'Improper secondary qualities are not *eteêi*: they are therefore unreal.' An easy gloss suggests itself: if improper secondary qualities can be accounted for by way of primary and proper qualities, then a complete account of the real world need mention no improper secondary qualities at all; for every fact expressible by a sentence of the form 'Macroscopic object M has Q^*' is equally, and more fundamentally, expressible by a sentence of the form 'Atoms A_1, A_2, . . ., having Q_1, Q_2 . . ., are arranged in pattern P'.

But *eteêi* contrasts with *nomôi*; and the contrast suggests a further, and equally Lockean, sort of 'unreality'. The classical contrast with *nomôi* is *phusei*, 'by nature'; and the doxographers deploy the contrast:

> The others say that perceptible things are by nature, but Leucippus and Democritus . . . [say that they are] *nomôi* (**258**: Aëtius, **67 A 32**).

> By nature nothing is white or black or yellow or red or bitter or sweet (**259**: Galen, **68 A 49**).

This, however, does not take us far: we have still to interpret *nomôi*. It is doubtless 'conventional' in some sense that we call sweet things 'sweet' and that the Greeks called them *glukea*; but it is no 'convention' that ripe plums taste sweet and green plums taste sour, nor can Democritus have thought that it was.

Sextus offers a more appealing gloss:

> I.e., perceptible things are thought (*nomizetai*) and believed to exist, but they do not exist in truth (**260**: *adv Math* VII.135 = **68 B 9**).

Galen hints at the same thought:

> Things are thought (*nomizetai*) by men to be white and black and sweet and bitter and all the rest, but in truth there is nothing but [atoms and void] (**261: 68 A 49**).

Let Q^* be an improper secondary quality of body: then Q^* exists *nomôi*, i.e., people think that some things have Q^* but in truth none do. We might compare Democritus' view on 'mixture' or *krasis*:

> He says that in truth things simply are not mixed, but that what is thought (*dokousan*) to be a mixture is a close juxtaposition of bodies which each preserves its own appropriate nature (**262**: Alexander, **68 A 64**).

Things seem to be mixed; they are not—and a microscopic inspection would reveal the fact. Similarly, things seem to be red or warm or bitter or soft; they are not—and a microscopic inspection would reveal the fact.

But that will not do. It is simply absurd to say that fire is only *thought* to be hot, grass only *thought* to be green, sugar only *thought* to be sweet. And what are we to make of Democritus' laborious and detailed accounts of such qualities as heat, greenness and wetness if those qualities are never actually instantiated? Aristotle unwittingly brings home the absurdity:

> That is why he [sc. Democritus] says that colour does not exist—for things are coloured by position (*tropêi*) (**263**: *GC* 316a1 = **68 A 123**).

'Grass is green in virtue of such and such an atomic structure; *ergo* grass is not green.' Could there be a crasser inference than that?

A better gloss on *nomôi* is to hand: improper secondary qualities are not 'natural' because they are mind-dependent:

> [They are] *nomôi*, i.e., they are in belief and by virtue of our affections (**264**: Aëtius, **67 A 32**).

> For '*nomôi*' means the same as 'in thought (*nomisti*)' or 'relative to us', not in virtue of the nature of the objects (**265**: Galen **68 A 49**).

The view is found in Theophrastus: Democritus says that

> Of none of the other sensible objects is there a nature (*phusis*), but they are all affections of perception, as it alters and imagination comes from it; for there is no nature of the hot and the cold, but the shape (*schêma*) alters and works the change in us (**266**: *Sens* §63 = **68 A 135**).

'Sweetness and Whiteness', as Locke puts it, 'are not really in Manna' (II.viii.18); they are not *in* manna, because they are relations between manna and the mind of some sentient creature. Thus 'there would . . . be no more Light, or Heat in the World, than there would be Pain if there were no sensible Creature to feel it, though the Sun should continue just as it is now, and Mount *Ætna* flame higher than ever it did' (*Essay*, II.xxxi.2).

Qualities divide into two groups: those which are *eteêi* or real, and those which are *nomôi* or mind-dependent: 'square', 'heavy', 'at rest' name intrinsic properties of objects; 'smooth', 'red', 'sweet' are, as Sextus put it 'names of our own feelings' (*adv Math* VIII.184). Atoms, the fundamental items of the world, possess only real qualities; and those qualities are either primary qualities, qualities which every body as a matter of necessity possesses, or else proper qualities, determinate forms of primary qualities. All improper secondary qualities are explicable by way of *eteêi* qualities; and the explication reveals that they are all mind-dependent.

I shall not attempt to assess the merits of that complex thesis; but it is perhaps worth indicating what any assessment must look to. First, there is the distinction between *eteêi* and non-*eteêi* qualities itself. It is, I think, plausible to believe that the class of *eteêi* qualities can be accurately defined by way of the notion of a primary quality; and it is plausible to believe that the *eteêi* properties of body will constitute a scientifically important sub-class of the class of bodily qualities.

Second, there is the Abderite list of *eteêi* qualities: it needs to be asked just what qualities satisfy the definition of *eteêi*. And it may well be that this question proves unexpectedly difficult; at any event, philosophers have not agreed on any list of primary qualities of body.

Third, there is the status of non-*eteêi* qualities. Are all these qualities in fact explicable by way of *eteêi* qualities? And would such an explication yield a logical or a causal dependence between *eteêi* and non-*eteêi* qualities? (It is often noticed that Locke fails to distinguish clearly between a causal thesis, that secondary qualities are *produced* by primary qualities, and a logical thesis, that secondary qualities are *analysed* into primary qualities; the observation, which I have stated crudely, leads to some difficult and intriguing questions.) And, finally, are non-*eteêi* qualities really mind-dependent? And is that dependency logical or causal?

(i) *The philosophy of Abdera*

The Abderite philosophy of matter began from the notion of *being*, of primary beings, substances or *ousiai*. Substances, they held, are solid and unitary bodies, ungenerable, indestructible, immutable, indivisible, everlasting. These basic items of the physical world are infinitely numerous and exhibit an infinite variety of shape and size; they are in constant motion, and their collisions and colligations form the macroscopic and changing world of phenomenal reality. The qualities they possess are those qualities which every body logically must possess, or at least determinate forms of those qualities.

The phenomenal world reveals a vast range of qualities not included in the list of atomic characteristics. But those qualities exist only 'by convention': they are mind-dependent, and their existence is to be explained in terms of the properties of the fundamental atomic traits. That assertion raises various difficult questions; and the value of the Abderite theory remains uncertain until they are answered. But it is, I hope, very plain that the theory began a line of thought whose influence upon philosophy and upon science was of unparalleled consequence.

XVIII

Philolaus and the Formal Cause

(a) *Pythagorean numerology*

The Pythagoreans sailed their intellectual boats on the ocean of anonymity. One name stands out: Philolaus, according to a reliable tradition, was the first Pythagorean philosopher to publish his views; and his book *Concerning Nature* for the first time congealed the fluid oral tradition of the school (Demetrius, *apud* Diogenes Laertius, VIII.85 = **44 A 1**).[1] A malicious and silly rumour insinuated that Plato in his *Timaeus* plagiarized the work of Philolaus (Timon, fr. 54 = **A 8**; Hermippus, *apud* Diogenes Laertius, VIII.84 = **A 1**); if the gossip has a basis in truth, and Plato was influenced by Philolaus, then that adds an extrinsic interest to the book.[2]

Several fragments of Philolaus' book have been preserved. A majority of scholars has found them spurious, adding them to the vast library of pseudo-Pythagorean literature; but the arguments for scepticism are not very solid, and I am persuaded by those scholars who think that some at least of the texts are genuine productions of Philolaus' pen. It would be pointless to rehearse the published arguments, and I have no new thoughts to contribute to the debate: I shall proceed on the assumption of authenticity, and let the interested or sceptical reader prove the assumption himself.[3]

Philolaus is sometimes taken as a mere mouthpiece: the views he expounds are not his own inventions; they are the common wisdom of his fellow Pythagoreans. And it has been judged that Philolaus' book was 'unscientific and without real understanding of the doctrines it reports'; it reveals 'a thinker of no great stature, whose interest is peripheral'.[4] The later part of this chapter will, I hope, show that Philolaus is a philosopher of some merit; but before turning to that task I shall spend a few pages on Philolaus' anonymous colleagues whose views he allegedly parroted.

If Philolaus was an inaccurate parrot for Pythagorean views, then we need an accurate account of those views against which to measure his mouthings.[5] Such an account is to be found in Aristotle's *Metaphysics*. Aristotle's remarks on the Pythagoreans in *Met* A 5 are intricate and obscure; but three generalities can be essayed with some confidence. First, the Pythagorean views that Aristotle reports belong as a whole to the fifth century.[6] Second, Aristotle is not reporting a single philosophy, but several variations on the broad Pythagorean theme. Third, some of Aristotle's account bears a resemblance to the views expressed in the Philolaic texts.

Aristotle does not name Philolaus in *Met* A 5. Sceptical scholars think that the fragments are part of a post-Aristotelian production designed to repair and defend the Pythagorean philosophy which Aristotle has mauled; others think that the fragments are the wreckage of Aristotle's main source for Pythagorean doctrine.[7] I do not accept the former view, and I think that there are sufficient differences between the fragments and Aristotle's account to rule the latter out of court. For what it is worth, I imagine that Aristotle is reporting the major orthodoxies of Pythagorean thought, and that Philolaus represents a heterodoxy: his heresy was, I suppose, deemed too slight by Aristotle to warrant special treatment. The matter lies beyond our knowledge; but it seems clear that we cannot justly interpret Philolaus' texts by way of Aristotle's reports. (And I shall spare the reader the profound *ennui* which an extended treatment of those reports would surely induce.)

The foundation and the distinguishing mark of the Pythagorean philosophy is number: according to Sextus

> The Pythagoreans say that reasoning [is the criterion of truth]—not reasoning in general but that which comes about from mathematics, as Philolaus said (**267: A 29**).

Plutarch says that in Philolaus' view

> Geometry is the principle and mother-state (*mêtropolis*) of the other disciplines (*mathêmatôn*) (**268: A 7a**).[8]

An old *acousma* runs: 'What is wisest?—Number'; and the primacy of number is a striking feature of Aristotle's account of Pythagoreanism (e.g. *Met* 985b23 = **58 B 4**; 986a15 = **58 B 5**). In the case of Philolaus himself, **B 4** (= **280**) illustrates the same thesis; and Archytas, the leading Pythagorean of the generation after Philolaus, wrote this:

> The mathematicians seem to me to have attained a fine knowledge, and it is not absurd that they should think aright about each of the things that are; for, having a fine knowledge about the nature of everything, they were likely to have a fine discernment too about the particular things that there are (**269: 47 B 1**).

The question of Pythagorean mathematics is a notorious thing. Once upon a time, scholars gave the Pythagoreans most of the credit for the astonishing advances in mathematics made in Greece during the fifth century. Now a contrary scepticism is fashionable; and most, I guess, will assent to the judgment that 'in its essence, mathematics is not Pythagorean but Greek'.[9] Hippasus of Metapontum did not discover the irrationals; Pythagoras' theorem is not Pythagorean; and there was no great Pythagorean mathematician before Archytas of Tarentum.[10]

It is hard to dissent from that negative opinion; but it would be an error to infer from it that the Pythagoreans were not mathematically inclined. Aristotle's testimony is explicit:

> At the same time as these men [sc. the Atomists] and before them, those called the Pythagoreans touched on mathematics and were the first to bring them forward; and being brought up in them, they thought that their principles were the principles of everything (**270**: *Met* 985b23–5 = **58 B 4**).

> The Pythagoreans, having devoted themselves to mathematics, and admiring the rigour of its arguments, because it alone of the studies men undertake contains proofs, and seeing it agreed that the facts of harmonics are due to numbers, thought that these and their principles were in general the causes of existent things (**271**).[11]

Aristotle's testimony is backed by Eudemus, who ascribes a few of the theorems contained in our Euclid to the Pythagoreans (cf. **58 B 18, 20, 21**). In the case of Philolaus we have a general notice that he was well-versed in the mathematical sciences (Vitruvius, **44 A 6**), and detailed evidence of his work in harmonics (**B 6**; Boëthius, **A 26**). Philolaus' mathematical abilities were not, perhaps, great: a recent scholar accuses him of 'mathematical inconsistencies' and 'gross errors';[12] and we may well imagine that the Pythagoreans, as a group, were students rather than professors of the mathematical arts.

In any case, it is not for their technical but for their philosophical contribution to mathematics that the Pythagoreans win our interest.

Aristotle (**270**) puts it very clearly: the Pythagoreans only 'touched on (*hapsamenoi*)' mathematics, in the technical sense; but they 'were the first to bring them forward (*proêgagon*)' in a philosophical context.[13]

What philosophical use did the Pythagoreans make of mathematics? The cynical will speak dismissively of number mysticism, arithmology, and other puerilities. And it is undeniable that a great quantity of Pythagorean 'number philosophy' is a 'number symbolism' of the most jejune and inane kind. According to Aristotle, the Pythagoreans 'say that things themselves are numbers' (*Met* 987b28 = **58 B 13**), or that 'existent things are by imitation of numbers' (*Met* 987b11 = **58 B 12**);[14] elsewhere he particularizes:

> The Pythagoreans, because they saw many of the attributes of numbers belonging to sensible things, assumed existing things to be numbers (**272**: *Met* 1090a20–22);

thus:

> Such and such an attribute of numbers is justice, such and such soul and mind, another opportunity, and so on for everything else (**273**: *Met* 985b29–31 = **58 B 4**).

Alexander says that justice was 4, marriage 5, opportunity 7 (*in Met* 38.8–20); comparable assertions are attested for Philolaus;[15] and his younger contemporaries, Lysis and Opsimus, are said to have proclaimed that God is an irrational number (Athenagoras, **46 A 4**).[16]

The Pythagoreans swore by the *tetraktus*. This was a graphic representation of the number 10:

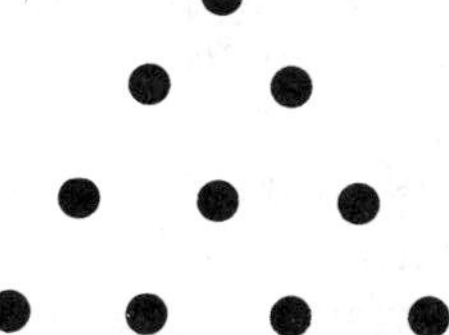

And it exhibited in a vivid fashion some of the qualities of that number; for 'the number 10 seems to be perfect and to embrace the whole nature of number' (*Met* 986a8 = **58 B 4**).[17] 'Touching on' arithmetic, the Pythagoreans were impressed by certain properties of the number 10; alas, their impression degenerated into a sort of mysticism: amazement, the nurse of philosophy, soon has her milk soured and turns into silly reverence and superstition. Those with a taste for intellectual folly will have their appetite sated if they go through the *Theologoumena Arithmeticae*. That Pythagorean work is a late compilation; the earliest examples of such symbolism are found in the *acousmata* and probably date from the time of Pythagoras himself: from first to last the Pythagoreans engaged in arithmology.

The mumbo-jumbo would not bear exposition but for the fact that certain Pythagoreans attempted to place a rational foundation beneath it.

> They believed that the elements of numbers are the elements of everything that exists (**274**: *Met* 986a1–2 = **58 B 4**).

Aristotle's short statement can be illustrated from the *Pythagorean Memoirs* preserved by Alexander Polyhistor:

> The principle of all things is a monad, and from the monad comes an indefinite dyad, to play matter to the monad's cause; and from the monad and the indefinite dyad come the numbers; and from the numbers the points; and from these the lines, from which come the plane figures; and from the planes come the solid figures, and from these the perceptible bodies. (**275**: Diogenes Laertius, VIII.25 = **58 B 1a**).

Alexander's account is influenced by Plato; but it is reasonable to believe that the Platonizing version is based on an earlier theory. Aristotle points to some such theory, and I assume that the fifth-century Pythagoreans did, in some sense, 'generate' the sensible world from the principles of number.[18] And that 'generation' would license or explain the crude assertions of arithmology: if horses, say, are ultimately 'generated' from the principles of numbers, then in an intelligible sense horses *are* numbers.

The 'generation' of things from the principles of numbers may, I fear, seem no less absurd than the primitive number symbolism I have just dismissed: how can men 'come from' numbers? How can abstract principles give birth to solid stuffs? If the 'generation' is construed literally, as a sort of cosmogony, then it surely is absurd; yet cosmogony is easily confused with analysis (witness Plato's *Timaeus*); and if we listen to the 'generation' system as a faltering attempt to play an analytical tune, unhappily transposed into the cosmogonical key, then we may hear something of modest interest.

The generation system becomes an abstract ontology. The thesis of this ontology is simple: the only ultimate entities in the world are the 'principles of number'. The ontology relies on three reductive analyses. First, the numbers can be reduced to a few basic principles. This rudely anticipates the insights of Leibniz and Peano: the number system can be built up from the unit (or monad) and the successor-operator (or 'indefinite dyad'). The ontology of arithmetic is reduced to a minimum. Second, geometry is arithmetized: the truths of geometry can be expressed in purely arithmetical terms; and geometrical objects can be constructed from numbers. That claim, I suppose, adumbrates the Cartesian discovery of analytic geometry. Finally, physical objects are reduced to geometry. There are two ways of effecting the reduction: first, each object has a characteristic shape; it is determined by, and can thus be identified with, some three-dimensional solid; second, the elemental stuffs which constitute the physical world are atomically structured, and their atoms have a characteristic stereometrical configuration. The former reduction will occupy us again; the latter is familiar from the *Timaeus*.

All truths of science are ultimately truths of arithmetic; all scientific entities are ultimately arithmetical. The generation system points to an ontological desert that is clean and arid even by the obsessively puritanical standards of American pragmatism; and at the same time it holds out the heady prospect of a rigorously mathematical approach to every branch of science. Yet if the Pythagorean ontology is stimulating, it is also wholly vague and programmatic; and I sympathize with the reader who remains unimpressed.

(b) *The philosophy of Philolaus*

Philolaus' book came to possess the traditional Ionian title *Concerning Nature*. And it seems probable that its contents followed the old Ionian models: we know that it elaborated an astronomy, a biology and an embryology (Menon, **44 A 28**; cf. **B 13**), and a psychology; and it is a plausible guess that it covered most of the traditional topics of the *phusiologoi*.

In a later chapter, I shall say something of Philolaus' psychology; here I may briefly describe his revolutionary astronomy. For Philolaus was the first thinker who dared displace the earth from its central position in the universe, and to suggest that, contrary to appearances, the earth was not stationary (Aëtius, **A 21**). In the Philolaic system, the centre of the cosmos was occupied by a mass of fire; around the fire circled the sun, the spherical earth, the moon, the planets, and that celebrated invention of Pythagorean astronomy, the *antichthôn* or counter-earth (cf. Aristotle, *Cael*, 293a17–27 = **58 B 37**; Aëtius, **44 A 16**). The system contained a few grotesqueries. (The moon is inhabited, like the earth; and lunar creatures 'are fifteen times as powerful [as their terrestrial counterparts], and do not excrete' (Aëtius, **A 20**).[19]) Some judge it harshly: it was not 'a scientific astronomy' but 'a *mélange* of myth and *phusiologia*'; it was 'a superficial conglomeration of heterogeneous elements and naive speculation, not an attempt to find a deeper penetrating explanation of the phenomena'.[20] Those judgments are unfair: the fact is that we do not know what considerations led Philolaus to propound his startling innovations; and without such knowledge we cannot pass judgment. Astronomically, of course, the Philolaic system is inadequate; but so are all the admirable astronomical systems of antiquity.

However that may be, Philolaus' views did not catch on. In the fourth century, Hicetas of Syracuse allowed the earth to move (Theophrastus, *apud* Cicero, **50 A 1**); but Hicetas' system was geocentric.[21] It was not till Aristarchus that the earth was again pushed from the centre of things; and since Aristarchus customarily wins credit for his heliocentric innovation, it is only decent to remember that the innovation was not an entirely unprecedented intellectual accomplishment.

If the superstructure of Philolaus' account of the world was Ionian in tenor, its foundations were characteristically Pythagorean.[22] The marriage of these two traditions (if I may change metaphors) was bound to produce curious offspring: how the consummation was effected must be discovered from the first six fragments of Philolaus' work.

Like the other neo-Ionians, Philolaus began by confronting the Eleatic challenge; and his starting point was, in one respect, even closer to Elea than theirs. For, like Parmenides, Philolaus approached metaphysics from epistemology: Parmenides' initial question was: What conditions must any object of scientific inquiry satisfy? Philolaus began by asking what things must be like if they are to be known; and the connexion between being and knowledge remains prominent in the development of his ideas.

According to Diogenes, Philolaus' treatise opened thus:

> Nature in the universe[23] was harmonized from both unlimited and limiting things—both the universe as a whole and everything in it (**276: B 1**).

That initial statement was backed up by argument. It will be convenient to begin with **B 6**, which reads thus:

> And about nature and harmony things stand thus:—[i] The being (*estô*) of the objects, being eternal, and nature itself, admit divine and not human knowledge—[ii] except that none of the things that exist and are known by us could have come into being if there did not subsist (*huparchousas*) the being of the objects out of

> which the universe is compounded, both of the limiting things and of the unlimited. [iii] And since the principles subsisted being neither similar nor of the same tribe, it would have been thereby impossible for them to be arranged into a universe (*kosmêthênai*) if a harmony had not supervened, in whatever fashion it did come about. [iv] Now things that were similar and of the same tribe had no need of harmony; but those that were dissimilar and not of the same tribe and not of the same order (?)—it was necessary for such things to have been locked together by harmony if they were to be held together in a universe (**277**).[24]

The text of **277** is in several places uncertain; and interpretation is always hard. I shall deal with sentences [iii] and [iv] later on; sentence [i] is a conventionally sceptical or pious exordium (see above, p. 137): it is sentence [ii] which engages immediate attention.

The curious phrase 'the being of the objects (*ha estô tôn pragmatôn*)' must, I suppose, mean something like 'the existents *par excellence*'; at all events the phrase clearly denotes the same thing as 'the principles (*hai archai*)' of sentence [iii]. Of these principles we can know very little: first, that they are 'eternal'; second, that they consist of limiters and unlimiteds; third, that they require, in some cases at least, a harmonizing force. Why our knowledge is thus restricted Philolaus does not say: he implicitly rejects all Presocratic attempts to say what stuff or stuffs are primary, but he does so without argument. Perhaps he means only that a complete, and hence humanly impossible, knowledge of the present world would be required if we were to grasp just what types of principle were needed to generate it.

The eternity of the principles is presumably the *probandum* of sentence [ii]: 'the being of the objects subsists (*huparchein*)' means 'the principles are eternal'. The nerve of Philolaus' argument is constituted by two propositions:

(1) If *a* exists and is known to us, then *a* came into being.

(2) If *a* came into being, then the principles of *a* are eternal.

That (1) and (2) have an Eleatic background is plain enough; how precisely they relate to that background is a harder question to answer.

I take it that (1) is meant as an empirical observation: entities in the familiar world about us do, as a matter of fact, all have origins, near or remote. The epistemological *motif* which some have seen in (1) is only apparent: Philolaus does not mean that our knowing something requires that it be generated; he means only that the ordinary things that we do know are in fact generated.[25]

Epistemology proper does not enter until **B 2** and **B 3**.

Premiss (2), on the other hand, fits easily into the box of neo-Ionian answers to Elea: things cannot come into being *simpliciter*, Philolaus avers, but they may spring from eternal, ungenerable and incorruptible, principles. The roots of Empedocles, the 'things' of Anaxagoras, and the atoms of Leucippus and Democritus are all eternal; and their eternity is generally regarded as a concession to Elea. Philolaus, in (2), makes an analogous concession; how useful these concessions are will be discussed in a later chapter.

Thus far nothing of a peculiarly Pythagorean character has emerged from 277: it is the reference to 'limiters' and 'unlimited' things that gives the fragment its characteristic flavour; I shall approach this by way of **B 3** and **B 2**:

> For there will not even be anything that will be known if all things are unlimited (**278: B 3**).

> [v] It is necessary for the things that exist to be all either limiting or unlimited or both limiting and unlimited. [vi] But they could not be only unlimited [or only limiting]. [vii] Since, then, the things that exist are evidently neither from things all of which are limiting nor from things all of which are unlimited, it is clear then that both the universe and the things in it were harmonized from both limiting and unlimited things. [viii] And the facts too make this clear; for some of them, coming from limiting things, limit; and others, coming from both limiting and unlimited things, both limit and do not limit; and others, coming from unlimited things, are evidently unlimited (**279: B 2**).

The logical form of Philolaus' argument is fairly clear. Let *P* abbreviate 'All existing things are limiting', *Q* 'All existing things are unlimited', *R* 'All existing things are both limiting and unlimited'. Then [v] asserts:

(3) *P* or *Q* or *R*.

[vi] asserts:

(4) not-*P* and not-*Q*.

and [vii], inferring *R*, makes the further deduction that:

(5) Existing things were harmonized from both limiting and unlimited things.

Why does Philolaus expect us to assent to this curious argument? Premiss (3) is, I suppose, meant as an exhaustive disjunction, a logical truth. It is natural to read *R* as 'everything is both limiting and unlimited'; but that is ruled out by sentence [viii], which plainly places among 'the facts' the existence of some unlimited limiters and of some unlimiting unlimiteds. Hence if **279** is to be consistent, *R* must be read as: 'Some things are limiting and others are unlimited'. The reading is confirmed by the fact that it makes (3) a logical truth: the disjuncts are indeed logically exhaustive.

278, I take it, argues for not-*Q*: if we know anything, then not-*Q*; and we do have knowledge. The truth of **278** cannot be assessed until we have come closer to grips with the notion of a 'limit'. The first conjunct of (4), not-*P*, is a conjectural addition to the text; but not-*P* is plainly necessary to Philolaus' argument. No argument for not-*P* survives, but one is readily invented: surely if *a* is limiting, then *a* limits something; limiters logically require limitees. And again surely limitees are themselves intrinsically unlimited; if *a* limits *b*, then *b* is *per se* unlimited. But in that case the argument in **278** only needs a slight prolongment to prove not-*P* as well as not-*Q*.

The conclusion (5) is familiar from **276** and **277**; and it is the kernel of Philolaus' ontology. The thought that carries Philolaus from *R* to (5) is simple: what is itself a limiter cannot be compounded purely from unlimited things; no conjunction of unlimiteds will produce a limit. And conversely, what is unlimited requires unlimited constituents: a set of limiters will never give the unlimited its constitutional freedom. Thus (3) is a truth of logic; epistemology guarantees (4); (3) and (4) yield *R* by elementary logic; and *R* produces (5).[26]

(c) *Shape and number*

The 'facts'[27] alluded to in sentence [viii] are intended to convince us of the truth of (5): their form is logically appropriate but their content is obscure. Indeed, I fear that the fastidious reader will long ago have given up Philolaus in distaste: perhaps **279** contains a formally clear argument; but its substance is certainly misty and probably mystical. If that natural and entirely commendable feeling is to be dispelled we must discover what Philolaus has in mind when he talks of 'limiters' and 'unlimiteds'.

The fragments give no elucidation and no concrete illustration of 'limiters' and 'unlimiteds'; and the slim doxography is helplessly silent. Some scholars point to a notorious passage in Plato's *Philebus* which speaks of limits and the unlimited;[28] but that dialogue's gross obscurities give no help to a mind puzzling over Philolaus. Others read infinite divisibility into the 'unlimited' and speak of limiting atoms; but that will hardly fit the text. We are reduced to conjecture; but conjecture is not difficult, for an obvious interpretation is to hand: to apply a limiter to an unlimited is to give specific shape or form to a mass of unformed stuff. The 'facts' appealed to in [viii] will then consist of elementary examples of that type of operation: a potter moulds a wedge of clay into a pot; a sculptor casts a mass of bronze into a statue; a baker pats his dough into a loaf; a carpenter shapes a table from rough timber: all these artists apply a shape to a stuff, a limiter to an unlimited. Shapes are essentially limiting: anything shaped in such and such a way has, *eo ipso*, limits beyond which it does not extend; it is determined and circumscribed by its shapely boundaries. Stuffs, on the contrary, are essentially unlimited; clay and bronze, dough and wood, have no shapes. Any particular parcel of clay does, of course, possess some shape, however irregular or unaesthetic; but clay as such has no shape: 'What shape is clay?' is a nonsense question.

If we look at 'the facts', we find an abundance of cases in which things 'come from both limiting and unlimited things'; and they 'both limit and do not limit', i.e., they are compounds of a limiting shape and an unlimited stuff. But the 'facts' are also supposed to give us examples of compounds made exclusively from limiters, and of compounds made exclusively from unlimiteds. The former set of examples must, I imagine, be geometrical: a geometer may construct a square by conjoining two triangles, or a cube by adding two pyramids. Here two limiters are put together, and the result is a limiter; two shapes, conjoined, yield a third shape. Unlimiteds, too, are compounded: a metalworker may pour copper and tin together to make bronze; a cook mixes oil and vinegar; a painter blends one pigment with another. Such familiar operations are compoundings of one stuff from other stuffs, of one unlimited from other unlimiteds.

That interpretation seems to me to fit the Philolaic texts better than any other; and it gives Philolaus an original and important role in the development of philosophy.[29] The early Ionians, as Aristotle rightly insists, concentrated their attention on 'the material cause'; they inquired into the stuff of the universe, and supposed that one or two fairly simple operations on that *Ur*-stuff would suffice to generate our well-formed world. Empedocles and Anaxagoras also focussed their minds on matter: it was the diversity of stuffs rather than the diversity of substances which drew their attention and which they aspired to vindicate in the face of Eleatic objections. Atomism, it is true, pays some attention to form: the atoms have shapes, and are indeed referred to as *schêmata* or *ideai*; but there is no evidence that the Atomists placed any particular stress on the diversity of forms in the world, or that they went out of their way to account for the shape as well as the stuff of things.

Philolaus stands in strong contrast to that long tradition: he recognizes stuffs, but he insists equally on shapes. His fundamental tenet, expressed at the outset of his book in **276**, is that both matter and form are required in any analysis or explanation of the phenomena; we have to account not only for the diverse materials present in the mundane world, but also for the diverse ways in which those materials present themselves to us: we live in a material world, but the material is informed. And that, after all, is the essence of Aristotle's judgment on the Pythagorean contribution to natural philosophy: they 'began to talk about what a thing is, and to make definitions' (*Met* 987a20 = **58 B 8**); in other words, they began to investigate form as well as matter.

'But', Aristotle continues, 'they treated the issue too simply.' To see how Philolaus treated the issue we must look at two further fragments:

> And indeed all the things that are known have a number; for it is not possible for anything to be thought of or to be known without this (**280: B 4**).[30]

> Number indeed has two proper kinds, odd and even [and a third from both mixed together, even-odd];[31] and of each kind there are many forms (*morphai*) which each thing in itself signifies (**281: B 5**).

These two fragments stand in an intelligible relationship to **279**. The two 'kinds' of number are the odd and the even; and a strong tradition connects limit with odd numbers and unlimitedness with even numbers: in the *Metaphysics* Aristotle briefly delineates two Pythagorean views:

> These evidently believe that number is a principle . . . and that the elements of number are the even and the odd, and of these one is unlimited, the other limited; and the unit is from both these (for it is both even and odd). . . . Others of the same group say that there are ten principles, set out in a column:
> limit and unlimited
> odd and even
> one and plurality
> right and left
> male and female
> resting and moving
> straight and bent
> light and darkness

good and bad
square and oblong
(**282**: 986a15–26 = **58 B 5**; cf. Aristotle, fr. 203).

There is much in that column of 'principles' to excite the curiosity. Here I observe simply that odd associates with limit, even with lack of limit. (And there are explanations, of a vaguely arithmetical sort, for those associations.[32])

It is easy to suppose that Philolaus, who has limiting and unlimited principles, and who refers to the two 'kinds' of number, made the same association between the members of these two pairs: Philolaic limiters are odd numbers; Philolaic unlimiteds are even numbers. I do not believe the interpretation. The main argument against it is that it does not, as far as I can see, lead to any clear overall understanding of Philolaus' theory of principles, whereas the alternative interpretation which I shall shortly offer gives Philolaus a fairly coherent philosophy. Two small points tell in the same direction: first, **280** suggests that 'having a number' is a sufficient condition for knowability; but if even numbers characterize the unlimiteds, then the unlimiteds too will be knowable—*contra* **278**. Second, the numbers, both odd and even, are said to be 'forms (*morphai*)'; that surely connects having a number with having a shape; but 'the unlimiteds' have no shape. I conclude that Philolaus differs from those Pythagoreans who assimilated odd and even to limited and unlimited. (That, indeed, is my chief reason for doubting that Philolaus was a main source for Aristotle's account of fifth-century Pythagoreanism.)

The 'forms' of **281** are presumably the natural numbers themselves: 2,4,6 . . . are the forms of the kind *even*; 1,3,5 . . . are the forms of the kind *odd*. 'Each thing in itself signifies' one of the natural numbers in that each thing is essentially determined by a natural number: what is known must have or be a limit or form; forms are expressed by numbers; hence whatever is known 'has a number'.

An explicit account of this sort of thing is ascribed to Eurytus, a pupil of Philolaus (cf. Iamblichus, **45 A 1**). Archytas told how Eurytus 'used to set out some pebbles, and say that *this* is the number of man, *this* of horse, *this* of something else' (Theophrastus, *Metaphysics* 6a19 = **45 A 2**). Aristotle refers to the same practice (*Met* 1092b8 = **45 A 3**), and a commentator explains it at length:

> Suppose for the sake of argument that the number 250 is the definition of man, and 360 of plant. Positing this, he used to take

> 250 pebbles—some green, some black, some red, and in general coloured in all sorts of hues; then, smearing the wall with plaster and sketching a man and a plant, he would stick these pebbles on the drawing of the face, these on that of the hands, others elsewhere, and he would complete the drawing of the pictured man by means of pebbles equal in number to the units which he said defined man (**283**: pseudo-Alexander, **45 A 3**).[33]

That sounds intolerably puerile; and puerile it doubtless was. Yet it is not quite as frivolous as it is sometimes imagined to be: Eurytus was not just 'drawing pictures with pebbles'; nor did his pebbles represent physical—or atomic—constituents of man.

Rather, he must have started from a geometrical observation: three points, however disposed, determine a triangle; and any triangle is determined by three points; four points determine a quadrilateral, and any quadrilateral is determined by four points. In general, then, geometrical and stereometrical figures will be determined by natural numbers; and since men and plants are stereometrical figures, they too will have their defining numbers. Eurytus' task was to work out 'the minimum number of points necessary to ensure that the surfaces formed by joining them would represent a man and nothing else';[34] and his pebble-dashing provided a striking if crude analogy to that grand scientific task. Philolaus, I assume, anticipated Eurytus; and in **278** and **279** we have the theoretical statement of the view which Eurytus' pebbles illustrate.

Is all this mere comical arithmology? or is it the first scrabbling essay towards a quantitative and mathematically-based science? Surely it is both of those things. Scientific theorems must be mathematical in their expression if they are to have the precision and utility we require of scientific knowledge: the early Milesian theories were largely unquantitative (above, p. 48), and their neo-Ionian successors seem to have done little better in that respect; even the Atomists made no attempt to apply arithmetic or geometry to scientific knowledge. Philolaus and Eurytus saw their failing, and attempted to meet it: the shapes of things are essential to them (we recognize things by virtue of their shapes); shapes can be expressed arithmetically; and the consequent arithmetical definitions of substances may be expected to function as the foundations of a mathematical physics.

In aim and scope the Philolaic project is admirable; in practice it is, inevitably, jejune. Shapes are not determined by natural numbers in the way Philolaus apparently imagined: does 4 determine a quadrilateral or a tetrahedron? does 8 determine an octagon or a hexahedron? Natural numbers alone will not do: if geometry is to be 'reduced' to arithmetic, the reduction must be carried out by more sophisticated means. Again, however important shapes may be in our recognition of substances, it is plain that they do not constitute the essence of substances. A poodle is not simply a mass of stuff formed in such and such a shape; it is a thing with certain powers and dispositions; decoy ducks and waxwork men, however cleverly modelled, are not ducks and men. Conversely, it is hard to imagine that there is *a* shape of man, let alone of dog or of plant: men come in different shapes and sizes; species of dog differ considerably in outline; and any attempt to distinguish the shape of a plant would be laughable.

Finally, stuffs have no shape—they are essentially unlimited; yet we surely do have knowledge of stuffs. Philolaus' fundamental assumption that 'there is no knowledge of the unlimited' seems to be a baseless prejudice; and it is implicitly contradicted by the third type of 'fact' to which the end of **277** appeals. No doubt genuine knowledge of stuffs must be in some sense quantitative: we do not have genuine knowledge if we only 'know' that tin and copper alloy to bronze; we need to know that a mixture of *n* per cent tin and *m* per cent copper yields bronze. But even if knowledge is thus connected with quantity and number, there is no connexion with shape or form, and we are left, it seems, with knowledge of 'the unlimited'. Some may feel that this point is at once so evident and so strong that it rules out my whole interpretation of Philolaus' philosophy. That feeling engages my sympathy; yet I still incline to accept the interpretation, and its consequent inconcinnity: no alternative fares any better, and Philolaus, I fear, is not wholly consistent or clear-minded.

(d) *The harmony of things*

Limiters and unlimiteds do not exhaust Philolaus' conceptual resources: these principles, by themselves, would not have sufficed for a universe 'if a harmony had not supervened, in whatever fashion it did come about' (**277**); and the 'harmonizing' of the principles is adverted to again in **276**, **279** and **B** 7.

'Harmony' translates—or rather transliterates—'*harmonia*'; and the word, familiar to us from Heraclitus (see p. 600, n. 13), may mean no more than a conjoining or fitting together. It is thus tempting to read no more than a tautology into sentence [iii] of **277**: if there were no *harmonia*, then, quite trivially, limiters and unlimiteds could not have been fitted together. But sentence [iv] makes it plain that Philolaus meant more than that: *harmonia* is required not for any compounding, but for the compounding of things that are dissimilar or 'not of the same tribe'.

The dissimilar things are limiters and unlimiteds: why should conjunctions of limiter and unlimited require a *harmonia* when conjunctions of limiter and limiter, or of unlimited and unlimited, do not? Any two limiters may be fitted together: limiters are shapes, shapes are numbers, and any two numbers can be added together. What is more, their compound is eternally stable: the truths of arithmetic are indestructible. Again, most stuffs can be mixed or amalgamated into a moderately stable compound; such, at least, was the implicit assumption of all the Presocratic cosmogonies, and if a few trite examples tell against it (oil and vinegar proverbially separate), then either Philolaus ignored them or he supposed that they are not 'of the same tribe' even though they are 'similar': similar *qua* unlimited, they do not belong to the same kind of unlimiteds.

On the other hand, it is a clear empirical fact that not every shape can be fitted to every stuff: you may fashion a sphere of wood or metal, but you will not impose a spherical form on water or fire; the characteristic form of flames cannot, or cannot easily, be matched in wood; sand will form dunes but not pinnacles; mercury, globules but not cubes. Of the innumerable matchings of form and stuff that are possible, few are actual; and therefore some explanation is required for those matchings that do occur. In short, there must be a harmony between certain shapes and certain stuffs which accounts for their felicitous association. To say that there is a harmony is not to offer an explanation; it is to point out the need for an explanation. Just as the terms 'limiter' and 'unlimited' are schematic designations of types of principle, so the term 'harmony' is a schematic designation for a type of explanation: we cannot know what the essential nature of limiters and unlimiteds is; nor can we know how, in concrete terms, shape and matter cohere. What we do know is, first, that there must be both shape and matter; and second, that there must be an explanatory harmony of their conjunction.

Harmonia is not a static thing: it is introduced in a dynamic cosmogonical context. Nature 'was harmonized (*harmochthê*)' (**276**); the universe 'was compounded (*sunesta*)' (**277**); things were 'arranged into a universe (*kosmêthênai*)' (**277**); 'everything comes about (*gignesthai*) by necessity and harmony' (Diogenes Laertius, VIII.84 = **A 1**). Two fragments of the cosmogony survive. One says merely that:

> The first thing to be harmonized in the middle of the sphere is called the hearth (**284: B** 7).[35]

The other is longer; I quote it for its interesting attempt to deal with the notions of 'up' and 'down':

> The universe is one, and it began to come into being at the middle, and from the middle upwards in the same way as downwards. And what is upward is over against the middle from the point of view of those below; for to those below the lowest part is like the uppermost part, and similarly for the rest. For both have the same relationship to the middle except that their positions are reversed (**285: B 17**).[36]

This fragment coheres well enough with the Philolaic astronomy, and it might easily come from a cosmogony in the traditional Ionian style; but the fact is that we know almost nothing of Philolaus' cosmogonical speculations.

A naive interpretation of Philolaus would imagine a pre-cosmic state of things in which on the one side there rose a vast mass of completely shapeless stuffs, and on the other side there stood a tailor's shop of forms: at the cosmogonic moment, something caused a suit to be taken from the shop and fitted harmoniously to the first fortunate lump of clay; and cosmogony proceeded, in orderly fashion, in the same general way, pre-existing forms being successively wrapped around suitable lumps of pre-existing stuff.

Aristotle makes two criticisms of the Pythagoreans which seem to tell against Philolaus even if they were not expressly aimed at him. First, he says that:

> They did not think that the limited and the unlimited and the one are different natures—e.g., fire or earth or something else of that sort, but that the unlimited itself and the one itself are the substance (*ousia*) of the things they are predicated of; and for that reason number is the substance of everything (**286**: *Met* 987a15–9 = **58 B 8**).

Second, he says that:

> These men evidently think that number is the principle for existing things both as matter and as affections and properties (**287**: *Met* 986a15–17 = **58 B 5**).

Does not Philolaus in his cosmogony treat limiters, and hence numbers, as physical components of things? And does he not also treat the unlimiteds and the limiters as substances rather than attributes?

One part at least of the Aristotelian criticism does not touch Philolaus: he does not deny that the limiters and the unlimiteds are 'different natures'; that is to say, he does not assert that there are things which are *simply* unlimited and not unlimited fire or water or whatever. He does not imagine that the phrase 'the unlimited' picks out some peculiarly abstract kind of stuff; rather, he means that the original principles, whatever they are, are some of them limiters and some of them unlimited.[37]

The core of Aristotle's criticism, however, remains. Philolaus plainly holds, first, that limiters and unlimiteds are eternal, and second, that their cosmogonic harmonizing was an historical, or pre-historical, event. It follows that at some time there existed limiters or shapes that limited nothing or were shapes of nothing; and also that there existed shapeless, unlimited, masses of stuff. Moreover, the claim that the universe was 'compounded' from limiters and unlimiteds does powerfully suggest a picture in which the formal element in the compound is treated 'as matter'.

Some sort of a defence can be found for Philolaus: his shapes or limiters are, after all, essentially numbers; and the 'Platonist' view that numbers are eternal substances is not to be abandoned merely on Aristotle's ukase. There are deep waters here on which Philolaus may, for a time at least, contrive to float. Again, Philolaus' pre-cosmic masses need not, perhaps, be literally devoid of form: Philolaus might have contented himself with the suggestion that the pre-cosmic form of stuffs was 'form' only in an etiolated sense—shape, but not intelligible shape, not mathematically determinable shape. Cosmogony, thus conceived, is the imposition of intelligible form on unintelligible matter. And finally, the crude conception of form as a quasi-constituent, and of information as a quasi-material colligation, can be purified or replaced by an unobjectionable notion.

I do not intend to follow up those vague suggestions: to do so would impose an anachronistic syncretism on Philolaus, uniting a Platonic account of mathematics with an Aristotelian position on form and matter. I prefer to end by underlining Philolaus' essential mistake. Rightly observing that a bronze sphere could be analysed into form (sphericity) and matter (bronze), Philolaus wrongly conflated that sort of analysis with the analysis of bronze into copper and tin. Bronze is compounded or put together from copper and tin; in much the same way, he supposed, a bronze sphere is compounded or put together from bronze and sphericity. In the latter case, to be sure, the components are 'dissimilar and not of the same tribe'; but the notion of compounding is the same in the two cases.

But the analyses and the compoundings are quite different: a chemical or physical analysis shows that bronze is made of tin and copper; a logical or conceptual analysis shows that a bronze sphere is made of sphericity and bronze. The former analysis, in Aristotelian jargon, breaks a thing down into its real parts, the latter into its logical parts: no physical process will separate the bronze from sphericity, and no logical penetration will reveal the chemical components of bronze. The distinction is not easy to articulate or expound; and the difficulties are increased by the fact that the same language is customarily used for both notions. Aristotle's commentators regularly fell into the confusion I am ascribing to Philolaus; and Aristotle himself only avoided it by the skin of his logical teeth.

Was Philolaus a great wit, or a ninny? We do not possess a vast amount of evidence, and the evidence we do have is of contested value. Certainly there are naive elements in Philolaus' thought; but equally certainly there are elements of bold originality, both in speculative science and in philosophy. I for one am prepared to credit Philolaus with the discovery of Aristotelian 'form'; and to claim that such a discovery was no insignificant achievement.

XIX

The Logic of Locomotion

(a) *Empedocles and antiperistasis*

The neo-Ionian defence of science against Eleatic metaphysics rests at bottom on their vindication of locomotion: if things can move, science is possible; if locomotion is impossible, science falls with it. All three Eleatics argued against locomotion: Parmenides in **156**. 26–33, Melissus in **168**, Zeno by way of his four or five paradoxes. The neo-Ionian defence takes on only Melissus: Parmenides' obscure lines are justifiably ignored; and nothing is said against Zeno. I have no explanation of the latter omission: perhaps the paradoxes were unknown to the neo-Ionians; perhaps they were despised as sophisms or set aside as insoluble problems. With an adequate chronology some of that puzzlement might evaporate; but we have no adequate chronology (above, pp. 305–7). At best, then, the neo-Ionians will achieve a partial success: however powerful their arguments in Melissan country, they have still to fight on Zeno's territory.

We have considerable evidence for the Atomists' attitude to locomotion; we possess a few straws pointing to the position of Empedocles and of Anaxagoras; we know nothing of Philolaus. In this section I deal with Empedocles and Anaxagoras.

Empedocles 'says in general that there is no void' (Theophrastus, *Sens* §13 = **31 A 86**). Aristotle gives the same report (*Cael* 309a19 = **59 A 68**); and we have Empedocles' own word for it:

> Nor is any part of the universe (*tou pantos*) empty, nor yet overfull (**288: B 13**).

> It . . . is not empty, nor yet overfull (**289**).[1]

The clause 'nor yet overfull (*perisson*)' is not casual: an empty space would contain no body; an overfull space would contain more than one body. Melissus' argument against motion needs to deny both emptiness and overcrowding (above, p. 226); and Empedocles is perfectly aware of the fact.

According to Anaxagoras, too, 'nothing is empty' (Aristotle, *Resp* 471a2 = **59 A 115**); Aristotle repeats the assertion (*Cael* 309a19 = **A 68**), and it reappears in the *MXG* (976b20), in Lucretius (I.843 = **A 44**), and in Hippolytus (**A 42**). We have no first-hand evidence for the ascription, but the doxographical tradition is unanimous and indisputable. Anaxagoras, it is true, held that 'the dense and the rare' could be found in the world (**B 15**); and 'there are some who think it evident from the rare and the dense that there is void' (Aristotle, *Phys* 216b22). But the examples of Descartes and of Aristotle himself (*Phys* Δ 9) show that a philosopher may deny the existence of void and still assign different degrees of density to different stuffs; and that position is, I judge, logically consistent.

It is regularly supposed that both Empedocles and Anaxagoras offered empirical arguments to show that 'nothing is empty'. The source of the supposition is Aristotle:

> Those who attempt to prove that it [sc. the void] does not exist do not refute what men mean by void but only what they erroneously say; e.g., Anaxagoras and those who refute it in that fashion. For they show that the air is something, by twisting wineskins and proving that the air is strong, and by capturing it in clepsydras (**290**: *Phys* 213a22–7 = **59 A 68**).

We know that Anaxagoras talked about the clepsydra (pseudo-Aristotle, *Prob* 914b9 = **59 A 69**), and Aristotle (despite his plural 'they') may have Anaxagoras alone in mind in this passage. It is, however, regularly connected with a celebrated fragment of Empedocles (**31 B 100**). That fragment attempts to explain the phenomena of respiration by means of an elaborate analogy with the clepsydra, an ancient device for transmitting liquids from one vessel to another, similar in function and action to the modern chemist's pipette.[2] It is often alleged that the fragment describes an experiment, and that the experiment was designed to disprove the existence of empty space. I shall not try to elucidate **B 100**, which has aroused a busy hum of commentary. But it is, I think, perfectly plain that no 'experiment' is described in the fragment;[3] that if the fragment incidentally implies the corporeality of the air, it was certainly not meant to demonstrate it; and that the whole piece says nothing whatever about the void. Empedocles' clepsydra is a red herring: let us return to the *Physics*.

Air pressure forces liquid out of the pipette and holds liquid in it; the force or 'strength' of the air is tangible in an inflated balloon or a twisted wineskin. There is no reason to doubt that Anaxagoras made these observations, and that he used them to confirm the long familiar fact that air is corporeal. Quite evidently, such observations do not prove the non-existence of the void: some scholars infer that in the *Physics* Aristotle merely misrepresents the purpose of Anaxagoras' remarks.[4] But Aristotle cannot be dismissed so lightly; and we may readily connect Anaxagoras' observations to the void without ascribing any childish error to him. Partisans of the void will have tried to establish their case simply by pointing to the air; 'for the air seems to be empty' (Aristotle, *An* 419b34). Against such people, Anaxagoras' observations are pertinent: they do not show that there is no void, nor were they meant to; but they do refute a simple-minded argument for the existence of empty space.

Why, then, did Empedocles and Anaxagoras reject the void? I suppose that they adopted a Melissan argument.

There is no void. Melissus inferred the impossibility of motion; Empedocles and Anaxagoras believed in locomotion: how did they justify their defiant opinion?[5] Of Anaxagoras we know nothing. He allows that the world contains 'the dense' and 'the rare' (**59 B 15**); and he presumably had some answer to Melissus' assertion that 'the rare is thereby more empty than the dense' (**168**). But what answer he might have given I do not know; nor can I invent any connexion between degrees of density and locomotion.

Empedocles' fragments are equally silent; but in his case the doxography comes to our aid:

> Similarly Empedocles too says that the compounds are always moving continually for all time, but that nothing is empty; saying that 'of the whole nothing is empty: whence, then, might anything come?'; and when they are compounded into one form so as to be one, 'it', he says 'is not empty in any respect nor overfull'. For what prevents them from travelling and circulating (*peristasthai*) into one another, if at the same time one always changes into another and that into another and another into the first? (**291**: *MXG* 976b22–9 = **30 A 5**).

The doctrine ascribed to Empedocles in this passage is that of counter-circulation or *antiperistasis*:

Nature that hateth emptiness,
Allows of penetration less:
And therefore must make Room
Where greater Spirits come.

Abhorring emptiness and penetration alike (**288**), Empedoclean nature must 'make room' if it is to encompass locomotion. The *MXG*'s mode of expression implies, perhaps, that Empedocles did not make his doctrine fully explicit; but he did, I think, come fairly close to it:

> Empedocles said . . . that all [the elements] take one another's places (*metalambanein*) (**292**: Aëtius, **31 A 35**);

> He says that they give way to each other (*antiparachôrein*) (**293**: Achilles, **31 A 35**).

The doxographers rely ultimately on the Empedoclean phrase that occurs more than once in the fragments: the elements, he says, 'run through one another (*di' allêlôn . . . theonta*)' (**B** 17.34 = **B 21**.13 = **B 26**.3). In the context, it is entirely reasonable to take the repeated phrase as a first, imprecise, formulation of the theory of *antiperistasis*.[6]

What exactly was the theory? And how does it answer the Eleatic challenge? Melissus' argument against motion relied on the following principle (above, p. 219):

(1) If *a* moves to *p* at *t*, then immediately prior to *t p* is empty.

A mobile opponent will not grant (1). First, he might suggest that prior to *t p* is occupied by a body, *b*, which is compressible: at *t a* compresses *b* by the force of its trajectory and thus comes to occupy a region formerly occupied by a part of *b*. But that will not trouble Melissus, who has argued that no bodies are compressible: being 'full', bodies are not 'dense and rare'. The opponent turns to a second suggestion: up to *t p* is occupied by *b*, but at *t*, just as *a* enters *p*, *b* moves to a new position p_1.

Melissus will still remain unshaken: instead of (1) he will offer:

(2) If *a* moves to *p* at *t*, then immediately prior to *t* some place or other must be empty.

Admittedly, *p* may be occupied up to *t*; but its occupant, *b*, must move at *t*; and there must be some empty place or other for *b* to move into. Proposition (2) will do all the work Melissus required of (1); and it turns the opponent's second suggestion.

Yet why should a proponent of locomotion accept (2)? Motion, he will say, does not require ***any*** vacancies. Let *b* occupy *p* up to *t*: then *a* may move to p at t provided that there are two series of bodies, $c_1 \ldots c_n$ and $d_1 \ldots d_m$ such that, first, the places occupied by a, b, each c_i and each d_i are all identical in shape and size, and, second, a is contiguous with c_1, c_1 with c_2, ... c_{n-1} with c_n, c_n with b, b with d_1, d_1 with d_2, ... d_{m-1} with d_m, and d_m with a. Then a may move to p at t, provided that each of the contiguous bodies moves, at the same time and the same speed, to fill its neighbour's position. Imagine a card circle, divided by two diameters into quarters labelled a, c, b, d. At t revolve the circle through 180°; then a comes to occupy the place of b; and at no time is any part of the circle empty.

That is the theory of *antiperistasis*; and it is that by which Empedocles hoped to vindicate locomotion. The theory had an illustrious life: Plato formulated it clearly (*Timaeus* 80C); and Aristotle produces it as his own answer to the Melissan challenge: 'For it is possible for things to yield place to one another at the same time, even though there is no separable interval [i.e. no empty space] apart from the moving bodies. And this is clear in the case of whirls of continuous things, just as it is in the case of those of liquids' (*Phys* 214a29–32).[7] Aristotle illustrates *antiperistasis* by pointing to children's tops and water eddies; the best known illustration was first produced by Straton of Lampsacus, head of the Peripatetic school in the third century BC: 'Straton's example offers a more suitable escape from these difficulties; for if you put a pebble into a jar full of water and turn the jar upside down while holding the stopper over the mouth, the pebble will move to the mouth of the jar as the water moves around (*antimethistamenon*) into the place of the pebble' (fr. 63 W = Simplicius, *in Phys* 659.22–6).

Those modern thinkers who held that the universe is a *plenum* accepted the ancient theory of *antiperistasis*. Thus Descartes: 'The only possible movement of bodies is in a circle; a body pushes another out of the place it enters, and that another, till at last we come to a body that enters the place left by the first body at the very moment when the first body leaves it'.[8] I see no logical objection to *antiperistasis*. Russell once observed that 'it should . . . be obvious, even to the non-mathematical, that motion in a closed circuit is possible for a fluid. It is a pity that philosophers have allowed themselves to repeat [the argument that motion presupposes a vacuum], which a week's study of hydrodynamics would suffice to dispel'. It has been asserted that 'the plenum theory inevitably implies the existence of instantaneous physical actions, that is, of actions spreading in space with infinite velocity';[9] for the force transmitted, in my schematic example, from a to c_1 must pass in an instant about the 'circle' of bodies to b. But that is not so, as the case of the spinning top demonstrates; moreover, it does not seem to me to constitute a logical objection to *antiperistasis*. Melissus' principle (2) is not a logical truth; and locomotion within a *plenum* is a logical possibility.

(b) *The Atomists and the void*

The Atomists did not move by counter-circulation: motion, they held, took place through a void; and there *is* a void.

> Leucippus and Democritus . . . [said] that there is void not only in the universe but also outside the universe (**294**: Simplicius, **67 A 20**).

The world contains interstitial void between its component atoms; and the world itself is separated from other atomic conglomerates by acres of extra-mundane vacuity. 'In truth, there are atoms and void' (**68 B 125**): in that famous fragment, and in countless doxographical reports, void has a place alongside the atoms as one of the twin pillars of the Abderite universe.[10]

Melissus' rejection of vacancy depended on the premiss that what is empty is non-existent, or nothing (above, p. 218). The Atomists boldly accepted his premiss:

> Leucippus and his associate Democritus say that the full and the empty are elements, calling one existent and the other non-existent; the full and solid is the existent, the empty and rare the non-existent. That is why they also say that what exists exists no more than what does not exist—because the empty [exists no less than] body (**295**: Aristotle, *Met* 985b4–9 = **67 A 6**).

> What exists subsists no more than what does not exist; and both alike are explanations for what comes into being (**296**: Simplicius, **67 A 8**).

The void is non-existent; the void exists: hence the non-existent exists.

The void is also nothing. And Plutarch quotes a passage from Democritus

> in which he asserts that 'the thing exists no more than the nothing'—calling body thing and the void nothing—on the assumption that this latter too possesses a certain nature and substance of its own (**297: 68 B 156**).

We need not delay over the order of the phrases in this quotation: '*a* exists no more than *b*' and '*b* exists no more than *a*' both mean no more than '*a* and *b* alike exist'; the relative order of *a* and *b* has at most a stylistic point. Nor need the phrase 'the thing' detain us: 'nothing' in **297** translates '*mêden*'; *mê* means 'not'; subtract *mê* from *mêden* and you get *den*, and that is the word I translate 'thing'. Subtract 'not' from 'nothing' and you get 'hing'; and some scholars proudly offer 'hing' as their translation of *den*. But 'hing' is a nonsense word, *den* is not: it occurs once elsewhere, in a fragment of Alcaeus (fr. 130 LP), and was, it seems, a rare word meaning '*chrêma*' or '*pragma*'—'thing'.[11] Clearly, *den* in **297** is present only for its rhetorical effect: the fragment says no more than that nothing, no less than existent things, exists.

Melissus in **168** uses 'nothing (*mêden*)' to mean 'non-existent (*mê on*)'; and Democritus in **297** is, I suppose, simply following Melissus, Even so, 'the non-existent exists' does not seem much more promising as an axiom of science than '(the) nothing exists': the axiom looks flatly self-contradictory. It is tempting to dismiss the remark as a piece of *ad hominem* abuse: 'The void exists, and if Melissus chooses, absurdly, to call the void non-existent, why then, the non-existent exists. But we Atomists will not be outfaced by such a trivially verbal manoeuvre.' Yet Melissus, I have argued, did not simply mishandle the notion of non-existence; and our texts give no hint that, in asserting the existence of the non-existent, the Atomists were merely indulging in raillery.

If we are to take seriously the assertion that 'the non-existent exists', we must make it something more than a simple self-contradiction; and the only way of doing that is to posit two different senses for 'exist'. Democritus, we know, was alive to the possibility of ambiguity (cf. **B 26**); but there is no evidence that he saw an ambiguity in '*einai*'. Nonetheless, I am inclined to think that the Atomists were feeling towards such an insight: at all events, without that supposition we must leave them in the gloomy depths of blank contradiction.

Frege has familiarized us with the distinction between *Esgibtexistenz* and *Wirklichkeit*. In English, the normal phrase for expressing *Esgibtexistenz* is 'there is (are)', and a standard way of expressing *Wirklichkeit* is by means of the predicate 'real'. But both notions can be put across by the verb 'exist'; and similarly in Greek both notions are customarily expressed by the one verb '*einai*'. There are horses, and horses are real (they exist, whereas unicorns do not exist—they are fictional, not real); there are numbers, but numbers (in my book at least) are not real—they do not exist. When 'exist' signifies reality it is a predicate, and the formula '*a* exists' is well-formed; when 'exist' signifies *Esgibtexistenz* then it is not a (first-order) predicate and '*a* exists' is not well-formed.

Let us distinguish the reality sense of 'exist' as 'exist$_1$' and the *Esgibtexistenz* sense as 'exist$_2$'. Then I suggest that the proper sense of 'the non-existent exists' is given by 'the non-existent$_1$ exists$_2$'; i.e., by 'There are things which are not real'. Atoms and void exist; i.e., atoms and void exist$_2$, there are atoms and empty spaces. The void does not exist; i.e., the void does not exist$_1$, the void is unreal.

Now to exist$_1$ or to be real is to be a space-filler; and it is therefore a necessary truth that atoms exist$_1$: atoms are bodies, and bodies exist$_1$. On the other hand, 'void exists$_1$' is necessarily false; for only bodiless places are void. Thus 'the void is non-existent$_1$' is necessarily true, even though it is an axiom of physics that there are empty spaces or that the void exists$_2$. The Atomists can be given a consistent thesis; moreover, their thesis has, to my mind, a considerable plausibility: if we agree with Locke, and several of the ancients, that 'to be (i.e. to exist$_1$) is to be somewhere (i.e. to occupy a space)', then bodies and atoms do necessarily possess a being that empty space necessarily lacks. To pursue that hare further would lead to some of the more horrid thickets of philosophical logic: I shall assume that I have given the Atomists' slogan at least a *prima facie* plausibility, and proceed to the existence$_2$ of the void.

In the *Physics* Aristotle offers a list of arguments which had been used to show the existence of the void: local motion requires void, and so do rarefaction and condensation; growth presupposes a void; a jar full of ashes will hold as much water as the same jar when empty of ashes (213b2–29 = **67 A 19**). Some scholars ascribe those arguments to the Atomists;[12] and the argument from locomotion was canonical in Epicureanism: 'If there were not that which we call void and place and intangible nature, bodies would not have anywhere in which to be or through which to move—and they evidently do move' (*ad Hdt* §40; cf. §67; fr. 272 Us.). Evidently, bodies move; locomotion demands void: *ergo* there is void. Yet no ancient source attributes any of the arguments of the *Physics* to the Atomists; and the arguments are dialectically inapposite: Melissus rejects the void, and therefore motion; the Atomists, seeking to rehabilitate motion, restore the void. If they do so merely because motion requires it, their argument falls shamefully flat.

Metrodorus of Chios, a pupil of Democritus, said that:

> Everything that anyone thinks of (*noêsai*) exists (**298: 70 B 2**).

The sentiment is Eleatic in substance and form; and an easy

conjecture has Metrodorus attacking Elea with its own weapons: we can think of the void (for we can readily imagine vast oceans of empty space); thus, by the Eleatic principle that thinkability implies being, the void exists. I like to think that Metrodorus used that argument; but no text explicitly mentions it, nor is the Eleatic principle ascribed to Metrodorus' master.

To establish the void, the Atomists used, I believe, their own *Ou Mallon* Principle: Democritus said that 'the thing exists no more (*ou mallon*) than the nothing' (**297**); and *ou mallon* is used in the same context by Aristotle (*Met* 985b8 = **67 A 6**) and by Simplicius (**67 A 8**). The phrase *ou mallon* does not in itself prove the presence of the *Ou Mallon* Principle: '*a* is *ou mallon F* than *b*' may simply mean '*b* is just as *F* as *a* is'. And in **297** it is possible to take *ou mallon* in that way: 'the void is just as existent as the atoms are'. But I dislike that interpretation: the phrase 'more existent' grates on the logical ear; and if Democritus thinks that atoms $exist_1$ and $exist_2$ whereas the void $exists_2$ but does not $exist_1$, then it is false to say that void exists just as much as atoms. Thus I read the *Ou Mallon* Principle into **297**, and thereby discover the Atomists' argument for introducing the void: 'there is no more reason for there to be occupied than for there to be unoccupied areas of space'; 'there is no more reason for the $existence_2$ of atoms than for the $existence_2$ of void'. And since atoms $exist_2$, so too does void.

The argument rests on two premisses. First, it assumes that Melissus' argument *against* the void has no power; for otherwise there would be 'more reason' for the $existence_2$ of atoms than for the $existence_2$ of void. Second, it assumes the truth of the *Ou Mallon* Principle itself. I shall discuss those two premisses at a later stage of my argument: for the nonce, I leave the Atomists in possession of the field.

(c) *Anaxagoras and mind*

If the neo-Ionians are to succeed in their endeavours, motion must be more than a logical possibility: it must be an actual feature of the world. Parmenides objected to generation by asking, rhetorically, 'what *need* would have aroused it to come into being later or sooner?' (**156**. 9–10); and the same question can be applied to motion: nothing will move unless there is some explanation of its movement; yet what *need* impels things to move? *Aitiologia* or the giving of explanations, is in any case a part of the scientist's art: even without the prick of Parmenides' spur the neo-Ionians would have searched for explanations; goaded by it they only galloped faster. In the remaining sections of this chapter I shall look at some of the results of their search for explanation; and I begin with the most celebrated of them.

> [Anaxagoras] was the first to add mind to matter, beginning his book, which is pleasantly and grandly written, thus: 'All things were together; then mind came and arranged them' (**299**: Diogenes Laertius, II. 6 = **59 A 1**).[13]

Anaxagoras' invention earned him the nickname of 'Mind' (Timon, fr. 24 = **A 1**) and it won him rare praise from Aristotle:

> Someone said that mind is present as in animals, so in nature as the explanation of the universe (*kosmos*) and of the whole order of things; he appeared as a sober man compared to his predecessors who spoke at random (**300**: *Met* 984b15–18 = **A 58**).

What was Anaxagoras' mind? How was it related to the ordinary stuffs of his world? And how did it operate in and on the world?

Mind (*nous*) is a stuff, or at least stuff-like. The term 'mind' generally functions in Anaxagoras' fragments as a mass-noun, like 'gold' or 'flesh', and not as a count-noun, like 'ingot' or 'arm'. Moreover, mind 'is the finest of all things and the purest' (**B 12**): the reference to the rareness or 'fineness' of mind is often thought to represent an attempt, only partially successful, to express the thin notion of incorporeality. But mind is certainly extended in space (**B 14**), and I am inclined to think that Anaxagoras, far from hinting at mental incorporeality, was bent on the opposite tack: 'mind' is not, after all, a very stuff-like term in its ordinary behaviour; Anaxagoras, given to an ontology of stuffs, was determined to ascribe to mind a material existence and nature which by no means evidently belongs to it.

Since mind is a stuff we might expect it to act like other Anaxagorean stuffs, to have a share of everything and to be in everything; that is, we should expect the following two propositions to hold:

(1) If *a* is a piece of mind, then for any stuff, *S*, *a* contains a portion of *S*.

(2) For any stuff *S*, if *a* is a piece of *S*, then *a* contains a portion of mind.

But mind is no ordinary stuff: its peculiar features are expressed in four fragments:

> In everything there is present a portion of everything, except mind; and in some things mind too is present (**204: B 11**).

> The other things share a portion of everything; but [i] mind is unlimited[14] and independent (*autokratês*) and has been mixed with no thing but alone is itself by itself. For [ii] if it were not by itself but had been mixed with something else, it would share in all things if it had been mixed with anything (for [iii] in everything there is a portion of everything, as I have said earlier); and [iv] the things commingled with it would obstruct it so that it would not control (*kratein*) any thing in the same way as it does when being actually alone by itself. For [v] it is the finest of all things and the purest; and [vi] it has every knowledge about everything, and greatest power; and [vii] mind controls all the things that have soul (*psuchê*), both the greater and the smaller. [viii] And mind controlled the whole revolution (*perichôrêsis*), so that it revolved at the beginning. And [ix] first it began to revolve in a small way, but it revolves more, and it will revolve more. And [x] the things that commingle and those that separate off and those that separate out: mind knew them all. And [xi] what was to be and what was and is not now and what is now and what will be—all these mind ordered, and this revolution in which now revolve the stars and the sun and the moon and the air and the aether that are separating off. But the revolution itself made them separate off. And the thick is separating off from the thin, and the hot from the cold, and the bright from the dark, and the dry from the wet. And [xii] there are many portions of many things; but nothing is altogether separating off or separating out one from another, except mind. And [xiii] all mind is homogeneous, both the greater and the smaller. And nothing else is homogeneous; but each single thing is and was most clearly those things of which most are present in it (**301: B 12**).

> And when mind began to move things, it separated off from everything that was moved; and whatever mind moved, all that was separated out. And as things were moving and separating out, the revolution made them separate out much more (**302: B 13**).

> Mind . . .[15] is now where all other things are: in the surrounding multiplicity and in what are conjoined and in what are separated off (**303: B 14**).

At first blush, **204** seems to deny proposition (2), and sentences [i] and [xii] of **301** seem to deny proposition (1). I begin with (2).

'In some things mind too is present': Anaxagoras is simply stating the common-sense fact that some things have minds and others do not; the things that do are presumably those creatures with a soul or *psuchê* which mind 'controls' (**301**, [vii]); the things that do not are stocks and stones.[16] Can we infer from that common-sense proposition to the metaphysical thesis that some stuffs contain no portion of mind? and hence that (2) is false? It would be a rash inference: Anaxagoras might consistently maintain both (2) and the thesis of **204**; after all, when I drink a glass of gin, a 'mindless' stuff, my spirits revive—perhaps I extract a little mind from my drink.[17] And **303** does appear to imply (2): if mind is 'in the surrounding multiplicity' and in everything else, then surely every piece of stuff must contain a portion of mind? That easy interpretation is not inevitable; but as far as I can see it is both intelligible in itself and consistent with everything else that Anaxagoras has to say. And I conclude that Anaxagoras in fact assents to (2).

Mind, of course, is pure, unmixed, and by itself; but to say that is to deny (1), not to deny (2); more precisely, it is to assert the contrary of (1):

(3) If *a* is a piece of mind, then for no stuff *S* does *a* contain a portion of *S*.

Why does Anaxagoras maintain (3)? Some see it as an inference from the negation of (2); but Anaxagoras does not deny (2); the inference is plainly invalid; and Anaxagoras himself tells a different tale. In sentences [ii]—[iii], **301** explicitly infers (3) from the negation of (1); and the inference, given Anaxagorean physics, is correct. Given that every stuff contains a portion of every stuff, it follows that if mind does not contain every stuff, it does not contain any stuff.

Why, then, does Anaxagoras reject (1)? Why cannot pieces of mind, like any other bits of stuff, be omnivorous in their appetites? If they were, the characteristic powers of mind would be 'obstructed' according to sentence [iv], and it would lose 'control'. Sentence [v] explains sentence [iv] by reference to the 'fineness' of mind. Perhaps mind's fineness explains why mixture would obstruct its powers: mind is, as it were, a fine penetrating oil; and its penetrative powers, to which it owes its ability to control and know all things, would be inhibited by any commingling with grosser matter. But there is no reason to suppose that commingling would inhibit mind's penetrative capacities: in Anaxagorean physics, 'everything is in everything' and even the grossest body may penetrate the finest of stuffs. Fineness will not explain why mind should be obstructed; and I suppose that sentence [v] justifies the last part of [iv]: fineness explains mind's control 'when being actually alone by itself'. (Thus Diogenes of Apollonia held that *psuchê* was air, the 'most fine-bodied of all things', and that *psuchê* is 'mobile *qua* finest': Aristotle, *An* 405a21–5 = **64 A 20**.)

A different argument has been offered against (1): mind, alone of stuffs, has motive powers; hence mind must be distinguished from other inert stuffs; and the only mode of distinction is the denial of commixture to mind. But that argument has no textual basis. In any case, every other stuff has powers or properties of its own, yet those stuffs contain portions of everything else: why should mind alone lose its characteristic powers if it were not pure?

A man is made of flesh and blood and bone and mind; the universe contains earth and air and fire and water and mind. Those are platitudes. But, as Aristotle stressed, mind is not on a par with the other stuffs of the world: when we talk of a man's mind we are not speaking of any physical constituent, nor even of a quasi-physical constituent; we are referring, in a collective way, to his powers and his dispositions. If mind is treated as a constituent, physical or non-physical, of a man, confusion is likely to follow. I guess that Anaxagoras half saw that: mind is not like the other things of the world; its defining functions, knowledge and control (cognition and volition in a later argot), reveal the fact. Yet Anaxagoras could not grasp the full implications of his insight: he made mind pure, unmixed, and so on; but he deliberately construed it as a stuff. By accepting (2), he strongly affirmed its stuff-like nature; by denying (1), he hoped, vainly, to preserve its special status as a cognitive and active force.

What, then, are the powers of mind? and how does it operate in the world? The second half of **301** answers those questions. The details of mind's cosmic activity are of no philosophical interest; and I shall note only the main heads under which that activity can be subsumed: they are four.

First, mind knows everything. Perhaps, like the Homeric Muses, Anaxagorean mind knows everything because it is everywhere (**303**); or perhaps mind knows everything because it ordered everything and thus foresees all events in the world's history. (In the same way, some Christian theologians connect God's omniscience with his creativity.) Second, mind ordered or arranged everything: it planned the blueprint for cosmogony and determined how the primordial mass should be articulated into a world. Third, mind controls some things: some of the events in the present world are brought about by thought or ratiocination; and these, trivially, are the work of mind. Fourth, mind moved the *Ur*-mass; it set the stuffs into a whirl and thus began assembling a cosmos according to its blueprint.

That summary of mind's functions raises several questions. In this section I consider only the most obvious feature of mind: it is, above all, a 'moving cause', a source of locomotion and of change: 'he makes it a principle of motion' (Aristotle, *Phys* 256b25 = **A 56**); 'he linked the artist to the matter' (Aëtius, **A 46**); 'he filled out the missing explanation' (Simplicius, **A 41**).[18] Why did the mass of homoiomeries ever begin to whirl and form a cosmos? Because of mind. Why do the heavenly bodies now pursue their ordered courses? Because of mind. The general formula of explanation is this: 'Mind brought it about that *P*'. What is this 'mind'? Some think of a cosmic mind, a vast mass of pure mind which dreamed up and executed the cosmic plan.[19] But **302** implies that there was, at the cosmogonic starting point, no large central mass of mind; and no other text implies that such a mass ever existed. Nor are the ordinary events which mind controls plausibly assigned to any cosmic mind. Perhaps, then, 'mind' refers to the totality of mind stuff, the whole collection of mind portions; and to say that 'mind brought it about that *P* and mind brought it about that *Q*' is not to ascribe two acts to a single subject: water surrounds New Zealand and water flows from Oxford to London, but no one bit of stuff does both these things. For 'Mind brought it about that *P*' we should read: 'Some piece of mind brought it about that *P*'.

'Some', said Berkeley, 'have pretended to account for appearances by *occult qualities*, but of late they are mostly resolved into *mechanical causes*, to wit, the figure, *motion, weight*, and such like qualities of insensible particles: whereas in truth there is no other agent or efficient cause than *spirit*' (*Principles*, § 102). If a facile comparison sets Anaxagoras on Berkeley's side in this dispute, conjecture readily suggests Democritus as the ancient representative of the proponents of mechanical causes; and there is, I think, a distinction here that is worth bringing out.

Some philosophers, concerned to understand the notion of causation, take the performances of rational agents (in particular, of themselves) as paradigms of causal activity: when I observe myself or another man striking a billiard ball or driving a motor-car, then I am attending to a plain piece of causation. This attitude suggests that causes are *agents*, and that the causal structure of the world is tied together by powers and capacities to act and be acted upon. The canonical formula for causal propositions is: 'Agent *a* brings it about that *P*'.

Other philosophers look outward: causation is the cement of the universe, the adhesive which binds event to event; and we should seek it in the external universe and not in ourselves. When I observe one billiard ball strike and move another, or when I study the intricate mechanism of an internal combustion engine, then I am in the presence of causality. This attitude suggests that causes are antecedent *events*, and that the causal structure of the world is primarily a matter of regularity. The canonical formula for causal propositions is: 'Event E_2 occurs because event E_1 occurs'.

I shall call the first of those approaches to causation Berkeleian, the second (with some historical impropriety) Humean; and I suggest that Anaxagoras adopted a Berkeleian approach to causation, and the Atomists a Humean approach.

I have talked, somewhat feebly, of different approaches: do the approaches point to different theories of causation, or offer rival accounts of the notion of causation, or show that we have at least two distinct concepts of what it is to cause something to happen? Let us start by expanding the Humean approach: as well as events, we sometimes cite states of affairs as causes (the glass broke because it was brittle, and the man died because he was old). Since every true proposition describes either an event or a state of affairs, the canonical formula for the expanded Humean notion is simply: 'P_1 because P_2'.

The Berkeleian approach admits of a similar expansion: objects as well as agents are designated as causes (Pompeii was destroyed because of Vesuvius, the cricket ball brought about the death of the sparrow). Thus the canonical formula of Berkeleianism is: '*a* brings it about that P_1' (where *a* names any object or agent).

It seems plausible to suppose that '*a* brings it about that P_1' is true if and only if some proposition of the form 'P_1 because *a* is ϕ' is true: Pompeii was destroyed because of Vesuvius, i.e. because Vesuvius erupted; the sparrow was killed by the cricket ball, i.e. because the cricket ball struck it. In general, Berkeleian causation is explicable in terms of Humean causation; for Berkeleian formulae are merely abbreviations of Humean formulae. '*a* brings it about that P_1' is equivalent to a special type of the formula 'P_1 because P_2', viz. 'P_1 because *a* is ϕ'.

Now even if that unpolished account has some truth at its foundation, there remains an important way in which Berkeleian causation differs from Humean. For in cases where *a* is an agent, the translation of '*a* brings it about that P_1' into Humean language will always include a reference to *a*'s mind—to his intentions, his desires, his beliefs. 'Brutus', we say, 'killed Caesar.' And that causal hypothesis may be put into canonical Berkeleian form: 'Brutus brought it about that Caesar died.' That sentence is expandable to a Humean sentence of the form: 'Caesar died because Brutus ϕed'; and that in turn must expand into something like: 'Caesar died because Brutus stabbed him and wanted him to die and believed that if he stabbed him he would die.' Thus even if Berkeleian causes in some sense reduce to Humean causes, they still mark an important sub-class of Humean formulae, viz. those in which P_2 is a complex proposition including a reference to intentions, desires or beliefs. Let us call that sub-class of formulae the Berkeleian formulae: then Anaxagoras, I suggest, held that science required Berkeleian formulae; the Atomists that it did not.

(d) *Causas cognoscere rerum*

> [Democritus said that] he would rather find a single causal explanation (*aitiologia*) than gain the kingdom of Persia (**304: 68 B 118**).[20]

We possess a quantity of Democritean explanations; many of them are preserved by Theophrastus (**A 135**), from whom I have already quoted (above, p. 373). If we ask, on a more abstract level, how Democritus conceived of causation, we have less information; but a clear and consistent picture emerges.

Epicurus says of the Abderites that:

> Though they were the first to give adequate explanations, and far surpassed not only their predecessors but also their successors many times over, yet here, as in many other places, they did not realize that they were making light of grave matters in ascribing everything to necessity and the spontaneous (**305: 68 A 69**).[21]

For the moment let us ignore 'the spontaneous'; then Epicurus charges that all phenomena in the Atomists' world are necessitated.

> Refusing to mention the final cause (*to hou heneka*), Democritus reduces everything that nature handles to necessity (**306**: Aristotle, *GA* 789b2 = **68 A 66**).

> Everything happens by fate, in the sense that fate applies the force of necessity (**307**: Cicero, **68 A 66**).

> Everything comes about by necessity, since the whirl, which he calls necessity, is the cause of the generation of everything (**308**: Diogenes Laertius, IX.45 = **68 A 1**).

These reports bear on Democritus; but Leucippus held the same view. Only one Leucippan fragment survives. It reads thus:

> Leucippus says that everything occurs by necessity and that that is the same as fate; for he says in *On Mind*: No thing comes about in vain (*matên*); but everything for a reason and by necessity (*ek logou kai hup' anankês*) (**309**: Aëtius **67 B 2**).

Leucippus appears to be stating some version of a principle which we have already met, the Principle of Causality (above, pp. 24–6).[22] He talks of things 'coming about (*ginetai*)', but he presumably means to encompass all events in that term and not merely generations; and it will not be absurd to allow that states as well as events were probably in his mind. Thus **309** asserts that all states and events are explicable by reason and necessity; and I gloss that by:

(1) For any proposition *P*, if *P* is the case, then there is some *Q* such that the fact that *P* is necessitated by the fact that *Q*.

In (1) *Q* is the *logos* or reason for *P*; and the 'necessity' of **309** is expressed by the link of necessitation between *Q* and *P*.

It is, of course, in atomic nature that we must seek the proper explanations of things:

> The reason why the substances [i.e. the atoms] stay together with one another up to a point, he finds in the overlappings and interlockings (*epallagai kai antilêpseis*) of the bodies. . . . Thus he thinks that they hold on to one another and stay together for a time, until some stronger necessity comes upon them from their surrounding, shakes them about, and scatters them apart (**213**, Aristotle).

The 'stronger necessity' is created by atomic clashings; and thus it is the atomic 'whirl' which ultimately causes all change, and which can therefore be called 'necessity' (**308**). We are, I think, entitled to particularize proposition (1), and say that: every macroscopic state is explicable by way of some atomic state; every macroscopic event by way of some atomic event. Every atomic state is determined by the properties of its atomic constituents; every atomic event is explained by the locomotion of its atomic constituents. Every atomic locomotion is explained by way of atomic collisions; and atomic collisions depend on the velocity, size and shape of the colliding corpuscles. In that way, the world is explained; and if a complete aetiology of the universe is for ever beyond our powers, at least it is in principle possible.

The Atomists are Humean, in the loose sense in which I use that adjective: they do not talk of agents; and the formula '*a* brings it about that *P*' does not figure in their aetiologies. Were the Atomists

Humean in a more historical sense of the term? Humean causes are prior and contiguous to their effects; and they adhere to their effects with a necessity which Hume explains (or explains away) in terms of regularity. The Atomists are concerned with two different kinds of explanatory hypothesis. First, a macroscopic state or event, M_1, is explained by way of a microscopic state or event, M_2. ('The kettle of water is cold, because its constituent atoms have such and such a structure'; 'The kettle is coming to the boil, because its constituent atoms are moving in such and such a way.') Here M_2 is not prior to M_1, but simultaneous with it; M_2 is not contiguous to M_1, but identical with it; and M_1 and M_2 do not illustrate a merely Humean regularity: rather, M_2 necessitates M_1 (in a somewhat Pickwickian sense); for, being identical with M_2, M_1 cannot but occur when M_2 occurs.

Second, a microscopic state or event, M_2, is explained by reference to an atomic collision, *C*. Here *C* is presumably prior to M_2. In a loose sense we can say that *C* is contiguous to M_2, if we suppose that only collisions involving the constituent atoms of M_2 can result in M_2. And *C* necessitates M_2. Is that necessitation to be explained *à la* Hume, by way of regularity? Do the Atomists think that states or events like M_2 come about whenever collisions like *C* occur? and that such regularity is all that there is to *C*'s necessitating M_2? Our evidence is silent. That the Atomists believed in causal regularity is not implausible in itself, and it is perhaps implicit in Leucippus' use of the word *logos*. But nothing suggests that the Abderites took a Humean view of necessity.

(e) *Agents and purposes*

'No thing comes about in vain (*matên*)' (**309**): the sentiment is Aristotelian in expression; and when Aristotle asserts that 'God and nature do nothing in vain (*matên*)' (*Cael* 271a33), he means to subscribe to a teleological theory of nature. That cannot, however, be Leucippus' meaning; and we must take *matên* in **309** to mean 'without cause', not 'without purpose'. For the Atomists rejected all teleological or purposive explanation:

> Leucippus and Democritus and Epicurus [say that the universe is] neither animate nor governed by purpose (*pronoia*), but by a sort of irrational nature (*phusis alogos*) (**310**: Aëtius, **67 A 22**).

> Is there a providence which looks after all things, or is everything created and governed by chance? The latter opinion was propounded by Democritus and corroborated by Epicurus (**311**: Lactantius, **68 A 70**; cf. Aëtius, **67 A 24**).

Humean explanations do not rule out purposive or teleological explanation; but they do not require it. Berkeleian explanations do not entail purposive explanation; but they suggest it. And Anaxagoras for one is generally thought to have fallen in with the suggestion: the issue is celebrated, and it warrants rehearsal at some length.

Socrates bought a second-hand copy of Anaxagoras' book in high hopes; here was a thinker who, unlike his materialistic predecessors, was wise and bold enough to give intelligence a part in the formation of the world. But:

> Proceeding and reading on, I see the man making no use of mind, nor indicating any explanations for the ordering of things, but making explanations of airs and aethers and waters and many other such absurdities (**312**: *Phaedo* 98 B = **59 A 47**).

Aristotle makes the same point more pregnantly:

> Anaxagoras uses mind as a theatrical device (*mêchanê*) for his cosmogony; and whenever he is puzzled over the explanation of why something is from necessity, he wheels it in; but in the case of other happenings he makes anything the explanation rather than mind (**313**: *Met* 985a18–21 = **A 47**).

And the point is constantly repeated (e.g., Eudemus, fr. 53W = **A 47**; Clement, **A 57**). 'Mind,' the objection runs, 'is not systematically applied: it is used to explain the initial cosmic whirl; and it is later used to account for one or two otherwise inexplicable interactions in the course of nature; but apart from that, it has no function: mind is not invoked to account for the circulation of the blood or the shape of an oak tree, for the functioning of the nitrogen cycle or the design of a spider's web.'

The point, we might hastily judge, is right in substance but wrong in evaluation. On the one hand, **301** says that mind moves and controls some but not all things: it sets the whirl in motion; but after that, the revolution itself, by its own unmeasurable speed and force (**B 9**), suffices to bring things about. Mind is the cosmic starter, initiating action by its own intrinsic powers; but once it has imparted motion to the cosmic masses, natural events proceed in a purely mechanical way. That is Anaxagoras' view; and Socrates and the rest represent him correctly. On the other hand, the Socratic criticism is misplaced: the vast majority of cosmic happenings do not require an explanation in terms of mind; most natural events are in fact explicable in a mechanical fashion, and a reference to mind would be an absurd solecism in a treatise on chemistry or meteorology.

Anaxagoras was right, Socrates and Aristotle wrong; for Anaxagoras wished to banish teleology from science, and they desired to recall it from its exile. As Simplicius saw, Anaxagoras advocates 'the method proper to natural science' (*in Phys* 177.9).

That flattering portrait of Anaxagoras may be embellished. According to Aristotle,

> Anaxagoras says that man is the cleverest of animals because he has hands; but it is reasonable to hold that he acquired hands because he is the cleverest; for hands are a tool, and nature (like a clever man) always distributes each thing to those who are capable of using it (**314**: *PA* 687a7–12 = **A 102**).

How pleasantly Anaxagoras' assertion contrasts with Aristotle's superstitious speculation. An anecdote in Plutarch presses the point home:

> It is said that the head of a single-horned ram was once brought from the fields to Pericles, and that Lampon the seer, when he saw that the horn grew strong and firm from the middle of the forehead, said that of the two power groups in the state—that of Thucydides and that of Pericles—control would come to the one to whom the sign was brought. But Anaxagoras had the skull split open and showed that the brain had not filled out its position, but had drawn together to a point, like an egg, at the very place in the cavity where the root of the horn began (**315: A 16**).

Anaxagoras' explanation is wholly naturalistic; Lampon indulges in a childish superstition. And our admiration for Anaxagoras is scarcely tempered by the fact that Lampon's prediction turned out true.

But that admiration is perhaps hasty: after all, Anaxagoras does not 'banish teleology from science', he merely limits its scope. And those who dislike teleology will be distressed by a cosmogony which rests firmly on teleological principles. Yet perhaps we can alleviate their pain? At all events, several scholars have heroically urged that Anaxagoras gave no teleological explanations at all.[23]

Aristotle's teleology is, in a sense, impersonal: he explains the form and operation of an animal's organs in terms of the function of those organs, not in terms of the purposes of an Author of Nature. Why do cows have a fourth stomach? In order to digest their cud. Why do men blink? In order to moisten their eyes and sharpen their vision. Good digestion is not the purposed end of the cow; for cows do not deliberate. Moist eyes are not my purpose in blinking; for my blinking is a reflex act. Nor is bovine digestion or human sharp-sightedness the goal of some superhuman or superbovine artificer. Teleology, thus construed, posits a *telos* or end; but it does not imply that the *telos* is the goal of any purposive act.

If we look for Aristotelian teleology in Anaxagoras we shall not find it: as far as we know, Anaxagoras did not attempt to explain anything by way of impersonal ends. (For my part, I put that down to Anaxagoras' credit; but the question is controversial, and I have no space to broach it.) Yet there are personal as well as impersonal ends, and a reference to purpose, aim or design will often figure in our explanations: why do men take exercise? In order to keep fit. Why do men learn Greek? In order to raise themselves above the vulgar herd and reach positions of considerable emolument.

Roughly speaking, an impersonal teleological explanation will be expressed in the form:

(1) *a* is *F* because being *F* leads to being *G* and it is in *a*'s interest to be *G*.

A personal teleological explanation will be expressed by:

(2) *a* is *F* because *b* wants *a* to be *G* and believes that being *F* leads to being *G*.

Now proposition (2) is a Berkeleian explanation; and since Anaxagoras was a Berkeleian, he was thereby given to personal teleological explanation.

Personal teleology is not normally a feature of natural science; yet it will enter the world of nature if natural phenomena are viewed as the operations of an intelligent artificer. Anaxagoras took just such a view; and it is merely perverse to deny that he was a teleologist in that perfectly intelligible sense. Simplicius puts it clearly:

> He seemed to say that all things were together and at rest for an unlimited time, and that the cosmogonical mind, wanting to separate out the kinds which he calls homoiomeries, created motion in them (**316: A 45**).

Mind 'wanted (*boulêtheis*)' to make a world: the existence of the cosmos is explicable as the aim of an intelligent actor. If the word 'want' does not occur in Anaxagoras' fragments, the verbs 'know' and 'order' do: mind ordered or arranged things, and it knew what was to be. There is, surely, no doubt about the teleological import of all this; and indeed, the very enterprise of setting up mind as a cosmic force is hardly to be detached from a teleological view of cosmic history.

'And what was to be, and what was and is not now, and what is now and what will be—all these mind ordered' (**301**, [xi]). The difficulty with Anaxagoras' view is now the very opposite of the difficulty Socrates discovered: Socrates objected that mind did too little work—the danger is rather that mind does too much. What room is there in Anaxagorean physics for natural causes? If mind arranges everything, what can the 'revolution' do?

Anaxagoras distinguishes between ordering (*diakosmein*) and controlling (*kratein*): mind orders everything but controls only some things. The following explanation suggests itself. Take any causal chain, E_1, E_2, . . ., E_n, in which each E_i accounts for its immediate successor. We may say, using a convenient Aristotelian distinction, that E_i is the *proximate* cause of E_{i+1}, and that E_1 is the *ultimate* cause of each subsequent E_i. According to Anaxagoras, E_1 will always be an act of mind, and it will be expressible by the formula 'Mind arranges that E_2 shall occur'. Now since all events hinge on an initial arrangement by mind, we may say that mind arranges everything; for E_1 is the ultimate cause of each E_i. But only E_2 is immediately linked to E_1; only for E_2 is an act of mind a proximate cause. And if we say that mind controls E_i only if mind is a proximate cause of E_i, then mind will not control everything. Anaxagoras' teleology is now reconciled with the possibility of naturalistic explanations: by attending to Anaxagoras' distinct terms, 'order' and 'control', we can give mind overall responsibility for the world while leaving room for natural necessity.

There is a vulgar objection to that sort of theory: 'The *real* cause of E_n is E_1; E_{n-1} is only a seeming or spurious cause. For if E_1 causes E_2, E_2 E_3, . . . and E_{n-1} E_n, then it is E_1 which is the true cause of E_n. Thus if E_1 is an act of mind, then naturalistic explanation has no room; for the real cause of *everything* is E_1, and E_1 is supernaturalistic.' That strangely persuasive line of argument involves an inconsistency and a false presupposition. The inconsistency is palpable; for the argument asserts both that E_{n-1} causes E_n and also that E_{n-1} does not cause E_n. The false presupposition is that in any causal chain there is some one item which is 'the' cause (or the 'real' cause) of any E_i. In fact, as the distinction between ultimate and proximate causes shows, every E_i (for $i > 2$) will have several causes; for each E_j (for $j < i$) is a cause of E_i. The noun 'cause' is the evil genius here: instead of talking of causes, we might well stick to the connective 'because': E_n occurs because E_{n-1} occurs; E_{n-1} occurs because E_{n-2} occurs; hence E_n occurs because E_{n-2} occurs. There is no temptation to make the absurd inference that, since E_n occurs because E_{n-2} occurs, E_n does not occur because E_{n-1} occurs.

(f) *Chance and necessity*

According to the Atomists, necessity governs the world; yet I have already quoted two passages which ascribe great influence to chance. Chance and necessity are surely polar opposites: is not the atomist account of explanation simply contradictory? A similar question arises over Empedocles; and I shall return to the Atomists after running quickly through the Empedoclean material.

At first glance, Empedocles' explanatory mechanism seems simple enough: in addition to the four 'roots' or elements that constitute the world, there are two forces which control their congresses and separations. These forces are denominated Love (*Philia*) and Strife (*Neikos*):

> And dread Strife apart from them [sc. the roots], balanced in all directions,
> and Love amongst them, equal in length and breadth (**317: 31 B** 17.19–20).

Love accounts for elemental conjunction, Strife for elemental separation:

> Now by Love all coming together into one,
> now again each carried apart by the enmity of Strife (**194: B 17**, 7–8).

How are Love and Strife to be conceived? Aristotle, for one, thought that Empedocles' conception of them was hopelessly muddled (e.g., *Met* 1075b2–4; cf. Simplicius, **A 28**).

First, Love is frequently treated as an internal moving cause:

> [Love] is thought innate in human limbs,
> by which men think loving thoughts and accomplish fitting deeds,
> calling her Joy by name and Aphrodite (**318: B** 17.22–4).

Nor in human limbs alone; for the elements

> come together in Love, and desire one another (**319: B 21**.8)

Elements, like animals, unite because they are in love.[24]

Second, Love and Strife are sometimes treated as material constituents of natural bodies. The treatment is implicit in **317**, where Strife is 'apart from' the roots and Love 'amongst' them; and it is plain in **B 109** which enumerates the four roots and the two forces without indicating any ontological distinction between them. Thus:

> [Love] gathers together and sets together and holds together [the elements], thickening them by consortings and friendships
> As when rennet pegs and binds white milk (**320: B 33**).

In its material form, Love functions as a sort of catalyst: earth, air, fire and water, taken together, will not of themselves unite; pour in a little Love and the reaction will take place.

Most frequently Love is an external force, a divine or semi-divine agent.[25] Thus:

> The divine Aphrodite fitted together the tireless eyes (**321: B 86**; cf. **B 73, B 87**);

and in general:

> They first grew together under the hands of Cypris [= Love] (**322: B 95**).

Strife too is an agent; for at the start of the cosmogony

> Strife still held [some things] aloft (**323: B 35**.9).

As an internal force, Love wears a Newtonian aspect, being the counterpart of attraction or gravitation; as a material constituent, Love appears in a chemical role; and in its third form, Love is an agent, comparable to Anaxagoras' mind. The ancient commentators, having broken Empedocles' single pair of causes into three disparate fragments, do not desist from their attack; for beside Love and Strife they find three more 'causes' in Empedocles' science.

First, the elements themselves are sometimes endowed with powers of their own.

> [Plants] root downwards because the earth [in them] naturally moves thus, and they grow upwards because the same goes for the fire [in them] (**324**: Aristotle, *An* 415b29–30 = **A 70**).

The same point is made anecdotally:

> The natural philosophers actually arrange the whole of nature by taking as a principle the thesis that like goes to like; that is why Empedocles said that the bitch sits on the tiles because she contains a great deal of like matter (**325**: *EE* 1235a10–12 = **A 20a**).[26]

And we might cite **B 62**.6:

> Fire sent them up, longing to come to its like (**326**),

or **B 90**:

> Thus sweet seized on sweet, bitter jumped on bitter,
> sharp climbed on sharp, and (?) salty rode upon salty (?) (**327**).

Second, there is necessity: according to Aristotle,

> Empedocles would seem to say that the alternate domination and moving of Love and Strife belong to things from necessity (**328**: *Phys* 252a7–9 = **A 38**).

Plutarch reports that Empedocles gives the name of necessity to 'Love and Strife together' (**A 45**); and many more *testimonia* give necessity a niche in the Empedoclean system.[27] From the fragments there is only one reference:

> There is an oracle of necessity, an old edict of the gods,
> eternal, bound by broad oaths (**329: B 115**.1–2).[28]

Third, there is chance. Aristotle complains that his predecessors said nothing about chance:

> That is absurd, whether they did not believe it to exist or supposed it to exist and ignored it—and that though they sometimes use it, as Empedocles says that the air is not always separated off upwards, but as it may happen. (At any rate, he says in his cosmogony that: 'running, it met up then in this way, but often in other ways [= **B 53**]'), and he says that the parts of animals mostly come about by chance (**330**: *Phys* 196a19–24).

Commenting on this passage Simplicius quotes six further verses to show the power of chance in Empedoclean physics, and he observes that 'you might find many similar passages from Empedocles' *Physics* to set beside these' (*ad* **B 85**).[29]

We have an *embarras de richesse*. As explanatory powers Empedocles offers us: (a) Love and Strife as physical forces; (b) Love and Strife as catalysts; (c) Love and Strife as semi-divine agents; (d) the natural strivings of stuffs; (e) necessity; and (f) chance. Can we discover a seemly frugality behind this seeming prodigality?

First, (d) and (e) are not in conflict; indeed, it is easy to take (d) as a specification of (e): events occur by natural necessity, and in particular by virtue of the natural powers of the world's constituent stuffs. Nor, second, are (d) and (a) at odds; for, again, (a) is a specification of (d); the natural powers of stuffs are attractions and repulsions. In a syntactically difficult couplet Empedocles observes, it seems, that:

> The things that are more suitable for mixture
> are likened to and loved by one another by Aphrodite (**331: B 22**.4–5).

The lines suggest that the natural striving of like for like is explicable by the action of Love. Again **327** employs sexual metaphors to account for the conjunction of like stuffs: like goes to like because like loves like. Thus (d) does indeed reduce to (a).

Third, we may ask how (a) is to be explained: what is it to act 'from Love'? An answer is given by (c): Love is one of the material constituents of any substance, *a*; and for *a* to move 'from Love' is simply for *a*'s motion to be caused by the catalytic action of its connate portion of Love. Moreover, once Love is thus materialized, it is readily deified: before cosmogony has intermingled the roots, Love was present in a great and separate mass; it will not then have worked as a catalyst, but rather as an agent or an artificer goddess. Thus (a), (c), (d) and (e) are reconciled; and (b) is given a natural and reasonable explanation.

The possibility of such a reconciliation explains how Empedocles could offer so many different explanatory notions without blush or apology: the notions are, to a large degree, different ways of expressing one idea. But the reconciliation will not quite do: there is potential conflict between (b) and (e). It is indicated in **B 116**, which says that *Charis* (Grace or Love) 'hates unbearable necessity'; and Aristotle finds it in a second fragment:

> And at the same time he gives no explanation of the change itself [i.e. of the change from the period of Love to the period of Strife] except to say that it occurs thus by nature:
>
> But when Strife grew great in the limbs,
> and rose to office as the time was accomplished
> which had been fixed in alternation for them by a broad oath
> [**B 30**]
>
> —that it is necessary for the change to occur; but he gives no explanation for the necessity (**332**: *Met* 1000b12–17).

The operative times of Love and Strife are determined by a broad oath, and hence (cf. **329**) by necessity: that explains why Love hates unbearable necessity; for necessity fixes the range of Love's affairs. The doxographers, for what it is worth, imply that necessity has a status superordinate to Love and Strife (cf. Aëtius, **A 32, A 45**).[30]

Anaxagoras gives a controlling position in the universe to agent-like causation, and he subordinates natural necessity to the arrangements of mind; the Atomists give universal power to natural necessity and profess to find no domain of agency in the world. Empedocles, it seems, was not so clear: on the one hand, Love and Strife are the supreme causes, and they work as agents; on the other hand, some bond of necessity controls everything, even the workings of Love and Strife.

I have not yet mentioned (f), chance; and some will find in (f) the deepest flaw in Empedocles' explanatory system. The same flaw, as I said at the beginning of this section, is found in the Atomists.

First, let us consider more closely the evidence that chance played a part in Empedoclean and Abderite physics. Of the passages which Simplicius assembles to prove the prevalence of Chance in Empedocles, four contain the verb '*sunkurein*' and two '*tunchanein*': Simplicius evidently interpreted the words as 'chance across' and 'happen to occur'; but both verbs are standardly used in the sense of 'come about', 'actually happen', and they do not by themselves point to chance. But chance cannot be eliminated from Empedocles' system by cunning translation. **B 53**, which Aristotle quotes in **330**, countenances infrequent conjunction, or coincidence.[31] And one fragment appeals explicitly to Dame Fortune:[32]

> Thus by the will of chance everything possesses thought (**333: B 103**).

For the Atomists we possess no first-hand texts; but the doxography is rich and unanimous:

> From them [sc. the atoms] the earth and the universe are made . . . by a certain chance concurrence (**334:** Cicero, **67 A 11**).[33]

> He sets up chance as mistress and queen of universal and divine things and says that everything happens in accordance with it (**335**: Dionysius, *ad* **68 B 118**).

> Democritus too, in the passage where he says that a whirl of every sort of form was separated off from the whole [cf. **B 167**] (he does not say how or by what cause), seems to generate it spontaneously and by chance (**336**: Simplicius, **68 A 67**).

In his discussion of chance in the *Physics* Aristotle reports the following theories:

> Some . . . say that nothing comes about by chance, but that there is some determinate explanation for everything which we say comes about spontaneously or by chance (**337**: 195b36–196a3 = **68 A 68**).

> There are some who make the spontaneous the cause both of this world and of all the universes; for they say that it is spontaneously that the whirl comes about, i.e. the dissociative motion which sets everything into its present order . . . saying that animals and plants neither exist nor come to be by chance, but that either

> nature or mind or something else of that sort is their cause . . . but that the heavens and the most divine of visible things come to be spontaneously and that there is no cause for them of the sort there is for animals and plants (**338**: 196a24–35 = **68 A 69**).

Simplicius identifies the second group of men as the Atomists (**68 A 69**); and on the authority of Eudemus he connects the first view too with Democritus:

> For even if in his cosmogony he seems to have used chance, yet in particulars he says that chance is the cause of nothing, and refers them to other causes (**339: 68 A 68**).

The identification in the second passage is certain (though the reference to 'mind or something else of that sort' indicates that Aristotle does not have the Atomists uniquely in his thoughts); and the identification in the first passage is corroborated by Diogenes of Oenoanda, who criticizes Democritus for 'saying that the atoms have no free (*eleuthera*) motion' but that 'everything moves necessarily (*katênankasmenôs*)' (**68 A 50**).

At first sight those passages seem to import a horrible muddle. As we have already seen, Democritus is committed to:
(1) Everything happens by necessity.
Eudemus and Diogenes now give him:
(2) Nothing happens by chance.
But the doxography offers:
(3) Everything happens by chance.
and Simplicius produces:
(4) Some things happen by chance and others are caused.
Surely (1)–(4) are flatly inconsistent, and the Atomists foolishly confused?

The confusion is, I think, purely verbal.[34] Plato helps to clear it up:

> They say that fire and water, and earth and air, all exist by nature and chance, and none of them by art (*technêi*), and that as to the bodies that come next in order—earth, and sun, and moon, and stars—they have been created by means of these absolutely inanimate (*apsucha*) existences. The elements are severally moved by chance and some inherent force according to certain affinities among them: of hot with cold, or of dry with moist, or of soft with hard, and according to all the other things which are mixed by the mixture of opposites in accordance with chance from necessity (*kata tuchên ex anankês*). In this way and in this manner the whole universe was created, and everything in the universe, and animals too and all plants; and all the seasons come from these elements,

> not because of a mind, they say, nor because of some god or by art, but, as we said, by nature and chance only (**340**: *Laws* 889 BC trans. Jowett = **31 A 48**).[35]

There are obscurities of detail in this paragraph; but one moral emerges quite plainly from it: '*E* happens by chance (*tuchêi*)' and '*E* happens of necessity (*ex anankês*)' are not, as we might incautiously think, incompatible. Plato plainly ascribes to his opponents the view that everything happens *both* by nature or necessity *and* by chance; and the sense he gives to 'by chance' indicates how he can do so. '*E* happens by chance' means '*E* happens and *E* was not brought about by design'; no mind, no god, no art planned or executed the event. That is a normal sense of 'chance' in English, and evidently it was a normal sense of '*tuchê*' in Greek: in that sense, every event in a wholly deterministic world might occur by chance.

Empedocles' bow to Dame Fortune in **333** is thus perfectly compatible with his reverence for stern necessity (though it is not compatible with a strictly agent-like interpretation of Love and Strife); and the Atomists' proposition (3), which simply reflects their denial of *pronoia* (Aëtius, **67 A 22**), sits in happy concord with (1).

But 'by chance' does not only denote the absence of purpose: it may also denote the absence of causality or natural necessity. '*E* happened by chance' may mean not only '*E* happened and was not purposed' but also '*E* happened and was not necessitated'. And in that sense, (2) follows at once from (1), and is perfectly compatible with (3). Aristotle knows that in this sense chance and necessity are oppugnant; and that is why he objects to Empedocles' use of chance. His own analysis of chance in *Physics* II 5–7 is intricate; but it is worth pulling out one relevant strand of it here. Chance is standardly construed by Aristotle as coincidence: if *E* occurs by chance, then *E* is a conjunctive event, described by a formula of the form '*Fa* and *Ga*'; and *E* occurs by chance if and only if neither all nor most *F*s are *G*. Chance contrasts with regularity: a chance event is a rare event, a freak or extraordinary occurrence. Whether or not that is a decent account of chance I do not ask; I mention it only to draw attention to one obvious feature: a fully deterministic world may, on this analysis, be riddled with chance events. If E_1 is necessitated and E_2 is necessitated, then the conjunctive event $E_1 + E_2$ is necessitated; yet that event may be a coincidence. *a*'s being *F* and *a*'s being *G* may be necessary, even if few *F*s are *G*.

Thesis (4) remains to be accounted for. According to Aristotle, 'some think that chance is a cause, but one unclear to human intelligence, being something divine and somewhat demonic' (*Phys* 196b5 = **68 A 70**): when we say '*E* occurs by chance' we may mean only 'We cannot tell why *E* occurs' That use is, I think, found in English; and I assume that Aristotle speaks with authority for Greek. If we apply it to (4), then (4) is rendered consistent both with (2) and with (3); and it becomes an honest confession of the weakness of the human mind—a weakness which, as we shall see, Democritus was quick to notice and to emphasize.

For the sake of clarity, then, we may rewrite (1)–(4) as follows:

(1*) All states and events are causally determined.
(2*) No states or events lack a necessitating cause.
(3*) No states or events are the results of purposive agency.
(4*) Of some states and events the causes are accessible, of others they are not.

Together, (1*)–(4*) form a consistent theory of the possibility of explaining natural phenomena. And they form a popular and a plausible theory: here, too, the Abderites prove themselves hard-headed and influential philosophers of science.

XX

The Neo-Ionian World Picture

(a) *Scientific explanation*

The Eleatic philosophers had argued that nothing can ever be generated or destroyed, that nothing can ever alter, that nothing can ever move—and that, were change possible, there would be no reason why it should ever occur. In this chapter I shall discuss the neo-Ionian response to those perturbing conclusions; and I begin with the last: could the neo-Ionians explain change, if change should prove to be possible?

The Peripatetics gave the verdict to Elea. Of Empedocles Aristotle writes:

> And at the same time he gives no explanation of the change itself [i.e. of the change from the rule of Love to that of Strife], except to say that it occurs thus by nature (*houtôs pephuke*):
> But when Strife grew great in the limbs,
> and rose to office as the time was accomplished
> which had been fixed in alternation for them by a broad oath [**B** **30**]
> —that it is necessary for the change to occur; but he gives no explanation for the necessity (**332**: *Met* 1000b12–17).[1]

> Eudemus faults Anaxagoras not only because he says that motion which did not before exist begins at a certain time, but also because he omits to say anything about its continuing or future cessation, though the matter is not evident. 'For,' he says, 'what prevents mind from determining at some time to stop all things,

> just as, according to him, it determined to move them?' (**341**: Eudemus, fr. 111 W = **59 A 59**).

And of the Atomists:

> About motion—whence or how it belongs to existent things—these men too, like the others, lazily shelved the question (**342**: *Met* 985b19 = **67 A 6**).

> Whence the principle of natural motion comes, they do not say (**343**: Alexander, **67 A 6**).

In detail these criticisms presuppose Peripatetic doctrine, but behind them there lies a simple question: *Why* does Strife give way to Love and vice versa? *Why* does mind start the cosmogony rolling? *Why* do the atoms move?

The case of Empedocles is complicated, and it raises no issue which does not arise in the other two cases; hence I shall consider only the criticisms of Anaxagoras and of the Atomists. According to Anaxagoras, all things were motionless up to the cosmogonical instant t; then, at t, mind began to move stuffs and to create the cosmos. Eudemus' question, which has evident Eleatic ancestry, is just this: Why t? The question is ambiguous: it may mean either 'What feature of the world before t brought it about that mind acted at t?' or else 'What feature of the world at t gave mind its reason for creating at t?' But on both interpretations the question seems fatal: before t, there was no change and there were no events; any two times, t_1 and t_2, prior to t were quite indistinguishable. Suppose, then, Anaxagoras suggests that the state S, holding at t-n, caused mind's creation at t, or was mind's reason for creating at t; then, by way of an argument already familiar, we can infer the absurdity that for any t_i prior to t, mind created at t_i. For S obtains at every instant up to t; hence it obtains at t_i-n; and if S's obtaining at t-n brings it about that mind creates at t, then S's obtaining at t_i-n brings it about that mind creates at t_i.

The argument is not, in fact, lethal. Anaxagoras has more than one answer.[2] First, he may deny that there is any time earlier than t at which mind could have created things: take a Peripatetic leaf from your opponents' book, and hold that time implies change; infer that before t, the first instant of change, there was no time: how, then, could mind have created the world before t? The state S at t itself caused mind to embark on its cosmogonical operation; and since there was no t_i prior to t, the *reductio* argument does not begin. Was there a time before the creation? The question was hotly debated by later philosophers, and it is too deep and difficult to be discussed here. It is worth saying, however, that many philosophers have taken the view I have offered to Anaxagoras, and that it is not simply silly.

Second, Anaxagoras may reject the Universalizability of Explanation. Suppose that S at t-n explains creation at t; why infer that S at t_i-n requires creation at t_i-n? Why not take it as a brute fact that S is effective at t-n but not at t_i-n? A cigarette lighter sometimes flames when the cap is flicked, and when it does, the flicking causes the flaming. But not every flicking, as ordinary experience confirms, causes a flaming. This second answer of Anaxagoras' has also had adherents: it, too, raises difficult questions; and it, too, is far from being captious or silly.

Third, Anaxagoras may reject the Principle of Causality: that 'every event has a cause' is an unargued dogma; it has no basis in experience where, for all that we know, countless events and states are uncaused; and it is not an *a priori* truth, for we can easily conceive of an undetermined event. (Physicists who believe in sub-atomic indeterminacy conceive of such events daily; and if their belief is true then a myriad of events do really lack causes.) Elea asks: Why does cosmogony start at t? Anaxagoras answers: Mind moves things at t. The Peripatetics come to the defence of Elea: 'You explain why cosmogony *starts*, but not why it starts *at t*; for why does mind begin its operations at t?' And Anaxagoras in effect, says: For no reason. I can see nothing philosophically disreputable in his retort.

The Atomists are committed to the Principle of Causality and cannot countenance uncaused events. How, then, can they explain 'whence and how motion belongs to the things that exist'?

Their explanation is simple: atom *a* moves because it was struck by moving atom *b*. An infinite regress opens up; for if there were a first moment of motion, then the first atomic motion would be inexplicable, since it could not have been occasioned by collision with a moving atom.[3] But the regress is not vicious; and it was explicitly embraced by the Atomists:

> Leucippus and Democritus say that the primary bodies [i.e. the atoms] are always moving in the unlimited void (**344**: Aristotle, *Cael* 300b8 = **67 A 16**);

and in the doxography eternal motion is a standing characteristic of the atoms (see above, p. 365). Since the atoms are always in motion, each atomic trajectory was preceded by, and may be explained in terms of, an atomic collision: *a* moves because *b* hit it; *b* moved because *c* hit it; and so on. And that is all there is to say; every atomic locomotion, and hence every natural change, is equipped with an explanation.

Aristotle was not satisfied.

> They should say what motion it is and what is their natural motion (**345**),

he grumbles in the *de Caelo* (300b9–10 = **67 A 16**). But the Atomists do say a fair amount about the nature of atomic motion; and they implicitly deny that atoms have any 'natural' motion: all atomic motion is, in Aristotelian jargon, violent, *biaios*. The *Metaphysics* adds another criticism:

> Some—e.g., Leucippus and Plato—suppose an eternal activity; for they say that motion always exists. But they do not say why or what, nor the explanation of why it is thus or thus (**346**: 1071b31–3 = **67 A 18**).

It is the first 'why' that bears the weight; it is repeated in the *Physics*:

> In general, to think that it is a sufficient principle to say that it always is or comes about thus, is to hold a mistaken belief; Democritus reduces the causes of nature to this state, saying that earlier things also happened thus, but he does not think to look for a cause of the 'always' (**347**: 252a32–b1 = **68 A 65**; cf *GA* 742b17–29).

There are, I think two ways of construing Aristotle's criticism. The first fits **346** better: 'Any individual atomic motion can perhaps be explained; but the explanation implies eternal atomic motion: and why do atoms move eternally?' To that question Democritus has an entirely adequate answer, and his answer has an important generalization. All atoms move eternally provided that every sentence of the form '*a* moves eternally' is true; and '*a* moves eternally' is true provided that every sentence of the form '*a* moves at *t*' is true. Now every sentence of this last form is, by hypothesis, true; and the fact it expresses is in every case explicable by way of some sentence of the form '*b* struck *a* in fashion ϕ at *t-n*'. In this way the eternity of atomic motion is explained; for every fact necessary for the occurrence of eternal motion has been explained.

It is worth looking at the argument schematically. The *explanandum* is:

(1) For every object, *x*, and time, *t*, *x* is moving at *t*.

For every case of (1), there is available, in theory, a truth of the form:

(2) *a* moves at t_i because *Q*.

Hence (1) itself is explained. In general, we explain why everything is

ϕ if we explain, in the case of every individual, why it is ϕ: All the people I invited to the party stayed away. Why? One was ill, one forgot, one couldn't stand the thought of another party, and so on; once individual explanations for each invited friend are given, the complete vacuity of my party is explained. It is absurd for me to accept all these individual excuses and still ask why *everyone* stayed away, as though that were a further question. The case is analogous to the explanation of conjunctive facts: Why is the grass so long and wet that the mower won't cut it?—It is long because it hasn't been cut for two weeks; it is wet because last night's dew has not had time to evaporate. There is no room for the further question: Why is it long *and* wet?

The second interpretation of Aristotle's criticism seems to fit the *Physics* passage quite neatly. Suppose that atom *a* moves with velocity v at t. Why so? Because, Democritus answers, *b* collided with it at t-n, and the velocities of *a* and *b* at t-n were v^a and v^b. But what makes that an *explanation* of *a*'s velocity at t? Well, 'it always . . . comes about thus'; i.e., whenever an atom of the same type as *b* moving at v^b strikes an atom of the same type as *a* moving at v^a, its subsequent velocity is v. But why is *that* the case? Democritus offers no answer: 'he does not think to look for a cause of the "always"'.

That is an entirely different criticism from the former one. In effect, Aristotle ascribes to Democritus a regularity theory of explanation; and he rejects it as inadequate. Democritus explains individual causal links in terms of universal regularities; but he does not think to explain those regularities. *E* occurs because *C* occurs. Behind this there lies a regularity: every *C*-type event is followed by an *E*-type event. That regularity may, in a sense, be explained; for it may be subsumable under a higher regularity: every *C*-type event is a C_1-type event; and every C_1-type event is followed by an *E*-type event. And C_1 may give place to C_2, and so on. But the regress cannot be infinite; for the ways of specifying atomic events are finite. Thus there will be some ultimate regularity which evades explanation.

Aristotle may mean no more than that Democritus did not push his explanations far enough: he was satisfied with low-level regularities and did not attempt to construct high-level laws. And that criticism was doubtless justified. But I suspect that Aristotle intends a more profound criticism: regularity as such, he thinks, requires explanation; and Democritus cannot satisfy that requirement, since he has nothing but regularities to appeal to. No doubt Aristotle requires a teleological account of natural regularities: things regularly happen thus because it is good that they should so happen. But here again, the Atomists are right: even if teleological explanation has a place in natural science, it is far from clear that every natural regularity is teleologically grounded; and I see no reason for believing that there is anything ultimately unsatisfying about the notion of an inexplicable regularity.

The first round goes to the neo-Ionians: even with Aristotle on their side, the Eleatics lose the fight.

(b) *Locomotion*

Empedocles and Anaxagoras accepted the Eleatic *plenum* and attempted to insinuate locomotion into it; the Atomists boldly defended a universe riddled with vacancies, and thereby dulled the edge of Melissus' logical razor: has Melissus any reply to either of their suggestions?

Antiperistasis does, I believe, show that locomotion in a *plenum* is possible; and to that extent Melissus' arguments fail. And if the Atomists are successful in their defence of the void, then the arguments are inapplicable. But Melissus, I think, should not have been unduly dismayed by either of these facts; for his arguments constitute what is, logically speaking, an unnecessarily devious manoeuvre. Consider any volume of space, V, whether full or pitted with void; and suppose that some of the occupants of this space move between t_1 and t_2. Suppose that, at t_1, the occupants are arranged in a pattern P_1, and that at t_2 they are arranged in P_2. Now it may be that $P_1 = P_2$; and indeed, it may be that at every instant t_i between t_1 and t_2, $P_i = P_1$: locomotion does not strictly imply any change in pattern, as Aristotle's spinning tops indicate. But such a changeless locomotion is no good to the neo-Ionians: if the only locomotion the universe may undergo is of that sort, then plainly locomotion cannot lead to the minglings and collisions which in neo-Ionian physics explain the diverse appearances of the world. Moreover, if V is the whole of space, and if at any t_i $P_i = P_1$, then it is plausible to infer that the occupants of V do not move at all; for none of them ever changes its position relative to anything else.

If locomotion entails change of relative position, Melissus is home. Formally, his argument runs like this: 'Suppose, as before, that there is locomotion in V between t_1 and t_2. Then there must be some volume V^1, whose inhabitants are rearranged between t_1 and t_2; i.e., there must be some t_i between t_1 and t_2 such that $P^1_i \neq P^1_1$. But rearrangement, or *metakosmêsis*, is a kind of alteration; and the general argument against alteration shows, as Melissus explicitly points out, that *metakosmêsis* is impossible. Therefore locomotion is impossible. Void or no void, motion involves rearrangement; void or no void, motion is logically absurd.'

I do not know whether Melissus saw that point: he does not make it expressly, though his particular attention to *metakosmêsis* leads me to suppose that it was not far from the surface of his mind. I do not think that any neo-Ionian got a glimpse of the danger, or took any evasive action. And evasive action is necessary: if the neo-Ionians hope to do away with alteration and retain locomotion, then Melissus has thwarted their hope before it was expressed; and if they intend to admit alteration by grounding it on locomotion, then Melissus has proved their intention topsy-turvy—before they can vindicate locomotion they must defend alteration. In either case, victory goes to Melissus: only if the neo-Ionians can defeat him on alteration will they obtain their mobile world.

What of the void? The Atomists argued that there is empty space, on the grounds that there is no more reason for there to be body than for there to be space. Melissus will hardly accept that: after all, he has provided a reason against the existence of the void, and the Atomists have done nothing to discountenance it. The Atomists agree with Melissus that no substance has vacuous parts: Abderite bodies, like Melissan bodies, are full, massy, or solid. But Melissus has argued that any existent body is spatially infinite; hence there is no empty space outside his body. And if vacancy can be found neither within nor without body, vacancy cannot be found at all. Melissus may accept the distinction between existence$_1$ and existence$_2$ (above, p. 404); but he has no reason to accept the existence$_2$ of void.

Here, too, Melissus wins the fight. But here his victory is only a technical one: the Atomists should have attacked his argument for the spatial infinity of body; they did not do so, but they could have done so with little difficulty. For that argument is perhaps the weakest link in Melissus' deductive chain.

(c) *Alteration*

Alteration, it might appear, is the key to the neo-Ionian treasure chest: give them that, and they will show us again the familiar world of changing phenomena; withhold it, and they cannot even describe a mobile world. Alas, the neo-Ionian attitude to alteration yields no satisfaction at all: either they were discreetly taciturn, or fate has chosen to hide their wisdom from us; at all events, we can learn remarkably little about this crucial issue. I shall briefly survey the few facts that do present themselves.

First, Anaxagoras. According to Aristotle,

> He states that coming to be and being destroyed are the same as alteration (**348**: *GC* 314a13 = **59 A 52**).

Some scholars find an original fragment lurking in this sentence; but that is improbable.[4] In any case, the purport of the sentence is quite obscure: does it mean that Anaxagoras held on to alteration and explained generation in terms of it? Or does it rather imply that, in conflating generation and alteration, he abandoned the latter along with the former? Some look to **B 10** for a general rejection of alteration; but the fragment cannot be taken in that way (below, p. 437). Nor will general considerations of Anaxagorean physics help us. Take a pint of water and freeze it: has it, according to Anaxagoras, lost one set of qualities and acquired a new set? Is there something which was fluid and is now solid? which was transparent and is now opaque? Or is it rather the case that the stuff has had all its qualities all along, now manifesting one set, now another? And if that is so, is not its coming to manifest a different set of qualities in itself an alteration in the stuff? There is no advantage in pursuing these questions: as far as we know, they were never posed by Anaxagoras.

The Abderites fare a little better: atoms are unequivocally immutable (above, p. 346); so that if there is any alteration in the Abderite world, it can only occur at the macroscopic level. And atomic motions are said to account for macroscopic changes:

> Democritus and Leucippus, having made their shapes, make alteration and generation from them: generation and destruction by association and dissociation, alteration by order and position (**349**: Aristotle, *GC* 315b6–9 = **67 A 9**).

The Atomists ascribe locomotion to their atoms:

> and this is the only *kinesis* they give to the elements, reserving the others for the compounds; for they say that things grow and diminish and change and come into being and perish as the primary bodies congregate and separate (**350**: Simplicius, **68 A 58**).

But what exactly are these macroscopic changes? Does freezing water change from being transparent to being opaque? Does grass in high summer change from green to brown? Transparency and opacity, green and brown are not 'real' qualities; they exist only 'by convention' (above, pp. 370–77). Then perhaps the changes are similarly unreal, occurring only 'by convention'. Does the world contain *apparent* changes from green to brown, or *genuine* changes from apparent green to apparent brown? As far as I can see, the

Abderites did not pose these questions; nor did they grasp the importance of alteration in the neo-Ionian answer to Elea.

Of Empedocles we hear a little more; but that little is hardly satisfying. Once, Empedocles seems to allow that his 'roots' may alter:

> . . . running through one another,
> they become different-looking (*alloiôpa*): such is the change that mixture makes (**351: 31 B 21**.13–14).

But the corresponding lines in **B 17** are significantly different:

> . . . running through one another,
> they become different things (*alla*) at different times and are always absolutely homogeneous (**352: B** 17.34–5).

Aristotle perhaps has this last phrase in mind when he argues that, according to Empedocles, the elements are 'preserved (*sôzomena*)' when they mingle to form compounds (*GC* 337a29 = **A 43**). And Philoponus expands the point critically:

> He contradicts the phenomena when he does away with alteration which evidently occurs, and himself when he says on the one hand that the elements are immutable and that they do not come from one another but the other things come from them [= **B** 17.35], and on the other hand he says that when Love is in power they all become one and form the Sphere which is qualityless [cf., e.g., **B 35**.5], since in it is preserved the characteristic property (*idiotês*) neither of fire nor of any of the other [elements], each of the elements losing its own form (**353: A 41**).

There are thus two related criticisms of Empedocles: he expressly makes his elements 'always absolutely homogeneous' or immutable; yet first he holds that at the time of the cosmic Sphere there is just *one* mixed stuff in the universe; and, second, he says that during the periods of cosmic growth and decay the elements 'become different-looking'. I think that Empedocles is undeniably confused on both these counts; and I see no plausible answer to the first charge of inconsistency. But it is the second charge that is more interesting here: what should Empedocles have said about the status of macroscopic alteration?

First, he might have said that his elements, like Abderite atoms, never alter: no quantity of fire ever loses any of its characteristic qualities or ever gains any extra properties; masses of fire may split or coagulate, mix, mingle and associate with other elements; but no bit of fire ever alters. When Empedocles says that fire 'becomes different-looking' or 'different things', he is speaking with the vulgar, not with the learned (cf. **B 9**.5), and we should not charge him with strict inconsistency.

Yet that defence leaves us uneasy: what, after all, happens when we vulgar speakers say that Socrates grows pale? Not, admittedly, an alteration in any constituent element of Socrates; but surely the mixed mass of elements which we vulgarly call a man alters? Surely that particular volume of stuff, considered as a whole, changes in colour? Does Empedocles mean to deny this? Would he say that Socrates does not really change at all? and would he explain this by a theory of sensible qualities Abderite in tone? Again, we simply do not know.

These animadversions on the neo-Ionian attitude to alteration may seem a trifle crotchety or at least ungenerous. Yet it does appear to be the case that the neo-Ionians were careless and cavalier in their account of alteration: locomotion and generation engaged their close attention; but they failed to see the strength and cohesion of the Eleatic position—of the Melissan version in particular—and they made no attempt to come to grips with the neat argument by which 'change in bright colour' was allegedly abolished.

But after all, the Eleatic rejection of alteration is firmly based on their rejection of generation; and it will be said, reasonably enough, that if the neo-Ionians saw a route to the defence of generation they may properly have taken the defence of alteration for granted. I turn, therefore, to generation.

(d) *Generation*

Empedocles is forthright and plain:

> [Mortal men are] fools; for their thoughts are not deep,
> since they think that what before did not exist comes into being,
> or that something dies and is completely destroyed (**354: 31 B 11**).

That Eleatic conclusion was based on Eleatic reasoning; for **354** must originally have been followed by **B 12**:

> It is impossible for anything to come into being from what is not;
> and it is unattainable and unaccomplished for what exists to perish;
> for wherever anyone ever takes a stand, there it will always
> be (**355**).[5]

The argument is cribbed from Parmenides, **156**.7–9. (Empedocles' argument against destruction is presented in a corrupt text: no emendation I know of gives a sense which is both clear and interesting.)

Anaxagoras holds the same Eleatic view: 'No thing comes into being or is destroyed' (**59 B 17**). And he too probably adopted the Parmenidean argument; for

> He held the common opinion of the natural scientists to be true—that nothing comes into being from what is not (**356**: Aristotle, *Phys* 187a27–9 = **A 52**; cf. Aëtius, **A 46**).

Some scholars catch the Eleatic scent in **B 10** which asks, rhetorically, 'How could hair come into being from non-hair, or flesh from non-flesh?' (**212**). Aristotle appears to connect the view implicit in **B 10** with 'the common opinion of the natural scientists'; and we can make sense of the connexion. Suppose that the general principle lying behind **B 10** is:

(1) If something *F* comes into being from *a*, then *a* is *F*.

Evidently, (1) is closely related to the Principle of Synonymy which I have already discussed (above, pp. 88, 118). A special case of (1) is:

(2) If something existent comes into being from *a*, then *a* is existent.

And (2) can be read as bearing on the Parmenidean problem of 'absolute' generation; for it effectively denies the possibility of generation 'from what is not'.

Unfortunately the application is un-Eleatic and pointless. It is un-Eleatic because in (1) the phrase 'from *a*' marks *a* as the *source* of the *F* product; and in the Eleatic argument 'from *a*' is taken in a different sense. It is pointless because there is no way of moving from (2) to a rejection of generation; indeed, (2) comes uncomfortably close to rehabilitating generation. The purpose of (1) is to indicate that *F*s are produced from other *F*s; why, then, cannot (2) be taken to indicate that generation is possible, provided that existents are produced from other existents? At the very least Anaxagoras needs to argue that generation 'from what is' is impossible; and there is no hint in our texts that he ever did that. Thus I do not believe that **B 10** has any bearing on generation (for my reading of it see above, p. 333); and I suspect that Anaxagoras, like Empedocles, simply adopted the orthodox Parmenidean argument for his own.

In two respects, however, the accounts of generation in Anaxagoras and Empedocles do go beyond anything in Parmenides. First, they both reject 'epigenesis', the theory that there might come into being new things in addition to the present ungenerated furniture of the world. Here is Anaxagoras' argument:

> And when these things are separated out in this way, you must know that all of them are in no respect less nor more (for it is not possible to have more than all), but all are always equal (**357: B 5**).

Thus: 'There can never be more than all the things there are; so things will always be equal in number.' Both the premiss and the conclusion of this argument are 'untruisms' (above, p. 167). The premiss may be glossed by either of:

(3a) For any time t, if there are exactly n things at t, then there are no more than n things at t.

(3b) For any times t and t', if there are exactly n things at t, then there are no more than n things at t'.

And the conclusion may be glossed by either of:

(4a) For any time t, the number of things existing at t = the number of things existing at t.

(4b) For any times t and t', the number of things existing at t = the number of things existing at t'.

Anaxagoras is certainly not entitled to (3b), so it is natural to take his parenthetical premiss as (3a); he is hardly interested in the trivial conclusion (4a), so it is natural to take his conclusion to be (4b). Now (3a) does not entail (4b); but (3b) does: Anaxagoras surreptitiously mates the truth of (3a) with the powers of (3b), and produces a logical monster.

Empedocles' argument against epigenesis goes like this:

> And in addition to these [sc. the four roots, (?) and Love and Hate], nothing comes into being or declines.
> For if they perished outright they would no longer exist.
> And what could increase this totality? And whence could it come?
> And where could it be destroyed, since nothing is empty of these?
> (**358: B 17**.30–3).

The argument is not pellucid;[6] but the following gloss seems possible. 'Suppose that at t some new root R comes into existence, and suppose that there is an empty space for R to occupy at t. Since at present the four roots occupy all the space there is, some of them would have to have perished before t to make room for R; and it is impossible for the roots to perish. Hence there is no empty space at t for R to occupy; thus R cannot be added to the universe at t; nor, for that matter, can it come *from* anywhere or pass away *to* anywhere.'

The argument presupposes Empedocles' rejection of 'the void' or empty space (**287**); and its last two clauses are jejune, reminiscent of Epicharmus' satire rather than of Parmenides' philosophy. But those points apart, the argument is sound; and it makes a mildly interesting addition to the Eleatic armoury. What is its purpose? Why argue specifically against epigenesis when you have a general argument against generation as such? Perhaps Empedocles indulged in the following train of thought: 'Parmenides' argument shows that if *a* exists, then *a* was not generated, and hence that none of the present furniture of the world can have come into being; but he has omitted to show that the present furniture cannot be augmented; and I shall repair the omission.' But that is a poor line of thought: Parmenides' argument does not apply simply to present existents.

The second respect in which Empedocles and Anaxagoras went beyond Parmenides reflects their greater consideration for the common man and his common language.[7] I have already quoted a sentence from **59 B 17**; here is the whole fragment:

> The Greeks do not think correctly[8] of coming into being and being destroyed; for no thing comes into being or is destroyed, but it is from existing things that things are commingled and separated out. And in this way they would correctly call coming into being commingling and being destroyed separating out (**359**).

In place of the generation of new items Anaxagoras offers us the rearrangement of old items; instead of the destruction of existent items Anaxagoras offers us the rearrangement of their parts.

There is a similar passage in Empedocles:

> I will tell you another thing: there is birth (*phusis*) for none of all
> mortal things, nor is there an end in doleful death;
> but there is only mixing and interchange of what is mixed
> —and the name of birth is applied by men to this (**360: 31 B 8**).[9]

Again:

> And when they [sc. the four roots] are mixed in the shape of a
> man† and come into the light,†
> or in the shape of a kind of wild beast or of plants
> or of birds, then (?) they say that this comes into being (?);
> and when they [sc. the roots] are separated apart, this again [they
> call] wretched fate:
> (?) they do not name them as is right (?) but I too myself
> comply with the custom (**361: B 9**; cf. **B 10, 15, 35**).

The text of **361** is desperately corrupt;[10] but its general drift is clear enough: like Anaxagoras, Empedocles is offering us comminglings and separations in place of generations and destructions.

Men talk of 'generation' and 'destruction': according to

Parmenides, such talk is mere verbiage (**156**. 40); Anaxagoras and Empedocles agree that the talk is necessarily false, but they assert that it is readily translated into an unobjectionable idiom: replace '*a* is generated' and '*a* is destroyed' by 'comminglings and separations of such and such a sort occur'. And Empedocles at least is prepared to 'comply with the custom' and speak with the vulgar: 'It is impossible, even in the most rigid of philosophic reasonings, so far to alter the bent and genius of the tongue we speak, as never to give a handle for cavillers to pretend difficulties and inconsistencies. But a fair and ingenuous reader will collect the sense from the scope and tenor and connexion of a discourse, making allowance for those inaccurate modes of speech which use has made inevitable' (Berkeley, *Principles* §52).[11]

Philolaus and the Atomists differ from Empedocles and Anaxagoras in the matter of generation. In **277**, Philolaus asserts that 'the things that exist . . . have come into being'; and nothing forbids us to take this text at its face value. Leucippus set up his system precisely in order to defend generation and destruction; for:

> He thought he had arguments which, by saying what agreed with perception, would not do away with either generation or destruction or motion and the plurality of existent things (**362**: *GC* 325a33–5 = **67 A** 7).

Philolaus' principles, and the Abderites' corpuscles, are ungenerated and indestructible; but the macroscopic objects of the world which come from the principles and are constituted by the corpuscles can and do come into existence and cease to exist.

In Philolaus' system, macroscopic entities are generated by a harmonizing (*harmozein*) or arranging (*kosmein*) of the elements; and it is reasonable to suppose that he hoped to immunize generation against the Eleatic disease by explaining it in terms of the interconnecting of the ungenerated elements. Thus '*a* is generated' may be true; but its truth conditions are given by some proposition of the form 'b_1 and b_2 are harmonized'. The same account is explicitly ascribed to the Atomists:

> If generation is the association of atoms and destruction their dissociation, then generation will be alteration (**363**: Simplicius, **68 A** 37).

> These atoms, separated from one another in the unlimited void and differing in shapes and sizes and position and order, travel in the void and overtake and strike one another; and some rebound

> wherever it chances, but others catch onto (*periplekesthai*) one another by virtue of the symmetry of their shapes and sizes and positions and orders, and stay together (*summenein*), and in this way the generation of composites is achieved (**364**: Simplicius, 67 A 14).

Empedocles and Anaxagoras deny that anything is ever generated: the process we habitually call generation is, they say, in fact a commingling of ungenerated stuffs. Philolaus, Leucippus and Democritus, on the other hand, hope to save generation: things, they say, certainly are generated and destroyed; but generations and destructions are in fact comminglings and dissolutions of one sort or another. Consider the two sentences: *P*—'an *F* is generated'; *Q*—'*a*, *b*, *c*, . . . commingle in such a way as to take on an *F*-like appearance'. According to Anaxagoras and Empedocles, *P* is always false, *Q* sometimes true; and *Q* in fact describes the type of event men typically mean to refer to when they use *P*. According to Philolaus and the Atomists, *Q* is sometimes true; and *P* is equivalent to *Q*; so that *P*, too, is sometimes true.

That distinction may seem fairly trifling: after all, both parties 'reduce' generation to comminglings (and hence to locomotion); for both claim to account for the phenomena we usually refer to as generations by way of comminglings.[12] Yet there are at least two significant differences between the parties: one will emerge in the next section; the other I state briefly now. The Atomists' analysis of generation has certain formal similarities to Aristotle's; in particular, they, like Aristotle (above, p. 197), make generation *ex nihilo*, or creation, a self-contradictory notion. For *a* to be generated is for pre-existent entities to rearrange themselves: the sentence form '*a* was generated at *t* and nothing existed before *t*' is inconsistent. Now Empedocles and Anaxagoras are equally opposed to generation; and they too think that creation is logically impossible. But the impossibility in their case has Parmenidean roots: sever the stem of the Eleatic argument, show the objections to 'not-being' misguided, and creation becomes possible. If Elea were refuted, Empedocles and Anaxagoras might countenance creation: the refutation would have no such liberating consequence for the Atomists.

What, finally, would Melissus have said to all this? He would not have been impressed: 'Empedocles and Anaxagoras deny generation but accept locomotion; they thereby commit themselves, whether they like it or not, to alteration; and alteration entails generation. Their position is tediously inconsistent. Philolaus and the Atomists accept generation for non-elementary objects, and defend it by analysis in terms of commingling. They do not explain how their analysis constitutes a defence; and they do not indicate where they think the Eleatic arguments against generation fail. Their position may not be internally contradictory; but it amounts to no more than an unargued rejection of Eleatic metaphysics.'

I have sympathy with Melissus' hypothetical retort; and I believe that the neo-Ionians never apprehended the power of the Eleatic deduction. Empedocles and Anaxagoras must drive a wedge between '*a* becomes *F*' and '*a*'s *F*ness comes into being'. I do not see how they can do that. Philolaus and the Atomists must point to the flaws in Parmenides' argument: flaws there certainly are; but no Presocratic put his finger upon them. The neo-Ionians threw off the intellectual paralysis with which Parmenides had threatened Greek thought: they manfully attempted to tread again the scientific road, and they took many progressive steps even if their feet remained shackled by Elea. And of course the neo-Ionians are more right than the Eleatics: things do move, they do alter, they are generated. For all that, the neo-Ionian revival is fundamentally a flop: it does not answer Elea.

(e) *Ontology*

Generation and existence are connected by the tightest of conceptual bonds: to be generated is to come into existence; if *a* is generated at *t*, then *a* exists immediately after *t*. Thus anyone who holds that '*a* is generated' is always false must maintain that '*a* exists' is true only if *a* is eternal—ungenerated and indestructible. Now philosophers, evidently, are not eternal; nor can they be generated, according to Empedocles and Anaxagoras: hence no philosophers exist. Do men, horses, trees, clouds, chairs, books exist? Empedocles and Anaxagoras must answer: No.

As far as we know, Anaxagoras did not recognize this consequence of his views; Empedocles perhaps did. At **31 B 17**.34 (= **B 26**.3) he says of the four roots:

> But these themselves exist; and running through one another they become different things at different times and are always absolutely homogenous (**365**; cf. **352**).

The words 'these themselves exist' translate '*aut' estin tauta*': one permissible paraphrase of the Greek is: 'these alone exist'.[13] If that paraphrase is right, Empedocles assigns existence to his roots and to nothing else. At least one ancient critic seems so to have understood Empedocles: Colotes, Plutarch's Epicurean opponent, asserted that in Empedocles' view men do not exist (Plutarch, *adv Col* 1113 AB).

And it is worth quoting a fragment of Empedocles' younger contemporary, Ion of Chios. His philosophical work, the *Triagmos*, began as follows:

> The beginning of my account is this: all things are three, and there is nothing more or less than these three things (**366: 36 B 1**).[14]

We know almost nothing of Ion's philosophical stance; and it would be rash to put much weight on these words. Yet the obvious interpretation is this: apart from the basic primordial entities, nothing at all exists.

But can we really believe that Empedocles or Ion meant to deny the existence of chalk and cheese? Of course not: Empedocles means that there are no *elemental* stuffs other than the four roots; and Ion means that everything is made from just the three things that constitute his elements. Empedocles surely did not see what he was committing himself to in denying generation.

Philolaus and the Atomists have not the same need for a parsimonious ontology: macroscopic objects are generated; they may be ephemeral and yet existent. Philolaus explicitly asserts that macroscopic objects do exist; indeed, they are paradigmatically *ta eonta* (cf. **277**). Yet Philolaus distinguishes, I think, between the ontological status of his elements and that of their compounds. At all events, he uses, in **277**, the ordinary verb '*einai*' for the existence of ordinary things, but applies '*huparchein* (subsist)' to the elements; and while ordinary objects are designated *ta eonta*, the elements are *ta pragmata*. The difference in terminology may, I suppose, be merely an accident of style; yet I am inclined to think that it is deliberate: the difference in language is employed to signal a difference in fact. To see the point of this we may turn to the Atomists.

In discussing the Abderite divide between what exists *nomôi* and what exists *eteêi* I considered only the status of qualities on the *nomôi* side of the fence (above, pp. 370–7). And indeed all our authorities, with the exception of Plutarch, make *nomôi* entities exclusively qualities. Plutarch adds *sunkrisis*, 'combination', to the *nomôi* list. A *sunkrisis* is a macroscopic body, or atomic conglomeration: '*sunkrinein* (to combine)' is regularly used for the formation of complex bodies from the elementary corpuscles (e.g., **213**, Aristotle; Sextus, **68 A 59**); and elsewhere those bodies are called *sunkrimata* (e.g., Diogenes Laertius, IX.44 = **68 A 1**; Galen, **A 49**) or *sunkriseis* (e.g., Aëtius, **A 105**). Plutarch's gloss on *sunkrisis* is thus correct:

> And when [the atoms] come close to one another or fall together or intertwine, of the conglomerated masses one seems to be water, one fire, one a plant, one a man; and the atoms, which he calls *ideai*, are all that exist; nothing else does (**367: 68 A 57**).

Stuffs and macroscopic substances only *seem* to be (*phainesthai*); atoms alone really exist: water and men, fire and plants, stand on the *nomôi* side of the great divide.

The obscure philosopher Cleidemus gave the following account of lightning:

> There are some who, like Cleidemus, say that lightning does not exist but is an appearance (*phainesthai*), suggesting that the occurrence is similar to what happens when one strikes the sea with a stick; for the water appears (*phainetai*) as flashing in the night. In this way when the moisture in the clouds is struck, the appearance (*phantasia*) of brightness is the lightning (**368**: Aristotle, *Meteor* 370a10–15 = **62 A 1**).

Cleidemus' point is this: when water is struck with an oarblade, it cannot be supposed to undergo a genuine change of colour, or to emit a tongue of flame or the like; all that happens is that the water *appears* differently to the striker. Similarly, the lightning flash is not a substance in its own right, nor yet a coloration of the clouds: what happens is simply that the cloud *appears* differently.

Why Cleidemus advanced this view we do not know; nor am I interested here in Cleidemus' meteorology. I cite the passage because it is echoed in the doxography on Leucippus:

> All things happen in accordance with *phantasia* and *dokêsis* and none in accordance with truth; but they seem (*phainesthai*) in the way of the oar in the water (**369**: Epiphanius, **67 A 33**).

The report is not clear, and the reporter is not worth much; yet behind his words there may lie an account of macroscopic items similar to the one which Plutarch ascribes to Democritus—they do not really exist.

At all events, the Atomists have a good argument for denying reality to macroscopic ephemera—not the Eleatic argument, which they cannot employ, but a reasoning of their own.

> Democritus says . . . that it is impossible for one thing to come from two or two from one (**223**: Aristotle, *Met* 1039a9 = **68 A 42**).

Thus the interweaving (*periplokê*) of the atoms

> makes them touch, and be next to one another but does not generate any genuinely single nature whatever out of them; for it is absolutely silly to think that two or more things could ever become one (**213**, Aristotle).

Anything that truly exists is *one* thing, a unity; macroscopic objects are conglomerations of atoms; no conglomeration of objects can ever constitute *one* thing, a unity; hence macroscopic objects do not truly exist. That, I suppose, is the metaphysical foundation of the Atomists' view that macroscopic objects are unreal.

But why suppose that 'two or more things cannot become one'? As it stands, that proposition seems to be a trivial falsehood. Two or more things do frequently make one: a nib and a penholder make a pen; four limbs, a head and a torso make a body; engine and bodywork make a motor-car; and—in just the same way—many million corpuscles make a desk or a tree or a cloud. Most of the things we see are compounds in an evident way. That does not derogate from their unity: my pen is *one* thing, viz. one pen; it is a cohesive item with a unifying function; it shows no tendency to fall apart, atomize, or disintegrate. What could be more unitary than that?

Yet it would be wrong to dismiss the Atomist principle out of hand. Let us approach it obliquely. There is a classical conception of substance, originating with Aristotle, according to which substances are ultimate subjects of predication: things are said of them, they are not said of anything else. Substances are ontologically indispensable objects. In a more up-to-date jargon: 'If a complete account of what there is would need some substantival expression referring to the *F*s, then the *F*s are substances; but not otherwise'.[15] Non-substances may be said to exist or to 'have being'; but their existence is essentially parasitic upon the existence of substances. Pride, doubtless, exists: there is such a thing as pride. But all talk about pride can be analysed, one would imagine, into talk about proud men; and for pride to exist is simply for there to exist men who are proud. Prejudice exists; but truths about prejudice are presentable as truths about men who prejudge matters; for prejudice to exist is simply for there to be men who are thus given to prejudging.

Pride and prejudice are non-substances. A further type of non-substance is an aggregate: aggregates are the sums of their parts; any truths about aggregates can be expressed as truths about those parts, and all facts about aggregates are no more than facts about their parts. The meteorological truths about clouds dissolve into truths about their constituent water-particles; anatomical facts are facts about the constituent cells of the body; and, in general, macroscopic facts are facts about the constituent atoms of macroscopic bodies. Clouds exist just in so far as water droplets congregate; there are bodies only if cells are suitably harmonized; and, in general, for macroscopic bodies to exist is for atoms to be collected together.

We can now give a more plausible sense to Democritus' assertion that two things cannot be one: no aggregate of two or more real things or substances is itself a real thing or substance. Aggregates are not substances; hence aggregates of substances are not substances. Since all macroscopic objects are atomic conglomerates, no macroscopic object is a substance: no such object exists *eteêi*.

Anaxagoras and Empedocles, it might be thought, are not far from the Atomists here: they make certain stuffs eternal and substantial, and they are committed to denying real existence to everything else. They differ from the Atomists only in a certain conceptual poverty: denying existence to men and clouds, they were obliged to say that, in strictness of speech, there are no men and there are no clouds; the Atomists, availing themselves of a distinction between two senses of 'exist' (above, p. 404), can say that men and clouds do exist$_2$ but do not exist$_1$. There are men and clouds; but men and clouds are not real. In Philolaic terminology, men and clouds exist (*einai*), they do not subsist (*huparchein*).

However that may be, it is only the Atomists from among the neo-Ionians whose ontology and philosophy have had any influence on later scientific ages. That philosophy can be briefly stated as follows: 'The proper language of science is thin and meagre: the only objects it names are atoms; the only predicates it contains are those denoting primary or proper qualities of bodies, and those denoting certain elementary spatio-temporal relations between objects. All facts can be expressed in this language; for any sentence in our ordinary language can be uniquely paired with a scientific sentence which has the same truth conditions as it has: "grass is green", "bread is nutritious", "ink dries quickly", can each be paired with a sentence mentioning only atomic structures and atomic predicates. Ordinary language is, ordinarily, indispensable; but for the purposes of science—that is to say, with regard to the pursuit of truth—it is grotesquely ornate, and a plain, severe style is preferable.'

Scientifically, Atomism is ancient history. No scientist believes anything that Democritus said; and the modern successors to atomism have long ago repudiated the primitive image of a world of billiard balls rolling about on a vacant three-dimensional cloth. Philosophically, on the other hand, the Atomist system remains an interest and a challenge: as the first exercise in reductive ontology, it is the ultimate source of a popular pastime of modern philosophical logicians. The questions 'What *really* is there?' and 'What *must* there be?' still trouble and perplex; and some at least of the modern answers to them have a complexion curiously reminiscent of Abdera. Again, as the first fully conscious attempt to provide a thoroughgoing materialist account of the world, Atomism remains alive: to that issue I shall turn in a later chapter.

XXI

The Sophists

(a) *Anthropology*

Gorgias of Leontini has already made an appearance on the Presocratic stage. Gorgias was a Sophist; and his fellow Sophists will have a larger part to play in this and the following chapters. Who, then, were these Sophists? They do not constitute a school, like the Milesians and the Eleatics, bound together by a common philosophy; rather, they are a group of outstanding individuals—Protagoras, Gorgias, Hippias, Prodicus, Antiphon, Thrasymachus—who are associated not by any common doctrines but by a common outlook on life and learning. The term 'sophist (*sophistês*)' was not originally a term of abuse: when Herodotus calls Solon and Pythagoras sophists (I.29; IV.95) he is praising them as sages and men of wisdom (*sophia*) (cf. Aristides, **79 A 1**). But '*sophistês*' became connected not with '*sophia*' but with '*to sophon* (cleverness)'; and *to sophon ou sophia*. Thus Plato offers us six uncomplimentary 'definitions' of the sophist as a tradesman in cleverness (*Sophist* 231 D = **79 A 2**); and Aristotle defines the sophist as 'a man who makes money from apparent but unreal wisdom' (*Top* 165a 22 = **79 A 3**). Xenophon, that stuffy old prig, put the classical view clearly:

> The sophists speak to deceive and they write for their own gain, and they give no benefit to anyone; for not one of them became or is wise, but each is actually content to be called a sophist—which is a term of reproach in the eyes of those who think properly. So I urge you to guard against the professions of the sophists, but not to dishonour the thoughts of the philosophers (**370: 79 A 2a**).[1]

The sophist sells his cleverness: he is an intellectual harlot; and, not inappropriately, he adopts a meretricious intellectual pose (Xenophon, *Mem*. I.vi.13).

A Protagorean anecdote is apposite. Protagoras taught rhetoric for cash; and, confident of his tutorial abilities, he stipulated that his legal pupils need not pay him until they had won their first lawsuit. A pupil, Euathlus, had not paid his fees, and Protagoras took him to court. Euathlus argued that he had not yet won a case: Protagoras retorted that if he, Protagoras, won the present case, then clearly Euathlus must pay the tutorial fee; and if Euathlus won, then by the terms of the tutorial, he must equally pay the fee (Diogenes Laertius, IX.56 = **80 A 1**).

A spurious cleverness, and a love of cash: those are the marks of the sophist in the unflattering portrait painted by Xenophon and Plato. I shall not trace out the somewhat tedious dispute among modern scholars over the reasons for Plato's judgment and its fairness. Certainly, the Sophists taught for money; but no modern scholar will dare to hold that against them (cf. Philostratus, **80 A 2**). Certainly, they were clever; but cleverness is not an intellectual vice. In some cases their seriousness is in doubt; but only the solemn will find fault with that. And it is an indisputable fact that many of the Sophists were men of wide interests and vast knowledge; the most cursory perusal of their remains will convince any reader of that.[2] I shall not attempt a rounded picture of the contribution to philosophy of the Sophists, nor even a portrayal of any individual Sophist: to do so would require a volume in itself. But in this and the following two chapters I shall discuss several of the larger and more interesting theses ascribed to one or another of those men; and some rough idea of the nature and value of the sophistic movement will, I hope, emerge.

> About gods I cannot know either that they are or that they are not. For many things prevent one from knowing—the obscurity, and the life of man, which is short (**371: 80 B 4**).

Later generations reported those resounding words with a frisson of pious horror, and alleged that they caused the Abderite Protagoras to be expelled from Athens, that bastion of liberty, and his books to be publicly burned (e.g., Diogenes Laertius, IX.52 = **A 1**).[3] Protagoras was listed among the ancient *atheoi* (e.g., Eusebius, *ad* **B 4**); but **371** is not atheistical: as Philostratus (**A 2**) correctly observes, it indicates *aporia* or agnosticism (cf. Cicero, *de natura deorum* I.42.117). Diogenes of Oenoanda, it is true, offers an atheistical interpretation:

> He said he did not know if there are any gods, and that is the same as to say he knew that there are no gods (**372**: fr. 11 Ch = **A 23**).[4]

But Diogenes crassly conflates a profession of knowledge, ('I know that not-*P*') with a confession of ignorance ('I do not know that *P*'). To the believer, agnostics may be as bad as atheists; but to the atheist agnostics are not much better than believers.

Agnosticism is an interesting stance; but Protagoras' reasons for adopting it are disappointing. The term 'obscurity (*adêlotês*)' recalls Xenophanes; and we wonder if Protagoras developed arguments of the sort he found in Xenophanes' poem. But the second of the 'many things [that] prevent one from knowing' suggests that Protagoras offered no such support for his agnosticism: *vita brevis*—theology is dismissed with a shrug.

The significant part of 371 is the part we do not possess: the fragment begins '*peri men theôn* . . . (About gods on the one hand . . .)'; the word *men*, we may guess, had its answering *de*: 'On the other hand'. A further guess has it that the *de* sentence asserted the possibility of knowledge about men: 'Of the gods I know nothing; about men I speak thus'.[5] If we presume to scan god we shall observe nothing; theology is to be adjured, and replaced by anthropology.

And anthropology, in a broad sense of the term, was, as we know from Plato, an interest of Protagoras: the origins of man, and more particularly, the origins of human skills, of human customs, and of human social and moral conventions, were for him an object of speculative study. The long story put into his mouth in Plato's *Protagoras* (320C–322E = **C 1**) is doubtless Plato's own production; but it was produced on the basis of a Protagorean original.[6] The subject was popular in Abdera; for Democritus also offered an anthropology. A few fragments survive:

> Democritus says that music is a younger art, and he gives the reason, asserting that necessity did not separate it off but it came about from superfluity (**373: 68 B 144**),

and thus anticipating the familiar Aristotelian account of the origin of the arts and sciences (*Met* 981b13–25). Again:

> In the most important things we became learners: of the spider in weaving and healing, of the swallow in building, of the songbirds—swan and nightingale—in imitative song (**374: B 154**; cf. Aelian, **A 151**).

These are pitiful remnants of a grand work. In a passage of Diodorus (**B 5**) many scholars see a comprehensive epitome of that original; but their view is on the whole unlikely to be true.

In scope and in emphasis Democritus' work and its Protagorean offspring represent a new departure; but behind them lies the old

Ionian ideal: a complete and systematic account of the generation, growth and present state of the universe. Democritus' anthropology was probably set within a cosmogony (cf. Censorinus, etc. **A 139**): the universe began; life was formed; man, and human institutions, were founded. Anaximander or Xenophanes might have written the work; all that is new in Democritus is the anthropological slant: instead of the natural world it is the human world which absorbs his interest; instead of a history of the stars a history of human culture fires his intellectual imagination. (Or so at least it seems: we are dealing with fragmentary reports, and inference to the emphasis and focus of a work from a few fragments is a chancy thing.)

I shall not attempt to outline the speculations of Democritus or of Protagoras, nor yet to fit them into their historical contexts: both tasks are exceedingly intricate, and in any case I find anthropology—especially armchair anthropology—a fearful bore.[7] Instead, I shall expand a little upon two topics included in the Democritean anthropology which do possess some philosophical interest. And the first of these, paradoxically, is theology.

(b) *The origins of atheism*

I begin, not with Democritus, but with Critias, a man of black fame: 'he seems to me the worst of all men who have a name for evil' (Philostratus, **88 A 1**). He was one of the Thirty who overthrew the Athenian democracy in the last desperate years of the Peloponnesian War, and who in turn received a swift and fatal overthrow. By all accounts he was an unlovely character, cruel, cynical, overbearing. He was also the scion of a noble house, and a literary dilettante: we possess fragments of occasional poems, of verse comedies, and of prose 'constitutions' full of recondite trifles. Critias was no philosopher; nor was he a sophist in the Protagorean or Gorgian mould; indeed, his nearest connexion to philosophy was by blood, for Plato was his nephew. He might well be left for the historians and literary scholars to write upon; but one long fragment has won him, by accident, a place in the history of thought, and the fragment is amusing enough to bear transcription. It comes from a satyr play, *Sisyphus*:

> There was a time when the life of men was unorganized,
> and brutish, and the servant of force;
> when there was no reward for the good,
> nor again any punishment came to the bad.
> And then I think men set up laws

as punishers, in order that justice might be ruler
[of all alike], and hold violence a slave.
And anyone who might transgress was penalized.
Then, since the laws prevented them
from performing overt acts by force,
but they performed them secretly, then it seems to me
[for the first time] some man, acute and wise in mind,
invented the fear of the gods for mortals, so that
there might be some terror for the bad even if in secret
they do or say or think anything.
Hence, then, he introduced divinity,
saying that 'There is a spirit enjoying undying life,
hearing and seeing by its mind, thinking and
attending to everything, carrying a divine nature;
and he will hear everything said among men
and will be able to see everything done.
And if in silence you plan some evil,
that will not escape the gods; for thinking
belongs to the gods.' Saying these words
he introduced the pleasantest of teachings,
hiding truth with a false account.
And he said that the gods dwell there, where
he might most confound men by naming,
whence he knew fears came to men
and toils in their wretched life
—from the celestial orbit where he saw
the lightnings were, and the terrible crashings
of thunder, and the starry shape of heaven,
fine embroidery of the wise craftsman Time,
and whence the bright mass of the star steps
and the damp rain travels to earth.
Such fears he set about men,
because of which in his account he fairly housed
the spirit in a fitting place—
and extinguished unlawfulness by fears.

Thus first I think someone persuaded
mortals to believe that a tribe of spirits exists (**375: B 25**).

This is a speech from a play, and a semi-comedy at that: it is not a theological tract; nor need the view it expresses coincide with the sentiments of its author. For all that, its content is worth taking seriously, even if it was designed only to outrage or to entertain.

'Some clever man, dismayed at the inability of human laws to curb human evil, invented the gods: by persuading them of the existence of a divine law and divine judges, he succeeded, to some extent, in making social life less nasty and less brutish.' Such is the message of the *Sisyphus* speech. I shall use it, in this and the following section, to introduce two issues in philosophical theology. The first issue concerns divine justice.

In the *Sisyphus*, the *raison d'être* of the gods is a moral, or at least a social, matter: the gods are invented to supplement the laws; and by their invention the god-giver 'extinguished unlawfulness by fears'. The notion that the gods punish malefactors is ancient and ubiquitous; in Greek literature its *locus classicus* is an elegy by the Athenian statesman Solon: Zeus, he proclaims, punishes all transgressors; and if justice sometimes proceeds at a limping pace, it is for all that unrelenting and inevitable (fr. 1. 25–32 D).[8]

Not all Greeks were equally convinced of the efficacy of divine justice. Against Solon's solid affirmation we may set a poem in the collection ascribed to Theognis: the gods, he says, ought indeed to love the just and to hate and punish the unjust; but alas, they do not; for the unjust evidently prosper (Theognis, 731–52).[9] Thrasymachus drew an unpalatable moral:

> The gods do not observe human affairs; for they would not pass over the greatest of human goods, justice; for we see that men do not use justice (**376: 85 B 8**).

'O Zeus, what shall I say? That you do not observe mankind?' (Euripides, *Hecuba* 488).[10] The gods, lovers of justice, could not overlook the myriad unjust successes which Theognis laments; hence they cannot observe them—the gods are not omniscient.

Later, from a different perspective, Epicurus drew a different conclusion: 'The statements of most men about the gods are not cognition but false suppositions, according to which the greatest harms befall the bad from the gods, and the greatest benefits the good' (*ad Men* §124). Unlike the Thraymachean divinities, Epicurus' gods do observe our miserable lives; but they do not care: omniscient, they are not practically benevolent.

The prevalence of successful malefaction provoked a third reaction. The ancient doxographers possessed a traditional catalogue of *atheoi*, godless men or atheists.[11] The *atheos par excellence* was Diagoras of Melos who 'made the downright assertion that god does not exist at all' (Athenagoras, III, 9 J).[12] We know little about Diagoras, and that little is confused. He lived in the second half of the fifth century; 'he committed verbal impieties about foreign rites and festivals [i.e. the

Eleusinian mysteries]' (pseudo-Lysias, VI. 17 = I. 5 J); and as a result he was prosecuted in Athens and forced to flee the country. Some scholars judge that the offending work—if indeed Diagoras really put his offensive thoughts to paper—was only 'a sensational pamphlet published by an otherwise insignificant man'; and that 'nowhere do we find evidence of an intellectual defence of atheism'. Perhaps, indeed, Diagoras was an *atheos* only in the old sense of an 'ungodly' man; he was not, properly speaking, an atheist. To other more generous scholars Diagoras appears as one of 'the leaders of progressive thought' in Athens.[13]

We lack the evidence to determine this dispute; but a few straws indicate a mildly philosophical breeze. If we find no 'intellectual defence' of atheism ascribed to Diagoras, we do find two or three rationalistic anecdotes. Cicero reports that Diagoras' friends, attempting to convince him of the existence of the gods, pointed to the numerous votive tablets set up by mariners saved from the storms of the sea; Diagoras replied that there would be many more tablets had the drowned sailors survived to make their dedications (*de natura deorum* III. 89 = III. 12 J). Sextus reports that Diagoras became an atheist when an opponent of his perjured himself and got away with his perjury (*adv Math* IX. 52 = V. 5 J): the Suda makes the opponent a rival poet who had plagiarized Diagoras' work (s.v. Diagoras = III. 3 J), and a scholiast on Aristophanes' *Clouds* has the opponent refuse to return a deposit entrusted to him by Diagoras (III. 4 J). The anecdotes bring out, in a personal form, the same point which Theognis and Thrasymachus expressed more generally: injustice thrives. And it is suggested that Diagoras used that truism as a basis for atheism.[14]

That very inference was made in Euripides' *Bellerophon*. One of the fragments of this lost drama reads thus:

> Does someone then say that there are gods in heaven?
> There are not, there are not, if a man will
> not in folly rely on the old argument.
> Consider it yourselves; do not build your opinion
> on my words. I say that a tyranny
> kills many men and deprives them of their possessions,
> and breaking oaths destroys cities;
> and doing this they are more happy
> than those who live each day in pious peace.
> And I know of small cities that honour the gods
> which obey greater and more impious ones,
> overcome by the greater number of spears. (**377**: fr. 286 N)

Euripides' fragment, the anecdotes of Diagoras' conversion to atheism, and the judgments of Thrasymachus and of Epicurus, all converge on an issue which Christian theology knows as the Problem of Evil.

The Problem concerns an apparent incompatibility between the existence of an omniscient, omnipotent and benevolent god, and the prevalence of badness in the world. There is no unique statement of the Problem, and therefore no single answer to it. One version of it runs like this: Assume:

(1) Unjust actions often go unpunished.
(2) God loves justice.
(3) God observes all human actions.
(4) God can intervene in mortal affairs.

Here (2), (3) and (4) reflect the benevolence, the omniscience, and the omnipotence of God; and (1) is the mournful observation of Theognis. Now it is argued that (1)–(4) are mutually incompatible: suppose, by (1), that an unjust action *A* goes unpunished. Then, by (3), God observes *A*; by (2), he dislikes *A* and wishes it punished; and by (4) he has power to punish *A*. But if God—or anyone else—wants to ϕ and has the power to ϕ, then he will ϕ. Hence God does punish the perpetrator of *A*. But, by hypothesis, *A* is unpunished. An almighty and omniscient god, who loves justice, cannot, logically, allow the unjust to thrive: if injustice is seen to thrive, that fact provides a conclusive disproof of the existence of any such god.

Different thinkers will react to that argument in different ways. Some, following in Solon's footsteps, will deny (1), and take the position pilloried in Voltaire's *Candide*. Heraclitus, in effect, adopts such a view (above, p. 131); and its most celebrated adherent is Leibniz. Modern philosophers have exercised their imaginations to provide reasons for rejecting (1): I assert, dogmatically, that (1) is a plain and patent truth.

Epicurus in effect denied proposition (2): his gods have no particular concern for justice. And the same denial is implicit in Theognis. Thrasymachus preferred to reject proposition (3). Both (2) and (3) may seem undeniable to those educated in a Christian tradition; and to many Greeks they will have carried the same air of self-evidence. But the Homeric gods were not remarkable for their love of justice, nor were they all omniscient; and a religion can, I suppose, survive the observation that its gods are neither all-knowing nor utterly devoted to the good of mankind.

Diagoras, and the speaker in the *Bellerophon*, take (1) for what it is: a platitude. And they implicitly accept (2)–(4): gods, they suppose, are by definition lovers of justice, possessors of knowledge, and repositories of power. Their conclusion is atheism: there are no gods.

I hold no brief for theism; but Diagoras has too easy a victory here. Doubtless there is a logical connexion between divinity and a love of justice; yet Diagoras requires a remarkably strong connexion: he must take it as a logical truth that gods wish for justice at any price. But a benevolent ruler, ardently desiring the prevalence of justice in his kingdom, may deliberately let some unjust acts go unpunished: the consequences of a constant intervention in the name of justice may be even less desirable than a state wherein injustice occasionally triumphs. It is a platitude of political philosophy that justice and liberty frequently conflict. In theology the same conflict is found; and Christian apologists who explain the existence of 'moral evil' by reference to the free will of man are urging, in effect, that liberty is not always inferior to justice. Nor does that argument seem bad; proposition (2) is true, but in a sense too weak to yield any atheistical conclusion: God loves justice, but he also loves liberty.

I conclude that the Problem of Evil, in its original form, does not lead to atheism. It does not follow that the Problem holds no embarrassment for theists: first, the ascription of liberty to humans is itself hard to reconcile with many popular forms of theism; and second, other versions of the Problem, which refer to natural rather than to 'moral' evil, are not so easily evaded. If Diagoras failed to refute theism, he did at least invent an argument whose more sophisticated and subtle forms still cause the acutest difficulties for many types of contemporary theism.

(c) *The aetiology of religious beliefs*

I turn now to the second issue raised by the fragment of Critias' *Sisyphus*. One of the *atheoi* in the ancient catalogue was Prodicus of Ceos, another sophistical contemporary of Critias. Atheism was ascribed to him on the basis of a fairly innocent assertion:

> The ancients thought that sun and moon and rivers and springs, and in general everything that benefits the life of men were gods, because of the benefit coming from them (**378: 84 B 5**).

Something very similar was said by Democritus:

> The ancients, seeing what happens in the sky—e.g., thunder and lightning and thunderbolts and conjunctions of stars and eclipses of sun and moon—were afraid, believing gods to be the cause of these (**379**: Sextus, **68 A 75**).

According to Sextus, this passage offers an aetiology of religious belief: fear, inspired by a contemplation of celestial pyrotechnics, led men to postulate a divine pyrotechnician. The interpretation is plausible; and it receives some support from a fragment of Democritus' treatise *On the Things in Hell* (cf. **B O c**):

> Some men, ignorant of the dissolution of mortal nature, but conscious of the miseries of their life, crawl, during their lifetime, in troubles and fears, inventing falsehoods about the time after their death (**380: B 297**).

Men are mortal, but they will not acknowledge their mortality: doomed to a wretched life, they invent stories of *post mortem* bliss. There is an evident parallelism between this account of eschatological belief and the religious aetiology described by Sextus in **379**.[15]

We may possess an actual fragment of Democritus' aetiology:

> Of the sage men, a few raising their hands to what we Greeks now call air, said: 'Zeus is everything; and he knows everything, and gives, and takes away; and he is king of everything' (**381: B 30**).[16]

Some scholars compare these wise men to Critias' god-giver: cleverly and for political ends, they invent a ruler who knows everything and has supreme power of giving and taking. Others, more plausibly, take the reference to 'wise men' ironically, thus: 'some *soi-disant* sage, impressed by the weather, called the common air Zeus, and gave it divine powers'. Either interpretation will offer some sort of illustration of **379**; for each gives an aetiology of religious belief. But scholars dispute over **381**; and against those who find a cynical or contemptuous aetiology in the fragment there are others who find it a beautiful and touching assertion of faith: 'Those old, wise, men piously stretched out their hands; and rightly divinized the air'. In the absence of any context such a reading cannot be excluded: **381** must leave the arena; it cannot help us to understand Democritus' theology.

Critias, Prodicus and Democritus all offer anthropological aetiologies of religious beliefs: Critias and Prodicus are listed as *atheoi*, Democritus is not.[17] Is that fair?

The *Sisyphus* speech implies that all present religious belief can be traced back to the pronouncement of the original god-giver. And that pronouncement was false (**375**. 26); the gods are an invention (**375**. 13).[18] The speech is thus overtly atheistical, but its atheism is so far ungrounded. Xenophanes, I argued (above, p. 142), held that an inappropriate causal ancestry might deprive a belief of the title to knowledge; in particular, our beliefs about the gods, being causally explicable in terms of our local environment, fall short of knowledge. In effect, then, Xenophanes offered an anthropological aetiology of religious belief, and inferred that religious belief is unrational. Critias, I suggest, did just the same: all religious beliefs, he imagines, are explicable ultimately by reference to the god-giver's pious fraud; that fraud has a purely social explanation—hence the religious beliefs it grounds are unrational.

The same thought occurs more cleanly in Prodicus. In itself, **378** is innocent of sceptical implications;[19] but Prodicus meant more than **378** says:

> [He] attaches all human cults and mysteries and rites to the needs of farming, thinking that both the conception of gods and every sort of piety came to men from here (**382**: Themistius, *ad* **84 B 5**).

All religious beliefs are explicable in terms of agricultural fears and hopes; those farming feelings are, plainly, irrelevant to the question of whether or not there are any gods: religious beliefs are therefore irrational.

What is irrationally believed is not thereby falsely believed. Why were Critias and Prodicus atheists? or were they called *atheoi* not for rejecting the gods outright but for a gentle Protagorean agnosticism? Suppose (truly) that very many very clever men have for many years searched for reasons for believing in the existence of gods; suppose (again, truly) that all their researches have failed to produce a single argument of any substance. Then, I suggest, we are entitled to lean towards atheism. The common inference from 'There is no reason to believe that *P*' to 'not-*P*' is puerile; the less common inference from 'Extensive inquiry has produced no reason to believe that *P*' to 'Probably not-*P*' is sound. Atheism is a negative position in two ways: first, it is essentially of the form not-*P*; and second, the strongest indication of its truth is the failure of all attempts to prove its contradictory. Did Critias or Prodicus glimpse something of that? Did they reflect that long generations of religious believers had produced no rational account of a position which remained causally tied to an old fraud or an ancient superstition? And did they infer that religion was not only groundless but also false? It would be beautiful to think so; but beauty, alas, is not truth.

Democritus remains, and his texts pose far greater problems. Comparison with Prodicus and Critias leads us to expect an atheistical or at least an agnostic stance; but certain fragments and reports appear to make Democritus a theist. First, in several of his ethical fragments Democritus refers, unapologetically, to gods and things divine:

> He who chooses the goods of the soul chooses the more divine; he who chooses those of the body, the human (**383: 68 B 37**).

> It is best for a man to live his life with the most good cheer and the least grieving; and that will happen if he takes his pleasures not in mortal things (**384: B 189**).

> They alone are dear to the gods, to whom injustice is hateful (**385: B 217**).

But popular moralizing may appeal to the divine without committing itself seriously to theism; and we cannot ascribe theism to Democritus on the basis of a few disjointed platitudes.

Second, there is a confusing set of doxographical reports:

> Democritus [says that] god is intelligence (*nous*) in spherical fire (**386**: Aëtius, **68 A 74**).

> Democritus imagines that the gods arose with the rest of the heavenly fire (**387**: Tertullian, **A 74**).

He thinks that 'our knowledge (? *sententia*) and intelligence', or 'the principles of mind' are divine (Cicero, **A 74**). The reports are uninspiring: Aëtius is corrupt, Cicero uses a hostile source, Tertullian is a Christian. Perhaps Democritus said that the fiery soul-atoms constitute the 'divine spark' in us; more probably, such a view was generously ascribed to him on the basis of his moral fragments. This second group of texts will not make Democritus a godly man.

The third and final set of evidences is of far greater importance.

> Democritus says that certain *eidôla* approach men, and that of these some are beneficent, some maleficent—that is why he even prayed (*eucheto*)[20] to attain felicitous *eidôla*. These are great, indeed enormous, and hard to destroy though not indestructible; and they signify the future to men, being seen and uttering sounds. Hence the ancients, getting a presentation of these very things, supposed that there was a god, there being no other god apart from these having an indestructible nature (**388**: Sextus, **B 166**).[21]

The passage has been interpreted in a variety of contradictory ways: does it offer an atomistic aetiology of religious notions? does it reduce gods to mere figments of the common fantasy? Or does it attempt to justify religious belief? and are its *eidôla* genuine divinities?

Cicero poses one of the problems: Democritus, he complains,

'seems to nod over the nature of the gods', treating the *eidôla* sometimes as being themselves divine, sometimes as images produced by the gods (**A 74**). The latter view is taken by Clement, who says that '*eidôla* fall on men and brute animals from the divine substance' (**A 79**); it interprets the term '*eidôla*' in the psychological sense of '*deikela*' or '*aporrhoiai*', 'films' or 'effluences' (see below, p. 477). The former view is taken by Hermippus, who says that Democritus 'naming them [sc. daemons] *eidôla*, says that the air is full of these' (**A 78**). Pliny, who asserts, in evident allusion to **388**, that Democritus only admitted two gods, Penalty and Benefit, probably adhered to this interpretation (**A 76**); and Diogenes of Oenoanda may have accepted it.[22]

Some scholars attempt to conjoin those reports into a unified theology; but I am inclined to think that they all spring from one source, the original of **388**, and that that source has an atheistical tendency. **388** is talking about dreams: in praying for 'felicitous *eidôla*' Democritus was praying for happy dreams, in particular, I suppose, for dreams which 'signify the future'. These *eidôla*, then, will be the dream images whose functioning is described by Plutarch in **A** 77; and '*eidôlon*' has its psychological sense. (It will not do to object that images cannot utter sounds, or that they cannot be hard to destroy: to say that some dream images speak and are almost indestructible is simply to say that, in dreams, we imagine speaking and almost indestructible entities.)

Dreaming of huge and indestructible prophets, the ancients believed that they were perceiving gods: they looked behind their dream images for divine originals (cf. Lucretius, V. 1161–93). Democritus will, I suppose, have agreed that every *eidôlon* has an original; but he will not have allowed that divine-seeming *eidôla* require divine originals. Perhaps they are somehow 'compounded' or 'enlarged', by the process which gives us *eidôla* of chimaeras or giants; perhaps they are ordinary human *eidôla* which their observers fail to identify. (They are human in shape: Sextus, *adv Math* IX.42.) How can these *eidôla* 'signify the future'? Plutarch ascribes a sort of telepathic theory to Democritus: human dream *eidôla* will include *eidôla* of the thoughts and plans of their originals; for those thoughts and plans, being physical structures, will emit effluences. Consequently, a dreamer, in grasping an *eidôlon*, may sometimes apprehend the thoughts and plans of its original (cf. **A** 77). It has been suggested that the 'felicitous *eidôla*' of **388** are just such images: the dreamer grasps the intentions of others, and hence gains a knowledge of the future entirely analogous to his knowledge of his own future actions.[23] The suggestion is ingenious, but strained:

dream *eidôla* 'speak'; sometimes it happens that what they 'say' is true—and in that way, unexcitingly, they 'signify the future'. **388** does not imply that certain *eidôla* come overtly branded as truth-tellers, or that an attentive dreamer may distinguish good from bad dream utterances; it says only that some dream utterances will turn out true.

Thus, according to Democritus, religion arose first (as Prodicus suggested) from attention to natural phenomena (**379**), and second (his own contribution) from attention to the contents of the sleeping mind (**388**). **379** and **388** offer two complementary aetiologies of religion; neither is inconsistent with the other, and neither implies any adherence to theism.

388, indeed, seems to commit Democritus to atheism: if 'there is no other god apart from these' dream *eidôla*, then there are no gods at all: evidently, the *eidôla* themselves are not gods; and, so Democritus says, there is in fact no divine source or origin behind or apart from the *eidôla*.

A final fragment stands strongly against that conclusion:

> The gods grant men all good things, both in the past and now. But what is bad and harmful and useless, that neither in the past nor now do the gods donate to men; but they themselves strike against these things from blindness of mind and ignorance (**389: B 175**).

Does **389** make Democritus a theist? If so, we must credit him with an important distinction: **379** and **388** show that the *origins* of our religious beliefs are disreputable; but it does not follow that the beliefs themselves are irrational; a belief may overcome its low breeding. A full-blooded aetiologist will say that anthropology explains the origins of religious thought, and that all present beliefs are exclusively accountable for in terms of those origins; Democritus, we are now imagining, allows that anthropology explains the origination of religion but denies that all our present beliefs are explicable solely by reference to those origins. A rational theism may transcend its irrational childhood.

That is a consistent and an interesting view; and I hesitate to deny it to Democritus. Yet if it was his, it is strange that no explicit trace of it remains, and that no justification of religious belief is ascribed to its author. I incline still to an atheist Abderite. **389**, I guess, came from one of Democritus' literary pieces: it is not a piece of philosophy but an exegesis of a passage in Homer's *Odyssey* (I. 33). But the guess will not be found very appealing; and Democritus' stand on religious belief will remain shrouded in the fogs of the past.[24]

(d) *Poetics*

'First, as Prodicus says, you must learn about the correctness of words' (Plato *Euthydemus* 277E = **84 A 16**). Interest in language and the various disciplines associated with it was a feature of the Sophists. 'I agree', says Protagoras in Plato's dialogue, 'that I am a sophist, and that I educate men' (317B = **80 A 5**). The primary art by which the Sophists sought to educate, and which they sought to instil in their pupils, was rhetoric, 'the craftsman of persuasion' (*Gorgias* 453A = **82 A 28**).[25] Gorgias, 'the first to give the power and art of speaking to the rhetorical form of education' (Suda, **82 A 2**), wrote a treatise on rhetoric (Diogenes Laertius, VIII.58 = **A 3**) of which we possess a scrap or two (**B 12–14**); and in *Helen* he dilates with evident satisfaction upon the persuasive powers of his art (**B 11**, §§8–14; see below, p. 529).

The matter as well as the mode of education led to language: study of language is a part of literary criticism, and literary criticism was a great part of education in a land where 'from the beginning everyone learned from Homer' (Xenophanes, **21 B 10**). There is an example of the Sophist's literary art in the analysis and criticism of the verse of Simonides which Plato's Protagoras conducts (339A = **80 A 25**); and we know that Protagoras was famed for 'interpreting the poems of Simonides and others' (Themistius, *oratio* 23, 350. 20 D). Hippias (**86 B 6**) and Gorgias (**82 B 24–5**) engaged in literary studies; and the practice was no doubt widespread. The Sophists did not originate the studies of rhetoric and of literary criticism; but they were professed masters of those high arts.[26]

One part of their studies dealt with strictly linguistic matters. Protagoras has some claim to be called the inventor of syntax;[27] and Prodicus dabbled in semantics. Prodicus is credited with a 'nicety (*akribologia*) about names' (Marcellinus, **84 A 9**); and Plato's dialogues contain numerous examples of his subtle distinctions in sense: between 'strive' and 'vie' (*Protagoras* 337B = **84 A 13**), between 'enjoy' and 'take pleasure in' (ibid.), between 'wish' and 'desire' (ibid. 340A = **84 A 14**), between 'end' and 'limit' (*Meno* 75E = **84 A 15**). Some of Prodicus' distinctions are significant: Aristotle rightly availed himself of that between 'wish (*boulesthai*)' and 'desire (*epithumein*)', and he would have improved his account of pleasure had he attended to Prodicus' differentiation between 'enjoy (*euphrainesthai*)' and 'take pleasure in (*hêdesthai*)'. But there is no evidence that Prodicus himself saw any philosophical point in his linguistic diversions. If 'the Sophistic explanations of poetry foreshadow the growth of a special field of enquiry, the analysis of language', yet 'the final object is rhetorical or educational, not literary'—and still less philosophical.[28]

In two ways, however, the literary interests of the late fifth century did make a direct contribution to philosophy: the period was exercised by a problem about the nature and origins of language; and it saw the birth of that Cinderella of modern philosophy, aesthetics.

Gorgias had an aesthetic theory:

> Tragedy flourished and was famed, an admirable object for those men to hear and to see, and one which gave to stories and passions a deception (*apatê*), as Gorgias says, in which the deceiver is more just than he who does not deceive and the deceived wiser than he who is not deceived (**390**: Plutarch, **82 B 23**).[29]

In his *Helen* (**82 B 11**) Gorgias shows how speech, that 'great potentate', can 'persuade and deceive (*apatân*) the soul' (§8); and he illustrates his thesis from poetry:

> All poetry, as I believe and assert, is measured speech; and upon those who hear it there comes a fearful shuddering (*phrikê periphobos*) and a tearful pity (*eleos poludakrus*) and a mournful yearning; and for the misfortunes and calamities of the affairs and the bodies of other men, the soul, through words, experiences an emotion of its own (**391**: §9).

(I refrain from commenting on the connexion between this passage and Aristotle's account of the effects of tragedy in *Poet* 1449b27.) The *Dissoi Logoi* offers the following consideration in support of the thesis that 'the just and unjust are the same':

> In tragedy and in painting whoever deceives (*exapatai*) most by creating what is similar to the truth is best (**392: 90 A 3**, §10).

There is nothing original in the view that poets and artists are purveyors of falsehoods: *polla pseudontai aoidoi*. The Muses, according to Hesiod, 'know how to say many false things similar to the true' (*Theogony*, 27); and references to the deceptions of art are not infrequent in Greek literature.[30] Again, the gullibility of the vulgar, which leads them to believe in soap operas as well as soap advertisements, naturally breeds a puerile admiration for *trompe l'oeil* art and 'realistic' drama. Such phenomena were familiar enough in Greece: they are exhibited in the naive wonderment of the Chorus in Euripides' *Ion* (184–219), and in the conversations of Herodas' fourth *Mime*: 'What lovely statues, Cynno dear. . . . Look, dear, at that girl up there, looking at the apple: you'd say she'd pass away if she didn't get the apple' (IV. 20–9).

Gorgias' theory perhaps began from those commonplaces; but it goes far beyond them, and offers a genuine theory of art—or at least of literature and painting; for whether or not Gorgias intended the theory to extend to music and sculpture we do not know. Art essentially strives for illusion: the better the deception, the greater the art; and good artists will always try to deceive their public. As a dramatist, Sophocles is concerned to express, verbally and by action, a set of false propositions. As a good dramatist, Sophocles will regularly convince his audience that those falsehoods are true.

The theory had an enormous attraction; and it became a standard item of Philistine thought; for if Gorgias ironically asserted that a deceived audience would grow wiser by the deception, later men, condemning deceit, condemned art with it. Thus Macaulay: 'Poetry produces an illusion on the eye of the mind, as a magic lantern produces an illusion on the eye of the body. And, as the magic lantern acts best in a dark room, poetry effects its purpose most completely in a dark age. As the light of knowledge breaks in upon its exhibitions, as the outlines of certainty become more and more definite and the shades of probability more and more distinct, the hues and lineaments of the phantoms which the poet calls up grow fainter and fainter. We cannot unite the incompatible advantages of reality and deception, the clear discernment of truth and the exquisite enjoyment of fiction' (*Essays*, 'Milton'). Art, like all fiction, will gradually lose its power and its attraction as knowledge of truth advances.

Some thinkers deny that art is a deceiver on the grounds that art has no connexion with truth or falsity at all. In the arts, according to the *Dissoi Logoi*:

> Justice and injustice have no place; and the poets do not make their poems with a view to truth but with a view to giving men pleasure (**393: 91 A 3** §17).

Coleridge echoes the point: a notion of Wordsworth's, he maintains, 'seems to destroy the main fundamental distinction, not only between a poem and prose, but even between philosophy and works of fiction, inasmuch as it proposes *truth* for its immediate object, instead of *pleasure*' (*Biographia Literaria*, I. 104). Neither belief nor disbelief is an appropriate attitude to art; rather, we must experience 'that *illusion*, contra-distinguished from *delusion*, that *negative* faith, which simply permits the images presented to work by their own force, without either denial or affirmation of their real existence by the judgment' (ibid., I. 107). Frege assents: 'In hearing an epic poem, for instance, apart from the euphony of the language we are interested only in the sense of the sentences and the images and feelings thereby aroused. The question of truth could cause us to abandon aesthetic delight for an attitude of scientific investigation' (*Philosophical Writings*, 'On Sense and Reference').

That answer to the Gorgian theory has something to be said for it: certainly, it is silly to wonder whether Achilles really dragged Hector's corpse around the walls of Troy, or to ask how the Ancient Mariner really managed to steer his ship with a dead albatross hanging about his neck. Such things are fictions, and they are presented as fictions; they do not deceive or delude us, and the poet does not fail if we remain unconvinced. But it will not do to answer Gorgias by saying, simply, that artists do not aim at truth: first, that answer will not appease the Philistines—if art is no longer a criminal falsehood, it is something just as bad: an empty fantasy; and second, it is simply untrue to say that contemplators of art must refrain from putting 'the question of truth'. Many artists regularly aim at a fairly mundane sort of truth: portraiture is a species of painting; Gibbon's *Decline and Fall* is a work of literature. And many more artists aim, I guess, to convey a higher and less ordinary truth: the *Oedipus Rex* does not tell us a true history of a king of Thebes, but it does tell us some large truths about human destiny; *Pride and Prejudice* is not a journal or diary of events in an English country town, but it does make shrewd and true comments on human nature. Any reader will multiply those examples and give flesh to their skeletal frames: only the most insensitive philosopher will judge that there is no 'question of truth' in the *Iliad* on the grounds that Homer's account of the Trojan War is doubtful history.

Most generalizations about art are false. I do not suggest that all art purports to express truth (unaccompanied music cannot); I do not think that art can only be defended if it aims at truth; nor do I think that Macaulay's condemnation is just even in those few cases (mime, perhaps, is the best example) where deception and falsity are desired and attained. My aim in the last paragraph has merely been to recall the elementary truth that works of art very often do purvey truths, and the slightly less elementary truth that not all the sentences of a work of fiction are intended to be believed.

How, then, did Gorgias arrive at his false and influential theory? I suspect that he was led to it by puzzling over the emotive powers of art. **391** hints at an argument: when I attend to a work of art (Verdi's *Traviata*, say) I am affected by genuine emotions of a fairly strong variety; and my feelings are not capricious but seem an appropriate and rational response to the opera. Now if my feelings are rational, they must be backed by belief; hence if Verdi's aim is to arouse my passions, he must first instil some beliefs in me. And since his plot, like that of most dramatists, is a fiction, he must endeavour to instil false beliefs in me, or to deceive me. If a friend dies, you feel grief because you believe her to be dead; when Violetta dies you feel a grief of the same intensity and variety: that can only be because you believe, falsely, that Violetta is dead. Verdi is a great artist because he can move us; he can move us only if he can deceive us: art, therefore, is essentially deceptive.

I do not endorse that argument; but I do not think it despicable. And it does raise in a clear form the genuinely puzzling question of why Violetta's death infects us with grief: is the grief (and hence the opera) an emotional sham? or does it give us something to weep for? Gorgias saw that there were questions here to be asked.

(e) *Language and nature*

The second contribution of fifth-century linguistic studies to philosophy is due not to sophists but to Democritus. Diogenes' catalogue of Democritus' writings lists eight titles under the heading *Mousika* ('Literary Studies'): 'On rhythm and harmony', 'On poetry', 'On beauty of words', 'On consonant and dissonant letters', etc. (IX.48 = **68 A 33**). But the few fragments of these works that remain (**B 15–26**) are not of great interest. What is of interest, I think, is Democritus' contribution to the Greek debate on the status of human language: is language a natural or a social phenomenon? do words have their meaning by nature or by convention? is *phusis* the subtle *éminence grise* directing our speech, or are we rather governed by *nomos* or *thesis*? The classic text on the subject is Plato's *Cratylus*; and after Plato's time the debate rarely slackened. Aulus Gellius, writing in the second century AD, could say that 'it is ordinarily asked among philosophers whether names are by nature (*phusei*) or by legislation (*thesei*)' (X. iv. 2). The debate began in the fifth century BC.

There are two quite distinct questions involved: much of the literature confuses them. The first question concerns the *origins* of language, or of 'names': was language deliberately created and imposed by a 'name-giving' person of divine, heroic, or human status? or did language gradually evolve from brutish grunts and growls, without the intervention of any conscious agent? The former view is taken by the Book of *Genesis* and by the *Cratylus* (e.g. 388D). It posits a *thesis*, or laying down, of names; and since what is laid down is a *nomos*, the view may be stated by saying that words exist *nomôi*. But that statement is misleading; for the *thesis* theory need not hold that the name-giver set up purely conventional or arbitrary connexions between words and objects. The *thesis* theory was vigorously expressed by saying that 'words are by convention'. The view was vigorously and mockingly attacked by the Epicureans, who advanced the alternative, 'natural', account (Epicurus, *ad Hdt* §§75–6; Diogenes of Oenoanda, fr. 10 Ch; Lucretius, V. 1041–90).

The second question concerns the relation between language and the world: does language fit the world naturally, like skin on an animal? or is it an artificial matching, like clothes on an Edwardian *belle*? Are names fixed to what they name by a natural adhesive? or is the glue man-made? Metaphorically stated, the questions are impressive and imprecise; a major part of the interpretation of the ancient answers consists in understanding the ancient questions.

Four texts bear on the two issues. Diodorus' anthropology contains the following passage:

> Their sounds being without significance and confused, they gradually articulated their locutions; and by making signs for one another for each of the objects, they made their remarks about everything intelligible to one another. Such gatherings took place all over the inhabited world, and all did not have a similar-sounding language but each group ordered their locutions as it chanced; that is why there are all types of languages (**394**: I.viii. 3 = **68 B 5**).

Diodorus offers a 'natural' answer to my first question: language originated not with the *fiat* of a name-giver, but from the need, and the gradually increasing competence, of groups of men to communicate with one another.

Once a language has been rudely articulated within a group, some clever men may pose as a primitive *Académie Française*. But the Diodoran account of the first beginnings of language is surely true, and logically so: the existence of a name-giver presupposes the existence of a language; for he himself must have the names already articulated if he is to bestow them on his community. (Those philosophers who think that there can be no 'private languages'—languages intelligible only to one person—will go further and say that a communal dialect, of the sort imagined by Diodorus' source, must have preceded the activity of any name-giver.) Now if language is 'natural' in this way, then it is a product of specifically human nature; for the brutes do not in fact possess any articulated dialect. The mark of humanity is rationality; and rationality, if not thought itself, depends on language; for without language none but the simplest and crudest thoughts are possible. This amounts to a justification of the ancient and vain belief that humans are set apart from the other animals. Only a natural account of the origins of language will lead to that belief: on the *Cratylus* view, the divine name-giver might as well have bestowed his gift on apes or peacocks.

We cannot, however, rely on Diodorus, whose connexions with Democritus are unsure. My next two texts are genuine fragments of Democritus, but they are unreliable for different reasons. **B 145** reads simply:

> The word is shadow of the deed (**395**).

Some have read this as implying that names are naturally attached to the world; for shadows are naturally attached to the objects that throw them. But the fragment is an apophthegm out of context; and a thousand interpretations can be found for it. In **B 142** Democritus says that the names of the gods are their 'speaking images (*agalmata phônêenta*)'. Images are made by an image-maker, and they are usually tied to their originals by the natural relation of resemblance: the one word '*agalmata*' thus suggests both that the origins of language were unnatural and that words are naturally attached to the world. But it is absurd to read so much theory into a single word. A simpler explanation of *agalmata* suggests itself: from Homer onwards the Greeks liked to see significance in the etymologies, or purported etymologies, of proper names. Aeschylus provides the best-known example when he describes Helen as '*helenaus, helandros, heleptolis* (destroyer of ships, destroyer of men, destroyer of cities': *Agamemnon*, 689), and Democritus is known to have indulged in the sport: Tritogeneia is etymologized in **B 1** and '*gunê* (woman)' is repellently connected with '*gonê* (semen)' because a woman is 'a receptacle for semen' (**B 122a**). Some words are 'speaking images' by virtue of this etymological turn: a word may speak volumes.[31]

The fourth and last Democritean text comes from Proclus' commentary on the *Cratylus*. It reads thus:

> Democritus, saying that names are by legislation (*thesei*), established this by four arguments. From homonymy: different things are called by the same name; hence their name is not natural (*phusei*). From polyonymy: if different names will fit one and the same thing, [they will fit] one another too—which is impossible. From the changing of names: why did we change Aristocles' name to Plato, and Tyrtamus' to Theophrastus, if their names were natural? From the lack of similar names: why do we say 'think' from 'thought' but do not form a derivative (*paronomazomen*) from 'justice'? Hence names are by chance

(*tuchêi*) and not natural. And he calls the first argument polysemy, the second equipollence, [the third metonymy], the fourth anonymy (**396**: **B 26**).

Only the last sentence of this extract pretends to quote Democritus' own words: both form and content of the 'four arguments' are due to Proclus; and we do not know whether the form of the conclusion is Democritean or Proclan. What thesis can the arguments have been designed to establish?

Proclus believes (if I understand him aright) that Democritus is offering a *thesis* account of the origins of language: no *onomatothetês* laid down language; names evolved by nature. But on that view the four arguments are very feeble. Other scholars associate **396** with **B 142**: some, but not all, names are *agalmata phôneenta*: the original names of Plato and Theophrastus did not reveal the nature of their bearers; that is why we changed them to the more descriptive terms Flatfoot and Godspeaker. (The examples are post-Democritean: I do not know what instances Democritus himself might have cited.) But neither the second nor the fourth argument of **395** has any tendency to support that thesis.

A third interpretation of **396** encourages us to attend to a less trivial aspect of the relation between language and the world. 'Mean' in English, like '*sêmainein*' in Greek, can be used in at least two quite different contexts. On the one hand, spots mean measles; clouds mean rain; and a child's cry means hunger. Meaning, in such cases, is a matter of pointing to, indicating, being a sign of. On the other hand, 'measles' means measles; 'rain' means rain; and 'hunger' means hunger. In these cases meaning is the relation which links language to the world. The question: 'Are words by nature?' can be interpreted in terms of these two sorts of meaning; for it can be taken to ask whether or not the relation which links language to the world is the relation of pointing to, indicating, or being a sign of. To say that 'words are by nature' is thus to say that the word 'mean' in '"Measles" means measles' names the same, natural, relation as the word 'mean' in 'Spots mean measles'.

The first argument in **396**, from homonymy, now works well enough: if clouds mean rain, then if clouds appear rain will follow; natural signs are inevitably followed by what they signify. But though 'rain' means rain, not every utterance of 'rain' is followed by rain; and homonymy provides clear instances: not every utterance of 'mole' signifies the presence of a furry rodent (or of an idea or image or thought of such a rodent); for 'mole' may mean jetty. The third argument in **396** is even better: if a child's crying means hunger, no agreement or compact will make it mean anything else; if spots mean measles, we cannot, by *fiat* or convention, get them to mean intoxication. But the meaning of 'hunger' or 'measles' could be altered by consent: vague words regularly replace standard English; and marriage usually changes a woman's name as well as her nature.

The fourth argument is harder. I suspect that Proclus' 'paronyms' are an anachronistic illustration of his own, and that by 'anonymy' Democritus meant nothing more impressive than the fact that language does not contain a term for every natural object: we may come across a new element, an unknown species of bird, a fresh frisson to titillate our jaded minds. If those new objects are to have signs, we must bestow them; and we can bestow any sign we care to. Natural signs do not work like that: we do not instruct a hungry child to cry, or fix clouds to the heavens as a sign of rain.

Finally, there is the argument from polyonymy or 'equipollence (*isorrhopon*)'. Proclus' remarks here are very obscure. 'If different names will fit (*epharmozein*) one and the same thing, [they will fit] one another too'. Perhaps that means: 'If *A* means *C* and *B* means *C*, then *A* means *B*.' At least, that interpretation yields a truth; and I can find no other that does. For that 'is impossible'; i.e., 'that is impossible if words are natural'. Now if 'mean' is used in the 'natural' sense, then it is indeed false that if *A* means *C* and *B* means *C*, then *A* means *B*; for though a drought means poor crops, and a flood means poor crops, a drought does not mean a flood. If, on the other hand, 'mean' has its linguistic sense, then if *A* means *C* and *B* means *C*, then *A* does mean *B*.

The distinction between 'natural' and 'non-natural' meaning—between the way in which spots mean measles and the way in which 'measles' means measles—is not a trivial one: many classical theories of meaning founder on the failure to draw it, or on the assumption that the relation of a word to what it means is similar to that of a cloud to the rain it portends.[32] 396 is not a simple fragment to interpret; and perhaps no simple thought lies behind it. But I incline to believe that one of the points that Democritus was attempting to make was the one I have briefly mentioned; and if that is so, then Democritus stands at the head of a long line of thinkers who have laboured to uncover the meaning of meaning.

(f) *Gorgias on communication*

The third part of Gorgias' treatise on *What Is Not* (above, p. 173) attempts to show that even if what exists can be known, our knowledge cannot be communicated. The argument is a curiosity: I present it with no comment beyond the observation that it treats significance as a natural relation. Again, I follow Sextus' text, though here the *MXG* differs from and expands upon Sextus to a considerable degree.

(83) And even if it were grasped, it is incommunicable to anyone else. For if what exists is visible and audible and, in general, perceptible (I mean, what lies outside us), and if what is visible is grasped by sight, and what is audible by hearing, and not vice versa, then how can these things be signified to anyone else? (84) For that by which we signify is a formula (*logos*), and what lies outside us and exists is not a formula; therefore we do not signify to our neighbours what exists but a formula which is different from what lies outside us. Thus just as what is visible could not become audible, or the reverse, so, since what exists lies outside us, it cannot become our formula; (85) and if it is not a formula, it will not be signified to anyone else.

And a formula [, he says,] is constructed from the things which hit us from outside, i.e. from the objects of perception; for it is from meeting with a savour that the formula we utter about this quality is produced in us; and from the incidence of a colour comes the formula about a colour. And if this is so, it is not the formula which reveals the external object, but the external object which signifies the formula.

(86) And one cannot say that the formula lies outside us in the same way as the visible and the audible, so that, lying outside us and existing, it can signify what lies outside us and exists. For, [he says,] even if the formula lies outside us, yet it differs from the other things that lie outside us—and visible bodies differ very greatly from the formulae; for what is visible is grasped through one organ, the formula through another. Thus the formula does not reveal most of the external objects, just as they do not show the nature of each other (**397: 82 B 3**).

XXII

De Anima

(a) *Material beginnings*

The *psuchê* or animator is that part or feature of an animate being which endows it with life; and since the primary signs of life are cognition and mobility, the *psuchê* is the source of knowledge and the source of locomotion. That gives a formal or functional account of *psuchê*; but it leaves us to ask what the psychic nature consists in: what sort of thing is it that provides us with life? is it the same sort of thing in men, in animals and in plants? where (if anywhere) is it located in the body? is it separable from the body?

To those questions the early Presocratics had, by and large, no interesting answers. The doxography regularly deals with the question: What is *psuchê* made of?

> Anaximenes and Anaximander and Anaxagoras and Archelaus said that the nature of the *psuchê* is airy (**398**: Aëtius, **12 A 29**; cf. **13 B 2**; Philoponus, **13 A 23**).[1]

> Parmenides and Hippasus and Heraclitus [say that the *psuchê*] is fiery (**399**: Aëtius, **18 A 9**).

And a fragment of Epicharmus indicates that the fiery soul was familiar enough outside professional scientific circles (**23 B 48**). Water and earth, the other two canonical elements, had fewer backers; but Hippo went for water (Hippolytus, **38 A 3**), and late stories give souls of earth and water to Xenophanes (Macrobius, **21 A 50**).[2] In the physics ascribed by Diogenes to Zeno, 'soul is a mixture of [the hot, the cold, the dry and the wet], with none of them having dominance' (IX. 29 = **29 A 1**). The doxographers do not usually expand upon these unilluminating *dicta*.

Heraclitus at least had a little more to say. His views, painfully obscure to us, were mildly sceptical and unpretentious:

> You would not find in your journey the limits of soul, even if you travelled the whole road—so deep is its account (**133: 22 B 45 = 67 M**).

The crude report of Aëtius that Heraclitean souls are fiery appears in Aristotle as the suggestion that the soul is an 'exhalation' (*anathumiasis*: *An* 405a24 = **A 15**). The suggestion is repeated in the doxography (e.g., Aëtius, **A 15**; Arius Didymus, *ad* **B 12**), and it connects readily with **B 36 = 66 M**:

> For souls it is death to become water, for water it is death to become earth, from earth water comes to be, from water soul (**400**).

If souls are warm, moist exhalations, it is plausible to think both that they come from water (like steam from a kettle or mist from a morning lake), and also that they perish on becoming water (as the steam disappears when condensed). Three further fragments are enigmatic. Perhaps

> A dry soul is wisest and best (**401: B 118 = 68 M**)

because it is furthest from watery death. I do not know why

> Souls smell in Hades (**402: B 98 = 72 M**),[3]

or what Heraclitus meant when he said that the soul was

> A *logos* increasing itself (**403: B 115 = 112 M**).

A late source contains the following report:

> Thus the vital heat proceeding from the sun gives life to all things that live. Subscribing to that opinion, Heraclitus gives a fine simile comparing the soul to a spider and the body to a spider's web. 'As a spider', he says, 'standing in the middle of its web is aware the instant a fly breaks any one of its threads and runs there swiftly as though lamenting the breaking of the thread; so a man's soul when any part of his body is hurt hastily goes there as though intolerant of the hurt to a body to which it is strongly and harmoniously conjoined' (**404: B 67a = 115 M**).

The authenticity of this charming report is dubious; but it may contain some genuine echoes of Heraclitean thought. I imagine that the simile is intended to explain a puzzle about pain: pain is a mental affection yet it derives from a bodily harm; how can that be?

Heraclitus answers that the *psuchê* is immediately aware of bodily damage, runs to the scene of the harm, and grieves over it: psychic grief over corporeal damage is pain; and we suffer pain because our souls are immediately sensitive and sympathetic to our bodily condition. Even if **404** is Heraclitean at bottom, it cannot be pressed too hard: it appears to reveal the *psuchê* as a living, sensitive, independent substance, localized in some central part of the body but capable of moving about within its corporeal dwelling. It may be that Heraclitus had just such a picture in mind; but **404** is only a picturesque analogy, designed to explain a single psychic phenomenon.

If the spider is idiosyncratically Heraclitean, the notion of *anathumiasis* suggests a way of finding a common and intelligible element in the early accounts of the *psuchê*. The parallel between a warm, moist 'exhalation' and our warm, moist breath is evident; and it is a commonplace of classical scholarship that the word '*psuchê*' originally denoted a 'breath-soul'. We live just as long as we breathe; and the conjecture that our life-giving part is breath, or a breath-like stuff, is easy. The antiquity of the view is attested by Aristotle, who reports that in 'the so-called Orphic verses' it is said that 'the soul enters from the universe as we breathe, and is carried about by the winds' (*An* 410b29 = **1 B 11**); and it is referred to by Plato in the *Phaedo* (70A, 77D). Diogenes ascribes the view to Xenophanes (IX.19 = **21 A 1**); and Aëtius says, plausibly, that when Anaximenes refers to the *psuchê* as 'our air' he uses 'air' synonymously with 'breath' (**26: 13 B 2**). The *psuchê* is variously specified as air, fire or water; but those rival specifications have a common core: breath is airy, moist fire; or hot, wet air; or warm, airy water.

The 'breath-soul' is doubtless a 'primitive' notion; but it has a grounding in solid scientific fact: we live by breathing; our *psuchai*, therefore, are breathlike. Moreover, the 'breath-soul' seems to explain with admirable neatness the twin functions of any *psuchê*, cognition and locomotion:

> Diogenes [of Apollonia], like certain others too, [said that the *psuchê*] is air, thinking that this is the finest of all things and a principle. And that explains why the *psuchê* knows and moves things: in so far as it is primary, and the rest come from it, it knows; in so far as it is finest, it is motive (**405**: Aristotle, *An* 405a21–5 = **64 A 20**).

The Atomists' account of the *psuchê* is comparable to earlier doctrines, though it is, of course, expressed within the terms of their new-fangled physics. One quotation will suffice:

> Of these [shapes] the spherical form the *psuchê*; for such *rhusmoi* are especially able to pass through everything and to move other things while moving themselves—for they suppose that the *psuchê* is that which provides animals with motion. And that is why breath is the determinant of life; for as the surrounding matter compresses the bodies and squeezes out those shapes which provide animals with life because they themselves are never at rest, help comes from outside when other such [atoms] enter in breathing; for they actually prevent those inhering in the animals from being separated out, by restricting the compressing and fixing body; and animals live as long as they can do this (**406**: Aristotle, *An* 404a5–16 = **67 A 28**).

Since spherical atoms account for the perceptible quality of heat, the Atomists can also say that the *psuchê* is 'a sort of fire, and hot' (*An* 404a1 = **67 A 28**).[4] The atomist soul is hot breath: the thesis is explained in characteristically Abderite terms, but it is essentially traditional.

To the modern ear, attuned to a Christian or Cartesian notion of soul, one feature of these Presocratic accounts is striking: they are all thoroughly and uncompromisingly materialistic. The *psuchê* is made of some ordinary physical stuff: the matter of body is the matter of soul. A *psuchê* may be thin and ethereal; but it is for all that material: its thinness is the thinness of fire or air, not the insubstantiality of an unextended Cartesian spirit.

That conclusion is sometimes resisted: 'The concept of an immaterial being was not invented until the fourth century BC; and the contrast between materialism and dualism, between a physicalist and a Cartesian account of mind or soul, is a creature of modern philosophy. It is an impertinent anachronism to apply those modern categories to Presocratic philosophy: Anaximenes' assertion that the soul is air is not a materialist thesis—nor, of course, is it non-materialist; the terms are simply inapplicable.' It is worth stating what a miserable bit of argumentation that is. If our modern categories of materialism and dualism are well-defined, then *any* intelligible theory of the soul is either materialistic or dualistic, whenever it may have been framed. Of course, Presocratic theories may be too crude, or too vague, or too confused, to be categorized; but in that case they are too crude, or too vague, or too confused, to be understood and interpreted. If intelligible, they fall into one or other of our categories. (The distinction between valid and invalid arguments was discovered by Aristotle; for all that, we do not regard it as anachronistic to judge Presocratic reasoning by modern canons of validity.)

'But at least the Presocratics were only materialists *faute de mieux*: they adopted a materialistic stance because no other occurred to them; had they been offered spiritual substance they would gladly have accepted it.' That is a judgment difficult to assess; yet I am inclined to reject it. The materialism of the early Presocratics was, so far as our evidence goes, implicit: they do not expressly say that the *psuchê* is a body like any other body. But the Atomists made materialism explicit: Democritus' account of thought is, according to Theophrastus, 'reasonable for one who makes the *psuchê* a body' (*Sens* §58 = **68 A 135**; cf. Aëtius, **A 102**); and if Aristotle can say that fire, the stuff of Democritean souls, is 'the most incorporeal (*asômatos*) of the elements' (*An* 405a6 = **68 A 101**), he means only that the *psuchê* is very fine or rare (cf. Philoponus, **68 A 101**); '*asômatos*' is used loosely, as we might use 'insubstantial'.[5] We possess no original text from Democritus announcing the corporeality of the soul; but the Peripatetic insistence on it indicates some fairly explicit avowal, and it was, after all, no recondite implication of Atomist psychology.

The Atomists were self-conscious materialists in psychology; and their thesis was original, if at all, only in the explicitness with which it was held. Perhaps the Atomists insisted on materialism because they had found some immaterialist psychology to object to? did materialism become explicit only because an alternative theory had arisen? Many scholars believe that the Pythagorean doctrines of metempsychosis and immortality require an immaterial soul. Yet if the Pythagoreans were profoundly concerned about the cultivation and fate of their souls, they apparently remained reticent about the nature of *psuchê*. Pythagoras is credited with a lecture *On the Soul* (Diogenes Laertius, VIII.7 = **14 A 19**), and so is Archytas (**47 B 9**); but neither ascription is believed by scholars. A late source ascribes to 'Hippo of Metapontum' (i.e. Hippasus?) the judgment that

> The soul is one thing, the body quite another; when the body is at rest, the soul thrives, when the body is blind, it sees; when the body is dead, it lives (**407**: Claudianus, **18 A 10**).

The same Claudianus ascribes a similar view to Philolaus (**44 B 22**), from whom Clement quotes the following words:

> The old theologians and seers also bear witness that as a punishment the soul is yoked to the body and is buried in it as in a tomb (**408: 44 B 14**).

That evidence will bear little weight. Claudianus is confused, and is probably relying upon some late Pythagorean forgery;[6] and Clement's report is hard to reconcile with the rest of what we learn about Philolaus' psychology.[7] In any case, none of the three reports strictly implies an incorporeal soul: each is concerned to distinguish the *psuchê* from the human body; and such a distinction does not entail that the *psuchê* is not itself bodily. A *psuchê* distinct from the body it inhabits may be corporeal: human prisoners are distinct from their physical jails, but they are physical substances. Moreover, Aristotle says that

> Some of them [sc. the Pythagoreans] said that the motes in the air are a soul, or that what moves them are. It was said of them because they are seen to be continually moving even in a complete absence of wind (**409**: *An* 404a17–9 = **58 B 40**).[8]

That little analogy does not yield a 'theory of the *psuchê*'; but it does suggest a fairly crudely materialistic notion of soul.

There is, however, at least one other Pythagorean theory to be described; and that, in many scholars' opinion, will be a more probable target for Democritean attack than the minor *dicta* that I have just quoted. I hold the target back for a section.

(b) *Empedoclean psychology*

> Leucippus and Democritus say that perceptions and thinkings are alterations (*heteroiôseis*) of the body (**410**: Aëtius, **67 A 30**).

Democritus 'places perceiving in changing (*alloiousthai*)' (Theophrastus, *Sens* §49 = **68 A 135**): we perceive a poker or think of a theorem if our bodies, or certain parts of them, alter in certain ways. Alteration is a matter of atomic locomotion, so that mental events will occur when certain types of atoms clash in certain ways; that is how Aristotle can say that

> Democritus and most of the *phusiologoi* who speak of perception do something quite absurd; for they make all objects of perception objects of touch (**411**: *Sens* 442a29–30 = **68 A 119**).

As an illustration, take the atomist account of seeing. It is founded on the hypothesis of images (*eidôla*) or, in Democritus' language, *deikela*; and a *deikelon* is 'an effluence (*aporrhoia*) similar in kind to the objects [from which it flows]' (**B 123**). The full theory is somewhat complicated; here is Theophrastus' account of it:

> He has seeing occur by reflexion, but he gives an idiosyncratic account of this; for the reflexion does not occur immediately in the pupil, but the air between sight and the object of sight is given an impression as it is compressed by the object seen and the seer; for from everything there is always some effluence issuing. Then this [air], being solid and different in colour [from the eyes], is reflected in the moist eyes; and the thick part [of the eye] does not receive it, but the moist part lets it through (**412**: *Sens* §50 = **A 135**).

Thus an observer, *a*, sees an object, *b*, in the following fashion: 'effluences', or thin atomic films similar in form to their begetter, leave *b* continuously; the passage of the effluences compresses a volume of air against the eye of *a*, and impresses it with the form of *b*. That airy impression then causes a reflection of *b* in certain receptive portions of *a*'s eyes. And thus *a* sees *b*.[9]

The theory of sight was generalized to explain the phenomena of reflexion (Aëtius, **67 A 31**) and of dreaming (Plutarch, **68 A 77**; Aëtius, **68 A 136**). As it stands it contains nothing specifically atomistic; but it is a thoroughly materialist account. It has no room for any dubiously physical operations or entities, like imaging and mental images; there are physical operations of effluxion, compression and reflexion, and physical entities—nothing else. No doubt reflexion and effluxion were ultimately explained in terms of atomic motions; but that apart, the Democritean account of perception is highly unoriginal. Theophrastus explains his views on sight and hearing, and notes the few novelties they include; he adds:

> On sight and hearing this is what he says; the other senses he accounts for in a way pretty similar to most people (**413**: *Sens* §57 = **68 A 135**).

The evidence we possess bears out Theophrastus' judgment. Of Democritus' predecessors the most interesting is Empedocles, the earliest (from whom Empedocles probably borrowed) Alcmeon of Croton.

Alcmeon is said to have dissected an eye (**24 A 10**); and he believed, presumably on experimental evidence, that 'all the senses are connected in some way to the brain' (Theophrastus, *Sens* §26 = **A 5**). He gave a purely physical account of the senses; e.g.:

> We hear by our ears because there is a vacuum in them; for this echoes (it makes a sound by being hollow), and the air echoes back (**414**: ibid., §25 = **A 5**; cf. Aëtius, **A 6**).

The text of Theophrastus is corrupt;[10] but the general lines of Alcmeon's account are clear: we hear external sounds by virtue of the physical properties of certain echoing parts of our ear. That account can hardly be complete, though it is all that Theophrastus offers us: it does not mention the brain, but implies, as it stands, that hearing is a function merely of the ear. For a fuller treatment of Alcmeonic psychology we must turn to Empedocles.

Like Alcmeon, Empedocles was a doctor (e.g., Satyrus, *apud* Diogenes Laertius, VIII. 58 = **31 A 1**; Galen, **A 3**); and he is said to have written a medical treatise (Suda, **A 2**). To his pupil Pausanias, the addressee of *Concerning Nature*, he says:

> You will learn what medicines there are for evils, and a remedy against old age (**415: B 111**.1–2);

and in the *Katharmoi* he claims that crowds followed him about,

> . . . some wanting prophecies, some for sicknesses
> of every sort asked to hear a healing word,
> long ravaged by harsh pains (**416: B 112**.10–2).

These boasts were the seeds of the later legend, of which the celebrated story of Empedocles on Etna is only the final dramatic scene.[11] And the medical theories and practices by means of which Empedocles tried, apparently with success, to give substance to his words had a significant influence on later medical men.

From doctors we expect physiology; and Empedocles does not disappoint us. Plato gives a brief account of his general theory of perception:

> Do you agree with Empedocles that existing things give off a sort of effluence (*aporrhoia*)?
>
> Certainly.
>
> And that they have pores into which and through which the effluences travel?
>
> Yes.
>
> And of the effluences some fit some of the pores while others are too small or too big?
>
> That is right.
>
> And there's something you call sight?
>
> There is.

> From this, then, 'grasp what I say to you' as Pindar puts it: colour is an effluence of things which is fitted to (*summetros*) sight and perceptible (**417**: *Meno* 76C = **A 92**).

Theophrastus continues Plato's dialogue in plain prose:

> Empedocles speaks in the same way about all [the senses] and says that we perceive by things fitting (*enharmottein*) into the pores of each [sense]. That is why [the senses] cannot discriminate one another's objects; for the pores of some are too broad and of others too narrow relative to the percept, so that some slip through without touching and others cannot enter at all (**418**: *Sens* §7 = **A 86**).

The surviving fragments do not mention pores (*poroi*),[12] but they do contain a reference to *aporrhoiai*:

> . . . knowing that there are effluences of everything which has come into being (**419: B 89**);

and a corrupt text refers thus to the activities of hounds on the chase:

> Searching out with their nostrils the particles (*kermata*) of animal limbs . . . which their feet have left behind in the soft grass (**420: B 101**).

The hounds snuffle up the effluences of their quarry and thus track it down. Empedocles' *aporrhoiai* are plainly the fathers of Democritean *deikela*; but they should not be identified with them: first, *aporrhoiai* come to all the senses, *deikela* only to the eyes; second, nothing indicates that Empedoclean *aporrhoiai* are likenesses of their origins: the *aporrhoia* for sight is light (Philoponus, **A 57**) or perhaps colour (Theophrastus, *Sens* §7 = **A 86**).

The details of Empedocles' theory are uncertain and in some places controversial. A long fragment, **B 84**, describes the eye. Many scholars attempt to extract a theory of vision from it, but in fact the fragment means only to describe the structure of the eye. The doxography on vision is confusing rather than clarifying.[13] Here is Theophrastus' account of the other four senses:

> Hearing comes about from internal sounds; for when the air is moved by the noise, it echoes inside. For the ear is like a bell (?) of equal echoes (?)—he calls it a 'fleshy shoot'; and when the air is moved it strikes against the solid parts and makes an echo. Smelling comes about by breathing. That is why those creatures smell best whose breathing motion is most violent. Most smell flows from (*aporrhein*) the finest and lightest things. About taste

> and touch he says nothing in particular, neither how nor by what means they come about, but only the general thesis that perception occurs by things fitting (*enharmottein*) the pores (**420**: *Sens* §9 = **A 86**).

Streams of effluent flow from all bodies; their waters differ in outline and magnitude, some representing colours, some sounds, some smells, and so forth. When the streams strike against sentient creatures most of them are diverted; but some hit an appropriate sense organ, equipped with *summetroi* pores into which they can fit (*enharmottein*). Colour streams hit the eyes and fit the eye pores; and that is how we can see colours; sound streams fit the ears, and we hear; colour streams are asymmetrical with the ears, sound streams with the eyes—so we neither see sounds nor hear colours.

Perception is thus a purely physical occurrence: Empedocles' theory is expressed, crudely but firmly, in the language of physical science; and to that extent he is at one with the Atomists, and indeed with all Presocratic psychological speculation. Any such materialist theory lays itself open to an obvious objection; Theophrastus brings it against Empedocles, and repeats it for Anaxagoras and Diogenes (whose theories are only uninteresting variants on the Empedoclean tradition). Thus: 'one might wonder . . . first, how inanimate objects differ from the rest with regard to perception; for things fit into the pores of inanimate objects too' (*Sens* §12 = **A 86**; cf. §36 = **59 A 92**; §46 = **64 A 19**). If perception is just a matter of effluences fitting pores, why is the phenomenon so rare? In general, if perception is a purely physical interaction, why is it that only select physical objects perceive?

Some scholars reply boldly: perception, on Empedocles' theory, is widespread, if not universal; for he himself says that:

> Thus, then, everything has breathing and smellings (**422: B 102**).

And he ascribes understanding, which presupposes perception, to all things:

> Thus by the will of chance everything possesses thought (**333: B 103**).
>
> For know that everything possesses sense and a portion of thought (**423: B 110**.10).

But that reply is no good. First, the texts it cites give uncertain support: the word 'everything' in **422** and **333** has no context; and it may well have referred only to animate things (the two fragments probably come from Empedocles' zoogony). **B 110** is a difficult fragment: I shall argue later that line 10, read in its context, does not after all say that 'everything has thought' (below, p. 485).[14]

Second, even if Empedocles did ascribe perception to everything, that will not help him against Theophrastus' criticism. For not every fitting of effluences into pores is a case of perception. No one recognizes that more clearly than Empedocles himself: *aporrhoiai* and *poroi* are not only employed in the elucidation of perception; they account for the phenomena of reflexion (**B 109a**; Aëtius, **A 88**); for some aspects of breathing (Aristotle, *Resp* 473b1; cf. **B 100**); for magnetism (Alexander, **A 89**); for chemical mixture (**B 91, B 92**); and for the way in which certain trees lose their leaves in autumn (Plutarch, *ad* **B** 77).[15] Far from being a distinguishing mark of perception, the fitting of effluences into pores is a common feature of natural phenomena: *aporrhoiai* and *poroi* are general principles of physics, not special principles of psychology.

According to Theophrastus, perception in Empedocles comes about 'by likes' (*Sens* §1 = **A 86**; cf. §10); and Theophrastus asserts that

> He assigns knowledge to these two things, similarity and touch; that is why he uses the word 'fit (*harmottein*)'. So that if the less should touch the greater, there will be perception (**424**: §15).

The point is supported by a fragment:

> For by earth we see earth, by water water;
> by air bright air, and by fire brilliant fire;
> love by love, and strife by horrid strife (**425: B 109**).

For sight to occur, an *aporrhoia* must enter a *poros* in the eye; and it must 'fit' (*harmottein*): i.e., it must be of the right shape and size to fill the pore (it must 'touch'), and it must also be homogeneous with the walls of the pore (it must be 'like'). Thus I shall see red if a red *aporrhoia* (a ray of red light, perhaps) fits snugly into a red-edged pore in my eye. The lesser red touches the greater; and I perceive.

Will the 'likeness' principle thus eke out the theory of pores and defend Empedocles from Theophrastus? Hardly: how can auditory *aporrhoiai* be 'like' the ears they enter? or why suppose that the iron filings attracted by the magnet are 'unlike' it? Theophrastus reports that

> In general, likeness in his theory is done away with and commensurateness alone is enough. For he says that the sense organs do not perceive one another's objects because they have

> incommensurate pores; and whether the effluent is like or unlike he does not determine (**426**: *Sens* §15 = **A 86**).

The 'like by like' principle is vague; it solves nothing; it was not seriously used by Empedocles. (**425** fits a different context: see below, pp. 484–8.)

But Empedocles' theory is not dead yet: Theophrastus may show that it is not enough to talk of *aporrhoiai* and *poroi*, but he does not show that no modification can defend the theory. Empedocles' *aporrhoia* in the case of vision is light, his *poroi* are rods and cones: modern physiologists can doubtless tell us how the impact of light on rods and cones differs from its impact on the glass of a mirror or from the impact of air on the breathing passages; and they will thereby complete Empedocles' account and establish it as a full theory of visual perception.

'But surely such an account can only aspire to the status of a physiological description: it cannot tell us what perception really is; it cannot touch on the properly psychological side of sight, hearing and the rest. Physiology of perception is interesting enough; but it is no substitute for philosophy of perception.' Empedocles had no means of anticipating that objection; and he might well have been puzzled by it: what facts remain unaccounted for by the physical account? What opening or need is there for philosophy? 'There are illusions, hallucinations, after-images and other paraperceptual occurrences.' But surely the physical theory can be extended to account for them? 'Perception has a subjective or experiential side; and physiological theorizing necessarily ignores the felt qualities of sensation; it accounts only for what happens in our bodies, not for what we experience ourselves.' But *is* there an 'experiential' side to perception, distinct from the 'physical' side? What are its characteristics? and why cannot an Empedoclean account explain experience too?

There are modern materialists, of a sophisticated sort, who are at bottom Empedocleans; and it is by no means evident that their Empedoclean efforts to give a purely physiological account of the subjective elements in perception are unsound. In tacitly rejecting any non-physiological 'philosophy' of perception Empedocles is curiously modern.

If perception is materialistic, what of thought, that supremely Cartesian operation? According to Aristotle,

> The old thinkers said that perception and thought were the same; thus Empedocles said:

> For men's wit is increased by reference to what is present [= **B 106**];

and elsewhere:

> To the extent that they become different, to that extent always does thinking present different things to them [= **B 108**].[16]

(**427**: *An* 427a21–5; cf. *Met* 1009b17–20.)

Theophrastus qualifies Aristotle's judgment and offers a new text:

> He speaks in the same way about thought and ignorance; for thought is by likes and ignorance by unlikes, thought being either the same as or similar to perception. For having enumerated the way in which we recognize each thing by itself, he adds at the end that:
>
> > From these are all things fitted and formed,
> > and by these they think and feel pleasure and pain [= **B 107**].
>
> That is why we think especially with the blood; for in this of all parts are the elements especially mixed (**428**: *Sens* §10 = **A 86**).

Before his quotation of **B 107** Theophrastus summarizes **425**: clearly **425** immediately preceded **B 107** in Empedocles' poem, and 'these' in **B 107**.1 refers to the four 'roots' (together with Love and Strife) which are 'enumerated' in **425**.[17] Theophrastus' final sentence is also a paraphrase of a surviving fragment:

> . . . (?) turned (?) in seas of surging blood;
> and there especially is what men call thought
> —for the blood about the heart is thought for men (**429: B 105**).[18]

In **B 105–B 109** we have the passages upon which the Peripatetics based their account of Empedocles' theory of thought. Some modern scholars think that the Peripatetics should have attended also to **B 110**:

> For if you establish them (*sphe*) in your stout mind
> and guard them kindly with pure exercises,
> they will indeed all remain with you throughout your life,
> and you will gain many others from these; for they themselves increase
> each in its kind, as is the nature of each.
> But if you reach for different things such as among men

there are, innumerable, evil, which blunt the mind,
they will at once abandon you as their time is accomplished,
desiring to come to their own dear kind;
for know that they all have sense and a portion of thought (**430**; cf. **423**).

The interpretation of the fragment turns on the identity of 'them (*sphe*)' in the first line. Some scholars make 'them' the elements, and are then able to construe **430** as an account of thought.[19] But '*sphe*' in line 1 contrasts with 'many others' in line 4, and with the 'different things, . . . innumerable, evil' of lines 6–7: the elements have nothing to contrast with, for they embrace all the things that there are. Moreover, 'they' may 'abandon' Pausanias (line 8); but the elements could never do that.

Accordingly, we must find a different identity for *sphe*; and the orthodox view is that *sphe* are the axioms of Empedoclean physics. **430** then reads thus: 'Remember my words and keep them fresh in your mind; then you will possess not only them but also the consequences and implications to which they will lead you. But if you attend to other foolish philosophies, my thoughts will leave you; for they have more sense than to dwell in a mind given to un-Empedoclean views.' That construe is not easy: it takes lines 6–10 as a highly coloured statement of a fairly mundane possibility. But it is the best we can do in the absence of a larger context; and it removes **430** from the theory of perception and thought. (It also shows that line 10 does not commit Empedocles to the view that 'everything has thought': '*panta*' means not 'everything' but 'all [my words]'.)

What, then, was Empedocles' analysis of thought? Aristotle's statement that 'thinking and perceiving are the same' should not be taken *au pied de la lettre*: he argues only that thinking, in Empedocles' view, is, like perception, a physical process; he does not mean that thinking is exactly the same process as perception. Similarly, Theophrastus is concerned only to point out that the 'like by like' principle applies, in Empedoclean doctrine, to thought no less than to perception; and there is again no question of a strict identity between the two processes. 'The blood about the heart is thought for men' (**429**. 3): Empedocles does not say that it is the blood which thinks; nor does he say that the heart, or the heart's blood, is the *sole* organ or instrument of thought; the heart is of pre-eminent importance, but it is only the place where 'especially' we think.[20] Heart's blood is a peculiarly fine mixture of the elements; since, as **B 107** implies and **425** makes explicit, each of the elements is an organ or instrument of thought, then heart's blood is a peculiarly fine cognitive medium.

At this point I shall turn to discuss a Parmenidean fragment. The quatrain is of interest in its own right; and it is relevant here as it expresses, in a fuller and reasoned form, the theory of thought that Empedocles hints at. The lines run thus:

> For as on each occasion is the mixture of the much-wandering limbs,
> so does the mind stand in men. For the same
> as what it thinks of is the nature of the limbs for men,
> for each and for all; for what preponderates is thought
> (**431**: **28 B 16**).

The text of lines 1–2,[21] and the syntax of lines 2–4, are highly controversial; and my interpretation will inevitably be uncertain.

Theophrastus quotes the lines to show that 'he treats perceiving and thinking as the same' (*Sens* §3 = **28 A 46**; cf. Aristotle, *Met* 1009b12–25, also quoting **431**). Again, all that he means is that thinking, like perceiving, is treated as a physical change; and we need make no more of it. Equally, we may put aside a question that has troubled some critics: how, they ask, can Parmenides maintain the theory of **431** and still say what he does about the objects of thought in **148–9**? The answer is simple: **431** appears in the Way of Opinion; it represents Mortal Thoughts, not Eleatic doctrine.

What does Parmenides mean by 'limbs (*melea*)'? Some gloss the word by 'sense-organs'. 'Men', as Archilochus had observed, 'think the things they come across':[22] the first couplet of **431** means that we only think of the things we meet with in perception, thus precociously formulating the Aristotelian doctrine, *nil in intellectu nisi prius in sensu*. And since the 'limbs' are 'much-wandering', Parmenides is in effect offering a criticism of any epistemology built upon that doctrine: if the doctrine is correct, all our thoughts are based ultimately on our misleading and mischievous senses.[23] In **B 106** Empedocles presents the same Aristotelian theory: 'men's wit is increased by reference to what is present'; i.e., if the senses have presented something to a man, then, and only then, is he capable of thinking of it. But Empedocles drops the Parmenidean criticism.

That may be a correct interpretation of Empedocles, but it will not fit Parmenides. First, it must read into **431** not the Aristotelian doctrine, but the far stronger and wholly absurd thesis that we think only of the things we are actually perceiving ('Our thought *on any occasion* is given by the contents of our sense-organs on that occasion'). Second, it ascribes an impossible sense to '*melea*': 'limbs' is not naturally taken as 'sense-organs'; and the word nowhere else bears anything like that meaning.[24] If *melea* are not sense-organs, then there is no empiricist epistemology glanced at in **431**; nor, indeed, is there any theory of perception at all in the fragment: **431** offers an account not of perception but of thought.

The crucial sentence of **431** occupies lines 2b–3; in Greek it runs: *to gar auto estin hoper phroneei meleôn phusis anthrôpoisin*. The sentence is multiply ambiguous. *Melea*, 'limbs', may be glossed either by 'body' or by 'elements': the body is the sum and organization of the limbs; the elemental stuffs are the limbs of the universe.[25] '*To . . . auto*' may mean either 'the same thing' or 'that very thing'. *Hoper* may be either subject or object of *phroneei*. The last sentence of the fragment is also ambiguous: *to gar pleon esti noêma*. The traditional reading (cf. Theophrastus *Sens* §3 = **28 A 46**) takes *to . . . pleon* to mean 'the more', i.e. 'that which predominates'. Many modern scholars prefer 'the full'; and it has been proposed, ingeniously, to separate *to* from *pleon*: 'For that is full thought'.[26]

Permutation of those different readings yields a mass of conflicting construes of the fragment. More than one can be given a sort of plausibility; and none has any clear claim to superiority. I shall simply present the view I incline towards, leaving the reader to construct his own reading for himself. Thus I take *melea* to refer to the elements; I read *to . . . auto* as 'the same thing'; I make *hoper* object of *phroneei*; and I construe *to pleon*, with Theophrastus, as 'the preponderating [element]'. Lines 1–2 then paraphrase thus: 'The state of a man's thoughts at any time is determined by the elemental mixture [in his body].' The crucial sentence reads: 'The nature of the elements is the same as what they think of'; and since 'the nature of the elements' is merely a paraphrase for 'the elements', the sentence purveys the same thought as Empedocles, **425**: by means of element E_1 you can think only of E_1. Finally, the last sentence means: 'the element predominating in a man's body is what he thinks with'.[27] The three sentences that make up **431** are linked by *gar* ('for'); but it is not easy to give that particle its proper force. Perhaps the argument is this: 'Given, first, that by E_1 a man can think only of E_1, and, second, that if E_1 predominates in a man, then he thinks with it; it follows that what a man thinks of at any time is determined by the elemental predominance, and thus by the elemental mixture, in his body.'

If that interpretation of Parmenides is right, it gives us a little help with Empedocles; for in effect **431** infers Empedocles' **B 108** from his **425**. We think of elements by elements; hence (since thinking is determined by elemental predominance) as we change physically, so do the objects of our thought change. Moreover, Parmenides confirms the decidedly materialistic aspect of Empedocles' theory of thought: to think of E_1 is simply to have E_1 predominant in your body (or in some selected part of it); and to come to think of E_1 is for your physical constitution to change. Intellectual states are physical states, intellectual processes are physical operations. It is entertaining to find a materialist account of thought so self-consciously paraded by a Presocratic; but the account itself is too crude to contemplate, and I hasten on.

(c) *The soul as harmony*

'The fragments of Empedocles contain only a single occurrence of the word "*psuchê*" (**B 138**), and then it means "life": the fact is no accident; for, strictly speaking, Empedoclean psychology has no room for a *psuchê*. "Empedocles did not hold that the soul is composed of the elements; but what we call the activity of the soul he explained by the elementary composition of the body; a soul distinct from the body he did not assume".'[28] The view that Empedocles had no soul is now fairly common. It was not held in antiquity: the doxographers are ready enough to use *psuchê* in Empedoclean contexts,[29] and their sunny acceptance of Empedoclean souls suggests that the absence of the term *psuchê* from the fragments should be ascribed to chance. In any case, it seems to me that in **B 138** ('drawing off his *psuchê* with bronze'—i.e. 'slitting his throat') the word *psuchê* does mean 'soul'.

What was the Empedoclean *psuchê*? In the *Phaedo* Socrates refers anonymously to those who say that 'blood is that with which we think' (96B = **24 A 11**); and he surely has Empedocles' **429** in mind. According to Hippo, 'the fact that the semen is not blood refutes those who say that the *psuchê* is blood' (*An* 405b4 = **31 A 4**): Hippo, too, had Empedocles in mind.[30] The doxographers, however, pass on a slightly different interpretation of **429**:

> The regent part (*to hêgemonikon*) is neither in the head nor in the chest, but in the blood (**432**: pseudo-Plutarch, **A 30**; cf. Aëtius, **A 97**).

Theophrastus, perhaps, disagreed with Plato. And Theophrastus' master confessed his own puzzlement:

> And it is similarly absurd to say that the *psuchê* is the *logos* of the mixing; for the mixing of the elements which produces flesh and that which produces bone do not have the same *logos*. Hence it

> will follow that one has many *psuchai* throughout the whole body, if everything is composed of mixed elements and the *logos* of the mixing is {*harmonia* and}[31] *psuchê*. And one might also put the following problem to Empedocles: he says that each of them exists by some *logos*; then is the *psuchê* the *logos*, or is it rather as something else[32] that it comes about in the limbs? (**433**: *An* 408a13–21 = **A 78**).

Let us forget about the blood and consider the view that the *psuchê* is a *logos* of the mixing: what does that mean? and was Empedocles in fact committed to it? Aristotle compares this Empedoclean doctrine to the celebrated theory that 'the soul is a harmony': I shall look at the latter theory before returning to Empedocles.

> There is another opinion handed down about the *psuchê*. . . . For they say that it is a sort of harmony; for a harmony is a mixing and composition (*krasis kai sunthesis*) of opposites, and the body is composed of opposites (**434**: *An* 407b27–32 = **44 A 23**).

> Many of the wise men say—some that the soul is a harmony, others that it has a harmony (**435**: *Pol* 1340b18 = **58 B 41**).

Our main source for the view is Plato's *Phaedo*:

> For, Socrates, I think you are aware that we believe the soul to be something like this: our bodies are, as it were, tensioned and held together by hot and cold and dry and wet and other things of the same kind; and our souls are the mixture and harmony of these things when they have been well mixed in a correct *logos* (**436**: 86 B).

Aristotle leaves the harmony men in comfortable anonymity. The speech in the *Phaedo* is made by Simmias; and the whole discussion is reported by Echecrates, who explicitly says that the harmony theory was familiar to him (88D = **53 A 4**). Now Echecrates is listed as a Pythagorean (Iamblichus, **53 A 2**); and Simmias studied under Philolaus (*Phaedo* 61D). The obvious inference is that the harmony theory was Pythagorean, and, specifically, a doctrine belonging to Philolaus. The importance of *harmonia* in Philolaus' thought adds credibility to the conclusion; and there is external corroboration; three late sources explicitly ascribe the doctrine to the Pythagoreans;[33] and one asserts that:

> Pythagoras and Philolaus [say that the soul is] a harmony (**437**: Macrobius, **44 A 23**).

The 'opposites' do not, it is true, figure in what we know of Philolaus' physics; but we have no reason to deny him the Presocratic commonplace that animal bodies are compounds and that their constituents are in some respects 'opposite'. Again, the only genuine Philolaic fragment that explicitly mentions *psuchê* (**44 B 13**) says nothing of *harmonia*;[34] but that fragment is consistent with the *harmonia* theory, and has no particular reason to advert expressly to it. I conclude that the traditional ascription is correct: Philolaus held that 'the soul is a harmony'.[35]

To say that 'the *psuchê* is a harmony' is to say that a person has a *psuchê* just so long as his physical constituents are harmoniously arranged,[36] thus:

(1) *a* has a *psuchê* if and only if *a*'s physical parts are harmoniously arranged.

The essential point about (1) is this: it makes the *psuchê* non-substantial, a dependent entity, like a mood or a cold, not an independent part of a man, like a brain or a heart. There are filthy moods and bad colds if and only if someone is in a filthy mood or has a bad cold; there are harmonies if and only if something is harmoniously arranged; and there are souls if and only if something has a soul. If I say '*a* has a coat', I assert a two-place relation (the relation of *having*) between a man and his apparel; and the predicate '. . . has a coat' is formed from the relation '. . . has——' and the general term 'coat'. If I say '*a* has a filthy temper' I do not assert a two-place relation between a man and some other item; and the predicate '. . . has a filthy temper' is not compounded from a relation and a general term. According to (1), '*a* has a *psuchê*' is like '*a* has a temper' and unlike '*a* has a coat'.

The thesis that a *psuchê* is 'the *logos* of the mixing' has the same implication; and that is why Aristotle treats the two views together. '*Logos*' in this phrase hovers between 'proportion' or 'ratio' and 'definition'; but the difference is trifling, since a mixing is presumably defined by the ratio of the stuffs it mixes. Thus the thesis says that a person has a *psuchê* just so long as his physical constituents are mixed in the right proportion; or:

(2) *a* has a *psuchê* if and only if *a*'s physical parts are correctly mixed.

Evidently, the *psuchê* of (2) is non-substantial in exactly the same way as the *psuchê* of (1).

Psuchê is essentially defined in functional terms: a *psuchê* is that in virtue of which one lives. Similarly, we might define a temper as that in virtue of which one rants and rages; and a waterproof as that in virtue of which one remains dry in rainstorms. Given these formal definitions, we ask after the nature of the *psuchê*, the temper, the waterproof. Answers of very different types emerge for the two latter questions: a waterproof is a piece of oilskin or canvas or similar material; a temper is a disposition or inclination to act in such and such a way. '*a* has a waterproof' is true if and only if *a* possesses a piece of oilskin or the like: 'has' denotes a two-place relation; and the sentence might be symbolized, to bring that feature out, by the formula: $(\exists x)$ (x is a waterproof and a has x). '*a* has a temper' is true if and only if *a* is disposed to act in such and such a way: 'has' does not denote a two-place relation, and the sentence permits no symbolic formalization that parallels the waterproof formula. The *harmonia* theory and the *logos* theory bring *psuchê* to the side of tempers and separate it from waterproofs. The theories contrast both with run-of-the-mill Presocratic notions, which make the *psuchê* a part of a man's bodily stuff, and also with the Cartesian account, which makes the soul an incorporeal homuncule temporarily resident in the body.

Theories (1) and (2) are close to one another; the *Phaedo* perhaps conflates them. Aristotle, however, rightly distinguishes between them, and rightly points out the absurdity of (2): there is no one ratio which gives the 'correct' elemental mixture for all a man's physical constituents; different parts require different ratios, and there is no such thing as '*the logos* of the mixing'. The objection can be countered by rewriting the *definiens* of (2) as 'each of *a*'s physical constituents is correctly mixed'. The difference between (1) and (2) now diminishes; and both theories face a common question: What is a 'harmonious' arrangement, or a 'correct' mixing? What are the canons of harmony, the criteria of correctness?

A lyre is 'harmoniously' arranged if it is correctly strung and attuned for playing: its harmony or attunement consists in its aptitude for performance. Similarly, then, a body's harmony, or correct mix, is one which conduces to its functioning: the arrangement of the bodily parts is harmonious only if the body is capable of performing certain vital functions; and a mixture of bodily constituents is correct only if it is conducive to such performance. Thus (1) and (2) give place to:

(3) *a* has a *psuchê* if and only if *a*'s body is in a state such that *a* is capable of performing the vital functions.

The vital functions will vary from one species of creature to another; no doubt they will include, in the case of man, nutrition, reproduction, perception, locomotion, and thought.

I have deliberately developed the *harmonia* theory in an Aristotelian direction: indeed (3) constitutes as good an account as I can give of Aristotle's thesis that 'the *psuchê* is an *entelecheia* of a potentially living body' (*An* 412a26). Aristotle vigorously rejects the *harmonia* theory, and gives no hint that it approximated to his own view. His hasty dismissal of the theory is a pity; for if, as I incline to think, Aristotle's own view of mind is substantially correct, then it would be pleasant to know more about its first adumbration in the writings of Philolaus: had Aristotle praised the theory, later writers might have prized and preserved it.

(d) *Metempsychosis and immortality*

Philolaus held both a *harmonia* theory of the *psuchê* and a Pythagorean view on metempsychosis and immortality. Most scholars are worried by the conjunction, and some see a difficulty so great that they dissociate psychic harmony from Philolaus. There is, it is true, no direct evidence for transmigration or psychic immortality in Philolaus: scholars point to his alleged prohibition on suicide (*Phaedo* 61DE = **44 B 15**); and to the *mot* that the body is a tomb of the soul. But the prohibition has no bearing on the question; and the *mot* is ascribed to Philolaus by virtue of a misreading of the *Phaedo* (62B = **44 B 15**).[37] Thus if either *harmonia* or immortality must be denied to Philolaus, I should incline to deny him immortality. Yet such a rejection, in a Pythagorean, would have been remarkable; and since our sources do not remark upon it, we must work on the supposition that both *harmonia* and immortality are Philolaic.

In the *Phaedo* Simmias himself discovers an incongruity between harmony and immortality: 'If, then, the soul really is some kind of harmony, it is clear that when our bodies are unduly relaxed or tensioned by disease or some other evil, the soul must immediately perish' (*Phaedo* 86C). There cannot be separate souls; for it is an immediate consequence of the harmony theory that anyone who has a *psuchê* has a body. And souls cannot survive their owner's body; for any destruction of the arrangement of that body is *eo ipso* an end of the *psuchê*. Aristoxenus, who later developed a version of the *harmonia* theory, was perfectly clear that the *psuchê*, not being substantial, could not have a separate immortal existence (cf. frr. 119–20 W).

There are two distinct arguments to consider here. Before discussing them I have two preliminary points to make. First, even if the argument outlined in the last paragraph is correct, we need not suppose that Philolaus knew it or would have accepted it had he known it. Indeed, 'one has the impression that Plato, in this passage in the *Phaedo*, was the first to point out an embarrassing implication of the idea of the soul as a harmony'.[38] Even if harmony and immortality are inconsistent, Philolaus may well have embraced both doctrines, in blissful ignorance or erroneous belief.

Second, we must distinguish clearly between psychic insubstantiality and psychic incorporeality. To say that the soul is insubstantial, as (1)–(3) implicitly do, is to deny that the soul is an independent substance, or that 'soul' is an indispensable substantive (see above, p. 445). To say that the soul is incorporeal is to deny that souls are physical or that a complete account of psychology can be given in terms of physical theory. The distinction allows four types of view on the soul: (a) the soul is substantial and incorporeal—as Plato and Descartes held; (b) the soul is substantial and corporeal—as Democritus and most of the Presocratics held; (c) the soul is insubstantial and incorporeal ('soul' is not a substance word, but there are irreducibly non-physical predicates)—Aristotle, I think, held this view; (d) the soul is insubstantial and corporeal—as modern behaviourism and modern physicalism hold. Philolaus' harmony theory rejects (a) and (b); it does not, so far as I can see, plump definitely for (d) rather than (c). Thus Philolaus was not necessarily a full-blooded physicalist; and any difficulty there may be in reconciling his psychology with his eschatology is due not to materialism or physicalism, but to 'insubstantialism'.

What, then, of Simmias' difficulty? One argument is plain enough: the harmony theory entails the impossibility of independently existing souls. Aristotle saw the entailment clearly (*An* 413a3), and it is indeed obvious: there exists a *psuchê* only if '*x* has a *psuchê*' is true of something; and '*x* has a *psuchê*' is true of *a* only if *a* has a body. No soul without body. The conclusion is anathema to modern advocates of immortality. It does not, however, imply that the soul is mortal: I ignore the tedious and unreal possibility that *a*'s body may be immortal and point to the particular form of Pythagorean immortality: metempsychosis allows psychic immortality without requiring the existence of separate, disembodied, souls (see above, p. 111). My body perishes, certainly; and so my *psuchê* cannot achieve immortality by cleaving to this flesh. But other bodies survive, and my soul may fly to a new body on the destruction of mine; and if there is an infinite sequence of bodies, my soul may achieve a transmigratory immortality. Metempsychosis, in short, allows Philolaus to make his *psuchê* immortal, even though it cannot exist apart from a body.

The second argument against Philolaus seems to have failed along with the first: the second urges that if a body, b_1, ceases to be harmoniously arranged, then its harmony and its *psuchê* perish;

Philolaus replies that the harmony and *psuchê* need not perish, they may simply pass on to another body, b_2.

Philolaus' victory, however, is spurious. The suggestion is that two different bodies may have the same soul; and that a suitable succession of mortal bodies may support a single immortal soul. In a way the suggestion is correct: there is a perfectly clear sense in which Philolaus can say that b_1 houses the same soul as b_2. Two different lyres may have the same *harmonia*, for they may be attuned in exactly the same way; two different men may have the same bad temper, for they may be disposed to rage at the same things in the same ways; two different bodies may 'house' the same soul, for they may exhibit exactly the same harmonious arrangement. And it is logically possible (though no doubt physically improbable) that my soul should, in this sense, be immortal: at any time t, there exists a body exhibiting exactly the same harmonious arrangement that my body now exhibits.

But an immortality of that sort is eschatologically barren. Psychic immortality so construed does not guarantee personal immortality; psychic 'transmigration' (the word is hardly apposite) does not ensure that *I* survive my body's decay. Two different bodies existing at different times may have the same *psuchê*; but in exactly the same way, two different bodies existing at the same time may have the same *psuchê*. For all I know, my body and the body of the Prime Minister of Australia may be attuned exactly alike; hence, the Prime Minister and I have the same soul. But that does not mean that I am the Prime Minister of Australia. Similarly, it may happen that the Australian Prime Minister in 2075 will have the same soul as I have now; but that fact gives me no reason to expect a future Antipodean existence, or to anticipate a prime-ministerial salary. Psychic identity and personal identity fall apart; psychic immortality has no implications for personal immortality: Philolaus has no call to rejoice in the survival of his soul.

In a monogamous country, if a has the same wife as b, then a is the same person as b; in the present state of surgical accomplishment, if a has the same brain as b, then a is the same person as b. In general, if F is a substance term, and R a one-one relation, then if a and b bear R to the same F, a is identical with b. That is an elementary truth of logic. Now on the standard doctrine of metempsychosis, it is my soul that makes me the individual I am; consequently, only I can have my soul. Hence the relationship between myself and my soul is one-one; and if the Australian premier of 2075 has the same soul as I have, then I am he. Philolaus, however, cannot employ that argument: '. . . has a soul' is not a relational predicate in his view; consequently

I do not stand in any relation to my soul, and specifically I do not stand in a one-one relation to it. 'He has his father's soul' is perfectly intelligible; but it is not an assertion of metempsychosis, nor does it imply that he is his father. 'He has his father's soul' is, logically speaking, parallel to 'He has his father's temper': both are comments on the similarity of human nature; neither comments on the identity of human persons.

I conclude that Philolaus is at a loss: *harmonia* and psychic immortality are logically consistent; but together they entail the immortality of the body. If bodies rot, then either *harmonia* or psychic immortality is false. For all that, the harmony theory represents a signal advance in the philosophy of mind; and any discussion of the difficulties into which Philolaus unwittingly drove plunges at once into some of the thickest bush of modern philosophy.

(e) *Was Empedocles a centaur?*

My remarks on Empedocles' psychology have drawn exclusively on fragments traditionally assigned to his poem *Concerning Nature*; my earlier account of Empedocles' theory of metempsychosis drew exclusively on the *Katharmoi*. One of the standing problems in Empedoclean studies concerns the relationship between the two poems, and in particular between the doctrine of metempsychosis and the physiological psychology of *Nature*.[39] *Nature*, it is said, is thoroughly materialistic; the *Katharmoi* treats of the fate of an immortal and incorporeal soul: the two poems are thus in flat contradiction. Empedocles' 'two pictures of rationality remain not only heterogeneous but contradictory at crucial points; they admit of no rational or, for that matter, even imaginative harmony'; 'the Orphic piety of his *Purifications* . . . admits of no rational connexion with the scientific temper and doctrine of his work *On Nature*.' Some scholars generalize from the case of Empedocles: 'all through this period, there seems to have been a gulf between men's religious beliefs, if they had any, and their cosmological views': Empedocles was a 'philosophical centaur', in an age when such monstrosities were regularly spawned.[40]

An essay in intellectual biography may solve the paradox: philosophers change their views; and perhaps Empedocles' equine and his human features were not contemporaneous characteristics—the Ionian doctrines of *Nature* were forgotten or abandoned when the Pythagorean *Purifications* intoxicated Empedocles' mind. We have not an incongruous simultaneity of opinions, but a radical *volte-face*. Such changes are not unknown in the history of philosophy.

The fragments of Empedocles which we possess can be assigned to his different poems with some confidence;[41] moreover, we know the order in which the poems were written. **B 131** comes from the *Katharmoi*:

> If for the sake of any of the mortals, divine Muse,
> it pleased you to let my exercises pass through your mind
> now again stand by me as I pray, Calliope,
> and reveal a good argument about the blessed gods (**438**).

The earlier aid for which **438** thanks the Muse was surely given for the penning of *Nature*; hence *Nature* was penned before the *Katharmoi*.[42]

The biographical solution will hardly do. The *Katharmoi* gives no hint of a change in doctrine; on the contrary, there are well-marked connexions between the two poems. The *Katharmoi* contains constant linguistic echoes of *Nature*; **438** refers complacently to *Nature* at the opening of the later poem. And there are also close connexions of substance: thus **B 111**, from *Nature*, and **B 112**, from the *Katharmoi*, make very similar proclamations, and Clement intelligibly cites both fragments to prove a single point (cf. **A 14**). Hippolytus, who preserves **B 115** of the *Katharmoi*, intelligibly glosses it in the terms of *Nature*.

If we cannot seriously entertain the theory of a radical change in Empedocles' philosophical outlook, we cannot, by the same token, find a lack of 'imaginative harmony' between the two poems; at any rate, Empedocles' imagination, and that of his ancient critics, was broad and bold enough to encompass both poems. It was not unusual to find prophet and scientist united in one person in old Greece; and the religious physicist is no rarity today. I may be astonished to find that one man both has expertise in nuclear physics and practises as a lay preacher; but I can hardly doubt that there are such men, and that they manage to combine their apparently heterogeneous beliefs into an imaginative unity.[43]

There is just one Empedocles, the scientist of *Nature* and the moralist of the *Katharmoi*: we have no grounds for positing an intellectual revolution in his life, or for accusing him of imaginative schizophrenia. The main charge remains: are not the two poems simply inconsistent with each other? Is not the transmigratory soul of the *Katharmoi* incompatible with the psychology of *Nature*?

I begin with **B 15**, which scholars locate in *Nature*:

> A man wise in such matters would not think in his mind
> that while they live what they call life
> so long do they exist, and bad and good things face them,

> but that before they were put together as men and once they are
> dissolved they do not exist at all (**439**).

The fragment speaks of immortality; and Plutarch, who quotes it, plausibly takes it to be promising a personal immortality:[44] 'only a fool would think that his existence is limited to that short span which men call life'.

439 is not easy to integrate with the rest of *Nature*: strictly speaking (see above, p. 442), Empedocles cannot admit that men exist at all; for only the elements really exist. But **439** is not ascribing immortality to *men*: the things that are immortal are only men for a brief span in their existence. If **439** does announce a personal immortality, it must distinguish persons from men. Persons, of course, must be parcels of elemental stuff; but they need not always be parcels of human form. Thus **439** brings *Nature* into close doctrinal contact with the eschatological promises of the *Katharmoi*. That, I think, shows that in Empedocles' mind the two poems were consistent; it does not, of course, show that they are consistent in reality. We must now look at the incorporeal objects of the *Katharmoi* whose alleged existence breeds the inconsistency.

Four fragments need to be quoted; the first describes 'the divine (*to theion*)':

> We cannot bring it near to be approachable by our eyes,
> or grasp it with our hands, which is the greatest
> path of persuasion leading into men's minds (**440: B 133**).

The next fragment may well have been continuous with **440**:

> For its limbs are not fitted out with a human head,
> nor do two branches spring from shoulders,
> nor feet, nor swift knees, nor hairy chest;
> but it is only a holy and superhuman mind,
> darting with swift thoughts over the whole world (**441: B 134**).

The Byzantine scholar, Tzetzes, ascribes **441** to 'the third book of the *Physics*'; and some moderns accordingly place **441**, and with it **440**, in *Nature*.[45] From the present point of view the attribution is unimportant: if correct, it only strengthens the connexion between the two poems.

The next long fragment is expressly concerned with transmigration:

> There is a pronouncement of Necessity, an old decree of the gods,
> eternal, sealed with broad oaths:
> when anyone in wickedness defiles his dear limbs with bloodshed

—a *daimôn* who has been allotted long life—
thrice ten thousand seasons is he to wander apart from the blessed ones,
being born through that time in every kind of mortal form,
treading in turn the wretched paths of life.
For the force of the air pursues him into the sea
and the sea spits him up onto the threshold of the land, and the land into the rays
of the tireless sun, and that casts him to the whirls of the air:
one receives him from another, and all hate him.
This way I myself am now going, a fugitive and wanderer from the gods,
who trusted in mad strife (**442: B 115**).[46]

Finally, a single line reads:

. . . clothing it about in an alien cloak of flesh (**443: B 126**).

Plutarch makes the subject 'nature'; Porphyry says that 'nature' or '*daimôn*' is the tailor, and that her clients are 'souls'.[47]

These four fragments are together taken to show that the theory of transmigration uses an incorporeal soul: **442** makes the migrating soul a *daimôn* or godlike thing; **443** shows that *daimones* find flesh, and hence the four roots, foreign stuff; and **440** and **441** reveal that, in general, Empedoclean gods are pure, incorporeal minds.

That argument is wholly mistaken. First, the gods. **440** is quickly dismissed: it says that *we* cannot see or touch *to theion*. The point is epistemological: 'since we cannot have immediate perception of the divine, we must rely on inference or analogy or the like'. From that it scarcely follows that the divine is absolutely intangible and invisible; let alone that the divine is incorporeal. As for **441**, that is pure Xenophanes: as Ammonius observes, Empedocles' point is to 'castigate the stories told by the poets which treat of the gods as being anthropomorphic' (*ad* **B 134**). A denial of anthropomorphism does not entail incorporeality; and if the divinity is 'a sacred mind (*phrên*)', that will not secure incorporeality, for Empedocles is a psychological materialist.

In fact, Empedocles' theology is far denser and more difficult than the simple argument from **440** and **441** suggests. First, the four roots, together with Love and Strife, are given divine names (e.g., **B 6**);[48] those gods are, trivially, corporeal. Second, the cosmic Sphere is given divine status (e.g., **B 31**); and the Sphere too is a massy god. Third, there are the traditional gods named in **B 128**:

Nor was there among them any god Ares, nor Kudoimos,
nor King Zeus, nor Cronus, nor Poseidon,
but only queen Cypris . . . (**444**).

The main purport of these lines is to state that men of the Golden Age made love, not war; and the gods may be no more than rhetorical window-dressing. If we take the gods of **444** seriously, then they are to be placed among the fourth set of divinities, the created gods of **B 21**:

For from these [sc. the elements] comes everything that was and is and will be—
trees sprang up, and men and women,
and beasts and birds and water-dwelling fish,
and long-lived gods who are first in honour (**195**: cf. **B 23**. 5–8).

Like men, these gods are not eternal but at best long-lived (*dolichaiônes*): being elemental compounds, they cannot survive the complete elemental dissociation at the time of total Strife, nor the utter fusion in the years of the Sphere. Finally, and fifth, there are the *daimones* of **442**. They have a divine status; yet they are not eternal, their lot is 'long-lived life (*makraiôn biotos*)'. The *daimones* and the long-lived gods of **195** have much in common: parsimony suggests their identification.

If that identification is correct, it has some importance for **442** and **443**, to which I now turn. The orthodoxy sees in those two fragments a picture of the *daimôn* as a journeying *homunculus*, condemned to lodge in a succession of dirty doss-houses; the *daimôn* is, as it were, an incorporeal ghost of a thing, which properly exists untrammelled by any body, but whose sins condemn it to 30,000 seasons in physical clink. The picture suggests a Cartesian rather than a Presocratic artist. I do not think that it is entirely wrong; nor even that the Cartesian touches are all anachronistic. But in one point it is seriously unrepresentational: nothing at all in **442** implies that the *daimôn*, in its blessed state, is incorporeal; fallen, it puts on mortal forms; but that does not imply that unfallen it was wholly bodiless. Nor does **443** imply daemonic incorporeality: the word '*allogños*', which I translate 'alien', is unique. If the translation is right, **443** does not show that the *daimôn* is naturally incorporeal, or even that it is naturally fleshless; if I put on a strange suit of worsted at the tailor's, that does not mean that I entered the shop naked, nor even that I did not enter in my familiar worsted. If '*allognôs*' means rather 'making unrecognizable',[49] the same holds: men who put on disguises need not have been naked beforehand, nor even undisguised.

In short, we are at liberty to have our *daimôn* corporeal; and that liberty becomes a pleasant necessity if the *daimones* of **442** are identified, as I suggest, with the long-lived gods of **195**.

Of what stuffs is the material *daimôn* compounded? The natural answer is: of all stuffs. The response is implicit, I think, in **195**; and it is necessary if the *daimones* are going to have a knowledge of the world commensurate with their unfallen status; for 'by earth we see earth'. Some modern scholars give a different answer: first, they distinguish between two types of *psuchê*: the seat of cognition and consciousness, and the 'divine spark' or soul. Second, they connect the former *psuchê* with the materialistic psychology of *Nature* and the latter with the *daimôn* of the *Katharmoi*. Finally, they urge that the *daimôn* is not composed of the four roots, but solely of Love (and, perhaps, Strife); thus the *daimôn* is not exactly material, for Love and Strife are only quasi-matter.[50]

That modern theory is, I fear, a modern fantasy, engendered by the desire to give a transmigratory theorist an incorporeal soul. The desire is unwarranted; for transmigration does not require incorporeality. And the fantasy does not satisfy the desire; for Love and Strife are corporeal. No jot of evidence suggests that the *daimôn* is made of Love (and Strife). If the *daimôn* is separated from the psychology of *Nature*, then it is hard to see how the *daimones* will live their blessed life. And the distinction between two types of *psuchê*, if it is found in other Greek texts, is nowhere hinted at by any Presocratic.

Empedocles can now emerge with a coherent psychology-cum-eschatology. Let us replace the term '*daimôn*' by 'person', its nearest English equivalent. Persons are long-lived: they are created fairly early in the cosmic cycle, and destroyed or decomposed fairly late. They are essentially corporeal, being tightly-knit elemental compounds; and thanks to their elemental constitution, they are capable of cognition and of locomotion. In their original state, persons are not human in form, nor do they rely upon human organs of cognition or locomotion; and to that extent an Empedoclean person is a *res cogitans*, a 'sacred mind'.

In their original state persons have some sort of social life. The punishment for moral transgression in that life is severe: the person is obliged to take on human, animal and vegetable forms—to become a man, a horse, a marrow. Throughout these transmogrifications it remains a person, and the same person. Proteus-like, it changes form frequently and radically; like Proteus, it remains the same divine creature. And at last, its sins expiated, it reverts to its original state, and may again flit knowingly through the universe.

The account is doubtless implausible: Empedocles does not tell us how to identify a *daimôn*, or how to trace a daemonic substance from one mortal form to another; and if it is possible to think of ways in which his hypothesis might become scientifically testable, it is hard to think of a way which would not also lead to speedy refutation. But that is only to say what everyone believes: that transmigration does not happen. Logically, the hypothesis is impeccable: no inconsistency is generated by the supposition that one and the same physical *daimôn* passes through a succession of animal and vegetable phases; and those scholars who state that transmigration requires an incorporeal soul are simply in error.

Pedants will deny Empedocles' theory the name of metempsychosis, since it involves no wanderings of a *psuchê*; but if those ancient commentators who called the *daimôn* a *psuchê* were going beyond their evidence, the appellation was intelligible and harmless. Nor need we be puzzled, as Aristotle was, by Empedocles' failure to give a plain account of *psuchê*: he may, if he pleases, say that the soul is a mass of blood, or of whatever stuff is most appropriate to describe the daemonic composition; he may, that is to say, call the *daimôn* a *psuchê*. Alternatively, he may say that the *psuchê* is a '*logos* of the mixing': the *daimôn* has a *psuchê* inasmuch as its component stuffs are arranged thus and so. The two accounts are only verbally distinct.

Empedocles was no centaur: *Nature* and the *Katharmoi* do not state opposing philosophies uneasily coexisting in a single schizophrenic mind. On the contrary, as Hippolytus obscurely saw (*ad* **B 115**), *Nature* provides the physical foundation for the eschatology of the *Katharmoi*: a proper natural philosophy shows first, that the events we denominate by 'birth' and 'death' are in actual fact comminglings and separations of our elemental parts; and second, that our vital functions are, scientifically speaking, alterations in our physical constitution. Now 'birth' and 'death' evidently do not start from or end in pure elemental stuffs: the processes of association and dissociation are long drawn out. What, then, is more reasonable than to imagine that our selves have pre-existed and will survive those partial dissolutions and reminglings of our gross constituents which men habitually suppose to mark the terminal points of their lives? Natural philosophy does not imply an Empedoclean eschatology; but in a perfectly clear sense it provides the backcloth against which that drama can be played out.

(f) *The whirligig of time*

The gods of **195** are *dolichaiônes*, not *aidioi*; the *daimones* of **442** enjoy a *makraiôn biotos*; and **439**, strictly construed, promises not immortality but only survival of what is vulgarly called death. Moreover *Nature* is incompatible with an unbroken personal immortality: in the homogeneous Sphere, and again at the time of Utter Strife (and doubtless for some considerable periods at the beginning and at the end of the cosmogonical era) there is no place for persons. Men are shorter lived than *daimones*; but *daimones* are not immortal.

The *Katharmoi*, however, promises immortality: greeting the inhabitants of Acragas, Empedocles announces:

> I come to you an immortal god (*theos ambrotos*), no longer mortal (**445: B 112**.4);

and at the end of their punishment the *daimones*

> spring up as gods, highest in honours,
> sharing a hearth with the other immortals (*athanatois*) (**446: B 146**.3; **B 147**.1).

Do we not, after all, have a basic inconsistency between *Nature* and the *Katharmoi*? It is not that the former poem is materialistic, the latter spiritualistic; but that the former countenances no immortals but the elements, while the latter proclaims personal immortality.

The difficulty here is not serious: 'immortal' is a stock epithet of the Greek gods, and 'the immortals' comes to mean 'the gods', its literal sense ('those who never cease to exist') being at most a faint semantic undercurrent; it would be absurd to press the word '*athanatois*' in **446** and to insist that it ascribes literal deathlessness to the gods. It would be equally silly to make anything of '*ambrotos*' in **445**. At worst, Empedocles is speaking loosely: his thought is consistent, and it consistently yields gods and *daimones* who are long-lived but not immortal. Personal immortality is not, in fact, explicitly promised in Empedoclean eschatology.

Yet an ingenious suggestion seems capable, after all, of investing Empedocles' *daimones* with a sort of eternity. Dicaearchus ascribes to Pythagoras the view that 'at certain periods, what has happened once happens again' (**84: 14 A 8a**). The theory of Eternal Recurrence has had a strange hold on the human mind. In an enervated form it is embraced both by Plato and by Aristotle, and adopted by those who claim to find cyclical patterns in human history; in a strong form it was propounded by the Stoic sages, and raised by Nietzsche as the pinnacle of philosophy, the *Gedanke der Gedanken*. The view is ancient and has Eastern origins. Even if we do not believe Dicaearchus' ascription (though I do not see why we should not),

Eternal Recurrence was surely current in fifth-century Pythagorean circles; and it is clearly present in the cosmic cycle of Empedocles.

For Empedocles' universe, on the orthodox interpretation (above, p. 310), gives a perfect example of Eternal Recurrence: the Sphere yields to a cosmological period which ends in total Strife; after Strife comes a second cosmogony, symmetrical with the first; and then the Sphere returns, only to yield again to a cosmology. The cycles roll on infinitely, without beginning and without end; each cycle follows the pattern of its predecessor.

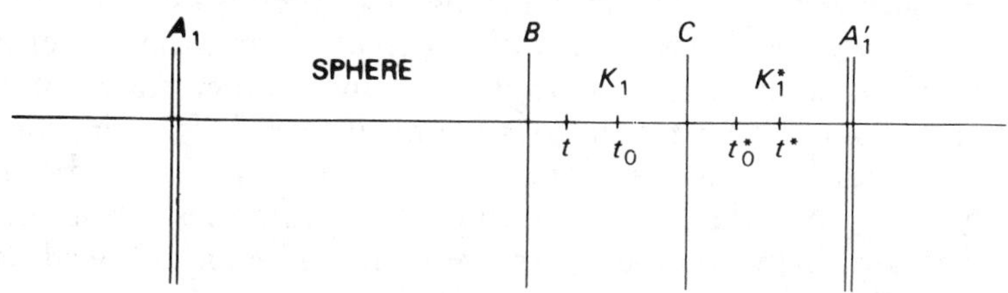

$A_1\ A'_1$ represents one cosmic cycle; within it $B\ A'_1$ is the period of the cosmos, divided at C by the instant of total strife. The state of the world at t in K_1 is exactly repeated at t^* in K^*_1, if $Bt = t^*A'_1$; and the history of K_1 from t to t_0 is exactly repeated, in the opposite direction, from t^*_0 to t^* in K^*_1 (if $|t\ t_0| = |t^*_0 t^*|$). Before and after $A_1A'_1$ there are infinitely many cycles, $A_iA'_i$; in each cycle there are cosmic periods $K_i + K^*_i$; and in each cosmic period the roll of events exactly mirrors the history of $K_1 + K^*_1$. Empedocles holds a theory of Eternal Recurrence in a remarkably strong form.

Why should anyone have embraced that bizarre theory? Two lines of argument are suggested. The first is scientific: we observe the movements of the heavens; and we see that they are strictly periodical; after a long span or 'Great Year' every heavenly body will be in exactly the same place as it is now. Since the heavens mirror, or even determine, sublunary events, we infer that the world as a whole has its Great Year: 'in the case of the motion of the heavens and of each of the stars, there is a circle: what then prevents the generation and decay of perishable things from being like this, so that these things are generated and decay again?' ([Aristotle], *Probl* 916a25–7). Above, the boarhound and the boar pursue their patterns as before: below, they are faced by the same destiny.[51]

The second line of argument is metaphysical. Crudely stated, it has a certain charm: the universe is finite, and it has finitely many different states; but time flows on infinitely, and every moment in time is the time of some state of the universe. Since the states follow one another in causally ordered succession, they are bound to recur:

the history of the universe is cyclical. More precisely: consider some state of the universe, s_1 (a description of s_1 will specify the total arrangement of the universe at some time). s_1 will cause s_2; s_2, s_3; and so on. Consider the series $s_1, s_2, \ldots, s_n, s_n + 1$. Suppose that there are just n different s_is: then $s_n + 1$ is identical with some s_i between s_1 and $s_n - 1$. Call it s_j. Then the series from s_j to s_n will repeat itself infinitely in infinite time; and since s_1 was caused by some s_i, s_1 was caused by s_n, so that the cycle s_j—s_n has already been infinitely repeated.[52]

The argument relies on the following large premisses: that time is infinite; that time cannot exist without change; that the universe is deterministic; that there are finitely many distinct states of the universe. None of those premisses is uncontroversially true. For all that, the argument is a rational construction: Nietzsche did not merely adopt, by superhuman intuition, a striking thesis. But alas, I doubt if any such argument ran through Empedocles' head (see above, p. 311).

So far Eternal Recurrence makes no reference to personal immortality. Nietzsche proceeds thus: '"Now I die and disappear," you would say; "in the totality of things I am nothing. Souls are as mortal as bodies." But the knot of causes in which I am bound up returns—it will create me again. I myself belong to the causes of the eternal recurrence. I come again with this sun, with this earth, with this eagle, with these snakes—*not* to a new life or a better life or a similar life: eternally again to this very same life, the same in largest and in smallest points; and I teach again the eternal recurrence of all things' (*Also Sprach Zarathustra III*, 'Der Genesende'). The Stoics had said the same: 'after our death, when certain periods of time have passed, we shall come to the state in which we are now'; 'this same I will be born again in the renascence'; 'after the conflagration, everything in the universe comes about again, the same in number (*ta auta . . . kat' arithmon*)'.[53] And the same point was explicitly made by the Pythagoreans; for, according to Eudemus, they hold that

> [Things will occur] again, the same in number (*ta auta arithmôi*), and I shall be holding my stick and lecturing to you sitting like that—and the same will go for everything else (447: fr. 88 W = 58 B 34).

Consider the present stretch of the cosmic cycle, $BC = K_1$. It consists of n successive world states, $S_1^1, S_1^2, \ldots, S_1^n$. Pythagoras' life is included in a subset of those states: it is constituted by the set of states P_1^k—P_1^n, where each P_1^i is a part of S_1^i. In the next stage of the cycle, $CA'_1 = K_1$, there is an analogous set of states, P_1^{k*}—P_1^{m*}, and in every one of the infinitely many K_is, there is a set of Pythagorean states, P_i^k—P_i^m. Thus Pythagoras lives in each K_i; and since there are infinitely many K_is, he enjoys an immortal existence. His existence is discontinuous; but it never ends. Such an immortality would be tedious if we had perfect memories; and it is, indeed, hard to see why anyone should find comfort in it. Yet Nietzsche certainly did; and so, I suppose, did the Stoa, Empedocles, and perhaps even Pythagoras himself.

The argument I have just presented, simple though it is, is worth setting out more formally. Call the man whose history is constituted by the successive states P_1^k—P_1^m, 'Pythagoras$_1$'. Each K_i will then contain a Pythagoras$_i$. Now every S_1^j is identical with each corresponding S_i^j. Consequently, for any j, $P_1^j = P_2^j$. Hence:

(1) For any property ϕ, Pythagoras$_1$ has ϕ if and only if Pythagoras$_2$ has ϕ.

But in general:

(2) If for any property ϕ, a has ϕ if and only if b has ϕ, then $a = b$.

Hence:

(3) Pythagoras$_1$ = Pythagoras$_2$.

In general:

(4) For any cycle K_i, Pythagoras$_1$ = Pythagoras$_i$.

Hence Pythagoras—our familiar Pythagoras—lives in every cosmic cycle; and he is therefore immortal.

The argument is open to objection from two sides. The first objection allows it validity but denies it any immortal significance. Eudemus places his report of the Pythagorean view in a philosophical context: 'If one believes the Pythagoreans, so that [things occur] again, numerically the same . . ., then it is plausible (*eulogon*) that the time too is the same, for it is [the time] of the same motion; and similarly, of many identical things the "earlier and later" are one and the same, and so, then, is their number. All things, then, are the same; so that the time is, too' (fr. 88 W = **58 B 34**). Eudemus expresses himself in terms of Aristotle's philosophy of time; but the main point of his argument stands out independently of that philosophy. Times are necessarily times *of events* (or 'motions'); one time is distinct from another, therefore, only if it is the time of a different event. Now since, by hypothesis, the state of the world S_1^j holding at t_j^1 in K_1 is exactly the same as the corresponding state S_2^j holding at t_j^2 in K_2, the two instants t_j^1 and t_j^2 are identical.

Stated more rigorously, the Eudemian argument runs like this: Take two instants of time, t_1 and t_2. Suppose that every event occurring at t_1 has a counterpart occurring at t_2, and *vice versa*; and suppose further that every event occurring at $t_1 + n$ (for any positive or negative n) has a counterpart at $t_2 + n$, and vice versa: then nothing distinguishes t_1 from t_2, and so $t_1 = t_2$. Now the instant t^1_j in our period K_1 has, by hypothesis, a counterpart instant t^i_j in every K_i; hence for every i $t^1_j = t^i_j$. Hence every cosmic period K_i is simultaneous with K_1 ('the time too is the same'). Pythagoras$_1$ lived from t^1_x to t^1_y; Pythagoras$_2$ lived from t^2_x to t^2_y. But $t^1_x = t^2_x$; and $t^1_y = t^2_y$. Pythagoras$_1$ and Pythagoras$_2$ are indeed identical; but their lifespan is not infinite, it is simply the three score years and ten between t^1_x and t^1_y.

Eternal Recurrence not only fails to produce immortality; it appears to produce a cyclical theory of time itself: take any state S_n occurring at t_n, and preceded at t_{n-1} by S_{n-1}. At some point, t_1, S_{n-1} will recur. By the preceding argument, $t_1 = t_{n-1}$. But t_{n-1} is, *ex hypothesi*, *before* t_n; and t_1 is, by construction, *after* t_n. Thus t_1 is both before and after t_n, and time is, as they say, circular. The cyclical theory of time is distinct from the thesis of Eternal Recurrence, though the two things are often confused. Some philosophers, insisting that time has a unique 'direction', would reject circular time out of hand; other philosophers allow that temporal circularity is at least a logical possibility. I cannot decide which view to adopt; and I leave the issue in the air.

For Eudemus, time is the 'measure of change'—not a medium in which events occur but an aspect of the organization of those events. Events necessarily occur in time; but there is no 'absolute' time, independent of events: instants of time are determined by the occurrence of events; periods of time are delimited by ends and beginnings of events. 'Time is a thought or a measure', not a substance (Antiphon, **87 B 9**). The Eudemian argument relies on that theory; but the theory does not go uncontested: according to Newton, 'absolute, true and mathematical time, of itself and from its own nature, flows equably without relation to anything external'; and Newton is not without followers. Perhaps Newtonian time can reconcile Recurrence and Immortality, and remove the threat of a circular chronology?

Alas, Newtonian time saves Pythagoras from Eudemus' frying-pan only to deposit him in the fire. The difficulty was adumbrated in antiquity. Pseudo-Aristotle asserts that 'it is silly to aver that those who are born are always the same in number' (*Probl* 916a29); and Simplicius says of the Stoics that 'they inquire, reasonably, whether I am one in number now and then (because I am the same in substance) or rather differ in virtue of my ordering in different cosmogonies' (*in Phys* 886.13 = *SVF* II.627). One salient feature of Pythagoras$_1$ is not, so far as we can tell, a feature of Pythagoras$_2$:

$Pythagoras_1$ taught eternal recurrence in 520 BC; $Pythagoras_2$ will teach it, but not until AD 29,480. Thus every $Pythagoras_i$ will differ from every other $Pythagoras_i$, at least in his teaching hours. Indeed, every $Pythagoras_i$ will differ from every other $Pythagoras_i$ in respect of countless predicates. For if time 'flows equably' along, independently of events, then t_x^1 is distinct from t_x^2; and '. . . is *F* at t_x^1' is a distinct predicate from '. . . is *F* at t_x^2'. Thus the theory of Eternal Recurrence does not lead to (3), nor to immortality.

'Absolute' time does not, of course, entail that Eternal Recurrence does not offer a hope of immortality: we may, I suppose, find some reason for identifying $Pythagoras_1$ and $Pythagoras_2$—perhaps $Pythagoras_2$ experiences a succession of otherwise inexplicable *déjà vus*;[54] and on the strength of that we might affirm that '. . . teaches at 520 BC' and '. . . teaches at AD 29,480' do in fact apply to the same person. The argument adduced in the last paragraph only exhibits a weakness in the reasoning for immortality; it does not provide an argument against immortality.

XXIII

Conduct Unbecoming

(a) *Antiphon and moral anarchy*

According to Aristotle, Socrates invented moral philosophy. Aristotle is hardly fair; for if the moral views associated with the earlier Presocratics are scanty and somewhat unstimulating, the men of the fifth century were much given to ethical speculations. The fragments of the Sophists and of Democritus, and the plays of Euripides, testify to a widespread and excited interest in moral matters; and that interest extended beyond the desire to preach or to enrage, and exhibited an admirable tendency to tunnel and to probe. The testimony is rich and my treatment in this chapter will be partial and selective. I choose two main topics, moral nihilism and systematic ethics—the former associated with the Sophists, the latter with Democritus. And I divide my first topic into three parts: moral anarchism; moral relativism; and moral irresponsibility.

In the nineteenth century the Sophists were generally denounced as immoral charlatans, teaching vice for cash, corrupting the minds and bodies of the young, and leading Athens (or Greece as a whole) into a dank cesspool of iniquity. Against that charge George Grote protested, in a celebrated chapter of his *History of Greece*: 'I know,' he wrote, 'few characters in history who have been so hardly dealt with as these so-called Sophists'; and in twenty brilliant pages he portrayed Protagoras and his crew in the implausible disguise of Victorian moralists, stern and upright men, educators, the ethical leaders of the Greek enlightenment. Grote had some right on his side: the pious homily of Prodicus' *Choice of Heracles* (**84 B 2**) can now be matched by the banalities of the 'Anonymus Iamblichi' (**89 A 1**), of which Grote knew nothing. But Grote overstated his case: the performances of Thrasymachus in the *Republic* and of Callicles in the

Gorgias; the speeches in Thucydides' Mytilenean debate and in his Melian dialogue (III. 37–48; V. 84–111); and the *agôn* between Just and Unjust *Logos* in the *Clouds*, are evidence enough of that.

Yet all that is philosophically uninteresting: the Sophists may have been demon kings or Prince Charmings, they may have preached sobriety or sin; I do not greatly care. This chapter is concerned with questions of a more theoretical nature: did the Sophists propound any general accounts of ethics? and if so, to what extent and in what direction might those accounts have influenced their substantive ethical judgments? If we have no complete theory of ethics from a Sophist's hand, we do possess three substantial pieces, each of which has been supposed to offer some general reflexions on ethics, and each of which has been suspected of immoral tendencies.

The first passage belongs to Antiphon. Of Antiphon's life nothing is known. Indeed, there is a standing dispute, of antique origin (Hermogenes, **87 A 2**), over precisely how many men Antiphon was. We hear of Antiphon the Sophist, who wrote *On Truth*; we possess speeches by the orator, Antiphon of Rhamnous; there is Antiphon the tragedian; and Antiphon the interpreter of dreams. There is no decisive evidence telling for or against the identification of any two, of any three, or of all four of these men; nor is the question of great moment.

The passage in question comes from Antiphon's *On Truth*. Its three parts, preserved on papyrus, were discovered at Oxyrhynchus and published in 1915 and 1922; I translate them in the order in which they are printed in Diels-Kranz, where they figure as **88 B 44**; for convenience I number them separately.[1]

. . . justice . . . consists in not I
transgressing the regulations (*nomima*) of
the state in which you are a citizen.
Hence a man will deal with justice in the way most
advantageous to himself if in the
presence of witnesses he holds the laws
high, and when isolated from witnesses the
dictates of nature (*ta tês phuseôs*). For the dictates of
the laws are imposed (*epitheta*), those
of nature necessary; and those of the
laws are agreed and not grown (*phunta*),
those of nature grown not agreed. Hence II
if in transgressing the regulations you escape
the notice of those who have made the agreement, you are
free of shame and of penalty; but

not if you do not escape notice. But if
para to dunaton you violate any
of the things which are connate with nature,
then if you escape the notice of all men,
the ill is no less; and if everyone sees, it
is no greater; for you are harmed not
in opinion but in truth. The
inquiry is for the sake of all these things,
because most of what is legally just
is inimical to nature: laws
have been made for the eyes, telling them
what they must see and what they must not; and III
for the ears, what they must hear and what they
must not; and for the tongue, what it must
say and what it must not; and for the hands,
what they must do and what they must not; and for
the feet, where they must go and where they must
not; and for the mind, what it must
desire and what not. 'On the contrary, by nature the things
these laws turn us from are no dearer or more
appropriate than the things they turn
us towards. For living and dying
belong to nature; and living is among
what is advantageous, dying among what
is not advantageous.' But of things advantageous IV
those laid down by the laws are chains,
those laid down by nature are free. Well, it is not true,
by a right account, that what pains
benefits nature more than what delights;
nor would what grieves be more
advantageous than what gives pleasure; for
what is truly advantageous cannot
harm but must benefit. Thus what is by
nature advantageous. . . . . . . and those V
who having suffered defend themselves and do not
themselves initiate action; and those who behave
well to their parents even if they are bad
to them; and those who allow others to tender an
oath but do not tender an oath themselves. And of the
things I have recounted you will find many
inimical to nature; and in them there
is the suffering of more pain when it is possible
to suffer less, and the getting of less pleasure when

it is possible to get more, and being treated
badly when it is possible not to be treated so.
Now if for those who submit to such things there
came any help from the laws, and
for those who do not submit but oppose them, some
penalty, then obedience to the laws would not be VI
unbeneficial; but in fact it seems that
the justice that derives from law is not
adequate to help those who submit to such
things; for, first, it allows the sufferer
to suffer and the agent to act, and it does
not there and then prevent the sufferer from
suffering or the agent from acting. (?) And
when it is referred to punishment, it
is no more partial to the sufferer than to the
agent(?); (?)for he must persuade those who
will administer punishment that he suffered, and
requires the power to win the case (?). And
these same things are left for the agent,
to deny. . . (**448**).

. . . we praise and honour; but those from II
a family that is not noble we neither
praise nor honour. And in this we
have become barbarians towards one another,
since by nature we are all in all respects similarly
adapted to be either barbarians or Greeks.
(?) We may consider this in the case of natural things,
which are necessary to all men (?) . . .
. . . and in all these things none
of us is marked off, neither barbarian
nor Greek. For we all breathe into
the air by our mouths and noses . . . (**449**).

. . . since what is just seems to be good, I
testifying truly concerning one another is
deemed (*nomizetai*) to be just and no less
useful for the practices of men.
Now he who does this is not just, if
not wronging anyone unless you have
been wronged yourself is just; for it
is necessary for him who testifies, even if
he testifies truly, nevertheless in a

> way to wrong another. And it is probable that he himself will be wronged later on. For this is possible, in so far as the man he testified against is condemned because of the things he testified to, and loses either his money or his life because of someone he in no way wronged. In this way, then, he wrongs the man he testifies against, because he wrongs someone who has not wronged him; and he himself is wronged by the man he testified against because he is hated by him for testifying truly—and not only II
> by hatred, but also because for all his life he must guard against the man he testified against; for he stands as an enemy to him, ready to say and do whatever ill he can to him. Now these wrongs are evidently not inconsiderable, neither those which he himself suffers nor those which he commits. For it is not possible both for these things to be just and for neither wronging at all nor being wronged oneself to be just. But it is necessary that either the one set of things is just or both are unjust. And it seems that to condemn and to judge and to arbitrate, however things are settled, are not just; for benefiting some harms others. And in this those who are benefited are not wronged, but those who are harmed are wronged . . . (**450**).[2]

Modern commentators are distressed by these fragmentary opinions: on the one hand, they applaud the 'cosmopolitanism' of **449**; on the other hand, they are appalled at the 'moral anarchism' in **448** and **450**. The two opinions, nice and nasty, are united by a common prescription: Follow nature, *phusis*; do not follow law or convention, *nomos*. Social and racial discord is based on conventional artifice: abandon convention and you enjoy the cosmopolitan harmony of nature. Ordinary morality is based on law and etiquette:

abandon convention and you may luxuriate in an advantageous immorality.

I have nothing to say about **449**: I suppose that it represents Antiphon's own views; and I suppose that Antiphon means to urge the claims of *phusis* above those of *nomos*. In that case, Antiphon becomes the father of what is surely the silliest of all arguments in political philosophy (a subject where folly spreads like bindweed, choking the few weak shoots of truth): 'By nature all men are equal; hence all men deserve equal treatment.' The evidently false premiss of natural egalitarianism yields, by an evidently invalid inference, the absurdity of moral egalitarianism. But more than one interpretation of **449** is possible; and we are not obliged to file a paternity suit for that argument against Antiphon.

The connexion between **448** and **450**—and between them and **449**—is quite uncertain: the papyrus gives no technical answer; and the content of the fragments does not help.[3] I shall therefore treat **448** and **450** in relative isolation, beginning with **448**.

448 divides into three main sections: first, I.6–II.23 argues that it is in a man's interest to obey the regulations in public and to follow nature when he can do so unobserved; then II.23–V.24 urges that the regulations normally show themselves inimical to nature; and finally V.25–VI.33 remarks that the regulations do not offer the advantages they pretend to. Antiphon uses '*nomima* (regulations)' and '*nomoi* (laws)' interchangeably: both terms, I take it, refer not just to the enactments of the legislature, but generally to the rules and customs, whether legally or socially sanctioned, by which any communal life is ordered. To follow the *nomima* is to conform, to do the done thing. By '*phusis*' Antiphon intends, primarily at least, human nature (cf. II.11). Among the constituents of human nature are certain desires, wants, longings and yearnings: to follow 'nature', or to obey 'the dictates of nature (*ta tês phuseôs*)' is to act on those natural inclinations: crudely, it is to do what you want to do.

Many scholars find in **448** an injunction or recommendation to 'follow nature' and to disregard the regulations, so long as you can do so with impunity: 'Join me, and do what's natural: play, and laugh, and think nothing is wrong' (Aristophanes, *Clouds* 1078). Other scholars, eager to clear Antiphon of so foul a crime, say that the thesis advanced in I.6–II.23 is not advanced *in propria persona*; rather, it represents a view which Antiphon is concerned to refute. That has no foundation in Antiphon's text; and in any case the suggestion that Antiphon is offering an immoral injunction is groundless: there is no word of injunction or recommendation in **448**; Antiphon does not say 'Follow nature when you can get away with it'; he asserts, as a statement of fact and not as a suggestion for action, that if you do follow nature and get away with it you will act in your own interest.[4]

Antiphon offers an argument for his statement: it is advantageous to follow your natural inclinations, because if you ignore them 'you are harmed not in opinion (*dia doxan*) but in truth' (II.21; i.e., 'you will surely be harmed, for the harm does not depend simply upon the beliefs which other men have about your action'). Thus the whole argument of I.23–II.26 runs as follows: 'Suppose ϕing is against the customs or laws; suppose that you want to ϕ; and suppose that you can ϕ unobserved. If you do not ϕ, you violate the dictates of your nature. But those dictates are "necessary (*anankaia*)" (I.26; i.e., it is not up to men to decide what they shall want and when) and they are inborn (*phunta*: I.32); consequently, the penalties attached to their violation are necessary and inborn, and "you are harmed . . . in truth" whether your law-abiding course is overt or covert. If, on the other hand, you do ϕ, you will violate a dictate of custom. Now such dictates are "imposed" and "agreed" (i.e., it is up to men to decide what acts shall be allowed by *nomos* and what forbidden). Hence the penalties they threaten depend on detection; and an undetected piece of ϕing is harmless.' The argument is clear and correct: if I can get away without paying my income tax, it is to my advantage to do so. If I do not pay, I suffer no harm, and gain the advantage of extra cash; if I do pay, I am harmed in truth, for my natural desire not to waste my substance is frustrated.

The second part of **448** runs from II.23 to V.24. Suppose that all *nomima* are in fact in line with nature: then, though it is still in my interest to follow nature when I can, the fact has no bite; for following nature and following *nomima* lead to the same actions. Antiphon shows that the supposition is false by arguing that 'most of what is legally just is inimical to nature' (II.26). 'Law,' as Hippias says in the *Protagoras,* 'is a tyrant of men and violates nature in many ways' (337D = **86 C 1**). Again, Antiphon has hold of a sober truth; he is not counselling anarchy but reporting a fact about the relation between law and nature: the purpose of a large part of the law and of many social customs is to curtail the exercise of natural desire; *nomima* would lose their point if they never clashed with *phusis*.

That truth is stated, in roundly rhetorical terms, at II.23–III.17, and repeated, with a different type of example, at IV.30–V.24. The intervening passage, III.17–IV.30, is obscure; I tentatively suggest that it first states and then answers an objection to Antiphon's truth: *me*]*n oun* at III.17 introduces the objection, and *de* at IV.2 the reply. Objection: '*Nomima* not only discourage, they also promote; and what they promote is just as advantageous to us as what they discourage; e.g., by discouraging murder they promote life.' Reply: '*Nomima*, even where they seem advantageous, are chains on our nature; they therefore involve pain, and things that pain us are not more advantageous than things that give us pleasure.' The reply is feeble; for surely the pain or frustration we suffer by having our liberty chained is outweighted by the advantage we gain from chaining the liberty of other human tigers?

The third part of **448** answers just that point. The tigers pounce with impunity: the law cannot prevent their pouncing; at best it will punish them after they have pounced; and punishment is far from certain if the tigers have honeyed tongues. Is that true? Or rather, was it true in Athens in the last quarter of the fifth century? I do not know; but Antiphon was in a better position to tell than we are.

448 thus argues that *nomima* are not advantageous to those who obey them: almost always, obedience will involve a frustration of natural inclinations; and the bonds of the social contract are not tight enough to constrain the determined criminal. What is the moral? We cannot tell: perhaps, as some believe, Antiphon was out to urge 'natural' behaviour; perhaps, as others assert, he wanted a reform of the laws in order to bring the balance of advantage down on the side of the just.[5] Perhaps he offered his observations with no practical recommendation in mind: his book, after all, is *On Truth*; it was not primarily a practical tract.

450 contains a clear and self-contained argument: men generally think *both* that it is unjust to wrong someone who has not wronged you, *and* that it is just to tell the truth in the witness box. Antiphon correctly points out that those two views will lead to conflict when, as often happens, truthful witnesses who have been unharmed send crooks to jail. And he correctly adds that in such circumstances the just witness may put himself in danger.

The verb 'wrong' translates '*adikein*', which literally means 'treat unjustly'. A defender of the general opinion might say that bearing true witness against a man cannot be a case of *adikein*: a witness may 'wrong' someone in the sense of harming him; but he cannot 'wrong' him in the sense of treating him unjustly. But that defence will not do; for if 'wrong' is construed as 'treat unjustly', then the first of the two general opinions is reduced to a tautology: 'It is unjust to treat a man unjustly unless he has treated you unjustly'. The opinion was plainly meant in a non-tautological sense: 'You should not act against a man's interests unless he has acted against yours'. That, I suppose, sounds like a decent moral principle. And Antiphon proves it untenable.

450 talks a lot about justice; and justice is mentioned in **448**. Many scholars feel that justice is the central concern of the fragments, thus: 'At I.6, **448** defines justice as obedience to the rules of society; at II.20, **450** defines justice as not wronging those who have not wronged you. The function of **448** is to reduce the legalistic account of justice to absurdity; the function of **450** is to substitute a moral account; and the overall aim of the two passages is the establishment of a sound theory of justice.'

I fear that will not wash. There is no definition of justice in **450**: II.20 merely offers the thesis that it is unjust to harm those who have not harmed you; and (if I am right) it implies that we should reject the thesis. There is no suggestion that **450** replaces views dismantled in **448**, and there is no suggestion in **448** that the definition of justice given at I.6 is absurd. **448** does offer a definition of justice; but the definition was a commonplace. It is reflected in Euripides and in Lysias; it was advanced approvingly by Xenophon's Socrates, and Aristotle recognizes it as giving one of the senses of 'just'.[6] In Antiphon's fragment it is neither new nor shocking; and it plays no role in the development of his argument: **448** argues that illegal and irregular conduct may be advantageous, and we may infer that unjust conduct may be advantageous; but Antiphon does not make the inference for us, and he cannot have felt it of great importance.

Fragments **448–50** of Antiphon contain the earliest essay written in the light of the distinction between *nomos* or convention and *phusis* or nature. To accept that distinction does not imply a preference for *phusis* and a leaning to anarchism: Antiphon's *Truth*, so far as I can see, contains no moral or political recommendations at all. It is, in part, a sociological work; but not even a sociologist need preach distasteful doctrines—for he need not preach at all.

(b) *The* Dissoi Logoi *and moral relativism*

The definition of justice, which Antiphon treats so lightly, can be used to promote a view more vigorous than anything he professed. Swiftly and fatally, the argument runs thus: 'What is just is what is *nomimon*; *nomima* are human creations, and vary from one culture and country to another: hence justice—and, in general, morality—is a relative thing.' The first premiss of the argument was a fifth-century commonplace; the second premiss was a familiar truth, classically illustrated by the experiment of Darius (Herodotus, III.38); and the conclusion seems to give the deathblow to morality.

> [Archelaus, Anaxagoras' pupil] composed a *Physiology* and believed that the just and ugly are so not by nature (*phusei*) but by custom (*nomôi*) (**451**: Suda, **60 A 2**).

Here we have the first appearance of the fatal argument. Aristophanes makes comic use of its elements: Pheidippides is proposing to beat his father, Strepsiades:

> STR: But it's nowhere the custom (*nomizetai*) for a father to suffer this.
>
> PH: Wasn't the person who first laid down this custom (*nomos*) a man, like you and me? And didn't he persuade the men of old by making a speech? Then is it any less possible for *me* now to lay down a new custom for sons—to beat their fathers back? (*Clouds* 1420–4).

And Plato spells the argument out: 'And about political things too—things fine and ugly, just and unjust, holy and the reverse—whatever any city thinks to be and lays down as lawful (*nomima*) for itself actually is so in truth for it; and in these matters no individual is any wiser than any other, and no city than any other. But on the question of laying down what is advantageous or not advantageous to it, here if anywhere it will agree that one counsellor is better than another and that the judgment of one city is better with regard to truth than that of another. And it would not dare to say that whatever a city thinks to be and lays down as advantageous to itself will actually be advantageous to it come what may. But in the case I am talking about—the case of the just and unjust, the holy and unholy—they want to insist that none of them has by nature any substance of its own, but that what is communally judged to be the case actually comes to be the case at the time when it is so judged and for as long as it is so judged' (*Theaetetus*, 172AB; cf. *Laws* 889E).

Plato ascribes the argument to Protagoras, and the *Theaetetus* here is sometimes taken to provide genuine Protagorean doctrine.[7] But it occurs at the end of Socrates' long and plainly unhistorical 'defence' of Protagoras; and the doctrine it expounds is not, in fact, very closely connected with Protagoras' epistemological relativism (see below, pp. 545–53). To discover a Sophistic expression of moral relativism we must turn to the *Dissoi Logoi*.

The *Dissoi Logoi* or *Double Accounts* is a strange document. An anonymous piece of some dozen pages, written in an odd dialect by a talentless author, it somehow became attached to the text of Sextus, and so survived along with his works. It is generally dated to about 400 BC;[8] and it is therefore supposed to breathe, in a puerile way, the air of Sophistic Athens. It is a contemporary document on the workings of the Sophistic movement, the more interesting in that it reflects a feeble layman's apprehension of things.

The work is divided into nine sections: 'On Good and Bad'; 'On Fine and Foul'; 'On Just and Unjust'; 'On True and False'; on the thesis that 'things are and are not'; 'On Wisdom and Virtue—whether they can be taught'; on the proper way of choosing state officials; on the relation between speech, knowledge and action; on memory. Some scholars think that the *Dissoi Logoi* is a compilation of two or more originally separate essays, and much effort has been expended in finding traces of the great Sophists in the work. The discussion is sadly inconclusive.[9] No less fruitless are the attempts to categorize the tract: is it a schoolboy's exercise? the notes of a pupil on his master's lectures? the lecture notes, or half-finished lecture, of the master himself? We cannot tell.

Section 1, on Good and Bad, opens thus:

> Double accounts are offered in Greece by those who philosophize about the good and the bad. For some say that the good is one thing, the bad another; others that they are the same—good for some, bad for others; and for the same man now good, now bad (**452: 90 A 1** §1).

First, the relativistic argument, that bad and good are the same, is offered (§§2–10); then the counter-argument, that good and bad are different, is produced (§§11–17). The author concludes:

> I do not say what the good is; but I attempt to teach this: that the bad and the good are not the same, but each is different[10] (**453**: §17).

The pattern of argument in sections 2, 3, and 4 is precisely analogous.

Here are samples of the relativistic arguments:

> Incontinence is bad for the incontinent, good for the sellers and hirers. Illness is bad for the sick, good for the doctors. Death is bad for the dead, good for the undertakers and funeral masons (**454: A 1** §3).

> For the Lacedaemonians it is fine for girls to exercise(?) without sleeves(?) and to walk about without tunics; for the Ionians it is foul. For the former it is fine for children not to learn music and letters; for the Ionians it is foul not to know all these things (**455: A 2** §§9–10).

> First I shall say that it is just to lie and to deceive. People would say that to do this to one's enemies [is fine and just], to do it [to one's friends] foul and wrong: [but how to one's enemies] but not to

> one's friends? Take your parents: if your father or your mother has to eat or swallow a medicine and doesn't want to, isn't it just to give it to them in their food or drink and to say that it is not there? Then it is [just] to lie to and deceive one's parents (**456: A 3** §§2–3).

All three ethical sections of the *Dissoi Logoi* begin by advancing a relativism; yet neither the author nor his modern commentators realize that three different relativisms are advanced. The relativist of section 1 in effect argues that '. . . . is good' is an incomplete predicate, elliptical for the overtly relational predicate '. . . is good for ——'. Goodness is understood as advantage: '*a* is good' means '*a* is advantageous'; and if we sometimes omit the *relatum* and say, simply, '*a* is advantageous', our saying always carries a tacit rider of the form 'for *b*'. Goodness is advantage; and advantage is relative in an obvious enough fashion. It follows that items and events cannot be divided up into the advantageous and the disadvantageous, the good and the bad: what is good for me is very likely bad for you, and vice versa. Everything advantageous is also disadvantageous; everything disadvantageous is also advantageous: in a word, 'the good and the bad are the same'.

The relativism of section 2 is less clear; but it probably intimates the thesis that '. . . is fine' is elliptical for '. . . is fine in culture——'. Sometimes, it is true, the relativist says that things seem (*dokei*) or are deemed (*nomizonti*) fine in certain cultures; but he does not distinguish between '*a* seems fine in *K*' and '*a* is fine in *K*'.

Section 3 does not imply that '. . . is just' is elliptical; rather, its message is that 'ϕing is always (un)just' is always false. Lying may be usually unjust, but it is sometimes just; returning a loan may be usually just, but it is sometimes unjust. 'The just and the unjust are the same' in a weaker sense: 'For any ϕ, some cases of ϕing are just if and only if some cases of ϕing are unjust.' Nothing is *both* just *and* unjust in the way in which some things, according to section 1, are *both* good *and* bad.

The author of the *Dissoi Logoi* produces a single line of argument against all his relativists. In the case of 'good' he gets nowhere:

> Tell me, have your parents ever done you any good?—Yes, many great goods.—Then you owe them many great evils, if the good is the same as the bad (**457: A 1** §12).

'*a* does *b* good; good and bad are the same: hence *a* does *b* evil.' The inference sounds right, but it ignores the proper meaning of 'good and bad are the same'; and it ignores the central fact that the relativist makes 'good' *relative*. The answer is a silly *ignoratio elenchi*.

That 'advantageous' is a relative term is plain; that 'good' means 'advantageous' is less clear. Yet I am inclined to let the relativist win on 'good': sometimes, at least, 'good' does seem to mean 'advantageous' or 'profitable'; when it has a different meaning it is likely to prove a synonym of 'fine (*kalon*)' or 'just (*dikaion*)'; so that the relativist of section 1 wins no significant victory unless he carries the day in sections 2 and 3 as well.

The author of the *Dissoi Logoi* fares no better in section 2: if fine and foul are the same, then

> In Lacedaemon it is fine for the girls to exercise, and in Lacedaemon it is foul for the girls to exercise (**458: A 2** §25).

That, again, is a mere *ignoratio elenchi*. But he almost grasps a better retort: answering the relativist claim that 'to wear ornaments and make-up and gold bangles is foul for a man, fine for a woman' (§6), he says that 'if it is fine for a woman to wear ornaments, then it is foul for a woman to wear ornaments, if foul and fine are the same' (§24). A neat point can be extracted from that clumsy remark: the relativist claims that 'ϕing is fine' is elliptical for 'ϕing is fine in *K*'; his opponent asserts that ϕing is fine in *K* if and only if ϕing-in-*K* is fine; and this latter use of 'is fine' is not elliptical. For women to parade naked is fine—'in Lacedaemon'. Then for women in Lacedaemon to parade naked is fine *tout court*. Culture may determine what is fine and what is foul; but the concepts of fineness and foulness are not culture-relative. The difference sounds small but is considerable: it is one thing to say that the *contents* of our value judgments must always refer to some culture, so that 'When in Rome do as the Romans do' becomes the supreme recommendation; it is quite another to claim that our judgments *themselves* are logically culture-bound, that we can no more talk of 'fine *simpliciter*' than we can of 'advantageous *simpliciter*'.

The relativist may fight the equation of 'ϕing is fine in *K*' with 'ϕing-in-*K* is fine'. An educated but prudish Athenian will know that naked female sport is fine in Sparta but will deny that naked female sport in Sparta is fine; and the same Athenian may hold that slave revolts in Sparta are fine without holding that such things are fine in Sparta. But in making this case, the relativist destroys himself; for he allows a non-elliptical use of '. . . is fine'. The Athenian does not deny that naked female sport in Sparta is fine *in Sparta*—he knows that to be true; nor does he deny that naked female sport in Sparta is fine *in some other culture*—for no other culture lays down canons for *Spartan* behaviour. What the Athenian denies is that naked female sport is fine, *simpliciter*. And that, I think, crumples the culture relativist: it is simply an error to maintain that 'fine' is an elliptical term, expandable to 'fine in culture *K*'.

The relativist of section 3 is an Aristotelian: 'We shall speak adequately if we are as clear as the subject matter allows; for rigour (*to akribes*) is not to be sought in all accounts alike any more than in all products of craft. And the fine and the just, about which political science inquires, contain great differences and divergences, so that they seem to exist by custom alone and not by nature. And good things too contain such a divergence because harm comes to many people from them (for men have died before now on account of riches, and others on account of bravery). Thus we must be content in arguing about such matters and from such principles to show the truth roughly and in outline—in arguing about what is for the most part and from such principles, to conclude in such a way too' (*EN* 1094b11–22). The details of that celebrated passage remain unclear; but its sophistic background is immediately discernible.

Aristotle seems to mean at least this: every sentence of the form 'ϕing is always wrong (right, just, unjust, fine, foul, good, bad, etc.)' is false. We can sometimes say, truly, 'For the most part, ϕing is wrong'; we can never say truly 'In all cases, ϕing is wrong'. And that is precisely the message of the relativist of the *Dissoi Logoi*: lying is not *always* wrong—it is all right to lie to your enemies; lying to your friends is not *always* wrong—it is all right to lie to your parents in order to get them to drink their medicine. No doubt lying is normally wrong; but it is not *always* so. And neither is anything else.

The view can be given a weak or a strong construction. Weakly, it points out that all the customary moral injunctions we daily parrot (Tell the truth, Be kind to your mother, and Brush your teeth after meals) allow exceptions. They are at best rules of thumb, not universally binding laws. That is, I take it, indubitably true; and since people, even philosophers, are sometimes extraordinarily rule-bound, there is something to be said for proclaiming the truth from time to time. From a pedagogic point of view, moral injunctions need to be neat and snappy; and if we issue and accept them with a pinch of salt or a *hôs epi to polu* we shall not do or suffer much harm. But only wretchedness or hypocrisy can result from taking universally and defending rigorously those nursery-room saws which constitute the rough bedrock of our moral beliefs.

A stronger interpretation, however, is surely intended both by Aristotle and by the *Dissoi Logoi* relativist: *every* universal moral judgment—not merely every simple moral saw—is, strictly speaking, false; for *all* ϕ, it is not the case that ϕing is always M (where M is any moral predicate). Moral education, according to some modern philosophers, consists in a progressive refinement and sophistication of our first crude and general moral principles: I reject 'Do not kill' in favour of 'Do not kill except in time of war'; that yields to 'Do not kill except in time of war, and then only kill combatants'; and so on. According to the Aristotelian doctrine, that process of education is incompletable: however complex and refined your moral principles may be, they are (strictly speaking) false; they may be replaced by other principles yet more complex and yet more refined, but the replacements will still be false.

The *Dissoi Logoi* rejects the view:

> That stealing your enemies' goods is just proves that that very thing is unjust too, if their account is true (**459: A 3** §16).

That again is an *ignoratio elenchi*; but it hides a clever point: the relativist, attacking the naive thesis that stealing is always wrong, must specify his exceptions to the rule; he must produce a thesis of the form 'Stealing in circumstances C is right'. But such a thesis is, according to the very view he is trying to advance, inevitably false: in arguing for his case, the relativist disproves it. The argument is clever but unsatisfactory: the relativist need only emend his exception clause to read 'Stealing in circumstances C is, at least sometimes, right'. However that may be, the Aristotelian relativist has, so far as I can see, no good argument for his position: in the *Dissoi Logoi* he simply claims to be able to find an exception to any moral generalization; the claim is illustrated by simple cases, and there is no reason at all to believe that every generalization can be so punctured. Aristotelians customarily talk of the 'infinite variety' of human circumstances: circumstances alter cases; and so many and so varied are the circumstances that no universal rule can govern them all. But circumstances, if varied, are not infinitely varied; nor is it clear that all their variations are of moral import. Rules must certainly be complicated; but nothing has yet shown that they are impossible.

These programmatic remarks do not exhaust the question: no doubt more can be said in favour of Aristotelianism. And more should be said; for if the theory is correct, its implications for morals, and for moral reasoning, are serious. The 'relativism' of section 3 of the *Dissoi Logoi* is the most interesting and the most dangerous of the Sophistic relativisms.

(c) *Gorgias and moral irresponsibility*

> A certain athlete accidentally struck Epitimos the Pharsalian with a javelin and killed him; and he [sc. Pericles] spent the whole day with Protagoras puzzling over whether, in the strictest account, one should hold responsible (*aitios*) for the accident the javelin or the thrower rather than the organizers of the games (**460**: Plutarch, **80 A 10**).

The story may be apocryphal; but issues of responsibility were certainly discussed and debated in Athens, a city where litigation was a popular hobby. Indeed, the second *Tetralogy* of Antiphon contains four speeches, two prosecuting, two defending, devoted to the very case that Protagoras allegedly debated with Pericles. A boy was practising the javelin; as he hurled it, another youth ran across the stadium, and was transfixed and killed. Who, Antiphon's speeches ask, was responsible (*aitios*) for the youth's death?

The English word 'responsible' is slippery: '*aitios*' in Greek is anointed with the same oil. Sometimes in saying of someone that he is responsible for a certain state of affairs, we mean to hand out blame: calling someone responsible is calling him guilty. '*Aitia*', according to Liddell and Scott, means '*responsibility*, mostly in the bad sense, guilt, blame, or the imputation thereof, i.e. *accusation*'. ('Haig was responsible for the slaughter at Paaschendaele'; 'The conductor is responsible for the ragged violin entries'.) Sometimes we use 'responsible' more generously, to saddle someone not with blame, but with a liability to be blamed: by saying 'he is responsible for so and so', we mean that any moral, political, aesthetic or other evaluation of so and so should be laid at his door, whether for good or for ill. ('Haig was responsible for the strategy on the Western Front'; 'The conductor is responsible for the ensemble playing'.)

Again 'responsible' may impute agency: if *a* brought it about that *P*, then *a* is responsible for the fact that *P*. ('My cat is responsible for the holes in the lawn'; 'I am responsible for the broken plate'.) Or 'responsible' may indicate causation: inanimate objects, and events, may be responsible without being agents; and animate creatures can sometimes be causally responsible at one or more removes from agency. ('Bad weather is responsible for the poor batting averages this season'; 'His great-grandfather is responsible for his Habsburg profile'.) Thus '*a* is responsible for *X*' may be used to pick out *a* as an agent or cause, and it may be used to blame *a* or to mark *a* as an appropriate object of appraisal: the phrase has a causal and an evaluative use.

It is easy to think that the evaluative and the causal uses are co-extensive, that I am causally responsible if and only if I am evaluatively responsible; and there is, of course, a close connexion between causal and evaluative responsibility: standardly, 'he is responsible' holds evaluatively only if it holds causally, and vice versa. But that is not always so: vicarious and collective responsibility yield cases in which the evaluatively responsible are not causally responsible (parents must pay their children's debts; the orchestra fails if the horns alone are out of tune); accidents and flukes yield cases in which the causally responsible are not evaluatively responsible (I knocked the jug off the window-sill, but liability for blame attaches to the fool who put it there; I won the rubber by making three no trumps, but the contract was made by way of an inadvertent squeeze).

It is easy to confuse the two uses of 'responsible'. Antiphon's defence counsel does so: he wishes to show that his unfortunate client is guiltless and not a suitable subject for blame and punishment, that he is not morally *aitios*. But he argues, bizarrely, that his client did not kill the youth at all (III.10; IV.4; cf. *Tetralogy* 3, II.6), that he is not causally *aitios*. The correct defence, that the boy is causally but not morally *aitios*, was apparently too subtle for Antiphon.

One sophistic document appears to deal *ex professo* and in philosophical depth with the issue of responsibility: Helen left her husband Menelaus and sailed to Troy with Paris, thereby launching a thousand ships and the Trojan War. The Greek poets liked to berate her for her indiscretions. Gorgias in his *Helen* sets out to defend her:

> I wish to give a certain reasoning (*logismos*) in my argument and so to remove responsibility (*aitia*) from her who has a bad repute and to remove stupidity from those who blame her by showing them up as liars and by proving the truth (**461: 82 B 11** §2).

Gorgias' defence has a lucid structure:

> She did what she did either by the wishes of Luck and the decision of the gods and the decrees of Necessity; or seized by force; or persuaded by arguments; or captured by love (**462**: §6).

Successive paragraphs argue that Helen bears no responsibility if her rape was due to the gods (§6), or to force (§7), or to persuasion (§§8–14), or to love (§§15–19):

> Then how can one think the blame of Helen just, who, if she did what she did either loved or persuaded by argument or seized by force or compelled by divine necessity, in any case escapes responsibility? (**463**: §20).

Gorgias ends his oration on a note of self-deprecation:

> I wished to write a speech that would be praise for Helen and a plaything (*paignion*) for myself (464: §21).

Scholars have disputed the seriousness of Gorgias' purpose: is his *paignion* a contribution to moral philosophy, or a rhetorical exercise? the expression of an intellectual position, or a clever speaker's exhibition piece?[11] We can hardly hope to answer the question: Gorgias' psychology is unknown to us, and his use of the term '*paignion*' signifies nothing. In any case, whatever Gorgias may have felt or intended, the *Helen* is the first detailed and challenging contribution to the vexed question of human responsibility; we may take Gorgias seriously whether or not he did so himself.

Nothing ties the argument of the *Helen* to its eponym: if the argument works at all, it lets every adulteress off the moral hook. Indeed, nothing really ties the argument to any particular type of action: if the argument works, it works for all agents and all actions, and no one is ever responsible for anything. I assume that Gorgias was himself aware, and intended his audience to be aware, of the general application of his argument. The speech, after all, is surely meant to shock; and no one is going to be shocked by an argument that applies only to an ancient and fictional delinquency.

Gorgias' argument relies on his fourfold classification of the springs of actions, and it cannot succeed unless that classification is exhaustive. I think that it is: if I ϕ, then either my ϕing was accidental (a fluke or quirk or freak occurrence) in which case it falls under 'divine necessity'; or my ϕing was forced upon me; or my ϕing was the result of thought, in which case I was 'persuaded by argument', my own or someone else's; or, finally, I ϕed impetuously, driven on by my feelings. No doubt many ϕings are complex in their causes, and will fall into more than one of these four categories; but no ϕing, I think, can miss all four pigeon-holes.

First, 'divine necessity': in this case, 'the responsibility must be assigned to Chance and God' (§6). Gorgias is confused: god and divine necessity are irrelevant (their place is in §7 under the heading of Force); and Chance cannot be ascribed responsibility at all. Yet many philosophers will find a serious truth behind Gorgias' confused façade: '. . . if it is a matter of pure chance that a man should act in one way rather than another, he may be free but he can hardly be responsible. And indeed, when a man's actions seem to us quite unpredictable, when, as we say, there is no knowing what he will do, we do not look upon him as a moral agent. We look upon him rather as a lunatic.'[12] Chance, as Gorgias says, removes responsibility.

Now if chance events are simply unintended events, then I may surely be both causally and morally responsible for what happens by chance. If I draw a bow at a venture and the arrow lands in your eye, you will plausibly hold me responsible for the event which I never intended; and if I affix a randomizing device to my bow, so that your transfixion is the immediate result of an uncaused event, you will again take me to task. Chance, *pace* Gorgias, does not in general exonerate. Yet clearly chance does somehow fight against responsibility. I suggest that the connexion is this: if I ϕ by chance, then I am responsible for ϕing only if I am responsible for bringing it about that I ϕ by chance. If I put myself, knowingly, in a position where chance will play a part, I bear responsibility for the effects of chance. Gorgias must, I think, allow that to be true; but he can immunize his position. Let him hold that if chance and chance alone plays a part in my ϕing, then I am in no sense responsible for ϕing.

That force (*bia*) excludes responsibility is a corner-stone of Aristotle's theory of responsibility (*EN* 1109b35–1110b17); and it is taken as axiomatic by modern moralists: what I am forced to do, I cannot help doing; what I cannot help doing, I am not responsible for doing. The argument seems impregnable; but it is ambiguous. One philosopher has argued thus: '. . . if the man points a pistol at my head, I may still choose to disobey him; but this does not prevent its being true that if I do fall in with his wishes he can legitimately be said to have compelled me. And if the circumstances are such that no reasonable person would be expected to choose the other alternative, then the action that I am made to do is not one for which I am held to be morally responsible.'[13] Force or compulsion, on this view, is consistent with choice; so that if I am forced to ϕ, I may still be causally responsible for ϕing. But I am not morally responsible. That seems wrong to me: the bank-clerk who opens the safe at pistol-point acts, I judge, with wisdom and prudence; in ascribing such virtues to him I am praising him (in a fairly mild way); and if I praise him, I deem him liable to praise and hence I deem him morally responsible. Had he refused to give in to the gunman I should have judged him foolhardy; and that judgment again presupposes responsibility. *Bia*, then, does not remove responsibility: it will, no doubt, affect our assessment of the agent, and it may cause us to think pity a more appropriate attitude than disapprobation; but to say that is to say nothing about responsibility.

Aristotle has a different view: 'A forced act (*biaion*) is one of which the principle is external [to the subject], being such that the agent or patient contributes nothing' (*EN* 1110a1–3). That is a contrived reading of '*bia*' or 'force': we *do* say that the bank-clerk was forced to open the safe, even though he did not 'contribute nothing' to the action; and so did the Greeks (e.g. *Odyssey* XXII.351). But the contrivance is intelligible and perhaps intelligent; and we may imagine that Gorgias adopted it. Given the contrivance, *bia* certainly removes causal responsibility. But even so, it does not remove moral responsibility; for the agent may be responsible for putting himself into the situation in which he is forced. (If a captain sails in spite of gale warnings and his ship founders, then he is responsible for the wreck even though it was brought about by *force majeure*.) We can, however, come to Gorgias' aid here in the same way as before: if *bia* and *bia* alone accounts for my ϕing, I am not responsible in either way for what I do.

I turn next to the fourth of Gorgias' arguments, leaving the third and most interesting to last. Gorgias claims that love is either 'a god, having the divine power of gods', or 'a human disease and an ignorance of the soul' (§19): in neither case is the victim of love to blame. He compares the action of love with that of fear:

> Some men on seeing fearful things have actually lost their present mind at the present time: thus fear extinguishes and expels thought (**465**: §17).

And he offers a psychological explanation of the effects of fear:

> We see, having the sight not that we wish but whatever chances; and through the sight the soul is actually moulded in its ways (**466**: §15).[14]

An easy generalization suggests itself: whenever we act from passion, we ourselves are not responsible; the object of passion strikes our senses; our senses directly move the soul; and the soul moves us. Thought (*to noêma*) is by-passed, and we are not involved essentially in the action. Gorgias does not say that the emotions always have this effect: 'many' and 'often', not 'all' and 'always', qualify his remarks in §§15–19; but where love and fear do not have these effects, thought has a place; and thought-induced acts fall to Gorgias' third argument.

Aristotle refers to the view that 'things pleasant and fine are compulsive (for they necessitate, being external)' (*EN* 1110b9–10). The view is found in Euripides: according to Jason 'Eros necessitated you [i.e. Medea] to save my body' (*Medea* 530–1); other tragic figures are 'conquered' against their will (fr. 220), for 'Aphrodite cannot be borne if she comes in force' (*Hippolytus* 443) and sometimes 'anger is stronger than my plans' (*Medea* 1079). Aristotle will have none of that. His arguments are on the whole pretty feeble (1110b9–15, 1111a24–b3), but his final comment deserves quotation: 'Irrational passions seem nonetheless to belong to the man, so that the actions done from anger and desire are the man's; hence it is absurd to make them involuntary' (1111b1–3). Euripides, in one passage, concurs:

> We know and recognize the good
> but do not do it—some through indolence,
> some preferring some other pleasure to the fine (*Hippolytus* 380–3).

What the *Medea* rhetorically ascribes to anger, the *Hippolytus* honestly attributes to the angry man: the passions through which we act 'belong to the man', they are *our* passions; and if they are ours, it is we who are responsible for actions done through them. Gorgias says that 'it was love which did all these things' (§15); but that is simply to say that it was the infatuated Helen who did them and was responsible for doing them. 'Love did it' is not incompatible with 'The lover did it'; on the contrary, the two sentences mean the same.

Aquinas develops the Aristotelian view. Actions done from fear, he says 'are, if one considers it rightly, rather voluntary than involuntary' (*Summa Theologiae* 1a 2ae 6.6 resp.); and 'we should say that lust does not cause the involuntary but rather makes something voluntary; for something is called voluntary from the fact that the will is carried towards it; and by lust the will inclines to willing that which is lusted after' (ibid. 6.7 resp.). Fear does not remove responsibility; lust only adds to it. But Aquinas allows a relaxation of his hard doctrine: 'if lust totally removes knowledge, as happens in those who become lunatic because of lust, it follows that lust removes the voluntary' (ibid. 6.7 *ad* 3); and the same, surely applies to those paralysed by terror. Love sometimes is 'unbearable'; and the strength of our emotions—or the power of their inevitable physical manifestations—may close to us all paths of action but one. Sometimes emotion overpowers us; and if that is so, and if we are not responsible for getting ourselves into that unfortunate situation, then (I suppose) we are not morally responsible for our passionate actions. Sometimes, at least, lovers and cowards, Casanova and Falstaff, are not to be blamed or praised.

So far I have endeavoured to defend Gorgias: deeds done exclusively by chance, or exclusively by force, or exclusively by passion, are not to be held against their perpetrator. But a vast range of actions remains; and if Gorgias' argument is to succeed, they must all fall under the third of his categories: persuasion. In §8, 'the sophist now enters his temple—we reach the very marrow of the pamphet';[15] *logos*, the rhetorical sophist's engine and delight, is 'a great potentate (*megas dunastês*)' (§8), and if it 'persuaded and deceived' Helen, then evidently she bears no responsibility for her actions;

> For the *logos* which persuaded, compelled the soul it persuaded both to obey what was spoken and to approve what was done (467: §12).

Logos is comparable to *bia* (§12);[16] it works on the soul as drugs work on the body (§14).

Gorgias refers to deceit, to falsehood, to persuasion; and it is customary to construe his remarks as bearing properly upon his own craft: §§8–14 argue that if Helen was deceived by a lying speech, she was not responsible for her betrayal of Menelaus. That construe gives sense to §§ 8–14, but removes all sense from the *Helen* as a whole; for it leaves open and untouched the evident possibility that Helen thought out and decided upon her betrayal by herself. The 'persuasive *logos*' is not just the wily speech of the professional orator, and the references to deception and falsity are inessential. *Logos* covers any ratiocination; and Gorgias means that if Helen was influenced by argument, then she was not responsible for her acts. Thus rationally explicable actions, the only type of act not embraced by §6, §7, or §§15–19, are stigmatized as irresponsible.

Gorgias is utterly correct in calling *logos* a *megas dunastês*; and his illustrations of the power of *logos* are apt and true. Yet how does the *logos* remove responsibility from the logical agent? To answer that question we must bring out a skeleton which has long been rattling its bones in the cupboard, the skeleton of causal determinism. Suppose that a ϕs, or Helen runs to Troy. Then, Gorgias assumes, there is some true proposition of the form 'b brings it about that a ϕs' or 'b brings it about that Helen runs to Troy'. If b brings it about that a ϕs, then b is causally responsible for a's ϕing; and if a is not causally responsible for his ϕing then he is not morally responsible either. Now a survey of the possible springs of action yields just four types of substituend for x in 'x brings it about that a ϕs': chance, a constraining agent, *logos*, passion. In every case, a, the ϕer, and b, the cause of a's ϕing, are distinct: b is causally responsible for a's ϕing; b is distinct from a; hence a is not causally responsible for a's ϕing; hence a is not morally responsible. Suppose that Helen read *Lady Chatterley's Lover* and was impressed by its argument: then the argument was causally responsible for Helen's flight; and Helen was guiltless.

In the cases of chance, force, and emotion it is possible to defend Gorgias' stance; I can find no defence for the case of *logos*. Moreover—and this is the important point—the general line of argument which Gorgias relies on is fatally flawed. Gorgias assumes that we can always find a cause for *a*'s ϕing; he argues that we can always find a cause for *a*'s ϕing distinct from *a*; he tacitly assumes that if there is a cause of *a*'s ϕing distinct from *a*, then *a* did not cause his own ϕing; and he implies that if *a* is not causally responsible for his ϕing then he is not morally responsible either. The schema is plausible; but we should not succumb to its attractions. I allow that if *a* ϕs then for some *x* distinct from *a* *x* brings it about that *a* ϕs. But I deny, first, that this entails that *a* does not bring it about that he ϕs: if *x* is *a*'s lust, say, then if *x* brings it about that *a* ϕs, *a* brings it about that *a* ϕs. And further I deny that causal irresponsibility entails moral irresponsibility.

Gorgias' *paignion* fails. Yet it is a signal piece of philosophy: it introduces the problem of determinism to moral philosophy; and it anticipates, *in nuce*, many of the bad arguments subsequently advanced with such force and at such length by the passionate opponents of human freedom.

(d) *Democritean ethics*

Of the three hundred surviving fragments of Democritus, some 220 are given to ethical matters.[17] Such an unparalleled treasury raises high hopes: we may surely expect to discover a systematic moral philosophy in Democritus; and to discern a close connexion between his moral and his physical philosophies. Both hopes will be dashed; yet it is worth briefly conning the fragments in order to see why and to what extent that is so. I begin with the quest for an ethical system.

> If anyone attends intelligently to these maxims (*gnômai*) of mine, he will do many things worthy of a good man and he will leave undone many bad things (**468: 68 B 35**).

The key word is '*gnômê*': the vast majority of Democritus' ethical fragments are maxims, brief and pithy sayings of an exhortatory and moralistic nature:

> He who chooses the goods of the soul chooses the more divine; he who chooses those of the body, the human (**383: B 37**).

> It is fine to prevent a wrongdoer; if not, not to do wrong with him (**469: B 38**).

> One should either be or imitate a good man (**470: B 39**).

Some of the maxims are, as it were, potentially interesting: thus Democritus stresses the moral importance of the will:

> It is not refraining from wrong-doing, but not even wishing it that is good (**471: B 62**; cf. **B 68, B 89, B 96**);

and he anticipates a doctrine of the 'mean':

> In everything the equal is fine: excess and deficiency do not seem so to me (**472: B 102**; cf. **B 233**).

And he sometimes shows a flash of wit:

> To speak sparingly is an adornment for a woman; and sparingness in adornment is a fine thing (**473: B 274**).

Most of the *gnômai* are trite,[18] but some reveal an idiosyncratic judgment: Democritus dislikes sex (**B 32**) and would not indulge in procreation (**B 275**: cf. Antiphon, **87 B 49**). His political pronouncements, whether or not they reveal a democratic inclination,[19] show him a severe and uncompromising judge; e.g., **B 260:**

> Anyone who kills any cutpurse or pirate, whether by his own hand, by ordering it or by voting for it, let him be free of penalty (**474**).

In his collection of *gnômai* we may perhaps discern a consistent outlook, but we shall look in vain for a systematic ethics.

> Many live in accordance with *logos* although they have not learned *logos* (**475: B 53**).

Perhaps the *gnômai* are guides for the many, and a *logos*, or systematic account, was provided for the intellectual few?[20] Democritus did set up a *telos* or 'end' of life, a goal for human striving:

> The Abderites too teach that there is an end; Democritus, in his book on the end, makes it *euthumia* which he also called *euestô*. And he often adds: 'For pleasure and lack of pleasure is the boundary' (**476**: Clement, **B 4**).

The word '*telos*', though the doxographers repeat it (Diogenes Laertius IX.45 = **A 1**; Epiphanius, **A 166**), is probably not Democritean; but the notion is, as **B 189** shows.

Democritus gave his *telos* various names: it is *euthumia* and *euestô*; *athambia* (Cicero, **A 169**; cf. **B 215, B 216**) or *athaumastia* (Strabo, **A 168**) or *ataraxia* (Stobaeus, **A 167**); *harmonia* or *summetria* (Stobaeus, **A 167**); *eudaimonia* (Stobaeus, **A 167**). *Euthumia* ('good heartedness') and *euestô* ('well-being') give nothing away. *Athambia* and *athaumastia* ('lack of wonderment') and *ataraxia* ('tranquillity') indicate an Epicurean penchant for the quiet life, undisturbed either by the startings and starings of superstition or by the jolts and jostlings of practical activity. And *summetria* and *harmonia* point in the same direction:

> [He says that] *euthumia* is the end, not being the same as pleasure (as some wrongly interpret it) but a state in which the soul lives calmly and in a stable fashion, not disturbed by fear or superstition or any other passion (**477**: Diogenes Laertius, IX.45 = **A 1**).

The state is achieved by not engaging in much business, either private or public, and by not trying to exceed one's capacities (**B 3**); it depends on one's mental and psychological state and 'does not live in cattle or in gold' (**B 171**; cf. **B 170**); to reach it you 'must not take your pleasures in mortal things' (**B 189**). Above all, you must practise moderation (**B 191**).

All that is very dull and depressing; but we may find a little more joy in the suggestion that 'pleasure and lack of pleasure is the boundary' (**476**); or rather, that

> Pleasure and lack of pleasure is the boundary of the advantageous and the disadvantageous (**478: B 188**).

For we should

> Deem nothing pleasant unless it is advantageous (**479: B 74**).[21]

If pleasure as such is advantageous—indeed the only advantageous thing—it does not follow that we should recklessly pursue all pleasures:

> Inopportune pleasures produce displeasures (**480: B 71**),

and some pleasures produce wretchedness (*kakotês*: **B 178**). Bodily pleasures in particular are followed by 'many pains' (**B 235**), and we should become masters of sexual pleasure and not be slaves to women (**B 214**). Well-being depends on a wise discrimination among pleasures (Stobaeus, **A 167**). Observe moderation in joy (**B 191**), for

> Temperance increases the enjoyable and makes pleasure greater (**481: B 211**).

> Great joys come from contemplating fine works (**482: B 194**: noble deeds? or beautiful works of art?).

It follows that:

> One should choose not every pleasure but that which has the fine as its object (**483: B 207**).

And we should find our pleasures not in 'mortal things' (**B 189**) but rather in the joys of the mind (**B 146**).

> A life without festivity is a long road without an inn (**484: B 230**),

but Democritean festivity will be a fairly sober and earnestly intellectual business, a symposium rather than a pub-crawl.

All that amounts, I suppose, to a moderately coherent plan of life; and we may, if we wish, call it a practical system. Lovers of anachronism (among whom I happily enrol myself) may begin to think of a Benthamite Utilitarianism: if he did not invent and advocate a felicific calculus, at least Democritus prepared the way for one, and Bentham's great moral system was adumbrated at Abdera. But that suggestion is wholly mistaken: Democritus' hedonism has nothing at all to do with morality; it does not pretend to tell us what, morally speaking, we ought to do, or how to live the moral life. It is a recipe for happiness or contentment, not a prescription for goodness: the system sets up a selfish end for the individual and counsels him on how to attain it; it does not set up a moral goal and offer advice on its achievement. If Democritus' *gnômai* offer an unsystematic set of moral maxims, his reflexions on *euestô* offer no moral speculations at all; instead, they offer a systematic theory of prudence.

There is nothing particularly objectionable in presenting a recipe for personal well-being: there is no reason why all practical advice should be moral advice. Yet I confess that I find Democritus' recipe, like that of Epicurus after him, peculiarly unappetizing. Calm and placidity are tedious virtues; moderation in all things leads to a confoundedly dull life. I do not hate the Persian apparatus; and *nil admirari* is a prescription for *ennui*. We can hardly take Democritus seriously.

So much for the homiletic side of Democritean 'ethics'; I do not care for it. What, next, of the other great question? How does Democritus the practical philosopher fit with Democritus the physicist? Scholars are radically divided:[22] some see a coherent and self-conscious unity in Democritus' work; some discern only a loose compatibility; others detect downright inconsistencies. A brief and negative survey must suffice.

Of the systematists, some interpret the practical *telos* of *euestô* in an Aristotelian vein as the 'theoretical' or philosophical life; they then pronounce Democritus the natural philosopher to be the living embodiment of Abderite ethics. At best that is a very weak way of interlocking practical and theoretical philosophy; and in any case the evidence for taking *euestô* to consist in 'theorizing' is tenuous. Others point out that *euestô*, being a state of the soul, must be determined by some arrangement of its atomic constituents. That is no doubt true; but there is no reason to think that Democritus the scientist speculated about the precise nature and cause of *euestô*, nor, again, would such speculations constitute much of a connexion between ethics and physics. Others, finally, turn from atomism to anthropology: Democritus, they say, tried to ground morals on nature or *phusis*; in particular, certain features of animal behaviour, by revealing what *phusis* really is, point a moral for men. (Camels do not copulate in public: neither, then should we.)[23] Again, the evidence that Democritus offered any such view is nugatory; nor would it unite, in any significant way, his natural and his practical philosophy.

A different sort of connexion has been sought between ethics and physics: there seems to be a parallelism, of which Democritus was conscious (cf. **B 69**),[24] between the role of pleasure in ethics and the role of perception in physics. In ethics the unreflecting man goes all out for immediate pleasure; in physics he believes his senses. In ethics, reason replaces pleasure while yet relying indirectly upon it; in physics, reason replaces perception while yet relying indirectly upon it. I find it hard to care much about that: the parallelism between ethics and physics is not as neat as my brief sentences suggest; and in any case the parallelism hardly amounts to a systematic connexion between physics and ethics.

Democritus' practical philosophy has no metaphysical or physical basis. Nor should we really expect it to have one. For what, after all, would a physical basis for ethics look like? Ethics and physics, so far as I can see, have no systematic interconnexion at all; in many boring little ways a man's natural philosophy will rub off on his moralizing, but no general or systematic influence is even conceivable. The long scholarly discussion of the possible 'materialistic foundation' of Democritus' ethics is empty: it follows a will-o'-the-wisp.

Physics and ethics can, however, be inconsistent; and many scholars find an inconsistency at least potentially present in Democritus: physically, Democritus is a thorough-going determinist (above, pp. 323–6); yet 'his moral precepts are given on the assumption that man is free to act as he will'.[25] Epicurus was acutely conscious of the dilemma:

> If someone makes use of the theory of Democritus, saying that there is no free movement in the atoms because of their collisions

> with one another, whence it is clear that everything is moved necessarily, we shall say to him: Do you not know, who ever you are, that there *is* a kind of free movement in the atoms which Democritus did not discover but which Epicurus brought to light, being an inherent swerve as he proves from the phenomena? The most important point is this, that if destiny is believed in, all advice and rebuke is done away with (**485**: Diogenes of Oenoanda, fr. 32 Ch. = **68 A 50**).

There is no trace of the scandalous swerve in Democritus: 'by the time of Democritus this great question was apparently not even simmering and he proceeds to lay down his directions for the moral life with a simple *naïveté*, unconscious of the problem which he himself had raised by his insistence on the supremacy of "necessity" in the physical world'.[26]

But by Democritus' time the 'great question' *was* simmering: the briefest reflexion upon Heraclitus' philosophy would suggest it, and we know that Democritus was a student of Heraclitus; Gorgias had raised it explicitly in his *Helen*; and it was implicit in many of the problems canvassed on the Euripidean stage. Yet no fragment and no doxographical report indicates any discussion of the question by Democritus. He may have held that the emission of moral precepts does not require a 'free will'; he may, alternatively, have held that determinism and free will are compatible. Both views have, after all, been defended by eminent thinkers. But had Democritus sketched any such view, we should surely hear of it; and I incline to the sombre conclusion that physics and ethics were so successfully compartmentalized in Democritus' capacious mind that he never attended to the large issues which their cohabitation produces.

XXIV

The Bounds of Knowledge

(a) *Neo-Ionian empiricism*

Eleatic scepticism was philosophically barren; for it was fundamentally a metaphysical rather than an epistemological thesis, resting wholly upon Eleatic metaphysics and not at all upon any speculation proper to epistemology. Thus once it was believed that the foundations of Elea were undermined, there can have seemed no need to devote critical attention to the superstructure: fragment **191** of Melissus offers no challenge to the philosopher who believes that he has vindicated an Ionian world. That fact, I think, explains why it took a second attack on the possibility of objective knowledge to elicit a neo-Ionian epistemology: Democritus was spurred to thought by Protagoras; Empedocles and Anaxagoras had no such sharp incentive.

For all that, I shall devote a few pages to Empedocles and Anaxagoras. Both men say something of an epistemological nature; and the former is usually misunderstood, the latter usually mispraised.

Sextus made Empedocles a sceptic:

> He talks about the fact that the judgment of truth does not reside in the senses in the following way:
>
> For narrow hands are scattered over the limbs;
> and many wretched things impede, which blunt the thoughts.
> And gathering a poor part of life in their lives,
> swift to die, rising like smoke, they fly away,
> persuaded only of that which each meets
> as they drive everywhere. And who boasts that he has found the whole?

In this way these things can neither be seen by men, nor heard,
nor grasped in their mind [**31 B** 2.1–8].

And as to the fact that the truth is not utterly unattainable, but is attainable to the extent that human reason reaches, he makes that clear in the next lines, continuing:

But you, since you have come here
will learn—more, human wit has not achieved [**B** 2.8–9].[1]

And in the following lines, having attacked those who pretend to know more, he asserts that what is grasped by each sense is reliable, if reason oversees it—although earlier he has run down their reliability. He says:

But, gods, turn away their madness from my tongue,
and channel from me a pure spring of holy words;
and you, much famed white-armed maiden Muse,
I beg—what things it is right for mortals to hear,
send me, driving the well-reined chariot of Piety.
Nor will *you* be forced by the flowers of well-reputed honour
at the hands of mortals to pluck them at the cost of saying more than is holy
in boldness, and then indeed to sit at the heights of wisdom.
But come, gaze with every hand, in the way in which each thing is clear,
nor hold any sight in greater trust than what comes by hearing,
or resounding hearing above the clarities of the tongue,
nor in any way from any of the other limbs by which there is a way for thinking
take away trust, but think in the way in which each thing is clear
[**B** 3][2] (**486**).

Empedocles' language is flowery: partly he is indulging in the poetical vocabulary appropriate to an exordium; partly he is hampered by *patrii sermonis egestas*; thus the curious reference to 'hands (*palamai*)' shows only that Empedocles possessed no general term for 'sense-organs'.[3] Amid the luxuriant rhetoric, Sextus discerned his own dear bloom of scepticism—and then contrary evidence of a naive trust in the senses.

Yet **B 2** is hardly a sceptical fragment: lines 1–7 attack pretensions to knowledge; but they do not make a general assault on human cognitive powers. Lines 1–6 observe merely that ordinary men, flitting from one experience to the next, do not gain the knowledge that their 'narrow hands' can supply them with: '*in this way*' truth is not to be apprehended. (Fragment 68 D of Archilochus is plainly alluded to in line 5.) Sextus' interpretation is doubly false: **B 2** is not sceptical; nor does it attack, specifically, the *senses*; for ordinary men, as line 8 indicates, are no better at using their minds than their perceptive faculties. The contrast in **B 2** is not between sense and reason but between benighted mortals and Pausanias: by following Empedocles' advice, Pausanias will 'find the whole', or achieve a synoptic appreciation of natural phenomena.[4] In short, **B 2** offers a systematic science in place of the partial and disorderly beliefs of unscientific men.

The first eight lines of **B 3** also contain a contrast; and again, the contrast is between types of thinker, not between the senses and reason. Empedocles piously requests a 'holy' knowledge and dissociates himself from the 'madness' of some anonymous students. There is nothing more in these lines than the familiar deprecation of superhumanly ambitious aspirations.

Thus **B 2** and **B 3** show that Empedocles was no sceptic of sense-perception. All the senses, if appropriately used and systematically deployed, yield trustworthy evidence; and the path to scientific knowledge runs through their separate provinces. That, no doubt, is true enough; and it was worth saying to men who had read Melissus or Parmenides and were prepared to reject perception wholesale. Yet it does not amount to anything like an epistemology; it is a statement, not an argued case; and it offers no objection to any critic of perception.

Nor did Anaxagoras pursue those matters. Sextus reports a statement of Diotimus:

> Diotimus said that according to him [sc. Democritus] there are three criteria: for grasping what is unclear (*ta adêla*), the phenomena—for the phenomena are the sight of what is unclear, as Anaxagoras, whom Democritus praises for this, says . . . (**487: 76 A 3 = 59 B 21a**).

Opsis tôn adêlôn ta phainomena, 'the phenomena are the sight of what is unclear'; we can come to know what we cannot perceive (*ta adêla*) by way of the things we do perceive (*ta phainomena*). That celebrated *mot* has seemed to some scholars to contain a significant contribution to epistemology and scientific methodology: in it Anaxagoras explains and justifies the procedure of analogy and induction which his scientific predecessors had been unselfconsciously using. Anaxagoras is not, indeed, the only ancient to have formulated the general principle (it can be found in Herodotus (II.33) and in the Hippocratic corpus (*vet med* 22; *vict* I.12)); but he was probably the first to do so, and his formulation was certainly the most elegant.[5]

The earlier Ionians had used analogy; and their methods had been adopted by Empedocles and the medical writers. Things unclear and unfamiliar—either by reason of their celestial distance from us or by virtue of their microscopical size—could be illuminated and made intelligible by a sort of extrapolation and extension from the middle-sized data that surround us on earth; and the microscopic features thus apprehended could be offered in explanation of the observed phenomena. That methodology was no doubt welcomed and embellished by Anaxagoras; after all, his whole physics, though founded on empirical observations, goes far beyond the limits of perception in its effort to account for the phenomena. The *adêla* are revealed by *ta phainomena*—and then advanced in their explanation.

We can, I suppose, guess at some of the particular applications of his 'method' that Anaxagoras made; but the fragments and the doxography give little or no solid evidence. Here, for what it is worth, is the sole report that has any near connexion with **487**:

> The fine scientist Anaxagoras, attacking the senses for their weakness, says: 'by their feebleness we cannot judge the truth'. And he gives as evidence of their unreliability the gradual change of colours; for if we take two colours, black and white, and then pour one into the other, drop by drop, our sight will not be able to discriminate the gradual changes, even though they subsist in nature (**488**: Sextus, **59 B 21**).

There are some natural distinctions too fine for our gross senses; some things we cannot discriminate. Yet we can, for all that, know that they are distinct: common observation tells us that if we mix a pint of black paint with a gallon of white, the result is grey; and further observations indicate that the darkness of the grey is proportional to the amount of black added to the original white gallon. A gentle generalization, by way of **487**, allows us to infer that each drop of black, when added to the white, changes its hue to a slightly darker grey, even though these little changes are individually unobservable.

The example is not, perhaps, of great importance; nor is it wholly convincing: why, for example, does Anaxagoras suppose that colour is an intrinsic property of things, existing independently of any observer? Does it make sense to talk of real but indiscriminable differences in colour? Again, why suppose that the colours are *continua*? why does every drop of black turn the mixture a shade greyer? why not suppose (as Aristotle did) a finite number of real shades, and chromatic quantum jumps from one shade of grey to the next? But these are niggling objections; and the grand principle of **487** does not suffer by criticism of its minor application in **488**.

The objections to **487** are of a larger and more abstract order: the methodological principle there enunciated is hopelessly vague and entirely unjustified. It is vague in that it offers no criteria for the admissibility of analogical argument: what comparisons are scientifically fruitful and what are not? It is unjustified because it makes no attempt to exhibit itself as a rational principle: why, after all, think that the *phainomena* guide us to the *adêla*? Why not approach the *adêla*, as many Presocratics did, by way of abstract reasoning? Or why embrace, promiscuously, 'the' *phainomena*? Why not single out some senses above others, or some observers over others? I do not deny that from **487** we can construct some theory that is interesting and even true: my point is simply that **487** does not, in itself, contain any such theory. It is a *bon mot*, an aphorism neatly summing up the general spirit and optimistic hope of Ionian science; it is not a piece of serious philosophizing.

Anaxagoras is also said to have been a sceptic; before leaving him for epistemologically more interesting pastures I shall review the evidence for that assertion. There are two fragments and half a dozen bits of doxography to examine. The fragments can be dismissed instantly: **488**, to which Sextus characteristically gives a sceptical interpretation, states only that some distinctions in nature are too fine for our unaided senses to perceive; and **208** (see above, p. 330), while excepting one area from the range of our knowledge, does not remotely suggest a general scepticism.

Cicero idiotically enrolls Anaxagoras among those who say that 'nothing can be apprehended, nothing perceived, nothing known' (**A 95**); and Aëtius echoes him (**A 95**). Sextus reports that

> We oppose what is grasped by the mind (*ta noumena*) to what is grasped by the senses (*ta phainomena*), as Anaxagoras opposed the fact that snow is white by saying that snow is frozen water, water is black, therefore snow too is black (**489: A 97**).

The argument, which is referred to more than once (Cicero, **A 97**; Scholiast to Homer, **A 98**; Scholiast to Gregory, **B 10**), seems to Sextus to have a sceptical moral: either mind trumps perception, or each faculty neutralizes the other. But it is more plausible to connect the argument with the Anaxagorean doctrine that 'Everything is in everything': snow seems purely white; yet reason assures us that there is darkness in it; for snow is frozen water, and water is black. The black in the water cannot be destroyed; it must, therefore, reside somehow in the white snow.

Finally, there is an anecdote in the *Metaphysics*:

> A remark of Anaxagoras to some of his friends is preserved: Existent things will be for them such as they take them to be (**490**: 1009b25 = **A 28**).

I leave the reader to make what he will of that.

(b) *Protagoras: man the measure*

Protagoras, the first of the Sophists, hailed from Abdera. Our sources make him a 'hearer' of Democritus, his fellow-citizen (e.g., Diogenes Laertius, IX.50 = **80 A 1**); there is no particular reason to doubt the story and there are visible links between various aspects of Democritean and Protagorean thought. According to Plutarch, Democritus attacked Protagoras' views on knowledge (**68 A 156**); and for that reason I shall consider Protagoras' epistemology before that of Democritus.

> Of all things a measure is man—of the things that are, that they are; of the things that are not, that they are not (**491: 80 B 1**).[6]

That notorious statement, which Plato, Sextus, and Diogenes all quote, opened Protagoras' tract on *Truth* or *Knockouts* (*Alêtheia* or *Kataballontes*: Diogenes Laertius, IX.51 = **A 1**; Sextus, *ad* **B 1**). The Germans compendiously refer to the statement as the *Homomensurasatz*; and I shall adopt their convenient and portentous name, sometimes abbreviating it to a humble *H*.

The *Homomensurasatz* has only one uncontroversial feature: opacity. Protagoras' words are surely transmitted; but their sense is a matter of dispute. The *Satz*, as befits an exordium, is grand and allusive rather than clear and prosaic. Fortunately, we possess a detailed ancient interpretation: Plato, in the *Theaetetus*, offers a reading which, though fanciful in detail, is, I think, correct in its central contention. That central contention reads as follows:

> Doesn't he mean something like this: 'As each thing seems (*phainetai*) to me, so it is for me; and as to you, so again for you—and you and I are men'? (**492**: 152A = *ad* **B 1**).

The same gloss is repeated in the *Cratylus* (385E = **A 13**); and its main point is almost universally accepted: in saying that 'of all things (*chrêmatôn*) a measure (*metron*) is man', Protagoras means that what *seems* to be, *is*. Set a man against a thing and he will provide a measure or accurate assessment of it; for it is as he takes it to be. Man is a measure: seeming is being. That is the philosophical core of the *Homomensurasatz*.

The core remains vague; and to clarify it we must come more closely to grips with the wording of the fragment. First, 'man': Socrates objects that Protagoras might just as well have said 'pig' or 'jackal' (*Theaetetus* 161C = **A 1**); and that suggests that 'man' here is used generically: whatever seems to mankind, is. The suggestion is apparently supported by Sextus:

> Thus according to him man (*ho anthrôpos*) becomes the criterion of the things that are; for everything that seems to men (*tois anthrôpois*), actually is; and what seems to no man, is not (**493**: **A 14**).

Mankind, not the individual man, is the measure of things. Plato, however, does not intend that interpretation: his paraphrase of **491** explicitly refers to individual men, to you and me. Sextus in his introduction to **491** takes the same view; and so does Aristotle (*Met* 1062b12–15 = **A 19**). There is, to be sure, no independent check on that interpretation; and it may be that in accepting it we accept a Platonic travesty not a Protagorean original. But almost all the evidence favours individual men, little speaks for mankind; and we should, therefore, interpret 'Man is the measure . . .' as 'Each individual man is the measure. . .'.[7]

After 'man', 'measure'. Following Plato, I have taken '*a* is a measure of *b*' to mean '*b* is as it seems (*phainetai*) to *a* to be'. How are we to understand '*phainetai*' here? *Phainesthai* in Greek, like 'seem' in English, is ambiguous: it has a judgmental and a phenomenological sense. 'It seems to me that . . .' often means, roughly, 'I incline to believe that . . .'; and 'He seems to me to have been misled' means 'I judge that he has been misled'. But '*a* seems *F*' also has a different sort of sense, roughly equivalent to '*a* presents itself as *F* to the senses'; thus 'Your face seems yellow' means 'Your face is yellow to the sight', and 'The trumpet seems flat' means 'The trumpet is flat to my ear'. Judgmental seeming and phenomenological seeming are distinct: your face seems yellow phenomenologically but not judgmentally—I do not judge it to be yellow; he seems guilty judgmentally but not phenomenologically—his boyish face radiates innocence. Is Protagoras' seeming judgmental or phenomenological?

Plato explicitly gives a phenomenological interpretation: 'and "it seems (*phainetai*)" means "he perceives (*aisthanetai*)"?—It does' (*Theaetetus* 152A = *ad* **B 1**). Some of the doxographers follow Plato (cf. Hermias, **A 16**; Eusebius, **70 B 1**); but Sextus talks of 'everything which *phainetai* or *dokei* to anyone' (*ad* **B 1**) and '*dokei*' means 'it seems' in the judgmental sense only. Aristotle, too, uses *dokei* in the same context (*Met* 1007b21 = **A 19**); and there is evidence that the judgmental account is earlier even than Plato.

> No one can say that all *phantasia* is true, because of the *peritropê*, as Democritus and Plato taught us in their attack on Protagoras; for if every *phantasia* is true, then even the proposition that not every *phantasia* is true, being itself subject of *phantasia*, will be true, and thus it will turn out false that every *phantasia* is true (**494**: Sextus, **A 15** = **68 A 114**).

The *peritropê*, or about-turn, is suffered by the *Homomensurasatz* because it is self-refuting. The argument requires that 'every *phantasia* is true' be interpreted by way of the judgmental sense of *phainesthai*; thus, 'If *phainetai* to *x* that *P*, then it is true that *P*' must be written as:

(H1) For any proposition *P*, and any man, *x*, if *x* judges that *P*, then it is true that *P*.

From (H1) it follows at once that:

(1) For any man *x*, if *x* judges that not-*H*, then it is true that not-*H*.

But many men reject the *Homomensurasatz*, or judge that not-*H*. It follows that it is true that not-*H*, and hence that *H* itself is false. Thus the *Homomensurasatz* suffers an about-turn: it marches to its own ruin.

I shall return to the *peritropê* in a later section. My reason for quoting it here is to show first that Democritus accepted the orthodox paraphase of *H* in terms of *phainesthai*; and, second, that he interpreted *phainesthai* in its judgmental and not in its phenomenological sense.

According to Sextus, Plato as well as Democritus used the *peritropê* against Protagoras; and Sextus was right (cf. *Theaetetus* 171A). Use of the *peritropê* implies a judgmental *phainetai*; and in his allusions to *H* Plato sometimes explicitly uses the purely judgmental *dokei* (e.g., *Theaetetus* 161C). Moreover, much of the argument against Protagoreanism which Plato develops in the *Theaetetus* implicitly assumes *dokei* rather than *aisthanetai*. The phenomenological interpretation given at *Theaetetus* 152A is thus not consistently adhered to by Plato.

The weight of the evidence tells, I think, for a judgmental interpretation.[8] The contrary evidence probably all derives from *Theaetetus* 152A; and we may guess that Plato's concern there with the thesis that 'knowledge is perception' encouraged him to give a temporary and unhistorical phenomenological interpretation to Protagoras' *Satz*. At all events, I propose to follow the judgmental view.

Many scholars write as though the dispute between phenomenological and judgmental *phainetai* was only one of scope: is *H* restricted to matters of perception, or does it extend to all judgments? That is mistaken: phenomenological or Φ-seeming, and judgmental or J-seeming, differ not in range but in kind. J-seeming turns *H* into a thesis about the judgments, beliefs or opinions of men—all such judgments are true. Φ-seeming turns *H* into a thesis about perceptual seemings: whatever strikes the senses as such and such, is such and such. An example of Aristotle's brings out the difference: a man, looking at the sun, may judge that the sun is several thousand miles across; yet the sun may *look* to him about a foot in diameter (cf. *An* 428b3). If we interpret *H* by way of J-seeming we shall give truth to the man's judgment, not to the content of his sense experience; if we interpret it by Φ-seeming, we shall give truth to the experiential content, not to the judgment.

So much for 'man' and 'measure'. Next, 'of the things that are (*tôn ontôn*), that they are (*hôs estin*)'. What does '*esti*' mean here? Some scholars say 'exist'. The *Homomensurasatz* can then be tied to the coat-tails of Elea: if anyone judges that a thing exists, then it does exist, for judgment involves thought, and thought requires existent objects. The interpretation has a superficial attraction: and it is perhaps supported by Hermias, **A 16**; but I do not see how *einai* can be taken existentially in the second, negative, clause of the *Satz*.

Plato takes *einai* to be predicative: 'of the things that are, that they are' means 'of whatever is (*F*), that it is (*F*)'. And having glossed *H* in terms of 'such' and 'so', Plato illustrates it thus:

> Sometimes when the same wind blows, one of us shivers and the other doesn't; or one of us mildly, the other violently.—Yes indeed—Then shall we say that the wind is in itself cold or not cold? (**495**: *Theaetetus* 152B = **B 1**).

The wind is one of 'the things that are'; and what it 'is' is cold. Plato's predicative interpretation is tacitly adopted by Aristotle (e.g., *Met* 1007b20 = **A 19**) and by Sextus (e.g., **A 14**); and I have no hesitation in following them.

Thus 'man is a measure . . . of the things that are, that they are . . .' means that if a man judges an object to be *F*, then it is *F*. Man is also a measure 'of the things that are not, that they are not': analogy suggests the meaning that if a man judges an object not to be *F*, then it is not *F*. And that interpretation is clearly implied by Aristotle:

> If the man seems to someone not to be a trireme, then he is not a trireme (**496**: *Met* 1007b21 = **A 19**).

Sextus has a different gloss: 'Everything that seems to men, actually is; and what seems to no man, is not' (**493: A 14**). If no one judges that a thing is *F*, then it is not *F*. Protagoras may have embraced that thesis; but he does not state it in *H*.

Things[9] are *F* or not *F* just in so far as some man 'measures' them, or judges them to be so. The *Homomensurasatz*, then, invites the following formulation:

(H2) For any man, *x*, and object, *O*, if *x* judges that *O* is *F*, then *O* is *F*; and if *x* judges that *O* is not *F*, then *O* is not *F*.

The *Homomensurasatz* is outrageous: was Protagoras' *Truth* an exercise in irony? or a virtuoso display of cleverness? Did the *Satz* aspire merely to shock and to excite? Or was *Truth* serious, and the *Satz* an effort to enlighten and instruct, to surmount some philosophical hurdle? I think that the *Satz* is the keystone of a systematic and sophisticated epistemology, and that it represents one part of an original, and not uninteresting, contribution to philosophy. I shall try to make that view plausible by a somewhat circuitous argumentative route.

(c) *Knowledge and relativity*

> [Protagoras] was the first to say that there are two *logoi* about everything, opposite to one another (**497**: Diogenes Laertius, IX. 51 = **A 1** = **B 6a**; cf. Clement, **A 20**).

Logoi here are arguments, or perhaps, more generally, reasons; for Seneca enlarged upon Diogenes' report:

> Protagoras says that on every issue it is possible for it to be argued (*disputari*) with equal force (*ex aequo*) on both sides (**498: A 20**).

For any proposition *P* there is an argument for *P* and an argument of equal strength for not-*P*. If you claim that the argument for *P* is in fact stronger, Protagoras will fulfil his wicked promise 'to make the weaker argument stronger' (Aristotle, *Rhet* 1402a23 = **B 6b**). All sticks are straight: show me a warped lath, and I will bend it straight. All arguments are equal: show Protagoras a feeble reason and he will strengthen it to par. In all things there is an intellectual equilibrium; for any thesis there is an equipollence of argument *pro* and *contra*.

Such paired and equipollent arguments were, it seems, a stock-in-trade of Protagoras' sophistry; and his two books of *Antilogies* (cf. Diogenes Laertius, IX. 55 = **A 1**) doubtless contained a selection of them. Alas, none has survived, and the *agôn* between Just and Unjust Logos in Aristophanes' *Clouds*, which scholars deem a parody of Protagorean sophistry, is too much of a caricature and too unclever to permit any safe inference about the nature or plausibility of its probable patterns.

For all that, it is not difficult to guess at the areas in which Protagoras hunted for his equipollences. First, ethical argument, in which he is known to have had an interest, must have been a rich quarry. By the second half of the fifth century the differences in moral belief from one culture and age to another were familiar enough; and a Protagorean equipollence would be suggested by them, and corroborated by the actual ease with which ethical argumentation reaches an *impasse*. The *Dissoi Logoi* provides copious illustration. Second, there are the deliverances of the senses: the *Theaetetus* illustrates the *Homomensurasatz* by an example which may well have been taken from Protagoras' own treatise. The wind makes me shiver and leaves you unmoved: is it cold?—Yes; it makes me shiver. No: you do not twitch. That is a simple example: the rich treasury of cases illustrating the relativity of sense perception began to be stocked in Protagoras' time; and we need not doubt that he found material there with which to support his equipollence thesis.

Such examples suggest a generalization: any predication can be supported by argument, and attacked by argument of precisely equal weight. Protagoras was a clever man; and a little ingenuity would enable him to give some initial plausibility to his general thesis even in areas where it seemed wholly inapplicable. Surely mathematics provides innumerable examples of sound argumentation for a theorem where no countervailing considerations can be adduced? But Protagoras, we are told, 'refuted the geometers' (Aristotle, *Met* 998a4 = **B** 7). 'The facts are unknowable and the language unpleasing, as Protagoras says of mathematics' (Philodemus, **B** 7a: Diels-Kranz II.425). The details of Protagoras' 'refutation' of the geometers are unknown; but they can be guessed at. 'The circle does not touch the ruler at a point' (*Met* loc. cit.):[10] geometry is about physical objects; if it does not apply to physical objects it is an empty game and not a science; if it does apply, then the geometers' proofs are subject to empirical checks. Take any *a priori* argument, say for the theorem that the angles of a triangle sum to 180°. Draw and measure a triangle: you will get a result differing from 180°. Any *a priori logos* can be matched by an equipollent *logos* based on empirical observation. Thus even among the apparent certainties of mathematics the Principle of Equipollence holds sway.

If the Principle is to fit into Protagoras' epistemology it must be stated in a slightly more restricted form than the one Seneca gives. I take it to assert that for any object *O* and apparently objective predicate *F*, any reason for judging that *O* is *F* can be matched by an equally strong reason for judging that *O* is not *F*. The point of this formulation, and the sense of 'apparently objective predicate', will emerge shortly.

The wind blows cold on the shorn lamb and warm on its woolly brother: 'should we say that the wind is in itself cold or not cold, or shall we be persuaded by Protagoras that it is cold for the shiverer and not for the other?' (*Theaetetus* 152B = **B 1**). If we have equal reason to believe *P* and *Q*, we cannot rationally accept *P* and reject *Q*, or vice versa. That fundamental axiom of rationality, coupled with the Principle of Equipollence, forbids us to accept '*O* is *F*' and reject '*O* is not *F*', and also to reject '*O* is *F*' and accept '*O* is not *F*'. Equipollence of argument requires equality of assent.

Three courses are open. First, we might reject both '*O* is *F*' and '*O* is not *F*'. But it is paradoxical to *reject* '*O* is *F*' when we have good arguments in its favour. Second, we might retreat to a forlorn scepticism: no doubt just one of '*O* is *F*' and '*O* is not *F*' is true, but we cannot possibly know which. But again, it is paradoxical to withhold assent from propositions for whose truth we have excellent evidence: if the wind feels cold to me, what more could I wish for by way of evidence that it is cold? Third, we can embrace both '*O* is *F*' and '*O* is not *F*'. That is the Protagorean path.

Surely, though, that is a 'path beyond all tidings'? Even if the Principle of Equipollence is true, we can hardly follow Protagoras' argument and deny the Law of Contradiction. Now just such a denial is in any case demanded by the *Homomensurasatz*: nothing prevents men from making opposite judgments; if I judge that the wine is corked and you deem it excellent, you contradict me. But according to (H2) both our judgments are true. Aristotle puts the point clearly enough: 'but if this is the case [i.e. given *H*], it follows that the same thing is and is not—is bad and good, and the rest of the so-called opposing phrases; because often this seems fine to *these* men and the opposite to *those*, and what seems to each is the measure' (*Met* 1062b15–9 = **A 19**). The Principle of Equipollence may have encouraged Protagoras to embrace both '*O* is *F*' and '*O* is not *F*'; but such intellectual troilism is in any case forced upon him by his *Homomensurasatz*.

Did Protagoras, then, knowingly and cheerfully deny the Law of Contradiction? According to Diogenes,

> He was the first to advance the thesis (*logos*) of Antisthenes which attempts to prove that it is not possible to contradict (*antilegein*), as Plato says in the *Euthydemus* (**499**: Diogenes Laertius, IX.53 = **A 1**).

Plato says:

> And *this* thesis [sc. that it is not possible to contradict] I have often heard from many people, always with astonishment. The Protagoreans used it vigorously, and it was used even earlier; but it always seems quite astonishing to me and to upturn (*anatrepein*) both other theses and also its own self (**500**: 286BC = **A 19**).[11]

Plato takes the thesis that 'it is not possible to contradict' to be a denial of the Law of Contradiction; and it is therefore liable to 'upturn itself'. This self-*anatropê* is surely equivalent to *peritropê*: having attacked *H* by *peritropê*, Plato now uses the same manoeuvre against the further Protagorean thesis, that *antilegein* is impossible. 'Call the thesis *A*. Let Protagoras assert *A*. Then Plato maintains not-*A*. But according to *A* not-*P* does not contradict *P*; hence not-*A* is compatible with *A*. Hence, for all Protagoras has said, not-*A* is the case: hence *A* is not the case.' That, at least, is the best I can do for Plato; and it is not good enough. The fundamental misapprehension is, I think, the assumption that Protagoras 'denies the Law of Contradiction' in rejecting the possibility of contradiction: to say that contradiction is impossible is not to assert that a proposition and its contradictory may both be true at the same time; it is to assert the perfectly distinct thesis that you cannot contradict me.

Suppose I judge that *O* is *F* and you that *O* is not *F*. Then, according to Protagoras, I have not yet contradicted you; and if we are not *antilegontes*, the truth of what I say is compatible with the truth of what you say. Thus the denial of *antilegein*, far from opening Protagoras to a peculiarly damning charge of inconsistency, is actually designed to protect him from that charge: the clouds of contradiction which lour over *H* and over the Principle of Equipollence are evaporated by the thesis that 'it is not possible to contradict'.

'But that is a hollow victory: Protagoras' thesis is false; for you and I patently do contradict one another: what more obvious contradiction could one desire than "*O* is *F* and *O* is not *F*"? Mere *fiat* cannot abolish contradiction: "*O* is not *F*" contradicts "*O* is *F*", whatever Protagoras may choose to ordain.'

It is an elementary truth that not every pair of sentences of the form '*O* is *F*' and '*O* is not *F*' express contradictory propositions. Of the many exceptions one is peculiarly apposite here: I may say 'The Marx Brothers make me laugh'; you may say, 'The Marx Brothers do not make me laugh'. In a loose sense you have contradicted me; but the loose sense of 'contradict' is not the technical logical one: the truth of what you say is not incompatible with the truth of what I say. The reason for the compatibility is plain: in my sentence, 'me' refers to me; in yours, 'me' refers to you; we are talking about different people, not saying opposing things about one man.

Let us call 'subjective' any sentences containing a word which refers to whoever utters the sentence and whose reference therefore varies from one utterance of the sentence to another. ('I', 'me', 'the speaker', etc. will make sentences subjective in this sense.) And let non-subjective sentences be called 'objective'. Consider, now, the sentence: 'The Marx Brothers are funny'. That is an objective sentence, none of its words refers to whoever utters it. (If the Marx Brothers chorus it, 'the Marx Brothers' refers to the sentence's utterers; but 'the Marx Brothers' does not refer to whoever utters the sentence.) But it is not wildly implausible to suggest that '. . . is funny' means '. . . amuses me'; so that 'The Marx Brothers are funny' is synonymous with the subjective sentence: 'The Marx Brothers amuse me'. If an objective sentence has a subjective synonym, I call it crypto-subjective. English contains many crypto-subjective sentences: 'Condor Flake is nauseating' (it makes me sick); 'Aristotle is fascinating' (he interests me); 'Rock-climbing is terrifying' (it frightens me); 'Irish politics are boring' (I find them tedious).

Many philosophers claim that crypto-subjective sentences are more common than we like to believe. Ethics provides the most familiar case: '. . . is good' has been analysed as '. . . is approved of by me', '. . . excites moral feelings in my breast', and so on. Protagoras, I think, was the first philosopher to plough that furrow, and he ploughed it deep. He suggested that *all* objective predications are in fact crypto-subjective: every sentence of the form '*O* is *F*' is synonymous with some relational sentence '*O* is *R* to *S*', where '*S*' refers to whoever utters '*O* is *R* to *S*'.

That is an ancient interpretation: Sextus says that Protagoras 'introduces the relative (*to pros ti*)' (**A 14**), adding that this is because 'he posits only what seems to each person' (ibid.). Again: 'everything which *phainetai* or *dokei* to anyone thereby is so—*relative to him*' (*ad* **B 1**). And the interpretation is Plato's: 'as each thing seems to me, so it is *for me*' (*Theaetetus* 151E = **B 1**).

I suggested that, according to Protagoras, '*O* is *F*' is synonymous with '*O* is *R* to *S*'. Plato's words suggest a more specific formulation: '*O* is *F*' is synonymous with '*O* is *F* for *S*': 'the wind is cold' means 'the wind is cold for the speaker'. Plato's formulation has one great advantage: it enables us to provide, in any given case, the overtly subjective counterpart of a crypto-subjective judgment. It has one disadvantage: 'Cold for me', 'funny for me' and the like are artificial and unnatural predicates. The disadvantage is easily overcome: 'The

Marx Brothers amuse me' can be replaced without change of sense by, say, 'The Marx Brothers are funny to my way of thinking' or 'I find the Marx Brothers funny'. We may reasonably take 'the Marx Brothers are funny' to be elliptical for one of those synonyms of 'The Marx Brothers amuse me'; and the artificial sentence 'The Marx Brothers are funny for me' is an intelligible, if inelegant, way of expressing the thought captured by those natural synonyms.

The generalization is plain: every apparently objective predicate '*F*' is to be taken as elliptical for '*F* to——'s way of thinking' or '*F* for——'. Protagoras suggests that '*O* is *F*' always means '*O* is *F* for *S*'.

How does that suggestion, which I shall call the Relativity Thesis, bear upon the other Protagorean theories I have endeavoured to express? First, Equipollence: that Principle maintains that any apparently objective predication is precisely as well or as badly supported as its negation. Protagoras should, I think, say this: for any sentence '*O* is *F*', there are judges *a* and *b* such that *a* has just as good grounds for judging that *O* is *F* as *b* has for judging that *O* is not *F*. Hence we must be prepared to countenance '*O* is *F* and *O* is not *F*'. The thesis that Contradiction is Impossible now relieves the discomfort of that conclusion: '*O* is *F*' does not contradict '*O* is not *F*'; for contradiction is impossible. The Relativity Thesis then explains the impossibility of contradiction: '*O* is *F*' expresses the fact that *O* is *F* for *a*, and '*O* is not *F*' expresses the compatible fact that *O* is not *F* for *b*.

Finally, that happy result not only frees the *Homomensurasatz* from the taint of contradiction, but actually provides it with a proof. For suppose that someone judges that *O* is *F*; say:

(1) *a* judges that *O* is *F*.

By the Relativity Thesis, that amounts to:

(2) *a* judges that *O* is *F* for *S*.

Now since in the present case *S* is *a*, we may express (2) by:

(3) *a* judges that *O* is *F* for *a*;

or in other words:

(4) *a* judges that *O* is *F* in *a*'s judgment.

Now from (4) we can surely infer:

(5) *O* is *F* in *a*'s judgment,

for how could *a* possibly misjudge the contents of his own judgments? But (5) expresses the content of the judgment ascribed to *a* by (1). Hence we infer:

(6) If *a* judges that *O* is *F*, then *a* judges truly.

Finally, generalizing, we get:

(H3) For any proposition *P* and man *x*: if *x* judges that *P*, then *x* judges truly.

And that is a version of the *Homomensurasatz*. (The differences between (H1), (H2), and (H3) are not entirely trivial; but there is not space to explore them adequately.)

Such is Protagoras' epistemology: surprisingly little of it is known to us at first-hand, and the second-hand doxography is thin: *Truth*, despite the extrinsic interest Plato bestowed on it, was destined to almost total oblivion. Yet the few remains allow us, I think, to reconstruct an original concatenation of thoughts. Protagoras was an epistemologist of some ingenuity. Keen to categorize, scholars have assigned to him a variety of modern isms: the ascriptions are not anachronistic in any vicious sense; but neither are they particularly illuminating. Protagoras was certainly a relativist, a subjectivist and an idealist; equally, he was not a sceptic in the philosophical sense, and to that extent can be called an objectivist. But those labels are old, tired, and multivocal; we shall grasp Protagoras' ideas by studying his four central contentions: the Principle of Equipollence, the thesis that Contradiction is Impossible, the Relativity Thesis, the *Homomensurasatz*; labelling those doctrines as isms may be a helpful (or a misleading) mnemonic device—it is nothing more.

Protagoras' epistemology is a *tour de force*: is that all? It seems to me plausible to represent it as an attempt to come to grips with the rigorous requirements of empiricism. From this point of view, the Relativity Thesis is of fundamental importance: if, as common sense seems to suggest, all our concepts are ultimately taken from experience and all our judgments are ultimately based upon experience, then some relativity may seem inevitable; for the experience on which *my* knowledge rests can only be *my* experience. If my cognitive beginnings are tied to my own experiences, how can I ever escape from myself? And if I cannot escape from myself, is not Protagoreanism the only possible epistemology? My complex judgments are only functions of my primitive judgments; and my primitive judgments are reports of my own experiences. If I say, primitively, 'the wind is cold' or 'the grass is green' or 'the tobacco is tart', my sentences have an objective air; but since those primitive reports report my experiences they are crypto-subjective; they say how things are *for me*.

Modern empiricists start from the self-centred position; and a constant item in empiricist thought has been the attempt to found genuinely objective judgments on these subjective foundations. Protagoras did not make the attempt; instead he trod the lonely path of idealism, and it led him to an idiosyncratic epistemology. It would be idle to pretend that his views constitute a full and clear version of extreme empiricism; and inane to urge that they give a competent and satisfactory account of human knowledge. But I am more concerned to applaud Protagoras for trying than to hiss him for his failings; and in any event, a serious assessment of Protagoreanism would require a lengthy study of the foundations of knowledge. In order to compensate a little for my cowardly refusal to offer such an assessment, I shall end by looking again at the Democritean *peritropê*: after all, the *peritropê* is an ingenious objection; and if it works, Protagoras' main thesis is shown up as logically intolerable.

The relevant portion of text **494** reads thus: '. . . if every *phantasia* is true, then even the proposition that not every *phantasia* is true . . . will be true; and thus it will turn out false that every *phantasia* is true.' Assume that (H3) is true. Now it is indisputable that:

(7) Some men have judged that *H* is false.

From (H3) we infer:

(8) If anyone judges that *H* is false, he judges truly.

And from (7) and (8) it surely follows that:

(9) *H* is false.

Thus if (H3) is true, it is false; and therefore—by the Lex Clavia (above, p. 277)—(H3) is false. The *peritropê* or about-turn is a species of self-refutation.

How does that argument fare? I shall not consider it in any detail; rather, I shall simply list three lines of argument which any defender of Protagoras might expect to develop. I do not know if any of the lines is successful; but I think that each is worth exploration.

First, then, Protagoras might simply deny the applicability of the *peritropê*: its use involves an *ignoratio elenchi*. For (he might say) sentence (H3) is not an adequate representation of the *Homomensurasatz*: it ignores the fact, plainly set down in (H2), that *H* is a thesis about objects and properties, about judgments of the form '*O* is *F*'. Now *H* itself is patently not of the form '*O* is *F*', and neither is the negation of *H*. The sentence '*H* is false', which appears as a component of (7), does indeed appear to be of the required form; but a short course of reading in modern philosophy will convince any Protagorean that that appearance is deceptive. '*H* is false' does not predicate anything of *H*; it is simply a ponderous way of expressing the negation of *H*. And since the negation of *H* is not of the form '*O* is *F*', neither is '*H* is false'. Thus *H* does not refute itself; for it is a thesis about propositions of the type '*O* is *F*', a type to which it does not itself belong.

Second, Protagoras might question the inference from (7) and (8) to (9). The inference certainly seems to be valid; for if *a* judges that *P*, and *a* judges truly, it surely follows that *P*. To say that he judges truly is simply to say that what he judges is true, i.e. that *P* is true; and if we can infer '*P* is true', we can surely infer the simpler '*P*'? Now all that is, I think, almost indisputable, given our ordinary understanding of true judgment. But it is not clear that Protagoras will, or ought to, grant us that ordinary understanding. (Suppose that *a* judges truly that *O* is *F*: can I infer that *O* is *F*? No, given the Relativity Thesis; for if I infer that *O* is *F*, I judge that *O* is *F for me*; and that conclusion cannot be warranted by the premiss that *a* judges truly that *O* is *F*.)

Third, Protagoras might allow that (9) is indeed validly inferred from (H3); but he might question the significance of the inference for *H*. After all, he will suggest, the predicate '. . . is false', like any other objective predicate, is crypto-subjective; and (9), the conclusion of the *peritropê*, is of course elliptical for:

(10) *H* is false for *S*.

Falsity—and truth—is, like everything else, a relative and subjective manner. No doubt *H* is false for some men. But that hardly refutes *H*; for *H* remains true; true, that is to say, for other men; and in particular, true for Protagoras. 'But then *nothing* can be refuted, and all judgments are equally true or false.'—'Not exactly: some judgments may have more backers than others, and be truer; and some judgments may have a far better property than truth: they may be advantageous to believe.'

(d) '*Isonomia*'

According to Plutarch, Democritus attacked Protagoras' epistemological stance (**68 B 156**); and we know that he applauded Anaxagoras' empiricist aphorism (Diotimus, **76 A 3**). Yet the fragmentary reports of his attitude to human knowledge, its scope and limits, indicate both that he developed the Protagorean Principle of Equipollence, and also that he toyed with a Pyrrhonian scepticism. Democritus' epistemology is perplexing, paradoxical, and perhaps inconsistent; and Democritus himself was ruefully aware of the fact (**B 125**). Our evidence is, again, a tangled skein; and I do not know how best to unravel it. But here at least there is reason to think that the tangles are original, and not due to the accidents of history.

I begin with what I have called the *Ou Mallon* Principle (it was later called the Principle of *Isonomia*, or Balance).[12] '*Mallon* . . . *ê* . . .' means 'Rather . . . than . . .'; and '*ou*' (for which '*mê*', '*ouden*', and '*mêden*' are common substitutes) is simply the negation sign. Thus '*Ou mallon P ê Q*' means 'Not rather *P* than *Q*'. Properly speaking, 'Not rather *P* than *Q*' is compatible with '*Q* rather than *P*'; but in Greek idiom *ou mallon* appears to ascribe an equal status to *P* and to *Q*, so that '*ou mallon P ê Q*' marks a sort of indifference, equipollence, or equivalence between *P* and *Q*.

According to Sextus, '*ou mallon*' was a constant refrain (*epiphthegma*) in the Abderite song (*Pyrr Hyp* I.213). And we have already heard the refrain thrice. First, in **238** (above, p. 363):

> If the region outside the heavens is unlimited, so too, it seems, are body and the worlds; for why should it be here rather than here (*entautha mallon ê entautha*) in the void?

Second, in **236** (above, p. 361):

> . . . the unlimited quantity of the shapes among [the atoms] because nothing is rather such than such (*ouden mallon toiouton ê toiouton*).

And third, in **297** (above, p. 402):

> The thing exists no more than (*ou mallon*) the nothing.

The first argument is ascribed to Democritus. The second is given to Leucippus in **236**; but Simplicius attributes it to Democritus too (**68 A 38**). **297** is a Democritean fragment: its argument is given to Leucippus by Aristotle (*Met* 985b8 = **67 A 6**) and by Simplicius (**67 A 7**).

Aristotle reports a fourth occurrence of the refrain. Our senses, he observes, are at odds with one another in a variety of familiar ways; and the variations in our sense experience may well lead us to conclude that

> which of them is true or false is unclear; for the ones are no more (*ouden mallon*) true than the others but to a similar degree; that is why Democritus says that either none is true or it is unclear to us (**501**: *Met* 1009b9–12 = **68 A 112**).

Nausiphanes, pupil of Democritus and teacher of Epicurus, said much the same:

> Of the things which seem to be, none is rather than is not (**502**: Seneca, **75 B 4**).

Seneca's Latin phrase '*nihil magis*' translates the Greek '*ouden mallon*'.

That last application of the *Ou Mallon* Principle perhaps suggests an epistemological interpretation of the 'equivalence' involved in *ou mallon*. One perceptual judgment is 'no more true' than another just in so far as the *evidence* for each judgment is equally good; '*ou mallon P ê Q*' will be true, then, just in case any evidence in favour of

P is matched by evidence in favour of *Q*, and vice versa. Let us abbreviate '*ou mallon P ê Q*' to '*E* (*P*, *Q*)', where '*E*' may be imagined to stand for 'equivalent' or 'equipollent'. Then Protagoras' Principle of Equipollence can be written compendiously as:

(1) For any proposition *P*, *E* (*P*, not-*P*).

And in **501** and **502** we may discern a restricted version of (1). If *S* is any sensible property (redness, roughness, roundness), then Democritus and Nausiphanes hold:

(2) For any object *x*, *E*(*x* has *S*, *x* does not have *S*).

Consider Protagoras' sentence, 'The wind is cold'. Democritus, I imagine, thought that the only evidence I could have for the truth of that sentence must consist in the fact that the wind seems cold to me or makes me shiver. But what seems cold to me, seems warm to you; so my evidence for thinking that the wind is cold is balanced by your evidence for asserting that it is not. Hence *E* (the wind is cold, the wind is not cold). I ignore the incautious assumptions made in that argument in order to concentrate on its logical form. Let *R* (*P*) abbreviate 'there is sufficient evidence to believe that *P*'; and let '*P*' here stand for 'the wind is cold'. Then my shivering testimony gives Democritus:

(3) *R* (*P*),

and your stoical report allows him to hold:

(4) *E* (*P*, not-*P*).

But it seems to be true that:

(5) It is impossible that both *P* and not-*P*:

Now that triad of propositions, (3)–(5), is not formally inconsistent; but an inconsistency can be derived if it is enlarged by two additions:

(6) If *R* (*P*) and *R* (*Q*), then *R* (*P* and *Q*).

(7) If it is impossible that *P*, then not-*R* (*P*).

For (3) and (4) yield:

(8) *R* (not-*P*).

And (3), (8) and (6) give;

(9) *R* (*P* and not-*P*).

But (5) and (7) give:

(10) not-*R* (*P* and not-*P*).

That schematic argument represents the background both to Protagoras and to Democritus: both men accepted (4); and they would doubtless have accepted (6) and (7). (6) is evidently true; (7) is, I think, false as it stands; for we can have sufficient reason for believing false mathematical propositions. But some suitable modification of (7) will surmount that difficulty: we surely cannot have sufficient reason to believe overt impossibilities. Protagoras, accepting (3), rejected (5) and safeguarded his reputation for consistency by reinterpreting '*P*' by way of his Relativity Thesis. What did Democritus do?

According to Aristotle, 'he says that either none is true or it is unclear to us' (**501**). Did Democritus give that disjunctive conclusion, or did he rather plump for one of the disjuncts? Some scholars argue as follows: 'Presumably Democritus holds that not both *P* and not-*P*; for he will not reject (5) and the Principle of Contradiction. Consequently, he must either reject both *P* and not-*P*, or else come to the sceptical conclusion that we cannot tell which of *P* and not-*P* is true. Now Democritus cannot have been prepared to countenance "neither *P* nor not-*P*" but not "both *P* and not-*P*"; for those two propositions are logically equivalent. And it is charitable to infer that Democritus in fact mentioned the first of Aristotle's disjuncts only as an evident impossibility, and intended to commit himself to the second, sceptical disjunct.'[13]

If that is true, it is strange. According to Sextus,

> [Protagoras] says that the explanations (*logoi*) of all the appearances lie in the matter, so that the matter is capable in itself of being everything which it seems to anyone (**503: 80 A 14**).

Sextus' account is an implausible interpretation rather than a report; but the account might well have been given by Democritus. For according to the Atomists,

> The truth is in the appearing (**504**: Aristotle, *GC* 315b8 = **67 A 9**).[14]

That is to say, all the diverse phenomena are explicable in terms of the atomic structure of matter: their *logoi* 'lie in the matter'. Thus if the wind feels cold to me, that is because certain constituents in the air react in certain ways with some of my constituent atoms; and its feeling warm to you is explained by the different reaction that occurs between the air's atoms and yours. Protagoras accepts (5) and gives a relativistic interpretation to 'cold'. We might expect Democritus to have done exactly the same: temperature is not an intrinsic property of atoms or atomic conglomerates, and *P*, scientifically construed, is after all compatible with not-*P*.

Perhaps, then, Democritus does want to conclude that 'none is true', that neither *P* nor not-*P*. The grass looks green to you, brown to me: which colour is it really? Neither: for colours exist only *nomôi*, nothing is intrinsically coloured. The wine tastes corked to me, clear to you: it is neither, for savours exist *nomôi*. But not all qualities exist only *nomôi*: shape is real; and so are size and motion. If the wind seems a light breeze to you and a gale to me, at most one of us can be right; for the wind, or the atomic conglomerate which forms it, really does have an intrinsic velocity.

I conclude that Aristotle means what he says: Democritus asserted a disjunction: 'Either both P and not-P are false (if P involves a *nomôi* quality),[15] or else we cannot know which, if either, of P and not-P is true (if P involves an *eteêi* quality).' Thus Democritus differs from Protagoras at two points: first, he admits scepticism in certain cases;[16] second, he refuses to relativize sensible qualities.[17] The former difference is more significant than the latter.

The details of that argument should not obscure its essential structure: whatever may be thought about Democritus' attitude to sensible qualities, his use of the *Ou Mallon* Principle displays a subtle and conscious appreciation of a central feature of the notion of rational belief: if $E\ (P,\ Q)$, then it is unreasonable to accept one and reject the other of P and Q.

So far, '*ou mallon*' has shown itself as a destructive weapon. Its more interesting applications are constructive; and I shall now turn to them. Suppose that for some pair of propositions, P and Q, we have:

(11) $R\ (P)$.

(12) $E\ (P,\ Q,)$.

(13) Possibly both P and Q.

That triad threatens no inconsistency; and indeed, given (11), we should believe that P; and given (12), that Q. Consider, then, the application of *ou mallon* to the problem of atomic shapes. There is an infinity of possible shapes, S_1, S_2, ... Let P_i represent the proposition that there are atoms of shape S_i; then the infinite conjunction of the P_is is a logical possibility. But we have (let us grant) sufficient reason to believe that there are atoms; and since every atom has some shape, we have reason to believe that there are atoms of some shape. But we have no reason to believe in, say, spherical atoms rather than in, say, cubic atoms; hence all the P_is are rationally on a par; hence we have reason to believe that there are atoms of every shape.

The argument is confused. The Abderites need the following two premisses:

(14) There is some atomic shape, S_i, such that $R\ (P_i)$.

(15) $E\ (P_1,\ P_2,\ \ldots)$.

But they have not established a title to (14); for the argument I assigned to them yields only:

(16) R (there is some shape S_i, such that P_i).

But (16) does not imply (14). Indeed, the Atomists have no reason for believing in atoms of any particular shape; they may be saddled with the contradictory of (14), viz.:

(17) For no atomic shape, S_i, R (P_i).
And even though (17) yields (15), that will not, so far as I can see, give them their desired conclusion, that there are atoms of every shape.

The second constructive use of *ou mallon* fares no better. Let '*P*' now represent 'there are atoms'; '*Q*', 'there is void'. And suppose (what again was not uncontroversial) that (13) is true. The Abderites then require both (12) and also either *R* (*P*) or *R* (*Q*). No doubt they claimed *R* (*P*). Yet how are they entitled to *E* (*P, Q*)? No Atomist text gives any grounds for holding *E* (*P, Q*), nor can I invent any.

Perhaps this interpretation construes *ou mallon* in too narrowly epistemological a fashion: a broader interpretation may be thought to serve the two positive applications better. First, let '*E* (*P,Q*)' represent not epistemological, but what we might call nomological equivalence: 'Necessarily, *P* if and only if *Q*'. Then it might seem that the existence of atoms and the existence of void are mutually implicative; there cannot physically be atoms unless there is void, and vice versa. Thus '*E* (*P,Q*)' yields 'if *P*, necessarily *Q*'; and that, with *R* (*P*), does lead to *R* (*Q*). The inference is, I think, again a valid one; but again I do not think that the Atomists are entitled to *E* (*P,Q*). Nor will this version of *ou mallon* apply to the case of atomic shapes.

Second, let '*E* (*P,Q*)' embrace what I may call explanatory equivalence: 'For any *R*, *P* because *R* if and only if *Q* because *R*'. Consider again the atomic shapes. We have granted the Atomists' proposition (16). Now a generous interpretation of text **309** (Leucippus, **67 B 2**), will give us:

(18) For any proposition *P*: if *P*, then there is some proposition *Q* such that *P* because *Q*.

We may now infer to:

(19) *R* (there is some *Q*, and some atomic shape S_i, such that P_i because *Q*).

And then, given (15) and the explanatory reading of '*E*', we may conclude to:

(20) *R* (for any atomic shape S_i, P_i).

It is reasonable to believe in an infinity of atomic shapes.

The inferential apparatus here is interestingly complex; and I am inclined to think that it is valid. But, again, *E* (P_1, P_2, . . .) still seems a groundless hypothesis: why on earth suppose that all atomic shapes are explanatorily equivalent? Plato would urge that some shapes are physically and theologically superior to others; a modern atomist, if he allowed his atoms shape at all, would prefer a single atomic shape, and probably deny the need to explain why that shape alone should exist.

I shall not pursue these matters further. In conclusion, I say first, that the epistemological *Ou Mallon* Principle is a sound and important principle of reasoning; second, that certain other *Ou Mallon* Principles, which the Atomists may possibly have confused with it, are equally interesting, though more in need of elucidation; and thirdly, that the few verses of the *ou mallon* song which we possess are less melodious than the refrain which punctuated them.

(e) *Democritean scepticism*

Metrodorus of Chios, a pupil of Democritus (e.g., Clement, **70 A 1**) who held solidly to the main tenets of atomism (e.g., Theophrastus, **A 3**), purveys an extreme scepticism which foreshadows, in its ingenious comprehensiveness, the most extravagant claims of Pyrrho: at the beginning of his book *Concerning Nature* Metrodorus said:

> None of us knows anything, not even that very fact whether we know or do not know; nor do we know what not to know and to know are, nor, in general, whether anything is or is not (**505: B 1**).[18]

Of Metrodorus' book little else survives and nothing tells us what his scepticism rested upon, or why he wrote *Concerning Nature* at all. His scepticism, however, like his atomism, was inherited. For according to Democritus,

> In reality (*eteêi*) we know nothing; for truth is in a pit (**506: 68 B 117**).

Our main source for Democritus' scepticism is Sextus; and I quote the chief Democritean fragments in their Sextan setting:

> Democritus sometimes does away with what appears to the senses. . . . In the *Buttresses*, though he had promised to ascribe the power of conviction to the senses, he is none the less found condemning them; for he says:
>
> > We in actuality grasp nothing firm, but what changes (*metapipton*) in accordance with the contact (*diathigên*)[19] between our body and the things which enter into it and the things which strike against it [= **B 9**].
>
> And again he says:
>
> > Now that in reality (*eteêi*) we do not grasp of what sort each thing is or is not, has been made clear in many ways [= **B 10**].

And in *Concerning Forms* he says:

A man must know by this rule that he is separated from reality (*eteê*) [= **B 6**].

And again:

This argument too makes it clear that in reality (*eteêi*) we know nothing about anything; but belief (*doxis*) for each group of men is a reshaping (*epirhusmiê*) [= **B 7**].

And again:

Yet it will be clear that to know what sort each thing is in reality (*eteêi*) is inaccessible [= **B 8**].

In those passages he pretty well destroys apprehension in its entirety, even if he explicitly attacks only the senses. But in the *Canons* he says that there are two kinds of knowing (*gnôseis*), one via the senses, one via the intellect (*dianoia*); he calls the one via the intellect 'legitimate (*gnêsiê*)', ascribing to it reliability for the judgment of truth, and he names that via the senses 'bastard (*skotiê*)', denying it inerrancy in the discrimination of what is true. These are his words:

Of knowledge (*gnômê*) there are two forms, the one legitimate, the other bastard; and to the bastard belong all these: sight, hearing, smell, taste, touch. And the other is legitimate, and separated from that.

Then, preferring the legitimate to the bastard, he continues:

When the bastard can no longer see anything smaller, or hear, or smell, or taste, or perceive by touch, † but more fine † [= **B 11**].

Thus according to him too, reason, which he calls legitimate knowledge, is a criterion (**507**: *adv Math* VII. 135–9).

Fragments **B 7** and **B 10** show that Democritus' scepticism was not merely a glum asseveration of intellectual impotence, but the melancholy conclusion of a set of arguments. Two of Democritus' arguments can, I think, be reconstructed.

First, there is *doxis epirhusmiê* of **B** 7. I suppose that '*doxis epirhusmiê*' means 'belief is a rearrangement of our constituent atoms', i.e. 'coming to believe that *P* is having certain parts (e.g., cerebral parts) of one's atomic substructure rearranged' (cf. Theophrastus, *Sens* §58 = **A 135**).[20] Belief, then, cannot ever amount to knowledge, because it is never anything more than an atomic rearrangement. I guess that Democritus is supposing, if only tacitly, that knowledge is essentially reasoned belief: opinion not arrived at by rational considerations cannot qualify as knowledge. But if every belief is simply a cerebral alteration (caused, no doubt, by our changing relation with other atomic conglomerates), then no belief can be rational. To put it crudely, causally determined cerebral mutations cannot be identical with rationally accepted beliefs.

The argument has connexions with Xenophanes (above, p. 142); but it is less subtle and less persuasive than Xenophanes' argument. According to Xenophanes, certain types of causal chain prevent a caused belief from counting as knowledge; according to Democritus, any belief, being the physical result of a causal chain, is disqualified from knowledge. Democritus, I think, is simply wrong: my belief that *P* may constitute knowledge even if it is itself a physical state (a state of my nervous system) and even if it stands at the end of a causal chain (as surely it does). Roughly speaking, the belief is knowledge if the physical state which embodies it was caused, mediately or immediately by the fact that *P* (i.e., if it is true that because *P* I believe that *P*); and the belief is rational if the physical state which embodies it was caused by certain other beliefs (i.e., if because I believe that *Q* I believe that *P*, where *Q* in fact gives good grounds for *P*). If a causal theory of knowledge can be worked out in detail, then Democritus' argument for scepticism in **B 7** must be rejected.

Second, there is **B 9**. Sextus evidently thinks that Democritus means 'perceive' by 'grasp (*sunienai*)'; and he may be right. But Democritus is not simply 'condemning' the senses: he is offering an argument. The point, I think, is this: cognitive processes are interactions between observers and objects of observation; the processes, atomically construed, consist in the impingement of atoms from the object on the body of the observer. Now any such process involves a change in the object; for it loses at least those atoms which impinge upon the observer. Consequently, we can never know the state of any object; for any attempt to discover it thereby changes it. We grasp nothing 'firm'; for our very grip disturbs. Knowledge alters the known; and therefore knowledge is impossible.

According to modern physical theory, we discover the position and characteristics of an object by way of some physical interaction with it: in the simplest case, I see where the cat is by shining a torch on it and receiving the reflected rays. What goes for cats goes for sub-atomic particles; to tell where a particle is I must fire a ray at it and receive it on the rebound. But sub-atomic particles are delicate things, and when a ray hits them they are shaken; thus the reflected ray will not give me the information I want. It cannot tell me where the particle is and how it is travelling; for the impact, without which I can know nothing of the particle, will change the particle's trajectory. (That is meant as a kindergarten version of the reasoning behind Heisenberg's Indeterminacy Principle; science for the infant is usually bad science, but I hope that the point of my parallel is not wholly blunted by my puerile exposition.)

Atomic structures cannot be known; for the process of acquiring knowledge necessarily distorts those structures. The quest for knowledge is like the search for the end of the rainbow: we can never discover the pot of gold; for our journey towards the rainbow's end in itself moves the rainbow to a different and ever distant location.

The argument that I have dredged from **B 9** is not *a priori*: it depends on Democritean physics and psychology. I guess that it may present a plausible deduction from those Atomist theories, though I doubt if there is enough evidence for us to test its validity. In any case, there is no philosophical way of attacking it: it fails if the physics and psychology are false (and I assume that they are).

> Metrodorus of Chios said that no one knows anything: the things we believe we know we do not strictly (*akribôs*) know; nor should we attend to our senses. For everything is by belief (**508**: Epiphanius, **70 A 23**).

Leucippus insists that we have belief, but no more (Epiphanius, **67 A 33**); and in many of the fragments I have quoted, Democritus denies that we have genuine knowledge. Many sceptical philosophers seem to be making what is little more than a verbal point: we do not, strictly speaking, *know* anything, but we can, of course, have reasonable beliefs. Such thinkers set the canons of knowledge artificially high: knowledge must be certain, or infallible, or necessary, or indubitable, or whatever. If the canons are set high, then knowledge is indeed beyond us; but ordinary men are quite happy with relaxed canons, and those sceptics who allow reasonable belief in fact allow precisely the thing that ordinary men call knowledge.

The Atomists, however, do not even allow reasonable belief: their arguments against knowledge, in so far as we know them, are equally arguments against reasonable belief. We have beliefs: that is an incontestable empirical fact. Our beliefs do not amount to knowledge: that is the argument of the Abderites. Yet our beliefs are not even reasonable: being atomically caused, they are not founded on reason; and the physics of the cognitive processes assures us that no impressions of external reality are accurate. If there is no room for knowledge, by the same token there is no room for reasoned belief: 'everything is by belief'—but that, far from being a consolation, is only a cause for despair. The urbane scepticism of Locke allows a decent wattage to the human candle: our light extends as far as we need, but not as far as we like to boast. Abderite scepticism is Pyrrhonian: the light of the mind is an *ignis fatuus*.

That conclusion did not please Democritus; indeed, as Sextus observes, his fragments do not exhibit consistency. Fragment **B 11** tails off into corruption; but the general sense of Democritus' remarks is clear enough: 'the bastard way of knowing (*skotiê gnôsis*)' will not carry us to the finest or ultimate constituents of stuff; for that, 'the legitimate way of knowing (*gnêsiê gnôsis*)' is needed. That coheres with Democritus' approval of the Anaxagorean slogan: *opsis tôn adêlôn ta phainomena*—what the senses cannot apprehend must be grasped by the intellect. There seems, then, to be an empiricist Democritus rising in revolt against the sceptic.

And perhaps the sceptical fragments have been misread: the Heisenbergian argument, after all, at most shows that we cannot directly apprehend the atomic elements of things; it does not show that we may make no inferences from perceptible things to their elemental structure. **B 9** and **B 10** consistently say that we cannot 'grasp' things in their reality; but that only means that atoms are not open to perceptual knowledge.[21] Thus we may find a positive epistemology for Democritus: 'All knowledge rests on perception: and perception will not, directly, yield knowledge of what exists *eteêi*. But by perception we may come to know about what is *nomôi*, and intellectual attention to those sensual pronouncements will enable us to procure an inferential knowledge of genuine reality.'

Alas, that happy picture is mistaken. The *doxis epirhusmiê* argument is resolutely sceptical; and **B 6, B 7, B 8**, and **B 117** leave no room for any knowledge at all. Moreover, Democritus recognized that the empiricist intimations of **B 11** were misleading:

> Having slandered the phenomena . . . he makes the senses address the intellect thus: 'Wretched mind! Do you take your evidence from us and then overthrow us? Our overthrow is your downfall' (**509: B 125**).

In a puckish mood, Russell once observed that naive realism leads us to accept the assertions of modern science; and that modern science then proves realism false. Realism is false if it is true; hence it is false. And if science rests on realism, then it is built upon sand. The parallel with Democritus is plain: the observations of the senses give us a set of facts upon which an atomistic science is reared; the science then proves the irrationality of all belief and the unreliability of the senses. If the senses are to be trusted, they are not to be trusted; hence they are not to be trusted. And if atomism rests upon the senses, then atomism is ill founded.

Did the mind answer the senses? Had Democritus any solution to the problem which **509** candidly poses? There is no evidence that he had; and I am inclined to think that he had not. It is, I suppose, a tribute to Democritus' honesty that he acknowledged his plight; but it derogates somewhat from his philosophical reputation that he made no move to escape from the *impasse* he found himself in.

EPILOGUE

XXV

The Last of the Line

(a) *Diogenes the eclectic*

Diogenes of Apollonia was no great original. He was a medical man whose views appear to have had some considerable influence on his contemporaries and successors; and Aristotle has preserved for us his detailed account of the human blood vessels (**64 B 6**; cf. **B 9**). Like earlier doctors, he engaged in natural philosophy, writing, by his own account, a work *Concerning Nature*, a *Meteorology*, a treatise *On the Nature of Man*, and a book, *Against the Sophists* (Simplicius, **A 4**).[1] The philosophy he expounded was conceived on the old Ionian pattern; and Theophrastus held him to be the last of the *phusiologoi* (Simplicius, **A 5**). By common scholarly consent, he was least as well as last: he worked eclectically rather than creatively, and 'does not seem to have attempted original thought'; indeed, he represents a positive regression, for his 'general level of philosophical awareness suggests the age of Anaximenes, not that of Anaxagoras and the sophists'.[2]

A few voices have spoken for Diogenes: he was affected by Heraclitus, a pupil of Leucippus and Anaxagoras, and a significant influence on Melissus—in short, a man of some historical importance. Or he was a teleologist, and indeed the inventor of teleological explanation; or else, *pace* Aristotle, he was the first 'material monist'. But those voices do not convince. Chronologically, the first suggestion is implausible; Anaxagoras was a teleologist before ever Diogenes wrote; and the Milesians were, as Aristotle says, material monists. In the last quarter of the fifth century Diogenes appears to have stood in Athenian estimation as the very type and paradigm of Ionian *phusiologia*: he is a common butt of comedy and he had an influence on Euripidean tragedy.[3] Such a reputation implies not stature and novelty but rather the reverse; it is unoriginal men who are thus representative.

Three reasons, I think, justify the expense of a few pages on this essentially second-rate man: first, though aware of Eleatic arguments he remained a material monist, evidently thinking that the pluralistic accounts of his fellow neo-Ionians were not necessary to evade the Eleatic snares; second, we know far more of him than of the Milesian monists, and in his fragments we find arguments which have not come down to us under any earlier name; third, our knowledge of his teleology is much fuller than our knowledge of Anaxagoras' earlier theory. If the man was a bore, his fragments (partly for accidental and extrinsic reasons) still command interest.

Diogenes was aware of Eleatic metaphysics, and defended an old Milesian monism in its face. The evidence for the first part of that statement is in fact thin, though it will hardly be imagined that a *phusiologos* writing at the end of the fifth century could have been unaware of Parmenides' writings. Diogenes Laertius reports:

> He held that . . . nothing comes into being from what does not exist, nor perishes into what does not exist (**510**: IX.57 = **A 1**).

The report is perfunctory and formulaic, but there is no reason to doubt its accuracy, or to reject the obvious suggestion that it states an acceptance of the Eleatic position on generation and corruption.

Diogenes' adherence to a Milesian monism is attested in his own words. *Concerning Nature* began, according to Diogenes Laertius, thus:

> When beginning any account, one must, it seems to me, provide an indisputable starting point (*archê*) and write in a simple and noble style (**511: B 1**).

It is not, perhaps, entirely fanciful to see a serious methodological point here: in the second half of the fifth century, the Greek geometers had been developing an axiomatic way of presenting their study; and Diogenes, in requiring an 'indisputable starting point', is, I imagine, striving to imitate the geometers and to found something like an axiomatized physics. But it would be foolish to lay much weight on that; and my present interest is in the content of Diogenes' *archê*. 'Immediately after the preface', Simplicius says, 'he writes thus:

> It seems to me, to state it comprehensively, that all existing things change from the same thing and are the same thing (see **515: B 2**).

That this is material monism is clear enough; and most of the doxographers identify Diogenes' *Urstoff* as air.

From the *Urstoff* Diogenes developed the world. We have no first-hand fragments; but the doxography supplies the want:

> He says that the nature of the whole is air, unlimited and eternal; and from it, as it is condensed and rarefied and changed in its affections, the form of other things comes into being (**512**: Simplicius, **A 5**).

> He makes the cosmos thus: as the whole is moved, and becomes rare here and dense there . . . (**513**: pseudo-Plutarch, **A 6**).

Motion of the original stuff introduces variation in density; and those variations account for the different forms that the world assumes. The system is traditional; indeed, it is so far indistinguishable from Anaximenes' cosmogony.

How did Diogenes reconcile an Anaximenean cosmogony with an Eleatic denial of generation?

> The others say that perceptible things are by nature (*phusei*); but Leucippus and Democritus and Diogenes say that they are by convention (*nomôi*), i.e. in opinion (*doxêi*) and in our affections (*pathesi*) (**514**: Aëtius, **A 23**).

Aëtius is not the best of authorities; and his testimony is isolated.[4] Yet it can, I think, be supported from **B 2**. After the general assertion of monism that I have already quoted, Diogenes proceeds thus:

> And that is quite clear; for if the things that now exist in this universe—earth and water and air and fire and the other things which appear (*phainetai*) as existing in this universe—if any of these were different from the others (different in its proper nature) and were not the same as they changed in many ways and altered, they could in no way mingle with one another (see **515: B 2**).

The 'proper nature (*idia phusis*)' of any stuff is the same as that of every other stuff; and a proper nature cannot change. Everything is, really, the same; nothing, really, changes. What, then, are the alterations to which **515** refers? Some of them are specified in **B 5**; speaking of air Diogenes says:

> For it is of many types (*polutropos*)—hotter and colder, drier and moister, stabler and having a sharper motion; and there are many other alterations in it, both of taste and of colour, unlimitedly many (see **527**).

515 implies that cosmic change is somehow extrinsic to things; the examples of **527** confirm the implication; they are all alterations which can comfortably be construed as relational: if air becomes hotter, that is only to say that it appears differently to us; if the air moves faster, that is only to say that its parts alter their spatial relations to one another. Such changes are extrinsic or relational; they are not intrinsic or real.[5]

Change is a matter of gain and loss: we change by gaining one property and losing another; and a simple-minded definition of change might read thus:

(D) *a* changes at *t* if and only if for some ϕ *a* is not-ϕ before *t* and *a* is ϕ after *t*.

But (D), as Plato realized, will not do: if Cebes grows until he overtops Socrates, then according to (D) Socrates, as well as Cebes, has changed; for the predicate 'is shorter than Cebes' comes to be true of him. Cebes, no doubt, has changed; and as a result of Cebes' change a new predicate comes to hold of Socrates. But that is not enough to make us say that Socrates has changed; and definition (D) must be abandoned.

Occurrences which count as changes by (D) but which are not genuine changes have been called Cambridge changes. In the example of Socrates and Cebes, Socrates undergoes a Cambridge change because Cebes suffers a genuine change. But Cambridge change is not always parasitic upon genuine change: if Socrates is alone in his room until Cebes enters, then at the time of Cebes' entry the predicate 'shorter than someone in the room' comes to hold of Socrates. But neither Socrates nor Cebes (nor the room) has changed.

Diogenes, I suggest, wanted us to regard all apparent alterations in the world as Cambridge changes. He adopted the Abderite account of *nomôi* qualities, making them relational and mind-dependent; and he developed that account in an intelligible way. There is reason to think that he borrowed the void from Leucippus (cf. Diogenes Laertius IX.57 = **A 1**); and that the void allowed him locomotion, and condensation and rarefaction. Those operations will explain all apparent changes: yet they do not constitute intrinsic or real change in the *Urstoff*, for they are essentially relational operations. Things alter only in the sense that there are appearances of alteration to be accounted for. Similarly, locomotion, condensation and rarefaction underlie all generation; yet they do not constitute any intrinsic or real generation of things or stuff, for they are essentially relational operations. Things are generated only in the sense that there are appearances of generation to be explained. And the appearances, both of alteration and of generation, can be explained in a way that does no violence to Eleatic logic.

(b) *Monism revived*

Diogenes argued for his monism; he did not merely assert it. I begin by copying out the whole of **B 2**, the first half of which I have already quoted.

> It seems to me, to state it comprehensively, that all existing things change from the same thing and are the same thing. And that is quite clear; for if the things that now exist in this universe—earth and water and air and fire and the other things which appear as existing in this universe—if any of these were different from the others (different in its proper nature) and were not the same as they changed in many ways and altered, they could in no way mingle with one another, nor would advantage and harm come to one from another, nor would plants grow from the earth, nor animals, nor anything else be born, if things were not so put together as to be the same. But all these things, being alterations from the same thing, become different at different times and return to the same thing (**515**).

Theophrastus sums the fragment up in a sentence:

> There would be no acting or being acted upon if everything were not from one thing (**516**: *Sens* §39 = **A 19**).

Material monism is necessary to account for change: if everything is not at bottom one substance, then alteration is not possible. That is, at first blush, an implausible assertion. How can Diogenes have defended it? I offer two interpretations.

First, consider the following reports about Democritus:

> He says that what acts and what is acted upon must be the same or similar; for it is not possible for distinct and different things to be acted upon by one another; but if they *are* distinct and act in some way upon one another, that happens to them not in so far as they are distinct but in so far as some one thing belongs to them both (**517**: Aristotle, *GC* 323b11–15 = **68 A 63**).

> It is impossible, he says, for things which are not the same to be acted upon [by one another]; but if though different they actually act [on one another], they do so not in so far as they are different, but in so far as some one thing belongs to them both (**518**: Theophrastus, *Sens* §49 = **A 135**).

If X and Y interact, then X and Y must be somehow 'the same'. Classical dualism discovered a problem in the interaction between body and soul: how, they wondered, can a corporeal stuff act upon a spiritual, or a spiritual upon a corporeal? Descartes asserted that interaction occurred but was inexplicable. Leibniz allowed that '*the way of influence* [i.e. of interaction] is that of the common philosophy; but as we cannot conceive material particles or immaterial species or qualities which can pass from one of these substances into another, we are obliged to give up this opinion'; and Leibniz advances instead his own theory of the 'pre-established harmony'.[6]

Descartes' difficulty and Leibniz' argument rest upon a specification of the Democritean Principle:

(1) If a acts upon b, then a is of the same stuff as b.

Since soul and body have no stuff in common, soul and body cannot interact. Was this classical application of the Democritean principle also its original application? The Abderite world is homogeneous—all agents are indifferent atoms; but the neo-Ionian world of Anaxagoras is not. In Anaxagorean physics, mind is the supreme agent, and mind is distinct in nature from all other stuffs. I wonder if Democritus had Anaxagoras in his sights when he formulated principle (1).

However that may be, the first interpretation of **515** bases monism on the Democritean Principle. In addition to that Principle, Diogenes needs a premiss to the effect that all things interact with one another. That premiss requires a precise statement. Let us say that a interacts with b if either a acts upon b or b acts upon a; and let us say that a is linked to b if there is some ordered set of objects, $\langle c_1, c_2, \ldots, c_n \rangle$, such that a interacts with c_1, c_1 interacts with c_2, . . ., c_n interacts with b. Then Diogenes' premiss is:

(2) For any objects x and y, either x interacts with y or x is linked to y.

From (1) and (2) we can readily infer monism. Take any two objects, a and b. By (2) either a and b interact or they are linked. If they interact, then by (1) they are of the same stuff; if they are linked, then a is of the same stuff as c_1, c_1 as c_2, . . ., c_n as b; so that, again, a is of the same stuff as b. Generalize the argument, and you have material monism.

Assumption (2) is, I think, a highly plausible hypothesis. Diogenes' argument fails if the Democritean principle is false. And although that principle has been immensely popular, I know of no argument in its favour: the principle is not (as far as I can see) a logical truth; and I do not think that it is confirmed by empirical observation.

I find a different interpretation of **515** in Aristotle:

> Diogenes rightly says that if everything were not from one thing, then things would not act and be acted upon by one another; e.g., the hot become cold, and this again become hot. For it is not the heat and the coldness that change into one another, but (evidently) the underlying subject (**519**: *GC* 322b12–17 = **A 7**).

Aristotle is not thinking of the Democritean principle, but of a theorem on change which he himself accepts: if at t an F becomes a G, then there must be some one thing, persisting from some time before t to some time after t, which is first F and later G. Change is change *in* or *of* something; it requires a unity in diversity; it occurs when some one thing assumes (or appears to assume) different aspects at different times.

The Aristotelian principle may be written as:

(3) If an F becomes a G at t, then there is something which was F before t and G after t.

Diogenes, I think, needs a strong version of (3), viz.:

(4) If an F becomes a G at t, then there is some stuff S such that a piece of S was an F before t and a G after t.

In addition to the Aristotelian principle, Diogenes requires a premiss to the effect that everything becomes everything. In order to state that premiss precisely, let us say that *F*s connect with *G*s if either some F becomes a G or there is an ordered set $\langle H_1, H_2, \ldots, H_n\rangle$ such that some F becomes an H_1, some H_1 an H_2, . . ., some H_n a G. Diogenes' premiss then is:

(5) For any ϕ and ψ, ϕs connect with ψs.

The parallelism between linking and connecting, between (2) and (5) is evident.

Take any two properties, *F*ness and *G*ness. By (5), *F*s and *G*s connect. Hence either some F becomes a G, in which case (by (4)) *F*s and *G*s are made of the same stuff; or else some F becomes an H_1, some H_1 an H_2 . . ., in which case *F*s and H_1s are of the same stuff, H_1s and H_2s are of the same stuff . . ., so that again *F*s and *G*s are of the same stuff. Generalize the argument, and again you have monism.

Assumption (5) is less plausible than assumption (2); but it has evident connexions with Anaxagorean physics (above, p. 330), and I imagine that Diogenes may have adopted it from his neo-Ionian predecessor. Aristotle's principle (3) is surely true—indeed, it is a logical truth about alteration. It may be expressed by saying that alteration implies a persistent substrate; and in a trivial sense any such substrate is an Aristotelian 'matter' or *hulê*—if '*hulê*' is defined as that which persists through change (cf. *Met* 1042a32–b8). But must *hulê* then be a stuff or material? Lot's wife changed into a pillar of salt and Niobe was turned into stone: if we regard those phenomena as alterations, then the persistent substrate is form, not stuff. What links Lot's wife and the pillar, Niobe and the rock, is the shape or form of their different constituent stuffs. Normally, perhaps, a material continuity underlies formal alteration; but in odd cases formal continuity may underpin material change. And if that is so, it is neither a necessary nor even a contingent truth that alteration presupposes some persisting stuff, and proposition (4)—Diogenes' version of the Aristotelian principle—is false.

In any case, as I have stated the argument it contains a logical flaw: given that an *F* becomes a *G*, we can infer, by (4), that *that F* and *that G* are made of the same stuff; but we cannot infer—as the argument would have us do—that *all* Fs and *all* Gs are made of the same stuff. In order to reach that universal conclusion we must supplement the argument with a further premiss, a Principle of Homogeneity:

(6) If any *F* is made of a stuff *S*, then every *F* is made of *S*.

Now that Principle is perhaps Diogenean; for Diogenes supposes that everything that is *F* must have some one 'proper nature'; and may not that 'proper nature' consist in, or at least include, being constituted by some stuff, S^F? But the 'proper nature' of Lot's wife or of Niobe does not include a constituent stuff; and in general, if alteration can occur by formal rather than material change, then 'natures' do not determine stuffs. Nor need we look to such *outré* occurrences: it is plainly untrue that everything *F* ('humaniform', 'green', 'sour', 'six feet long') is made of a single stuff S^F.

Neither interpretation of Diogenes' fragment gives him a sound argument for monism; and that is hardly surprising. Yet **516** indicates some cogitation on the logical features of alteration; and from it we may elicit plausible and influential propositions. The fragment is not devoid of philosophical charm.

(c) *The matter of the universe*

If there is a single stuff, what is it?

> And [Diogenes] too says that the nature of the whole is air, unlimited and eternal. . . . That is what Theophrastus reports about Diogenes; and the book of his entitled *Concerning Nature* which has come into my hands clearly names as air that from which all other things come to be (**520**: Simplicius, **A 5**).

Theophrastus' account is repeated by the doxographers (Diogenes

Laertius, IX. 57 = **A 1**; pseudo-Plutarch, **A 6**; Aëtius, **A 7**); and it accounts for the tradition that Diogenes was a follower of Anaximenes (Simplicius, **A 4**; cf. Antisthenes, *apud* Diogenes Laertius, IX. 57 = **A 1**). Theophrastus, however, did not win universal support.

> The research of the majority asserts that Diogenes of Apollonia, like Anaximenes, makes the primary element air; but Nicolaus in his book *On Gods* reports that he takes as his principle something between fire and air (**521**: Simplicius, **A 4**).

Simplicius notes that Porphyry adhered to Nicolaus' interpretation (cf. **63 A 1**) and he says that:

> I too, on reading these initial remarks [i.e. **515**], thought that [Diogenes] took the common substrate to be something other than the four elements [and hence something distinct from air] (**522**: *ad* **64 B 2**).

Simplicius offers an argument for taking air as the material *archê*: 'These men thought that the ease with which air is acted upon and altered (*to eupathes kai euallolôton*) made it susceptible to change' (**A 5**); but he does not ascribe that to Diogenes by name, and he produces no textual evidence to support such an ascription. He does, however, quote from Diogenes to prove Theophrastus' opinion right and Nicolaus' wrong: after copying the passages we list as **B 3**, **B 4** and **B 5** he says:

> Here, then, [Diogenes] evidently says quite clearly that the stuff which men call air is the principle (**523**: *ad* **B 6**).

Simplicius is out to make a case, and he possessed Diogenes' treatise: if we cannot find in **B 3–5** the statement that air is the *archê*, we shall have no reason to ascribe it to Diogenes at all.

I shall later quote those three fragments in full. Here it is enough to say that **B 3** does not mention air at all; and that while **B 4** proclaims that 'men and the other animals that breathe live by air; and this is both soul and thought for them', it makes no mention of an *archê*. It is, I suppose, the following sentence from **B 5** on which Simplicius principally relies: 'And there is not a single thing which does not share in this [sc. air]; but there are many types both of air itself and of thought. For it [i.e. air] is of many types . . .'. Diogenes is not doing cosmology here; nor is he talking of a material substrate. Rather, he is concerned with psychology: that air is 'of many types (*polutropos*)' is advanced to show not that it is a suitable substratum, but that it can constitute souls and thoughts of radically different varieties.

There is, then, no evidence for Theophrastus' interpretation of Diogenes' *archê*; and there is some evidence against it. **515** lists air alongside earth, water, fire and the rest; the collocation implies that air is non-elemental just as they are, and nothing is done to cancel that implication. Nicolaus' assertion that the *archê* is 'something between fire and air' fares no better than Theophrastus: there is no textual evidence in its favour. Yet if we reject both Theophrastus and Nicolaus, what remains? Only, I think, **B 7**:

> And this itself is a body, both eternal and deathless; and of the rest, some come into being, others depart (**524**).[7]

Is that Diogenes' final characterization of his material substrate? Is it simply body (*sôma*)—'stuff' or, in the Scholastic jargon, 'prime matter'?

Since water visibly changes into air, and the change is an alteration not a destruction-*cum*-generation, both water and air are modifications of some underlying stuff. But that underlying stuff cannot be characterized by any perceptible properties; for any such characterization would identify it with one of the four elements, or with an elemental compound. Consequently, it is pure, unqualified, stuff. The conclusion will offend philosophers as a nonsense (did not Locke unwittingly explode the notion of 'substance in general', that 'something we know not what'?); and it will offend scholars as an anachronism (prime matter was invented by Aristotle, if not by later Aristotelians). Neither offence is justified, and a single argument will do for both: Diogenes is applying to Milesian stuff precisely the account which the Abderites gave to their atoms. Atoms are bodies (*sômata*); they occupy space and they have motive powers; but they have no perceptible qualities, they are *apoia*, without qualities (above, pp. 368–70). That is a coherent notion; and it is virtually identical with the notion of 'prime matter'. Diogenes, I suggest, married Anaximenes with Leucippus; and the marriage produced an Aristotelian offspring: his *archê* is not air, and it is not a mysterious fifth element between air and fire; it is matter, stuff.

(d) *Immanent will and its designs*

> For things could not have been parcelled out (*dedasthai*) in this way without thought (*noêsis*), so that there are measures of everything: of winter and of summer, of night and of day, of rains and of winds and of fine weather. And the other things, if one wishes to think about them, one would find to have been disposed in the finest (*kallista*) way possible (**525: B 3**).

In this brief fragment we find the first extant exposition of the Teleological Argument for the existence of God, or the Argument from Design. We may conjecture that Anaxagoras had employed it, though no evidence directly supports the conjecture; and we find it elaborated in two passages in Xenophon's *Memorabilia*;[8] but if it was current at the end of the fifth century and not an innovation of Diogenes, it is to the despised Diogenes that we must now look for its first statement.

The Argument was canonized by Aquinas as the fifth of his Five Ways to God. According to Kant, it 'is the oldest, the clearest, and the most accordant with the common reason of mankind. It enlivens the study of nature, just as it itself derives its existence and gains ever new vigour from that source. . . . It would . . . not only be uncomforting but utterly vain to attempt to diminish in any way the authority of this argument. Reason, constantly upheld by this ever-increasing evidence, which, though empirical, is yet so powerful, cannot be so depressed through doubts suggested by subtle and abstruse speculation that it is not at once aroused from the indecision of all melancholy reflection, as from a dream, by one glance at the wonders of nature and the majesty of the universe—ascending from height to height up to the all-highest, from the conditioned to its conditions, up to the supreme and unconditioned Author' (*Critique of Pure Reason*, A 624).

Kant's high praise for the Argument derives from Hume; in Hume's *Dialogues on Natural Religion*, Cleanthes advances the Argument and asserts that 'it requires time, reflection and study, to summon up those frivolous, though abstruse objections, which can support Infidelity. . . . To what degree . . . of blind dogmatism must one have attained, to reject such natural and such convincing arguments?' I am, I confess, a blind dogmatist by Cleanthes' reckoning; but I shall not try here to justify my dogmatism, limiting my task to the exposition and criticism of Diogenes' version of the Argument.

Diogenes' argument is splendidly simple. He starts from the premiss:

(1) Everything is arranged in the finest possible way;

and he concludes to:

(2) There is an intelligent arranger of everything.

The premiss is a truth of experience: we observe that 'there are measures of everything'; and the conclusion follows at once. From the conclusion it is easy to infer the existence of an almighty, everlasting, and merciful God.

I shall ignore the final, theogonical, step in the argument. Hume demonstrated with wit and cogency that the Argument from Design cannot establish the existence of a god with the traditional Christian attributes: infinity, eternity and benevolence cannot be squeezed from the Argument. But Diogenes was not a Christian; and he does not claim that his designing intelligence has the Christian attributes. In any case, the argument from (1) to (2) is interesting in its own right.

The premiss (1) contains two uncertainties. First, the word 'everything' can be taken either collectively ('the whole sum of things') or distributively ('each thing'). The latter sense seems intended in **526**, and it is certainly suggested by Xenophon and by most of the orthodox modern versions of the argument. Suppose, now, that we accept the principle:

(3) If *a* is finely arranged, then there is an intelligent arranger of *a*.

Even so, we cannot infer (2) from (1). The premiss entails that everything has its arranger, i.e.:

(4) $(\forall x)\ (\exists y)\ (y$ is the arranger of $x)$;

but it does not entail that there is an arranger of everything, i.e.:

(5) $(\exists y)\ (\forall x)\ (y$ is the arranger of $x)$.

Kant anticipated the objection: having concluded that 'there exists, therefore, a sublime and wise cause (or more than one)', he proceeds to argue that 'the unity of this cause may be inferred from the unity of the reciprocal relations existing between the parts of the world, as members of an artfully arranged structure'. Kant's recipe, in effect, is to read 'everything' in (1) in the collective and not the distributive sense; and (5) rather than (4) is the result. But Hume had already countered that move: 'And what shadow of an argument . . . can you produce, from your hypothesis, to prove the unity of the Deity? A great number of men join in building a house, or ship, in rearing a city, in framing a commonwealth: why may not several deities combine in contriving and framing a world?'

That criticism is, I think, fatal to any Christian use of the Argument; yet it is not so damaging to Diogenes, who does not seem to have shown any particular interest in proving a unique deity. The second uncertainty in (1) brings us nearer to a fatal blow. The traditional Argument speaks of order or design; Diogenes talks of a fine parcelling out or arrangement. These terms may cover two distinct notions. First, the underlying notion may be aesthetic: order, thus construed, is pattern, regularity, symmetry, or in general some aesthetically satisfying and economical arrangement of things. Second, the underlying notion may be one of purpose or plan: order, thus construed, is the appearance of direction, of intention, of purposed or planned progress. A snowflake and the solar system show aesthetic order (of different magnitude and to different degrees): they are intricately patterned, arranged in simple and satisfying regularities. The human digestive track and the maggot show purposive order: their activities appear directed to some goal or end. Snowflakes do not appear to have a purpose; and the intestines are aesthetically disgusting: pattern and purpose regularly fall apart (functional architecture is almost invariably ugly); but they sometimes combine, in the spider's web, the bee's honeycomb, or the elegant root of the parsnip.

Does everything exhibit pattern? does everything exhibit purpose? do we find things 'to have been disposed in the finest way possible'? Let me be brutally dogmatic. First, not all features of the world exhibit the beauty of the snowflake; even in the natural world, untouched by human hand, there is much that is messy, crude, and ugly. Nor, in my judgment, is the universe as a whole a thing of aesthetic value. Second, the universe as a whole does not seem, to me at any rate, to evince or exhibit purpose; it does not look as though it were planned or contrived for some end. And if some of the parts of the natural world do seem purposive, most of inanimate nature does not: there is no appearance of intention in the course of the comets, no goal in the ebb and flow of the tides.

But those reflexions are perhaps a trifle subjective; others may spy pattern and purpose where all I see is heartless, witless Nature. Third, then, I assert that (3) is false. It is certainly not a *logical* truth that patterned objects were planned by a designer or that the apparent goals of natural processes are the actual goals of some instigator of those processes. Nor is (3) a well-grounded empirical hypothesis. Defenders of the Argument regularly call upon analogy: the eye has the same pattern and appearance of function as the telescope; the latter was designed by a human artificer; hence the former was designed by a divine artificer. The analogy is frail: it starts from a very small number of cases, and it implies a false degree of similarity between natural objects and artefacts. Every day we are faced with a thousand attractive or purposive things, none of which bears any mark of the designer's hand. Proposition (3) is grotesquely implausible: experience suggests something quite different: that fine arrangements arise, for the most part, without the plan or intervention of any fine arranger.

The Argument from Design is, I guess, the most appealing of all the traditional arguments for the existence of God; and of all those arguments it is (in my view) the least plausible. At any event, Diogenes' version of it has no probative force.

Having argued for a cosmic intelligence, Diogenes proceeds to inquire into its nature. He argues that it is air; and he implies that it is divine. For that conclusion, which delighted the comic poets (e.g., Philemon, **C 4**) and is frequently reported in the doxography,[9] we have Diogenes' own words:

> Again, in addition to this there are these great signs too: man and the other animals that breathe live by air; and this is both soul (*psuchê*) and thought (*noêsis*) for them (as will clearly be shown in this treatise), and if this is taken away they die and thought leaves them (**526: B 4**).

The promise of **526** is fulfilled in **B 5**, which I here quote in full:

> [i] And it seems to me that what has thought is that which men call air; and that by this all are governed, and it controls all. For (?) the custom of this very thing seems to me to be (?) to have penetrated everything, and to dispose everything, and to be in everything. [ii] And there is not a single thing which does not share in this; but no one thing shares in the same way as another, but there are many types both of air itself and of thought. For it is of many types—hotter and colder, drier and moister, stabler and having a sharper motion; and there are many other alterations in it both of taste and of colour, unlimitedly many. [iii] And the soul of all animals is the same: air, hotter than the external air in which we exist but much colder than the air by the sun. And this warmth is not alike in any of the animals (since not even in men is it the same from one to another), but it differs—not greatly but in such a way as to be similar. [iv] Now none of the things that change can become utterly similar to another, without becoming identical. Thus inasmuch as the alteration is of many types, animals too are of many forms, and many, alike one another neither in form nor in way of life nor in thought, because of the quantity of the alterations. Nevertheless it is by the same thing that all live and see and hear, and all have their other thought from the same thing (**527**).

The argument of this long fragment is far from clear in detail; and I shall not attempt a full exegesis. The chief *probandum*, I take it, is the identification of air as the medium of thought, and in general of life; and part [i] offers the argument for that conclusion: air is the penetrating oil *par excellence*; it is therefore the stuff that can govern and control; and hence it is to be identified as the bearer of thought. The argument is thoroughly Anaxagorean; and it requires no special commentary here.

The function of parts [ii]–[iv] is negative. It seems an objection to Diogenes that there is so vast a variety of life and intelligence; for how can one stuff, air, underlie so many thoughts? Part [ii] answers this by reference to the vast variety of forms of air; and [iii] states how thought can indeed be 'the same' in all animals, and yet 'different'. (In [iv] Diogenes adduces a logical principle which seems to amount to:

(6) If for any ϕ, if a is ϕ then b comes to be ϕ, then b comes to be a.

The principle has evident affinities with Leibniz' doctrine of the Identity of Indiscernibles; but it is not the same as that doctrine, and I do not understand how Diogenes intends it to be applied.)

527 has Anaxagorean connexions. The doxographers notice the fact (cf. Simplicius, **A 5**), but they do not make Diogenes a 'pupil' of Anaxagoras: Anaxagoras' pupil, in the standard histories, is Archelaus (e.g., Simplicius, **60 A 5**), the first Athenian philosopher. Archelaus followed Anaxagoras' physics on most points, but on the status of *nous* he differed:

> He says that some mixture inheres in mind essentially (**528**: Hippolytus, **60 A 4**).

> [He held that] air and mind are god—but not the cosmogonical mind (**529**: Aëtius, **60 A 12**).

Anaxagoras' mind is 'pure': Archelaus identifies it with air; and hence he is obliged to treat it as a stuff alongside other stuffs, containing a 'mixture' or a portion of everything. And, being a stuff, mind too will be in everything:

> He thought that everything was constituted in such a way that mind too, he said, inhered (**530**: Augustine, **60 A 10**).

The authorities are late and confused; yet the picture they present is not wholly implausible: in much the same way as Anaximenes gave substantial form to Anaximander's abstract *apeiron*, Archelaus made Anaxagoras' *nous* an intelligible part of the cosmos by identifying it as ordinary air, a familiar stuff capable of figuring in hard-headed physics. If *nous* is divine, and *nous* penetrates everything, then Archelaus has on his hands a panpsychism and a pantheism; and Augustine perhaps indicates as much.

Many scholars find Archelaus' view in Diogenes: **527** contains in [i] a statement that air is god; and in [ii] an assertion of panpsychism. From those two premisses, pantheism follows immediately. The relative chronology of Diogenes and Archelaus is unknown; but whether Diogenes borrowed from Archelaus or Archelaus from Diogenes, both men propounded the same revision of Anaxagoras' doctrine of *nous*.

That view may well be correct; but it rests on insecure foundations. First, the reader may well wonder how god is discovered in [i]: the answer is, by scholarly conjecture. The clause that I have embraced with question marks is textually corrupt; the most popular emendation makes it read: 'And this very thing seems to me to be god'.[10] Palaeographically the suggestion is neat; yet it does not fit particularly well into the argument of **527**, and other emendations which ignore god are possible. But however that may be, air is certainly divinized in the doxography; and that does give some force to the first premiss in the argument for Diogenean pantheism.

What of the second premiss, panpsychism? **527** says in [vi] that 'there is not a single thing which does not share in this [i.e. in air]'; and in [i], air is 'in everything'. That amounts to panpsychism provided that 'everything' means literally everything, and that air always bestows thought or intelligence. The first proviso may be true; but it is possible that 'all' and 'everything' are throughout **527** limited to animate objects. (In the clause 'all are governed', 'all' is restricted to men, as its gender shows.) The second proviso is almost certainly false: thought, according to **527**, is carried by fairly hot, moist air. To say that 'what has thought is that which men call air' is not to say that every bit of air is intelligent: air is the stuff of thought; but only in one of its modifications does air actually support thinking.

On the orthodox view of Diogenes' philosophy, air is both the omnipresent substratum of change and the omnipresent divinity: stuff and creator coincide, and material monism becomes a form of pantheism. I have preferred to separate both the substratum and god from air: the substratum is 'body' (*sôma*), and air is just one of its forms; the creative intelligence is not air as such, but a modification of air.[11] Diogenes' philosophy may thus be outlined as follows: the phenomena of change show that there is an underlying substrate more primitive than earth or water or fire or even air; it is pure stuff or 'body', and it has the essential characteristics of Abderite atoms. But the substratum logically required by change need not be identified with the *Urstoff* physically employed in cosmogony. It is possible that the cosmogonic *Urstoff* is air, one of the manifestations of body: in Diogenes' thought, as in that of Anaxagoras (**59 B 1**) and of Archelaus (Sextus, **60 A** 7), air plays an important role in cosmogony without being the general fundament of change. The *Urstoff* is moved, and the cosmogonical processes are begun, by the action of thought. And since what thinks is air, the cosmos is thus, in the final analysis, self-starting and self-created.

Diogenes of Apollonia was not a thinker of vast innovatory power:

the monistic insight of the early Milesians, the bold and intricate physics of Anaxagoras, and the profoundly influential speculations of the Atomists, cannot be matched by any grand Apolloniate thought. Diogenes was an eclectic and a synthesizer. Yet to say that is not to damn him: he was, I think, a judicious eclectic and a bold synthesizer. He ignored the intricacies of Anaxagorean mixture, but accepted the simple thesis of *nous*, supporting it by what was destined to become a classic argument; he ignored the untestable hypothesis of the Atomists and did not speak of minute corpuscles swimming in the void, but he took from them their characterization of stuff, and perhaps their account of change. He was conscious of the Eleatic pother and familiar with the neo-Ionian solutions. His own attempt at a solution is in many respects primitive: he does indeed breathe the air of Anaximenes. His primitiveness, however, is neither a weakness nor an indication of ignorance. Rather, grasping the importance of the central Milesian structure of material monism, he attempted to defend it against Eleatic assault, to buttress it with a few neo-Ionian stones, and to reveal its intrinsic strength and majesty.

After Diogenes, science and philosophy took a new turn; and the achievements of Plato, and then of Aristotle, temporarily eclipsed the light of Presocratic thought. For us that light is fitful but not dim: few rays emerge from the clouds of time; but they are brilliant and penetrating. And they will, I think, convince any doubters of the truth of the old platitude, that the history of thought begins with Thales and his Presocratic successors. Those ancient thinkers understood the nature of man long before Aristotle expounded it to the world at large; and they acted upon their understanding. For

What is a man,
If his chief good and market of his time
Be but to sleep and feed? A beast, no more.
Sure he that made us with such large discourse,
Looking before and after, gave us not
That capability and god-like reason
To fust in us unus'd.

Appendix A Sources

Our knowledge of the Presocratic philosophers is almost entirely indirect; for even where we possess their actual words, those words are preserved, fragmentarily, as quotations in the works of later authors. The sources we rely upon for *testimonia* and fragments span two millennia: they differ widely, one from another, in their literary aims, their historical competence, and their philosophical interests.

This appendix lists *in chronological order* the ancient authors I have quoted from or alluded to in the text and the notes. Some of the authors are (from a Presocratic point of view) of minor or minimal importance. A single asterisk is prefixed to the names of the more freely flowing sources; and those few gushing streams are marked by a pair of stars. Each name is followed by a date, often roundly given, and the briefest of biographical sentences. When a 'principal work' is named, that is not necessarily the author's major *opus*, but rather the book which holds most interest for students of the Presocratics.

Where no edition of the ancient text is mentioned, the reader may assume that I have used only the excerpts printed in Diels-Kranz. In citing editions I use these abbreviations:

CIAG *Commentaria in Aristotelem Graeca* (Berlin, 1881–1909)
OCT Oxford Classical Texts
SdA *Die Schule des Aristoteles*, ed. F. Wehrli (Basel, 1967–9[2])

HERODOTUS: *c.*485–*c.*430; the father of history. Edition: OCT, Hude.

HIPPOCRATES: *c.*470–*c.*380. The Hippocratic *corpus* is a compilation of works of various dates and of a medical character; perhaps none of them was written by the great Hippocrates himself. Abbreviations:
cord *de corde*

morb *de morbo*
morb sacr *de morbo sacro*
nat puer *de natura puerorum*
vet med *de vetere medicina* (ed. Festugière [218])
vict *de victu*
Edition: Littré, Paris, 1839–61.

ISOCRATES: 436–338; orator, statesman, and opponent of the Academy. Edition: Teubner, Benseler and Blass.

XENOPHON: *c*.430–*c*.355; general, historian, and pupil of Socrates. Principal work: *Memorabilia*. Edition: OCT, Marchant.

*PLATO: 427–347; his dialogues contain numerous references to his Presocratic predecessors. Edition: OCT, Burnet.

SPEUSIPPUS: *c*.410–340; Plato's nephew and successor as head of the Academy; only fragments of his writings survive. Edition: Lang, Bonn, 1911.

XENOCRATES: fl. second half of fourth century; pupil of Plato who succeeded Speusippus as head of the Academy. Only fragments remain. Edition: Heinze [311].

**ARISTOTLE: 384–322; son of a doctor, pupil of Plato, and master of those who know. Abbreviations and editions:
An *de Anima* (OCT, Ross)
APst *Posterior Analytics* (OCT, Ross)
Cael *de Caelo* (OCT, Allan)
EE *Eudemian Ethics* (Teubner, Susemihl)
EN *Nicomachean Ethics* (OCT, Bywater)
fr. *Fragmenta* (Teubner, Rose)
GA *de Generatione Animalium* (OCT, Drossaart Lulofs)
GC *de Generatione et Corruptione* (Joachim, Oxford, 1922)
HA *Historia Animalium* (Louis, Paris, 1964–9)
Met *Metaphysics* (OCT, Jaeger)
Meteor *Meteorologica* (Fobes, Cambridge Mass, 1919)
PA *de Partibus Animalium* (Loeb, Peck)
Phys *Physics* (OCT, Ross)
Poet *Poetics* (OCT, Kassel)
Pol *Politics* (OCT, Ross)
Resp *de Respiratione* (in *Parva Naturalia*, Ross, Oxford, 1955)
Rhet *Rhetoric* (OCT, Ross)
Sens *de Sensu* (in *Parva Naturalia*, Ross, Oxford, 1955)
Top *Topics*, including *Sophistici Elenchi* (OCT, Ross)
Pseudo-Aristotelian works:
lin insec *de lineis insecabilibus* (Timpanaro Cardini, Milan, 1970)
MM *Magna Moralia* (Teubner, Susemihl)
MXG *de Melisso, Xenophane, Gorgia* (Teubner, Apelt)

Prob *Problems* (Teubner, Ruelle)
HERACLIDES PONTICUS: *c*.390–*c*.310; Platonist and Pythagorean, renowned as a dandy. Only fragments survive. Edition: SdA VII.
*THEOPHRASTUS: 371–287; Aristotle's greatest pupil and his successor. Only fragments survive. Abbreviation:
Sens *de Sensibus*
Edition: Diels [4].
ARISTOXENUS: b. *c*.370; pupil of Aristotle, musical theorist with Pythagorean interests. Edition: SdA II.
DICAEARCHUS: b. *c*.370; Aristotelian philosopher, only fragments of whose writings are preserved. Edition: SdA I.
*EUDEMUS: fourth century; pupil of Aristotle, philosopher, and historian of mathematics. Edition: SdA VIII.
MENO: fourth century; pupil of Aristotle, and author of history of medicine.
EPICURUS: 342–270; founder and eponym of Epicureanism, a philosophy strongly influenced by Democritus. Principal work: *Letter to Herodotus*. Abbreviations:
ad Hdt *Letter to Herodotus*
ad Men *Letter to Menoeceus*
Edition: Arrighetti, Turin, 1960.
HERMIPPUS: third century BC, follower of Callimachus; sensational biographer.
SATYRUS: third century BC, peripatetic biographer.
TIMON: *c*.320–230; sceptic philosopher and poet. Edition: Diels [3].
ERATOSTHENES: *c*.280–200; geographer, scholar, and librarian at Alexandria.
CRATES OF MALLOS: mid-second century; scholar and librarian at Pergamum.
SOTION: second century BC, Peripatetic historian of philosophy.
ARIUS DIDYMUS: first century BC; philosopher, teacher of Augustus.
ALEXANDER POLYHISTOR: *c*.105–*c*.25 BC; a Greek who became a Roman prisoner of war and then a polymath.
DEMETRIUS OF MAGNESIA: flourished *c*.50 BC; a source for Diogenes Laertius.
CICERO: 106–43 BC: statesman, orator, master of prose, poet *manqué*, and amateur philosopher.
LUCRETIUS: 97–55 BC; Roman interpreter of Epicureanism in rough hexameters. Work: *de Rerum Natura*. Edition: OCT, Bailey.
PHILODEMUS: *c*.80–*c*.35 BC; Epicurean philosopher, fragments of whose works were discovered in the lava of Vesuvius.
NICOLAUS OF DAMASCUS: fl. second half of first century BC; historian and polymath, who wrote commentaries on Aristotle.

DIODORUS SICULUS: fl. *c*.35 BC; author of a *Universal History*. Edition: Teubner, Vogel and Fischer.

DIONYSIUS OF HALICARNASSUS: fl. end of first century BC; historian, and leading literary critic.

VITRUVIUS: fl. end of first century BC; leading Roman authority on architecture.

STRABO: 64 BC–AD 20; Romanophile Greek geographer.

AGATHEMERUS: ? first century AD; geographer.

OVID: 43 BC–AD 18; amatory poet. Principal work: *Metamorphoses*. Abbreviation and edition:

Metam *Metamorphoses* (Ehwald and Albrecht, Zürich, 1966)

PHILO: *c*.10 BC–*c*.AD 40. Jewish theologian and philosopher.

SENECA THE YOUNGER: 4/1 BC–AD 65: politician, Stoic philosopher, playwright. Principal works: *Quaestiones Naturales; Letters.*

PLINY THE ELDER: 23–79: minor politician and omnivorous observer, killed while scrutinizing the eruption of Vesuvius. Work: *Naturalis Historia*.

*PLUTARCH: 45–*c*.120. Biographer and philosopher, whose numerous philosophical essays are known collectively as the *Moralia*. Abbreviations and editions:

adv Col *adversus Colotem* (Teubner, Pohlenz and Westman)
aud poet *de audiendis poetis* (Teubner, Bernardakis)
comm not *de communibus notitiis* (Teubner, Pohlenz)
exil *de exilio* (Teubner, Bernardakis)
Plat quaest *Platonicae quaestiones* (Teubner, Hubert)
soll anim *de sollertia animalium* (Teubner, Hubert)
tranq *de tranquillitate animae* (Teubner, Bernardakis)

*AËTIUS: fl. *c*.100. Eclectic philosopher, whose doxography (the *Placita* or *Opinions*) was reconstructed by Diels from Stobaeus and pseudo-Plutarch (2). Edition: Diels [4].

NICOMACHUS OF GERASA: *c*.100; Platonist and mathematician.

FAVORINUS: *c*.80–*c*.150, hermaphrodite, favourite of Hadrian, friend of Plutarch, polymath.

JULIUS SORANUS: fl. 100–140; leading physician and author of history of medicine.

PTOLEMY: fl. *c*.150. Geographer, mathematician and astronomer. Principal work: *Syntaxis mathematica*—the '*Almagest*'. Edition: Teubner, Heiberg.

THEON OF SMYRNA: first half of second century; Platonist mathematician.

ARISTOCLES: second century, teacher of Alexander of Aphrodisias and historian of philosophy.

GALEN: 129–199; the most celebrated doctor of the age, and a copious author.

HERMOGENES: *c*.160–225; orator and rhetorician.

TERTULLIAN: fl. 196–212; Christian polemicist and theologian, whose wide interests included philosophy.

AULUS GELLIUS: second century, antiquarian and grammarian; his *Noctes Atticae* is a philosophico-legal miscellany.

JULIUS POLLUX: second century; successful teacher of rhetoric. Work: *Onomasticon*.

DIOGENES OF OENOANDA: second century; Epicurean, who had his philosophy inscribed on stone. Edition: Teubner, Chilton (several new fragments not yet collectively published).

HARPOCRATION: ? second-century lexicographer.

PSEUDO-PLUTARCH (1): mid-second century, author of *Stromateis*, a doxographical compilation. Edition: Diels [4].

*PSEUDO-PLUTARCH (2): mid-second century, author of an *Epitome* of the *Placita* (see Aëtius). Edition: Diels [4].

TATIAN: second half of second century, Christian apologist and rhetorician.

*CLEMENT OF ALEXANDRIA: *c*.150–215, the first major Christian philosopher. Principal work: *Stromateis*.

AELIAN: fl. second half of second century, author of miscellaneous natural histories.

ATHENAGORAS: fl. *c*.180, Athenian philosopher and Christian apologist.

*SEXTUS EMPIRICUS: fl. 180–200, massive compiler of sceptical *topoi* and our main source for ancient scepticism. Abbreviations and Editions:

adv Math *Against the Mathematicians* (Teubner, Mau)

Pyrr Hyp *Outlines of Pyrrhonism* (Teubner, Mau).

ALEXANDER OF APHRODISIAS: fl. *c*.200, seminal commentator on the works of Aristotle. Abbreviation:

quaest nat *quaestiones naturales*

Edition: CIAG.

ATHENAEUS: fl. *c*.200, author of the anecdotal miscellany, *Deipnosophistae*.

*HIPPOLYTUS: d. 235: presbyter of Rome, opposed to the Establishment. Principal work: *Refutatio Omnium Haeresium (Ref. Haer)*. Edition: Wendland, GCS.

**DIOGENES LAERTIUS: ? third century; scissors and paste historian of philosophy. Work: *Lives of the Philosophers*. Edition: OCT, Long.

PHILOSTRATUS: fl. *c*.220, sophist and author of *Lives of the Sophists*.

CENSORINUS: grammarian. Principal work: *de die natali* (written in 238).

HERMIAS: ? third to sixth century, author of *Gentilium Philosophorum Irrisio*. Edition: Diels [4].

PLOTINUS: *c.*205–70, the principal philosopher of the period between Aristotle and Aquinas. Work: *Enneads.*

DIONYSIUS OF ALEXANDRIA: bishop of Alexandria 247–264, opponent of atomism.

PORPHYRY: 234–*c.*303, Neoplatonist pupil of Plotinus. Abbreviations and editions:

de Abst *de Abstinentia* (Teubner, Nauck)

VP *Vita Pythagorae* (Teubner, Nauck)

ACHILLES: ? third-century astronomer and mathematician.

EUSEBIUS: *c.*260–340, bishop of Caesarea and leading churchman; principal work: *Praeparatio Evangelica* (*PE*).

ANATOLIUS: fl. 280. Bishop of Laodicea, saint, Aristotelian, and mathematician.

CALCIDIUS: fl. early fourth century, Christian philosopher; his Latin commentary on Plato's *Timaeus* had enormous influence on later ages.

IAMBLICHUS: *c.*250–320, Neoplatonist. Abbreviations and editions:

comm math sc *de communi mathematica scientia* (Teubner, Festa)

VP *de Vita Pythagorica* (Teubner, Deubner)

LACTANTIUS: fl. *c.*320, prolific Christian author, influenced by the Platonic and hermetic traditions. Principal work: *de Ira*.

THEMISTIUS: 317–388, Constantinopolitan orator and philosopher, who paraphrased Aristotle's works.

EPIPHANIUS: *c.*315–403, bishop of Salamis. Edition: Diels [4].

AUGUSTINE: 354–430, saint and church father, author of *Confessions* and *City of God*.

SERVIUS: fl. *c.*400, grammarian and author of celebrated commentary on Vergil.

MACROBIUS: early fifth century, author of the literary symposium, *Saturnalia*.

*STOBAEUS: early fifth-century excerptor with particular interest in philosophy. Work: *Florilegium*. Edition: Diels [4].

HESYCHIUS: fifth-century lexicographer.

THEODORETUS: 393–466, Bishop of Cyrrhus, Christian apologist.

BOETHIUS: d. 522, the last of the Romans; author of the *Consolatio Philosophiae* and numerous more professional works.

MAMERTUS CLAUDIANUS: d. 474, Neoplatonist. Principal work: *de statu animae*.

PROCLUS: 412–485, leading Neoplatonist philosopher and author of valuable commentaries on Plato's dialogues. Abbreviations and editions:

in Parm *Commentary on the Parmenides* (Cousin, Paris, 1864)

in Tim *Commentary on the Timaeus* (Teubner, Diehl)
PSEUDO-GALEN: *c*.500, author of *Historia Philosopha*. Edition: Diels [4].
EUTOCIUS: fl. *c*.530, mathematician who wrote commentaries on Apollonius and Archimedes.
AMMONIUS: second half of fifth century. A pupil of Proclus and leading Platonist of the Alexandrian school; commentator on Aristotle and influential teacher. Edition: CIAG.
PHILOPONUS: *c*.480–570, Christian pupil of Ammonius; author of commentaries on Aristotle. Edition: CIAG.
SIMPLICIUS: first half of sixth century; Ammonius' greatest pupil, and a major source for early Greek philosophy. Edition: CIAG.
OLYMPIODORUS: *c*.500–570, pupil of Ammonius and commentator on Plato.
ELIAS: sixth century, pupil of Olympiodorus and commentator on Aristotle. Edition: CIAG.
SUDA: tenth-century, a large Byzantine lexicon, formerly known as Suidas.
HISDOSUS: fl. *c*.1100, wrote on Plato's psychology.
TZETZES: *c*.1110–85, leading Byzantine scholar.
ALBERTUS MAGNUS: *c*.1200–80; St Albert the Great, teacher of Aquinas and Parisian exponent of Aristotle.
SCHOLIASTS on various authors: the margins of many ancient manuscripts contain notes or 'scholia'; the dates and identities of most scholiasts are unknown.

Appendix B Chronology

Our evidence for Presocratic chronology is scrappy, confused and unreliable: few thinkers can be dated with any precision; and monumental dispute governs all. My chronological table, then, has no high aspirations: its sole aim is to provide the reader with a rough and approximate idea of the temporal relationships that hold among the Presocratic philosophers. The table is tentative (broken lines indicate uncertainty); and it represents orthodoxy (in so far as any view here is orthodox). The reader who is hungry for more information should begin by consulting the relevant pages of Guthrie [25] or of Zeller-Mondolfo [26].

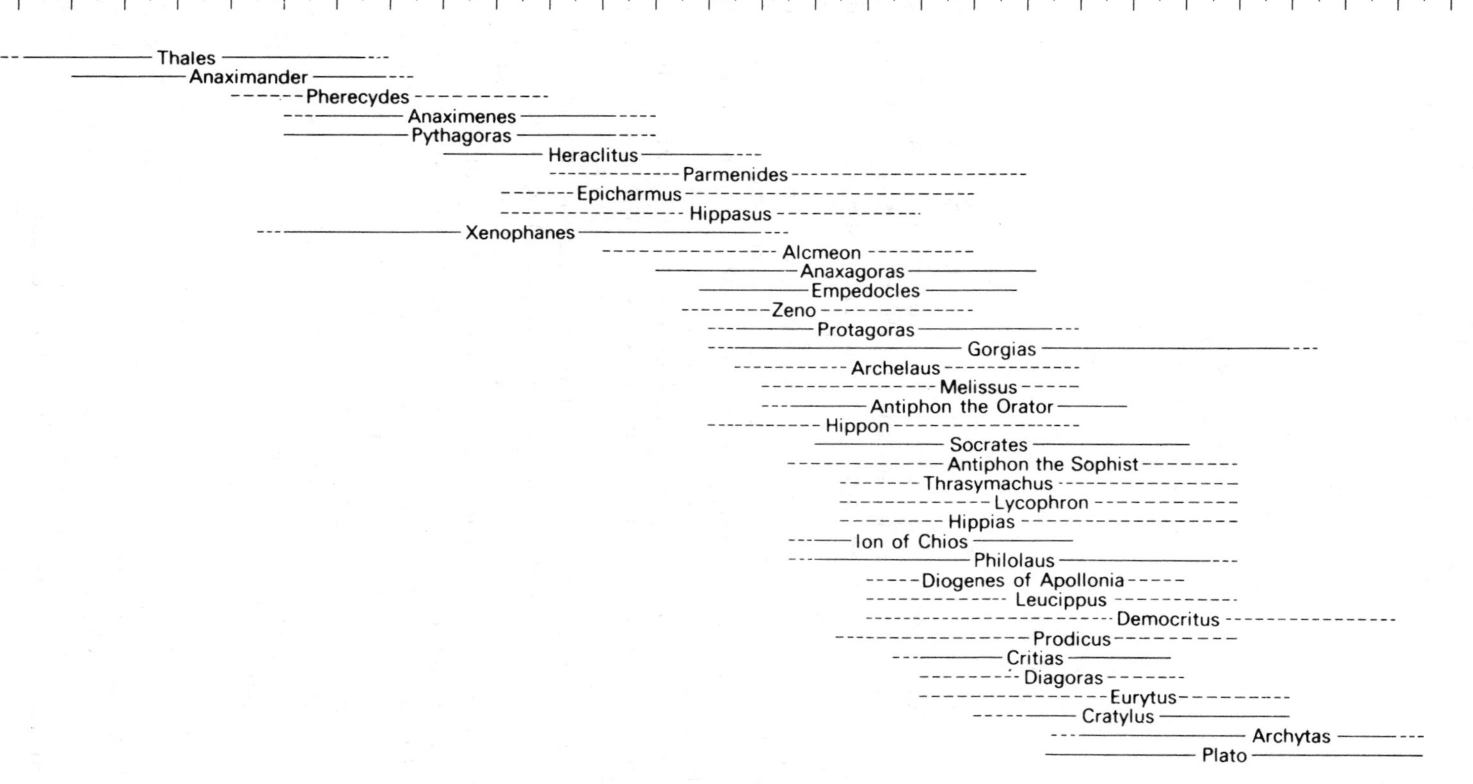

BC 620 610 600 590 580 570 560 550 540 530 520 510 500 490 480 470 460 450 440 430 420 410 400 390 380 370 360 350
Thales
Anaximander
Pherecydes
Anaximenes
Pythagoras
Heraclitus
Parmenides
Epicharmus
Hippasus
Xenophanes
Alcmeon
Anaxagoras
Empedocles
Zeno
Protagoras
Gorgias
Archelaus
Melissus
Antiphon the Orator
Hippon
Socrates
Antiphon the Sophist
Thrasymachus
Lycophron
Hippias
Ion of Chios
Philolaus
Diogenes of Apollonia
Leucippus
Democritus
Prodicus
Critias
Diagoras
Eurytus
Cratylus
Archytas
Plato
BC 620 610 600 590 580 570 560 550 540 530 520 510 500 490 480 470 460 450 440 430 420 410 400 390 380 370 360 350

Notes

The text of the book is intended to be self-sufficient; and the reader who ignores these notes should not find the main narrative broken or its arguments enthymematic. The notes are designed to serve four subsidiary functions.

First, they supply additional references to the ancient texts. (For the abbreviations used see the Note on Citations, and Appendix A.)

Second, the notes broach issues too technical or too narrow to justify inclusion in the body of the book.

Third, they explain (and sometimes attempt to justify) disputed readings, translations, or interpretations which the main narrative adopts without comment.

Fourth, there are some selected references to the secondary literature. (References consist of the author's name; a numeral, in square brackets, keying the work to the Bibliography; and, usually, a page or chapter number.) It is customary in scholarly works to compile references, pious and polemical, to authors who agree and disagree with a given interpretation. That practice is a pedantic pleasantry, of little value to the reader; and, apart from acknowledgments of direct quotations, I only provide references where they are likely to yield a useful supplement to my own remarks. The reader who seeks bibliographical assistance will find it, I hope, in the Bibliography.

I The Springs of Reason

1 On Hippias as a source for Aristotle see esp. Snell [13]; also Stokes [56], 50–60. Democritus also wrote about Thales: Diogenes Laertius, I.11 = **68 B 115a**.

2 Cf. e.g., Epicharmus, **23 B 4**.5; Anonymous Iamblichi, **89 A 4**.3.

3 See Alexander, *quaest nat* II.23, a text which includes Empedocles, **31 A 89**; Anaxagoras, **59 A 98a**; Diogenes, **64 A 33**; Democritus, **68 A 165**.

4 Propositions (4) and (5) are also found in Diogenes Laertius, I.27 = **A 1**; Scholiast to Plato, **A 3**; Simplicius, Servius, **A 13**; etc. (see Classen [88], 939). The two theses may conceivably have formed parts of a full cosmogony and cosmology (thesis (5) was used in the explanation of earthquakes: Seneca, **A 15**) see West [87], 172–6; [59], 208–13.

5 Stokes [56], 283, n. 113, suggests that the analogy with wood was intended to show only the *possibility* of the earth's floating on water; Kirk-Raven [33], 88, think that the analogy may have been supplied by Aristotle and doubt that Thales ever considered the problem of the earth's stability. Neither view is plausible.

6 Some scholars are content with the explanation that Thales was adopting an Egyptian myth: see especially Hölscher [91], 40–8 (the explanation is already in Plutarch, **A 11**, and Simplicius, **A 14**). Thales' tour of Egypt (Proclus, **A 11**, etc.) is of dubious historicity.

7 On Alcman see West [87] and [108]; on poetico-mythological cosmogony see Stokes [109]; Kirk-Raven [33], 24–72; Hölscher [91], 49–82; Schwabl [107], 1437–74.

8 West [59], 75. On Pherecydes see especially West [59], chh. 1–2; Kirk-Raven [33], 48–72. Some scholars have thought that Pherecydes' aim was to interpret the old mythological cosmogonies in the new Milesian spirit (see Jaeger [48], 67–72; *contra*: Vlastos [161], 106–10).

9 So, e.g., Guthrie [25], I.46–9; the scepticism of Dicks [42], 298, etc., is excessive.

10 References in Classen [88], 941–3 (mathematics), 943–5 (astronomy). Extreme scepticism in Dicks [86]; extreme credulity in van der Waerden [58], 86–90; a balanced view in Burkert [173], 415–17. (Note that Herodotus did not credit the stories of Thales' engineering feats: they are 'the common tale of the Greeks'. For late Thalean romance see Classen [88], 931-5.) Thales is the archetypical geometer for Aristophanes: *Birds*, 995, 1009; *Clouds*, 215. Three of the books ascribed to Thales concern astronomy (**B 1**, **B 2**, **B 4**); but all the ascriptions are almost certainly wrong.

11 On this report see especially Gladigow [89].

12 According to Proclus, Thales 'is said to have called equal angles "similar" in the archaic fashion' (**A 20**): this may come from Eudemus, and Eudemus' source may have been Hippias (cf. **86 B 12** = Eudemus, fr. 133 W). But we cannot infer that either Eudemus or Hippias possessed, or claimed to possess, a written work by Thales.

13 But (a) the central portion of Parmenides' poem has survived entire (see above, p. 155); (b) Gorgias' *Helen* is complete, and I shall treat it as a piece of philosophy (see above, pp. 523–30); and (c) some of the fifth-century works in the Hippocratic canon have a strong philosophical bias (see above, p. 139).

14 Fragments in Diels [4], 473–527. The long fragment on perception is edited by Stratton [14] who gives (51–64) a useful appreciation of Theophrastus' faults and merits. Most scholars, following Diels, hold that the *Phusikôn Doxai* was a comprehensive history of early Greek thought; and they infer that the Presocratic material extracted from that work has a better evidential standing than the stuff we quarry from Aristotle's treatises. Steinmetz [5] argues that the title '*Phusikôn Doxai*' was given to the collection of studies on individual Presocratics listed in Diogenes Laertius, V.42–7; that those studies were used by Theophrastus in his *Physics*; and that it is that latter work which formed Simplicius' main source. If Steinmetz is right, then the Theophrastan material is exactly comparable to the doxographical notices which we read in the Aristotelian treatises.

15 For the case against Aristotle see Cherniss [6]; McDiarmid [7] completes his companion study of Theophrastus by asserting that he 'is a thoroughly biased witness and is even less trustworthy than Aristotle' (133). The best defence of Aristotle is still that in Guthrie [8] (but see Stevenson [9]); the best defence of Theophrastus is in Mondolfo-Tarán [131], CXCIII–CXCVIII.

16 The classic study is Diels' magisterial *Doxographi Graeci*. There is a useful summary of Diels in Burnet [31], and a detailed illustration in Stokes [56], ch. 3.

II Anaximander on Nature

1 An epitome (or perhaps the work itself) survived to the time of Apollodorus; Anaximander may have gone to press at the age of 64 (see Diogenes Laertius, II.2 = **12 A 1**; cf. West [59], 76, n. 1). On Theopompus' report (Diogenes Laertius, I.116 = *FGrH* 115 F 71 = **7 A 1**) that Pherecydes 'was the first to write about nature and the birth of the gods', see Kahn [90], 6, n. 2; 240.

2 For a fine sketch of Anaximander's intellectual range see Kahn [90], 82–4; a main thesis of Kahn's book is the domination of later Presocratic speculation by Anaximander's conception of science.

3 See especially Kahn [90], 58–63; cf. Tannery [29]; Rescher [97] ('an intellect . . . audacity': Rescher, 731).

4 On *metabiônai* see Kahn [90], 67; Kahn shows (70–1) that Plutarch's story in **A 30** is mere romance.

5 See, e.g., Anaxagoras, **59 A 42**; Democritus, **68 A 139**; Diodorus Siculus, I.7.

6 On Xenophanes' theory see Guthrie [25], I.387–90. The observations were repeated in the fifth century by Xanthus of Lydia, *FGrH* 765 F 12.

7 First quotation from Kahn [90], 97; second from Popper [35], 140. There is a splenetic attack on Kahn's 'monstrous edifice of exaggeration' in Dicks [65], which Kahn [66] answers. Both authors are unconvincingly extreme: see Burkert [173], 308–10.

8 Cf. Diogenes Laertius, II.1 = **A 1**; Suda, **A 2**; Simplicius, *in Cael* 532.14.

9 A version of the Principle may have been used by Parmenides (see below, p. 187); it is employed at *Phys* 203b25–8, a passage which may have Milesian origins (cf. Hussey [34], 18).

10 Kahn [90], 77.

11 Aristotle, *Cael* 295a16–b9 = **31 A 67**; see Bollack [349], III.242–4.

12 See *Phaedo* 108E; *Timaeus* 62D. The ascription to Empedocles is probably a loose reference to **31 A 67**; that to Parmenides, an inference from the spherical symmetry of his world (**28 B 8**.42–4); that to Democritus a plain error (cf. *Cael* 294b13). *Pace* Robinson [98], there is nothing in the argument which exceeds Anaximander's capacities or conflicts with the rest of his astronomy.

13 Some scholars think that Xenophanes' earth was not literally of infinite depth and that he was not seriously tackling Anaximander's problem (e.g., Kirk-Raven [33], 175–6); but see Stokes [56], 75; 286, nn. 18–19. Empedocles **31 B 39** is generally taken as a criticism of Xenophanes (see *Cael* 294a25); *contra*: Bollack [349] III.242.

14 Anaximenes, Anaxagoras, Democritus (*Cael* 294b13 = **13 A 20**); Xenophanes (Simplicius, **21 A 47**); Empedocles (*Cael* 295a15 = **31 A 67**). Eudemus, fr. 145 W = **12 A 26**, has Anaximander's earth move: either Theon has garbled Eudemus (Kahn [90], 54), or the text is corrupt (Burkert [173], 345, n. 38).

15 Sweeney [57], ch. 1, gives a full account of the voluminous publications on this topic from 1947 to 1970. The most distinguished contribution is Kahn [90].

16 Cf. Simplicius, *in Phys* 465.5–10, who probably alludes to Anaximander, though he names no name. (*in Cael* 615.15 names Anaximander; but that is in connexion with quite another argument.)
17 Kahn [101].
18 See Hölscher [91], 10–12; and especially Schwabl [99], 60–4; *contra*: Kahn [90], 37–8.
19 The precise extent of the fragment is uncertain: see especially Kahn [90], 168–78; and, more sceptically, Dirlmeier [100].
20 For controversy see McDiarmid [7], 138–40, n. 46; Kahn [90], 30–2; Kirk [92], 324–7. I follow Stokes [56], 28–9; 274–6.
21 The role of the 'opposites' in Anaximander's thought is obscure: see especially Lloyd [64], 260–70; Kahn [90], 40–1; Hölscher [91], 31–2. For a detailed account of the 'opposites' in early Greek thought see Lloyd [50], ch. 1.
22 Conflationists have been worried by the plurals in [iv] (*ex hôn . . . tauta . . .*), covertly making them singular or else asserting that 'the unlimited' is a mixture and hence a plurality. The grammatical difficulty vanishes once it is seen that [iii] and [iv] need not belong together. Kahn [90], 181–3, argues that 'the things that exist' in [iv] cannot be the ordinary furniture of the world but must be the elements 'from which' and 'into which' those things come and go. That makes for a tortuous construe.
23 This interpretation is strongly advocated by Schwabl [99]. He sets out from [vi], where he alleges that 'them (*auta*)' must refer to 'generation' and 'destruction' in [iv]. That gives a good sense to '*legôn auta*' ('calling them thus by . . .'), but it is otherwise implausible. Most interpreters take '*auta*' in [vi] to have the same reference as '*auta*' in [v], i.e. the elements. That gives a good sense to [vi], but it puts a great strain on the Greek. I suspect that '*auta*' in [vi] should be changed to '*autos*' ('himself speaking thus . . .') or else excised.
24 Kirk-Raven [33], 116–17, suggest that Anaximander actually used the Homeric formula 'immortal and ageless (*athanatos kai agêrôs*)', and that Aristotle and Hippolytus have each preserved a half of it.
25 A lucid account in Kirk-Raven [33], 110–12; cf. Gottschalk [104], 40–7. On the *metaxu* passages see Kahn [90], 44–6; Hölscher [91], 34–7. On *migma* see Vlastos [111], 76–80; Seligman [102], 40–9; Hölscher [91], 16–17.
26 See **59 B 12**; cf. Dicks [42], 57; Guthrie [25], II.296.
27 **B 3** is generally rejected as spurious, and the language shows that it cannot be a *verbatim* report; but it may well be a fair paraphrase of Anaximenes (see West [59], 100, n. 3). The first 'and' in the quotation may belong to Olympiodorus, so that he preserves two fragments rather than one; certainly, the two parts of **B 3** hang only loosely together.
28 If argument (*B*) does not belong to Anaximander, I guess that in **A 14** Aëtius has written 'Anaximander' by mistake for 'Anaximenes'.
29 The etymology is entertained and rejected by Kahn [90], 231–3; see further Solmsen [103], 123–4; Classen [94], 44–5 (cf. Aristotle, *Phys* 204a2,13). On '*apeiros*' in general see Guthrie [25], I.85–7.
30 'Like a fog-bank': Rescher [97], 719.

III Science and Speculation

1 See Hippolytus, **A 7**; Aristotle, *Meteor* 354a28 = **A 14**; Aëtius, **A 12**, **A 14**, **A 15**; Pliny, **A 14A**. The report of Eudemus, fr. 145 W = **A 16**, that Anaximenes first saw that the moon shines with borrowed light, is unreliable (see Guthrie

[25], I.94, n. 2). On Anaximenes' meteorology see Aristotle, *Meteor* 365b6 = **A 21**; Aëtius, **A 17**, **A 18**; Galen, **A 19**.

2 See Simplicius, **59 A 41**; Diogenes Laertius, IX.57 = **64 A 1**. 'In the eyes of his contemporaries, and for long after, Anaximenes was a much more important figure than Anaximander' (Burnet [31], 78).

3 See especially Stokes [56], 30–65. McDiarmid [7], 92, asserts that 'it is an obvious historical impossibility that any Presocratic should have held this concept [sc. of *hulê*], for the concept implies a grasp of the notion of identity and of the distinction between subject and attribute'. That argument barely deserves refutation.

4 Jaeger [48], 24.

5 A passage from Simplicius has puzzled commentators:

> Anaximenes says that when thinned the air becomes fire, when condensed, wind. . . . For in his case alone Theophrastus in his *History* [i.e. in the *Phusikôn Doxai*] speaks of rarefaction and condensation. But it is clear that the others too used rareness and denseness (*in Phys* 149.30–150.1; cf. **A 5**).

Elsewhere, in passages presumably derived from Theophrastus, Simplicius and the other doxographers use '*manôsis*' and '*puknôsis*' of many Presocratic cosmogonies. (See, e.g., *in Phys* 202.32–203.5; 1266.33–8; 1319.17–27; cf., e.g., Aristotle, *Phys* 187a15; *GC* 330b10.) Simplicius does not report (*pace* Cherniss [6], 13, n. 55) that according to Theophrastus only Anaximenes used rarefaction and condensation; nor (*pace* Stokes [56], 273, n. 22) can he mean that Theophrastus used the words '*manôsis*' and '*puknôsis*' only in connexion with Anaximenes. Perhaps he means that in his *History*, as opposed to his *Physics*, Theophrastus speaks of rarefaction and condensation only in the case of Anaximenes. If so, then we shall infer that Simplicius' principal Theophrasten source was not the *History* (see above, p. 313, n. 14); and we may wonder how Theophrastus described non-Anaximenean cosmogonies in the *History*. Klowski [106] argues that the operation of condensation and rarefaction was an invention of Theophrastus, falsely fathered by him on the Presocratics; Stokes [56], 43–8, argues that condensation and rarefaction do not imply an Aristotelian interpretation of Anaximenes' air. Neither argument appeals.

6 Sambursky [53], 10–11; cf. Guthrie [25], I.126–7. It should in fairness be added that, in Sambursky's opinion, 'it is a far cry from the speculative teaching of Anaximenes to the extremely abstract calculations of the physicist and mathematician of today' (11).

7 The term 'felting' for condensation ('*pilêsis*', '*pilousthai*': Hippolytus, **A 7**; pseudo-Plutarch, **A 6**) has been thought Anaximenean; but it is common in the doxographers (see Diels-Kranz [1], III.352b).

8 But the point is controversial: Guthrie [25], I.131, n. 1.

9 Burnet [31], v; cf. 24–8. Popper [35] gives a strong statement of Burnet's thesis, on grounds diametrically opposed to those of Burnet.

10 See especially Cornford [114]. According to Raven [178], 175, Presocratic thought tends to rely 'on dogmatic reasoning alone' and shows 'a cheerful ignorance of the conditions of scientific knowledge'.

11 Vlastos [115], 53.

12 See Sambursky [53], 283–41. On the vagueness endemic in Presocratic science see especially Vlastos [115], 51–3; Dicks [42], 60–1.

13 Lloyd [113] gives an excellent account of the place of experiment in early Greek thought; the best examples are in Hippocrates, *morb* IV.39; *nat puer* 17.
14 Jones [49], 44.
15 Sambursky [53], 89, is mistaken when he says that experiment is 'now the final arbiter of every theory' and contrasts this modern notion with that of the Greeks. At 231–8 he argues in detail that lack of experimentation gravely impeded the advance of Greek science; but at 235 he observes that 'the heavenly phenomena display all the ideal qualities of a laboratory experiment'.
16 Kahn [66], 112. 'The apparently bizarre speculations of the early thinkers are rarely entirely divorced from observation, but sometimes depend on rather extravagant extrapolation from it' (Guthrie [25], II.188). But note first, that the word 'extrapolation' implies an hypothesis about Milesian procedure which we cannot test; and second, that the 'extravagance' is not shown by reliance on a paucity of data, but rather by a carefree connexion between data and theory. Dicks [65], 36, affirms that the Presocratics '*were not scientists*—and actual observation seems to have played a very minor part in their astronomical theories'. Of course, it does not matter a hang whether the Presocratics made their own observations (like Kepler), or simply worked from reports of others (like Newton).
17 Examples collected in Kranz [121]; Lloyd [50], part II. See also Baldry [122], and the celebrated paper by Diller [120], who judges that Anaximenes marks 'the birth of the analogical method' (35).
18 Text and interpretation are disputed: see Guthrie [123], Longrigg [124], and especially Schwabl [125].
19 A full examination of **26** in Alt [127], who concludes (unconvincingly) that it is a fragment of Diogenes of Apollonia. Although **26** contains anachronistic vocabulary (Alt [127], 129–30) and has been judged a fabrication (especially Reinhardt [30], 175), I side with those who find it Anaximenean in content (see Guthrie [25], I.131–2). Most scholars take '*hoion* . . . *kai* . . .' for an inferential construction: 'just as . . . so . . .'. (For different ways of construing the inference see Kirk-Raven [33], 158.) It is better to read '*hoion*' as 'e.g.', the doxographer's introduction to the quotation which follows; and I guess that the '*kai*' is doxographical, conjoining two quotations. See especially Longrigg [126].

IV The Natural Philosophy of Heraclitus

1 Popper [137], I.17; Hegel [27], 279. On Heraclitus' early followers see Diogenes Laertius, IX.6 = **A 1**; for early exegetes, *id.*, IX.15 = **A 1**; Antiphanes, fr. 113 K. An exhaustive discussion of the traditions and controversies surrounding Heraclitus' life in Marcovich [140], 246–56.
2 On Hippolytus see Reinhardt [30], 158–63; Hershbell [17]; on Clement see Reinhardt [135]; on the Stoics see Hölscher [79], 150–3; Marcovich [140], 315–17.
3 Note that Pythagoras was incarnated as a Delian diver: above, p. 108.
4 Numerals succeeded by '**M**' refer to the fragments in the edition of Marcovich [129]; whether or not that arrangement is correct, it is vastly superior to that of Diels-Kranz.
5 On Heraclitus' 'Orakelstil' see especially Hölscher [79], 136–41.
6 Some scholars deny that Heraclitus wrote a book and suppose instead a disjointed set of aphorisms (e.g., Kirk [136], 7). That view explains the ordering of the fragments in Diels-Kranz: the nature of Heraclitus' effusions prohibits systematic

arrangement, and Diels took the alphabetical order of the quoting authorities as a suitably arbitrary schema within which to print the fragments. There are ancient references to Heraclitus' book (Aristotle, *Rhet* 1407b16 = **A 4**; Diogenes Laertius, IX.1,5, 6, 7, 12 = **A 1**); but that book might have been an anthology of saws. But fragment **33** = **B 1** = **1 M** both by its form and by its content promises a continuous and systematic treatise (see, e.g., Guthrie [25], I.406–8; Kahn [139], 189–91).

7 See, e.g., Guthrie [25], I. 420–4; Hölscher [79], 130–43; Marcovich [129], 2–11; and, for a clear exposition of the right view, West [59], 124–9.

8 See, e.g., Snell [144], 139; West [59], 113–14. That will explain the initial 'and (*de*)' in **33**, if explanation is needed.

9 See the useful table in Kirk [136], 47.

10 Cf. **B 64** = **79 M**:

> The thunderbolt steers all things (cf. **B 41** = **85 M**).

But the connexion between the *logos* and the thunderbolt is uncertain: see Kirk [136], 356–7; West [59], 142–4. On **B 114** see p. 132.

11 For the text of **34** see Marcovich [129], 125. I take 'conjunctions' to mean 'composite things', i.e. to denote the ordinary furniture of the world; and I suppose that the first three clauses of the fragment say that 'all composite things are both unities and diversities' (see, e.g., Snell [146]; Kirk [136], 173–7).

12 For the text see Ramnoux [142], 461–3. Kirk [136], 70, thinks that **35** presents an inference from the *logos*; Stokes [56], 102, says that 'it is apparent from **B 50** that the unity of all things is the principal content of the Logos'. Neither view is in the text.

13 '*Palintonos harmoniê*' or '*palintropos harmoniê*'? 'Back-stretched connexion' or 'back-turning connexion'? For the controversy see Marcovich [129], 215–16. On *harmoniê* see also Stokes [56], 94–7; on *-tonos* and *-tropos*, Hussey [34], 43–5. I doubt if anything turns on the textual dispute: even if we could decide between *-tonos* and *-tropos*, it is not clear that they need bear significantly different senses; even if they do, it is not clear how far we may press the analogy with bow and lyre; even if we squeeze the analogy dry, we have no reason to take **36** as the key statement of the *logos* and to force the other fragments into its mould.

14 On text and interpretation of **40** see Jones [149]. I agree that the fragment must be read in two parts (Clement does not quote it as a continuous piece), and that the final '*ê genesthai gên*' should be excised.

15 Against *ekpurôsis* see especially Reinhardt [135] and [30], 163–201. For *ekpurôsis* see especially Mondolfo-Tarán [131], CLXXVII–CXCIII, 109–18. Mondolfo convinces me that at *Phys* 205a1–4 and *Cael* 279b12–17 = **A 10** Aristotle ascribes *ekpurôsis* to Heraclitus; he fails to show that the ascription is correct.

16 **B 76** = **66**(e) **M** carries the implication more clearly; but that fragment is probably a Stoic perversion of **B 36**. See Marcovich [140], 264.

17 I quote Guthrie [25], I.438–9; Kahn [139], 190. See also Hölscher [79], 139–40, 148–9 (but Hölscher's view is unclear to me: at 139–40 he says that in Heraclitus analogies take the place of proofs; at 145 he implies that analogies are a form of proof); von Fritz [62], 230–4, who says that in Heraclitus *nous* is pure insight; Cleve [37], 108 ('he is no proving and arguing philosopher. . . . Presenting no proof whatsoever, he appeals to faith and hope, pronouncing his Logos dogma like a prophet').

18 See especially Fränkel [145]; cf. Reinhardt [134], 72–5.

19 See especially Reinhardt [30], 206–7; Snell [144], 130–1; Kirk [136], 244, 366. Reinhardt denies that Heraclitus held a 'Flusslehre'; but he says that 'Heraclitus' fundamental idea . . . is the most perfect conceivable opposite of the Theory of Flux: stability in change; constancy in alteration; . . . unity in duality; eternity in ephemerality' (207). But that describes, in high-flown language, something very like the Theory of Flux.

20 References in Marcovich [129], 194–205.

21 On the *de victu* see especially Joly [153] (date, *c.*400: 203–9; influence from Heraclitus: 19–91); see also Wasserstein [152]; Mondolfo-Tarán [131], 231–4. Epicharmus **23 B 2** (above, p. 106) has been held to show acquaintance with the Theory of Flux: see especially Bernays [133]; Mondolfo-Tarán [131], XLII–LXIV; *contra*: Reinhardt [30], 120–1. Melissus **30 B 8** may hint at the Theory.

22 On Plato's doxographical talents see especially Mondolfo-Tarán [131], LXXXIV–CXVIII; on Plato and Heraclitus, ibid., CXVIII–CLVIII.

23 See Marcovich [129], 206–14, with references. Bollack-Wismann [143] accept all three quotations as genuine and independent fragments (87–8, 173–4, 268–9); most scholars pick upon one as the original.

24 Plutarch quotes **45**; his text continues as follows:

> It is not possible to step into the same river twice, according to Heraclitus, nor to touch twice a mortal substance the same in its character; but with a sharpness and celerity of change *it disperses and gathers together* again (or rather, not again or later, but at the same time it comes together and disintegrates), and *it approaches and departs*.

Some scholars claim the italicized words for Heraclitus (but see Marcovich [129], 207–14); if they are right, the Flux interpretation of the river fragment is assured.

25 Popper [137], I.11; [151], 159 (italics Popper's); Hegel [27], 287. For a different comparison between Heraclitus and Wittgenstein's *Tractatus* see Hussey [34], 59.

26 Reinhardt [30], 220; cf. Popper [35].

27 Another possibility is:
(3*) $(\forall\phi)\ (\forall x)\ (\phi x$ if and only if $\phi' x)$:
'opposites' are one in that they are mutually implicative. That, I suspect, is as suitable an interpretation as (2); but it raises all and only the problems raised by (2).

28 Kirk [136], 70.

29 See Stokes [56], 90–100, who distinguishes five relations involved in the Unity Thesis: opposites may be (i) logically indistinguishable, (ii) ascribed to the same object, (iii) mutually successive, (iv) mutually validating, and (v) 'the kind exemplified by **B 61**'. Now (iv), exemplified in **B 23** = **45 M** and **B 111** = **44 M**, has nothing to do with the Unity Thesis; and the cases Stokes lists under (i), (iii) and (v) can all be accommodated under (ii).

30 See Kirk [136], 139–48; Reinhardt [134], 91, n. 31 (whose reading, *taúto de ge zôn* . . ., I accept); cf. Plato, *Cratylus* 440A.

31 See Stokes [56], 93, who concludes with the romantic hypothesis that Heraclitus 'was only a step from knowing that there was something wrong somewhere in the argument; only he could not lay his finger on the flaw and continued to proclaim the paradoxes with his unique vigour'.

32 Plato, *Euthydemus* 293B 'may be the first extant text in which it is implicitly recognized that the factors of *respect* and *time* must be taken into account in deciding whether two assertions in which contrary attributes are predicated of a single subject contradict one another' (Lloyd [50], 138).

33 **B 48** = **39 M**:

> A name of the bow is life (*bios*), its function death.

(*Bios* means both 'bow' and 'life'.) See, e.g., Snell [144], 141–5. But there is no call to take that quip as philosophy. On **B 23** = **45 M**, sometimes taken to illustrate the Unity Thesis, see especially Mouraviev [130], 114–17.

34 Sextus, *Pyrr Hyp* I.210–1, II.63, explicitly ascribes this type of argument to Heraclitus.

35 See Stokes [56], 97–8; completely different interpretations in, e.g., Hölscher [79], 153–6, and Mouraviev [130], 122–5.

36 I side with those scholars who see no cosmological significance in **55** (see, e.g., Kirk-Raven [33], 190–1; *contra*: e.g., West [59], 121–3). On the sense of *anô katô* see Reinhardt [135], 62. The puzzle still troubled Aristotle: *Phys* 202b12–6.

37 According to Philo, A 6a, Heraclitus offered 'immensa atque laboriosa argumenta' for his *logos:* the surviving *argumenta* are usefully catalogued in Marcovich [140], 286–91.

38 Guthrie [25], I.461; contrast ibid. II.246: 'we can only study these philosophers in the light of our own conceptions, nor would the study be of much value if we did not'. Stannard [119], 198, n. 19, suggests that it is silly to accuse Heraclitus of violating the Law of Contradiction since 'there was no "Law of Contradiction" prior to Aristotle's formulation of logical rules'. Perhaps that is a joke.

39 *Ta enantia* and *ta antia* do not appear in the fragments (Kranz' change of *tauta* into *tdntia* in **B** 23 = **45 M** is implausible; *antion* appears as a preposition in **B 120** = **62 M**). Text **35** and **B 67** = **77 M**, taken in conjunction with Hippolytus' glosses, suggest that Heraclitus never spoke of 'the opposites'.

V The Divine Philosophy of Xenophanes

1 There are two exceptions to this generalization: Democritus (Diogenes Laertius, IX.41 = **68 B 5**; see p. 307); and Gorgias (Olympiodorus, **82 A 10**). On Aristotle, *Met* 984a11 = **31 A 6**, see p. 306.

2 For the Milesian aspect of Xenophanes' work see especially Heidel [160], 268–72 (*contra*: Fränkel [215], 339–40). According to Theophrastus, Xenophanes had 'heard' Anaximander: Diogenes Laertius IX.21 = **A 2**.

3 Sextus, Galen, and Simplicius could not find copies of Xenophanes' works (**A 35**, **A 36**, **A 47**): Aristotle's cutting appraisal (*Met* 986b21–5 = **A 30**) may have dulled interest in Xenophanes' thought.

4 A poem *Concerning Nature*: Crates of Mallos, *ad* **B 30**; Pollux, *ad* **B 39**; Stobaeus, **A 36**. For the majority view see especially Burnet [31], 121–6 (I quote 116); Steinmetz [159], 54–68; *contra*: see especially Untersteiner [156], CCXLII–CCL.

5 Cherniss [32], 18; similar judgments are legion.

6 On the sentence from the *Sophist* see especially Stokes [56], 50–2; for the issue in general, ibid., ch. 3. Mondolfo-Taran [131], C–CXIV, offer a spirited defence of the doxography. According to Simplicius:

> Theophrastus says that Xenophanes . . . supposes that the principle is one, or that what exists is one . . ., but he [i.e. Theophrastus] agrees that the account of his [i.e. Xenophanes'] opinion belongs to an inquiry other than that into nature (**A 31**).

Theophrastus did not say (*pace* Jaeger [48], 40) that Xenophanes was not a *phusiologos*; rather, he said that Xenophanes' alleged monism was not a 'physical' opinion (he probably gave Xenophanes a physical theory of elements: Diogenes Laertius, IX.19 = **A 1**). The inquiry to which Xenophanes' monism belongs is theology (see Diels [4], 480 n, recanting the view he expressed at 101–10): Xenophanes' theological monotheism was lightheartedly construed by Plato as an ontological monism; Theophrastus solemnly indicates that Plato is romancing. It is another question whether Parmenides was in any sense a 'pupil' of Xenophanes (Aristotle, *Met* 986b22 = **A 30**; Simplicius, **A 31**; etc.).

7 Vlastos [161], 92; contrast Burnet [31], 13–15, on 'the secular character of the earliest Ionian philosophy'. Where religiosity is concerned I am tone-deaf: it is certain that many of the Presocratics had something to say about the gods; whether or not they were religious men I cannot tell.

8 Nietzsche [28], 385; Jaeger [48], 49, 92. Cf. Kirk-Raven [33], 171; Cleve [37], 27–8; *contra*: Reinhardt [30], 100: 'the tradition compels us to replace Xenophanes the mystic by Xenophanes the dialectician'.

9 That the major gods were ungenerated was clear to Pherecydes, **7 B 1**; and note the apophthegm ascribed to Thales: 'What is divine?—That which has neither beginning nor end' (Diogenes Laertius, I.36 = **11 A 1**).

10 Note the strange phrase '*theoi aeigenetai*' (e.g., *Iliad* II.400; III. 296); Callimachus, *Hymn to Zeus* 1–10, says that Zeus was born, 'but you have not died; for you exist forever'.

11 The section of the *MXG* on Xenophanes is usually dismissed as worthless (e.g., Jaeger [48], 51–4; Guthrie [25], I.367–8); but the old arguments in Reinhardt [30], 89–96, still convince me that the *MXG* relies on Theophrastus and hence has some historical value (cf. Steinmetz [159], 49–51; von Fritz [158], 1548–52). (On the other hand, the attempt in Untersteiner [156], XVII–CXVIII, to date the *MXG* to *c*.300 BC is feeble and confused.)

12 On Epicharmus see especially Berk [172]. For his philosophical interests see Diogenes Laertius, VIII.78 = **23 A 3** (cf. Berk [172], 80–5). Some make him a Pythagorean (Diogenes Laertius, VIII.78 ≐ **A 3**; Iamblichus, **A 4**); but see Burkert [173], 289, n. 58; Thesleff [175], 84. That he criticized Xenophanes is attested by Aristotle (*Met* 1010a5 = **21 A 15**; cf. Alexander, *in Met* 308.12; and see especially Reinhardt [30], 122–5). Of the many fragments collected in Diels-Kranz, most are forgeries (see Athenaeus, **A 10**; Diels-Kranz I.193–4). **B 1–B 6** are quoted by Alcimus, a fourth-century historian of Sicily: he argued against Plato's pupil Amyntas that Platonism was in all essentials anticipated by Epicharmus. **B 1** and **B 2** seem to be genuine (Berk [172], 88–93); and **B 5** probably is too (ibid., 98–9).

13 See e.g. Kirk-Raven [33], 170. On 'polar expressions' see Wilamowitz [18], III.230–1; Lloyd [50], 90–4. Aristophanes, *Clouds* 573–4, may be a reminiscence of **B 23**.1; but his expression is not 'polar'.

14 See especially Stokes [56], 76–9, who thinks that this view gives the 'plain, ordinary meaning' of the Greek (83). A survey of interpretations in Untersteiner [156], XLIII–XLIX.

15 Euripides imitates Xenophanes in fr. 282 = **C 2** (cf. **B 2**, and see Athenaeus, *ad* **C 2**); see Nestle [459], 560–3; Dodds [43], 197, n. 20.

16 *orthôs*: for the logical sense of the word see Wilamowitz [18], III.18–19 (the MSS. read *ontôs*—an accurate gloss). Cf. *MXG* 977a31–3 = **A 28**: 'the divine is by its nature (*pephukenai*) not mastered'.

17 Diogenes Laertius, IX.19 = **A 1**, adds 'and does not breathe'; and the addition may be genuine (see Kahn [90], 98, n. 2).

18 Cf. Anaxagoras, **59 B 12**; Diogenes, **64 C 3** (pseudo-Hippocrates) and **C 4** (Philemon); and Critias, **88 B 25**. 17.

19 Cf. *MXG* 977b27 = **A 28**: 'Again, he assumes that god is most masterful (*kratistos*), meaning by this most powerful and best'. For the essential goodness of gods see especially Aristotle, *Cael* 279a30–5, and Euripides, fr. 292.7 ('if gods do anything evil, they are not gods').

20 See Antiphon, **87 B 10**:

> For this reason it lacks nothing and takes nothing from anything, but is unlimited and unlacking.

(Antiphon is almost certainly talking about god.) Socrates thought that 'to lack nothing is a divine characteristic . . . and what is divine is most powerful' (Xenophon, *Memorabilia*, I.vi.10). So too Diogenes the Cynic: 'It is proper to gods to lack nothing' (Diogenes Laertius, VI.105). *MXG* 977b27–30 = **A 28** objects that Xenophanes' almighty god is not conventional (*kata nomon*) (cf. Adkins [207], 26, n. 4). But Xenophanes 'everywhere starts from the definitions of the nature of the gods given by popular religion' (Drachmann [164], 19); rather, he forms his concept of the divine from the core of characteristics essential to the gods of popular thought.

21 'He remains in the same state' translates *en tautôi mimnei* (cf. Epicharmus, **23 B 2**.9; Euripides, *Ion* 969); thus line 1 of **62** asserts immutability, and line 2 adds immobility. But *en tautôi mimnei* may rather mean 'he stays in the same place'; in which case *oude* in line 2 may have the force of 'for . . . not . . .', so that **62** asserts immobility in line 1 and justifies the assertion in line 2.

22 Cf. 886D; 889A–890A; [Hippocrates], *morb sacr* 1–5; Plutarch, *Nicias* 23; see Guthrie [25], III.227–8. There is a long-standing controversy over the identity of the atheist philosophers attacked in *Laws* X: see especially Tate [167]; Guthrie [25], III.115–16; de Mahieu [168].

23 For the ascription, see especially Jaeger [48], 31–2, 203–6, n. 44 (comparing Diogenes, **64 B 5**); *contra*: e.g., Vlastos [161], 114, n. 75.

24 See especially Guthrie [25], I.376–80; Untersteiner [156], LXX–LXXVI, CXC–CCIV.

VI Pythagoras and the Soul

1 On Pythagoras' life see especially Guthrie [25], I.173–81; Burkert [173], ch II.2 ('There is not a single detail in the life of Pythagoras that stands uncontradicted': ibid., 109). On the extreme difficulty of getting to grips with Pythagoreanism see the wise words of Guthrie [25], I.146–56; Burkert [173], 1–14.

2 See Diogenes Laertius, VIII.6–8 = **14 A 19**; Iamblichus, **A 17**; Galen, **A 18**; see especially Burkert [173], 218–20 (who deals adequately with Ion, **36 B 4**, and Heraclitus, **22 B 129**, texts which appear to ascribe writings to Pythagoras).

3 See the list in van der Waerden [408] (cf. Aristoxenus, **58 D 6**, § 198); a full account of the pseudepigrapha in Thesleff [174] and [175].

4 Mathematics: e.g., Proclus, **58 B 1**; Aristoxenus, **B 2**; Diogenes Laertius, VIII.11. (Pythagoras' theorem: Proclus, **58 B 19**; Diogenes Laertius, VIII.12. See especially Burkert [173], 409–12, 428–9.) Astronomy: e.g., Aëtius, **41 A 7**; Diogenes Laertius, VIII.48 = **28 A 44**. Harmonics: e.g., Xenocrates, fr. 9 H; Iamblichus, *VP* 115. (Harmonics and astronomy as sister sciences: Archytas, **47 B 1**; Plato, *Republic* 530D. Music of the spheres: Aristotle, *Cael* 290b12–

291a28 = **58 B 35**. See especially Burkert [173], 350–7; West [108], 11–14.) Metaphysics: Aristoxenus, **58 B 2**.

5 In what follows I rely heavily on Burkert [173] (see also Reinhardt [30], 131–6; Heidel [406], 350–4); for critical comment on Burkert's scepticism see van der Waerden [408], 277–300; de Vogel [181], ch. 3; Kahn [177].

6 Our sources for Pythagoreanism fall into five classes (see especially Burkert [173], ch. II.1; Philip [180], 8–23): (a) the genuine fragments of Philolaus and Archytas (see chapter XVIII); (b) a handful of pre-Aristotelian reports, most of which are mentioned in the present chapter (see Burkert [173], 109, n. 64; Morrison [182], 136–41); (c) fourth-century accounts, mostly fragmentary (in general see von Fritz [183], 173–9), including Aristotle (see especially Guthrie [25], I.214–16; Philip [413], and [180]), Dicaearchus, Eudemus, Heraclides, Timaeus, Speusippus; (d) neo-Pythagorean writers such as Porphyry, Iamblichus and Nicomachus; (e) the usual compilers, such as Diogenes Laertius.

7 Iamblichus, *comm math sc* 76.16–78.8 (cf. *VP* 81, 87–9); see Burkert [173], 193–7, 206–7 (*contra*; Philip [180], 28–9).

8 For the *acousmata* see **58 C**, with Burkert [173], ch. II.4. Aristoxenus, **58 D**, contains a lot of sensible stuff about ethics, political theory and education; but it is probably a fourth century version of the *acousmata* (Burkert [173], 107–9).

9 Pythagoras is sometimes called a shaman (e.g., Burkert [173], 162–5; cf. Dodds [43], ch. 5); but I doubt if the phenomenon of shamanism sheds any light on early Greek philosophy (see Philip [180], 158–62; Kahn [177], 30–5).

10 The passage is from Porphyry, *VP* 19; for the attribution to Dicaearchus see Burkert [173], 122–3.

11 'Metempsychosis' is the orthodox name for the view later and more accurately referred to as '*palingenesis*' or '*metensômatôsis*' (Servius, *ad Aen* III.68).

12 See *Meno* 81AD; *Phaedo* 70A; etc. (see especially Long [188], 65–86).

13 References in Burkert [173], 126, n. 38; cf. Herodotus, II.18; Hellanicus, *FGrH* 4 F 73. Reinhardt tried to find cyclical transmigrations in Heraclitus (Reinhardt [30], 191–9); some scholars find them in Parmenides' Way of Opinion (cf. Simplicius, *ad* **28 B 13**). For Egyptian origins of Pythagoreanism see also Isocrates, *Busiris* 28 = **14 A 4**; Suda, **7 A 2**; and see Philip [180], 189–91; Burkert [173], 126.

14 Numerals followed by '**Z**' refer to the order of the fragments in Zuntz [193]. The fish in **86** is a dolphin: Wilamowitz [194], 635–6.

15 **B 129** is often mistranslated; for the correct version see, e.g., Zuntz [193], 208–9. Most scholars see a reference to Pythagoras (see Burkert [173], 137–8); but that is far from certain. Ion, **36 B 4**, ascribes some doctrine of survival to Pythagoras, but does not explicitly refer to metempsychosis; so too Herodotus, IV.95–6 = **14 A 2**.

16 There is no reason to doubt Diogenes' reference to Pythagoras (see Burkert [173], 120, n. 1), though Diogenes is of course wrong to refer to Pythagoras' *own* incarnations. Reference to later Pythagorean texts on metempsychosis in Thesleff [175], Subject Index IV; but some later Pythagoreans played the doctrine down (see Burkert [173], 124). I have nothing whatever to say about Orphism (see, e.g., Burkert [173], 125–33).

17 I note the probable answers of Empedocles to my peripheral questions. Hippolytus, **31 A 31**, implies that all *psuchai* transmigrate, but **B 112**.4 and **B 113**.2 suggest that transmigration is limited to an *élite* (but see Burkert [173], 136–7). As far as we can tell, all animals and at least some plants receive *psuchai*. There is a cycle of transmigration with a fixed time-table (**B 115**) (on a

Pythagorean time-table see Diogenes Laertius, VIII.14; Thesleff [175], 171, n. 21); and transmigrations are hierarchically arranged (see Zuntz [193], 232–4). There is no evidence for gaps between incarnation or for *post mortem* Judgment. A moral theory is erected on the doctrine (above, pp. 122–6).

18 E.g., *Iliad* XIX.350–4; *Odyssey* X.229–40; see especially Bacigalupo [189], 267–76.

19 Metempsychosis is ascribed to Pherecydes (Suda, **7 A 2**; see, e.g., Vlastos [161], 110, n. 60); for Epimenides see Dodds [43], 143. Note that Heraclitus **22 B 129** accuses Pythagoras of plagiarism.

20 See, e.g., Long [188], 2; Jaeger [48], 84–5. Burnet [185], 257, claimed that the personal *psuchê* was an invention of Socrates, and many scholars have believed him. But see, e.g., Zuntz [193], 270; Lloyd-Jones [51], 8–10. There is no standard Greek terminology for personhood (see especially Dodds [43], 138–9); but we can hardly say that 'strictly speaking, a doctrine of personal immortality could scarcely be developed without a word for "person"' (Kahn [493], 13, n. 24). The notion of an occult, non-personal self seems to figure in the doctrine of Pindar, fr. 116 B (see Burnet [185], 249–51; Kahn [493], 12–13), but that has nothing to do with the orthodox Pythagorean doctrine.

21 This argument, the *auxanomenos logos*, has had a long history. For the ancient part of the story see Plutarch, *Moralia* 1083AD and Bernays [198]; for the modern part see R. Hall 'Hume's Use of Locke on Identity', *Locke Newsletter* 5, 1974, 56–75. **88** has often been connected with Pythagoreanism for the absurd reason that the debtor's opening remarks refer to a Pythagorean 'Lehre vom Geraden und Ungeraden'.

22 Burkert [173], 136.

23 Burkert [173], 136.

24 According to Plutarch, Empedocles denied that we can remember our earlier incarnations (*ad* **31 B 116**); but Empedocles certainly claimed some such memories. In Plato the connexion between pre-existence and recollection is familiar. Further texts on Pythagorean mnemonics: Cicero, *Cato* 11.38; Proclus, *in Tim* 124.4–13; Porphyry, *VP* 40; Diodorus, X.viii (see Burkert [173], 213, n. 19; Gladigow [187], 412–14). But memory was cultivated in Greece, and a good memory is an advantage even to the non-Pythagorean sage (see, e.g., Aristophanes, *Clouds* 129, 414; Plato, *Republic* 486D).

25 I think that this argument lies behind the remarks in Diogenes of Oenoanda, fr. 34 Ch (cf. new fr. 2: M. F. Smith, 'New Readings in the Text of Diogenes of Oenoanda', *CQ* n.s. 22, 1972, 162); see Chilton [22], 85–8; 128–30.

26 Kahn [177], 167.

27 Cf. Herodotus, II.123 = **14 A 1**; Alexander Polyhistor, *apud* Diogenes Laertius, VIII.28 = **58 B 1a**; Cicero, **7 A 5**.

28 See especially Guthrie [25], I.351–7; Mugler [201], who argues ingeniously that men die and their *psuchai* survive because their physiological cycles break down and their psychic cycles are eternal. With **93** compare Heraclitus, **22 B 103**; [Hippocrates], *de victu* 19 = **22 C 1** (see Reinhardt [134], 76–80).

29 On *aeikinêton* ('ever-moving') and the variant *autokinêton* ('self-moving') see especially Robinson [202], 111–12, with references; on the sense of *pasa psuchê*, ibid., 111 (see also Hackforth [203], 64–6; Robinson [205]). This argument for immortality was one of the most quoted passages of Plato: see references in Moreschini's edition of the *Phaedrus*.

30 See, e.g., Skemp [204], 5–6; Burkert [173], 296, n. 97. The argument was

connected with Alcmeon by Simplicius: *in An* 32.1–13. See further Stella [200], 276–7, for other Platonic references.

31 So too Philoponus, *in An* 71.6; Sophonias, *in An* 11.25.

VII The Moral Law

1 Pythagorean abstention was a standard butt of comedy (see **58 E**); but the nature and extent of the practice was hotly debated from the time of Aristoxenus (see especially Burkert [173], 180–3).

2 Zuntz [193], 183.

3 Omitting line 4 with Wilamowitz [194], 634, and Zuntz [193], 194–6.

4 In line 2 I translate Zuntz' *oiktra toreunta*: that emendation makes sense, the MSS. text does not.

5 Burkert [173], 180; a more careful assessment in von Fritz [183], 195–7. For Theophrastus, see Porphyry, *de Abst* III.26 (Burkert [173], 122, n. 6); for Xenocrates, fr. 98 H (cf. Hippolytus *ad* **31 B 115**; Diodorus, X.vi.1). Note also the Empedoclean sentiments in the speech of Ovid's Pythagoras (*Metam* XV.75–175, 457–78; on Ovid's sources here see van der Waerden [184], 854–5).

6 P. D. Singer, 'Animal Liberation', *New York Review of Books*, *XX*.5, 1973, 18.

7 Cf. Diogenes Laertius, IX.12 = **22 A 1**:

> Some entitle Heraclitus' book *Muses* [cf. Plato, *Sophist* 242D = **A 10**], others *Concerning Nature*; Diodotus calls it
> A certain Steering to a Balanced Life,
> others *Judgment* [*gnômê*: cf. **B 41**), *Manners* [*êthê*: cf. **B 78**], *Turnings* [*tropai*: cf. **B 31**], *One Universe for All* [cf. **B 89**].

The MSS. text is corrupt, and I have tacitly emended it in places; at any event, it is plain that more than one ancient scholar found moral philosophy at the core of Heraclitus' book.

8 I quote only the second half of **B 5**: the first half, though on the related topic of ritual observances, seems to be a separate fragment. See also **B 14** = **87 M**; **B 15** = **50 M**.

9 Heraclitus' views on psychology and death are controversial (see especially Marcovich [140], 303–5; Nussbaum [477]). I offer a brief sketch of one possible reconstruction: 'Souls are fiery (Aëtius, **18 A 9**), and the drier they are the better (**B 118** = **68 M**; cf. **B 119** = **69 M**); "for souls it is death to become water" (**B 36** = **66 M**: cf. **B 76** = **66** (e) **M**; **B 77** = **66** (d) **M**; and perhaps **B 12** = **40 M**). But **B 36** does not imply that all souls do in fact become wet and die; and there may well be survival for some. Thus something unexpected awaits us after we die (**B 27** = **74 M**; cf. **B 98** = **72 M**); and the fate we meet with then depends upon the life we lead now (**B 25** = **97 M**; **B 136** = **96** (b) **M** (see Kirk [213]; West [214]); cf. **B 63** = **73 M**; **B 24** = **96 M**). Souls are immortal (Aëtius, **A 17**); and perhaps they undergo a cyclical series of incarnations (**B 88** = **41 M**)'. See further, pp. 473–4.

10 See also: **B 29** = **95 M**; **B 66** = **82 M** (but see below, n. 20). Other moralizing fragments: **B 43** = **102 M**; **B 95** = **110 M** (perhaps to be connected with **B 117** = **69 M**); **B 110** = **71 M**.

11 'What must be', *chreôn*, is in fact an emendation. See also **B 137** = **28** (d) **M**; Aëtius, I.28.1; pseudo-Galen, 42.

12 See Aëtius, Censorinus, **A 13** = **65 M**; Aëtius, **A 18**; Plutarch, Philo, Censorinus, **A 19** = **108 M**; cf. **B 100** = **64 M**. See especially Reinhardt [134], 75–83; Kirk [136], 295–305.

13 This interpretation of **109** is taken from Cleve [37], 83–7; see further Marcovich [140], 309–10.
14 On early uses of *nomos* see especially Ostwald [211], 20–54; he ends by distinguishing no less than thirteen senses of the word.
15 Clearly descriptive *nomoi*: Aeschylus, *Choephori* 400; Sophocles, *Antigone* 613; Euripides, fr. 346. Clearly prescriptive *nomoi*: Aeschylus, *Supplices* 670; Sophocles, *Antigone* 450; Euripides, *Hippolytus* 1328. See also Dover [206], 256–7.
16 Vlastos [111], 56; cf. Jaeger [48], 115–16; Lloyd [50], 210–32. Cornford [40], 21, says that 'the word "law" is missing from the vocabulary of Greek science. "Law" suggests a rule of behaviour, an enactment associated with the notions of cause and effect, of action and its consequences.' Cornford here seems to confuse prescriptive and descriptive laws; and he is quite mistaken in saying that legislative vocabulary was foreign to Greek science.
17 *Kata to chreôn*: some scholars see a normative notion in the phrase—'what should be' rather than 'what must be' (see especially Fränkel [230], 187–8). Even if that is right, Anaximander exhibits the confusion between descriptive and prescriptive laws which I am labouring here.
18 Justice figures in other Heraclitean fragments: on **B 23** = **45 M** see Mouraviev [130]; on **B 28** = **20** + **19 M** see above, p. 145; on **B 66** = **82 M** see below, n.20.
19 For the conjunction of **B 114** and **B 2** see Marcovich [129], 91–2. **B 114** may have followed close upon **33** (so West [59], 117; cf. Sextus, **A 16**), thereby giving prominence to the ethical content of Heraclitus' book. The text of **B 2** is uncertain. Sextus' MSS. read:

> Going on a little, he adds: For that reason one should follow what is *koinos*, for what is *koinos* is *xunos*; yet . . .

Diels-Kranz print:

> Going on a little, he adds: For that reason one should follow what is *xunos* (that is, what is *koinos*—for the *koinos* is *xunos*); yet . . .

I adhere to the orthodox opinion, which accepts this text and treats the parenthesis as an un-Heraclitean gloss on the rare word *xunos*. West [59], 118, begins the quotation at the word 'yet', ascribing the preceding clause to Sextus (cf. Bollack-Wismann [143], 65); that is implausible.
20 **B 66** = **82 M** reads:

> Fire, coming upon them, will judge and convict all things.

Its authenticity is defended by, e.g., Marcovich [129], 435; but Reinhardt [135], 64–7, argues—to my mind cogently—that it is Hippolytan, not Heraclitean. **B 33** = **104 M** reads:

> It is a *nomos* too to obey the will of one.

Some take 'one' to refer to God; but the presence of 'too' (*kai*) is against this. The fragment should rather be connected with **B 49** = **98 M** and **B 121** = **105 M**.

VIII The Principles of Human Knowledge

1 I follow the text suggested by Wachtler [199], 34–8 (cf. Stella [200], 237, n. 1).
2 *Iliad* II.484–6 (trans. Chapman); cf. Theognis, 141–2; Pindar, *Nemean* VI.1–6;

Herodotus, VI.50; Heraclitus, **22 B 78** = **90 M**, **B 79** = **92 M**; Philolaus, **44 B 6**. See especially Snell [55], ch. 7.

3 Lloyd-Jones [51], 35.

4 But Xenophanes was not a pure sceptic in Sextus' opinion: see *Pyrr Hyp* I.223–5 = **A 35**; II.18; III.219; *adv Math* VII.48–52. See also Aristocles, **A 49**, and Diels [3], 45. I am not sure how Xenophanes' rejection of divination (Cicero, Aëtius, **A 52**; pseudo-Galen, 105) connects with his scepticism.

5 In line 1 I read *iden* rather than *genet'* (see Fränkel [215], 342–3). An alternative translation of line 2 runs: '. . . and concerning what I say about everything'. In line 3, *tuchoi* may mean '. . . if he should happen . . .' rather than '. . . if he should actually manage . . .'. In line 4 I take *pasi* to be masculine; if it is neuter, the line reads: 'but in the case of all things, there is only belief'. The fragment is frequently cited or alluded to: see references in Diels [3], 45.

6 See especially Heitsch [217] 208–16.

7 See also Varro, *apud* Augustine, *Civitas Dei*, VII.17:

> sed ut Xenophanes Colophonius scribit, quid putem, non quid contendam, ponam. Hominis est enim haec opinari, dei scire.

8 For the phrase, used to refer to Ionian science, see, e.g., Plato, *Apology*, 18B; cf. Aristophanes, *Clouds* 187–95 (see Mejer [529]).

9 So Sextus, *adv Math* VII.48–52; Epiphanius, III.9. Timon reproaches Xenophanes for 'dogmatizing' about God (frr. 59–60 = **A 35**); and some scholars hold that Xenophanes' positive theology rules out a sceptical interpretation of **121** (e.g., von Fritz [158], 1557–8; Rivier [216], 55–7). But I do not see that Xenophanes' theology is 'dogmatic'; and I suppose that **124** is Xenophanes' anticipatory response to Timon's charge.

10 *adv Math* VII.48–52; 326. Plato, *Meno* 80D, perhaps suggests the same interpretation (see Fränkel [215], 344).

11 Clement paraphrases Xenophanes; Diels' tentative restoration of the original verses has become canonical, but it is speculative.

12 See **B 40** = **16 M**; **B 57** = **43 M**; **B 106** = **59 M**; **B 129** = **17 M**; **B 81** = **18 M** (see Reinhardt [219]); **B 42** = **30 M**.

13 See the table in Kirk [136], 47. With **128** compare *Odyssey* XVIII.130–7; Archilochus, fr. 68 D. I read *hokoiois* (Bergk) for *hokosoi*.

14 Cf. Archytas, **47 B 3**:

> . . . to discover without inquiring is difficult and rare, with inquiry it is plain sailing and easy—but impossible if you do not know how to inquire.

15 I follow, doubtingly, Mouraviev [130], 118–22.

16 Plutarch, *adv Col* 1118C, interprets **136** differently: 'I probed myself' (cf. **B 116** = **23** (e) **M**); see Westman [15], 295–7. Cf. Epicurus, fr. 117 Us.; *contra*: Dio Chrysostom, 54.2.

17 **137** is imitated by Democritus, **68 B 64** (cf. **B 65**); with **138** contrast Ion, **36 B 4**. For a related distinction between polymathy and wisdom see Anaxarchus, **72 B 1**; Plato, *Laws* 819A; see Pfeiffer [24], 138.

18 See especially Archytas, **47 B 3**; Plato, *Phaedo* 99C; cf. Xenophanes, **21 B 3**.1; Pindar, *Olympian* II.86–8 (see Ramnoux [142], 324–5); Parmenides, **28 B 1**.32; Empedocles, **31 B 14**. For Heraclitus see **B 17** = **3 M**; **B 55** = **5 M**; and note *didaskein* in **B 40** = **16 M**.

19 Some translate: 'The things of which there is sight, hearing, perception

(*mathêsis*)—these I prefer' (see Marcovich [129], 21); but that does not agree with Heraclitus' use of *manthanein*.

20 So Fränkel [145], 271–2; Cherniss [32], 15. For the obvious interpretation see Diogenes Laertius, IX.7 = **A 1**. Note that the heavenly bodies are carried about in *skaphai* or basins (Diogenes Laertius, IX.9 = **A 1**; Aëtius, **A 12**).

21 **B 46** = **114 M** reads thus:

> He used to say that thinking was a sacred disease (*hieros nosos*: epilepsy), and that sight deceives.

(cf. **B 131** = **114** (d) **M**). The second clause of **B 46** is surely derived from **B 107** = **13 M**. The first clause is presented as an apophthegm, not as a quotation. Its meaning is anyone's guess. **B 46** does not require a sceptical interpretation.

22 Many scholars feel that there is an incompatibility between **141** and **137**. On my interpretation of **137** there is evidently no incompatibility; but neither is there on the orthodox interpretation. For on that interpretation, **137** denies that polymathy is a sufficient condition for wisdom, while **141** asserts that it is a necessary condition. On the pre-philosophical background to **141** see Stokes [56], 88–9.

23 Nussbaum [477], 10.

24 Alcman, fr. 125 P reads:

> Experience (*peira*) is the beginning of learning.

Lanza [223], argues cogently that 'Alcman' here is a mistake for 'Alcmeon'. (The same mistake is certainly made at Theodoretus, *curatio* V.17). Note that the fragment fits well with the *Phaedo* theory. Cornford [114], 34, says that 'in the practical art of medicine we find the root of empirical epistemology'; but he is right only *per accidens*: Alcmeon's epistemology has no logical connexion with his medical practice. Vlastos [115], 47–8, finds no empiricist epistemology before *Phaedo* 96B (in which, by implication, he sees no Presocratic traces).

IX Parmenides and the Objects of Enquiry

1 See the condemnatory judgments of Plutarch, **A 16**, Proclus, **A 17**, **A 18**, and Simplicius, *in Phys* 7.3, 21.19. On Parmenides' style see Diels [224], 4–11; Mourelatos [237], ch. 1.

2 In line 29 I read *eukukleos*; for the variant, *eupeitheos* ('persuasive'), see, e.g., Diels [224], 54–7. In line 31, 'these' (*tauta*) are the mortal opinions (*contra*; Schwabl [243]; Reale [269], 226–34). In lines 31b–32, which are among the most disputed in Parmenides' poem, I incline to take *perônta* (read *perôntas?*) as masculine, and to accept Diels' *dokimôs'* for *dokimôs*; thus I translate:

> . . . you will learn . . . the way in which men were bound to judge the things that seem to be, since they always journey through them all.

i.e., 'You will learn how men who always have appearances thrust upon them could not help believing them to be real.' But the sentence does not have the importance some would ascribe to it: the central problem of the relationship between the Way of Truth and the Way of Opinion can be securely established without reference to lines 31b–32. The arrangement of the verses at the end of **B 1**, and their connexion with **150** and **156**, are disputed (see Bicknell [228]); I follow the orthodoxy of Diels-Kranz. But Bicknell [229] plausibly puts **B 10** after **B 1**.

3 It contained some interesting astronomy (see **A 37–44**; **B 10–15**): Parmenides is said to have identified the Morning Star with the Evening Star (Diogenes Laertius, IX.23 = **A 1**; Aëtius, **A 40a**), and to have been the first upholder of a spherical earth (Diogenes Laertius, IX.21 = **A 1**; VIII.48 = **A 44**). On the contents of the Way of Opinion see especially Hölscher [227], 106–23, who suggests connexions with the later theories of Empedocles and Philolaus.

4 For this translation see, e.g., Tarán [226], 41–4, with references. The traditional translation is: 'Thinking and being are the same' (e.g., Kahn [253], 721–4); but I can make no sense of that unless it is glossed in such a way as to make it equivalent to the translation I prefer. Full details of interpretations of **149** in Untersteiner [225], CII–CVI.

5 The grammar is horrid: should we read *legei te noei t'*, taking *to* as a relative pronoun? Then translate: 'It is necessary for what one says and thinks to be being'. Other interpretations documented in Untersteiner [225], CIX, n. 29.

6 See especially Verdenius [233], 65–6; Mourelatos [237], 68–70. Kahn [253], 713, n. 18, and Mourelatos [251], render *phrazein* in **148**.8 by 'point out' and gloss *legein* and *phasthai* by 'say truly'; but that gloss is unacceptable. In this context reference is often made to von Fritz [62]. But I do not know what von Fritz thinks he has shown. Originally, perhaps, *nous* referred to insight or intuitive knowledge. But even in Homer and Hesiod, *nous* is not always veridical; i.e., you can *noein* that *P* though *P* is false. Hence *nous* is nearer to thought than to knowledge. By the fifth century, *nous* covers reflective thought and intellect in general (see also Furley [186], 8–10).

7 Kahn [253], 703, n. 4, offers a different account of **148**. 2: *noêsai* is 'loosely epexegetical . . . with *hodoi*'; i.e. 'what ways of enquiring there are that lead to thought'.

8 The reference of *tautês* in **150**.3 has caused some difficulty (see especially Stokes [56], 112–15); but as far as I can see that word refers simply enough to the Road discussed in **148** and **150**.1–2 (see Cornford [242], 99–100).

9 The second half of **148**.3 is syntactically ambiguous: the *esti* in *ouk esti mê einai* may be either 'personal' or 'impersonal' ('It is not for not being' or 'It is not possible for it not to be'). Line 5 proves that the *sense* is: 'It cannot not be'; and I take it that either syntax will yield that sense.

10 See especially Kahn [255]; there is a useful table on p. 82 presenting a summary classification of the roles played by *einai*.

11 Eudemus, fr. 43 W = **A 28**, says that the Eleatics ignore different uses of *einai*; but the Peripatetic and the modern accusations are quite distinct. Furth [257] maintains that the notions of existence and of the copula are 'impacted or *fused* in the early Greek concept of being' (243). He cites no evidence; and he does not explain the difference between fusion and confusion. Kahn [255], 320–3, argues that existential *einai*—his Type VI—was invented in the fifth century; but I cannot distinguish Type VI from the early Type I.

12 '. . . negative judgments (*hoi apophatikoi logoi*), as Parmenides says, fit principles and limits' (Scholiast to Euclid, **A 22a** in Untersteiner's edition); but the sense and reliability of the report are uncertain.

13 The veridical use of *einai* is discussed in Kahn [252], and applied to Parmenides in Kahn [253]. Kahn's view is complicated by the fact that he maintains first that the veridical use of *einai* involves both the existential and the predicative uses ([253], 712), and second, that Parmenides' *esti* means both 'it is the case' and 'it

exists' (ibid., 336). Mourelatos [237], ch. 2 and Appendix 2, claims to follow Kahn; but he says that *esti* is the 'is' of 'speculative predication' (predication which gives insight into the identity of something or says what it is). That is not a special sense of *esti*; nor can I give any account of the three Roads in terms of it. Hölscher [227], 79 and 98, holds that *esti* is neither existential nor predicative: it means 'seiend sein', 'Bestand haben', 'wahr sein'. Jones [258], 290–1, thinks that Parmenides is proposing a new sense of *einai*, which he explains in **149**. None of these modern suggestions has any linguistic or interpretative plausibility; and none is worth considering unless there are grave objections to the existential construe of *esti*.

14 Some scholars talk vaguely of an 'indefinite' subject. Loenen [238], 12–14, emends line 3 to read: . . . *hopôs esti ti kai hôs* . . . ('that something (*ti*) is . . .'). Untersteiner [225], LXXV–XC, takes the subject of *esti* to be *hê* [*hodos*], 'the one [road]'; and **156**.17–18 supports the suggestion. But that gives Parmenides grammar at the cost of sense.

15 Reinhardt [30], 60, supposes a lost line before **148** in which Parmenides refers to *to eon*; Cornford [231], 30, n. 2, emends line 3 to read: *hê men hopôs eon esti* . . .

16 Tugendhat [256], 137, says that 'what Parmenides is dealing with is that (i.e. "the Whole") which previous philosophers had always dealt with'; so that the philosophically educated reader will grasp the subject of the poem at once (cf. Verdenius [233], 32: Verdenius, 73–5, argues that the poem was explicitly entitled *Concerning Nature*). The Milesians had indeed described the universe as a whole; but they had not, in any very obvious sense, made statements about 'the Whole'.

17 See especially Owen [244]; I quote from Stokes [56], 119–22.

18 As well as (4), (3) yields:
(4a) If *O* can exist, then *O* can be thought of
—there are no unthinkable mysteries. Parmenides does not need (4a) for his argument; for some reflexions on it see Anscombe [250], 128–32.

19 Parmenides had an ancient reputation for criticizing his predecessors (Simplicius, **A 19**; Plutarch, *adv Col* 1124C); but no details survive. For references to the modern controversy over the mortals of **150** see Untersteiner [225], CXII–CXVII; Mondolfo-Tarán [131], XLVI–LXIV.

20 *Pantôn* is usually taken as neuter; then 'the path of all things is backward turning' is part of mortal opinion. For the translation adopted in the text see Stokes [56], 116–17; Ballew [267], 194–5.

21 Parallelism with **156**.40 supports it; comparison with **B 8**.57–8 suggests that 'the same and not the same' means 'the same as itself and not the same as other things'.

22 See further J. Barnes, *The Ontological Argument* (London, 1972), 39–45.

23 Basson [265], 83.

24 Gorgias worked by 'putting together what others had said' (*MXG* 979a14); the *MXG* specifically mentions Melissus and Zeno (979a22; b22–5).

25 So Diels-Kranz, who do not even print the *MXG*.

X Being and Becoming

1 Diels [224], 25–6, guessed that we possess nine-tenths of the Way of Truth and one tenth of the Way of Opinion. On the status of **B 4** see above, p. 213.

Loenen [238], 75–7, discovers three new fragments of the Way of Truth, of which he thinks we have only a small portion. He has convinced no one.

2 Discussion of **155** in Jameson [266] (sceptical) and Ballew [267] (over-elaborate). Hölscher [227], 77, locates **155** between **B 1** and **148**, and supposes that the goddess means only that the order of the two Ways is indifferent.

3 Owen [244], 322.

4 For 'signs' (*sêmata*) see **B 8**.55, which indicates that the 'signs' are the characterizing properties of what exists and not proofs that what exists has those properties.

5 Diels-Kranz, and many others, print *esti gar oulomeles* . . . (cf. Untersteiner [225], XXIX). Their source is Plutarch, *adv Col* 1114C. But Plutarch is quoting from memory; and the words *esti gar* are plainly Plutarch's and not a part of his quotation (see Westman [15], 236–9). *Oulon mounogenes*, which I translate, has the support of Simplicius, Clement and Philoponus; it was the standard text in late antiquity; and most modern scholars now accept it.

6 *Ateleston* is defended by Untersteiner [225], XXX–XXXI; most scholars emend to *êde teleion* or the like ('and complete'). (References in Tarán [226], 88–93). For *atalanton* see Empedocles, **31 B** 7.19 (cf. T. J. Reilly, 'Parmenides, Fragment 8.4: a correction', *AGP* 58, 1976, 57).

7 Numerals followed by '**R**' refer to the edition of Melissus by Reale [269].

8 See Reale [269], 31–2; Jouanna [270], 314–23.

9 Melissus is talking about 'whatever is' (**B 1**); equivalently, he is supposing that 'something is' and asking what follows from that supposition (Simplicius *ad* **B 1**; *MXG* 974a2 = **A 5**). His subject is not 'the Whole' or 'Nature' or 'Being' or any of those odd things.

10 After (T 12), the *MXG* adds:
(12a) *O* is not mixed
(974a24–b2 = **A 5**). See especially Reale [269], 305–8.

11 'Not existing, it exists': *esti mê on*. Most scholars translate 'it is non-existent', gratuitously importing into the text a confusion between existential and predicative *einai*.

12 In his paraphrase Simplicius says:

> Melissus begins his treatise on generation and destruction thus: 'If it is nothing, what could be said about this as if it were something existent?' (*ad* **B 1**).

Reale [269], 34–6, 368–9, prints this as a genuine fragment (cf. Burnet [31], 321, n. 5). But *MXG* 975a34–5 implies that Melissus produced no such argument. If he did, he was of course only epitomizing Parmenides.

13 The MSS. read *ho ti ên* ('whatever was'): I accept the conjecture of Loenen [238], 144–7, *ho ti esti* (but see Reale [269], 59, n. 60; 370).

14 Note that Parmenides deals with generation and destruction together: Melissus probably does not deal with destruction until **B 7**.

15 See Wiesner [273]: Diels took lines 7–9a to be directed against generation, 9b–10 against growth. Calogero took 7–11 to be against generation, 12–13 against growth. For the colourless use of 'grow' (*auxanesthai*) see, e.g., Empedocles **31 B** 17.1.

16 The dilemmatic interpretation pairs 'Neither . . .' (*oute* . . . in line 7) with 'Nor . . .' (*oud'* . . . in line 12). It is tempting to emend *oud'* to *out'*. My interpretation pairs *oud'* with the *de* of line 9.

17 Aristotle's commentators find the dilemma in Melissus (**A 10aR**); but the text of

Melissus nowhere hints at a dilemma, and the *MXG* implies that there was none (see especially 975a22–32 = **A 5**). There is a dilemma in Gorgias, **157** § 71; but it is a bastard: in the disjunction, *ek mê ontos* or *ex ontos*, the first *ek* introduces a generator, the second does not. Aristotle also refers to the dilemma (*Phys* 191a23); but in his dilemma, *ek* does not introduce a generator at all.

18 See especially Stokes [56] 253–5: Anaxagoras and Empedocles attempted to answer Parmenides' argument, and they saw in it no more than the claim that every generation requires an instigating cause (against their answers Aristotle later applied the Principle of Sufficient Reason: *Phys* 252a4).

19 Lloyd [50], 103–6, observes that the disjuncts in line 11 are not exhaustive, and he faults Parmenides for relying on a false 'principle of Unqualified Exclusion'; but the 'principle' of line 11 is the conclusion of an argument, not an assumption.

20 See especially Reinhardt [30], 39–42; further references in Tarán [226], 95–102. Stokes [56], 310, n. 78, notes a number of places where scribes have erred over negation signs.

21 I translate the MS. text; many emend (references in Tarán [226], 104–5).

22 Thus I doubt if line 5 rests on two premisses: *homou pan*, proved in 6b–21, and *suneches*, proved in 22–5 (Schofield [275], 118–19); nor am I sure that the *suneches* of line 6a should be linked to that of line 25. Certainly, *hen, suneches* does not repeat *oulon, mounogenes* (Stokes [56], 308, n. 68). On *hen* in the sense of *suneches* see Stokes [56], 13–15.

23 Adherents of (a) must gloss line 5 thus: 'it is the case neither that *O* used once to exist [but does so no longer], nor that *O* will exist [but does not yet]'. Against that gloss see especially Owen [274], 320–2; but see Schofield [275], 122–4.

24 See Owen [274], 318–19; criticized by Schofield [275], 128–9.

25 I prefer *esti de* to Diels-Kranz' *esti te kai* ('Since it did not come into being, it both is and always was . . .'); and I take 'unlimited' in a temporal sense (*contra*: Reale [269], 82–6, but the point has no substantial significance). Raven [178], 82–4, refers to Aristotle, *Cael* 268a10 = **58 B 17**, and to Ion, **36 B 1**; he conjectures that Ion and the Pythagoreans objected against Parmenides that his 'One', like everything else, would be a plurality of beginning, middle and end, and he supposes that Melissus in **159** was out to scotch that objection.

26 For the temporal use of *pan* see **B** 7.3. Most scholars take *pan* spatially. Reale [269], 86–98, argues that his interpretation saves Melissus from Aristotle's objection; similarly Cherniss [6], 67–71, and Verdenius [278]. But at best those interpretations displace the fallacy, and do not avoid it; and the spatial reading of *pan* introduces a foreign element, and a wholly disputable premiss, into Melissus' argument.

27 *Top* 167b13–20; 168b35–40 = **A 10**. The details of Aristotle's accusation are not clear: see Reale [269], 73–7.

XI Stability and Change

1 References in Reale [269], 77–9; cf. *MXG* 975b38–976a13. Gorgias certainly made the inference (**157** §§ 68–9; cf. *MXG* 979b21–3: 'if it is ungenerated, he [sc. Gorgias] assumes, by the axioms of Melissus, that it is unlimited': but see Nestle [260], 555); so too did Metrodorus, **70 A 4** (pseudo-Plutarch).

2 See especially Reale [269], 98–104; he treats the last sentence of **162** as a fragment of Melissus, and infers that the fallacious deduction of spatial infinity

'should be considered a closed chapter in the history of the interpretation of Melissus'.

3 At line 49 I read *toigar* (Wilamowitz); the MS. reading, *hoi gar* gives the wrong logical connective.

4 For the use of *mallon hêtton* see [Plato], *Minos* 313B.

5 For the doxography see, e.g., Hippolytus, **A 33**; Aëtius, **A 31**.

6 References in Untersteiner [225], CLXIII, n. 174; cf. Simplicius, **A 20**:

> If he says that the one existent is 'like the bulk of a well-rounded ball', do not be surprised; for because of his poetry he also indulges in a sort of mythical fiction.

7 'But a plurality of spheres could not be close-packed.' (a) In the *Timaeus* Plato invents a vacuumless world of close-packed figures, which geometry will not allow to pack close enough: Parmenides may have made the same mistake. (b) Did Parmenides ever reject vacuums? (above, p. 222) (c) A very clever person might toy with the idea of packing the interstices between the spheres with infinitely many ever smaller spheres.

8 For the insertion of 'unlimited' see Reale [269], 121, n. 51. **B 5** reads:

> If it was not one, it would be limited against something else.

I guess that this is a paraphrase of **164** rather than a separate fragment.

9 Kirk-Raven [33], 300.

10 The dots mark the omission of '*en hôi pephatismenon esti*'. I adopt the translation suggested by Hölscher [227], 99–100, paraphrasing thus: 'If you think, your thought bears on that existing thing, whatever it may be, which makes the utterance conveying your thought something more than a mere "name".' But that is difficult; and the phrase has suggested numerous different interpretations.

11 Woodbury [283], argued for the reading *onomastai* instead of *onom' estai*, translating: 'with reference to it (sc. *to on*) are all the names given that mortals . . .' (cf., e.g., Mourelatos [237], 180–5). But that gives a remarkably feeble sense. For the orthodoxy, to which I adhere, see, e.g., Tarán [226], 129–36.

12 On homogeneity see especially Reale [269], ch. V. I accept the interpretation of *homoios* given by the *MXG* (976a14–8 = **A 5**); and I suppose that the argument in the *MXG* is Melissan (*contra*: e.g., Stokes [56], 151; Solmsen [282], 9, nn. 18–19).

13 Owen [244], 92, takes *homoion* adverbially: 'it all exists to a similar extent'; but that does not seem to me to affect the argument. Owen, ibid., finds the premiss of lines 22–5 in line 11; Stokes [56], 136, finds it in line 16.

14 *Leusse d' homôs apeonta noôi pareonta bebaiôs*. Diels-Kranz read *homôs* as 'nevertheless'; I prefer to take it for *homoiôs* (see Bollack [284], 56, n. 3). The point of the adverb is this: 'Don't make any distinction between the absent and the present'. *Noôi* is often connected with *apeonta . . . pareonta* ('things absent and things present to your mind': cf., e.g., *Iliad* XV.80); it might go both with *leusse* and with *apeonta . . . pareonta*; it might go just with *leusse . . . apeonta*. And a little ingenuity will conjure up a dozen different construes of the line. On *kata kosmon* in line 4 see Tarán [226], 47–8.

15 The suggestion is from Hölscher [227], 117–18. Bicknell [228], 47–8, puts **167** between **151** and **156**; for attempts to insert **167** into **156** see Untersteiner [225], CXLVI, n. 107.

16 Covotti proposed *apolluoi ti* ('nor would it lose anything') for *apoloito* (see Reale

[269], 388). That gives a neater contrast between (T8) and (T9); if it is accepted, we may suppose Melissus to have taken destruction as the limiting case of loss.

17 Accepting Heidel's emendation (*metakosmêtheiê ti tôn eontôn* for *metakosmêthentôn eontôn ti ê*); see Reale [269], 389–90.

18 Omitting *to hugies kai*, with Gomperz. The MS. text reads: 'for what is healthy and what is would perish'.

19 Sentences [i]–[xviii] and [xix]–[xxvii] may be independent fragments (see Solmsen [282], 10). For various attempts to elucidate **168** see Reale [269], 386–8.

20 Cf., perhaps, Empedocles, **31 B 17**.31: 'If they were destroyed continually, they would not exist': 'if there is any destruction, destruction will continue; and so, in the course of infinite time, all will be destroyed'. I translate *toinun* as 'again'; the normal translation, 'therefore', does not help; and *toinun* is not inferential in Melissus (cf. **158**, **159**; and see J. D. Denniston, *The Greek Particles* (Oxford, 1954^{2}), 574–7).

21 A *kosmos* is an arrangement or structure; *metakosmêthênai* must mean here 'change structure', 'be rearranged' (see Diller [540], 363; cf. Reale [269], 164–70).

22 I follow Loenen [238], 162–4. The rival translations of the first sentence are equivalent, given (T4). For the import of *ouk oun . . . ge . . .* in the third sentence see Dennison, *op. cit.*, n. 20 (above), 422–5.

23 We may smell the old Melissan fallacy in sentence [xxiii]; but if it is there, it does not infect the main argument of the passage.

24 The second clause of **169** admits of different translations: 'If it moves, it does not exist'; 'It cannot be a moving thing'; 'If it moves, it is not [full]'. Fortunately, those variants make no difference to the argument.

25 For *houneken* meaning 'because' see especially Fränkel [230], 191–2; further references in Untersteiner [225], CLV, n. 140.

26 I read *epidees· mê eon de,* which was certainly Simplicius' text (see Coxon [287], 72–3) ; and I follow Hölscher [227], 53, in translating *mê eon* by 'otherwise'. Other suggestions listed in Untersteiner [225], CLVI, n. 145.

27 Lines 22–5 do not reject vacuums as such (*pace* Guthrie [25], II.33), but at best only internal vacuums. According to Raven [178], 29, 'there is . . . no need to argue that these lines [sc. **156**.7–9] are simply a rejection of the Void'; but the lines say nothing at all about the void. **167** rejects intra-mundane void, but leaves open the possibility of extra-mundane void. In any case, none of this helps the argument of lines 30–2.

28 *Principles of Philosophy* II.40 (*Oeuvres*, ed. Adam and Tannery, VIII.65); cf. II.4 (*Oeuvres*, VIII.42); letter to More of 1649 (*Oeuvres*, V.267 = *Philosophical Letters*, ed. Kenny, 237–45). See also Capek [390], 54–8.

29 In these paragraphs I draw heavily on D. H. Sandford, 'Locke, Leibniz and Wiggins on Being in the Same Place at the Same Time', *PR* 79, 1970, 75–82.

30 I append a pleasant curio:

> There are some who think it evident from the rare and dense that there is void. For if nothing is rare and dense, nothing can come together and felt up. And if that cannot happen, either motion will simply not occur or the universe will swell like the sea, as Xuthus said (Aristotle, *Phys* 216b22–6 = **33 A 1**).

Did Xuthus, whom Simplicius calls a Pythagorean and who may have lived in the second quarter of the fifth century, imagine a full and finite universe in which motion nevertheless took place? (The internal convolutions would produce ripples or waves on the outer surface of the world.) If so, was he objecting to a finite and motionless Parmenidean sphere? And did Melissus invent an infinite universe partly to combat that suggestion? Speculation is seductive (see Kirk-Raven [33], 301–2).

31 According to Aristotle, Parmenides and Melissus do not admit the existence of non-perceptible things (*Cael* 298b21 = **28 A 25**; cf. Alexander, *apud* Simplicius, *in Cael* 560.5–10).

32 The text of **B 9** in Diels-Kranz runs together **170** and **171**. For the argument see above, p. 240, on Zeno; Plato, *Sophist* 244E–245A.

33 Simplicius, *ad* **160**, refers to 'limitlessness in respect of sublimity'; see also Loenen [238], 157–8; Vlastos [289], 34–5. *Contra*: e.g., Guthrie [25], II.110, n. 2.

34 Gomperz [288] argued that *asômatos* means the same as *leptos*: not 'incorporeal' but 'fine, not dense'; Guthrie [25], II.110–13, holds that it means 'non-finite and imperceptible' (cf. Reale [269], 211–20). Gomperz and Guthrie suggest that *pachos* is not solidity but 'palpable density'.

35 Incorporeality is not ascribed to *O* by the *MXG*; and *MXG* 976a10–13 and 28–31 = **A 5** imply that Melissus made no explicit statement about the corporeality of *O*.

36 According to Cherniss [32], 21, Parmenides thinks that his argument 'precludes the possibility of any characteristic [sc. of what is] except just *being*' (cf. Furth [257], 264–7). That view—which is a *communis opinio*—is surely absurd.

37 So Popper [35], 79; Mourelatos [237], xi.

XII Zeno: Paradox and Plurality

1 Russell [316], 347; cf. Russell [318], 175: 'They are not . . . mere foolish quibbles: they are serious arguments, raising difficulties which it has taken two thousand years to answer, and which even now are fatal to the teachings of most philosophies.' It is Russell's advocacy which has spurred modern philosophers to take Zeno seriously; but it should be said that Russell himself acknowledges that the decisive turn in Zeno's fortunes was due to the work of the Frenchmen, Tannery, Noël, and Brochard. For the history of Zeno's reputation see Cajori [295].

2 The reports, mostly worthless, about Zeno's life are discussed by von Fritz [298], 53–5. The curious will read the Arabic life of Zeno by Mubaššir, printed in Jacoby [457].

3 Aristotle discusses four paradoxes of motion; Elias says there were five (**A 15**: see Untersteiner [293], 68), and Simplicius thinks there may have been more than four (*in Phys* 1012.27–9). Bicknell [342], 103–5, suggests that the argument in Diogenes Laertius, IX.72 (above, p. 276), may have been the fifth paradox.

4 'He wrote *Disputes, Account of Empedocles, Against the Philosophers, Concerning Nature*' (Suda, **A 2**). *Disputes* and *Against the Philosophers* may be the forty *logoi*; for the Empedoclean title, see below, n. 6. Some natural science is ascribed to Zeno in Diogenes Laertius, IX.29 = **A 1** (cf. Aëtius, I.7.27–8); but the value of the report is uncertain (see Untersteiner [293], 14–17; Longrigg [300]). The report that Zeno wrote dialogues (Diogenes Laertius, III.48 = **A 14**) is merely confused (Untersteiner [293], 62–3).

5 A complex architecture was first suggested by Tannery [29], ch. 10, and developed by Noël and Brochard (see Cajori [295]); it was revived by Owen [307], whose view is tellingly criticized by Stokes [56], 188–93.

6 The literature is immense: for the view that Zeno is reacting against Pythagoreans see especially Tannery [29], ch. 10; Raven [178], ch. 5; *contra*; e.g., Burkert [173], 285–8, with references. The ancient assertions that Zeno was a Pythagorean (Proclus, **28 A 4**; Strabo, **28 A 12**) are worthless. Gaye [340], 106–16, argues that the Stadium was aimed against Empedocles (see Suda, **A 2**, above, n. 4); but he does not convince.

7 But Protagoras is said to have written against the monists (Porphyry, **80 B 2**); and some scholars (e.g., Nestle [260]) think that Gorgias, **82 B 3**, is a skit on Eleaticism.

8 In a passage designed to show that 'excessive subtlety produces great evil and is hostile to truth', Seneca asserts that 'Zeno . . . says that nothing exists'; and 'if I believe Parmenides, there exists but one thing—if Zeno, not even one' (*Epistle* 88.44–5: cf. **A 21**). Dillon [294] draws attention to Proclus, *in Parm* 862.25ff: Proclus says that Zeno used the argument of *Parmenides* 131B3–6, to prove that 'the many share in some one thing, and are not deprived of one even if they stand very far apart from one another'. Dillon wonders if that comes from a positive Zenonian argument for monism; but I am sceptical.

9 Alexander's view is uncertain: at 138.3–30 Simplicius says that Alexander shared Eudemus' opinion and borrowed it from him; at 99.12–16 he says that Alexander wrongly argued that Eudemus did not ascribe an attack on monism to Zeno.

10 Numerals followed by '**L**' refer to the arrangement in Lee [292].

11 According to Owen [307], 140–1, 'Zeno's major question is: if you say there are many things in existence, how do you distinguish your individuals?' But that view rests on one among several readings of the Eudemus fragment; and no reading will show that this little anecdote enshrines Zeno's 'major question'.

12 Aristotle, fr. 65 R^3 = **A 10** (see especially Fränkel [308], 199 n. 1); cf. Diogenes Laertius, IX.25 = **A 1**; Suda, **A 2**; Philostratus, **A 9**. For different interpretations of Aristotle's remark see Lee [292], 7–8, 113–19; von Fritz [298], 78.

13 According to Alcidamas, Zeno later in life 'philosophized on his own account' (Diogenes Laertius, VIII.56 = **31 A 1**; *contra*: pseudo-Plutarch, **29 A 23**).

14 *Antilogikos*: Plato, *Phaedrus* 261D; Plutarch, **A 4**; *eristikos*: Epiphanius, III.11; pseudo-Galen, 3. Modern advocates of an antilogical Zeno include Bayle [299], note B; Fränkel [308]; Solmsen [301]. Against them, see especially Vlastos [303].

15 I guess that the two conjuncts of (Z) are what Plato calls the 'hypotheses' of Zeno's *logoi*; so that the 'first hypothesis of the first *logos*' (*Parm* 127D) will be (Z1a).

16 Proclus, *in Parm* 619.34–620.3 adds 'equal and unequal'; Isocrates X.3 adds 'possible and impossible'. See also the suggestions in Cornford [231], 58.

17 Proclus, *in Parm* 721.25–726.27, has a long and tedious discussion; clearly, he had no textual evidence. For some guesses at Zeno's reasoning see, e.g., Untersteiner [293], 47–51.

18 It is disputed how much of Zeno's work Simplicius had access to: see Guthrie [25], II.81, n. 3; Vlastos [309], 137, n. 7. The course of Simplicius' argument in 138.3–141.10 is controversial (see especially Solmsen [301], 128–31); but this is not the place for an analysis.

19 In [vi] I retain the MSS. reading *esti* for Diels' *estai*. In [vii] I accept Fränkel's palmary emendations: *apeiron* for *apeirôn*; *ek tou* placed after *pollôn*. The general sense of Simplicius' report is uncontroversial.

20 Gomperz emends *oute* to *hôste* in [xiii]; his text translates: '. . . for no part of

it will be last in such a way that there will not be another part related to another'. That expresses the same sentiment as the MSS. text, but more elegantly.

21 The argument for (Z2b) in no way depends on that for (Z2a) (*pace* Fränkel [308], 211–12, 216, n. 2); nor can **B 1** be read as a self-standing argument for (Z2) (*pace* Solmsen [301], 131–7).

22 So, e.g., Fränkel [308], 212; Vlastos [309], 119–20. See also Xenocrates, fr. 44 H = Simplicius, *in Phys* 138.10–13.

23 Fränkel [308], 217–20, finds 'a very great difference' between 'what is added is nothing' and 'what is added does not exist', and he suggests that Zeno passed from the former to the latter by way of the Polypheman fallacy. I cannot see that the fallacy infects Zeno's argument.

24 For the geometrical interpretation see especially Grünbaum [313], ch. III, who holds that Zeno's arguments 'were designed to show that the science of geometry is beset by paradox' (3). Salmon [296] opines that 'the force of this argument is geometrical' (13); but he recognizes that Zeno's paradoxes 'are—so to speak—paradoxes of applied mathematics. No theory of pure mathematics can fully resolve them' (34).

25 'That no physical cut or fission is intended here is quite obvious' (Vlastos [309], 125): Zeno is certainly not thinking of cuts which an engineer can make 'with his present tools'; but he is certainly thinking of physical bodies, and claiming that they have physical parts.

26 See further Xenocrates, frr. 43–9 H. Plato too believed in atomic lines (Aristotle, *Met* 992a22; Alexander, *in Met* 120.6); but we are not told why (and Vlastos [401], 125, n. 28, doubts the report). The ancient evidence is confusing. (a) The argument of Zeno's which precipitated atomic lines is usually identified as the Dichotomy (see especially [Aristotle], *lin insec* 986a17–28 = Xenocrates, fr. 42 H = **A 22**), but sometimes as the present argument against pluralism (see Alexander, **A 22**: cf. Furley [387], 81–3). (b) Aristotle, *Phys* 187a1–3, says that 'some' gave in to the 'dichotomy' and posited atomic magnitudes: he probably refers to the Abderite atomists (see Ross [12], 479–80; Furley [387], 81–3), but all his ancient commentators refer to Xenocrates.

27 See especially Grünbaum [313], 40–64. On Epicurus' spatial atomism see Luria [398], 148–72; Mau [402]; Vlastos [401].

28 This, the classical solution, is plainly stated by Descartes in a letter to Clerselier of 1646 (*Oeuvres*, ed. Adam and Tannery, IV.445-7 = *Philosophical Letters*, ed. Kenny, 196–9); see further Cajori [295], 79–80. Fränkel [308], 226–7, attempts to pre-empt it by denying that (Z2b) states that the many things will be infinite in magnitude; but see Furley [387], 68–9. Zeno's 'hidden premiss' was set down as a luminous truth by Epicurus (*ad Hdt* 57: cf. Furley [387], 14–16), and generally adopted by the later tradition (e.g., Sextus, *Pyrr Hyp* III.44; Simplicius, *in Phys* 141.15–16; 459.25–6; *in Cael* 608.12–15; 635.11–26: cf. Vlastos [297], 370b–371a). See below, n. 30.

29 'He' in Porphyry's text, which Simplicius quotes *verbatim*, refers to Parmenides; but Simplicius is right in maintaining that the dichotomy argument belongs rather to Zeno.

30 Aristotle, *Phys* 206b7–9, knows that (9) is not unrestrictedly true. I incline to speculate that Zeno imagined that (9) held without restriction; that Aristotle scotched that supposition; and that Epicurus saw that a restricted version of (9) was defensible. Later subscribers to Zeno's 'hidden premiss' tacitly suppose the Epicurean version of it. Vlastos [309], 131–3, thinks Zeno assumed that any infinite sequence must have a smallest member. If that assumption were true,

then (9) would hold unrestrictedly. But the assumption is false; and there is no evidence that Zeno made it.

31 Vlastos [297], 371b. Vlastos says that only a Cantorian sophistication can pinpoint Zeno's error; but we do not need the 'diagonal method' to show how Zeno errs. The concept of one-one correspondence is expounded most famously by Gottlob Frege (*Foundations of Arithmetic*, §63); but, as Frege points out, it is already present in that most unsophisticated of mathematicians, David Hume.

32 See especially Simplicius, *in Phys* 96.15–99.31, quoting Alexander and Eudemus; Philoponus, *in Phys* 42.9–45.15 (cf. **A 21** and **3–5 L**).

33 For *plêthos henadôn* see, e.g., Philoponus, *in Phys* 42.21; 24 (cf. *sunthesis tôn kath' hen* in Gorgias, **157** § 74). For the sense of *henas* see, e.g., Plato, *Philebus* 15A: *henas* does not mean 'arithmetical unit', and it is a mistake (*pace* Raven [178], 71–2) to invoke any 'Pythagorean' theory about arithmetical units.

34 Simplicius is quoting Alexander's quotation of Eudemus; and Simplicius says that the argument Alexander retails is not in Zeno's book (*in Phys* 99.18). Eudemus is hardly inventing: either the argument fell out of Zeno's book in the millennium separating Eudemus from Simplicius; or else Simplicius means only that the argument does not occur *verbatim* in Zeno.

35 Solmsen [301], 128, n. 38, connects *katêgorikôs* with the Aristotelian categories. But the rest of the quotation shows that '*a* is many *kategorikôs*' simply means '*a* is many in virtue of the predicates (*katêgoriai*) true of it'.

36 The ascription to Zeno is also made by Alexander (*apud* Simplicius, *in Phys* 96.22–30) and by Philoponus (see especially *in Phys* 42.24–8 = **8 L**, with an anachronistic illustration). For doubts about the ascription see, e.g., Lee [292], 27–9; Burkert [173], 286–8.

37 Lycophron tackled this, or a very similar, puzzle: pseudo-Alexander, **83 A 1**.

38 The main text is Simplicius, *in Phys* 562.1–564.13; further references in Lee [292], 36. Diels-Kranz, I.498, accept Calogero's suggestion that *in Phys* 562.3–6 is an actual fragment of Zeno; but Simplicius himself makes it clear first that he does not possess Zeno's own words here, and second that he does not believe that the form of the argument given at 562.3–6 is authentic.

39 Philoponus, *in Phys* 513.8–12, did not know what point Zeno was trying to make; Cornford [231], 148–9, constructs a slightly different dilemma.

40 So too Plato, *Timaeus* 52 B. Zeno's premiss is used by Gorgias, **157** §§ 69–70 (*MXG* 979b25 explicitly ascribes to Gorgias this use of 'Zeno's argument about place'); it appears at *Parmenides* 145E, 151A; according to Aristotle, *Phys* 208a30, it was a commonplace (cf. Kahn [255], 237: it was 'firmly grounded in the idiomatic expression of existence').

XIII Zeno: Paradox and Progression

1 Texts collected in Lee [292] (**19 L–36 L**, with supplementary references). The Greek commentators say that Achilles' rival was a tortoise (the tortoise is not in Aristotle; Plutarch races a tortoise against a horse); apart from that, they add nothing (see Ross [12], 71). Aristotle probably found the arguments already numbered; he refers to previous attempts at a solution (*Phys* 239b11); and he remarks upon a non-Zenonian version of the Dichotomy (above, p. 263). (Aristotle may have composed a monograph on Zeno (Diogenes Laertius, V.25; cf. Untersteiner [293], 74); Heraclides Ponticus did (Diogenes Laertius, V.17).) Favorinus said that 'Parmenides and many others' raised the Achilles paradox (Diogenes Laertius, IX.29 = **A 1**).

2 'The Dichotomy' derives from *Phys* 239b22 = **L 26** (on 187a3 = **A 22**, see above, p. 337, n. 26); 'the Stadium' derives from *Top* 160b8 = **A 25**. Aristotle himself probably knew no title for the paradox (see Vlastos [321], 95, n. 2).

3 Cf. *Phys* 239b18–20 = **A 26** = **26 L**; and note that the 'counting' version requires this diagram. See, e.g., Fränkel [308], 204, n. 3; Vlastos [321], 95–6.

4 Cf. *Phys* 263a6–11; *lin insec* 968a18–b4; see Furley [387] 70–1; Grünbaum [313], 70 (Zeno is 'enticing us to attempt a one-by-one contemplation in thought' of all the temporal parts of the runner's task). On the counting paradox itself see Grünbaum [313], 90–2; Black [326], 100–8.

5 Cf. Black [326], 108, who distinguishes between 'the finite number of real things that the runner has to accomplish and the infinite series of numbers by which we describe what he actually does' (cf. Grünbaum [313], 73–8; and especially Wisdom [328]). Some scholars discuss the Dichotomy in terms of 'making infinitely many runs'; they declare that the term 'run' has two senses; and they find an equivocation in Zeno (see especially Grünbaum [313], 73–8; Vlastos [321]). I cannot find two relevant senses of 'run'; nor does Zeno himself say anything about 'making infinitely many runs'.

6 E.g., C. S. Peirce: 'This ridiculous little catch presents no difficulty at all to a mind adequately trained in mathematics and in logic' (*Collected Papers*, VI.122). Peirce is talking of the Achilles; but his remarks apply equally to the Dichotomy.

7 For Strato see fr. 82 W = Sextus, *adv Math* X.155; on the thesis he adopts see Grünbaum [313], 50–2.

8 But Ross [12], 73–4, argues strongly that Aristotle's objection in Z 9 is cogent *ad hominem*, and hence that Zeno himself did mention the finitude of *T*; and Grünbaum [313], 52, thinks it is the temporal aspect of the Dichotomy which 'constitutes the heart of the conviction' which it often carries (cf. Ushenko [314], 157).

9 The lamp was introduced into the literature, with far more finesse than in my sketch, by Thomson [331].

10 For Aristotle's discussion see *Phys* 234a24–b9; 235b6–32; 236a7–27; 236b32–237b22; 238b36–239b4; 263b15–264a6. My argument in the text abstracts from those remarks and is not an interpretation of them.

11 This argument is adapted from some subtler remarks in Bostock [322].

12 Diodorus' dilemma is designed to show that *atoms* do not move (fr. 123 D = Sextus, *adv Math* X.86–90; cf. frr. 116–24 D); he also offered, apparently as a distinct argument, something answering to Aristotle's non-dilemmatic text (Sextus, *adv Math* X.112).

13 On the text of *Phys* 239b5–7, see especially Ross [12], 657–8, whom I follow.

14 See especially Vlastos [335], 3, n. 2 (Fränkel [308], 209, n. 5, and Untersteiner [293], 149–51, offer different explanations). The 'space equal to itself' is the *place* of an object, in the strict Aristotelian sense (*Phys* 209a33; 211a2); it is that notion of place which is employed in the Paradox of Place. The Arrow is presented in characteristically Aristotelian terminology; but it is fruitless to attempt to recover Zeno's phraseology.

15 Russell [316], 347, 350; [317], 65. Epicurus, fr. 278 Us, and Diodorus Cronus, frr. 121–9 D, advance theories of motion interestingly similar to Russell's (see Furley [387], 131–5).

16 Bergson [320], 63.

17 Adapted from Black [338], 138–9; Black's own conclusion is that there are two senses of 'move'.

18 Vlastos [335], 11.

19 At 240a5–7 the MSS. offer a choice of readings: '*A*', '*AA*', '*AAA*', '*AAAA*', etc.; Ross rightly plumps for '*AA*', but that does not mean that Aristotle had precisely two *A*s in mind: '*ta AA*' means simply 'the *A*s'.

20 Palaeographically there is nothing to choose between '*to B*' and '*to prôton B*' (abbreviated to '*to a B*'); and one MS. reads '*to a B*' (see Ross [12], 665). Bicknell [341], 43, defends '*ta B*'.

21 Thus I retain sentence [x], which many editors excise (see especially, Ross [12], 665).

22 The Greek at 240a1 ('half the time is equal to its double') may mean either '$\frac{1}{2}T = T$' or '$\frac{1}{2}T = 2T$'; see, e.g., Lee [292], 88; Gaye [340], 100–1; Stokes [56], 329, n. 31.

23 A classical example in Bayle [299], n.F; a modern example in Bicknell [341] (but Bicknell [342], 81, recants).

24 (i) Defenders of *fig. 5* must change the text at 240a6: they must either (a) omit 'of the *A*s (*tôn A*)' after 'starting from the middle'; or else (b) add 'of the Bs (*tôn B*)' after 'starting from the end'. One MS. offers '*tôn B*', several omit '*tôn A*' (see Ross [12], 663). (ii) At 240a11 most MSS. and the Greek commentators read '*ta A*', which I translate; two MSS. read '*ta B*'. Adherents of *fig. 5* have a choice: either (a) they accept '*ta B*' instead of '*ta A*' and interpolate '*ta A*' later in the sentence ('the *C* had passed all the *B*s and the *B* half the *A*s')—so Diels-Kranz; or else (b) they omit '*ta A*' ('the *C* has passed all, and the *B* half'), and gloss the resulting sentence as 'the first *C* has passed all the *A*s and the first *B* has passed half the *A*s' (so Ross [12], 662). (ib) is tolerable, and (ia) may well be right; but both (iia) and (iib) are counsels of desperation, defensible only if *fig. 5* must at all costs be established.

25 The inventor of the sophisticated Stadium was Tannery [29], ch. 10 (further references in Guthrie [25], II.95–6); *contra*: e.g., Furley [387], 73–4; Stokes [56], 185–7. Sextus, *adv Math* X.144–7, preserves an argument similar to the Stadium which explicitly uses *minima*; see also Bayle [299], n. G.

XIV The Ports of Knowledge Closed

1 So Cornford [231], 32, referring to [Hippocrates], *de victu* I.23; Verdenius [233], 55, referring to **156**.38–41; cf. Antiphon, **87 B 44** (Diels-Kranz, II.348.6).

2 I do not translate *homoureôn* (*homou rheôn*?), the sense of which is obscure.

3 The bracketed sentence makes no sense here, where it stands in Simplicius' text. Karsten transposed it to follow '. . . from water' at the end of [iii], and most scholars accept his transposition. But the sentence is inapposite at the end of [iii]. Moreover, it is linguistically objectionable: *hôste* and *sumbainein* are used in a sense that is not Presocratic; we have *ta onta* for *ta eonta*; and *gignôskein* misinterprets *sunienai*. The sentence is a marginal gloss written in a later jargon.

4 Melissus refers simply to 'men' (*hoi anthrôpoi*): he is attacking the *communis opinio*, not any particular philosophical school (see Reale [269], 242–52). Mourelatos [237], 362–3, says that Melissus 'does not, of course, intend the paradoxical and self-contradictory thesis that *this* to which I point (the earth, the sea) does not exist. The verb "to be" here has a special sense'. The thesis is not self-contradictory, and Melissus surely did intend it: it is paradoxical—but what is Eleaticism if not paradoxical?

5 I.e. '$a_1, a_2, \ldots, a_n$ seem to be real, but in fact are not so' (see Loenen [238], 133–4). The usual translation reads: '. . . those things do not correctly seem to be many'.

XV The Ionian Revival

1 For Anaxagoras' dates see especially Diogenes Laertius, II.7 = **59 A 1** (cf. Guthrie [25], II. 322–3). Euripides: Strabo, A 7; Diodorus, A 62; etc.; Pericles: Isocrates, **A 15**; Plutarch **A 16**; etc. For the trial see, e.g., Plutarch, **A 17**, **A 18** (see Derenne [345], 13–41). Gershenson-Greenburg [361], 346–8, argue that the whole story of the trial is an invention based on Plato, *Apology* 26D = **A 35** (see also Jacoby [457], 41, n. 159).

2 On *Met* 984a11 see esp. O'Brien [348], with copious references.

3 See also Diogenes Laertius, VIII.46 = **44 A 4**; IX.38 = **A 2** (see, e.g., Burkert [173], 228–9).

4 He is also called an Abderite (e.g., Diogenes Laertius, IX.30 = **67 A 1**). Probably Miletus was his birthplace; 'Eleatic' and 'Abderite' were applied to him for his philosophical connexions (see Bailey [383], 66–7). For convenience I shall frequently refer to Democritus and Leucippus as 'the Abderites'.

5 The Greeks dated the fall of Troy variously between 1334 and 1136 (see F. Jacoby, *Das Marmor Parium* (Berlin, 1904), 146–9); we cannot tell what date Democritus favoured. The only other publication date for a Presocratic that we possess is given by Olympiodorus, who asserts that Gorgias wrote his treatise *Concerning Nature* in the 84th Olympiad, 444–1 BC (**82 A 10**). If we believe Olympiodorus, we shall date Melissus' treatise to the early 440s at latest; unless, of course, we hold that Melissus was defending Parmenides against the ridicule of Gorgias (see Nestle [260], 561). In any case, Olympiodorus' report is suspect: see Untersteiner [434], 100, n. 96 = [435], I.167, n. 98. Democritus was a widely travelled polymath: on his travels see Guthrie [25], II.387, n. 1; on his learning, see Steckel [385], 212–21.

6 See especially O'Brien [351], 129–44; Bollack [349], III.49–80. Hölscher [356], 201–9, makes **194** a biological fragment; Mansfeld [357] offers a heterodox reading of lines 3–5.

7 I.e. 'the elements' (see line 18); but Bollack [349], III.50 offers a different construe.

8 I.e. 'the one type of generation and destruction': see especially Stokes [56], 154–5 (but *contra*: Bollack [349], III.53–4).

9 Accepting Panzerbieter's palmary emendation ('*threphtheisa*' for '*thruphtheisa*'): see Bollack [349], III.55–7 (who, however, makes a different proposal).

10 Line 9 is interpolated from **B** 26.8: both sense and syntax require it (but see Bollack [349], III.59–60).

11 On Empedoclean atomism see Aristotle, *GC* 334a18–25 = **A 43**; *Cael* 305a1 = **A 43a**; Aëtius, **A 43**, **A 44**. Atomism is accepted by Longrigg [359]; but it was clearly disposed of by Reinhardt [491], 111–13.

12 On the problems caused by these appellations see especially Bollack [349], III.169–85, who quotes a host of doxographical texts omitted from Diels-Kranz.

13 It is hotly disputed whether there were periods of rest between worlds. In the end, everything turns on **B 27**.4 = **B 28**.2: 'a round Sphere, exulting in its joyful (?) *moniê*'. Some connect *moniê* with *monos* ('alone') and translate 'solitariness' (e.g., Bollack [349], III.137–8); others—to whose view I subscribe—connect *moniê* with *menein* ('rest') and translate 'rest' (e.g., Jaeger [48], 237, nn. 56–9).

14 Aristotle praised Empedocles' poetry in his early work, *On Poets* (fr. 70 R^3 = **A 1**), but later denied him the title of poet (*Poet* 1447b18 = **A 22**). The later judgment became canonical (e.g., Dionysius, **A 25**).

15 Millerd [352], 21.

16 Already noted by Theophrastus (Diogenes Laertius, VIII.55 = **A 1**); according to Alcidamas, Parmenides 'taught' Empedocles (Diogenes Laertius, VIII.56 = **A 1**).

17 So Aristotle, *Phys* 187a25 = **59 A 46**; Simplicius, **A 64**; Aëtius, **A 63** (see, e.g., Guthrie [25], II.313–15). Two fragments have been thought to bear on the question. In **B 8** Anaxagoras says that:

> The things in the one world (*ta en tôi heni kosmôi*) have not been separated from one another.

That has been taken to prove that Anaxagoras believes in a unique cosmos. I doubt if the phrase will bear that weight; but I am not sure what precisely it does mean.

Second, there are the references to what happens 'elsewhere' in **B 4** (quoted above, p. 319, as texts **199–201**). **B 4** has been taken to imply: (a) the coexistence of many—perhaps infinitely many—different worlds (e.g., Gigon [364], 25–6); (b) different stages in the development of the unique world (e.g., Simplicius, *in Phys* 157.17); (c) different inhabited parts of the earth's surface, as in Plato, *Phaedo* 109B (e.g., Kahn [90], 52–3); (d) an inhabited moon (cf. Diogenes Laertius, II.8 = **A 1**; Aëtius, **A 77**); (e) another inhabited earth (see references in Burkert [173], 345–8); (f) the counterfactual hypothesis that in every cosmogony there *would* be an inhabited world like ours (Fränkel [362], 288–91). I think that (b), (c), (d) and (f) can be ruled out: they do not fit the text closely enough. (e) is less ambitious than (a); but Democritus embraced (a), and the fact that he explicitly denied that all the other worlds have a sun and a moon suggests that Anaxagoras had asserted that they did (Hippolytus, **68 A 40**). See Vlastos [372], 53–4.

18 O'Brien [351], 244; see especially Bollack [349], I.169–73.

19 Guthrie [25], II.140; see especially Cornford [231], 15. The view is found in Nietzsche [28], 395–6.

XVI Anaxagoras and the Nature of Stuffs

1 Lanza [360], 187.

2 I should perhaps mention the heterodox opinion of Gershenson-Greenburg [361], 378: 'these so-called fragments cannot be used as the basis of a reconstruction of Anaxagoras' theory. . . . They can be assigned no more importance than their late chronological position relative to the time of Anaxagoras indicates. . . . The so-called fragments are assuredly far from direct quotes from Anaxagoras' book'. That view is deliciously wicked, but quite implausible; and the arguments on which it rests are worthless. It must be admitted, however, that the texts in Diels-Kranz are tidier than they should be: some of the fragments are patchworked from various pages of Simplicius (see below, n. 5), and the text of none is wholly free from doubt.

3 I take 'quantity (*plêthos*)' in a numerical sense: Lanza [360], 190–1, construes it as 'mass'; but that loses the contrast with *megethos* in **196**.

4 'Contained' renders *kateichen*: see Guthrie [25], II.294, n. 1; Lanza [360], 191–3. I construe 'contain' metaphorically, to amount to 'predominate over' (above, p. 325).

5 Diels-Kranz print **199**, **200** and **201** continuously. Burnet [31], 259, n. 1, claims responsibility, falsely stating that Simplicius thrice quotes the remarks continuously. The true situation is set out by Fränkel [362], 287, n. 1; but it is

worth repeating the salient facts. *In Phys* 34.21–6 quotes '*prin . . . chrêmata*' (Diels-Kranz, II.34.17–35.5); *in Phys* 34.29–35.9 quotes '*toutôn . . . allêi*' (II.34.5–16); *in Phys* 156.2–4 quotes '*toutôn . . . hêdonas*' (II.34.5–8); *in Phys* 156.4–9 quotes '*prin . . . heterôi*' (II.34.17–35.3); *in Phys* 157.9–16 quotes '*eneinai . . . chrôntai*' (II.34.5–14); *in Cael* 608.24 quotes '*en tôi sumpanti . . . chrêmata*' (II.35.4–5); *in Cael* 609.5–11 quotes '*toutôn . . . hêmin*' (II.34.5–12).

I doubt if we can make any safe inferences about the arrangements of Anaxagoras' words in the text which Simplicius used; and there is in any case a general opinion that Simplicius was using not a complete text of Anaxagoras but an epitome first prepared by Theophrastus (see Lanza [360], VIII–IX). Fränkel, *loc. cit.*, finds three separate fragments: (a) II.34.5–16; (b) II.34.17–35.3 (*heterôi*); (c) II.35.4–5 (according to Fränkel, the phrase '*toutôn de houtôs echontôn*' at II.35.3 belongs to Simplicius, not to Anaxagoras). My three fragments run thus: **199**: II.34.5–8; **200**: II.34.8–16; **201**: II.34.17–35.5. For other suggestions see Lanza [360], 199–200.

6 Aëtius, **A 46**, gives an unorthodox sense to *homoiomereia* (accepted by, e.g., Bailey [383], 554–5; Peck [376], 62); but I do not think that we can get anywhere by abandoning the Aristotelian notion of homoiomereity.

7 See, e.g., Guthrie [25], II.325–6.

8 See, e.g., Peck [371], 28–31; Reesor [367], 33, n. 3; but I see no reason to restrict the stuffs to 'organic' stuffs (Peck), or even to natural stuffs (Reesor).

9 Why not simply say that Anaxagorean things are both stuffs and qualities? (So Peck [371], 31–3; Reesor [366], 4, relying on *Phys* 187a24, b4–7 = **A 52**). But then Anaxagoras' theory is inelegant; and *he* gives no hint that his 'things' fall into two classes. No doubt the qualities (and the stuffs proper?) were conceived of in terms of 'powers' or *dunameis* (see especially Vlastos [372], 470–3).

10 I ignore the term '*panspermia*' (*GC* 314a29 = **A 46**); its sense and origin are alike obscure (see Lanza [360], 77).

11 There is a massive literature on *spermata*: see especially Vlastos [372], 461–5.

12 **201** speaks of 'seeds unlimited in quantity and not like one another'. Cornford [369], 22, glosses: 'there is a large number of different *kinds* of seeds' (but Anaxagoras says 'unlimited' not 'large'). I prefer to read 'unlimited in quantity' in the same way as I read the phrase in **197**.

13 According to some scholars, *apokrinesthai* is a biological term, referring to organic growth or formation (see Lanza [360], 195).

14 The particulate interpretation comes from Aristotle; he says that things are generated 'from what exists and inheres but which, because of the smallness of the bodies (*onkoi*), is imperceptible to us' (*Phys* 187a36–b1). The word *onkoi* commits Aristotle to a particulate interpretation of Anaxagoras (*pace* Lanza [360], 104—but the word may only be a carelessness); and the passage is a prime source for the doxography.

15 An *atomist* theory is, of course, immediately ruled out by (B); but you can, I suppose, be a corpuscularian without being an atomist.

16 'Anaxagoras was really striving after the idea of a union closer than mere mechanical juxtaposition, and more like our notion of chemical fusion, a union in which things are not merely placed side by side, but are, as it were, completely merged in a new substance' (Bailey [383], 545; Bailey owes the view to J. A. Smith).

17 Cornford [369], 14; *contra*: see especially Kerferd [378], whose main aim is to show that 'there is no logical inconsistency between the major doctrines

attributed to Anaxagoras in antiquity' (129).

18 Aristotle is defended by, e.g., Raven [373], 132–3; Kerferd [378], 134–6. **B 15** is sometimes taken to show that earth is non-elemental; but that construe depends upon an uncertain emendation (see Lanza [360], 237; Stokes [365], 218–21). Simplicius, *ad* **B 16**, tries to find a distinction between element and compound in that fragment; but see, e.g., Stokes [365] 16–19.

19 Thus in the view of Vlastos [372], 484–6, *x* contains *S* if and only if *x* possesses all those powers that are constitutive of *S*.

20 What of allomorphs? Anaximenes in effect treats all stuffs as allomorphs of air; and Empedocles is the first man explicitly to introduce the notion of a compound: the element/allomorph distinction is different from the element/compound distinction; but there is no evidence that Anaxagoras heeded the difference.

21 Charges of incoherence in, e.g., Cornford [369], 91; Guthrie [25], II.290.

22 The MSS. read '*ouden estin homoion oudeni* (nothing is like anything else)'. Wasserstein [363] excises *oudeni*, rightly. (The verbal parallel to the MSS. text at **201** is no use, *pace* Guthrie [25], II.274, n. 1; Lanza [360], 232; the contexts of the two fragments are quite different.)

23 'We have to assume that Anaxagoras' substance words, both particular and generic, are systematically ambiguous' (Strang [374], 102; *contra*: Stokes [365], 2–4). Strang fears an infinite regress: 'Suppose *x* is predominantly *S*. Consider that predominant *S*-portion: presumably *it* is *S* only because *S* predominates in it; then consider *that* predominant *S*-portion . . .' (cf. Cornford [369], 93; Vlastos [372], 51). The regress does not arise once we distinguish carefully between *pieces* of *S* and *portions* of *S*.

24 'The "portions" must be thought of as proportions that cannot be directly located or directly measured' (Hussey [34], 137; cf. Strang [374], 102–3): they cannot be located at all, since they have no location; they can be measured, but only indirectly.

25 Cornford [369], 90, observes that at *Phys* 203a23 Aristotle signals (by the word *eoike*, 'it seems') that his argument for (A) is a conjecture; and Cornford adds that 'Simplicius, after loyally searching Anaxagoras' book for every text that could support the interpretation based upon it by Aristotle, ends by rejecting that interpretation'. As for Simplicius, he may not have had a complete text of Anaxagoras (above, n. 5); and in any event, he does not reject Aristotle's interpretation but only modifies it. Nor, I think, does Aristotle indicate that (1) is conjecturally ascribed to Anaxagoras: what was unclear was the precise connexion between (1) and (A). Finally, (A) is indubitably Anaxagorean; and if we drop (1) we leave (A) unsupported.

26 The last clause is obscure, and no satisfactory account of *ekchôreousi* is to hand (see Guthrie [25], II.301, n. 1). I agree with Stokes [365], 229–44, that **211** deals with changes in the present world and not with cosmogony.

27 See especially Kucharski [379]; Longrigg [63]; Müller [52], 69–72, 126–37. Jaeger [48], 156–7, stresses Anaxagoras' empiricism; but there is nothing innovatory about that. The connexions between the *vet med* and Anaxagoras are especially strong: see Longrigg [63], 158–67.

28 Cornford [369], 18, finds (1) 'grotesquely superfluous and uneconomical'—and he would no doubt say the same for (C). 'Economical' is a slippery word: it seems to me that in a fairly clear sense (C) is the *most* economical hypothesis that Anaxagoras could have excogitated to explain the facts he observed.

29 See especially Schofield [380], 14–24, who suggests Eudemus as the ultimate source of the scholion.

30 Fraser, quoted with reference to Anaxagoras by West [23], 323.

31 Raven [373], 129 (cf. Strang [374], 102, n. 8) stresses the word *moira*, 'portion', which he contrasts to *meros*, 'part'; unfortunately, *moira* in Greek may mean 'part' as well as 'portion' (see Stokes [365], 12–13).

32 Guthrie [25], II.289. But later, 298, n. 2, Guthrie suggests that if we ascribe an understanding of infinite divisibility to Anaxagoras we will 'look back at Anaxagoras from Aristotle, whereas he was starting from Parmenides and Zeno'.

33 So Gigon [364], 14–15, who likewise connects sentence [iii] to Zeno B 1. A verbal similarity: much of Anaxagoras' language 'echoes' that of Zeno; it does not follow, and I do not think it is true, that Anaxagoras is trying to answer—or even thinking of—Zeno's arguments.

34 Reesor [366], 2; Guthrie [25], II.289, n. 2.

35 The proper comparison is not with Zeno but with Parmenides, **151**.1. Zeller's conjecture in [ii] (*tomêi* for *to mê*: 'for what is cannot not be by cutting') gives the wrong sense; and it is in any case poorer grammar than the MS. text whose grammar it was designed to improve.

36 This interpretation was suggested to me by John Guiniven.

37 E.g.: 'A large portion of *S* and a small portion of *S* contain as many stuffs—for they contain all the stuffs' (Burnet [31], 260); 'A large portion of *S* and a small portion of *S* contain stuffs in the same ratio' (Vlastos [372], 46, n. 64); 'For every larger there is also a smaller' (Reesor [366], 2); 'A large portion of *S* and a small portion of *S* are equal in extent, for size is relative' (Lanza [360], 199).

38 An understanding beyond the reach of Plutarch, who argued that if $a > b$, then a must have more parts than b (*comm not* 1079AB). But what of the end of **197**? 'These are *the greatest . . . in quantity*': if air is greater in quantity than anything else, how can everything be infinite in quantity? We must assume a slight infelicity of expression here: Anaxagoras means, I suppose, that in the present world there are more discrete, macroscopic, portions of air than of anything else; there are lungfuls of air in every creature, bubbles of air in the water, pockets of air underground, and so on. In any case, the weight of the argument falls on the last phrase: 'These are the greatest . . . *in magnitude*'.

39 I take *dunaito* impersonally (Lanza [360], 214): it is implausible to make 'the least' its subject.

40 *Kai* means 'even' here (*pace* Lanza [360], 214–15): the translation 'and' gives a strange syntax and an odd argument.

41 Reesor [367], 30; cf. [366], 3.

42 It is worth listing Anaxagoras' vocabulary:
apokrinesthai: **197**, **200** (twice), **201**, **202**, **B 7**, **B 9**, **B 12** (five times), **B 13**, **B 14**, **211** (twice).
perichôrein: **B 9**, **B 12** (eight times), **B 13**.
diakrinesthai: **B 5**, **B 12** (twice), **B 13** (twice), **B 17**.
kinein: **B 13** (four times).
summignusthai: **B 12** (twice), **B 17**.
sumpêgnusthai: **200**, **211** (twice).
sunkrinesthai: **199**.
proskrinesthai: **B 14**.
sunchôrein: **B 15**.

43 Anaxagoras' cosmogony and cosmology, which I shall not itemize, was wholly Milesian in spirit: see especially Stokes [365], 217–50 (a heterodox view in Bargrave-Weaver [368]).

XVII The Corpuscularian Hypothesis

1 Heisenberg [394], 7, 32.

2 I speak usually of 'the Atomists', not distinguishing between the views of Leucippus and those of Democritus. I doubt if our texts will sustain any systematic distinction: the best attempt to make it remains Bailey [383].

3 But McDiarmid [395], 293, n. 1, holds that this comes from Aristotle, *Phys* 265b25, and is not genuinely Abderite.

4 The doxography regularly uses *sômata* or *prôta sômata* ('bodies', 'primary bodies') to refer to the atoms (**68 B 141**; **B 156**; *Phys* 203a33 = **A 41**; and see Diels-Kranz, III.419a15–27). Epicurus states the first axiom of his philosophy by way of *sôma*: '. . . the universe is body (*sôma*) and place' (*ad Hdt* §39). He says that *perception* shows there are bodies (*ad Hdt* §39); but nothing we perceive has those properties (e.g., solidity, immutability) which are characteristic of the Atomists' bodies. Perhaps we perceive *sômata*: we surely do not perceive *prôta sômata*.

5 But Epicurus appears to have adhered to the Eleatic argument (*ad Hdt* §§54–5).

6 Cf. Theophrastus, **68 A 132**; Simplicius, **67 A 13**; *in Phys* 82.1–3; Diogenes Laërtius, IX.44 = **68 A 1**. In **68 A 49** Galen appears to assimilate impassivity to indivisibility, and to sever it from immutability. On the sense of '*apatheia*' see, e.g., Aristotle, *Met* 1019a26–32, 1073a11–3.

7 It is often said, vaguely enough, that Atomism is Elea minus monism (see, e.g., Burnet [31], 328; Bailey [383], 45, 71); but see Guthrie [25], II.392, for some apposite qualifications.

8 Simplicius, *in Cael* 609.17, probably means to ascribe both (C) and (D) both to Leucippus and to Democritus. Galen, **68 A 49**, ascribes (C) to the Epicureans and (D) to the Leucippans, and he implies that Leucippus did not use (C); but the passage is muddled.

9 So, e.g., Bailey [383], 204. But Furley [387], 95–6, suggests that the ascription of large atoms to Democritus is a careless inference from this text of Epicurus (cf. Lucretius, II.481–521).

10 Reading '*ho*' for '*hon*' (see Ross [11], II.211).

11 Cf. Lucretius, I.599–634; and see, e.g., Vlastos [401]; Furley [387], 7–43.

12 So, e.g., Furley [387], 97–9; *contra*: Luria [398], 172–80 (but Luria is driven to the unpalatable conclusion that Democritus recognized two different sorts of atom).

13 See especially Furley [387], 81–2 (see above, p. 619, n. 26).

14 Atoms are also said to be 'partless' (*amerê*) by Aëtius, **68 A 48**; cf. [Aristotle] *lin insec* 969a21.

15 Repeated by Simplicius, *in Cael* 649.1–9; 665.6–8; Philoponus, *in GC* 164.20–4.

16 Democritus was 'too good a mathematician' to believe in mathematically indivisible atoms, according to Heath [19], I.181; other scholars assert that if atoms have magnitude they cannot be mathematically indivisible (e.g., Burnet [31], 336). Heath echoes the reaction of Philoponus to Plato's geometrical atomism (*in GC* 210.12) and of Simplicius to Xenocrates' (*in Phys* 142.16). On Democritean mathematics see Guthrie [25], II.484–8.

17 For *minima* see, e.g., Luria [398], 138–41; against: e.g., Nicol [312], 120. On **233** see especially Hahm [403], with references at 206, n. 3.

18 *Contra*: Luria [398], 145–6; he quotes Plutarch, *Plat quaest* 1003F, which shows that, in the view of the ancient commentators, Plato held that a sphere was compounded of cubes.

19 Furley [387], 102, n. 17, concedes that 'Aristotle seems to have believed that the infinite divisibility of the geometrical continuum entails the infinite divisibility of matter'. But he adds: (a) that theoretical divisibility is definitely needed if Democritus is to counter Zeno's arguments; (b) that Aristotle cannot simply have overlooked a Democritean distinction between physical and theoretical indivisibility; and (c) that Democritus was probably 'no clearer' about the relation between physical and theoretical indivisibility than Aristotle was. I answer (a) later. On (b), I do not suppose that Democritus ever made the distinction; rather, the question of theoretical divisibility never explicitly arose for him. And as to (c), Democritus may have been as unclear as Aristotle without sharing Aristotle's views.

20 Furley [387], 95, dismisses Simplicius' mention of the parts of Democritean atoms (*in Phys* 82.1) as a 'hasty inference': I should as soon see a hasty inference in **229**.

21 See especially Mau [399], 25–6; *contra*: Luria [398], 129, who thinks that the *GC* contains 'a genuine fragment of Democritus'. That Philoponus calls the argument 'Democritean' (*in GC* 38.28, etc.) is neither surprising nor significant.

22 Furley [400], 92–3. The argument is accepted by Locke, *Essay* II.xiii.20.

23 Furley [400], 92–3, conflates this argument with Archytas' argument and also with Aristotle's fifth argument (*Phys* 203b22–5); and he ascribes the amalgam to Democritus.

24 Cf. Lucretius, I.1014–20; Diogenes of Oenoanda, fr. 19 Ch.

25 Simplicius, *in Phys* 467.16; Philoponus, *in Phys* 405.23; cf. Lactantius, *de Ira* X, 10. See especially Luria [398], 37–40.

26 'Now logically, of course, infinite differences in shape imply infinite differences in size' (Bailey [383], 127; cf. Marx [388], 56). Bailey wrongly ascribes his own error to Epicurus. Klowski [424], 232, argues that if there are infinitely many phenomena and only finitely many possible combinations of atoms, then there must be infinitely many atomic shapes. But why suppose the combinations finite?

27 See especially Müller [52], 85–90, with references. To say that atoms have weight is not to say that they have a 'natural' motion 'downwards': that view is Epicurean, not Abderite.

28 '*eikontos kai mê antitupountos*': cf. Plato, *Cratylus* 420D. Sambursky [396], argues that the phrase is Democritean: it is more likely that Simplicius is echoing—consciously or unconsciously—the Platonic phrase. (*Antitupos* was an Epicurean and Stoic technical term for the resistance or solidity essential to body.)

29 *Peripalassesthai* has been restored at Theophrastus, *Sens* §66 = **68 A 135**; *peripalaxis* ibid.; Aristotle, *Cael* 303a8; Simplicius, *in Cael* 609.25 (where two MSS. give it). McDiarmid [395] rejects all those emendations, and prefers *periplekesthai* in 246; Bollack [397], 38–42, allows the term only in 246. The translation 'vibrate' is favoured, e.g., by Bailey [383], 88; Liddell and Scott give 'collide' (following Hesychius); Bollack [397], 42, prefers 'éclabousser'; the atoms are 'spattered about in the void' as the brains of a dead warrior spatter the ground. Epicurean atoms vibrate (*ad Hdt* §§43, 50). The Epicurean term is '*palmos*'; and Aëtius reports that:

> Democritus maintained one sort of motion to be that by *palmos* (**68 A 47**).

It is possible that a Democritean theory of atomic vibration lies behind Aëtius' report, but Aëtius may merely be reading an Epicurean idea into Democritus.

30 In the third clause, editors restore the old form of zeta, 'ⵊ', and consequently

read 'H' for 'N'; then we should read 'H', 'HA' and 'AH' earlier in the sentence. In the Roman alphabet, 'N' is required.

31 The MSS. of Plutarch, *adv Col* 1110F = **68 A 57**, read '*ousias atomous kai diaphorous*'; Diels-Kranz print the emendation '*kàdiaphorous*' ('and indifferent'), which makes Plutarch report the view I am describing. But Westman [15], 266–7, plausibly prefers '*kai adiaphthorous*' ('and indestructible').

32 For the text see Westman [15], 253–4. The saying is also quoted by Sextus (**B 9**), Galen (**B 125**; **A 49**), and by Diogenes Laertius (IX.72, *ad* **B 117**); cf. Diogenes Laertius, IX.45; Diogenes of Oenoanda, fr. 6 Ch. The differences among these quotations all lie in the listing of the *nomôi* items.

33 I follow the text and interpretation of McDiarmid [404]; the controversy is about details, and the general point I am illustrating is not in doubt. If 'to us the whole theory seems almost a play of fantasy; yet we must not forget that to its author it was a serious attempt, on the most scientific and common-sense lines at that time known, to account physically for these sensations' (Beare [39], 164).

XVIII Philolaus and the Formal Cause

1 For the text of Diogenes see Burkert [173], 241 n. 10.

2 The evidence is dissected by Burkert [173], 224–7; von Fritz [411], 456–60.

3 I follow, in almost all respects, the masterly account of Burkert [173], ch. III.

4 Philip [180], 116, 32.

5 Many scholars have tried to reconstruct Pythagoreanism from its conjectured influence on other fifth-century philosophies; I agree with Burkert [173], ch. III.3, that all such attempts are doomed to failure.

6 See, e.g., Guthrie [25], I.232–3.

7 See especially Burkert [173], ch. III.1 (cf. 234, n. 83); Burns [412]; *contra*: e.g., Philip [180], 121–2; de Vogel [181], 84–5.

8 For this meaning of *mathêma* see Burkert [173], 207, n. 80. Plutarch continues in a Platonizing vein, and his anecdote is not wholly trustworthy.

9 Burkert [173], 427; cf. especially Heidel [406]. On the other side see especially van der Waerden [58], 92–105; [408], 271–300.

10 On Hippasus see the classic paper by von Fritz [407]—rejected (rightly) by Burkert [173], 456–65. Archytas worked at arithmetic (Boethius, **47 A 19**) and geometry (Diogenes Laertius, VIII.82 = **A 1**; Proclus, **A 6**; Eutocius, **A 14**); and he more or less invented mechanics (Diogenes Laertius, VIII.82 = **A 1**; Eratosthenes, **A 15**, Vitruvius, **B 7**: see Burkert [173], 331). He built a child's rattle (Aristotle, *Pol* 1340b26 = **A 11**) and a mechanical dove (Gellius, **A 10a**). On Archytas' contribution to harmonics see **B 2**; Ptolemy, **A 16**; Porphyry, **A 17**; etc. cf. Burkert [173], 379–80. It is surely significant that Proclus, in his epitomic history of early Greek mathematics, mentions no Pythagorean prior to Archytas.

11 Iamblichus, *comm math sc* 78.8–18: Burkert [173], 50, n. 112, convincingly argues that this comes from Aristotle's *Protrepticus*.

12 Burkert [173], 399.

13 (a) *proêgagon* is usually taken to mean that they 'advanced' mathematics, in a technical way; that goes against the facts, and fits Aristotle's argument ill. (b) *prôtoi* is often taken with *hapsamenoi*: that gives quite the wrong sense.

14 I agree with Burkert [173], 44–5, that there is no significant difference between these two ways of specifying the relation between numbers and things.

15 See **B 5**; **B 7**; **B 19**; pseudo-Iamblichus, **A 12** (but see Burkert [173], 247); Proclus, **A 14**; etc.

16 But the report is rejected by Burkert [173], 461, n. 71.
17 See the elaborations in Speusippus, fr. 4 = **44 A 13** (Burkert [173], 246); Theo of Smyrna, 93.17–99.23; Sextus, *adv Math* IV.3; Aëtius, I.3.8; [Aristotle], *Problems* 910b36 = **58 B 16**.
18 On the *Hypomnemata* see especially Festugière [410]; Burkert [173], ch.I.3. Burkert concludes (82) that 'the "derivation system" is an achievement of Plato and the Academy, a genuine *transposition platonicienne* of an older, Pythagorean number philosophy'. I prefer to believe in a pre-Platonic system, later modified by the Platonists. On the 'derivation system' see especially Raven [178], chh. X–XI; Guthrie [25], I.240–82.
19 Cf. pseudo-Galen, 71. Perhaps moon creatures do not excrete because they live off smells (Aristotle, *Sens* 445a16 = **58 B 43**). Pythagoras did not excrete (Diogenes Laertius, VIII.19). For an inhabited moon see also Xenophanes, **21 A 47**, and perhaps Anaxagoras (above, p. 625, n. 17).
20 Burkert [173], 342, 350; von Fritz [411], 474.
21 Van der Waerden [408], 293–4, ascribes the Philolaic system to Hiketas, because 'Philolaus was . . . no logical mathematician'. The little we know of Hiketas' astronomy precludes that suggestion.
22 Anticipated, perhaps, by Hippasus, a Pythagorean who adopted a *phusiologia* in the Milesian style (Simplicius, **18 A 7**). But we know virtually nothing about Hippasus.
23 Retaining '*en tôi kosmôi*' (Burkert [173], 250, n. 58): Heidel proposed '*tô kosmô*' ('the nature of the universe').
24 **277** continues with an analysis of the musical intervals: two independent passages from Philolaus have been fortuitously conjoined in our source. For the text see Burkert [173], 250–1, nn. 59–65. I follow him on all but two points. (a) He defends *isotachê* ('of equal speed'); but I can make no sense of that, and I adopt Heidel's emendation *isotagê* ('of the same order'). (b) In the last sentence I translate Burkert's text, but prefer a slight anacoluthon to his proposal to begin a new sentence at '*ananka*'.
25 'Being (*estô*) is a condition not of knowledge, but of the origin of this world of ours' (Burkert [173], 251, n. 62). The text of sentence [ii] is usually emended to read: *ouch hoion t' ên ouden tôn eontôn kai gignôskomenon huph' hamôn ga genesthai* ('none of the things that exist could even become known, by us at least, if . . .'). The emendation makes Philolaus' argument epistemological; but it is unnecessary.
26 Why did Philolaus not say, more simply, that what is known is limited, and that what is limited must consist of a limiting and an unlimited component? Perhaps he did not believe that everything that is known is limited. The Pythagoreans held that 'entities can neither exist apart from number nor in general be known, but numbers are known even apart from the other things' (Aristotle, fr. 203): Philolaus' limiters will turn out to be shapes, and hence numbers; so that he may have held that only limiters and limiteds, numbers and numbered things (*arithmoi* in both senses of the word) can be known.
27 I take '*erga*' quite generally: other interpretations in Burkert [173], 254, n. 79.
28 See especially *Philebus* 23C; cf. Raven [178], 180–6.
29 See Cornford [231], 3. Burkert [173], 255–6, rejects the attempt to find an Aristotelian form/matter distinction in Philolaus. Some scholars identify the being (*estô*) of things with 'the unlimited' and hence with matter, and they assimilate limit, form and harmony. Others identify the unlimited matter with the even numbers, and the limiting form with the odd numbers. Burkert rightly

rejects these views; but they are distinct from the interpretation I offer, and I do not think that Burkert's objections tell against it.

30 The same thought is embroidered in **B 11**; but the fragment is probably spurious (Burkert [173], 273–5; *contra*: de Vogel [181], 43–54).

31 According to one definition, a number is even if it is divisible into equal parts, odd if it is divisible only into unequal parts: the number 1, not being divisible at all, is thus neither odd nor even, but falls into a kind of its own: the 'even-odd' (see Aristotle, *Met* 986a20; fr. 199; fr. 203; cf. Raven [178], 116–18). There is no evidence that Philolaus adopted those definitions of even and odd; the 'third kind' of number plays no part in his system; and the phrase I translate 'of each kind' (*hekaterô eideos*) means literally 'of each-of-the-two-kinds'. I conclude that the clause introducing the even-odd into Philolaus' text is a later interpolation.

32 See, e.g., Burkert [173], 32–4, 51–2.

33 **A 3** may be 'of dubious authenticity' (Burkert [173], 41, n. 69); but it is surely a fair representation of what Eurytus did. 'Plaster' translates *asbestos*—more suitable for sticking pebbles on than Guthrie's 'whitewash'. 'Sketching' is *skiagraphein*: Guthrie [25], I.274, n. 1, thinks that the sense is 'do a shaded drawing' (to give an illusion of solidity) rather than 'do an outline drawing'.

34 Guthrie [25], I.274; cf. Raven [178], chapter VIII.

35 The 'hearth' is the central fire of Philolaic astronomy (Aristotle, fr. 203; Aëtius, **A 16**). The text of **284** reads: *to praton harmosthen to hen* . . . ('the first thing to be harmonized, the one . . .'). I think that *to hen* is a dittography (see Burkert [173], 255, n. 83); but it is perhaps defended by **B 8**: 'He says that the one is a principle of everything' (i.e., 'cosmogony starts from the central fire, or the One'); and by Aristotle, *Met* 1080b20; 1091a15 (see de Vogel [181], 40–2). **B 8**, however, is hardly genuine; and Aristotle's Pythagoreans may be an orthodoxy from which Philolaus deviated. Even if *to hen* is retained, we cannot infer that 'the number one is itself a *harmosthen*, and is therefore not simply *perainon*' (Burkert [173], 255); for if things are determined by their numerical shape, they may clearly be designated by the names of their shapes: Eurytus might have said 'And then man, 250, is generated', without implying that the *number* 250 is not a limiter.

36 On text and translation of **285** see Burkert [173], 268–9; *achri tou mesou* is hard, but the sense must surely be: 'the cosmos began to be formed at the middle'.

37 De Vogel [181], 33, judges that the limited/unlimited theory described by Aristotle is older than Philolaus' view (cf. perhaps Alcman's *poros* and *tekmôr*: above, p. 12); von Fritz [411], 230, takes the opposite view. The important point is that they are quite different theories: more evidence that Philolaus' book was not Aristotle's prime source on Pythagoreanism.

XIX The Logic of Locomotion

1 *MXG* 976b26 = fr. 96 Bollack. Diels-Kranz amalgamate this with fr. 48 Bollack to make their **B 14**; but see Bollack [349], III.84–5, 140–1.

2 See the illustrations on plates 4 and 5 of Bollack [349], III.

3 **B 100** is 'one of the most important discoveries in the history of science' (Burnet [31], 229); it gives an 'implicit proof of the corporeality of the air', even though Empedocles 'knew nothing of the experimental method as it is now understood'

(Kirk-Raven [33], 342). O'Brien [417], 168–9, and Furley [415], 34, show clearly that there is no trace of an 'experiment' in **B 100**; see also Guthrie [25], II.224–6.

4 So Gigon [364], 21, rightly comparing Hippolytus, **A 42**.

5 Gigon [364], 20–2 (cf. Stokes [56], 337–8, n. 14) implies that the problem simply did not arise; for Melissus wrote after Empedocles and Anaxagoras, and before him no one had connected motion with the void. But why then should Empedocles and Anaxagoras have bothered to reject the void?

6 The *MXG* probably means to ascribe *antiperistasis* to Anaxagoras too; and that may be right. But I find no other evidence to support the ascription.

7 Aristotle frequently refers to the theory (see H. Bonitz, *Index Aristotelicus*, 65a19–21, a57–b24); on the later history of the theory see, e.g., Bailey [383], 658–9.

8 *Principles of Philosophy* II.33; cf. Leibniz, *Nouveaux Essais*, preface; see Capek [390], 111–17.

9 Russell, *The Philosophy of Leibniz*, 93 n. (quoted by Capek [390], 112); Capek [390], 113. The objections in Lucretius, I.370–97, are feeble.

10 See, e.g., Diogenes Laertius, IX.31 = **67 A 1**; IX.44 = **68 A 1**; Aristotle, *Met* 985b5 = **67 A 6**; *Phys* 265b24 = **68 A 58**; Alexander, **68 A 165**; Simplicius, **67 A 8**. See also Metrodorus of Chios **70 A 2** (Aëtius), **A 3** (Theophrastus), etc; Epicurus, *ad Hdt* §§39–40; fr. 75 Us.

11 'Thing' is not wholly satisfactory, since (unlike *den*) it is not a rare word; but had Democritus written in English he would certainly have used it, playing on 'thing' and 'no-thing'.

12 See, e.g., Ross [12], 582–3, who vainly refers to *GC* 325a23–32.

13 *Pace* Diogenes, these words are not taken verbatim from Anaxagoras.

14 Zeller proposed *haploon* ('simple') or *amoiron* ('portionless') for *apeiron*; Lanza [360], 226, renders *apeiron* as 'unlimited by anything else'. But if mind is everywhere (**B 14**), then it will be *apeiron* in the ordinary sense.

15 The text of **303** is hopelessly corrupt. Diels-Kranz print: *Ho de nous, hos aei esti, to karta* . . . ('Mind, which always is, in truth now is where . . .'); Sider [422] proposes: *Ho de nous hosa estin ekratêse*, . . . ('Mind controls the things that are, and now is where . . .'); Marcovich [423] suggests: *Ho de nous, hos aei ên kai estai, karta* . . . ('Mind, which always was and will be, in truth now is where . . .').

16 For Anaxagoras, as for Plato and Aristotle, plants have souls: [Aristotle] *de plantis* 815a15 = **A 117**.

17 The first sentence of **204** is ambiguous between: (a) 'All stuffs contain a portion of every stuff other than mind', and (b) 'All stuffs other than mind contain a portion of every other stuff'. I prefer (b).

18 I.e. the 'efficient' cause; but some take Simplicius to mean the 'final' cause (see Lanza [360], 47).

19 Aëtius (**A 48**) identifies mind as God (accepted, e.g., by Vlastos [161], 114, n. 76); but the testimony is frail.

20 See **B 11b–11i**: eight book titles, *Aitiai Ouraniai*, *Aitiai Aerioi*, etc.

21 Fr. [34] [30] (p. 352.3–15) Arr (I translate Arrighetti's text, which differs substantially from that in Diels-Kranz).

22 Gigon [364], 150, says of **309** that 'this sentence . . . can only mean the following: The activity of *nous* is rejected'. But **309** neither says nor implies that. On the Principle of Causality see especially Klowski [424]; but he denies the Principle to Anaximander (ignoring **12 A 11**), and to Parmenides (ignoring

156.10); he also denies the Atomists the notion of natural regularities (228–40).

23 Already in Nietzsche [28], 412–3.

24 Some infer from Aristotle, *Phys* 252a27–32, that Empedocles used an inductive argument to show that Love and Strife are the twin forces of nature. But the induction is Aristotle's and he does not ascribe it to Empedocles (though he may well have **B 17**.22 in mind, as Hölscher [356], 184, believes).

25 For the varied nomenclature of Love and Strife see especially Jaeger [48], 235, nn. 38–9.

26 Cf. *MM* 1208b11 = **A 20a**; Plato, *Lysis* 214B. At *GC* 334a5, Aristotle repeats his ascription; but his quotation of **B 54** is hardly apposite.

27 Cf. Aristotle, *Phys* 198b12; Hippolytus, *ad* **B 115**; Aëtius, **A 32**, **A 35**; Philo, **A 49**; Cicero, *de Fato* XVII.39; Plutarch, *soll anim* 964DE; Simplicius, *in Phys* 465.12, 1184.5.

28 Simplicius, *in Phys* 1184.9–10, quotes two verses: the second is **B 115**.2, and the first is very similar to **B 115**.1. Most scholars plausibly suppose that Simplicius' first verse is in fact a slight garbling of **B 115**.1; Bollack [349], I.153, n. 6, III.151–2, thinks it a distinct fragment, and he thus finds two separate appeals to necessity in Empedocles' fragments.

29 Simplicius quotes, in order: **B 59**.2 (but Bollack [349], III.226, sees a separate fragment here); **B 98**.1; **B 85**; **B 75**.2; **B 103**; **B 104**. Cf. pseudo-Plutarch, **A 30**; Philoponus, *in An* 261.17.

30 But Plutarch, **A 45**, says that Necessity is simply the union of Love and Strife (cf. Hippolytus, *ad* **B 115**).

31 That, and not the use of *sunkurein*, is why Aristotle quotes the line.

32 Bollack [349], III.453, says that *Tuchê* or Chance here stands for 'le bonheur de Philotès'; he has no argument for that strange suggestion.

33 The full text reads: '. . . are made not by any compelling nature (*nulla cogente natura*), but by a certain chance concurrence': either Cicero is confused, or else '*nulla cogente natura*' means 'without the compulsion of any natural agent'.

34 The point was firmly grasped by Marx [388], 43–5.

35 On **340** see above, p. 604, n. 22. On the equation of chance and necessity see also Gorgias, **82 B 11**, §§6, 19 (cf. Immisch [472], 16–19); and see Guthrie [25], II.415, n. 1.

XX The Neo-Ionian World Picture

1 I ignore Aristotle's other criticisms of Love and Strife: they are petty (see, e.g., *Met* 985a21–31 = **31 A 37**; *Cael* 295a29–61; and especially *GC* B6, on which see Bollack [349], I.43–8).

2 Simplicius suggests that the ordering of the world by *nous* is not a cosmogonical event but a pedagogical device (**59 A 64**: compare the similar interpretation of the *Timaeus*); Lanza [360], 114, 235, agrees that the activity of mind is extra-temporal. That is very far-fetched.

3 Strictly speaking, the Atomists need not posit eternal motion: they could, in logic, hold that there was no first moment of motion, even though motion has not gone on for ever (see above, p. 271).

4 E.g., Lanza [360], 102–3; Schofield [380], 17, n. 59; cf. *Phys* 187a29–30 = **A 52**.

5 On the text of **355** see Bollack [349], III.81–2: I translate his text; but the only significant problems are in the last line which is in any event incomprehensible.

6 Kirk-Raven [33], 329, mark a lacuna after line 32.
7 But the point was perhaps implicit in Parmenides' Way of Opinion: see Reinhardt [30], 75; Kahn [90], 154, n. 2.
8 *Ouk orthôs nomizousin*: many scholars say that *nomizein* here refers to the use of language (see Heinimann [445], 49; Fahr [163], 22–3). But Anaxagoras is saying not that the Greeks misuse words, but that they misdescribe events.
9 On *phusis* meaning 'birth' see, e.g., Guthrie [25], II.140, n. 1. For the contrary view, that *phusis* here means *ousia* or 'essence' see Aristotle, *Met* 1015a1 (cf. Burnet [31], 205, n. 4). Bollack [349], III.88, n. 1, has an idiosyncratic interpretation. See also Ovid, *Metamorphoses* XV.254–7.
10 For the text see Bollack [349], III.92–5. In the last line we should probably read *hê themis, ou kaleousi* . . . (see West [23], 274).
11 Müller [52], 167–73, argues that the neo-Ionian view of generation and destruction was not so far removed from ordinary conceptions of birth and death. See, e.g., Euripides, fr. 839: 'None of the things that come into being dies; but they are dissociated (*diakrinomenon*) one from another, and reveal a different form' (further references at 168, nn. 48–51).
12 Anaxagoras holds that:

> All the stuffs come into being and are destroyed in this way only: by association and dissociation. They neither come into being nor are destroyed in any other way, but persist, eternal (Aristotle, *Met* 984a14–6 = **59 A 43**; cf. Simplicius, **A 41**).

That is not a careful paraphrase of **359**: Aristotle assimilates Anaxagoras to the Atomists.
13 So, e.g., Kirk-Raven [33], 329; Guthrie [25] II.153. Different versions in O'Brien [351], 324, n. 1; Long [358], 404, n. 11, who holds that the 'roots' are not immortal.
14 On the text of **366** see von Blumenthal [427], 18–19. The 'three things' were air, fire and earth (Philoponus, **36 A 6**); and the *Triagmos* was a cosmological work (Scholiast to Aristophanes, **A 2**). Philosophically, Ion may have been close to Empedocles.
15 J. Bennett, *Kant's Dialectic* (Cambridge, 1974), 40; in these paragraphs I am indebted to Bennett's discussion (see especially, 54–6).

XXI The Sophists

1 On the history of the word '*sophistês*' see, e.g., Grant [208], 106–15; Guthrie [25], III.27–34. For the fees charged by sophists see Harrison [437], 191, n. 44.
2 If they were not primarily natural scientists in the Ionian tradition, the Sophists had certainly studied science: see, e.g., Prodicus, **84 B 3–4**; Hippias, **86 A 2** (Philostratus); Antiphon, **87 B 22**. Gomperz [433], especially ch. II, states in its most extreme form the thesis that the Sophists were above all interested in rhetoric.
3 I translate the text of **371** as it appears in Diogenes Laertius, IX.51 = **A 1**; other authors append to the first sentence the clause 'nor what they are like in form'. The addition is accepted by Diels-Kranz; but see Gomperz [439]. Versions of **371** appear in Plato, *Theaetetus* 162D = **A 23**; Timon, fr. 5 = **A 12**; Cicero, **A 23**; Sextus, **A 12**; Eusebius, *ad* **B 4** (see further Müller [440], 148, n. 4). On Protagoras' condemnation and the burning of his book see also Hesychius,

A 3; Eusebius, *ad* **B 4**; Sextus, **A 12**. Von Fritz [438], 910 (comparing Plato, *Meno* 91E) and Müller [440], 149–51, judge the whole tale a fabrication.

4 The continuation of Diogenes' text is uncertain (see Chilton [441]; [22], 56–7); but there is no way of getting Diogenes off the hook. His *gaucherie* is repeated by Epiphanius, III.2.9.

5 Müller [440], 144–7, suggests: 'Of the gods I *know* nothing, but this is what I *believe*: . . .' (cf. Fahr [163], 94–6); and he notes that Diogenes Laertius (IX.54 = **A 1**) and Eusebius (*ad* **B 4**) speak of a Protagorean work *Concerning the Gods*. There have been fanciful attempts to reconstruct Protagoras' *Peri Theôn* (see Untersteiner [434], 38, n. 47 = [435], I.69, n. 47); but I doubt if Protagoras ever wrote a theology. There is no evidence beyond the title in Eusebius and Diogenes; and Diogenes and Eusebius are simply using the first two words of **371** as a title for the work they begin (as we use *Pater Noster* or *Ave Maria*).

6 References to the discussion of this passage in Untersteiner [434], 72, n. 24 = [435], I.118.24; Guthrie [25], III.64, n. 1.

7 The main texts, apart from Democritus and Protagoras, are: Hesiod, *Works and Days* 109–201 (see Kleingünther [444], 11–15); Aeschylus, *Prometheus* 436–506 (see ibid. 66–90); Xenophanes, **21 B 18** (see especially Edelstein [446], 3–11); Hecataeus, *FGrH* F 15; Euripides, *Supplices* 195–249; [Hippocrates], *vet med* 1; Anaxagoras, **59 B 4**, **B 21a**, **A 102** (Aristotle); Archelaus, **60 A 4**; Xenophon, *Memorabilia* I.iv; IV.iii.

8 See, e.g., *Odyssey* XVII.485–7; Aeschylus, *Supplices* 381–6; *Persae* 827–8; fr. 530 M; Euripides, *Heraclides* 387–8; fr. 506; fr. 1131.

9 When the plague struck Athens in 430 BC, 'no fear of god or law of man restrained the people, who judged worship and no worship to be indifferent because they saw that all perished equally' (Thucydides, II.53.4).

10 Cf. *Phoenissae* 1726; *Hercules* 346–7; fr. 645. On Euripidean theology see Guthrie [25], III.232–4; and especially Nestle [459], 87–151. Thrasymachus' view is stated again by Aristodemus in Xenophon, *Memorabilia* I.iv.11; it is reported by Plato at *Laws* 885B and 888C, and argued against at 899E–903A.

11 On the list see Diels [4], 58–9; Müller [440], 151, n. 4.

12 Numerals followed by '**J**' refer to the arrangement in Jacoby [457] (Diagoras does not appear in Diels-Kranz). Diagoras is regularly called '*ho atheos*': e.g., Scholiast to Aristophanes, II.2 **J**; Suda, III.3 **J**; Cicero, *de natura deorum* I.63 = V.6 **J**. The explicit statement of atheism in Athenagoras is found again in Diogenes of Oenoanda, fr. 11 Ch. Editors of Diogenes restore his text so as to ascribe the statement about Diagoras to Eudemus; but the stone is fragmentary, and no letter of Eudemus' name appears on it.

13 'Sensational pamphlet': Jacoby [457], 25; no book: Woodbury [458], 207–8 (see Aristoxenus, fr. 127a W; Philodemus, III.5 **J**); no 'intellectual defence': ibid. 208 (cf. Guthrie [25], III.236); *atheos* means 'ungodly': ibid. 208–9; 'leader of progressive thought': Dodds [43], 189.

14 Following Jacoby [457], 37, n. 106, Woodbury [458] thinks that the anecdotes point to 'a problem of popular belief', not a philosophical issue; and they compare Solon, fr. 1.25–32; Hesiod, *Works and Days* 267–73; Aeschylus, *Prometheus* 1093; Theognis, 731–52. It is doubtless a popular puzzle that the good gods apparently let evil prosper; but Diagoras, I hope, raised that banal puzzlement to an intellectual level and used it to ground an argument for atheism.

15 Cole [448], 153–63, suggests that the later aetiologies of Euhemerus, Diodorus,

and Leo originate from a Democritean model; but those later views are perhaps closer to Prodicus than to Democritus.

16 On the text see Kahn [90], xiv; 148, n. 3. Air is perhaps divinized by Diogenes of Apollonia, **64 B 5** (below, p. 580); cf. the Derveni papyrus (quoted below, p. 647, n. 11); Aeschylus, fr. 70; Epicharmus, **23 B 53**. With **381** compare especially Herodotus, I. 131; Euripides, fr. 941 (cf. fr. 877).

17 The Suda (III.3 J) says that Democritus bought Diagoras as a slave. Derenne [345], 59, believes the story and thinks that Diagoras caught atheism from Democritus.

18 In line 13, *exheurein* might mean 'discover' rather than 'invent'; in line 26 *pseudês* might mean 'insincere' rather than 'false'. But no candid reader will seriously dispute my translations.

19 On Prodicus' religious views see also Sextus, *adv Math* IX.39, 41; Epiphanius, III.21 (see, e.g., Gomperz [433], 238–42; Untersteiner [434], 221, n. 9 and 222, n. 27 = [435] II.30, n. 9 and 32, n. 27).

20 Or 'wished': there is a long and somewhat pointless debate over the sense of *eucheto*: in the vernacular, even atheists pray that good will come to them.

21 For the text see J. Blomqvist, *Eranos* 66, 1968, 90–2.

22 See new fr. 1 (Chilton [22], 124–7) and new fr. 12 (see M. F. Smith, *American Journal of Archaeology* 75, 1971, 376–8): fr. 12 appears to link with **388**, and it may upbraid Democritus for giving truth and substance to empty *eidôla*; but (as so often) the crucial words of the fragment are scholarly restorations.

23 So Bicknell [464], 321–6.

24 Luria [514], 4–5, judges that **389** is spurious; Eisenberger [463], 150–2, makes it a politico-ethical fragment.

25 Scholars divide over the question of whether this definition is Gorgias' own; references in Untersteiner [434], 202, n. 7 = [435], I.312, n. 7.

26 On the pre-sophistic rhetoricians, Corax and Teisias, see Radermacher [471], 28–35 (texts on the rhetorical activities of the Sophists are conveniently assembled, ibid. 35–106). Note that Gorgias' teacher Empedocles was called the founder of rhetoric by Aristotle (fr. 65 = **82 A 1**; cf. Sextus, **31 A 19**). Literary studies began with Theagenes of Rhegium, a contemporary of Xenophanes, who wrote about Homer (Tatian, **8 A 1**; Scholiasts on Dionysius Thrax and Homer, **A 2a**, **A 3**). In the fifth century, Stesimbrotus and Glaucus followed Theagenes (e.g., Plato, *Ion* 530C = **61 A 1**), and so too did Anaxagoras (Diogenes Laertius, II.11 = **59 A 1**). See also the evidence on Anaxagoras' pupil, Metrodorus of Lampsacus: Plato, loc. cit.; Diogenes Laertius, loc. cit.; Porphyry, **61 A 5**.

27 Protagoras

> was the first to divide utterance (*logos*) into four types: prayer, question, answer, command . . . which he called the foundations of utterances (Diogenes Laertius, IX.53 = **80 A 1**).

Again:

> He divided up the types of names: male, female, and chattel (Aristotle, *Rhet* 1407b6 = **80 A 27**).

Both 'divisions' enabled him to criticize Homer for solecism (Aristotle, *Poet* 1456b15 = **A 29**; *Top* 173b18 = **A 28**), criticisms which delighted Aristophanes (*Clouds* 658–79 = **C 3**). Protagoras' thoughts are not syntax in any technical sense; but they do mark the beginning of syntactical studies.

28 Pfeiffer [24], 37; cf. Classen [466], 34–6. Mayer [469], 18, exaggerates when he says that Prodicus 'was the first to attempt consciously to give *a logical analysis* of the meanings of terms in ordinary language'.

29 Cf. Plutarch, *aud poet* 15D. The anecdote about Simonides ('Why don't you deceive the Thessalians?—They're too stupid': ibid. 15C) is ascribed to Gorgias by Untersteiner, on the authority of Wilamowitz; but see Rosenmeyer [474], 233.

30 See, e.g., Pindar, *Olympian* I.28–33; Parmenides, **28 B 8**.52; Aristophanes, *Frogs* 910 (but see *Aeschyli Vita* 7); Aristotle, *Poet* 1460a18–9. Reference to an aesthetic *theory* may perhaps be seen at: Plato, *Republic* 598E; Ephorus, *FGrH* 70 F 8; Polybius, II.56.11; Horace, *Epistles* II.1, 211; Josephus, *IA* VIII.56; Epictetus, I.iv.26. On *apatê* in general see especially Pohlenz [473], 154–62; Rosenmeyer [474]; Segar [475].

31 Prodicus objected to the Greek use of *phlegma* for 'mucus': *phlegma* is cognate with *phlegein*, 'to burn', but mucus is moist and wet (**84 B 5**; cf. Soranus, **68 A 159**). For Democritus' etymologizing see, e.g., Cole [448], 68, n. 17; for early essays in the same genre see Pfeiffer [24], 4–5.

32 These paragraphs draw heavily on H. P. Grice, 'Meaning', *PR* 66, 1957, 377–88.

XXII De Anima

1 Anaximander's name is omitted in Stobaeus' version of Aëtius, and none of the three versions of the report inspires much confidence (but see Kahn [90], 114).

2 **21 A 50** is probably an inference from **21 B 33**; it is contradicted by Diogenes Laertius, IX.19 = **21 A 1** ('soul is breath (*pneuma*)'). **28 A 45** (Macrobius) conflicts with **399**.

3 But see Tugwell [479]. Perhaps compare **22 B 85** = **70 M** ('It is hard to fight with spirit (*thumos*); for whatever it wishes, it buys at the cost of soul'); cf. Verdenius [478]. See also above, p. 607, n. 9.

4 Cf. Aristotle, *Resp* 471b30–472a25 = **68 A 106**; *An* 406b15–22 = **A 104**; Aëtius, **A 102**.

5 On *asômatos* see above, p. 617, n. 34.

6 On Iamblichus' different report of Hippasus' psychology (**18 A 11**), which is also wrong, see Burkert [173], 249, n. 50.

7 See Burkert [173], 247–8 (and above, pp. 186–90). **44 B 21** is spurious (ibid. 242–3); on later Academico-Pythagorean psychology, see ibid. 73–5.

8 Burkert [173], 73, n. 130, compares Alexander Polyhistor: 'The whole air is full of souls' (Diogenes Laertius, VIII.32 = **58 B 1a**); and he observes that mote-souls are 'rather compatible than otherwise with metempsychosis' (121, n. 3).

9 See also Alexander, **67 A 29**. Most scholars say that the eye of *a* emits effluences, and that the conjunction of eye-effluences with effluences of *b* compresses the air midway between *a* and *b*; the mid-air compression then causes *a* to see *b*. But our evidence does not support that bizarre theory (see Baldes [480]).

10 See Beare [39], 93, n. 2.

11 Note that Gorgias claims to have been present at Empedocles' magical operations (Diogenes Laertius, VIII.59 = **31 A 1**).

12 Alcmaeon used *poroi*, and some think that Empedocles borrowed them from him. But Alcmaeon's pores lead from the sense organs to the brain (e.g., Theophrastus, *Sens* §26 = **24 A 5**); Empedocles' lead from the surface of the body to the sensitive interior of ear and eye.

13 Aristotle read a theory of vision into **B 84** (*Sens* 437b23–438a5; cf. Alexander, *ad* **B 84**); and so he saddles Empedocles with two theories:

> Sometimes he says we see in this way [i.e. by rays leaving the eye], sometimes by effluences from the seen objects (*Sens* 438a4–5).

Some scholars follow Aristotle's interpretation of **B 84**, but attempt to construct a unified theory from the two theories which Aristotle distinguishes; and they thus make Empedocles anticipate the view of *Timaeus* 45B. But once we realize that **B 84** deals with the structure of the eye and not with vision (see especially O'Brien [417], 140–6, with full bibliography at 157–9), we may be sure that there are neither two theories nor one *Timaeus* theory in Empedocles. (Theophrastus probably grasped the matter aright: *Sens* §§7–8 = **31 A 86**).

14 Sextus, *adv Math* VIII.286, quotes line 10 by itself; Bollack [349], III.512, characteristically and implausibly supposes that the line occurred twice in Empedocles' poem. Note that according to Democritus, 'everything has a share in soul of some sort' (Aëtius, **68 A 117**; cf. Albertus Magnus, **A 164**).

15 Differing attempts to unravel the knots of **B 77** and **B 78** in Bollack [349], III.513–7, and Zuntz [193], 209–11.

16 For the translation of **B 108**.2 see Bollack [349], III.458–9. Simplicius and Philoponus (*ad* **B 108**) explain the fragment as an account of dreaming; but see Verdenius [233], 20.

17 Hence *opôpamen* ('we see') in **425**.1 is metaphorical for 'we think' (so Aristotle, *Met* 1000b5), and the fragment has nothing to do with perception. That reading is confirmed by **B 17**.21: 'Gaze at it [sc. Love] with your mind (*noôi*), and do not sit gawping with your eyes.'

18 'Turned', *tetrammena*, is the MSS. reading, accepted by Bollack [349], III.444–6, who takes the four roots to be the subject. Most scholars prefer the emendation *tethrammenê* ('nourished'), and suppose that *hê kardia* ('the heart') is the lost subject.

19 So Bollack [349], III.576–85. For different interpretations of **430** see especially Long [494], 269–73; Schwabl [486].

20 See Theophrastus, *Sens* §10 = **A 86**. Bollack [349], III.447, paraphrases **429**.2 by: 'where especially, but misleadingly, men call the elements thought'. Hardly plausible. On the importance of the heart in thinking see, e.g., [Hippocrates], *morb sacr* VI.392 L; *cord* IX.88 L.

21 I read *hekastot'*, not *hekastos*; *periplanktôn*, not *perikamptôn*; *krasis*, not *krasin*; *parestêken*, not *paristatai*. For discussion see, e.g., Müller [52], 18–25, with references.

22 Fr. 68.3 D. Fr. 68. 1–2 D is a version of *Odyssey* XVIII.130–7, but its connexion with fr. 68.3 is uncertain. On the related fragment of Heraclitus, **B 17** = **3 M**, see above, p. 144.

23 This interpretation is elegantly argued for by Popper [35], 408–13.

24 Popper argues (i) that Parmenides had no *general* word for 'sense-organ', and so had to invent or adopt one; and (ii) that *guia* which, like *melea*, means literally 'limbs', was used by Empedocles to refer to the sense-organs. Point (i) is true and interesting (cf. Burkert [173], 270, n. 154); point (ii) is false: *guia* at **31 B 2**.1 and **B 3**.13 refers to the body as a whole (*palamai*, literally 'hands', is Empedocles' word for 'sense-organs': **B 2**.1; **B 3**.9).

25 'Body', e.g., Guthrie [25], II.67; 'elements', e.g., Bollack [284], 67 (referring to **31 B 27a**, **B 30**.1, **B 35**.11).

26 So Loenen [238], 53; for further references see, e.g., Bollack [284].

27 '*noêma*' here means 'instrument of thought', as it does at Empedocles, **429**.3.

28 Hicks [10], 221; cf. e.g., Wilamowitz [194], 658–9.

29 E.g., Aristotle, *An* 404b8–15; Porphyry, *ad* **B 126**; Diogenes Laertius, VIII.77 = **A 1**; Hippolytus, **A 31**; Aëtius, **A 32**.

30 Unless he was thinking of medical men: cf. [Hippocrates] *morb* I.30; *morb sacr* 17. Critias held that the *psuchê* is blood (e.g., Aristotle *An* 405b5 = **88 A 23**); and Philoponus, **88 A 23**, quotes Empedocles **429**.3 as a line of Critias. Philoponus may simply have bungled; but it is possible that Critias quoted Empedocles, taking him to have said that the *psuchê* was blood.

31 The reference to *harmonia* is unwanted: I take *harmonia* to be a gloss on *logos tês mixeôs*.

32 I.e., 'or is it rather some substance distinct from the elements?' Aristotle may be thinking of the *daimôn*. But the phrase 'as something else' (*heteron ti ousa*) is Aristotle's normal way of talking about non-substances; does he mean here: 'Is the *psuchê* not a *logos* but some other non-substantial being'?

33 Plotinus, *Ennead* IV.7.8[4]; Olympiodorus, *in Phaedonem* 57.17; Philoponus, *in An* 70.5.

34 **44 B 13** is defended by Burkert [173], 269–70. **44 B 22** is spurious (Burkert [173], 247; *contra*: Gladigow [187], 417–18).

35 *Contra*: see especially Gottschalk [490]. Gottschalk objects (a) that the source ascribing *harmonia* to Philolaus is late; (b) that Aristotle shows an 'inability to name a single adherent' of the doctrine, and that the anonymity of his reference 'looks deliberate and pointed'; and (c) that the doctrine is inconsistent with metempsychosis. I shall deal with (c) later. There is no force in (b): anonymous references are frequent in Aristotle; they are not 'pointed' but merely assume an ordinary knowledge of history in their audience.

Point (a) is stronger: we may well suppose that all the later references to the Pythagoreans as *harmonia* theorists derive from the *Phaedo*, and that the *Phaedo* is no history book. The question then is this: does the *Phaedo* give us reason to ascribe *harmonia* to Philolaus? Well, Plato does, I think, strongly imply that the doctrine was Philolaic; he has no motive for falsification; and the ascription is inherently plausible. And after all, who else can have propounded the doctrine?

36 There is, of course, no question of a harmony of *psychic* parts, as Cornford [405], 146–9, supposed.

37 Athenagoras ascribes the *mot* to Philolaus (**B 15**); but he is merely confused. Clement, **408**, claims to be quoting Philolaus:

> The old theologians and seers also bear witness that as a punishment the soul is yoked to the body and has been buried in it as in a tomb.

Is Clement quoting a Philolaic forgery? Or did Philolaus report the views of the 'old theologians and seers' without assenting to them?

38 Burkert [173], 272; cf. Cornford [405], 146.

39 There is a helpful survey of opinions in Guthrie [25], II.124–8.

40 I quote, in order: Vlastos [161], 125; 93; Burnet [31], 250; Jaeger [47], I.295.

41 See especially Zuntz [193], 236–43, who argues cogently that by and large the arrangement in Diels-Kranz is correct and well grounded.

42 See especially Reinhardt [491], 104–11; Zuntz [193], 211–13, 241–2.

43 Cf. Jaeger [48], 132: 'We ought to be no more surprised [by Empedocles] than when we come upon a purely scientific rationalism combined with the religious spirit of Christianity in a man of our own times.'

44 Westman [15], 247, thinks Empedocles means that human *bodies* do not simply fail to exist before and after life; but he is hardly making that banal point.

Bollack [349], III.98–100, takes the subject of **439** to be the elements; but the mistaken beliefs described in lines 2–3 apply not to the elements but to people. **B 111**.9 promises Pausanias that: 'You will bring the strength of a dead man back from Hades.' Is that a metaphorical way of saying that Pausanias will be able to show people their immortality, or just the implausible promise that Pausanias will raise the dead? **B 2**.8 reads: 'You, then, since you have come here, will learn . . .' Zuntz [193], 406–7, glosses 'since you have come to earth as a man'; and thus he finds another reference to metempsychosis in *Nature* (but see Bollack [349], III.16–17).

45 At **440**.2 I read *hêper*, with the MSS., for Diels-Kranz' *hêiper*; at **441**.3 I follow Zuntz [193], 216, in preferring *stêthea* to *mêdea*.

46 Line 1: *chrêma* probably means 'pronouncement' (Bollack [349], III.151). Between lines 3 and 4 Diels-Kranz print an invented line: it should be omitted (Zuntz [193], 194–6). Line 5: *hôrai* ('seasons') probably means 'years', and the figure 30,000 simply marks a very long period of time (see, e.g., Zuntz [193], 197). Line 10: I read *akamantos*, not *phaethontos*. Line 12: for the reading *tên kai egô nun eimi* see Zuntz [193], 198.

47 Empedocles surely ascribed the tailoring to a female *daimôn*; and that was later (rightly?) interpreted as 'nature' or 'fate'. On clothes of flesh see Zuntz [193], 405–6.

48 **B 59** begins: 'But when to a greater extent *daimôn* mingled with *daimôn* . . .' Simplicius (*ad* **B 59**) says that the *daimones* are Love and Strife; some scholars think they are the four roots; O'Brien [351], 325–36, implausibly argues that they are to be identified with the *daimones* of **442**.

49 So Guthrie [25], II.254, n. 1. Cf. **B 148**: Empedocles called 'the body surrounding the soul "man-encircling earth"'.

50 In favour of the view O'Brien [351], 328–36, cites **442**; Aristotle, *An* 408a18–23; Plutarch, *exil* 607CE; *tranq* 474B. But I fear I can see nothing in any of those passages which supports him. Some scholars have the *daimôn* of **442** enter the world of Love and Strife from a higher, incorporeal realm (see, e.g., Zuntz [193], 252–8); but that is incredible: Empedocles knows no world beyond that of the four roots.

51 Main texts on the Great Year are Censorinus, *de die natali* 18; Aëtius, II.32; cf. Plato, *Politicus* 269C–271C; *Timaeus* 39CD. See especially van der Waerden [496].

52 The argument is adapted from Nietzsche: see especially I. Soll, 'Reflexions on Recurrence: a Re-Examination of Nietzsche's Doctrine, *die Ewige Wiederkehr des Gleiches*', in *Nietzsche*, ed. R. C. Solomon (New York, 1973).

53 Lactantius, *SVF* II.623; Simplicius, *in Phys* 886.12 = *SVF* II.627; Alexander, *SVF* II.624; cf. *SVF* II.625–31; I.109. See also Hume, *Dialogues concerning Natural Religion*, ch. VIII.

54 Soll, op. cit. 339–40, argues that 'there can be no accumulation of experience from one recurrence to the next. A person can have no direct memories of earlier recurrences'; and he infers that $Pythagoras_1$ is not identical with $Pythagoras_2$. But Soll's second statement does not follow from his first.

XXIII Conduct Unbecoming

1 **448** and **449** are fragments 1 and 2 of Pap. Oxy. 1364 (fragments 3–13 contain only a few letters each); **450** is Pap. Oxy. 1797. Harpocration proves that **448**, and hence

(presumably) **449**, belong to Antiphon (see Diels-Kranz, II.346, n.); on the ascription of **450** see, e.g., Guthrie [25], III.110, n. 1.

2 The papyrus has many lacunae; I translate the restorations accepted by Diels-Kranz, except where noted.
448: I.1: Diels reads *ou*]*n* ('justice, therefore, . . .'); Schöne proposed *d' ê*]*n* ('justice, we said, was . . .'). I.12: 'deal with' translates *chrêsthai*; the word is hard to render, but 'manipulate' (Guthrie [25], III.108) gives the wrong idea. I.25: *epith*]*eta*—perhaps rather *sunth*]*eta*, 'conventional' (but see Untersteiner [430], IV.76). II.13: for *para to dunaton* some give *per impossibile*, others 'as far as possible', others 'more than it [sc. nature] can bear'. No translation is wholly agreeable, and I do not know what to make of the phrase. II.24: reading *pantôn heneka toutôn*: see Kerferd [502], 28. III.25: reading *t*[*o gar*] (Hunt), rather than Diels-Kranz' *t*[*o d' au*] ('but'). III.30: I make *apo* partitive, with Guthrie [25], III.109, n. 1. IV.24: lines 25–31 are beyond restoration; for 30–31 Heinimann [445], 138, n. 48, proposes:

. . . di]*kaioi* [*no*
mizo]*ntai ka*[*i*

'. . . are thought to be just; and so are those who . . .'. That gives what is surely the right sense. VI.1–5 is fragmentary; but the sense of the lines is clear. VI.19: the text is not in doubt; but I cannot make any sense of it. VI.25–30: the text is again fragmentary: I translate Diels-Kranz' text, which gives a tolerable sense; see further Untersteiner [430], IV.89. Col. VII probably continues the catalogue of injustices begun at VI.25; but the papyrus is too lacunose to translate.
449: Only *frustulae* of col. I survive. II.10: Guthrie [25], III.153, translates: 'since by nature we are all made to be alike in all respects, both barbarians and Greeks'; but he allows that 'the Greek is rather unusual', and considers the translation I adopt to be 'more accurate'. II.16–20: the text is reasonably plain, but the sense is obscure; perhaps a line has been omitted after 16. II.20–2 are too fragmentary to translate.
450: I.12: reading *eipe*]*r* (Diels) for Diels-Kranz' *epeipe*]*r* (Hunt proposed *kai ga*]*r*). I.20: reading *eikos de*] (Hunt) for Diels-Kranz' *kai hama*] ('and at the same time'). I.21: reading *eis* [*huste/ro*]*n* · *ene*[*sti gar* (Hunt-Crönert), for Diels-Kranz' [*husteron/hô*]*n hene* [*ka eipen* ('. . . later on, on account of what he said'). II.20: as Kranz observes, we expect not *mêde auton adikeisthai* but *mêden auton adikoumenon* ('and for not wronging at all when one has not oneself been wronged at all . . .'). Perhaps the text is in error.

3 Untersteiner [434], 267, n. 127 = [435], II.98, n. 127, places **450** between **448** and **449**; in [430], IV.91, he inserts Pap. Oxy. 414 between **450** and **449**. But see Guthrie [25], III.110, n. 1.

4 'Not everything that is *phusei* is advantageous, and Antiphon's norm must be restricted to *ta phusei xumpheronta*' (Kerferd [502], 31. He translates *ta phusei xumpheronta* by 'what is advantageous *to* human nature'). But there is no 'norm' laid down in **448**; *ta phusei xumpheronta* contrast with the artificial advantages brought by *nomima*.

5 'The principal argument to be extracted with certainty from the fragments is a criticism of *nomos* that is essentially ethical, not anarchistic' (Moulton [504], 331); see ibid. 329, n. 1, for references to those scholars who find a 'radical critique' of morality in **448–50**.

6 Euripides, *Hecuba* 799–801; Lysias, II.19; Xenophon, *Memorabilia* IV.iv.12–3;

Aristotle, *EN* 1129a32–4; cf. Pindar, fr. 169; Plato, *Theaetetus*, 172A; Chrysippus, *SVF* III.314.

7 See especially Kerferd [525]; *contra*: e.g., McDowell [526], 172–3. I pass by the question whether Protagoras is presented as a moral relativist in the *Protagoras*: see Moser-Kustas [507].

8 **90 A 1** §8 says that the Peloponnesian War is the most recent war. The text is emended; the reference hardly does the chronological work required of it; and a detailed commentary is required before the piece can be dated with any certainty.

9 'The author places side by side, without connecting them organically, elements borrowed from different sophists, among whom Protagoras is pre-eminent both as to thought and as to the methods employed' (Levi [511], 302; cf. Gomperz [433], 138–92).

10 Reading *all' allo hekateron* (Blass; cf. §11; **A 2** §12), for the MSS. *all' hekateron*.

11 See, e.g., Adkins [207], 124–7 (who strangely states that 'the concept of moral responsibility is . . . unimportant to the Greek', ibid. 3). Compare Euripides' defence of Helen in *Troades* 914–1059.

12 A. J. Ayer, *Philosophical Essays* (London, 1954), 275. (For Greek attitudes to chance and responsibility see especially Dover [206], 138–41).

13 Ayer, op. cit., 279.

14 I translate *kai gar horômen echontes opsin ouch* . . . (Immisch); the text is very uncertain.

15 Immisch [472], 22.

16 The text is too corrupt for restoration (see Immisch [472], 39, n. 1); but it is clear enough that *logos* is assimilated to *bia*.

17 130 in Stobaeus, 80 under the name of 'Democrates': the authenticity of both sets of fragments has been doubted; see especially Guthrie [25], II.489–92.

18 Luria [514], 6–7, refers to **B 299** and holds that the trivial *gnômai* are translations from Achikar. On early Greek gnomic moralizing see Grant [208], 86–97. Nestle [460], 589–93, finds numerous parallels between Democritus' *gnômai* and the *sententiae* of Euripides' characters.

19 'A democrat' (Bailey [383], 211); cf. **B 251**. *Contra*: Aalders [518] (cf., e.g., **B 49**, **B 75**, **B 254**, **B 266**, **B 267**). If the Anonymus Iamblichi (**89 A 1**) is Democritean (see Cole [519]), then there is more evidence available to decide the dispute.

20 Democritus propounds 'the first rigorously naturalistic ethics in Greek thought' (Vlastos [513], 62); see Guthrie [25], II.492, n. 1, for other attempts to find an ethical system in Democritus. But 'Democritus' "ethics" hardly amounts to a moral theory; there is no effort to set the picture of the "cheerful" man on a firm philosophical basis' (Bailey [383], 522).

21 Scholars usually see an apparent contradiction between **478** and **479**, which they try in various fashions to reconcile. The contradiction arises from the standard mistranslation of **479** as: 'Accept nothing pleasant unless it is advantageous'.

22 References in Luria [514], 3–4.

23 So Luria [514], 9–13; cf. Aelian, **A 150a**; Stobaeus, **C 7** §3; Aristotle, *HA* 630b31; [Aristotle], *Mirabilia* 830b1; Xenophon, *Memorabilia* IV.iv.20; see further Heinimann [445], 145–7.

24 See Taylor [517], 16–27, who also refers to Diotimus, **76 A 1** (but see Bailey [383], 188–9).

25 Bailey [383], 188; cf. Luria [514], 7.

26 Bailey, loc. cit.

XXIV The Bounds of Knowledge

1 Line 3: I read *athroisantes* (*athrêsantes*, Diels-Kranz; *athroisantos* or *athrêsantos*, MSS.); and I accept, with little confidence *en zôêsi biou* (see Bollack [349], III.11). Line 6: the MSS. read, unmetrically, *to d' holon euchetai einai*; I translate Fränkel's *to d' holon tis ar' euchetai einai*; (Diels-Kranz prefer to insert *pas* after *holon* ('but everyone boasts . . .'): Bollack reads *ta d' hol' oudeis* . . . ('but no one boasts he has found the wholes'). No emendation is wholly satisfactory; but the import of the line is plain enough. Line 9: retain *ou pleion ge* (MSS.). Diels-Kranz read *ou pleon êe*, with no stop before *ou* ('you will learn no more than human wit achieves'). The emendation is needless, and it produces bathos.

2 Line 2: translation as in Bollack [349], II.8. Line 6: 'you' probably refers to the Muse of line 3; Pausanias is not addressed until line 9. But the sentiments of lines 6–8 are odd if put to a Muse: some scholars refer 'you' to Pausanias, and posit a lacuna before line 6.

3 *Contra*: Bollack [349], III.8, who refers to Empedocles' alleged theory that vision involves the eye in sending out rays and 'grasping' its object. But that theory is not Empedoclean (above, p. 639, n. 13).

4 Bollack [349], III.19–22, rightly connects **B 2** with the promise of **B 111**.

5 The Greek of **487** is, unfortunately, not unambiguous. Thus Mourelatos [245], 347, translates: 'What manifests itself to us is the look of things which are not themselves perceptible'; Gomperz [521], 342, gives: 'For the appearances are only the way in which what is unperceived presents itself to us'. Those readings are, of course, thoroughly consonant with Anaxagorean physics; and we can understand Democritus' admiration for the fragment. But Epicurus understood the apophthegm according to the orthodox interpretation which I follow in the text (Diogenes Laertius, X.32); and no doubt Democritus did too.

6 *hôs* means 'that', not 'how'. For excellent notes on text and translation see Guthrie [25], III.188–92.

7 So, e.g., McDowell [526], 118, who thinks that 152A6–8 may be a quotation from Protagoras; *contra*: e.g., Versenyi [522], 181 (who wrongly cites *Theaetetus* 170A, 170E, 171AC, in support of the collective sense).

8 McDowell [526], 120, takes 167A8 to imply that Protagoras 'denies the possibility of non-perceptual judgments'; that is implausible in itself, and it does not follow from the distinction between judgmental and phenomenological seeming.

9 'Man is the measure of "all things" (*pantôn chrêmatôn*)': *chrêma* means, quite generally, 'thing'; it is fashionable but futile to recall its etymological connection with *chrêsthai* 'use', and to talk of 'things with a special relation to our involvement with them' (Versenyi [522], 182).

10 Democritus perhaps attacked Protagoras at this point: see **68 B 11** .

11 A papyrus fragment refers the thesis to Prodicus (see Binder-Lieseborghs [530]); Isocrates refers to it (*Helen* 1); and cf. Plato, *Cratylus* 429DE.

12 The *Ou Mallon* Principle had a long history; but I ignore later uses of the Principle, which seem to me to differ considerably from the Abderite use.

13 So Weiss [538], 49, n. 1; von Fritz [438], 916.

14 [Democritus] says that soul and mind are simply the same; for what is true is what appears (Aristotle, *An* 404a28 = **68 A 101**).

Presumably that has to be explained by way of **504** (see Kapp [537], 166–7).

15 Cf. Sextus, **A 59**, **A 110**, **A 134**.

16 The 'new fragment' of Protagoras (see Gronewald [528]) makes him a sceptic:

> e.g., I see the moon, another man does not: it is unclear (*adêlon*) whether it exists or not.

But the 'fragment' is full of Stoic terminology and has no authority.

17 Plutarch distressingly contradicts Aristotle's report. Colotes, it seems, had ascribed to Democritus the restricted Principle of Equipollence; Plutarch vehemently retorts:

> So far is Democritus from thinking that each thing is no more (*mê mallon*) thus than thus, that he attacked Protagoras the sophist when he said this, and wrote many convincing things against him (**68 B 156**).

We know nothing more of Democritus' attack on Protagoras than the *peritropê*. Democritus attacked Protagoras on matters intimately connected to the Principle of Equipollence, and he drew quite un-Protagorean conclusions from the Principle: Plutarch, who is engaged in heated polemic, may have wrongly inferred that Democritus rejected the Principle outright. In any event, I prefer the testimony of Aristotle and Colotes to that of Plutarch.

18 Cf. Sextus, **70 A 25**; Philodemus, **A 25**; Epiphanius, **A 23**; Diogenes Laertius, IX.58 = **72 A 1**. The text of **505** is reconstructed in part from Cicero's translation, and the details are far from certain.

19 The MSS. read *diathêkên* ('disposition'); for the emendation see, e.g., Steckel [385], 207.

20 The word '*epirhusmiê*' itself has foxed the scholars; de Ley [539] plausibly suggests *ameipsirhusmiê* (cf. **B 139**), which would have the sense I give to *epirhusmiê*.

21 And some translate *idmen* in **506** as 'know by experience' (see especially Cleve [37], 428–31). Compare Fränkel's version of Xenophanes' sceptical fragment (above, p. 138). But *idmen* means no more than 'know'; and **B** 7 and **B** 8 are more than enough to impose a scepticism on Democritus.

XXV The Last of the Line

1 Diels-Kranz, II.59, think that these are different titles for (parts of) a single work; *contra*: Theiler [541], 6–7.

2 Hussey [34], 141.

3 See, e.g., Aristophanes, *Clouds* 225–36 = **C 1**; *Frogs* 892; Euripides, *Troades* 884–9 = **C 2**. And perhaps the pseudo-Hippocratic *de natura hominis* singles out Diogenes as the representative of Ionian science (see Jouanna [270], 307–14).

4 Some may suspect that **514** refers to Diogenes of Smyrna, who 'believed the same things as Protagoras' (Epiphanius, **71 A 2**).

5 'Diogenes agreed with the atomists in holding that sensations were subjective and relative', but 'this subjectivity . . . did not for him carry with it the denial of sensible qualities to the primary substance itself, as the atomic theory demanded' (Guthrie [25], II.377 and n. 3). That ascribes a strange view to Diogenes; and there is no textual evidence to show that he did not agree with the Atomists on both counts.

6 'Third Explanation of the New System', in Leibniz, *The Monadology*, ed. R. Latta (Oxford, 1898), p. 333.

7 Diogenes is presumably 'speaking with the vulgar', if he really denies generation and destruction.
8 The source of the passages (I.iv and IV.iii) is much debated: see especially Theiler [541], 14–54, who argues that they are in part based on Diogenes; Huffmeier [542], who strangely denies any teleological thoughts to Diogenes.
9 Air and thought: e.g., Theophrastus, *Sens* §§39, 44 = **A 19**; Aristotle, *An* 405a21 = **A 20**; cf. Aëtius, **A 30**. Divine air. e.g., Philodemus, Cicero, Aëtius, Augustine, **A 8**.
10 The MSS. read *apo gar moi touto ethos*, which makes no sense. Diels-Kranz, and most scholars, accept Usener's emendation: *auto gar moi touto theos*. I translate, hesitantly, Panzerbieter's: *auto gar moi toutou ethos*.
11 Two fragments tell against that interpretation:

> And this itself is a body, both eternal and deathless; and of the rest, some come into being, others depart (**525**).
>
> But this seems to me to be clear, that it is both great and strong and eternal and immortal and multiscient (**B 8**).

Simplicius quotes **B 8** immediately after **525**, and he takes the subject of both fragments to be the *archê*. Hence the *archê* is multiscient, and therefore (by the argument of **528**) it is air—and presumably also the divinity. But Simplicius found **B 8** 'elsewhere', i.e., not in the same context as **525**; and we are not obliged to associate the two fragments as he does. Compare also column 15, lines 1–3 of the Derveni papyrus:

> And since the things that exist are, each one, called after that which predominates (*epikratountos*), everything by that same argument was called Zeus; for the air predominates over everything to the extent that it wishes.

(Text in G. S. Kapsomenos, *Archaiologikon Deltion* 19, 1964, 17–25; discussion in Burkert [67]). Air is the divinity and the predominant element: and the connexions between this fragment and Anaxagoras and Diogenes are not far to seek. But there is no suggestion that air is also the *Urstoff* or material *archê*.

Bibliography (revised 1981)

The bibliography to the first edition of this book, assembled in 1976, was designed to fulfil two functions: it gave detailed references to the various books and articles cited in the Notes, and it attempted to provide an intelligible and articulated guide to the vast modern literature on the Presocratics. The second aim accounted for the arrangement of the bibliography; the first explained the inclusion of some fairly minor items.

The last five years have seen a steady flow of studies on the Presocratics, many of them of the highest quality. This revised bibliography incorporates a selection from that recent work: the new items have been interpolated at appropriate points, and they are identifiable by the fact that their reference numbers carry a literal suffix (e.g. [181A], [368B]). The additions may, I hope, save the bibliography from premature obsolescence; but I do not pretend to have produced a comprehensive list of new items–nor, indeed, can I even claim to have snouted out all the tastiest truffles.

I use the following abbreviations:

ABG *Archiv für Begriffsgeschichte*
AC *Acta Classica*
AGP *Archiv für Geschichte der Philosophie*
AJP *American Journal of Philology*
An *Analysis*
APQ *American Philosophical Quarterly*
BICS *Bulletin of the Institute of Classical Studies*
BJPS *British Journal for the Philosophy of Science*
CP *Classical Philology*
CQ *Classical Quarterly*
CR *Classical Review*
H *Hermes*

HSCP *Harvard Studies in Classical Philology*
JHI *Journal of the History of Ideas*
JHP *Journal of the History of Philosophy*
JHS *Journal of Hellenic Studies*
JP *Journal of Philosophy*
M *Mind*
MH *Museum Helveticum*
Mnem *Mnemosyne*
NGG *Nachrichten von der Gesellschaft der Wissenschaft zu Göttingen*
PAS *Proceedings of the Aristotelian Society*
PCPS *Proceedings of the Cambridge Philological Society*
Phlg *Philologus*
Phron *Phronesis*
PQ *Philosophical Quarterly*
PR *Philosophical Review*
QSGM *Quellen und Studien zur Geschichte der Mathematik*
RE Pauly-Wissowa's *Realenkyklopädie der klassischen Altertumswissenschaft*
REA *Revue des Études Anciennes*
REG *Revue des Études Grecques*
RhM *Rheinisches Museum*
RM *Review of Metaphysics*
SO *Symbolae Osloenses*
TAPA *Transactions of the American Philological Association*
WS *Wiener Studien*

A: GENERAL

I: Texts

The standard work on the Presocratics, a monument to scholarship and an indispensable aid, is:
[1] H. Diels and W. Kranz: *Die Fragmente der Vorsokratiker* (Berlin, 1960[10])
The fragments, but not the *testimonia*, are Englished in:
[2] K. Freeman: *Ancilla to the Pre-Socratic Philosophers* (Oxford, 1948)
For the poetical Presocratics it is worth consulting:
[3] H. Diels: *Poetarum Philosophorum Fragmenta* (Berlin, 1901)

The doxography is finely discussed, and the main texts printed, in another magisterial work by Diels:
[4] H. Diels: *Doxographi Graeci* (Berlin, 1879)

Editions of texts of individual Presocratics are listed under the appropriate heading in part B of the bibliography; editions of certain other ancient authors are mentioned in the next section, and in Appendix A.

II: Source Criticism

Most scholars accept the reconstruction of the doxographical tradition which Diels established in [4]; but there are some important qualifications in:
[5] P. Steinmetz: *Die Physik des Theophrasts*, Palingenesia I (Bad Homburg, 1964)
and some intemperate disagreements in Gershenson-Greenberg [361].

The historical value of the doxography is a matter of grave dispute. A lengthy denunciation of Aristotle was made in:
[6] H. F. Cherniss: *Aristotle's Criticism of Presocratic Philosophy* (Baltimore, 1935)
and Theophrastus was attacked in similar vein by:

[7] J. B. McDiarmid: 'Theophrastus on the Presocratic Causes', *HSCP* 61, 1953, 85–156 = Furley-Allen [70]
Most books on the Presocratics contain appreciations of the doxography. Against Cherniss see especially:
[8] W. K. C. Guthrie: 'Aristotle as an Historian of Philosophy', *JHS* 77, 1957, 35–41 = Furley-Allen [70]
Guthrie's paper has been examined in turn by:
[9] J. G. Stevenson: 'Aristotle as Historian of Philosophy', *JHS* 94, 1974, 138–43
A wealth of relevant material can be found in the classic commentaries of:
[10] R. D. Hicks: *Aristotle: de Anima* (Cambridge, 1907)
[11] W. D. Ross: *Aristotle's Metaphysics* (Oxford, 1924)
[12] W. D. Ross: *Aristotle's Physics* (Oxford, 1936)
And there is a brilliant paper on a nice detail by:
[13] B. Snell: 'Die Nachrichten über die Lehre des Thales und die Anfänge der griechischen Philosophie- und Literaturgeschichte', *Phlg* 96, 1944, 170–82 = Snell [82] = Classen [72A]
On Theophrastus see Steinmetz [5], and the Introduction to:
[14] G. M. Stratton: *Theophrastus and the Greek Physiological Psychology before Aristotle* (London, 1917)
Plutarch's testimony is analysed by:
[15] R. Westman: *Plutarch gegen Colotes,* Acta Philosophica Fennica VII (Helsinki, 1955)
[16] J. P. Hershbell: 'Plutarch as a Source for Empedocles Re-examined', *AJP* 92, 1971, 156–84
And on Hippolytus consult:
[17] J. P. Hershbell: 'Hippolytus' *Elenchos* as a Source for Empedocles Re-examined', *Phron* 18, 1973, 97–114
The major commentaries on the classical authors frequently shed incidental light on the Presocratics; I have found myself most often helped by:
[18] U. von Wilamowitz-Moellendorf: *Euripides: Herakles* (Berlin, 1895)
[19] T. L. Heath: *The Thirteen Books of Euclid's Elements* (Cambridge, 1926^2)
[20] C. Bailey: *Epicurus* (Oxford, 1926)
[21] C. Bailey: *Lucretius: de Rerum Natura* (Oxford, 1947)
[22] C. W. Chilton: *Diogenes of Oenoanda* (London, 1971)
[23] M. L. West: *Hesiod: Theogony* (Oxford, 1966)
Finally, no one should fail to peruse the opening chapters of:
[24] R. Pfeiffer: *A History of Classical Scholarship*, I (Oxford, 1968)

III: General Histories

English readers will find a treasury of humane scholarship in the first three volumes of:
[25] W. K. C. Guthrie: *A History of Greek Philosophy* (Cambridge, 1962, 1965, 1969)
Zeller's handbook, *Die Philosophie der Griechen,* has undergone several revisions since its first appearance in 1892; the fullest and most recent edition—still incomplete—is:
[26] E. Zeller and R. Mondolfo: *La Filosofia dei Greci nel suo sviluppo storico* (Florence, 1932-)
Philosophers will enjoy the relevant chapters of:
[27] G. W. F. Hegel: *Lectures on the History of Philosophy*, trans. E. S. Haldane and F. H. Simson (London, 1892; first publishing of German text, 1840)
and also:
[28] F. Nietzsche: *Die Philosophie im tragischen Zeitalter der Griechen*, in vol. III of Nietzsche's *Werke*, ed. K. Schlechta (Munich, 1956; first published in 1872)
Of other general accounts of Presocratic thought, the most influential have been:

[29] P. Tannery: *Pour l'histoire de la science Hellène* (Paris, 1887)
[30] K. Reinhardt: *Parmenides und die Geschichte der griechischen Philosophie* (Bonn, 1916)
([30] is, for my money, the most sparkling book in the whole field)
[31] J. Burnet: *Early Greek Philosophy* (London, 1930^4)
[32] H. F. Cherniss: 'Characteristics and Effects of Presocratic Philosophy', *JHI* 12, 1951, 319–45 = Furley-Allen [70] = Cherniss [73A]
There are sober introductions in:
[33] G. S. Kirk and J. E. Raven: *The Presocratic Philosophers* (Cambridge, 1962^4)
[34] E. Hussey: *The Presocratics* (London, 1972)
And a spirited introduction in:
[35] K. R. Popper: 'Back to the Presocratics', *PAS* 59, 1958/9, 1–24 = K. R. Popper: *Conjectures and Refutations* (London, 1969^3) = Furley-Allen [70]
See also:
[36] T. Gomperz: *Greek Thinkers* (London, 1901–12)
[37] F. M. Cleve: *The Giants of Pre-Sophistic Greek Philosophy* (The Hague, 1965)
[38] G. Calogero: *Storia della logica antica* (Bari, 1967)

IV: Monographs

I list here a number of books which bear upon particular aspects of early Greek thought: their titles on the whole are adequate guides to their contents.

[38A] L. Ballew: *Straight and Circular—a Study of Imagery in Greek Philosophy* (Assen, 1979)
[39] J. I. Beare: *Greek Theories of Elementary Cognition* (Oxford, 1906)
[40] F. M. Cornford: *The Laws of Motion in Ancient Thought* (Cambridge, 1931)
[41] F. M. Cornford: *Principium Sapientiae* (Cambridge, 1952)
[42] D. R. Dicks: *Early Greek Astronomy to Aristotle* (London, 1970)
[43] E. R. Dodds: *The Greeks and the Irrational* (Berkeley, Cal., 1951)
[44] H. Fränkel: *Early Greek Poetry and Philosophy*, trans. M. Hadas and J. Willis (Oxford, 1975)
[45] T. L. Heath: *Aristarchus of Samos* (Oxford, 1913)
[46] T. L. Heath: *A History of Greek Mathematics* (Oxford, 1921)
[47] W. W. Jaeger: *Paideia* (Oxford, 1939–45)
[48] W. W. Jaeger: *The Theology of the Early Greek Philosophers* (Oxford, 1947)
[49] W. H. S. Jones: *Philosophy and Medicine in Ancient Greece* (Baltimore, 1946)
[50] G. E. R. Lloyd: *Polarity and Analogy* (Cambridge, 1966)
[51] H. Lloyd-Jones: *The Justice of Zeus* (Berkeley, Cal., 1971)
[52] C. W. Müller: *Gleiches zu Gleichen—ein Prinzip frühgriechischen Denkens* (Wiesbaden, 1965)
[53] S. Sambursky: *The Physical World of the Greeks* (London, 1956)
[54] B. Snell: *Die Ausdrücke für den Begriff des Wissens in der vorplatonischen Philosophie*, Philologische Untersuchungen 29 (Berlin, 1924)
[55] B. Snell: *The Discovery of Mind* (Oxford, 1953)
[55A] B. Snell: *Der Weg zum Denken und zur Wahrheit*, Hypomnemata 57 (Göttingen, 1978)
[56] M. C. Stokes: *One and Many in Presocratic Philosophy* (Washington, DC, 1971)
[57] L. Sweeney: *Infinity in the Presocratics* (The Hague, 1972)
[58] B. L. van der Waerden: *Science Awakening*, trans. A. Dresden (New York, 1961)
[59] M. L. West: *Early Greek Philosophy and the Orient* (Oxford, 1971)
I append to this section a number of articles of a general scope. The first two are seminal pieces:
[60] W. A. Heidel: 'Qualitative Change in Pre-Socratic Philosophy', *AGP* 19, 1906, 333–79 = Mourelatos [72]
[61] W. A. Heidel: 'Περὶ Φύσεως A Study of the Conception of Nature among the Pre-Socratics', *Proceedings of the American Academy of Arts and Sciences* 45, 1910, 77–133

The next article is of wider scope than its title suggests, being a comprehensive account of early notions of cognition:

[62] K. von Fritz: 'Νοῦς, νοεῖν and their Derivatives in Presocratic Philosophy', *CP* 40, 1945, 223–42 and 41, 1946, 12–34 = Mourelatos [72] = Gadamer [71]

With Jones [49], compare:

[63] J. Longrigg: 'Philosophy and Medicine: some early Interactions', *HSCP* 67, 1963, 147–76

With Lloyd [50], compare:

[64] G. E. R. Lloyd: 'Hot and Cold, Dry and Wet, in early Greek Thought', *JHS* 84, 1964, 92–106 = Furley-Allen [70]

With Dicks [42], compare:

[65] D. R. Dicks: 'Solstices, Equinoxes and the Presocratics', *JHS* 86, 1966, 26–40

and the reply by:

[66] C. H. Kahn: 'On Early Greek Astronomy', *JHS* 90, 1970, 99–116

Finally, note the interesting piece on the Derveni papyrus by:

[67] W. Burkert: 'Orpheus und der Vorsokratiker', *Antike und Abendland* 14, 1968, 93–114

V: Anthologies

[68] V. E. Alfieri and M. Untersteiner (eds.): *Studi di Filosofia Greca* (Bari, 1950)

[69] J. P. Anton and G. L. Kustas (eds): *Essays in Ancient Greek Philosophy* (Albany, New York, 1971)

[70] D. J. Furley and R. E. Allen (eds.): *Studies in Presocratic Philosophy* (London, 1970, 1975)

[71] H. G. Gadamer (ed.): *Um die Begriffswelt der Vorsokratiker* (Darmstadt, 1968)

[72] A. P. D. Mourelatos (ed.): *The Presocratics* (Garden City, New York, 1974)

[72A] C. J. Classen (ed.): *Sophistik* (Darmstadt, 1976)

[72B] R. A. Shiner and J. King-Farlow (eds): *New Essays on Plato and the Presocratics, Canadian Journal of Philosophy* suppt 2 (Guelph, 1976)

VI: Collected Papers

[73] J. Bernays: *Gesammelte Abhandlungen* (Berlin, 1885)

[73A] H. Cherniss: *Selected Papers*, L. Tarán (ed.) (Leiden, 1977)

[74] F. M. Cornford: *The Unwritten Philosophy* (Cambridge, 1950)

[75] H. Diller: *Kleine Schriften zur antiken Literatur* (Munich, 1971)

[76] H. Fränkel: *Wege und Formen frühgriechischen Denkens* (Munich, 1960[2])

[77] K. von Fritz: *Grundprobleme der Geschichte der antiken Wissenschaft* (Berlin, 1971)

[78] O. Gigon: *Studien zur antiken Philosophie* (Berlin, 1972)

[79] U. Hölscher: *Anfängliches Fragen* (Göttingen, 1968)

[80] W. Nestle: *Griechische Studien* (Stuttgart, 1948)

[81] K. Reinhardt: *Vermächtnis der Antike* (Göttingen, 1966[2])

[82] B. Snell: *Gesammelte Schriften* (Göttingen, 1966)

[83] F. Solmsen: *Kleine Schriften* (Hildesheim, 1968)

[84] M. Untersteiner: *Scritti Minori* (Brescia, 1971)

VII: Bibliography

There are excellent bibliographies in Guthrie [25], Sweeney [57], and Mourelatos [72]; see also:

[85] G. B. Kerferd: 'Recent Work on Presocratic Philosophy', *APQ* 2, 1965, 130–40.

And of course most of the books and papers I list here contain a multitude of further references.

Bibliographies date quickly. The reader may keep abreast of the tide by consulting *L'Année*

Philologique, Repertoire bibliographique de la Philosophie de Louvain, and *The Philosophers Index*, periodicals which, taken together, catch all the new literature on the subject.

B: PARTICULAR

The second half of this bibliography is divided into sections that correspond to the chapters of the book. Items referred to in one section will often contain material relevant to other sections; and many of the works listed in part *A*—notably Guthrie [25]—will profitably be consulted in connexion with every chapter.

Chapter I

On Thales in general see:
[86] D. R. Dicks: 'Thales', *CQ* n.s. 9, 1959, 294–309
[87] M. L. West: 'Three Presocratic Cosmologies', *CQ* n.s. 13, 1963, 154–76
[88] C. J. Classen: 'Thales', *RE* suppt. 10, 1965, 930–47

Literature on the notion of *psuchê*, on the stability of the earth, and on early cosmogony, is given on later pages (below, pp. 658, 653, 654). On Thales' mathematical achievements see chapter 4 of Heath [46]; and:
[89] B. Gladigow: 'Thales und der διαβήτης', *H* 96, 1968, 264–75
For the sources see the items in part *A*, section II, especially Guthrie [8] and Snell [13].

Chapter II

The classic study of Anaximander's thought is:
[90] C. H. Kahn: *Anaximander and the Origins of Greek Cosmology* (New York, 1960)
(I might observe that Kahn's book is crammed with wise and stimulating thoughts on every aspect of early Greek philosophy.) Out of numerous general studies of Anaximander I pick:
[91] U. Hölscher: 'Anaximander und die Anfänge der Philosophie', *H* 81, 1953, 255–77 and 385–417 = Hölscher [79] = Furley-Allen [70]
[92] G. S. Kirk: 'Some Problems in Anaximander', *CQ* n.s. 5, 1955, 21–38 = Furley-Allen [70]
[93] C. J. Classen: 'Anaximander', *H* 90, 1962, 159–72
[94] C. J. Classen: 'Anaximandros', *RE* suppt. 12, 1970, 30–69

Anaximander's 'Darwinism' is discussed ably by:
[95] J. H. Loenen: 'Was Anaximander an Evolutionist?', *Mnem* s. 4, 7, 1954, 215–32
and it is worth reading:
[96] G. Rudberg: 'Empedokles und Evolution', *Eranos* 49, 1951, 23–30

Anaximander's mathematical astronomy has often been described: see in particular chapter 4 of Tannery [29], and chapter 4 of Heath [45]; and the dispute between Dicks ([65] and [42]) and Kahn ([90] and [66]). See also:
[97] N. Rescher: 'Cosmic Evolution in Anaximander', *Studium Generale* 11, 1958, 718–31 = N. Rescher, *Essays in Philosophical Analysis* (Pittsburgh, Pa., 1969)
And on the stability of the earth:
[98] J. Robinson: 'Anaximander and the Problem of the Earth's Immobility', in Anton-Kustas [69]

The best discussions of the Anaximandrian fragment are in Kahn [90] and in:
[99] H. Schwabl: 'Anaximander—zu den Quellen und seiner Einordnung um vorsokratischen Philosophie', *ABG* 9, 1964, 59–72
See also:
[100] F. Dirlmeier: 'Der Satz des Anaximandros', *RhM* 87, 1938, 376–82 = F. Dirlmeier,

Ausgewählte Schriften (Heidelberg, 1970) = Gadamer [71]
[101] C. H. Kahn: 'Anaximander and the Arguments concerning the ἄπειρον at *Physics* 203b4–15', *Festschrift Ernst Kapp* (Hamburg, 1958)
(Kahn thinks he has discovered a second fragment of Anaximander in the text of the *Physics*.)
[101A] M. C. Stokes: 'Anaximander's Argument', in Shiner-King-Farlow [72B]
There is a full-length study of Anaximander's 'unlimited' principle by:
[102] P. Seligman: *The Apeiron of Anaximander* (London, 1962)
and several useful papers including:
[103] F. Solmsen: 'Anaximander's infinite: traces and influences', *AGP* 44, 1962, 109–31 = Solmsen [83]
[104] H. B. Gottschalk: 'Anaximander's Apeiron', *Phron* 10, 1965, 37–53
[105] P. J. Bicknell: τὸ ἄπειρον, ἄπειρος ἀήρ and τὸ περιέχον', *AC* 9, 1966, 27–48

Chapter III

Less attention has been paid to Anaximenes than to Anaximander. In addition to the general histories, chapter 2 of Stokes [56], and a few studies of detail, I know only:
[106] J. Klowski: 'Ist der Aër des Anaximenes als eine Substanz Konzipiert?', *H* 100, 1972, 131–42
[106A] C. J. Classen: 'Anaximander and Anaximenes: the Earliest Greek Theories of Change?', *Phron* 22, 1977, 89–102
The topic of ancient cosmogonical thought has been far more intensely discussed; the most comprehensive piece is:
[107] H. Schwabl: 'Weltschöpfung', *RE* suppt. 9, 1962, 1433–1589
On Pherecydes see especially West [59], chapters 1–2; and on the tantalizing fragment of Alcman:
[108] M. L. West: 'Alcman and Pythagoras', *CQ* n.s. 17, 1967, 1–15
For Hesiod see West [23], and:
[109] M. C. Stokes: 'Hesiodic and Milesian Cosmogonies', *Phron* 7, 1963, 1–35, and 8, 1963, 1–34
[110] J. Klowski: 'Zum Entstehen der Begriffe Sein und Nichts und der Weltentstehungs- und Weltschöpfungstheorien im strengen Sinne', *AGP* 49, 1967, 121–48 and 225–54
Milesian cosmogony is also discussed in Kahn [90] and in Hölscher [91]; and in a classic paper by:
[111] G. Vlastos: 'Equality and Justice in early Greek cosmologies', *CP* 42, 1947, 156–78 = Furley-Allen [70]
Finally, read:
[112] F. Solmsen: 'Aristotle and Presocratic Cosmogony', *HSCP* 63, 1958, 265–82 = Solmsen [83]
The question of the scientific standing of Presocratic thought has produced a large literature. The best general survey is in Sambursky [53]; and there is an invaluable article by:
[113] G. E. R. Lloyd: 'Experiment in Early Greek Philosophy and Medicine', *PCPS* n.s. 10, 1964, 50–72
F. M. Cornford more than once advanced the extreme view that the Presocratics were not, and did not mean to be, scientists: see Cornford [41], [74], and:
[114] F. M. Cornford: 'Was the Ionian Philosophy Scientific?', *JHS* 62, 1942, 1–7 = Furley-Allen [70]
Against Cornford see especially:
[115] G. Vlastos: review of Cornford [41], *Gnomon* 27, 1955, 65–76 = Furley-Allen [70]
(And compare the dispute between Dicks and Kahn, above, p. 653).
At the other extreme, Sir Karl Popper has lavishly praised Presocratic science: see Popper

[35]. Against Popper:
[116] G. S. Kirk: 'Popper on Science and the Presocratics', *M* 69, 1960, 318–39 = Furley-Allen [70]
[117] G. S. Kirk: 'Sense and Common Sense in the Development of Greek Philosophy', *JHS* 81, 1961, 105–17
See also Popper [151]; and:
[118] G. E. R. Lloyd: 'Popper versus Kirk: a Controversy in the Interpretation of Greek Science', *BJPS* 18, 1967, 21–39
I mention too:
[119] J. Stannard: 'The Presocratic Origin of Explanatory Method', *PQ* 15, 1965, 193–206
And see now the splendid treatment in:
[119A] G. E. R. Lloyd: *Magic, Reason and Experience* (Cambridge, 1979)

Analogy has long been recognized as a characteristic of early Greek thought. See especially Part II of Lloyd [50];
[120] H. Diller: 'ὄψις ἀδήλων τὰ φαινόμενα', *H* 67, 1932, 14–42 = Diller [75]
and:
[121] W. Kranz: 'Gleichnis und Vergleich in der frühgriechischen Philosophie', *H* 73, 1938, 99–122
See also:
[122] H. C. Baldry: 'Embryological Analogies in Presocratic Cosmogony', *CQ* 26, 1932, 27–34
and compare Fränkel [145], and Regenbogen [520].

On Anaximenean details see:
[123] W. K. C. Guthrie: 'Anaximenes and τὸ κρυσταλλοειδές', *CQ* n.s. 6, 1956, 40–4
[124] J. Longrigg: 'κρυσταλλοειδῶς', *CQ* n.s. 15, 1965, 249–52
[125] H. Schwabl: 'Anaximenes und die Gestirne', *WS* 79, 1966, 33–8
[126] J. Longrigg: 'A Note on Anaximenes fragment 2', *Phron* 9, 1964, 1–5
[127] K. Alt: 'Zum Satz des Anaximenes über die Seele—Untersuchung von Aëtius περὶ ἀρχῶν', *H* 101, 1973, 129–64
[128] G. B. Kerferd: 'The Date of Anaximenes', *MH* 11, 1954, 117–21

Chapter IV

The fragments of Heraclitus are best studied in the edition of:
[129] M. Marcovich: *Heraclitus* (Merida, 1967)
That edition can be supplemented by:
[130] S. Mouraviev: 'New Readings of Three Heraclitean Fragments (B 23, B 28, B 26)', *H* 101, 1973, 114–27
[130A] S. N. Mouraviev: 'Heraclitus B 31[b] DK (53[b] Mch): an Improved Reading?', *Phron* 22, 1977, 1–9
All other texts pertaining to Heraclitus are collected and annotated in:
[131] R. Mondolfo and L. Tarán: *Eraclito—testimonianze e imitazione* (Florence, 1972)
For bibliography see:
[132] E. N. Roussos: *Heraklit-Bibliographie* (Darmstadt, 1971)

There are three landmarks in modern Heraclitean studies. First:
[133] J. Bernays: *Heraclitea* (Bonn, 1848) = Bernays [73]
(see also papers II–IV in [73]); second, the work of Karl Reinhardt:
[134] K. Reinhardt: 'Heraclitea', *H* 77, 1942, 225–48 = Reinhardt [81] = Gadamer [71]
[135] K. Reinhardt: 'Heraklits Lehre vom Feuer', *H* 77, 1942, 1–17 = Reinhardt [81]
as well as chapter 3 of Reinhardt [30]; and, third:
[136] G. S. Kirk: *Heraclitus: the Cosmic Fragments* (Cambridge, 1962[2])

The best general account of Heraclitus' thought is perhaps that in Guthrie [25], I, ch. VII. There is a stimulating piece which appears as chapter 3 of volume I of:

[137] K. R. Popper: *The Open Society and its Enemies* (London, 1966⁵)

See also:

[138] G. Vlastos: 'On Heraclitus', *AJP* 76, 1955, 337–66 = Furley-Allen [70]
[139] C. H. Kahn: 'A New Look at Heraclitus', *APQ* 1, 1964, 189–203
[140] M. Marcovich: 'Herakleitos', *RE* suppt. 10, 1965, 246–320
[141] W. J. Verdenius: 'Der Logosbegriff bei Heraklit und Parmenides', *Phron* 11, 1966, 81–99

There is now a comprehensive English edition by:

[141A] C. H. Kahn: *The Art and Thought of Heraclitus* (Cambridge, 1979)

Idiosyncratically French accounts may be read in:

[142] C. Ramnoux: *Héraclite, ou l'homme entre les choses et les mots* (Paris, 1959)
[143] J. Bollack and H. Wismann: *Héraclite ou la Séparation* (Paris, 1972)

See also:

[143A] M. Heidegger and E. Fink: *Heraklit* (Frankfurt am Main, 1970)

The peculiarities of Heraclitus' style have been analysed by:

[144] B. Snell: 'Die Sprache Heraklits', *H* 61, 1926, 353–81 = Snell [82]
[145] H. Fränkel: 'A Thought Pattern in Heraclitus', *AJP* 59, 1938, 309–37 = Fränkel [76] = Mourelatos [72]
[146] B. Snell: 'Heraklits Fragment 10', *H* 76, 1941, 84–7 = Snell [82]

and in Hölscher [79].

On Heraclitean fire see Reinhardt [135] and:

[147] G. S. Kirk: 'Natural Change in Heraclitus', *M* 60, 1951, 35–42 = Mourelatos [72]
[148] W. J. Verdenius: 'Heraclitus' Conception of Fire', in J. Mansfeld and L. M. de Rijk (eds), *Kephalaion: studies in Greek philosophy and its continuation offered to Professor C. J. de Vogel* (Assen, 1975)
[149] H. Jones: 'Heraclitus: Fragment 31', *Phron* 17, 1972, 193–7
[150] R. Mondolfo: 'The evidence of Plato and Aristotle relating to the ekpyrosis in Heraclitus', *Phron* 3, 1958, 75–82
[150A] A. A. Long: 'Heraclitus and Stoicism', *Φιλοσοφία* 5, 1975–6, 133–56

The Theory of Flux is denied to Heraclitus by Reinhardt and by Kirk; it is vindicated for him by Mondolfo-Tarán [131];

[151] K. R. Popper: 'Kirk on Heraclitus, and on Fire as the Cause of Balance', *M* 72, 1963, 386–92 = K. R. Popper, *Conjectures and Refutations* (London, 1969³)
[152] A. Wasserstein: 'Pre-Platonic Literary Evidence for the Flux Theory of Heraclitus', *Atti di XII Congresso Internazionale di Filosofia* (Florence, 1960), 11, 185–91

Wasserstein's brief discussion of the *de victu* can be supplemented by:

[153] R. Joly: *Recherches sur le traité pseudo-hippocratique du Régime* (Paris, 1960)

The Cratylan texts are examined by:

[154] G. S. Kirk: 'The Problem of Cratylus', *AJP* 72, 1951, 225–53
[155] D. J. Allan: 'The Problem of Cratylus', *AJP* 75, 1954, 271–87

Finally, on the Unity of Opposites, see the various works by Reinhardt and Kirk. And also:

[155A] C. J. Emlyn-Jones: 'Heraclitus and the Identity of Opposites', *Phron* 21, 1976 89–114

Items bearing on Heraclitus' moral theories and on his psychology can be found below, pp. 659 and 672.

Chapter V

There is an edition of Xenophanes by:

[156] M. Untersteiner: *Senofane—testimonianze e frammenti* (Florence, 1956)
For general accounts of Xenophanes' thought see chapter 2 of Reinhardt [30], chapter 3 of Stokes [56], and:
[157] K. Deichgräber: 'Xenophanes περὶ φύσεως', *RhM* 87, 1938, 1–31
[158] K. von Fritz: 'Xenophanes', *RE* 9A, 1967, 1541–62
[159] P. Steinmetz: 'Xenophanesstudien', *RhM* 109, 1966, 13–73
And on his Ionian interests see especially:
[160] W. A. Heidel: 'Hecataeus and Xenophanes', *AJP* 64, 1943, 257–77
There is a fine paper on Presocratic theology by:
[161] G. Vlastos: 'Theology and Philosophy in Early Greek Thought', *PQ* 2, 1952, 97–123 = Furley-Allen [70]
and useful material can be found in:
[162] O. Gigon: 'Die Theologie der Vorsokratiker', *Entretiens Hardt* 1, 1954, 127–55 = Gigon [78]
[163] W. Fahr: Θεοὺς νομίζειν', Spudasmata 26 (Hildesheim, 1969)
It is still worth reading:
[164] A. B. Drachmann: *Atheism in Pagan Antiquity* (London, 1922)
For Milesian theology see chapter 2 of Jaeger [48], and:
[165] D. Babut: 'Le Divin et le Dieu dans la pensée d' Anaximandre', *REG* 84, 1972, 1–32
and for Heraclitus see:
[166] H. Fränkel: 'Heraclitus on God and the Phenomenal World', *TAPA* 69, 1938, 230–44 = Fränkel [76]
The atheists of *Laws* X are rooted out by:
[167] J. Tate: 'On Plato: *Laws* X, 889CD', *CQ* 30, 1936, 48–54
[168] W. de Mahieu: 'La doctrine des Athées au Xᵉ livre des Lois de Platon', *Revue belge de philologie et d'histoire* 41, 1963, 5–24, and 42, 1964, 16–47
On Xenophanes' theology see especially chapter 3 of Jaeger [48];
and also:
[169] W. Pötscher: 'Zu Xenophanes frag. 23', *Emerita* 32, 1964, 1–13
[170] G. Calogero: 'Senofane, Eschilo e la prima definizione dell' onnipotenza di dio', in Alfieri-Untersteiner [68]
[171] H. A. T. Reiche: 'Empirical Aspects of Xenophanes' Theology', in Anton-Kustas [69]
[171A] S. M. Darcus: 'The Phren of the Noos in Xenophanes' God', *SO* 53, 1978, 25–39
On the Synonymy Principle (p. 88) see:
[171B] A. C. Lloyd: 'The Principle that the Cause is greater than its Effect', *Phron* 21, 1976, 146–55
Finally, the Epicharman material is all judiciously examined by:
[172] L. Berk: *Epicharmus,* diss. Utrecht (Groningen, 1964)

Chapter VI

The study of Pythagoreanism has been advanced to a new level of sanity and scholarship by:
[173] W. Burkert: *Lore and Science in Ancient Pythagoreanism* (Cambridge, Mass., 1972; first German edition, 1962)
The main problem of interpretation, that of distinguishing early from late doctrine, should be approached with the help of:
[174] H. Thesleff: *An Introduction to the Pythagorean Writings of the Hellenistic Age*, Acta Academiae Aboensis Humaniora XXIV.3 (Åbo, 1961)
[175] H. Thesleff: *The Pythagorean Texts of the Hellenistic Period*, Acta Academiae Aboensis Humaniora XXX.1 (Åbo, 1965)
and see also:
[176] H. Dörrie: 'Der nachklassische Pythagoreismus', *RE* 24, 1963, 268–77

There is an excellent introduction to early Pythagoreanism in:
[177] C. H. Kahn: 'Pythagorean Philosophy before Plato', in Mourelatos [72]
Of other general studies I mention:
[178] J. E. Raven: *Pythagoreans and Eleatics* (Cambridge, 1948)
[179] K. H. Ilting: 'Zur Philosophie der Pythagoreer', *ABG* 9, 1964, 103–31
[180] J. A. Philip: *Pythagoras and Early Pythagoreanism* (Toronto, 1966)
[181] C. J. de Vogel: *Pythagoras and Early Pythagoreanism* (Assen, 1966)
[181A] B. L. van der Waerden: *Die Pythagoreer* (Zurich, 1979)
For Pythagoras himself consult:
[182] J. S. Morrison: 'Pythagoras of Samos', *CQ* n.s. 8, 1958, 198–218
[183] K. von Fritz: 'Pythagoras', *RE* 24, 1963, 171–268
[184] B. L. van der Waerden: 'Pythagoras', *RE* suppt. 10, 1965, 843–64
And see also West [108]
Literature on Pythagorean science is given on p. 669.
On early Greek notions of the *psuchê* or soul see the celebrated study by Dodds [43]; and also:
[185] J. Burnet: 'The Socratic Doctrine of the Soul', *Proceedings of the British Academy* 7, 1915/16, 235–59
[186] D. J. Furley: 'The Early History of the Greek Concept of Soul', *BICS* 3, 1956, 1–18
[187] B. Gladigow: 'Zum Makarismos des Weisen', *H* 95, 1967, 404–33
[187A] D. B. Claus: *Toward the Soul* (New Haven, 1981)
There is a thorough survey of Greek texts on metempsychosis in:
[188] H. S. Long: *A Study of the Doctrine of Metempsychosis in Greece from Pythagoras to Plato* (Princeton, N.J., 1948)
and a wealth of material in:
[189] M. V. Bacigalupo: 'Teriomorfismo e trasmigrazione', *Filosofia* 16, 1965, 267–90
For Plato see:
[190] R. S. Bluck: 'Plato, Pindar and Metempsychosis', *AJP* 79, 1958, 405–14
and for Pindar:
[191] K. von Fritz: 'Ἐστρὶς ἑκατέρωθι in Pindar's Second *Olympian* and Pythagoras' Theory of Metempsychosis', *Phron* 2, 1957, 85–9
[192] D. McGibbon: 'Metempsychosis in Pindar', *Phron* 9, 1964, 5–12
The Empedoclean material is edited and discussed in:
[193] G. Zuntz: *Persephone* (Oxford, 1971)
who draws on the study by:
[194] U. von Wilamowitz-Moellendorf: 'Die Καθαρμοί des Empedokles', *Sitzungsberichte der preussischen Akademie*, 1929, 626–61 = Wilamowitz-Moellendorf, *Kleine Schriften* I (Berlin, 1935)
See also:
[195] O. Skutsch: 'Notes on Metempsychosis', in his *Studia Enniana* (London, 1968)
[196] M. L. West: 'Notes on newly-discovered fragments of Greek authors', *Maia* 20, 1968, 195–205
and pp. 112–27 of:
[196A] H. B. Gottschalk: *Heraclides of Pontus* (Oxford, 1980)
On the phenomenon of shamanism see Dodds [43], chapter 5; and:
[197] J. D. P. Bolton: *Aristeas of Proconnesus* (Oxford, 1962)
And for the *auxanomenos logos*:
[198] J. Bernays: 'Epicharmos und der αὐξανόμενος λόγος', *RhM* 8, 1853, 280–8 = Bernays [73]
Further material is listed on p. 673; and for Empedocles' natural philosophy see p. 666.
There are two long studies of Alcmeon:
[199] J. Wachtler: *De Alcmaeone Crotoniata* (Leipzig, 1896)

[200] L. A. Stella: 'Importanza di Alcmeone nella storia del pensiero greco', *Memorie della Reale Accademia Nazionale dei Lincei,* s.6. VIII.4, 1939, 233–87
On the argument for immortality see:
[201] C. Mugler: 'Alcméon et les cycles physiologiques de Platon', *REG* 71, 1958, 42–50
Plato's version is analysed in:
[202] T. M. Robinson: 'The Argument for Immortality in Plato's *Phaedrus*', in Anton-Kustas [69]
and there are helpful comments in:
[203] R. Hackforth: *Plato's Phaedrus* (Cambridge, 1952)
[204] J. B. Skemp: *The Theory of Motion in Plato's Later Dialogues* (Amsterdam, 1967²)
[205] T. M. Robinson: *Plato's Psychology* (Toronto, 1970)
Further literature on Alcmeon is given on pp. 660 and 673.

Chapter VII

The best introduction to early Greek thought on moral matters is:
[206] K. J. Dover: *Greek Popular Morality in the Time of Plato and Aristotle* (Oxford, 1974)
There is much of value in Dodds [43], Lloyd-Jones [51], and
[207] A. W. H. Adkins: *Merit and Responsibility* (Oxford, 1960)
And it is still worth reading Essay 2 in:
[208] A. Grant: *The Ethics of Aristotle* (Oxford, 1885⁴)

For Empedocles, see the works cited under Chapter VI, especially Zuntz [193].

Heraclitus is exhibited as a moralist in chapters 4–6 of West [59]; and the main fragment on his ethics is discussed by:
[209] H. Blass: *Gott und die Gesetze*, Schriften zur Rechtslehre und Politik 12 (Bonn, 1958)
[210] A. P. D. Mourelatos: 'Heraclitus, fr. 114', *AJP* 86, 1965, 258–66
The intricacies of the concept of *nomos* are unravelled by:
[211] M. Ostwald: *Nomos and the Beginnings of the Athenian Democracy* (Oxford, 1969)
and there is further material in Vlastos [111] and Popper [137]

On some matters of detail see:
[212] H. Fränkel: 'Heraclitus on the Notion of a Generation', *AJP* 59, 1938, 89–91 = Fränkel [76]
[213] G. S. Kirk: 'Heraclitus and Death in Battle (fr. 24 D)', *AJP* 70, 1949, 384–93
[214] M. L. West: 'A pseudo-fragment of Heraclitus', *CR* n.s. 18, 1968, 257–9

Chapter VIII

On the popular origins of scepticism see chapter 7 of Snell [55]. Xenophanes' epistemology is discussed in the studies listed under Chapter V, and in a fine piece by:
[215] H. Fränkel: 'Xenophanesstudien', *H* 60, 1925, 174–92 = Fränkel [76] = Mourelatos [72]
Fränkel is supported by:
[216] A. Rivier: 'Remarques sur les fragments 34 et 35 de Xénophane', *Revue de Philosophie* 30, 1956, 37–61
and ably criticized by:
[217] E. Heitsch: 'Das Wissen des Xenophanes', *RhM* 109, 1966, 193–235
[217A] J. H. Lesher: 'Xenophanes' Scepticism', *Phron* 23, 1978, 1–21
[217B] J. H. Lesher: 'Perceiving and Knowing in the *Iliad* and *Odyssey*', *Phron* 26, 1981, 2–24

The Hippocratic treatise *On Ancient Medicine* is edited by:
[218] A. J. Festugière: *Hippocrate: L' Ancienne Médicine* (Paris, 1948)
and it is discussed in Jones [49].

To the literature on Heraclitus given under Chapter IV I add two pieces on minor topics:
[219] K. Reinhardt: 'Κοπίδων Ἀρχηγός', *H* 63, 1928, 107–10 = Reinhardt [81]
[220] G. S. Kirk: 'The Michigan Alcidamas Papyrus; Heraclitus Fr. 56 D; The Riddle of the Lice', *CQ* 44, 1950, 149–67
The theory of the *Phaedo* was attributed to Alcmeon by:
[221] R. Hirzel: 'Zur Philosophie des Alkmäon', *H* 11, 1876, 240–6
See also:
[222] D. Lanza: 'L' ἐγκέφαλος e la dottrina anassagorea della conoscenza', *Maia* 16, 1964, 71–8
[223] D. Lanza: 'Un nuovo frammento di Alcmeone', *Maia* 17, 1965, 278–80

Chapter IX

The best edition of the fragments of Parmenides is still:
[224] H. Diels: *Parmenides' Lehrgedicht* (Berlin, 1897)
More recent editions include:
[225] M. Untersteiner: *Parmenide—testimonianze e frammenti* (Florence, 1958)
[226] L. Tarán: *Parmenides* (Princeton, N.J., 1965)
[227] U. Hölscher: *Parmenides: Vom Wesen des Seiendes* (Frankfurt am Main, 1969)
Further suggestions of an editorial nature can be found in:
[228] P. J. Bicknell: 'A New Arrangement of Some Parmenidean Verses', *SO* 42, 1968, 44–50
[229] P. J. Bicknell: 'Parmenides, fragment 10', *H* 98, 1968, 629–31
There are three classic studies of Parmenides: that in Reinhardt [30]; and:
[230] H. Fränkel: 'Parmenidesstudien', *NGG* 1930, 153–92 = Fränkel [76] = Furley-Allen [70]
[231] F. M. Cornford: *Plato and Parmenides* (London, 1939)
Comprehensive accounts of Parmenides' thought can also be found in:
[232] G. Calogero: *Studi sull' Eleatismo* (Rome, 1932)
[233] W. J. Verdenius: *Parmenides* (Groningen, 1942)
[234] A. H. Coxon: 'The Philosophy of Parmenides', *CQ* 28, 1934, 134–44
[235] W. Bröcker: 'Parmenides', *ABG* 9, 1964, 79–86
[236] U. Hölscher: 'Parmenides', in Hölscher [79]
[237] A. P. D. Mourelatos: *The Route of Parmenides* (New Haven, Conn., 1970)
See also chapter 5 of Stokes [56], and the heterodox views of:
[238] J. H. M. M. Loenen: *Parmenides, Melissus, Gorgias* (Assen, 1959)
And see:
[238A] K. Bormann: *Parmenides* (Hamburg, 1971)
[238B] J. Jantzen: *Parmenides zum Verhältnis von Sprache und Wirklichkeit*, Zetemata 63 (Munich, 1976)
[238C] E. Heitsch: 'Parmenides', *Gymnasium* 84, 1977, 1–18
[238D] *Parmenides Studies Today*, *The Monist* 62, Jan 1979
[238E] C. H. Kahn: review of Tarán [226], *Gnomon* 40, 1968, 123–53
[238F] L. Tarán: review of Mourelatos [237], *Gnomon* 48, 1977, 651–66
[238G] A. Graeser: 'Vier Bücher zur Eleatik' (reviews of Mourelatos [237], Heitsch [249], Bormann [238A], Newiger [264A]), *Göttingische Gelehrter Anzeiger* 230, 1978, 37–69
On the prologue to Parmenides' poem see:
[239] C. M. Bowra: 'The Proem of Parmenides', *CP* 32, 1937, 97–112
[240] W. Burkert: 'Das Proömium des Parmenides und die Katabasis des Pythagoras', *Phron* 14, 1969, 1–30
[241] D. J. Furley: 'Notes on Parmenides', in E. N. Lee, A. P. D. Mourelatos and R. Rorty

(eds), *Exegesis and Argument: Studies in Greek Philosophy presented to Gregory Vlastos, Phron* suppt. 1, 1973
[241A] J. Owens: 'Knowledge and *Katabasis* in Parmenides', *Monist* [238D]
The best discussion of the relation between the Way of Truth and the Way of Opinion is that in chapter 1 of Reinhardt [30]; see also:
[242] F. M. Cornford: 'Parmenides' Two Ways', *CQ* 27, 1933, 97–111
[243] H. Schwabl: 'Sein und Doxa bei Parmenides', *WS* 66, 1953, 50–75 = Gadamer [71]
[244] G. E. L. Owen: 'Eleatic Questions', *CQ* n.s. 10, 1960, 84–102 = Furley-Allen [70]
And compare:
[245] A. P. D. Mourelatos: 'The Real, Appearances and Human Error in Early Greek Philosophy', *RM* 19, 1965, 346–65
[245A] T. Calvo: 'Truth and Doxa in Parmenides', *AGP* 59, 1977, 245–60
[245B] F. D. Miller: 'Parmenides on Mortal Belief', *JHP* 15, 1977, 253–65
[245C] W. Bröcker: 'Parmenides' ἀλήθεια', *H* 106, 1978, 504–5
On the content of the Way of Opinion consult, e.g., Popper [35]; and
[246] J. S. Morrison: 'Parmenides and Er', *JHS* 75, 1955, 59–69
[247] A. A. Long: 'The Principles of Parmenides' Cosmogony', *Phron* 8, 1963, 90–107 = Furley-Allen [70]
The argument about the Three Roads is brilliantly analysed by Owen [244], who is criticized by:
[248] S. Tugwell: 'The Way of Truth', *CQ* n.s. 14, 1964, 36–41
See also:
[249] E. Heitsch: *Gegenwart und Evidenz bei Parmenides*, Abhandlungen der Akademie der Wissenschaft und Literatur (Mainz, 1970)
and the interesting paper by:
[250] G. E. M. Anscombe: 'Parmenides, Mystery and Contradiction', *PAS* 69, 1968/9, 125–32
Also:
[250A] T. M. Robinson: 'Parmenides on the Ascertainment of the Real', *Canadian Journal of Philosophy* 4, 1975, 623–33
[250B] R. Bosley: 'Monistic Argumentation', in Shiner-King-Farlow [72B]
[250C] A. Graeser: 'Parmenides über Sagen und Denken', *MH* 34, 1977, 145–55
[250D] J. Klowski: 'Parmenides' Grundlegung seiner Seinslehre B 2–7 (Diels-Kranz)', *RhM* 120, 1977, 97–137
On Parmenides' conception of *nous* or thought see Snell [54], von Fritz [62], and:
[251] A. P. D. Mourelatos: 'φράζω and its derivatives in Parmenides', *CP* 60, 1965, 261–2
The 'veridical' interpretation of *einai* is advanced in several papers by Charles Kahn:
[252] C. H. Kahn: 'The Greek Verb "to be" and the Concept of Being', *Foundations of Language* 2, 1966, 245–65
[253] C. H. Kahn: 'The Thesis of Parmenides', *RM* 22, 1968/9, 700–24
[254] C. H. Kahn: 'More on Parmenides', *RM* 23, 1969/70, 333–40
[255] C. H. Kahn: *The Verb* Be *in Ancient Greek* (Dordrecht, 1973)
[255A] C. H. Kahn: 'Why Existence does not Emerge as a Distinct Concept in Greek Philosophy', *AGP* 58, 1976, 323–34
And see Mourelatos [237]. Kahn is criticized by:
[256] E. Tugendhat: 'Das Sein und das Nichts', in *Durchblicke: Festschrift für Martin Heidegger zum 80. Geburtstag* (Frankfurt am Main, 1970)
[256A] E. Tugendhat: review of Kahn [255], *Philosophische Rundschau* 24, 1977, 161–76
[256B] U. Hölscher: *Der Sinn von Sein in der älteren Griechischen Philosophie*, Sitzber. Heidelberg. Ak. Wiss., phil.-hist. Kl. 1976. 3 (Heidelberg, 1976)
A 'fused' account of *einai* is propounded in:

[257] M. Furth: 'Elements of Eleatic Ontology', *JHP* 6, 1968, 111–32 = Mourelatos [72] and criticized by:
[258] B. Jones: 'Parmenides' "The Way of Truth" ', *JHP* 11, 1973, 287–98
See also:
[259] W. J. Verdenius: 'Parmenides B 2.3', *Mnem* s.4, 15, 1962, 237
[259A] A. P. D. Mourelatos: 'Determinacy and Indeterminacy, Being and Non-Being, in the Fragments of Parmenides', in Shiner-King-Farlow [72B]
[259B] D. Gallop: ' "Is" or "Is not"?', *Monist* [238D]
[259C] A. P. D. Mourelatos: 'Some Alternatives in Interpreting Parmenides', *Monist* [238D]
For Gorgias' treatise *Concerning What is Not* see, besides Calogero [232] and Leonen [238]:
[260] W. Nestle: 'Die Schrift des Gorgias "Ueber die Natur oder über das Nichtseiende" ', *H* 57, 1922, 551–62 = Nestle [80]
[261] O. Gigon: 'Gorgias' "Ueber das Nichtsein" ', *H* 71, 1936, 186–213 = Gigon [78]
[262] W. Bröcker: 'Gorgias contra Parmenides', *H* 86, 1958, 425–40
[263] G. B. Kerferd: 'Gorgias on Nature or that which is not', *Phron* 1, 1955, 3–25
[264] J. M. Robinson: 'On Gorgias', in E. N. Lee, A. P. D. Mourelatos and R. Rorty (eds), *Exegesis and Argument: Studies in Greek Philosophy presented to Gregory Vlastos, Phron* suppt 1, 1973
[264A] H. J. Newiger: *Untersuchungen zu Gorgias' Schrift Über das Nichtseiende* (Berlin, 1973)

Chapter X

There are general accounts of Parmenides' metaphysical deduction in most of the major studies cited under Chapter IX; see also:
[265] A. H. Basson: ' "The Way of Truth" ', *PAS* 61, 1960/1, 73–86
And on Parmenides' 'circular' logic consult:
[266] G. J. Jameson: ' "Well-rounded Truth" and Circular Thought in Parmenides', *Phron* 3, 1958, 15–30
[267] L. Ballew: 'Straight and Circular in Parmenides and the *Timaeus', Phron* 19, 1974, 189–209
The problems raised by Parmenides' prospectus in B 8.3–5 are discussed by, e.g., Owen [244], Schofield [275], and:
[268] J. R. Wilson: 'Parmenides, B 8.4', *CQ* 2 n.s. 20, 1970, 32–5
Melissus has been less well served than his master; but there is a first-rate edition:
[269] G. Reale: *Melisso—testimonianze e frammenti* (Florence, 1970)
and useful chapters in Calogero [232] and Loenen [238]. On Melissus' importance see:
[270] J. Jouanna: 'Rapports entre Mélissos de Samos et Diogène d'Apollonie, à la lumière du traité hippocratique de natura hominis', *REA* 67, 1965, 306–23
[271] J. Klowski: 'Antwortete Leukipp Melissos oder Melissos Leukipp?', *MH* 28, 1971, 65–71
Studies devoted to Parmenides' arguments against generation and destruction include:
[272] C. M. Stough: 'Parmenides' Way of Truth, B 8.12–3', *Phron* 13, 1968, 91–108
[273] J. Wiesner: 'Die Negation der Entstehung des Seienden', *AGP* 52, 1970, 1–35
And Eleatic views on time are discussed by:
[274] G. E. L. Owen: 'Plato and Parmenides on the Timeless Present', *Monist* 50, 1966, 317–40 = Mourelatos [72]
[275] M. Schofield: 'Did Parmenides discover Eternity?', *AGP* 52, 1970, 113–35
[276] J. Whittaker: *God, Time and Being*, *SO* suppt. 23, 1971
[276A] P. B. Manchester: 'Parmenides and the Need for Eternity', *Monist* [238D]
[276B] T. M. Robinson: 'Parmenides on the Real in its Totality', *Monist* [238D]
[276C] L. Tarán: 'Perpetual Duration and Atemporal Eternity in Parmenides', *Monist* [238D]

See also:
[277] W. C. Kneale: 'Time and Eternity in Theology', *PAS* 61, 1960/1, 87–109
And on Melissus B 2:
[278] W. J. Verdenius: 'Notes on the Presocratics VII', *Mnem* s.4, 1, 1948, 8–10

Chapter XI

The interpretation of Parmenides' ball or 'sphere' has much engaged scholars; for a selection of views see Coxon [234], Owen [244], and
[279] G. Rudberg: 'Zur vorsokratischen Abstraktion', *Eranos* 52, 1954, 131–8
[280] J. Mansfeld: 'Σφαιρῆς ἐναλίγκιον ὄγκῳ', *Akten des XIV Internationales Kongress für Philosophie* (Vienna, 1970), 5, 414–9
[281] J. Bollack and H. Wismann: 'Le moment théorique (Parménide fr. 8.42–9)', *Revue des sciences humaines* 39, 1974, 203–12
Eleatic monism has, surprisingly, been less discussed; in addition to the commentaries I note only:
[282] F. Solmsen: *The 'Eleatic One' in Melissus,* Mededelingen der koninklijke nederlandse akademie van wetenschappen 32.8 (The Hague, 1969)
[282A] J. Barnes: 'Parmenides and the Eleatic One', *AGP* 61, 1979, 1–21
(But on Parmenides B 8.34–41 see also:
[283] L. Woodbury: 'Parmenides on Names', *HSCP* 63, 1958, 145–60 = Anton-Kustas [69])
Fragment B 4 of Parmenides is scrutinized by:
[284] J. Bollack: 'Sur deux fragments de Parménide (4 et 16)', *REG* 70, 1957, 56–71
And the Parmenidean attack on motion is discussed in:
[285] M. C. Stokes and G. S. Kirk: 'Parmenides' Refutation of Motion', *Phron* 5, 1960, 1–22
[286] P. J. Bicknell: 'Parmenides' Refutation of Motion and an Implication', *Phron* 12, 1967, 1–6
See also:
[287] A. H. Coxon: 'The Manuscript Tradition of Simplicius' Commentary on Aristotle's *Physics* i–iv', *CQ* n.s. 18, 1968, 70–5
Finally, on the solidity or corporeality of Melissus' being see:
[288] H. Gomperz: 'ἀσώματος', *H* 67, 1932, 155–67
[289] G. Vlastos: review of Raven [178], *Gnomon* 25, 1953, 29–35 = Furley-Allen [70]
[290] N. B. Booth: 'Did Melissus believe in incorporeal being?', *AJP* 79, 1958, 61–5
[291] M. Untersteiner: 'Un aspetto dell' Essere melissiano', *Rivista critica di storia della filosofia* 8, 1953, 597–606 = Untersteiner [84]
[291A] R. Renehan: 'On the Greek Origins of the Concepts Incorporeality and Immateriality', *Greek Roman and Byzantine Studies* 21, 1980, 105–38

Chapter XII

The texts bearing upon Zeno have been edited by:
[292] H. D. P. Lee: *Zeno of Elea* (Cambridge, 1936)
[293] M. Untersteiner: *Zenone—testimonianze e frammenti* (Florence, 1963)
See also:
[294] J. Dillon: 'New Evidence on Zeno of Elea?', *AGP* 56, 1974, 127–31
[294A] J. Dillon: 'More Evidence on Zeno of Elea?', *AGP* 58, 1976, 221–2
The history of Zenonian scholarship is recounted in:
[295] F. Cajori: 'The History of Zeno's Arguments on Motion', *American Mathematical Monthly* 22, 1915, 1–6, 38–47, 77–82, 109–115, 143–9, 179–86, 215–20, 253–8, 292–7
And there is an anthology (with an excellent bibliography) by:
[296] W. C. Salmon (ed.): *Zeno's Paradoxes* (Indianapolis, Ind., 1970)

For a lucid introduction to Zeno and his problems see:
[297] G. Vlastos: 'Zeno of Elea', in P. Edwards (ed.), *Encyclopaedia of Philosophy* (New York, 1967)
Compare:
[298] K. von Fritz: 'Zenon von Elea', *RE* 10 A, 1972, 53–83
It is a pleasure to read:
[299] P. Bayle: 'Zeno of Elea', in his *Historical and Critical Dictionary*, trans. R. H. Popkin (Indianapolic, Ind., 1965)
See also, on a minor matter:
[300] J. Longrigg: 'Zeno's Cosmology?', *CR* n.s. 22, 1972, 170–1
The crucial passage from the *Parmenides* has recently been thrice examined:
[301] F. Solmsen: 'The Tradition about Zeno of Elea Re-examined', *Phron* 16, 1971, 116–41 = Mourelatos [72]
[302] K. von Fritz: 'Zeno of Elea in Plato's *Parmenides*', in J. L. Heller and J. K. Newman (eds), *Studia Turyniana* (Urbana, Ill., 1974)
[303] G. Vlastos: 'Plato's Testimony concerning Zeno of Elea', *JHS* 95, 1975, 136–63
On the aim of Zeno's paradoxes see:
[304] N. B. Booth: 'Were Zeno's Arguments a reply to attacks upon Parmenides?', *Phron* 3, 1957, 1–9
[305] N. B. Booth: 'Were Zeno's arguments directed against the Pythagoreans?'. *Phron* 3, 1957, 90–103
[306] N. B. Booth: 'Zeno's Paradoxes', *JHS* 78, 1957, 189–201
On the architecture of the paradoxes see especially:
[307] G. E. L. Owen: 'Zeno and the Mathematicians', *PAS* 58, 1957/8, 199–222 = Salmon [296] = Furley-Allen [70]
Owen's thesis is rejected by Stokes [56], chapter 7, and by Furley [387], chapter 5.
Discussion of the paradox of 'large and small' was put on a sound scholarly footing by:
[308] H. Fränkel: 'Zeno of Elea's Attacks on Plurality', *AJP* 63, 1938, 1–25 and 193–206 = Fränkel [76] = Gadamer [71] = Furley-Allen [70]
For further discussion see Owen [307], Furley [387], chapter 5; and:
[309] G. Vlastos: 'A Zenonian Argument against Plurality', in Anton-Kustas [69]
[310] W. E. Abraham: 'The Nature of Zeno's Argument against Plurality', *Phron* 17, 1972, 40–53
[310A] W. J. Prior: 'Zeno's First Argument Concerning Plurality', *AGP* 60, 1978, 247–56
[310B] N. B. Booth: 'Two Points of Interpretation in Zeno', *JHS* 98, 1978, 157–8
[310C] S. Peterson: 'Zeno's Second Argument Against Plurality', *JHP* 16, 1978, 261–70
On the issue of geometrically indivisible magnitudes see:
[311] R. Heinze: *Xenokrates* (Leipzig, 1892)
[312] A. T. Nicol: 'Indivisible Lines', *CQ* 30, 1936, 120–6
and the papers listed on p. 668.
Since Russell's persuasive advertisements modern philosophers have taken Zeno seriously. The most sophisticated and exhaustive modern treatment is:
[313] A. Grünbaum: *Modern Science and Zeno's Paradoxes* (London, 1968) = (in part) Salmon [296]
See also the Introduction to Salmon [296] and:
[314] A. P. Ushenko: 'Zeno's Paradoxes', *M* 55, 1946, 151–65
[315] H. N. Lee: 'Are Zeno's Paradoxes Based on a Mistake?', *M* 74, 1965, 563–70
[315A] R. Ferber: *Zenons Paradoxien der Bewegung und die Struktur von Raum und Zeit*, Zetemata 76 (Munich, 1981)

Chapter XIII

Bertrand Russell more than once gave crisp accounts of Zeno's four paradoxes of motion; see:
[316] B. Russell: *The Principles of Mathematics* (London, 1903), chapters 42–3
[317] B. Russell: *Mysticism and Logic* (London, 1917), chapter 5
[318] B. Russell: *Our Knowledge of the External World* (London, 1956^2) chapter 6 = Salmon [296]
Russell was influenced by the brilliant assessment in chapter 10 of Tannery [29], on which see also:
[319] F. Cajori: 'The Purpose of Zeno's Arguments on Motion', *Isis* 3, 1920/1, 7–20
Philosophers will enjoy chapter 4 of:
[320] H. Bergson: *Creative Evolution* (London, 1964) = Salmon [296]
And Grünbaum [313] again has much of value to say.

The best scholarly study of the first two paradoxes, the Dichotomy and the Achilles, is:
[321] G. Vlastos: 'Zeno's Race Course', *JHP* 4, 1966, 96–108 = Furley-Allen [70]

And on all four paradoxes the notes in Ross [12] are invaluable; on Aristotle's interpretation of Zeno see also:
[322] D. Bostock: 'Aristotle, Zeno and the Potential Infinite', *PAS* 73, 1972/3, 37–53
[322A] J. Immerwahr: 'An Interpretation of Zeno's Stadium Paradox', *Phron* 23, 1978, 22–6

There are numerous modern attempts to grapple with the complex issues that Zeno raises:
[323] C. D. Broad: 'Note on Achilles and the Tortoise', M 22, 1913, 318–19
[324] W. V. Metcalf: 'Achilles and the Tortoise', *M* 51, 1942, 89–90
[325] G. Ryle: *Dilemmas* (Cambridge, 1954), chapter 3
[326] M. Black: 'Achilles and the Tortoise', *An* 11, 1950/1, 91–101 = M. Black, *Problems of Analysis* (London, 1954)
[327] M. Black: 'Is Achilles still Running?', in M. Black, *Problems of Analysis* (London, 1954)
[328] J. O. Wisdom: 'Achilles on a Physical Racecourse', *An* 12, 1951/2, 67–73 = Salmon [296]
[329] R. Taylor: 'Mr Black on Temporal Paradoxes', *An* 12, 1951/2, 38–44
[330] J. Watling: 'The Sum of an Infinite Series', *An* 13, 1952/3, 39–46
[331] J. Thomson: 'Tasks and Supertasks', *An* 15, 1954/5, 1–13 = Salmon [296]
[332] P. Benacerraf: 'Tasks, Supertasks and the Modern Eleatics', *JP* 59, 1962, 765–84 = Salmon [296]
[333] J. Thomson: 'Comments on Professor Benacerraf's Paper', in Salmon [296]
[334] C. S. Chihara: 'On the Possibility of Completing an Infinite Process', *PR* 74, 1965, 74–87
[334A] R. Sorabji: 'Aristotle on the Instant of Change', *PAS* suppt 50, 1976, 69–89

On the third paradox, the Arrow, see especially:
[335] G. Vlastos: 'A Note on Zeno's Arrow', *Phron* 11, 1966, 3–18 = Furley-Allen [70]
[335A] F. R. Pickering: 'Aristotle on Zeno and the Now', *Phron* 23, 1978, 253–7
[335B] J. Lear: 'A Note on Zeno's Arrow', *Phron* 26, 1981, 91–104
Among modern studies I mention:
[336] P. E. B. Jourdain: 'The Flying Arrow—an Anachronism', *M* 25, 1916, 42–55
[337] L. Greenberg: 'A Note on the Arrow in Flight', *PR* 59, 1950, 541–2
[338] M. Black: 'The Paradox of the Flying Arrow', in M. Black, *Problems of Analysis* (London, 1954)
[339] V. C. Chappell: 'Time and Zeno's Arrow', *JP* 49, 1962, 197–213

Finally, for detailed analysis of the Stadium see:
[340] R. K. Gaye: 'On Aristotle *Physics* Z ix, 239b33–240a18', *Journal of Philology* 31, 1910, 95–116
[341] P. J. Bicknell: 'The Fourth Paradox of Zeno', *AC* 4, 1961, 39–46
[342] P. J. Bicknell: 'Zeno's Arguments on Motion', *AC* 6, 1963, 81–105

And on Diodorus' Zenonian arguments:
[342A] D. Sedley: 'Diodorus Cronus and Hellenistic Philosophy', *PCPS* 23, 1977, 74–120

Chapter XIV

For literature relevant to this chapter see the general studies under Chapter IX, and the items on post-Eleatic epistemology under Chapter XXIV.

Chapter XV

Neo-Ionian history and chronology are discussed in all the General Histories; see also:
[343] A. E. Taylor: 'On the Date of the Trial of Anaxagoras', *CQ* 11, 1917, 81–7
[344] J. A. Davison: 'Protagoras, Democritus and Anaxagoras', *CQ* n.s. 3, 1953, 33–45
[345] E. Derenne: *Les Procès d'Impiété intentés aux philosophes à Athènes au Vme et au IVme siècles avant J. C.* (Liège, 1930)
[346] J. Ferguson: 'On the Date of Democritus', *SO* 40, 1965, 17–26
[347] H. de Ley: 'Democritus and Leucippus: two notes on ancient Atomism', *L'Antiquité classique* 37, 1968, 620–33
[348] D. O'Brien: 'The Relation of Anaxagoras and Empedocles', *JHS* 88, 1968, 93–114
[348A] J. Mansfeld: 'The Chronology of Anaxagoras' Athenian Period and the Date of his Trial', *Mnem* s.4, 32, 1979, 39–69; 33, 1980, 17–95

For Anaxagoras, the Atomists and Philolaus see the bibliographies to Chapters XVI–XVIII.

The most recent edition of Empedocles' poem *Concerning Nature* is:
[349] J. Bollack: *Empédocle* (Paris, 1965–9)
The classic study is:
[350] E. Bignone: *Empedocle* (Turin, 1916)
And there is a full-scale treatment in:
[351] D. O'Brien: *Empedocles' Cosmic Cycle* (Cambridge, 1969)
See also:
[352] C. E. Millerd: *On the Interpretation of Empedocles* (Chicago, 1908)
[352A] N. van der Ben: *The Proem of Empedocles'* Peri Phuseôs (Amsterdam, 1975)
[352B] M. R. Wright: *Empedocles—the Extant Fragments* (New Haven, 1981)
[352C] D. O'Brien: *Pour interpréter Empédocle* (Paris, 1981)

The orthodox account of the cosmic cycle is stated at length in Bignone [349] and O'Brien [351], and more concisely by:
[353] D. O'Brien: 'Empedocles' Cosmic Cycle', *CQ* n.s. 17, 1967, 29–40
For various heterodoxies see Bollack [349]; and also
[354] E. Minar: 'Cosmic Periods in the Philosophy of Empedocles', *Phron* 8, 1963, 127–45 = Anton-Kustas [69]
[355] F. Solmsen: 'Love and Strife in Empedocles' Cosmology', *Phron* 10, 1965, 109–48 = Furley-Allen [70]
[356] U. Hölscher: 'Weltzeiten und Lebenzyklus', *H* 93, 1965, 7–33 = Hölscher [79]
[357] J. Mansfeld: 'Ambiguity in Empedocles B 17.3–5', *Phron* 17, 1972, 17–40
There is a judicious survey by:
[358] A. A. Long: 'Empedocles' Cosmic Cycle in the 'Sixties', in Mourelatos [72]

Finally, on Empedoclean atomism see Reinhardt [491], and:
[359] J. Longrigg: 'Roots', *CR* n.s. 17, 1967, 1–5

Chapter XVI

There is an edition of Anaxagorean texts by:
[360] D. Lanza: *Anassagora—testimonianze e frammenti* (Florence, 1966)

and the Greek is Englished in:
[361] D. E. Gershenson and D. A. Greenberg: *Anaxagoras and the Birth of Physica* (New York, 1964)
On textual matters see also:
[362] H. Fränkel: review of Ciurnelli, *La Filosofia di Anassagora*, *CP* 45, 1950, 187–91 = Fränkel [76]
[363] A. Wasserstein: 'A note on fragment 12 of Anaxagoras', *CR* n.s. 10, 1960, 4–6
There are comprehensive papers on Anaxagoras' thought by:
[364] O. Gigon: 'Zu Anaxagoras', *Phlg* 91, 1936, 1–41 = Gigon [78]
[365] M. C. Stokes: 'On Anaxagoras', *AGP* 47, 1965, 1–19 and 217–50
See also:
[366] M. E. Reesor: 'The Meaning of Anaxagoras', *CP* 55, 1960, 1–8
[367] M. E. Reesor: 'The Problem of Anaxagoras', *CP* 58, 1963, 29–33 = Anton-Kustas [69]
[368] D. Bargrave-Weaver: 'The Cosmogony of Anaxagoras', *Phron* 4, 1959, 77–91
[368A] D. J. Furley: 'Anaxagoras in Response to Parmenides', in Shiner-King-Farlow [72B]
[368B] M. Schofield: *An Essay on Anaxagoras* (Cambridge, 1980)
The problem of Anaxagoras' ontology has aroused a massive literature: see the Appendix to Bailey [383]; and:
[369] F. M. Cornford: 'Anaxagoras' Theory of Matter', *CQ* 24, 1930, 14–30 and 83–95
[370] I. R. Mathewson: 'Aristotle and Anaxagoras: An Examination of F. M. Cornford's Interpretation', *CQ* n.s. 8, 1958, 67–81
[371] A. L. Peck: 'Anaxagoras: Predication as a Problem in Physics', *CQ* 25, 1931, 27–37 and 112–20
[372] G. Vlastos: 'The Physical Theory of Anaxagoras', *PR* 59, 1950, 31–57 = Furley-Allen [70] = Mourelatos [72]
[373] J. E. Raven: 'The Basis of Anaxagoras' Cosmology', *CQ* n.s. 4, 1954, 123–37
[374] C. Strang, 'The Physical Theory of Anaxagoras', *AGP* 45, 1963, 101–18 = Furley-Allen [70]
[375] W. Schwabe: 'Welches sind die materiellen Elemente bei Anaxagoras?', *Phron* 20, 1975, 1–10
On homoiomeries in particular see:
[376] A. L. Peck: 'Anaxagoras and the Parts', *CQ* 20, 1926, 57–62
[377] D. Lanza: 'Le Omeomerie nella tradizione dossografica Anassagorea', *Parole del Passato* 18, 1963, 256–93
But the clearest and the best paper on the whole topic is:
[378] G. B. Kerferd: 'Anaxagoras and the Concept of Matter before Aristotle', *Bulletin of the John Rylands Library* 52, 1969, 129–43 = Mourelatos [72]
And see now:
[378A] W. E. Mann: 'Anaxagoras and the *homoiomerê*', *Phron* 25, 1980, 228–49
The biological slant of Anaxagoras' thought has often been remarked upon; see Vlastos [372], Müller [52], Longrigg [63];
[379] P. Kucharski: 'Anaxagore et les idées biologiques de son siècle', *Revue philosophique de la France et de l'Étranger* 89, 1964, 137–66
[379A] J. Mansfeld: 'Anaxagoras' Other World', *Phron* 25, 1980, 1–4
Finally note the detailed study of **B 10** by:
[380] M. Schofield: 'Doxographica Anaxagorea', *H* 103, 1975, 1–24
On *nous* see under Chapter XIX below.

Chapter XVII

Atomist texts have been edited (with a Russian commentary which may be of more use to some readers than it is to me) in:

[381] S. Luria: *Demokrit* (Leningrad, 1970)

On the vocabulary and style of Atomism see:

[382] K. von Fritz: *Philosophie und sprachlicher Ausdruck bei Demokrit, Platon und Aristoteles* (New York, n.d.)

There are general surveys of atomism by:

[383] C. Bailey: *The Greek Atomists and Epicurus* (Oxford, 1928)

[384] V. E. Alfieri: *Atomos Idea* (Florence, 1953)

[385] H. Steckel: 'Demokritos', *RE* suppt 12, 1970, 191–223

See also chapter 5 of Sambursky [53]; and:

[386] H. Langerbeck: *Δόξις ἐπιρυσμίη*, Neue Philologische Untersuchungen 10 (Berlin, 1935)

[387] D. J. Furley: *Two Studies in the Greek Atomists* (Princeton, NJ, 1967) = (in part) Mourelatos [72]

And it is still worth reading:

[388] K. Marx: *The difference between the Democritean and the Epicurean Philosophy of Nature*, in K. Marx and F. Engels, *Collected Works*, I (London, 1975)

On Abderite cosmology see:

[389] J. Kerschensteiner: 'Zu Leukippos A 1', *H* 87, 1959, 444–8

On the historical continuity of the philosophy of atomism see especially:

[390] M. Capek: *The Philosophical Impact of Contemporary Physics* (Princeton, NJ, 1961)

There is fascinating historical matter in:

[391] A. van Melsen: *From Atomos to Atom* (Pittsburgh, Pa., 1952)

[392] D. M. Knight: *Atoms and Elements* (London, 1967)

[393] R. H. Kargon: *Atomism in England from Hariot to Newton* (Oxford, 1966)

And read the essay by an eminent modern physicist:

[394] W. Heisenberg: *Natural Law and the Structure of Matter* (London, 1970)

Atomic motions are discussed by:

[395] J. B. McDiarmid: 'Phantoms in Democritean Terminology: *περιπάλαξις* and *περιπαλάσσεσθαι*', *H* 86, 1958, 291–8

[396] S. Sambursky: 'A Democritean Metaphor in Plato's Kratylos', *Phron* 4, 1959, 1–4

[397] J. Bollack: 'Deux figures principales de l' atomisme d' après Aristote: l' entrecroisement des atomes et la sphère du feu', in I. Düring (ed.), *Naturphilosophie bei Aristoteles und Theophrast* (Heidelberg 1969)

[397A] D. O'Brien: 'Heavy and Light in Democritus and Aristotle: two conceptions of change and identity', *JHS* 97, 1977, 64–74

[397B] D. O'Brien: 'L'atomisme ancien: la pesanteur et le mouvement des atomes chez Démocrite', *Revue philosophique de la France et de l'Etranger* 169, 1979, 401–26

The issue of theoretical indivisibility is subtly treated by:

[398] S. Luria: 'Die Infinitesimaltheorie der antiken Atomisten', *QSGM* B 2, 1932, 106–85

and the discussion was advanced by:

[399] J. Mau: *Zum Problem des Infinitesimalen bei den antiken Atomisten* (Berlin, 1954)

and by Furley [387], and:

[400] D. J. Furley: 'Aristotle and the Atomists on Infinity', in I. Düring (ed.), *Naturphilosophie bei Aristoteles und Theophrast* (Heidelberg, 1969)

See also Heinze [311], Nicol [312];

[401] G. Vlastos: 'Minimal Parts in Epicurean Atomism', *Isis* 56, 1965, 121–47

[402] J. Mau: 'Was there a Special Epicurean Mathematics?', in E. N. Lee, A. P. D. Mourelatos and R. Rorty (eds), *Exegesis and Argument: Studies in Greek Philosophy presented to Gregory Vlastos*, *Phron* suppt 1, 1973

[403] D. E. Hahm: 'Chrysippus' Solution to the Democritean Dilemma of the Cone', *Isis* 63, 1972, 205–20

[403A] D. Sedley: 'Epicurus and the Mathematicians of Cyzicus', *Cronache Ercolanesi* 6, 1976, 23-54

Finally, for a special study of one Abderite account of a sensible quality see:

[404] J. B. McDiarmid: 'Theophrastus *de Sensibus* 66: Democritus' Explanation of Salinity', *AJP* 80, 1959, 56-66

[404A] M. Okál: 'Le sens des expressions utilisées par Démocrite pour désigner les goûts', *Listy Filologické* 92, 1969, 208-22

[404B] R. W. Baldes: 'Democritus on the Nature and Perception of "black" and "white" ', *Phron* 23, 1978, 87-100

Later pages give reading on the Atomists' account of explanation (see Chapter XIX), of anthropology (XX), of the soul (XXII), of morals (XXIII) and of knowledge (XXIV).

Chapter XVIII

Of the scientific achievements—or alleged achievements—of the Pythagoreans by far the best account is that in Burkert [173]. There is also much of value in Heath [45], chapters 6 and 12; in Heath [46]. chapter 5; in van der Waerden [58], and in:

[405] F. M. Cornford: 'Mysticism and Science in the Pythagorean Tradition', *CQ* 16, 1922, 137-50 and 17, 1923, 1-12 = (in part) Mourelatos [72]

[406] W. A. Heidel: 'The Pythagoreans and Greek Mathematics', *AJP* 61, 1940, 1-33 = Furley-Allen [70]

[407] K. von Fritz: 'The Discovery of Incommensurability by Hippasus of Metapontum', *Annals of Mathematics* 46, 1945, 242-64 = von Fritz [77] = Furley-Allen [70]

[408] B. L. van der Waerden: 'Pythagoreische Wissenschaft', *RE* 24, 1963, 277-300

There is a clear account of 'number philosophy' in chapter 5 of volume I of Guthrie [25], a somewhat credulous account in Raven [178], and a hard-headed account in Burkert [173]. See also:

[409] A. Delatte: *Études sur la littérature pythagoricienne* (Paris, 1915)

[410] A. J. Festugière: 'Les mémoires pythagoriques cités par Alexandre Polyhistor', *REG* 58, 1945, 1-65

On Philolaus see, again, Burkert [173]; and also de Vogel [181], Kahn [177], and:

[411] K. von Fritz: 'Philolaus', *RE* suppt. 13, 1973, 453-84

[412] A. Burns: 'The Fragments of Philolaus', *Classica et Mediaevalia* 25, 1964, 93-128

[413] J. A. Philip: 'Aristotle's Source for Pythagorean Doctrine', *Phoenix* 17, 1963, 251-65

[413A] W. Hübner: 'Die geometrische Theologie des Philolaus', *Phlg* 124, 1980, 18-32

[413B] M. C. Nussbaum: 'Eleatic Conventionalism and Philolaus on the Conditions of Thought', *HSCP* 83, 1979, 63-108

Chapter XIX

Most of the literature relevant to this Chapter has already been cited under Chapters XV-XVI

On the central and fascinating notion of *antiperistasis* I know of no special literature; but the minor matter of Empedocles' account of the clepsydra has been massively studied. See e.g.:

[414] H. Last: 'Empedocles and his Clepsydra Again', *CQ* 18, 1924, 169-74

[415] D. J. Furley: 'Empedocles and the Clepsydra', *JHS* 77, 1957, 31-5

[416] N. B. Booth: 'Empedocles' Account of Breathing', *JHS* 80, 1960, 10-16

[417] D. O'Brien: 'The Effect of a Simile: Empedocles' theories of seeing and breathing', *JHS* 90, 1970, 140-80

The void, and motion therein, has been scarcely better treated than *antiperistasis*. See:

[418] A. C. Moorhouse: '*Δέν*' in Classical Greek', *CQ* n.s. 12, 1962, 235-8

[419] W. I. Matson: 'Democritus, fragment 156', *CQ* n.s. 13, 1963, 26-30

[420] D. McGibbon: 'The Atomists and Melissus', *Mnem* s.4, 17, 1964, 248–55.
And consult Klowski [272] and Jouanna [270].

The standard piece on Anaxagoras' *nous* is:
[421] K. von Fritz: 'Der νοῦς des Anaxagoras', *ABG* 9, 1964, 87–102 = von Fritz [77]
See also:
[421A] D. Babut: 'Anaxagore jugé par Socrate et Platon', *RÉG* 91, 1978, 44–76
On the textual problem of B 14 see:
[422] D. Sider: 'Anaxagoras Fr 14 DK', *H* 102, 1974, 365–7
[423] M. Marcovich: 'Anaxagoras B 14 DK', *H* 104, 1976, 240–1

The Atomists' notion of causation, and their adherence to the Principle of Causality, are discussed by:
[424] J. Klowski: 'Die historische Ursprung des Kausalprinzips', *AGP* 48, 1966, 225–66
And the role of chance and necessity in Abderite physics is examined in:
[425] L. Edmunds: 'Necessity, Chance and Freedom in the Early Atomists', *Phoenix* 26, 1972, 342–57

Chapter XX

I have already listed items that bear upon the neo-Ionian accounts of explanation, locomotion, alteration, and generation. On Empedoclean ontology I may add:
[426] F. Solmsen: 'Eternal and Temporal Beings in Empedocles' Physical Poem', *AGP* 57, 1955, 123–45
[426A] N. van den Ben: 'Empedocles' fragments 8, 9, 10 DK', *Phron* 23, 1978, 197–215

For Ion of Chios see:
[427] A. von Blumenthal: *Ion von Chios: die Reste seiner Werke* (Stuttgart, 1939)
[428] F. Jacoby: 'Some Remarks on Ion of Chios', *CQ* 41, 1947, 1–17
[429] G. Huxley: 'Ion of Chios', *Greek, Roman and Byzantine Studies* 6, 1965, 29–46

Chapter XXI

Texts bearing upon the Sophists have been edited by:
[430] M. Untersteiner: *Sofisti—testimonianze e frammenti* (Florence, 1949–62)
And they are translated in:
[431] R. K. Sprague: *The Older Sophists* (Columbia, SC, 1972)

The most celebrated account of the sophistic movement is the one in Chapter 67 of volume 7 of:
[432] G. Grote: *A History of Greece* (London, 1888)
There are two full-length studies, each somewhat bizarre in its general conclusions:
[433] H. Gomperz: *Sophistik und Rhetorik* (Leipzig, 1912)
[434] M. Untersteiner: *The Sophists*, trans, K. Freeman (Oxford, 1954)
There is an expanded version of [434]:
[435] M. Untersteiner: *I Sofisti* (Milan, 1967²)
For a full and sober description of the Sophists consult the second half of volume III of Guthrie [25]; and see the notes by:
[436] G. B. Kerferd: 'The First Greek Sophists', *CR* 64, 1950, 8–10
[437] E. L. Harrison: 'Was Gorgias a Sophist?' *Phoenix* 18, 1964, 183–92
See also:
[437A] F. Solmsen: *Intellectual Experiments of the Greek Enlightenment* (Princeton, 1975)

On Protagoras in general see:
[438] K. von Fritz: 'Protagoras', *RE* 23, 1957, 908–23
And on his attitude to the gods:

[439] T. Gomperz: 'Das Götterbruchstück des Protagoras', *WS* 32, 1910, 4–6
[440] C. W. Müller: 'Protagoras über die Götter', *H* 95, 1967, 140–59 = Classen [72A]
[441] C. W. Chilton: 'An Epicurean View of Protagoras', *Phron* 7, 1962, 105–9
There is much excellent matter on early anthropology:
[442] E. Norden: *Agnostos Theos* (Leipzig, 1913)
[443] W. von Uxkull-Gyllenband: *Griechische Kulturentstehungslehre* (Berlin, 1924)
[444] A. Kleingünther: Πρῶτος Εὑρετής, *Phlg* suppt. 26, 1933
[445] F. Heinimann: *Nomos und Phusis* (Basle, 1945)
[446] L. Edelstein: *The Idea of Progress in Classical Antiquity* (Baltimore, 1967)
[447] E. R. Dodds: *The Ancient Concept of Progress* (Oxford, 1973)
Democritus' views on the origins of man and the growth of civilization are expansively analysed in:
[448] T. Cole: *Democritus and the Sources of Greek Anthropology*, Philological Monographs 25 (n.p., 1967)
And on Protagoras see the notes in:
[449] C. C. W. Taylor: *Plato: Protagoras* (Oxford, 1976)
The special issue of the Diodoran anthropology has aroused passionate controversy; the most interesting items are:
[450] K. Reinhardt: 'Hekataios von Abdera und Demokrit', *H* 47, 1912, 492–513 = Reinhardt [81]
[451] G. Vlastos: 'On the Pre-History of Diodorus', *AJP* 67, 1946, 51–9
[452] W. Spoerri: *Späthellenistische Berichte über Welt, Kultur und Götter* (Basle, 1959)
[453] W. Spoerri: 'Zu Diodor von Sizilien I. 7–8', *MH* 18, 1961, 63–82
[454] A. Burton: *Diodorus Siculus, Book I* (Leiden, 1972)
On Critias there is a rare but good book by:
[455] D. Stephens: *Critias, his Life and Literary Remains* (Cincinnati, Ohio, 1939)
and a useful article by:
[456] A. Battegazzore: 'Influssi e polemiche nel fr (DK) 25 di Crizia', *Dioniso* 21, 1958, 45–58
[456A] A. Dihle: 'Das Satyrspiele "Sisyphos" ', *H* 105, 1977, 28–42
[456B] D. Sutton: 'Critias and Atheism', *CQ* n.s. 31, 1981, 33–8
The texts bearing on Diagoras of Melos are splendidly edited by:
[457] F. Jacoby: *Diagoras ὁ Ἄθεος*, Abhandlungen der Akademie der Wissenschaften, Berlin, 3, 1959
And Diagoran problems are discussed by:
[458] L. Woodbury: 'Diagoras of Melos', *Phoenix* 19, 1965, 178–213
On Euripides' theology there are two informative studies by Wilhelm Nestle:
[459] W. Nestle: *Euripides der Dichter der griechischen Erklärung* (Stuttgart, 1901)
[460] W. Nestle: *Untersuchungen über die philosophischen Quellen des Euripides, Phlg* suppt. 8, 1900
Some reading on ancient atheism has already been given under Chapter V: see especially Drachmann [164], Fahr [163], and de Mahieu [168].
Finally, on Democritus' attitude to the gods see:
[461] V. E. Alfieri: 'Il concetto del divino in Democrito e in Epicuro', in Alfieri-Untersteiner [68]
[462] D. McGibbon: 'The Religious Thought of Democritus', *H* 93, 1965, 385–97
[463] H. Eisenberger: 'Demokrits Vorstellung vom Sein und Wirken der Götter', *Rhm* 113, 1970, 141–58
[463A] A. Henrichs: 'Two Doxographical Notes: Democritus and Prodicus on Religion', *HSCP* 79, 1975, 93–123
And, on a related issue:
[464] P. J. Bicknell: 'Democritus' Theory of Precognition', *REG* 82, 1969, 318–26

The linguistic studies of the Sophists are the subject of a delightful paper by Hermann Diels:

[465] H. Diels: 'Die Anfänge der Philologie bei den Griechen', *Neue Jahrbuch für Philologie* 25, 1910, 1–25

More recent papers include:

[466] C. J. Classen: 'The Study of Language among Socrates' Contemporaries', *Proceedings of the African Classical Association* 2, 1959, 33–49 = Classen [72A]

[467] D. Fehling: 'Zwei Untersuchungen zur griechischen Sprachphilosophie', *RhM* 108, 1965, 212–29 = Classen [72A]

[468] W. Burkert: 'La genèse des choses et des mots', *Les études philosophiques* 1970, 443–55

And see also the early pages of Pfeiffer [24].

On Prodicus' invention of 'semantics' there are some helpful remarks in Taylor [449], and a monograph by:

[469] H. Mayer: *Prodikos von Keos und die Anfänge der Synonymik bei den Griechen* (Paderborn, 1913)

See also:

[470] K. von Fritz: 'Prodikos', *RE* 23, 1957, 85–9

Early rhetorical fragments are collected and edited in:

[471] L. Radermacher: *Artium Scriptores*, Sitzungsberichte der österreichische Akademie der Wissenschaft, 227, 1951

Under Chapter IX I listed some items touching on Gorgias' metaphysics, or antimetaphysics; his *Helen* is admirably edited by:

[472] O. Immisch: *Gorgiae Helena* (Berlin, 1927)

On the aesthetic theory of *apatê* see especially:

[473] M. Pohlenz: 'Die Anfänge der griechischer Poetik', *NGG* 1920, 142–78

Compare:

[474] T. G. Rosenmeyer: 'Gorgias, Aeschylus and ἀπάτη', *AJP* 76, 1955, 225–60

[475] C. P. Segal: 'Gorgias and the Psychology of the Logos', *HSCP* 66, 1962, 99–156

Finally, on Democritus B 26, on meaning, see:

[476] R. Philippson: 'Platons Kratylos und Demokrit', *Philologische Wochenschrift* 49, 1929, 923–7

Chapter XXII

Some bibliography on Presocratic psychology has already been given under Chapter VI; and the book by Beare [39] is uniformly informative.

There is a fine paper on Heraclitus by:

[477] M. C. Nussbaum: 'Ψυχή in Heraclitus', *Phron* 17, 1972, 1–16 and 153–70

On two points of detail see:

[478] W. J. Verdenius: 'A Psychological Statement of Heraclitus', *Mnem* s. 3, 11, 1943, 115–21

[479] S. Tugwell: 'Heraclitus: fragment 98 (DK)', *CQ* n.s. 21, 1971, 32

Democritus' theory of perception is discussed by:

[480] R. W. Baldes: 'Democritus on Visual Perception: Two Theories or One?', *Phron* 20, 1975, 93–105

[481] K. von Fritz: 'Democritus' Theory of Vision', in E. A. Underwood (ed.). *Science, Medicine and History* (Oxford, 1953) = von Fritz [77]

[481A] I. Avotins: 'Alexander of Aphrodisias on Vision in the Atomists', *CQ* n.s. 30, 1980, 429–54

[481B] M. M. Sassi: *Le teorie della percezione in Democrito* (Florence, 1978)

And on Democritean thought see:

[482] P. J. Bicknell: 'The Seat of the Mind in Democritus', *Eranos* 66, 1968, 10–23

[482A] L. Couloubaritsis: 'Considérations sur la notion de Νοῦς chez Démocrite', *AGP* 62, 1980, 129–45

Alcmeon, Empedocles and Parmenides may be taken together. On their physiological psychology see:

[483] F. Solmsen: 'Greek Philosophy and the Discovery of the Nerves', *MH* 18, 1961, 150–97 = Solmsen [83]

[484] J. Mansfeld: 'Alcmaeon: "Physikos" or Physician? With some remarks on Calcidius' "On Vision" compared to Galen, Plac, Hipp. Plat. VII', in J. Mansfeld and L. M. de Rijk (eds), *Kephalaion: Studies in Greek Philosophy and its continuation offered to Professor C. J. de Vogel* (Assen, 1975)

[485] W. J. Verdenius: 'Empedocles' Doctrine of Sight', in *Studia Carolo Guglielmo Vollgraff Oblata* (Amsterdam, 1948)

—but consult O'Brien [417]. On Empedocles B 110 see in particular:

[486] H. Schwabl: 'Empedokles Fr B 110', *WS* 69, 1956, 49–56

And on Parmenides B 16:

[487] G. Vlastos: 'Parmenides' Theory of Knowledge', *TAPA* 77, 1946, 66–77

[488] J. A. Philip: 'Parmenides' Theory of Knowledge', *Phoenix* 12, 1958, 63–6

[489] J. P. Hershbell: 'Parmenides' Way of Truth and B 16', *Apeiron* 4, 1970, 1–23.

And also Bollack [284].

For literature on Philolaus see above, under Chapter XVIII. The *harmonia* theory of the soul is discussed by:

[490] H. B. Gottschalk: 'Soul as Harmonia', *Phron* 16, 1971, 179–98

The commentaries of Hicks [10] and Bailey [21] contain remarks on the objections to the theory put forward by Aristotle and by Lucretius; see too Gladigow [187] and Gomperz [288].

Empedocles' intellectual schizophrenia has been widely discussed:

[491] K. Reinhardt: 'Empedokles, Orphiker und Physiker', *CP* 45, 1950, 170–9 = Reinhardt [81] = Gadamer [71]

[492] H. S. Long: 'The Unity of Empedocles' Thought', *AJP* 70, 1949, 142–58

[493] C. H. Kahn: 'Religion and Natural Philosophy in Empedocles' Doctrine of the Soul', *AGP* 42, 1960, 3–35 = Anton-Kustas [69] = Mourelatos [72]

[494] A. A. Long: 'Thinking and Sense-Perception in Empedocles: Mysticism or Materialism?', *CQ* n.s. 16, 1966, 256–76

[494A] F. Solmsen: 'Empedocles' Hymn to Apollo', *Phron* 25, 1980, 219–27

[494B] D. Babut: 'Sur l'unité de la pensée d'Empédocle', *Phlg* 120, 1976, 139–64

See also Wilamowitz-Moellendorf [194], and chapter 8 of Jaeger [48].

Empedocles' theology and 'demonology' are treated in several of the studies I have just listed; in addition see:

[495] M. Detienne: 'La "Démonologie" d' Empédocle', *REG* 72, 1959, 1–17

[495A] S. M. Darcus: 'Daimon parallels the holy *phrên* in Empedocles', *Phron* 22, 1977, 175–90

The accounts of the Cosmic Cycle catalogued on p. 666 will contain matter touching on the theory of Eternal Recurrence; for more detailed studies see:

[496] B. L. van der Waerden: 'Das Grosse Jahr und die ewige Wiederkehr', *H* 80, 1952, 129–55

[497] M. Capek: 'The theory of Eternal Recurrence in Modern Philosophy of Science', *JP* 57, 1960, 289–96

[498] M. Capek: 'Eternal Return', in P. Edwards (ed.), *Encyclopaedia of Philosophy* (New York, 1967)

[498A] J. Barnes: 'La doctrine du retour éternel', in J. Brunschwig (ed.), *Les stoiciens et leur logique* (Paris, 1978)

Chapter XXIII

Various studies in early Greek ethical theory have been given under Chapter VII: in particular, see Dover [206], Adkins [207], and Grant [208]. Chapter 6 of Lloyd-Jones [51] is useful too.

On Antiphon's personal problems see:

[499] J. Stenzel: 'Antiphon', *RE* suppt 4, 1924, 33–43

[500] J. S. Morrison: 'Antiphon', *PCPS* n.s. 7, 1961, 49–58

[501] S. Luria: 'Antiphon der Sophist', *Eos* 53, 1963, 63–7 = Classen [72A]

Antiphon's moral—or amoral—doctrines are examined by:

[502] G. B. Kerferd: 'The Moral and Political Doctrines of Antiphon the Sophist', *PCPS* n.s. 4, 1956/7, 26–32

[503] J. S. Morrison: 'The *Truth* of Antiphon', *Phron* 8, 1963, 35–49 = Classen [72A]

[504] C. Moulton: 'Antiphon the Sophist, *On Truth*', *TAPA* 103, 1972, 329–66

[504A] M. Gagarin: 'The Prohibition of Just and Unjust Homicide in Antiphon's *Tetralogies*', *Greek, Roman and Byzantine Studies* 19, 1978, 291–306

[504B] T. J. Saunders: 'Antiphon the Sophist on Natural Laws (B 44 DK)', *PAS* 78, 1977/8, 215–36

And a connexion between Antiphon and Democritus is discerned by:

[505] C. Moulton: 'Antiphon the Sophist and Democritus', *MH* 31, 1974, 129–39

On the alleged moral relativism of Prodicus see:

[506] G. B. Kerferd: 'The "Relativism" of Prodicus', *Bulletin of the John Rylands Library* 37, 1954, 249–56

On the moral relativism of Protagoras see:

[507] S. Moser and G. L. Kustas: 'A Comment on the "Relativism" of the *Protagoras*', *Phoenix* 20, 1966, 111–15

and refer to the general literature on Protagorean relativism cited under Chapter XXIV.

Out of various articles on the *Dissoi Logoi* I select:

[508] C. Trieber: 'Die Διαλέξεις', *H* 27, 1892, 210–48

[509] W. Kranz: 'Vorsokratisches IV', *H* 72, 1937, 223–32 = Classen [72A]

[510] A. E. Taylor: 'The *Dissoi Logoi*', in his *Varia Socratica* (Oxford, 1911)

[511] A. Levi: 'On Twofold Statements', *AJP* 61, 1940, 292–306

There is an edition of the tract in Untersteiner [430], and a translation in Sprague [431]; and see now the comprehensive edition by:

[511A] T. M. Robinson: *Contrasting Arguments—an edition of the Dissoi Logoi* (New York, 1979)

There are helpful remarks on Gorgias' account of responsibility in Immisch [472]; and it is worth consulting the relevant pages of Adkins [207]. See also:

[512] G. Calogero: 'Gorgias and the Socratic Principle *Nemo sua sponte peccat*', *JHS* 77, 1957, 12–17 = Anton-Kustas [69] = Classen [72A]

Democritean ethics are treated in Bailey [383], and in Langerbeck [386]; and there is a classic paper by:

[513] G. Vlastos: 'Ethics and Physics in Democritus', *PR* 54, 1945, 578–92 and 55, 1946, 53–64 = Furley-Allen [70]

and a monograph by:

[514] S. Luria: *Zur Frage der materialistischen Begründung der Ethik bei Demokrit* (Berlin, 1964)

See also:

[515] D. McGibbon: 'Pleasure as the "Criterion" in Democritus', *Phron* 5, 1960, 75–7

[516] S. Luria: 'Heraklit und Demokrit', *Das Altertum* 9, 1963, 195–200

[517] C. C. W. Taylor: 'Pleasure, Knowledge and Sensation in Democritus', *Phron* 12, 1967, 6–27

[517A] R. Müller: 'Naturphilosophie und Ethik im antiken Atomismus', *Phlg* 124, 1980, 1–17
And on Democritus' political viewpoint:
[518] G. J. D. Aalders: 'The Political Faith of Democritus', *Mnem* s.4, 3, 1950, 302–13
[519] A. J. Cole: 'The Anonymus Iamblichi', *HSCP* 65, 1961, 127–63

Chapter XXIV

Anaxagoras' 'methodology', *opsis adêlôn*, is treated in two classic papers: Diller [120] and:
[520] O. Regenbogen: 'Eine Forschungsmethode antiker Naturwissenschaft', *QSGM* B 2, 1930, 131–82
See also:
[521] H. Gomperz: 'ὄψις τῶν ἀδήλων τὰ φαινόμενα', *H* 68, 1933, 341–3
and Lloyd [50], part II.
On Protagoras' slogan, 'Man the Measure', consult:
[522] L. Versenyi: 'Protagoras' Man-Measure Fragment', *AJP* 83, 1962, 178–84 = Classen [72A]
[523] D. K. Glidden: 'Protagorean Relativism and the Cyrenaics', *APQ* monograph 9, 1975
[524] D. K. Glidden: 'Protagorean Relativism and Physis', *Phron* 20, 1975, 209–27
The reliability of Plato's report of Protagoras' views is discussed in:
[525] G. B. Kerferd: 'Plato's Account of the Relativism of Protagoras', *Durham University Journal* n.s. 11, 1949/50, 20–6
[526] J. McDowell: *Plato: Theaetetus* (Oxford, 1973)
[527] J. P. Maguire: 'Protagoras or Plato?', *Phron* 18, 1973, 115–39
On the 'new fragment' of Protagoras see:
[528] M. Gronewald: 'Ein neues Protagoras-Fragment', *Zeitschrift für Papyrologie und Epigraphik* 2, 1968, 1–2
[529] J. Mejer: 'The Alleged New Fragment of Protagoras', *H* 100, 1972, 175–8 = Classen [72A]
On the Impossibility of Contradiction consult:
[530] G. Binder and L. Lieseborghs: 'Eine Zuweisung der Sentenz οὐκ ἔστιν ἀντιλέγειν an Prodikos von Keos', *MH* 23, 1966, 37–43 = Classen [72A]
And on the *peritropê* or 'about-turn' see:
[531] M. F. Burnyeat: 'Protagoras and Self-Refutation in Later Greek Philosophy', *PR* 85, 1976, 44–69
[532] M. F. Burnyeat: 'Protagoras and Self-Refutation in Plato's *Theaetetus*', *PR* 85, 1976, 172–95
The Democritean *Ou Mallon* Principle is treated in:
[533] S. Luria: 'Zwei Demokrit-Studien', in J. Mau and E. G. Schmidt (eds), *Isonomia* (Berlin, 1964)
[534] C. Diano: 'Mallon Hetton e Isonomia', in J. Mau and E. G. Schmidt (eds.), *Isonomia* (Berlin, 1964)
[535] P. de Lacey: 'οὐ μᾶλλον and the Antecedents of Ancient Scepticism', *Phron* 3, 1958, 59–71
[536] P. de Lacey: 'Colotes' First Criticism of Democritus', in J. Mau and E. G. Schmidt (eds), *Isonomia* (Berlin, 1964)
Democritus' epistemology is discussed in the general studies of his thought. See in particular Langerbeck [386], and the criticisms in:
[537] E. Kapp: review of Langerbeck [386], *Gnomon* 12, 1936, 65–77 and 158–69 = E. Kapp, *Ausgewählte Schriften* (Berlin, 1968)

See also:
[538] H. Weiss: 'Democritus' Theory of Cognition', *CQ* 32, 1938, 47–56
[539] H. de Ley: '*Δόξις ἐπιρυσμ*—a critical note on Democritus Fr. 7', *H* 97, 1969, 497–8

Chapter XXV

Diogenes of Apollonia has not excited the scholars. But he is given a decent place in history by Jouanna [207] and by:
[540] H. Diller: 'Die philosophiegeschichtliche Stellung des Diogenes von Apollonia', *H* 76, 1941, 359–81 = Diller [75]
And his teleology is debated in Chapter 9 of Jaeger [48], and by:
[541] W. Theiler: *Zur Geschichte der teleologischen Naturbetrachtung bis auf Aristoteles* (Zurich, 1925)
[542] F. Huffmeier: 'Teleologische Weltbetrachtung bei Diogenes von Apollonia?', *Phlg* 107, 1963, 131–8

Indexes

Prepared by Beth Crabb and Larry Schrenk

(i) *Passages*

(ii) *Persons*

(iii) *Topics*

Concordance

Barnes	Diels-Kranz
1	**11 A 1**
2	**11 A 22**
3	**11 A 12**
4	**11 A 14**
5	**11 A 20**
6	**12 A 10**
7	**12 A 30**
8	**12 A 27**
9	**21 A 33**
10	**12 A 26**
11	**12 A 11**
12	**50 A 1**
13	**12 A 9 + B 1**
14	**12 A 15**
15	**12 A 16**
16	**12 A 15**
17	**12 A 1**
18	**13 B 3**
19	**13 A 7**
20	**21 B 29**
21	**21 B 33**
22	(Hippolytus, *ref haer* I.2)
23	**12 A 10**
24	**13 A 5**
25	**13 B 1**
26	**13 B 2**
27	**13 A 7**
28	**13 A 12**
29	**13 A 14**
30	**13 A 15**
31	**13 A 17**
32	(see Diels-Kranz, I.488.30–5)
33	**22 B 1**
34	**22 B 10**
35	**22 B 50**
36	**22 B 51**
37	**22 B 80**
38	**22 B 30**
39	**22 B 90**
40	**22 B 31**
41	**22 A 5**
42	**22 A 6**
43	**22 B 12**
44	**22 B 49a**
45	**22 B 91**
46	**22 B 125**
47	**22 B 126**
48	**65 A 4**
49	(see Diels-Kranz, I.491.39–42)
50	**22 B 88**
51	**22 B 57**
52	**22 B 61**
53	**23 B 5**
54	**22 B 26**
55	**22 B 60**
56	**22 B 103**
57	**22 B 59**
58	**22 B 15**
59	**22 B 123**
60	**22 B 54**

Barnes	Diels-Kranz
61	22 B 56
62	21 B 26
63	21 B 14
64	21 A 12
65	21 A 28
66	23 B 1
67	21 B 23.1
68	21 A 28
69	21 A 31
70	21 A 32
71	21 C 1
72	21 B 23.2
73	21 B 15
74	21 B 24
75	21 B 25
76	21 B 11
77	(Plato, *Laws* 967A)
78	21 B 32
79	11 A 1
80	11 A 22
81	13 A 10
82	21 A 30
83	21 A 35
84	14 A 8a
85	14 A 1
86	31 B 117
87	21 B 7
88	23 B 2
89	14 A 8
90	(Diodorus, X.6.2)
91	(Ovid, *Metam* XV.158–64)
92	11 A 1
93	24 B 2
94	24 A 12
95	(Eusebius, *PE* XI.28.9)
96	24 A 1
97	24 A 12
98	(Plato, *Phaedrus* 245C–246A)
99	31 B 135
100	31 B 115.3–6
101	31 B 137
102	31 B 136
103	22 B 5b
104	22 B 53
105	22 B 25
106	22 B 96
107	22 B 64
108	22 B 41
109	22 B 52
110	(Hesiod, *Works and Days* 276–85)
111	22 B 94
112	22 B 102
113	22 B 114 + B 2
114	22 B 44
115	22 B 16
116	22 B 28
117	22 B 17
118	22 B 112
119	24 B 1
120	21 B 34
121	(Hippocrates, *vet med* § 1)
122	21 B 18
123	21 B 36
124	21 B 35
125	21 B 16
126	21 B 38
127	(Hippocrates, *vet med* § 9)
128	22 B 17
129	22 B 104
130	22 B 111
131	22 B 79
132	22 B 78
133	22 B 45
134	22 B 28
135	22 B 101a
136	22 B 101
137	22 B 40
138	22 B 129
139	22 B 55
140	22 B 7
141	22 B 35
142	22 B 107
143	24 A 11
144	24 A 5
145	28 B 1.28–31
146	28 B 8.50–2
147	28 B 8.60–1
148	28 B 2
149	28 B 3
150	28 B 6
151	28 B 7.1–2
152	90 A 5
153	28 B 7.3–6

Barnes	Diels-Kranz
154	**82 B 3**.77–82
155	**28 B 5**
156	**28 B 8**.1–51
157	**82 B 3**.66–76
158	**30 B 1**
159	**30 B 2**
160	**30 B 3**
161	**30 B 4**
162	**30 A 8**
163	**47 A 24**
164	**30 B 6**
165	**28 A 24**
166	**30 A 5**
167	**28 B 4**
168	**30 B 7**
169	**30 B 10**
170	**30 B 9**
171	**30 B 9**
172	(Plato, *Parmenides* 127A–128E)
173	**29 A 16**
174	**29 B 2**
175	**29 B 3 + B 1**
176	**29 A 21**
177	(Simplicius, *in Phys* 139.27–32)
178	**29 A 21**
179	**29 A 21**
180	(Philoponus, *in Phys* 510.4–6)
181	**29 A 29**
182	**29 A 25**
183	**29 A 25**
184	(Aristotle, *Phys* 263a15–22)
185	(Aristotle, *Phys* 263b3–9)
186	**29 A 26**
187	**29 A 27**
188	**29 A 27**
189	(Epiphanius, *adversus haereticos* III.11)
190	**29 A 28**
191	**30 B 8**
192	**30 A 14**
193	**67 A 8**
194	**31 B 17**.1–13
195	**31 B 21**.9–12
196	**31 B 23**
197	**59 B 1**
198	**59 B 3**
199	**59 B 4**
200	**59 B 4**
201	**59 B 4**
202	**59 B 6**
203	**59 B 8**
204	**59 B 11**
205	**59 A 43**
206	**59 A 46**
207	**59 B 12**
208	**59 B 7**
209	**59 A 52**
210	**59 A 45**
211	**59 B 16**
212	**59 B 10**
213	**68 A 37**
214	**68 A 71**
215	**68 A 57**
216	**67 A 13**
217	**67 A 14**
218	**68 A 1**
219	**68 A 43**
220	**68 A 47**
221	**67 A 7**
222	**67 A 7**
223	**68 A 42**
224	(Aristotle, *GC* 326a1–3)
225	(Alexander, *in Met* 36.25–7)
226	(Aristotle, *Phys* 187a1)
227	(Aristotle, *GC* 316a10–14)
228	(Aristotle, *GC* 316b28–317a2)
229	**67 A 13**
230	**68 A 48a**
231	(Aristotle, *Cael* 271a9–11)
232	(Aristotle, *Cael* 303a20–4)
233	**68 B 155**
234	**68 B 155a**
235	**68 A 38**
236	**67 A 8**
237	(Aristotle, *Phys* 203b20–2)
238	(Aristotle, *Phys* 203b25–8)
239	**67 A 9**
240	**68 A 60**
241	**68 A 61**
242	**68 A 135**
243	**68 A 47**
244	**67 A 10**

Barnes	Diels-Kranz
245	(Lucretius II.114–22)
246	**68 A 58**
247	**68 A 47**
248	**68 A 47**
249	**67 A 6**
250	**67 A 6**
251	(Aristotle, *GC* 326a1–3)
252	**67 A 19**
253	**68 A 135**
254	(Plutarch, *adv Col* 1110E)
255	**68 A 125**
256	**68 A 126**
257	**68 A 135**
258	**67 A 32**
259	**68 A 49**
260	**68 B 9**
261	**68 A 49**
262	**68 A 64**
263	**68 A 123**
264	**67 A 32**
265	**68 A 48**
266	**68 A 135**
267	**44 A 29**
268	**44 A 7a**
269	**47 B 1**
270	**58 B 4**
271	(Iamblichus, *comm math sc* 78.8–18)
272	(Aristotle, *Met* 1090a20–2)
273	**58 B 4**
274	**58 B 4**
275	**58 B 1a**
276	**44 B 1**
277	**44 B 6**
278	**44 B 3**
279	**44 B 2**
280	**44 B 4**
281	**44 B 5**
282	**58 B 5**
283	**45 A 3**
284	**44 B 7**
285	**44 B 17**
286	**58 B 8**
287	**58 B 5**
288	**31 B 13**
289	(Aristotle, *MXG* 976b26)
290	**59 A 68**
291	**30 A 5**
292	**31 A 35**
293	**31 A 35**
294	**67 A 20**
295	**67 A 6**
296	**67 A 8**
297	**68 B 156**
298	**70 B 2**
299	**59 A 1**
300	**59 A 58**
301	**59 B 12**
302	**59 B 13**
303	**59 B 14**
304	**68 B 118**
305	**68 A 69**
306	**68 A 6**
307	**68 A 66**
308	**68 A 1**
309	**67 B 2**
310	**67 A 22**
311	**68 A 70**
312	**59 A 47**
313	**59 A 47**
314	**59 A 102**
315	**59 A 16**
316	**59 A 45**
317	**31 B 17**.19–20
318	**31 B 17**.22–4
319	**31 B 27**.8
320	**31 B 33**
321	**31 B 86**
322	**31 B 95**
323	**31 B 35**.9
324	**31 A 70**
325	**31 A 20a**
326	**31 B 62**.6
327	**31 B 90**
328	**31 A 38**
329	**31 B 115**.1–2
330	(Aristotle, *Phys* 196a19–24)
331	**31 B 22**.4–5
332	**31 B 30**
333	**31 B 103**
334	**67 A 11**
335	**68 B 118**
336	**68 A 67**
337	**68 A 68**
338	**68 A 69**
339	**68 A 68**
340	**31 A 48**
341	**59 A 59**

Diels-Kranz	Barnes
11 A 1	1, 79, 92
11 A 12	3
11 A 14	4
11 A 20	5
11 A 22	2, 80
12 A 1	17
12 A 9	13
12 A 10	6, 23
12 A 11	11
12 A 15	14, 16
12 A 16	15
12 A 26	10
12 A 27	8
12 A 30	7
12 A 33	9
12 B 1	13
13 A 5	24
13 A 7	19, 27
13 A 10	81
13 A 12	28
13 A 14	29
13 A 15	30
13 A 17	31
13 B 1	25
13 B 2	26
13 B 3	18
14 A 1	85
14 A 8	89
14 A 8a	84
21 A 12	64
21 A 28	65, 68
21 A 30	82
21 A 31	69
21 A 32	70
21 A 33	9
21 A 35	83
21 A 7	87
21 B 11	76
21 B 14	63
21 B 15	73
21 B 16	125
21 B 18	122
21 B 23	67, 72
21 B 24	74
21 B 25	75
21 B 26	62
21 B 29	20
21 B 32	78

Diels-Kranz	Barnes
21 B 33	21
21 B 34	120
21 B 35	124
21 B 36	123
21 B 38	126
21 C 1	71
22 A 5	41
22 A 6	42
22 B 1	33
22 B 2	113
22 B 5b	103
22 B 7	140
22 B 10	34
22 B 12	43
22 B 15	58
22 B 16	115
22 B 17	128
22 B 22	33
22 B 25	103
22 B 26	54
22 B 27	117
22 B 28	116, 134
22 B 30	38
22 B 31	40
22 B 35	141
22 B 40	137
22 B 41	108
22 B 44	114
22 B 45	133
22 B 49a	44
22 B 50	35
22 B 51	36
22 B 52	109
22 B 53	104
22 B 54	60
22 B 55	139
22 B 56	61
22 B 57	51
22 B 59	57
22 B 60	55
22 B 61	52
22 B 64	107
22 B 78	132
22 B 79	131
22 B 80	37
22 B 88	50
22 B 90	39
22 B 91	45
22 B 94	111

Diels-Kranz	Barnes
22 B 96	106
22 B 101	136
22 B 101a	135
22 B 102	112
22 B 103	56
22 B 104	129
22 B 107	142
22 B 111	130
22 B 112	118
22 B 114	113
22 B 123	59
22 B 125	46
22 B 126	47
22 B 129	138
23 B 1	66
23 B 2	88
23 B 5	53
24 A 1	96
24 A 5	144
24 A 11	143
24 A 12	94, 97
24 B 1	119
24 B 2	93
28 A 24	155
28 B 1	105
28 B 2	148
28 B 3	149
28 B 4	167
28 B 5	155
28 B 6	150
28 B 7	151, 153
28 B 8	146, 147, 156
29 A 16	173
29 A 21	176, 178, 179
29 A 25	182, 183
29 A 26	186
29 A 27	187, 188
29 A 28	190
29 A 29	181
29 B 1	175
29 B 2	174
29 B 3	175
30 A 5	166
30 A 8	162
30 A 14	192
30 B 1	158
30 B 2	159
30 B 3	160
30 B 4	161

Diels-Kranz	Barnes
30 B 6	164
30 B 7	167
30 B 8	190
30 B 9	170
30 B 10	169
31 A 20a	325
31 A 30	432
31 A 35	292, 293
31 A 38	328
31 A 41	353
31 A 48	340
31 A 70	324
31 A 78	433
31 A 86	418, 421, 424, 426, 428
31 A 92	417
31 B 3	486
31 B 8	360
31 B 9	361
31 B 11	354
31 B 12	355
31 B 13	288
31 B 15	439
31 B 17	194, 317, 318, 352, 358, 365
31 B 21	195, 351
31 B 22	331
31 B 23	196
31 B 27	319
31 B 33	320
31 B 35	323
31 B 62	326
31 B 86	321
31 B 89	419
31 B 90	327
31 B 95	322
31 B 101	420
31 B 102	422
31 B 103	333
31 B 105	429
31 B 106	427
31 B 108	427
31 B 109	425
31 B 110	423, 430
31 B 111	415
31 B 112	416, 445
31 B 115	329, 442
31 B 126	443
31 B 128	444

Diels-Kranz	Barnes
31 B 131	438
31 B 133	440
31 B 134	441
31 B 146	446
31 B 147	446
36 B 1	366
44 A 7a	268
44 A 23	434, 437
44 A 29	267
44 B 1	276
44 B 2	279
44 B 3	278
44 B 4	280
44 B 5	281
44 B 6	277
44 B 7	284
44 B 14	408
44 B 17	285
45 A 3	283
47 B 1	269
58 B 1a	275
58 B 4	270, 273, 274
58 B 5	282, 287
58 B 8	286
58 B 34	447
58 B 40	409
58 B 41	435
59 A 1	299
59 A 16	315
59 A 28	490
59 A 43	205
59 A 45	210, 316
59 A 46	206
59 A 47	312, 313
59 A 52	209, 348, 356
59 A 58	300
59 A 59	341
59 A 68	290
59 A 97	489
59 A 102	314
59 B 1	197
59 B 3	198
59 B 4	199, 200, 201
59 B 5	357
59 B 6	202
59 B 7	208
59 B 8	203
59 B 10	212
59 B 11	204

Diels-Kranz	Barnes
59 B 12	207, 301
59 B 13	302
59 B 14	303
59 B 16	211
59 B 17	359
59 B 21	488
59 B 21a	487
60 A 2	451
60 A 4	528
60 A 10	530
60 A 12	529
62 A 1	368
64 A 1	510
64 A 4	521
64 A 5	512, 520
64 A 6	513
64 A 7	519
64 A 10	516
64 A 20	405
64 A 23	514
64 B 1	511
64 B 2	515, 522
64 B 3	525
64 B 4	526
64 B 5	527
64 B 6	523
64 B 7	524
67 A 6	249, 250, 295, 342
67 A 7	222, 362
67 A 8	193, 236, 296
67 A 9	239, 349, 504
67 A 10	244, 343
67 A 11	334
67 A 13	216, 229
67 A 14	217, 364
67 A 16	344, 345
67 A 18	346
67 A 19	252
67 A 20	294
67 A 22	310
67 A 28	406
67 A 30	410
67 A 32	258, 264
67 A 33	369
67 A 37	363
67 A 47	247, 248
67 B 2	309
68 A 1	218, 308, 477
68 A 6	306

Diels-Kranz	Barnes
68 A 37	213
68 A 38	235
68 A 42	223
68 A 43	219
68 A 47	220, 243
68 A 48	265
68 A 48a	230
68 A 49	259, 261
68 A 50	485
68 A 57	215, 367
68 A 58	246, 350
68 A 60	240
68 A 61	241
68 A 63	517
68 A 64	262
68 A 65	347
68 A 66	307
68 A 67	336
68 A 68	337, 339
68 A 69	305, 338
68 A 70	311
68 A 71	214
68 A 74	386, 387
68 A 75	379
68 A 112	501
68 A 114	494
68 A 117	506
68 A 119	411
68 A 123	263
68 A 125	255
68 A 126	256
68 A 135	242, 253, 257, 268, 412, 413, 518
68 B 4	476
68 B 5	394
68 B 6–11	507
68 B 9	260
68 B 26	396
68 B 30	381
68 B 35	468
68 B 37	383, 469
68 B 39	470
68 B 53	475
68 B 62	471
68 B 71	480

Diels-Kranz	Barnes
68 B 74	479
68 B 102	472
68 B 118	304, 335
68 B 125	509
68 B 144	373
68 B 145	395
68 B 154	374
68 B 155	233
68 B 155a	234
68 B 156	297
68 B 166	388
68 B 175	389
68 B 188	478
68 B 189	384
68 B 194	482
68 B 207	483
68 B 211	481
68 B 217	385
68 B 230	484
68 B 260	474
68 B 274	473
68 B 297	380
70 A 23	508
70 B 1	505
70 B 2	298
75 B 4	502
79 A 2a	370
80 A 1	497, 499
80 A 10	460
80 A 14	493, 503
80 A 19	496, 500
80 A 20	498
80 A 23	372
80 B 1	491, 492, 495
80 B 4	371
82 B 3	397
82 B 11	391, 461–7
82 B 23	390
84 B 5	378, 382
85 B 8	376
87 B 44	448–450
88 B 25	375
90 A 1	452, 453, 454, 457
90 A 2	455, 458
90 A 3	392, 393, 456, 459